PERÓN

PERÓN

a biography

Joseph A. Page

Random House New York

Library of Congress Cataloging in Publication Data
Page, Joseph A.
Perón, a biography.
Bibliography: p.
1. Perón, Juan Domingo, 1895–1974. 2. Argentina—
Politics and government—1943–1955. 3. Argentina—
Politics and government—1955. 4. Argentina—
Presidents—Biography. I. Title.
F2849.P48P28   1983   982'.062'0924 [B]   82-40136
ISBN 0-394-52297-4

A los jóvenes argentinos,
quienes merecen más . . .

Preface

Juan Perón presents formidable obstacles to the biographer. He left behind relatively few reliable records of his long public career, perhaps under the conviction that he would fare better in the eyes of posterity if judgments about him did not rest upon hard fact. His many books, pamphlets, articles, speeches, letters and taped conversations are so permeated with contradiction, exaggeration and misstatement that they must be used with extreme caution.

Moreover, much of this material is inaccessible to researchers. Lengthy reminiscences he recorded while in Spain have not been made public. The personal archive of his first and second presidencies, at last report, was being eaten by rats in a storage room of a Buenos Aires courthouse. The extensive correspondence of his exile period either remains locked in his house in Madrid or disappeared along with his last private secretary, José López Rega. Even some secondary sources—books, newspapers, magazines and pamphlets—are now to be found only in widely dispersed private collections.

Of the countless eyewitnesses to the events of Perón's extraordinary career, a few refuse to talk, out of discretion, distrust or fear; some claim they will one day write memoirs of their own; others maintain an active political involvement that colors their testimony. All struggle, often in vain, with the overwhelming Perón mystique, which hopelessly confuses reality and illusion.

Death continues to claim key participants and observers. In the course of the preparation of this book, Domingo Mercante, Spruille Braden, José Gelbard, Héctor Cámpora and Ricardo Balbín were among those who passed away.

This biographer has sought to overcome these difficulties by combining the persistence of seven years' work, unaccountable good fortune in securing source materials and interviews, hundreds of documents released under the Freedom of Information Act by the Department of State, Federal Bureau of Investigation, Central Intelligence Agency and Defense Intelligence Agency, and, most importantly, the help of many individuals.

The controversial nature of the subject prevents me from acknowledging most of the Argentines who went out of their way to assist me. Their warmth and generosity I shall forever cherish. It would be unfair to thank some by name, but not all. Therefore, I should like to convey my heartfelt appreciation to those who permitted me to look at their private archives, libraries, correspondence and motion-picture films; who opened doors for me; who took me to Lobos, the presidential residence in Olivos, and Perón's homes in Puerta de Hierro and Vicente López; and to the intellectuals, politicians, students, labor leaders, businessmen, journalists and ordinary Argentine citizens who spent many hours explaining their country to me.

I should also like to convey my gratitude to the many U.S. government officials and employees, both in Argentina and in Washington, who aided me; to the foreign correspondents in Buenos Aires and Madrid who provided me with leads and insights; and to Professor Robert J. Alexander, who let me peruse his ample files.

I should like to recognize the intellectual debt I owe to Hugo Gambini, Félix Luna, Marysa Navarro, Robert Potash and Wayne Smith, whose lucid and balanced writings were indispensable sources.

A word of thanks is due James Buchanan for reading and criticizing portions of the manuscript; Martha Gil-Montero, whose sensitivity and eye for detail vastly improved the final draft; and the indefatigable word processors at the Georgetown University Law Center.

I must credit my Spanish teacher at the Boston School of Modern Languages, Professor Peña, who first made me aware of the drama of October 17, 1945; my editor, Jonathan Galassi, for conceiving the project and having the patience to see it through; my agent, Carl D. Brandt, for his encouragement; Dean David J. McCarthy, Jr., for his steadfast support; and the world's foremost Peronologist, Enrique Pavón Pereyra, whose unflagging enthusiasm kept my spirits buoyed.

Finally, I must emphasize that I take full and sole responsibility for all the judgments expressed in this book.

—Joseph A. Page
Washington, D.C.

Contents

Part IV: The First Presidency (1946–1952)

Part V: The Second Presidency (1952–1955)

Part VI: Exile (1955–1973)

Part VII: The Third Presidency (1973–1976)

Part I

Introduction

1

The San Juan Earthquake

On Saturday evening, January 15, 1944, a twenty-five-second earthquake leveled the Argentine city of San Juan.[1] It was the worst natural disaster to hit the country and one of the most devastating ever to occur in the Western Hemisphere, with the death toll exceeding 10,000. Buildings moved and chandeliers shuddered as far away as Buenos Aires, the capital, more than 1,000 kilometers (600 miles) east of the epicenter.

Reports detailing the dimensions of the tragedy did not reach Buenos Aires until late Sunday. On the state-controlled radio network, the strong, nasal voice of an army colonel made a dramatic appeal to the nation for medicine, clothing, food, money and blood.[2] As an Argentine magazine noted on the twenty-fifth anniversary of the event, the speech marked the beginning of "a lengthy monologue that was to last for a decade."[3]

While the president of Argentina, General Pedro P. Ramírez, ordered all places of public amusement closed and all radio stations to broadcast only news and sacred music, Colonel Juan Domingo Perón took charge of the relief effort on behalf of San Juan. Only a few months earlier, he had been named head of the National Department of Labor, an obscure appendage of the Ministry of the Interior, and had upgraded it to the status of a secretariat, nominally responsible to the president but in fact independent. The tragedy of San Juan provided the colonel and his new Secretariat of Labor and Social Welfare with instant national exposure.

The earthquake also served to galvanize a strong sentiment of unity in a nation long rent by social, economic and political divisions. Sympathy for the victims brought people together as had no other event in recent history. When Colonel Perón called for blood, more donors appeared than the facilities could handle.[4] When he urged the participation of all citizens, women as well as men volunteered to help. It marked the first time that large numbers of Argentine women acted as citizens at the national level.

Of course there were the inevitable cynics who accused the military government of using the sudden spirit of unity to fortify its shaky hold on the populace. But they missed the point, one which Perón saw clearly, that with proper stimulus and leadership, Argentines could work together to meet a challenge.

General Ramírez visited San Juan on January 19 and attended a mass for the survivors in the Plaza 25 de Mayo. The clock on what was left of the tower of the nearby eighteenth-century cathedral stood motionless at 8:48, a grim reminder which would remain until the badly damaged structure was demolished. As the president was introduced, an ominous rumble intruded. For a brief moment a stir of panic seized the crowd. Ramírez asked for calm, and the tremor subsided.[5]

Perón remained in Buenos Aires and mobilized the relief program. He met with representatives from private industry to stimulate the donation of funds. He utilized his position as secretary to the minister of war to coordinate military assistance to the stricken region. He set up in the office of the Secretariat of Labor and Social Welfare a center for the collection of foodstuffs, clothing and cash, and saw to it that the replica of a giant thermometer was attached to the base of the towering obelisk at the intersection of Corrientes Street and the broad Avenida 9 de Julio, to publicize the progress of the fund-raising campaign.

Among the groups upon whom Perón called for help were the nation's actors and actresses. He planned appearances by stage, movie and radio celebrities on the streets of Buenos Aires. The high point of the campaign was to be a collection taken up on Saturday, when large crowds of shoppers and strollers would normally be on the street. On the appointed day, resplendent in his gold-braided white uniform and flashing the infectious smile that would soon earn him the derogatory nickname Colonel Kolynos,* the tall, handsome widower led a procession of dazzling actresses and well-scrubbed military cadets. Despite the sticky summer heat, crowds buzzed about the colonel and his cohorts. The collection was an unqualified success.

Lost in the bevy of the stars and starlets accompanying Colonel Perón was a young actress named Eva Duarte. Though she was not beautiful, sexy or particularly talented, Eva Duarte (Evita to her friends) was blessed with a tenacity that had lifted her from an obscure, small provincial town to a career in theater, radio and film. On this day she was to link her destiny with that of Juan Perón. The energy unleashed by this union would change the history of Argentina.

Mythology now shrouds the precise circumstances of their initial en-

---

* Kolynos was a popular brand of toothpaste.

counter.[6] In taped conversations made during the early 1960s, Perón claimed that he first noticed Eva when she spoke up at a meeting of actors and actresses called to discuss the Saturday collection.[7] He subsequently averred that she caught his eye when she remained behind after the meeting to help in the actual organization of the event.[8] Whether or not he did in fact take note of her on this occasion, it is clear that the crucial conjunction occurred during a gala benefit for San Juan staged on Saturday evening, January 22, at Luna Park, the big indoor sports arena at the foot of Corrientes Street.

The doors opened in the early afternoon to throngs eager to obtain good seats. The show was to last until 2:00 A.M., with the final four hours to be broadcast on national radio. Many of the performers who had participated in the street collection volunteered their talents for the Luna Park extravaganza. An oppressive humidity failed to dampen the spirits of the crowd.

Perón arrived at 10:00 P.M. in the entourage accompanying President Ramírez. Eva Duarte was already sitting in the front row, next to her escort and old friend, Lieutenant Colonel Aníbal Imbert. Perón responded to the cheers of the audience with a wave of the hand and displayed his eternal smile. He greeted Colonel Imbert, who introduced him formally to Eva Duarte, probably at the latter's insistence. As he took his seat, he found the actress in the chair next to his.

Both President Ramírez and Colonel Perón made brief speeches. When the show ended and Perón left Luna Park, Eva Duarte clung to his arm. The chemistry that drew them together proved powerful stuff. Within a brief period of time, the twenty-four-year-old actress and the forty-nine-year-old colonel were living together. They were to remain virtually inseparable until her untimely death in 1952.

For Juan Perón, the San Juan earthquake was a godsend, imparting momentum to his roller-coaster ride to immortality. Within two and a half years he would be Argentina's constitutionally elected president, surviving an interim fall that might easily have destroyed him and inflicting a decisive defeat upon a strong, united opposition. He would serve in office for more than nine years as the authoritarian leader of a genuinely popular movement, only to flee the country in response to an uprising against his government in September 1955. He would suffer a prolonged exile which would ultimately take him to Madrid, where he would mastermind an unprecedented political comeback. And in 1973 at the age of seventy-eight he would assume the role of national savior and stage a triumphal return to his native land, which once again would invest him with the presidency. Within a year he would die and leave behind a bitterly divided nation.

He has marked Argentina as no one else has, forcing his fellow citizens to define themselves according to their attitudes toward him while remaining ever enigmatic and constantly defying convention. In a passionate country, he aroused emotions of volcanic intensity in others, but very seldom felt deeply himself. (As a Spanish journalist put it on the day of Perón's death, "He loved his dogs and was loved by a great part of his country."[9]) Within a culture suffused with machismo, he never fathered a child, turned his second and third wives into political figures, and often boasted of his nonviolent nature.

He has bedeviled political observers, who have tried to classify him as Fascist, personalist dictator, populist and even leftist. For policymakers in the United States he has taken on the varying hues of a neo-Nazi scourge to be excised from the continent at any cost, a president with whom North American business interests could profitably deal, one of a number of Latin dictators blemishing the free world, and in the end Argentina's last hope of avoiding a left-wing takeover or civil war.

Masterful in his use of contradiction, Perón raised political ambiguity to an art form. He preached revolution, yet revolutionized little more than expectations. Far ahead of his time in advocating Latin American unity and Third World nonalignment, he simultaneously sowed fears of Argentine expansionism and kept his country within parameters set by North American foreign policy. Cultivating the image of a serious thinker, he embraced anti-intellectuality all his life. Fully aware of the mediocrity of those with whom he chose to surround himself, he nonetheless permitted them to deify him with mindless adulation.

The dark shadow of violence, a constant factor in the development of Argentine history, followed Perón at a discreet distance. The depredation of the unbridled mob as well as the lightning stroke of political assassination often furthered his ends without staining him with direct responsibility. Some called him a saint, others believed him to be the devil incarnate. He viewed himself as transcending good and evil.[10]

Perón's closest North American counterpart is Huey Long, the colorful, controversial Kingfish, whose name and memory still mark Louisiana politics nearly half a century after his death.[11] Though there are more differences than similarities between the two populist leaders (one of the most intriguing was Perón's luck in avoiding the violent death that brought an untimely end to Long's career), they were both products of a unique cultural and social environment. One cannot understand Long without an appreciation of the roots from which he emerged. The same is true of Perón.

2

Perón's Argentina

The eighth-largest country in the world, and of the South American nations second in size only to Brazil, Argentina stretches from subtropical forest in the north to the windswept desolation of Tierra del Fuego at the southern tip of the continent; and from the majestic Andes on the western border with Chile to 4,000 kilometers (2,500 miles) of coastline on the Atlantic Ocean. The varieties of landscape are striking: an arid tableland, suggesting Arizona, in the northwest; Tucumán's moist hills, carpeted with sugarcane, not far away; the lowlands of the northeast, where *quebracho* trees yield hardwood of great commercial value; the mighty Iguazú Falls on the Brazilian frontier, to be compared only with Victoria and Niagara; the vast bleakness of Patagonia, where millions of sheep far outnumber the humans; the jewel-like lakes and mountains around San Carlos de Bariloche; and Argentina's greatest natural resource, the flat, fertile grasslands known as the pampa. The man-made contribution to this geographer's banquet is the sprawling metropolis of Buenos Aires, one of the great cities of the world, guarding the mouth of the Río de la Plata, or Silver River (not really a river but rather a broad estuary, and not silver, but tawny).

One-third of the population of Argentina clusters in and around Buenos Aires, a demographic phenomenon giving rise to megalocephaly in the extreme. The capital totally dominates the political, economic and social life of the country. As the distinguished British historian James Bryce noted in 1912, this concentration makes Buenos Aires "dwarf all the other cities and gives to it an influence comparable to that of Paris in France."[1] The superiority complex of the *porteño* (port-dweller), as inhabitants of the city are called, mirrors this preeminence, achieved after decades of civil struggle with the provinces and in turn resented by the rest of the Argentines.

The city's origins, however, were humble.[2] In the latter half of the six-teenth century, Spaniards coming from Perú, Bolivia and Chile in search of gold and silver descended into northwestern Argentina and founded a string of towns, such as Salta, Jujuy, Córdoba, Mendoza and San Juan, whose political and economic ties were with the older Spanish settlements on the Pacific Coast. An attempt to colonize the mouth of the Río de la Plata had foundered in 1536, when settlers crossing the Atlantic from Spain were unable to survive the environment and attacks by warlike Indians. The survivors fled northward and founded the town of Asunción (now the capital of Paraguay), which flourished in more amenable sur-roundings. It was not until 1580 that an expedition from Asunción man-aged to plant a permanent colony on the banks of the Río de la Plata.

For nearly two centuries, Buenos Aires enjoyed a precarious existence, hardly comparable in importance or wealth to the older cities of the in-terior and vulnerable to English and Portuguese marauders, as well as to hostile Indians. It formed a part of the Spanish Vice-Royalty of Perú, ruled by a viceroy living some 5,000 kilometers (3,000 miles) away in Lima. Legal restrictions imposed by the viceroy required that all com-merce within the Vice-Royalty pass through Lima and prohibited direct, sea-borne trade to and from the port of Buenos Aires.[3] This made the city a center of lucrative contraband, especially for British traders. By 1750 the population of Buenos Aires had reached 12,000.[4]

In 1776, apprehensive at the threat of Portuguese expansion from Brazil in the north, the Spanish crown transformed the town into the capital of a new vice-royalty and the following year instituted a system of free trade. The city's growth reflected its new status. In 1778 it counted 24,000 inhabitants; in 1790, 32,000; and in 1810, 44,000.[5] By repulsing two British invasions in 1806 and 1807, Buenos Aires gained a measure of self-confidence that has survived intact to the present day.

Between 1810, the date of the outbreak of the revolution ultimately freeing Argentina from Spanish rule, and 1852, when a long series of bloody civil wars ended, the city continued to grow, its population reach-ing 88,000, but it was not until the latter part of the nineteenth century that Buenos Aires enjoyed a spectacular expansion. A succession of strong presidents developed the pastoral and agricultural industries, attracted foreign capital for the construction of railways, docks and commercial facilities, increased the labor force through immigration and encouraged the extermination of the Indians.[6] The open society that emerged per-mitted the bloom of a vigorous cultural and intellectual life.

In 1890 an American traveler described Buenos Aires as "a great com-mercial mart, and its citizens seem wholly given to business. The number of stores and the variety and elegance of the goods displayed are aston-ishing. The retail shops of the street called Florida have a true Parisian splendor. Many of them are small, and devoted to a special product or article for which you would think there would be sufficient demand only in a large city like Paris or Vienna."[7]

By 1938, American poet Archibald MacLeish could write: "[Buenos Aires] is a great city as the ancients measured great cities; a strong town famous for the horsemanship of its men and the beauty of its women. It is a great city in the sense in which Paris and London are great cities. It is a cosmopolitan, twentieth-century metropolis with all the fixings, crowds, avenues, parks, subways, visiting pianists, confusion of tongues, screaming of brakes, shining of movie theatres . . . impudence of plaster-of-paris bosoms in the show windows of lingerie shops, cadenzas of jazz bands over the roofs of extinguished apartment houses at 2:00 A.M."[8]

Though lacking the natural splendor of Rio de Janeiro and the dynamism of São Paulo, Buenos Aires still reigns supreme among the cities of Latin America. With an opera house larger than La Scala in Milan and a central avenue broader than Paris' Champs Elysées, it pulses with a special kind of vitality. Yet as even porteños will admit in candid moments, Buenos Aires is not Argentina.

The heartland of Argentina is an oval-shaped plain comprising one-fifth of the country's total area and reaching inland from Buenos Aires in a great arc whose radius extends more than 800 kilometers (500 miles). Nature has crowned this vast absolutely flat expanse with fertile topsoil some three meters deep. One can cross it with a plow, as the popular saying goes, without ever encountering a stone.[9] The Argentines call it the pampa, an Indian word meaning level land or space.

When the Spanish first came to Argentina, the pampa was a wilderness of grass and flowers, thistles and clover. A few nomadic Indian tribes roamed over a region devoid of animal life save for a species of small ostrich and a llamalike creature known as the guanaco. But horses and cows brought from Europe by the Spaniards were turned loose on the plain and multiplied into great herds, creating two classes of men who would leave an indelible mark on the Argentine character.

A handful of aggressive individuals, lured by the promise of easy wealth, staked out claims to the pampa. The economies of scale as well as the Spanish tradition of large landholdings produced a concentrated ownership of enormous tracts of land. These properties were owned by ranchers, or estancieros, whose culture, spirit and economic interests were different from those of the outward-looking porteños. From the ranks of the estancieros came the local caudillos, or quasi-feudal overlords, who ruled in autocratic fashion during the turbulent early years of Argentine independence. Though often of modest origin, the descendants of these early estancieros gradually formed an oligarchic elite whose economic and political power would long dominate the nation.

The pampa also produced the gaucho, or Argentine cowboy. In the words of James Bryce, "He was above all things a horseman, never dismounting from his animal except to sleep beside it. . . . His dress was the poncho, a square piece of woolen cloth with a hole cut for his head to go through, and a pair of drawers. He could live on next to nothing and knew no fatigue. Round him clings all the romance of the Pampas, for he was taken as the embodiment of the primitive virtues of daring, endurance, and loyalty."[10] Courage, independence, courtesy and a willingness to do a favor have long graced the gaucho's image.

Of mixed Spanish and Indian blood, the gaucho resisted civilizing influences and fought against the Spanish crown as resolutely as against the merchants and intellectuals of Buenos Aires. His only allegiance was to the local caudillo strong enough to command his respect. The civil strife convulsing Argentina during the early part of the nineteenth century pitted these caudillos and their gauchos against the porteños, the former favoring loose confederation, the latter advocating a strong central government located in Buenos Aires and European-style modernization.

In 1835, after a period of increasing anarchy, a leader from Buenos Aires Province gained control of the federal government. Juan Manuel de Rosas was a legend in his own time, a larger-than-life caudillo whose physical prowess and skills as a horseman inspired the devotion of a large gaucho following. He gained political control of the entire nation and for seventeen years imposed his will with an iron hand. Within the context of a violent era, he made systematic and widespread use of terror, but he also held Argentina together. In 1852 a caudillo from the interior made common cause with the liberal intellectuals of Buenos Aires and led an uprising that sent Rosas in flight to England.

Those who looked upon Rosas as a bloody tyrant saw the struggle as one between the forces of civilization and barbarity. But this was an oversimplification at best. The followers of Rosas rejected the model of Europeanization pursued by Buenos Aires and exalted *criollo* (native) values and traditions. They resisted domination by frock-coated porteños, who in their view exploited the wealth of the pampa to purchase European imports that did not benefit the rest of the country, while the legitimate needs of the inhabitants of the interior remained unmet. The fall of Rosas did not really resolve the conflict; it merely shifted the balance of power.

Dramatic changes overtook the pampa after Rosas' defeat. The improvement of breeding techniques, the construction of railroads from the port of Buenos Aires to the interior and the development of refrigeration for oceangoing vessels converted Argentina into one of the great cattle-raising nations of the world. Immigrants from Italy and Spain helped increase the production of wheat, corn, alfalfa and linseed. Foreign capital and trade, mainly from and with England, provided vital stimuli. As English historian George Pendle observed, "by the end of the century . . . the pampa in fact had been tamed, organized and virtually harnessed to the economy of faraway Great Britain."[11] The few families monopolizing the nation's best land grew ultra-rich and gave to the outside world the stereo-type of the affluent Argentine (such as the expatriate estanciero who brought his own cows to Paris so that his children might have fresh milk).

Meanwhile, having virtually disappeared from the face of the pampa, the gaucho reemerged as a heroic figure in the pantheon of the Argentine psyche. In 1872, José Hernández published his epic poem *Martín Fierro*. Eventually recognized as a classic of Argentine literature, the saga of *Martín Fierro* depicts one gaucho's struggle for survival and self-respect against the repressive, corrupting constraints of authority. The poem romanticizes the rugged individualism of the gaucho and his passionate devotion to freedom, while deploring efforts by those in power to impose an alien form of civilization that perpetuated injustice in the name of progress.[12]

One other region of the country merits special mention. The southern cone, known as Patagonia, contains more than one-quarter of the nation's continental territory but only 1 percent of its population. It is a dry yet often foggy land lashed by winds rushing west across bleak plateaus toward the tapering peaks of the Andes. John Gunther has aptly referred to it as a "wool-and-mutton factory,"[13] where numberless sheep range mega-sized ranches.

Although many Argentines regard it as a sort of Siberia, Patagonia's natural beauty and remarkable fauna have begun to attract discriminating tourists. Lago Argentino, a rugged lake fed by huge chunks of ice from a glacier, and the internationally famous ski resort at Bariloche grace the southern and northern extremities of the region. Penguins and lumbering sea elephants enliven the Atlantic shores. The condor, a species of vulture combining great size, bodily elegance and the most repulsive of heads, glides majestically along the Andean cliffs.

The geographic isolation of Patagonia from the nation's population centers has long worried the Argentine government. Many of the region's inhabitants are from Chile, and the country's defensive posture has traditionally included plans to protect Patagonia against the contingency of Chilean expansionism. But no effort has been made to encourage settlement of the region by breaking up its large estates.

Among the salient characteristics setting the Argentine people apart from most of the rest of Latin America are underpopulation, race and the immigration factor. On a continent where the tocsin of overpopulation has long sounded, Argentina ranks behind only Paraguay and Bolivia on the list of least densely settled nations. In 1820 the total population of the country was reckoned at half a million. In the first national census, conducted in 1869, the total reached 1.8 million. Subsequent counts showed 4 million in 1895, 8 million in 1913, 16 million in 1947, 20 million in 1960, and 23 million in 1970.[14] From 1900 to 1965 the annual growth rate averaged 2.5 percent, but in the 1960–1970 period it had slowed to 1.5 percent.[15]

Urbanization, education and relatively high per capita income have been blamed for Argentina's slow population growth. Between the 1895 and 1914 censuses, the urban population increased from 37 percent to 53 percent of the total, and in 1970 it was estimated at 69 percent.[16] The educational system, greatly improved during the boom era of the late nineteenth century, has yielded a literacy rate of better than 90 percent. Per capita income in Argentina has long been the highest in Latin America. These factors have influenced city dwellers to start bearing offspring later in life than their rural counterparts, and hence to have fewer children.[17]

With the possible exception of Uruguay, no other South American nation has a higher ratio of whites in the general population than Argentina, the end result of a bleaching process that took two centuries to run its course. In the colonial period, Spaniards settling in what is now Argentina intermarried with the native Indian women, a practical necessity due to the fact that the original conquerors and colonists brought no women with them from the mother country. At the same time, the need for labor on the plantations stimulated the importation of black Africans. Buenos Aires became a focal point for the illegal but highly lucrative smuggling of slaves. By the end of the colonial era, the population of Argentina was 60 percent Spanish or *mestizo* (a mixture of Spanish and Indian), 30 percent Indian, and 10 percent black or *mulato* (black-white mix).[18]

During the nineteenth century, three demographic phenomena occurred. The blacks and *mulatos* were absorbed into the rest of the population and within a few generations all but vanished. Second, military campaigns against Indian tribes on the pampa liquidated virtually the entire native population. In the 1947 census, Indians constituted less than 5 percent of the population, and their numbers have declined steadily since that time.[19] Finally, in the latter part of the nineteenth century Argentina opened her doors to waves of immigrants, most of whom came from southern Europe. Between 1856 and 1896, the arrival of at least six million immigrants, mostly Italians and Spaniards, marked the acceleration of an influx that had its maximum effect in 1914, when persons born abroad comprised 30 percent of the Argentine population.[20]

Problems of definition make it difficult to ascertain what percentage of the Argentine people is white, but the figure must be well in excess of 90 percent. The nation's whiteness has fostered a feeling of superiority that has led Argentines to think of themselves not as Latin Americans but as Europeans. However, the country's economic and political development has not matched this somewhat exaggerated self-image and has in turn fostered a deep sense of self-doubt.

Immigrants took advantage of social and economic mobility to form the backbone of Argentina's substantial middle class. The Italians, who comprised about 42 percent of the total influx,[21] have noticeably affected the Argentine style, especially in Buenos Aires. Their impact is particularly evident in speech patterns and slang. Spanish immigrants, the second-largest group, fortified the bonds of *hispanidad*, or Spanishness, which provide a cultural, intellectual and sentimental attachment to the mother country.

Important immigrant groups also came from Germany and the British Isles. The Jewish community in Buenos Aires is the largest in Latin America and one of the largest in the world.[22] In 1930, Argentina closed her doors to massive immigration as a result of the Depression. After World War II the flow resumed, but the new immigrants were predominantly from the poverty-stricken lower classes of neighboring countries, attracted by the reputed economic opportunities of Buenos Aires.

The overwhelming majority of the Argentine people are baptized into the church and profess adherence to Catholicism. The church maintains a conspicuous presence in many ceremonial aspects of Argentine life and casts a strong influence upon social behavior, ethical standards and education. Argentine Catholicism is generally traditional and conservative, yet has displayed elasticity toward the rural lower classes, whose unorthodoxies, often of Indian derivation, enjoy benign tolerance.*

During the struggle for independence, the Argentine hierarchy sided with the Spanish crown, while local priests supported the revolution.[23] Despite the loss of prestige the church incurred from the posture of its high clergy, the constitution of 1853 did not diminish the church's privileged position. Although it guaranteed freedom of religion, the constitution provided that Catholicism would be the state religion and that the president of the republic must be a Catholic. The economic liberalism that spurred Argentine growth during the latter nineteenth century did contain an element of anticlericalism, but its only concrete manifestation was the enactment of the Education Law of 1884, banning religious education in the public schools.

The complexities of the collective personality of the Argentines would easily fill a volume in itself. Yet a brief sketch of certain common factors is an essential prerequisite to grasping the Perón phenomenon.

---

* Country folk who migrate to Buenos Aires cling to their devotion toward figures such as Ceferino Namuncurá (a pious Indian boy who died at the Vatican in 1905, shortly after being introduced to the Pope), and the Madre María, a healer whose tomb in Buenos Aires' La Chacarita Cemetery is still a mecca for large numbers of the faithful.

A characteristic profoundly impacting upon the political process is an excessive individualism stemming in large part from the obsession with personal dignity found in Latin cultures. Aggressive driving behavior (for years there were no traffic signals in Buenos Aires), unwillingness to stand in lines and a soccer style that exalts individual brilliance and improvisation to the detriment of team play are diverse manifestations of this tendency. Every Argentine has political opinions as well as an unswerving conviction of their soundness. The result is a refusal to compromise, along with a tendency to extremism in both rhetoric and behavior. These factors, added to the deep suspicion with which Argentines regard one another, severely limit the workability of democratic institutions and foster a predisposition toward authoritarianism.

Geographic isolation is another key element. Indeed, two isolating factors have shaped the Argentine psyche. Tremendous distances keep Argentina on the margin of western civilization.[24] Buenos Aires lies more than 9,000 kilometers (5,000 miles) from New York, and almost 11,200 kilometers (7,000 miles) from Paris. Argentines tend to view Europe and the United States through a magnifying glass that distorts the importance of both events and opinions abroad. This produces a loss of perspective and paranoid reactions when foreigners criticize or ignore them.

The second is the sense of solitude imposed by the vastness of the pampa. Thus, the porteño feels alone on the edge of a wilderness far from the centers of power and culture, while the inhabitant of the countryside feels lost in the flat emptiness of the endless pampa. The result is an impression of helplessness and inevitability, sadness and frustration, themes often tapped in the lyrics of the tango.

A deep sentimentality plays handmaiden to Argentina's spiritual loneliness. The Argentines love an underdog. Some of the politicians they most venerate were in their own time losers who fought unsuccessfully against long odds. The Boca Juniors, a soccer team from a working-class district of Buenos Aires and uncannily reminiscent of the old Brooklyn Dodgers, attract fierce devotion despite unpredictable, often erratic play. (A visit to Buenos Aires is incomplete without an afternoon at La Bombonera, the Boca stadium, in its way as quaint and colorful as Ebbets Field.) Tango singer Carlos Gardel, who died in an airplane crash in 1935, remains an idol of undiminished, if not increasing, popularity.* The powerful pull of sentiment combines with deviant aspects of Mediterranean Catholicism to produce an almost manic preoccupation, approaching necrophilia, with death. Argentines customarily hold memorials and hom-

---

* "Every day he sings better," they say of Gardel, whose tomb in La Chacarita Cemetery receives daily floral offerings from loyal fans. A nine-foot statue depicts him smiling, in a familiar pose, as though ready at any moment to burst into song. There is always a fresh carnation in the lapel. On my last visit, his hand held a burning cigarette.

ages on anniversaries of deaths; funerals have occasioned some of the great moments in Argentine history. Whether to permit the return of Rosas' body from England remains even today a bitterly divisive issue.

A final trait worthy of passing note is the value Argentines attach to appearance. How one looks is often considered an indication of social status, and therefore the Argentine (especially the porteño) devotes careful attention to matters sartorial.[25] Meticulous grooming is endemic. Speech patterns abound with gracious formalities that often seem excessive to the foreigner, but furnish the warp and woof of social intercourse.

Juan Perón was a distinctly Argentine phenomenon, incomprehensible except in the context from which he emerged. Most misperceptions of him stem from a failure to grasp this truth. Indeed, the relationship between the man and his country often seemed symbiotic. It may not be far from the mark to suggest that Perón was Argentina and Argentina was Perón.

Part II

The Making of a Leader

(1895–1942)

3

The Formative Years

There are few surprises on the oceanic plain that covers most of Buenos Aires Province, and Lobos is not one of them.[1] The small town sits unobtrusively 100 kilometers southwest of the capital. Horse-drawn carts still travel the dirt roads on its perimeter. Approaching its center one passes a new Mormon church and a little plaza dedicated to Carlos Gardel. TV antennas sprout in clusters from modest homes.

On a late Saturday afternoon a rough-hewn gaucho strolls across an intersection. Cigarette in hand, black boots carefully shined, broad belt studded with silver coins, red neckerchief set off against green-checkered shirt, he is ready for a night on the town. A woman with her hair in curlers rides by him on a bicycle.

In 1970 Lobos made news when some promoters tried to hold a spring rock-music festival on the grounds of the nearby country club. Suspicious of hippies, the provincial government thwarted their plans and Lobos lost its chance to become Argentina's Woodstock.[2] Yet the town did not need the notoriety of a counterculture extravaganza to assure its place in the nation's history books.

A small building at 1380 Buenos Aires Street, several blocks from the main square, houses a training school for teachers. Its doorway bears traces of plaques recently removed. They commemorated the birthplace of Juan Perón. Today there is nothing to mark the location. Occasionally, such as on the anniversary of his death, people put wreaths and baskets of flowers against the wall, but the authorities quickly remove them.

Juan Domingo Perón came into the world in Lobos on October 8, 1895. There is some evidence to suggest that his parents were not married at the time he was born. A baptismal certificate published in 1955 refers to him as a "natural child."[3] His birth certificate, which would establish his illegitimacy, is missing from his military dossier.[4] Certain traces of

resentment manifested by Perón later in life might derive from the circumstances of his birth.

The roots of Perón's father's family reached back to Sardinia, from where his great-grandfather emigrated to Buenos Aires.[5] He married a woman of Scotch origin. His grandfather, Tomás Liberato Perón, married an Uruguayan whose ancestors were French Basque. His mother, a country girl, was a creole of Spanish derivation, with some Indian ancestry possible among her forebears.

The only distinguished offshoot of the family tree was Perón's grandfather, Tomás Perón.[6] A physician who served in the Senate, president of the National Council of Hygiene, army doctor in the war between Argentina and Paraguay and professor of medicine, he traveled abroad and was said to be the first Argentine to develop an antirabies vaccine. None of these activities, however, brought financial rewards. After Dr. Perón died in 1889 at the age of fifty-five, the Argentine Congress voted a special pension for his widow.[7]

One of his sons, Mario Tomás, was studying medicine at the time of his death. Perhaps due to ill health and certainly from personal preference,[8] he decided to abandon his career and move to the countryside. He was twenty-three when he arrived in Lobos in 1890 to become a minor public functionary and a tenant rancher. There he met, fell in love with and later married Juana Sosa Toledo, a teenage farm girl. The couple produced two sons, Mario Avelino in 1891, and Juan Domingo four years later.

The town of Lobos owes its existence to a fort built in colonial times as part of a chain of outposts designed to ward off marauding Indians. A stop on one of the first railroads constructed by British capital linking pampa to port, by the end of the century Lobos could boast of a school, a post office, a justice of the peace and the branch office of a bank.

The few years that Juan spent in Lobos appear to have been stable and happy. There were the usual childhood traumas, such as falling into a well and being pulled out by his mother, who was terrified by the incident. More typical were pranks, such as frightening a servant with the skull of Juan Moreira, a legendary outlaw.[9] At a tender age Juan learned how to ride a horse and sip mate (a bitter Argentine tea) in the kitchen with ranch workers.

In 1899, as economic conditions worsened, Mario Tomás grew dissatisfied with the kind of rural life he was leading in Lobos. (His son later noted that "he said that [his ranch] was no longer countryside."[10]) He resolved to abandon Lobos and seek his fortune in the bleak expanses of Patagonia. Signing a contract with a Buenos Aires company that owned huge tracts of Patagonian land suitable for sheep-raising, he arranged for his workers and horses to make the trek southward on foot while he traveled by ship to meet them. Their final destination was a ranch called Chank Aike northwest of the city of Río Gallegos, at the southern tip of Patagonia. The rest of the family remained behind with relatives in a town near Lobos. This marked the first of several domestic dislocations for Juan.

One year after his departure, Mario Tomás was sufficiently settled in his new environment to send for his wife and sons. A naval vessel carried them on the 2,500-kilometer (1,600-mile) voyage to Río Gallegos, and from there they made the overland journey to Chank Aike.

For the two boys the trip opened up an invigorating new world full of unfamiliar sights and sounds, fraught with hardship and adventure. At his new home Juan received the first present his father ever gave him, a .22-caliber rifle, with which he learned to hunt. He also learned about sheep-raising and grew to appreciate the work of the ranch dogs. He would forever retain his high regard for the canine. He would also bear the effects of a tapeworm cyst transmitted by one of his father's dogs and lodged in his liver.[11]

The rural workers, or peons, lived under oppressive conditions in Patagonia. Many were Chilean (chilotes, as they were commonly called); some were immigrants from Europe. They found it all but impossible to acquire land of their own because of the concentration of ownership in the hands of a few corporations and families, nor did they enjoy legal protection against mistreatment by the owners and their agents.[12] There is no way to know how much of an impression this environment of social injustice made upon the young Juan.

The years at Chank Aike tested the Perón family. Patagonian winters were of exceptional length and severity. Snow and bone-chilling tempera-tures often accompanied the ceaseless winds. Indeed, Juan came close to tragedy on one occasion, when he suffered an exposure that froze two of his toes and caused the nails to fall off, but he recovered without permanent harm.[13] In 1904, a winter extreme even by Patagonian standards brought ruin to the ranch and convinced Mario Tomás to seek more amenable surroundings. He moved his family to the territory of Chubut in northern Patagonia, where he once again set out to make his living as a small rancher.

Perón's recollection of his mother during those arduous years suggests a formidable matriarch undaunted by the primitive life. "We saw in her the chief of the household, but also the physician, counsellor and friend of those in need. . . . We had no secrets from her, and when we smoked cigarettes on the sly, we didn't worry when she was present."[14] Her talent for the healing arts, which later led her to the vocation of midwifery, greatly impressed Juan. He occasionally assisted her when she provided first aid, which under frontier conditions approximated the practice of medicine. He would inherit her self-confidence in medical matters. A rugged horsewoman, she often joined her husband and sons on the hunt. Round-faced and heavyset, she represented to her younger child the dominant figure of the family.

Mario Tomás seems to have been a stern father, not reluctant to use the rod or his hands to rectify the behavior of his offspring. Perón referred to him as an "austere man."[15] From the sparse evidence available, it is difficult to detect any strong bonds or warmth between father and son. The distinguishing mark of Mario Tomás was his restless, apparently indolent pursuit of the rural life. In Chubut he moved from town to town before settling on a sheep ranch in the interior. By this time Juan had been sent away to school in Buenos Aires.

In the early years at Chank Aike, one of Mario Tomás' old friends had come to the ranch to tutor the boys, but to obtain a formal education, both Mario Avelino and Juan had to make the long trip back to Buenos Aires, a world away from their parents. In 1904, Juan enrolled in an elementary school in the center of the city and lived with relatives of his paternal grandmother. Later he studied at two different schools in the wealthy suburb of Olivos. His brother, meanwhile, contracted pleurisy and had to return home to Patagonia. He remained there, following in the footsteps of his bucolic father, while Juan persevered in the capital. Only during summer vacations could he rejoin the family in Chubut.

The difficult adjustment to city life, the transition from the unfettered life of the ranch to the discipline of the classroom, and the need to get by on his own without the support of his immediate family posed challenges for the boy, but he was equal to them. As he later reminisced, "At ten, my way of thinking was not as a child, but almost as a man. In Buenos Aires I managed alone, and the skirts of my mother or grandmother did not attract me as they did other kids my age. I endeavored to be a man and proceeded on that basis. It is logical that, being 2,000 kilometers from home, I would have many chances to prove myself."[16] The little gaucho grew into a strapping adolescent, big for his age, devoted to sports and barely passing his courses at school.

By his fifteenth year he seemed to be complying with his father's wish that he emulate his famous grandfather. The subjects he took in school would qualify him for admission to the study of medicine at the university, but then he changed directions by sitting for and passing the entrance examination for the Colegio Militar, the army's military academy. (The reason he later gave for the switch was that some schoolmates decided to become officers, and they persuaded him to join them.[17]) Mario Tomás gave his blessing, and on March 1, 1911, Juan Perón donned the uniform of a military cadet.

The army had recently undergone a series of reforms[18] designed to strengthen its capacity to defend the national boundaries and meet what was perceived to be a threat from Chile. In an effort to professionalize the officer corps, graduation from the academy became a prerequisite for regular commissions. Among other changes was the widespread utilization of German officers in training programs, resulting from a judgment that the military needs of Argentina could be better served by the German army's strategy of offensive warfare than by the concept of a static defense advocated by the French.[19] Until the outbreak of World War I, German instructors taught hundreds of officers and cadets. At the academy, close-order drill and the manual of arms were performed in the German style, and a German captain served as an attaché.

Military life posed no difficulties for the young Perón. Having survived Patagonia, he was hardly tested by the physical ordeals imposed upon cadets. The feature that most attracted him was the camaraderie of the barracks. He had never known a secure family environment, and the institution to which he now belonged furnished a substitute that filled the void. A middling student,[20] Perón received his commission as a second lieutenant on December 13, 1913, and entered the infantry.

This put him on one side of the keen rivalry between the two major branches of the army. The cavalry had a glorious tradition dating back to the war of independence and attracted upper-middle-class youths who had learned to ride horseback on their families' country estates, while the infantry tended to attract boys from the lower-middle class, often the sons of immigrant parents.[21] Political struggles within the officer corps would one day reflect this division.

The first phase of Juan Perón's military career lacked distinction. For five years he served with an infantry regiment in the northeastern river ports of Paraná and Santa Fe. His fitness reports[22] show ratings in the "very good" category, which was the third-highest grade given. They also record a series of minor infractions of unspecified rules. One of his superiors called him an "officer of the future," but the chief of the regiment expressed reservations due to his disciplinary problem. On December 31, 1915, he was promoted to lieutenant.

A brief stint at the war arsenal in Buenos Aires followed. His grades had slipped down to the "good" category (except for a "very good" in bayonet handling). However, he showed some improvement by the end of 1919 and his report contained the notation "He is an excellent instructor."[23]

In 1920 he was transferred to the school for noncommissioned officers at the big Campo de Mayo garrison outside the capital. Boys from all over the country, many of them lower-class in origin, trained there for careers in the army and a chance for admittance to the military academy. The assignment caused the young lieutenant to come into his own as a teacher and leader.

The comments of his chief of battalion depict a new Perón:

> He is robust, has good presence and a correct military attitude; animated and determined, he transmits his military fiber to the troops he instructs. He lives his profession intensely and is always ready to do more. An outstanding instructor and a very good leader of troops. Good at gymnastics and drawing. He is prolific in his work. . . . An excellent comrade.[24]

Carlos V. Aloé, later to become one of Perón's most loyal and sycophantic acolytes, entered the school in 1922 and was assigned to the lieutenant's company. "Perón had great magnetism," he recalled, "and really cared for his men. If some of them couldn't go into town on Sunday for lack of money, he'd lend them some."[25] Aloé confirmed Perón's total absorption in his work. "He lived not only a barracks' life, but also the life of his men and of his company. . . . He stayed in the barracks and went out only on Sundays and off-duty days. . . . He was a true father to us."[26] Another subordinate has testified: "He taught us how to eat. Many of us lacked good manners, and he educated us in this respect."[27] A natural talent for teaching and communication was emerging.

While at the school, Perón produced his first published work. He contributed illustrations to a translation of a German book of exercises for soldiers and a couple of chapters to a manual for aspiring noncoms. (One of them dealt with personal hygiene and offered such rudimentary advice as "Wash your hands."[28])

Two qualities that were to serve him well throughout his entire life began to assert themselves during this period. One was his capacity for long hours of intense work, the other a charismatic appeal. Attentiveness to the personal needs of others was an important component of the latter. Also contributing were, as Perón once put it in a moment of self-analysis, his "spontaneity and peasantlike way of improvising."[29] There was something refreshingly different about the earthy, unpretentious way he talked. Yet this capacity to attract coexisted with a need to keep people at a discreet distance. He virtually never used the second person singular in addressing people, which in Spanish connotes intimacy.

It was during this period that Perón's passion for sports proved useful to his career, as he made improvements and innovations in the physical-fitness programs at the school. He introduced basketball into the army and encouraged the practice of a wide range of sports. A U.S. embassy biographical sketch reported that "he used to make a practice of taking on the winners of track events and boxing matches among the men under his command and defeating them."[30] Photographs from this epoch show the handsome captain (promoted from lieutenant in 1924) towering over his trainees as he supervised them at play.[31]

Perón's favorite active sport was fencing, at which he attained great proficiency despite the fact that nature endowed him with arms that were short in proportion to the rest of his body. He was army champion and even participated in matches at the aristocratic Jockey Club in Buenos Aires.[32]

The manly art of self-defense was relatively new to Argentina and found a great enthusiast in Perón.[33] As a young officer, he participated in the founding of a boxing club in Paraná. In order to raise funds, he organized a match between one of his assistants and a visiting English sailor. The assistant took sick on the day of the fight and Perón agreed to substitute. He was much taller than the Englishman, who fought from a low crouch. The Argentine's first punch landed atop his opponent's head and resulted in a broken right hand. For the rest of the bout, Perón took a sound thumping. Afterward, instead of seeking medical treatment, he let nature take its course. The fractured metacarpal bone eventually healed, leaving a marked deformity that Gene Tunney was able to detect as a boxing injury when he met and shook hands with Perón many years later.[34]

On March 12, 1926, Perón drew an assignment to the war academy (Escuela Superior de Guerra). The academy had been set up in 1900 as part of the attempt to raise professional standards within the army.[35] It trained midlevel officers heading for leadership within the army establishment. Perón spent nearly three years of intensive study at the academy.

Several months after commencing his studies at the academy, Perón attended a reception for military officers in the Buenos Aires district of Palermo, where he met a seventeen-year-old girl from the neighborhood. Aurelia Tizón, or Potota, as she was nicknamed by her family, taught in a local elementary school. Blond (by Argentine standards, which apply the term to anything but the darkest shades of brunette), petite and wistfully pretty, she came from a respectable middle-class family. Her father, Cipriano Tizón, ran a photography shop. One hears only glowing descriptions of Aurelia. She played the guitar and the piano. According to a primary-school classmate, Julián Sancerni Jiménez (an eminent ward-boss politician in Palermo), she was "very distinguished, very proper."[36] Not long after their initial encounter, Perón and Aurelia Tizón became *novios* (a relationship somewhere between going steady and formal engagement), and on January 5, 1929, they were married.

Aurelia's youth and the fourteen-year age differential were not unusual factors in marriage by Argentine norms. Perón had displayed no prior interest in matrimony, nor had he involved himself in any notorious escapades of an amatory nature, presumably due to his total involvement in military life. However, it was common practice for military officers to marry into middle-class families and settle into stable lives. Perón was no doubt ready to follow the pattern.

Another noteworthy aspect of this period was the reappearance of his mother and father in Buenos Aires. Mario Tomás had finally given up on Chubut and had left his older son on the ranch to take care of things. Before his marriage, Perón alternated between staying at his parents' residence in the district of Flores and joining several comrades in a rented apartment closer to the center of town. Two months prior to the wedding and one day before his sixty-fourth birthday, Mario Tomás died, ending an interval of familial stability for his son.[37]

As the 1920s drew to a close, ripples from the Great Depression were making their way across the vast distances separating Argentina from the rest of the world. The country was about to undergo radical transformation, and Captain Juan D. Perón would watch from the front row.

4

Teacher, Author, Traveler

The crisis facing Argentina in 1930 ended a brief interlude of political democracy that had interrupted a long era of conservative rule. One year after the 1852 overthrow of Rosas, a national convention had adopted a constitution modeled in large part after the Constitution of the United States.[1] A series of elected presidents then embarked upon efforts to unify the nation, secure its borders and promote modernization.[2] The means used to develop the nation were economic liberalism, immigration and improvements in mass education. But real power never left the hands of an oligarchic elite that controlled the economy. Democratic forms belied the autocratic nature of a system based upon electoral fraud and coercion.

The middle class, whose ranks were expanding with upwardly mobile immigrants, found itself shut off from meaningful participation in politics. The first dramatic protest against this exclusion occurred in 1889, when a group of intellectuals formed an organization called the Civic Union and unsuccessfully attempted to overthrow the government by force. From the ashes of this failure came a new political party, the Radical Civic Union (a deceptive name, inasmuch as these middle-class reformers were hardly radical). Protests by the Radicals against the institutionalized sham and several aborted rebellions created so much pressure that in 1912 the Congress enacted a law providing for the secret ballot, compulsory male suffrage and honest registration of voters. The Radicals won the next presidential election four years later.

The leader of the party and new president was one of the most fascinating characters in modern Argentine history. Hipólito Yrigoyen was the illegitimate son of a Basque blacksmith.[3] By nature withdrawn and secretive, he cultivated these traits during the conspiratorial phase of the Radical Civic Union. He made no speeches and rare public appearances, but instead relied upon personal contact and face-to-face bargaining, which built up around him a large, loyal following. Not even his assumption of the presidency altered the ascetic lifestyle that had become his trademark. Sumner Welles, who served as chargé d'affaires at the American embassy in Argentina during the Yrigoyen era, found him to possess "a quantity of innate force and inherent greatness of character, which his peculiar physical characteristics—a pineapple-shaped head, a Mongolian mask with straggling threads on each side of his mouth which did service for a mustache, and an evasive gaze—could not dispel."[4] His nickname was El Peludo, the armadillo. When he took office, he was already sixty-four years old.

Aside from broadening the political process, the Radical victory did not herald any dramatic assaults on the existing power structure. The party had neither the will nor the imagination to translate its nationalistic impulses from rhetoric to effective action. The urban middle class, most of which worked at white-collar jobs, identified its economic prosperity with that of the elite. This meant that a government responsive mainly to middle-class needs would perpetuate an economic system that relied upon the export of grain and meat, the import of manufactured goods and infusions of foreign capital, rather than adopt policies to encourage the growth of local industry. In addition to stability, the Radicals provided the middle class with access to an expanding number of government jobs. The party had little of substance to offer urban workers.

El Peludo's style eventually precipitated a latent schism within the party and the formation of a Radical faction opposed to the personalism characteristic of his administration. The Argentine constitution provided for a six-year presidential term, with no immediate reelection permitted. In 1922, a so-called anti-personalist Radical won the presidency, but Yrigoyen refused to withdraw from politics. Six years later, at the age of seventy-six, he was again elected to the highest office. The approaching Depression proved more than his advanced age (or senility, as some said) could cope with, and opposition to his opaque maneuvers and increasingly autocratic methods gave birth to political chaos.

The Argentine army could not escape the turbulence of the times. The Yrigoyen government had deeply disturbed the military establishment with its unsubtle displays of political favoritism in the handling of promotions and other personnel matters.[5] The use of the army during provincial interventions* likewise disgusted the military. This in turn divided the officer corps into pro- and anti-government factions and made the latter receptive to the blandishments of the regime's political opponents, who were eager to enlist military support in efforts to oust Yrigoyen. El Peludo

---

* The Argentine constitution created a federal system but authorized the federal government to take over (or "intervene") provincial governments for vaguely specified reasons. Resort to intervention has proved irresistibly tempting to presidents as a method of not only resolving political disputes but also turning provincial confrontations to the political advantage of the party holding national power.

could call upon scant moral capital to counter these siren calls, since the Radicals themselves had tried to provoke military interventions against prior Conservative governments.

By early 1930, two groups within the army were seriously considering a military coup.[6] One was led by General José F. Uriburu, a dashing, highly respected cavalry officer who had received military training in Germany. A former Conservative deputy (congressman), he had family ties to the aristocracy. His faction reflected the influence of ultra-Catholic nationalists and those who advocated the abolition of political parties and the establishment of an authoritarian system of government based on theories currently in vogue in Italy, Spain and France. The other faction counted General Agustín P. Justo as its most distinguished member. Minister of war during the anti-personalist Radical interregnum (1922–1928), General Justo was a charismatic leader. His group sought to put the country back on a firm constitutional footing under civilian rule and to cure the ailing economy by administering even stronger doses of nineteenth-century economic liberalism.

Captain Juan D. Perón found himself in the midst of this turmoil when he graduated from the war academy and drew an assignment to the army's general staff on January 26, 1929. Although he claimed to have voted for Yrigoyen in 1916[7] and had married into a family mildly active in Radical politics,[8] the scent of conspiracy soon proved irresistible to him.[9]

In June 1930 a major he had known for years persuaded him to attend a private meeting at which General Uriburu was speaking to a group of officers. Perón found him to be a "perfect gentleman and a good man,"[10] and was much impressed. Although he understood perfectly the ultra-conservative political notions espoused by the general, his decision to support Uriburu did not rest upon any ideological commitment. What monopolized his interest were problems of tactics.

Throughout July and August, Perón worked to solidify and amplify the movement. His lack of progress thoroughly disheartened him, as did the incompetence and disorganization of the officers surrounding Uriburu. One of his tasks, to secure the participation of the school for noncommissioned officers, had been frustrated by countermeasures taken by the Ministry of War on behalf of the government. Perón saw little hope of support from the powerful Campo de Mayo garrison. On September 3, he presented his verbal resignation from active participation in the movement.

Perón's withdrawal lasted fewer than twenty-four hours. On the next day he met with officers with whom he had previously been in touch in efforts to unify the army behind Uriburu but who had remained with the more numerous anti-government faction led by General Justo. They favored the overthrow of Yrigoyen but had not readied themselves for a coup. Their main dispute with the Uriburu group was its plan to exclude civilians from the government they proposed to form, a step toward open-ended military rule that kept many officers from joining the conspiracy. Perón decided to recast his lot with the pro-Justo faction. Whether he switched because of a preference for Justo's political intentions or a desire to be on what he thought would be the winning side is not clear.

Although confusion and lack of preparation beset the Uriburu faction, events forced the conspirators to act. Yrigoyen's minister of war resigned because of conflict and indecision within the administration regarding the measures to be taken against the now-not-so-secret military plot. Student demonstrations and growing tension in Buenos Aires combined with uncertainties caused by an illness that confined the president to his home to create a propitious climate for bold action. On September 6, General Uriburu resolved to make his move.

The actual number of troops that marched on the capital on that day was rather modest. Uriburu led the cadets and officers from the Colegio Militar and a few other troops. But the Yrigoyen government could count upon no military support at all. The reactions of the units garrisoned in the city remained in doubt until the last moment. In addition, as the Uriburu column arrived in downtown Buenos Aires, it met with resistance from a handful of civilian snipers as it passed the palatial structure that houses the municipal sanitation works, and afterward as it approached the Congress building.

Captain Perón made a marginal contribution to the unfolding events. On the morning of the sixth he visited several of the military units in the area to urge them to remain in their barracks. He also secured the use of an armored car, and with gunfire reverberating in the vicinity of the Congress, inched his way through streets overrun by civilians welcoming the coup. His destination was the Casa de Gobierno, or Government House, in the historic Plaza de Mayo. The building, commonly known as the Casa Rosada (Pink House) for obvious reasons, rests on a slope on one side of the rectangular plaza. To its right stand the massive Bank of the Nation and the neoclassical cathedral. The Casa Rosada was originally constructed as an annex to a fort that fronted on the river, at a time when the muddy waters of the Río de la Plata extended much further inland.

As Perón approached the Casa Rosada and ventured outside the protection of the armored car, he found what he later referred to as an "arrogant mob" beating on its doors.[11] It was the first time he had ever set foot on the premises. Unruly elements were still roaming the halls. After helping to restore some semblance of order, he returned to the armored car and drove slowly up the Avenida de Mayo to the Congress, where scattered shots indicated that a few hard-core civilian supporters had not yet given up their defense of the government.

Perón spent the rest of the day and most of the night on security patrols charged with preventing civilian disturbances in the city. He claimed credit for saving several buildings, including a hotel, from fire. This first-hand experience would be forgotten several decades later when he would attempt to duck responsibility for failing to control mob behavior.

Perón's analysis of what came to be known as the Revolution of 1930 placed decisive weight upon the actions of the large numbers of porteños who took to the streets in support of the coup. In his view, General Uriburu faced deep trouble when the snipers held up his cadets near the Congress. "Only a miracle would save the revolution. The people of Buenos Aires, who in a human avalanche spilled into the streets shouting . . . 'Long live the revolution' . . . made this miracle."[12] The dubiousness of his conclusion is less important than its influence upon his attitudes toward mass mobilization.

The fall of Yrigoyen, who was removed to the island of Martín García in the mouth of the Río de la Plata, brought to an end a sequence of constitutionally (if at times fraudulently) elected presidents dating back to 1862. Several days after the revolution, the Argentine Supreme Court granted legal recognition to the new provisional government. An unfortunate precedent had been set. Even more ominous was the army's overt assumption of political power. Argentina has yet to recover from this corruption of its democratic process.

On the day after the revolution, Perón was appointed private secretary to the new minister of war. But the job did not last very long. General Uriburu, having declared himself provisional president, immediately purged from the administration pro-Justo elements, in whose ranks Perón was now numbered. On October 28, the president signed a decree removing him from the government and naming him a professor of military history at the war academy. Before assuming his new post, the young captain was required to do a two-month stint in 1931 as part of an army commission investigating charges that foreigners were penetrating Argentina's northern frontier.[13] Perhaps this was his penance for switching sides.

While Perón was patrolling the Bolivian border, President Uriburu tried without success to impose his notions of reform upon the Argentine people, but his ultra-right-wing policies and proposals aroused so much resistance that he was finally obliged to call elections for November 1931.[14] At the same time he proscribed the participation of the Radical Civic Union. The Conservatives reorganized themselves into an entity called the National Democratic party and developed an electoral alliance, known as the Concordancia, with the anti-personalist Radicals and some Socialists. They then nominated General Justo as their presidential candidate. As the police ignored widespread fraud at the polls, Justo defeated the coalition candidate of the Socialist and Democratic Progressive parties. This marked the start of what Argentines would refer to as the "Infamous Decade."

Juan Perón was promoted to major on December 31, 1931. His tour of duty at the war academy did not fully occupy him; he also served stints as adjutant to the chief of the general staff and aide-de-camp to the minister of war. His competent performance in these posts distinguished him among his contemporaries. But the most significant work he did during this period took place at the war academy, where he honed his teaching skills and published several books on military history.

The eminent British historian George Pendle has pointed out that "Perón was not a military man nor a politician, but rather a student and then a professor . . . and when he gained power he kept teaching, in his own way, giving lectures to the [Argentine] people."[15] Pendle's downgrading of Perón's political talents is open to dispute, but his insight into the didactic side of the Perón personality hits the mark nicely. The teaching experience at the academy was a crucial phase in Perón's preparation for a political career. It made him comfortable on his feet in front of audiences and effective in conveying his thoughts; he became skilled at extemporization. The military setting put no premium on the type of elaborate, elegant rhetoric valued by civilian politicians, many of whom had learned their debating techniques in the universities. Perón's straightforward style set him apart from them in a way that many people found positive. He was to spend much of his life lecturing to groups large and small, an aspect of his career observers have tended to overlook.

The academy years also marked the emergence of Perón the author.[16] His first literary venture of note had appeared in a military journal in 1928 and dealt with the 1810–1814 campaigns of the Argentine liberator, General José de San Martín, in what is now Bolivia. As a professor he published three books on military history: *El frente oriental de la guerra mundial en 1914* ("The Eastern Front in the World War in 1914"); *Apuntes de historia militar* ("Notes on Military History") one year later in 1933; and a two-volume study, *La guerra ruso-japonesa* ("The Russo-Japanese War") in 1933 and 1934. He would continue his work as a military historian after his departure from the academy and produce articles on various campaigns of San Martín and on the Franco-Prussian War of 1870.

Neither originality nor profundity graced Perón's professional writing. Borrowing heavily from other authors (usually foreigners), he refrained from imposing his own intellect upon his material. In criticizing his study of the war between Japan and Russia, one of his superiors noted that he merely recounted the various campaigns "without formulating personal appraisals of the leadership of the operations."[17]

On one occasion his derivative approach to scholarship got him into trouble. A general accused him and a coauthor (his teacher of military history at the war academy) of failing to cite him in the bibliography of an article they had written. Apparently they had used without attribution a publication by the general. A military tribunal of honor ordered Perón and his colleague to make an apology.[18]

By far the most revealing of his publications was *Apuntes de historia militar*, prepared specifically as a text for the military-history course at the academy. In it Perón expounded the theme of the "nation in arms." The source for this concept came from the 1927 Argentine edition of a Spanish translation of *Das Volk in Waffen* ("The Nation in Arms"), a book written by German General Colman von der Goltz in 1883.[19] Postulating the inevitability of war as a natural state of mankind, von der Goltz argued that nations must remain on a perpetual military footing in order to insure peace and tranquility as well as to carry out their international policies. Perón adopted this as "the most modern theory of national defense," requiring "integral mobilization and organization of every citizen."[20]

Although his professional interest consistently focused upon military history, Patagonia continued to fascinate him. He made several trips to the region, and in 1935 and 1936 published in book form a curious compilation entitled *Toponomia patagónica de etimología araucana* ("Patagonian Place Names of Araucanian [Indian] Origin"). While working for the minister of war he delivered a lecture stressing the strategic importance of the south, its vulnerability to Chilean expansion and its neglect by the federal government. Shortly thereafter (and perhaps as a result thereof), he was named military attaché to the Argentine embassy in Santiago, Chile.

Argentina's relations with her trans-Andean neighbor in 1936 were lukewarm, not only because of the latter's supposed designs on Patagonia but also as a result of a longstanding dispute over the Beagle Channel (both countries claimed several tiny islands at the eastern mouth of the Channel), and the slighting of Chilean sensitivities by Argentine efforts to bring to an end the bloody Chaco War between Bolivia and Paraguay.

Perón purchased a secondhand car for the long drive from Buenos Aires across the pampa to Mendoza, and then over the Uspallata Pass in the shadow of Mount Aconcagua, the highest point in the Western Hemisphere, to Santiago. During the trip he instructed Potota in the use of the pistol, not out of any practical necessity but rather to satisfy his pedagogical impulses. The couple reached their destination in late March.

At his new post, Perón utilized his pleasing personality and appearance to win friends among the Chileans, who nicknamed him Che Panamavida.* He traveled extensively, especially to the south, and visited the frontier

* There is no adequate translation for the uniquely Argentine expression Che. It is a nickname applied by friends to one another conversationally. Non-Argentine Spanish-speaking people often use it as a general sobriquet for individual Argentines. Panamavida was a brand of carbonated soft drink to which Perón was quite partial.

between Chile and Argentina, an excursion of more strategic than tourist interest. On December 31, 1936, he was promoted to lieutenant colonel.

It was not until long after his return to Buenos Aires in March of 1938 that the first shadows of suspicion began to fall upon his Chilean sojourn. When he emerged as a political figure in the early 1940s, his enemies gave currency to an accusation that the Chilean government had expelled him for espionage.[21] Exaggeration attended the story, and before long Perón was said to have been caught red-handed passing intelligence secrets to German agents in Santiago.[22]

The truth of the matter, spelled out in a 1943 Chilean magazine article[23] that corroborates a report written in 1938 by a U.S. military attaché,[24] is more complex as well as somewhat ironic. An integral part of an Argentine and Chilean attaché's job was to obtain by any possible means, including the theft of documents, intelligence about the military plans of his host country. No doubt following orders, Perón organized a small spy network to obtain secret information from the Chilean armed forces. His activities drew the attention of Chilean military intelligence, but they never moved against him. Instead, they waited for his successor, Major Eduardo Lonardi.

One explanation for the delay may derive from the political implications of the incident. A leftist government unsympathetic to the military's budgetary demands was then governing Chile. The discovery of an Argentine spy ring might help pressure the Chilean Congress to increase military expenditures. But its disclosure had to be timed carefully for maximum dramatic effect, and the most opportune moment may not have arrived until Perón had already returned to Argentina.[25]

According to the U.S. military attaché, "suspicion led the Chilean Military Intelligence Department, and their secret service, to take advantage of Lonardi, as a new arrival, and make a plan to trip him and his collaborators. Evidently they fell for the frame-up, hook, line and sinker. The plan was to offer the Argentine military attaché certain secret data (believed to be Chilean War Department plans of offensive and defensive action in case of war with Argentina) for 75,000 Chilean pesos."[26]

The Chilean officers allowed themselves to be recruited by Perón's inside contact, an ex-lieutenant in the Chilean army, and on Saturday afternoon, April 2, 1938, delivered the bogus documents to the apartment of an Argentine couple also involved in the Perón ring. Major Lonardi was photographing the papers with his Contax camera and had placed the cash payoff in a small handbag on the table when Chilean detectives burst into the room and arrested the conspirators. Major Lonardi was declared persona non grata and was recalled by his government. The affair did not adversely affect his military career, but it created bad blood between Perón and Lonardi, who had reason to believe his predecessor had suspected he was under surveillance but had failed to warn him. Two decades later Lonardi would have an opportunity to settle the score.*

A final intriguing aspect of the affair was that a special U.S. ambassador to a conference in Buenos Aires was furnishing the writer of the report with information about the spy ring. The special ambassador was a mining engineer-turned-diplomat named Spruille Braden, whose path would later cross Perón's in a much more dramatic fashion.

Perón's return to Buenos Aires was marred by the illness of Aurelia. In July she entered a sanatorium and underwent an operation for uterine cancer. On September 10, 1938, Perón became a widower. The marriage had lasted ten years and was by all accounts a happy one. It also seems to have been a very ordinary one, except for the couple's failure to produce offspring.

The loss of Aurelia left Perón at loose ends. He set out on an 18,000-kilometer (10,800-mile) odyssey by automobile through Patagonia. By early 1939 he was back in Buenos Aires at work on mundane administrative matters. He sought diversion by helping Father Antonio D'Alessio, an old friend, provide athletic facilities and other forms of recreation for neighborhood boys. At this point his life had sunk to an emotional low, but suddenly a deus ex machina in the form of an assignment to Italy rescued him.

Years later Perón would claim that the minister of war complained to him that Argentine military attachés in Europe had been submitting inadequate reports about the impending outbreak of hostilities; he directed Perón to go abroad as a military attaché and analyze the situation.[27]

This reminiscence betrayed one of his less attractive characteristics, a cavalier disdain for truth. Perón's initial assignment placed him with an Italian division training for mountain warfare. The slopes of the Alps could hardly be deemed a fit location for the gathering of useful intelligence.

Wearing a mourner's armband on the left sleeve of his uniform jacket, Lieutenant Colonel Perón bade a dockside farewell to Father D'Alessio, some of the neighborhood boys and various other friends, and on February 17, 1939, set out from Buenos Aires aboard the *Conte Grande*, an Italian liner bound for Europe. The two years he was to spend away from his native land would leave deep and lasting impressions.

Perón's dossier indicates that between July 1, 1939, and May 31, 1940,

---

* Perón never talked about the matter on the record, except for a carefully worded denial that he had ever been expelled from Chile for espionage. He did not, however, deny engaging in espionage. And he added that the person who had in fact been expelled was his successor, "Leonardi." (As a common practice Perón would mispronounce the names of people with whom he was displeased as a way of deprecating them.) T. Luca de Tena, *Yo, Juan Domingo Perón*, p. 189.

he served with various alpine units of the Italian army and attended a school for mountain warfare. His hosts sent back glowing fitness reports. From June 1940 until his return in December he assisted the military attaché at the Argentine embassy in Rome.[28]

Although his official record does not confirm it, there is some evidence that he traveled to Budapest, Berlin, Albania and the German-Russian border, which he briefly crossed into the Soviet Union at a time when the Hitler-Stalin pact was still in effect. He may also have visited France after its surrender to Germany.[29] He stood among the crowd in the Plaza Venezia in Rome when Benito Mussolini made the speech propelling Italy into the war on the German side.[30] Despite his subsequent claims that he met with Mussolini[31] (and even gave him advice[32]), this was the closest "contact" between Perón and Il Duce.

What he saw and heard in Europe moved him, but there is no contemporary evidence, either first- or secondhand, to establish what he actually felt and thought at the time. The organization and mobilization of the German and Italian peoples under Hitler and Mussolini fascinated him.[33] He saw the German and (especially) the Italian systems as working toward a genuine social "democracy" that seemed to him to represent the political wave of the future. He also claimed he first became aware of the importance of trade unionism as a result of courses he took in Turin.[34] It is likely that he noted with interest the role Italian unions played within a Fascist state.

Perón's stay in Europe probably influenced him in at least two other respects. Mussolini's use of mass spectacle as a political tool surely must have impressed him. In addition, his contacts in Italy, and perhaps also in Germany, must have exposed him to the virulent anticommunism that was providing much of the intellectual and emotional impetus behind the Fascist and Nazi movements.

Perón saw nothing morally repugnant about Nazi Germany or Fascist Italy. He viewed them through the prism of his military background and found many features of both systems of government admirable. The fact that trains ran on time counted for a great deal, while the absence of free speech did not disturb him. Thoroughly pragmatic, he would adjust his attitudes as the fortunes of war turned against Italy and Germany.*

On his return he passed through Spain, where he saw the devastation wreaked by the recent civil war. He would constantly evoke the horror with which these memories filled him as a justification of his own refusal to take action that might plunge Argentina into civil strife. Despite his

---

* Several years later, when frantic efforts were being made to discredit him, the U.S. embassy in Buenos Aires requested the State Department to investigate the training he received in Italy for indications of political indoctrination. Cabot to secretary of state, 835.00/12-545, December 5, 1945. There is no record of the results of such an inquiry, if in fact it ever took place.

claim that he spent six months there,[35] he made only a brief tourist's journey through Spain on the way to Lisbon, where he boarded a Portuguese vessel bound for Rio de Janiero.[36]

He reached Buenos Aires in the closing days of 1940, and on January 8, 1941, received orders to go to Mendoza, where he served as an instructor in an army school for mountain warfare. He later asserted that on his return from abroad he gave a series of secret lectures about his impressions of the situation in Europe; as a result he was "exiled" to Mendoza.[37]

In all probability, this explanation bears no relationship to the truth. The period between his return to Argentina and his assignment to Mendoza seems much too brief for a series of lectures, especially since Christmas and the midsummer holidays also fell during this interval. Moreover, a tour of duty at a school for mountain warfare would seem a logical next assignment for an officer who had just completed his studies at a similar school in Italy.

The tour in Mendoza lasted for a bit more than a year. Perón received his promotion to full colonel on December 31, 1941, and at the same time became commanding officer of a detachment of mountain troops. He conducted classes and exercises in his new specialties, mountain warfare and skiing. He also helped younger officers prepare for future study at the war academy. The personal ties he developed in Mendoza would prove most helpful to him at a later date. This was especially true in the case of two of his colleagues, General Edelmiro J. Farrell and Lieutenant Colonel Domingo A. Mercante.

The careers of Farrell and Perón evidenced remarkable similarity.[38] Farrell had served on the general staff and during the 1920s had been attached to an Italian alpine regiment. He was now the director of the instruction center for mountain troops. He liked to play the guitar, spent much of his life in Mendoza, was totally disinterested in political and social issues, and could never be accused of intellectual celerity.

Perón first met Mercante during his tour at the school for noncommissioned officers. They renewed their acquaintance in the west, where Mercante served under Farrell. Three years younger than Perón, Mercante impressed the colonel with his quiet intelligence, loyalty and capacity for hard work.

On March 18, 1942, Perón was shifted to the inspectorate of mountain troops in Buenos Aires, under the command of General Farrell. Within a short time Mercante received a similar transfer. The two men rapidly became enmeshed in a new military conspiracy against the government. It looked like a repeat of 1930, but this time history would take a different course.

Part III

The Colonel

(1943-1946)

5

The Revolution
of 1943

While Perón's military assignments took him to Chile, Italy and the slopes of the Andes, events at home and abroad would soon shake Argentine society to its roots. The ruling elite's use of fraud and force and its commitment to policies that kept the economy under foreign domination generated deep dissatisfaction. At the same time, the outbreak of World War II aroused divisive passions and brought to the surface a long-simmering feud with the United States.

The democratic process in Argentina had reached putrefaction during the Infamous Decade.[1] Despite the emotions unleashed by Yrigoyen's death in 1933 and the transformation of his funeral into a political demonstration of hitherto unwitnessed proportions,[2] the Radical party could not muster effective, principled resistance to the ruling Concordancia. The Radicals remained badly split, some defecting to the Concordancia, others abstaining from politics. The Socialists played the game according to rules that helped keep them permanently out of power, and thereby furnished a veneer of legitimacy to a corrupt system. The result was widespread loss of faith in democracy and party politics, especially among the young.

The economic policies followed by the Conservatives during the 1930s favored the wealthy ranchers. The Depression provoked some of the member nations of the British Commonwealth to press for an increased share in the English market, a proposal that would have greatly reduced imports of beef from Argentina and would have brought ruin upon an economy already badly hurt by the world crisis. Argentina's response was to negotiate a treaty tying its economy even closer to that of Great Britain; the British would continue to purchase beef from Argentina in return for a reduction of tariffs on imports from Britain. Argentine nationalists attacked the treaty as a classic example of imperialism, rendering Argentina's agricultural economy complementary to British industry. Feeding their resentment were incidents such as British opposition to a badly needed road-building program launched by President Justo, on the ground that it put the Argentine government in competition with the British-owned railroads.[3]

Foreign control of their economy was difficult for many Argentines to accept. Just prior to the outbreak of World War II, virtually all the Argentine railroads were owned by British capital, and nearly 45 percent of Argentine industry belonged to foreigners. U.S. and Swiss companies controlled the public utilities, the automobile industry was North American, and the best construction firms in Buenos Aires were German and Dutch. Non-Argentine corporations dominated the critical meatpacking sector of the economy. Foreigners not only held ownership of basic industries but administered them as well.[4]

The Argentine nationalism behind General Uriburu in 1930 and opposed to the Concordancia during the Infamous Decade displayed a distaste for democracy, a preference for authoritarianism, opposition to British imperialism, an abhorrence of Communism and a very conservative brand of Roman Catholicism. Its adherents took as their model Franco's Spain. While they could not in principle accept Nazi totalitarianism because of its incompatibility with Catholic doctrine,[5] this did not preclude tactical support for the Nazis. Anti-Semitism from time to time surfaced among these right-wing nationalists. It drew sustenance from the popular use of the word *ruso* (Russian) as a nickname for Jews, since most Jewish immigrants came from Russia, and anything Russian readily invoked the specter of international communism.[6]

The 1930s also witnessed the flowering of a more progressive brand of nationalism. A group called FORJA (Fuerza de Orientación Radical de la Joven Argentina, or Radical Orientation Force of Young Argentina) came into existence in 1935 as a result of the desire of a small nucleus of young Radical intellectuals to return their party to the nationalistic stance initiated by Yrigoyen. Members of FORJA attacked not only British imperialism but also the growing economic penetration from the "Yankee colossus of the North." They were increasingly disenchanted with the political maneuvering of their Radical elders and began to search for fresh leadership.

General Justo chose as his successor Roberto M. Ortiz, a former anti-personalist Radical.[7] Having served as attorney for the British railroads and as Justo's finance minister, Ortiz had the full backing of the landowners who comprised the dominant element of the Concordancia. His running mate, Ramón S. Castillo, was an antediluvian Conservative. The Ortiz-Castillo ticket won easily in a rigged election in 1937.

Upon assuming the presidency, Roberto Ortiz proceeded to shock his backers by intervening in provincial elections *because* they were fraudulent, rather than to perpetrate fraud. These and other hints of political liberalism might have threatened the status quo but for a serious illness that struck down the president. A diabetic, Ortiz began to lose his eyesight. In 1940 he had to turn the presidency over to Castillo on a provisional basis, and on June 24, 1942, he resigned because of failing health. He died soon afterward.

Castillo brought to a halt the democratic trend initiated by Ortiz. The new president resorted to federal intervention as a mechanism to corrupt provincial elections. The U.S. declaration of war after the Japanese attack on Pearl Harbor gave him a pretext for imposing a state of siege, which legally authorized him to use a range of politically restrictive measures.

Three months after the German invasion of Poland, World War II arrived on Argentina's doorstep. A squadron of British cruisers trapped the pocket battleship *Graf Spee* in the Río de la Plata, and on December 17, 1939, the German warship was scuttled by her crew outside the harbor of Montevideo, Uruguay. Although the incident occurred in Uruguayan waters, tugboats from nearby Buenos Aires rescued crew members and brought them to Argentina for internment. The spectacle furnished Argentines with an early warning that geographic isolation alone would not shelter them from the global conflict.

In the initial stages of the war in Europe, Argentine neutrality was perfectly consistent with U.S. hemispheric policy.[8] Only after the bombing of Pearl Harbor did relations between the two countries come under serious strain. At a meeting of American foreign ministers in Rio de Janeiro in January 1942, opposition by the Argentine and Chilean representatives frustrated U.S. attempts to secure continental unity on the issue of diplomatic relations with the Axis powers. The only way to achieve unanimity was to accede to Argentine demands that the conference resolve to recommend, rather than require, the rupture of relations. This compromise brought the wrath of U.S. Secretary of State Cordell Hull down upon the U.S. delegate to the conference, Undersecretary Sumner Welles, who advocated a more flexible, patient approach toward Argentina.[9]

As a result of the conference, Argentina and Chile became the only Latin American nations to maintain ties with Germany, Italy and Japan. Thus began the mini-cold war that kept the governments of the United States and Argentina jabbing and growling at each other for the better part of a decade.

The dispute brought to the surface bad feelings that Argentines had long been harboring. The various North American military interventions in Latin America during the days of the big stick and gunboat diplomacy had abraded the sensitivities of many Argentines. Strict nonintervention in the affairs of other nations had transcended mere international law to become an article of quasi-religious faith for them ever since the porteños fought off the British during the colonial era. The Good Neighbor Policy of Franklin D. Roosevelt had been welcomed as a positive step, but did not allay growing fears that U.S. capital would replace that of Britain as a dominant force affecting the Argentine economy. North American efforts to promote Pan-Americanism had always met with suspicion on the part of Argentina. A U.S. embargo on Argentine meat because of fear of contamination by hoof-and-mouth disease made matters even worse, since the Argentines were convinced that it was really a protectionist measure imposed by North American ranchers.[10]

Apart from the minor irritations suffered by U.S. diplomats as a result of Argentine behavior during the prewar years, the prevailing attitude of the great majority of North Americans toward Latin America in general, and Argentina in particular, was consummate disinterest. It took the emotional trauma of Pearl Harbor to convert apathy into worry. At a time when an Axis assault on the Western Hemisphere seemed not only feasible but, in the minds of some, imminent, North Americans could not help but look anxiously to their underbelly. When they did, they discovered that their priority problem was Argentina.

Despite the fact that the Castillo administration had tempered its neutrality with promises to cooperate in efforts to secure the hemisphere from outside attack, North Americans felt that Argentina in 1942 was beginning to tilt alarmingly toward a pro-Axis posture.[11] German agents were operating freely from the cover of their embassy and other fronts, and their espionage activities helped U-boats prey upon shipping in the South Atlantic. The German and Italian training many Argentine officers had received was no secret. Right-wing nationalists did little to disguise their antipathy toward the Allied war effort and appeared to constitute a budding political movement with Nazi or Fascist overtones. Rabidly pro-Nazi newspapers, obviously financed from Berlin, were hawked on the streets of Buenos Aires.

Because of Argentina's neutrality, Washington flatly rejected a bid by a military mission from Buenos Aires to make a deal for armaments. Then, in August of 1942, Brazil declared war on the Axis and began to receive massive arms shipments from the United States as part of a hemispheric defense program.[12] This in turn alarmed the Argentine military, because it shifted to Brazil's favor the balance of power in South America. Argentina looked to Berlin for help. The vicissitudes of war prevented the Germans from supplying weapons to the Argentine army, but the mere request caused the U.S. government to regard the Castillo administration with repugnance.

North Americans were viewing things in simplistic terms during this epoch. From the tabloid press to the pages of the *Harvard Law Review*,[13] commentators sounded shrill warnings against the growth of Fascism in America's own backyard. Yet no one seemed to mind that the Brazilian government receiving U.S. arms was a dictatorship with fascistoid features.

Pressure kept mounting on the State Department to abandon diplomatic niceties and *do* something about Argentina.

Little heed was paid to the complexities of the situation. For example, it was in the best interests of the United States' closest ally, Great Britain, to keep Argentina out of the war.[14] England still very much depended upon Argentine beef and did not want Castillo to jeopardize neutrality status for Argentine shipping. The British also feared that a break with the Axis might tie Argentina irrevocably to the Pan-American bloc of nations under U.S. hegemony and would end an economic dominance that was already slipping from Great Britain. Thus the policy of the Castillo administration promoted the interests of the traditionally pro-English oligarchy.

The assumption took hold in the United States that the great majority of the Argentines were pro-Allied, and that the failure of their government to join in the fight against the Axis was domestically unpopular. In truth, many Argentines sympathized with the Allies because of traditional ties with Great Britain and cultural identification with France. A relatively small number actively approved of the Axis, while a third group embraced opportunism and lined up with the apparent winning side. A substantial portion of the working class, both rural and urban, felt more concern about the day-to-day struggle to make ends meet and did not care who won the war. The overwhelming majority of Argentines supported neutrality as being in the best interest of their country. The widely held view that the war was nothing more than a global contest for economic power fortified this position.[15]

Argentines who protested against the trend toward Fascism in their country and whose accusations attracted publicity in the United States often acted from ulterior motives. Political opponents of Castillo were in the forefront of efforts to paint the administration as pro-Axis and did not hesitate to stretch the truth beyond recognition. Many were outs attempting to become ins, rather than principled adherents of the Allied cause and the democratic way of life. The Communist party of Argentina, following directives from Moscow, hammered away indiscriminately at public figures advocating neutrality, branded them as Fascists and exercised a disproportionate influence on international public opinion.

When Juan Perón relocated himself in Buenos Aires in March 1942, he found the military establishment both divided and restless. One faction lined up behind General Justo, preparing to run for the presidency in 1943 and apparently possessed of sufficient civilian and military support to challenge the Concordancia.[16] Officers supporting Justo were pro-Allied, either because they believed in the Allied cause or because they saw no other way to procure badly needed arms and equipment for the military. This group counterpoised a substantial number of Axis sympathizers who admired the German army or held ultra-conservative, anti-democratic political views. A third group, uncommitted to either side yet favoring neutrality for Argentina, watched from the sidelines. A pair of recent military plots against the government aborted, but conspiratorial winds continued to blow through Campo de Mayo. Out of this matrix emerged a secret military lodge known by the initials GOU.[17]

Secret societies within the military have a long tradition in Latin America. General Justo himself had formed one during the 1920s to oppose Yrigoyen's politicization of the army. Yet the GOU acquired a singular notoriety because of its supposed Nazi orientation and its domination by Juan Perón.

The GOU was so secret that for a long time no one could say with certainty what the three letters represented. Various interpretations have included: Gobierno, Orden, Unidad (Government, Order, Unity); Grupo Obra de Unificación (Group Working for Unification); Grupo Orgánico Unificado (Unified Organic Group); and finally, what has been accepted as the official name, Grupo de Oficiales Unidos (Group of United Officers).

Despite claims to the contrary by the colonel himself and others, Perón in all likelihood founded the GOU. This is the conclusion reached by Professor Robert A. Potash in his authoritative study *The Army and Politics in Argentina: 1928–1945*.[18] Potash relies upon the testimony of one participant, information that an organizer of the lodge was acting as Perón's representative and corroboration by Domingo Mercante.

Efforts to attract officers to the lodge stressed a variety of themes, such as: distaste for a political system based on fraud; the loss of prestige the army would suffer if it became identified with that system; the need to resist pressures to abandon Argentine neutrality; and the fear of a Communist-dominated "popular front" government that might result from free elections. These were arguments meant to appeal to divergent factions —progressive and reactionary, pro-Allied and pro-Axis, military professionals and political interventionists—and bring them together in the name of institutional unity. Skill at putting and holding together coalitions composed of heterogeneous elements would become a hallmark of Juan Perón's career.

The membership of the GOU carried with it one major weakness: most of the officers belonging to the lodge had administrative jobs rather than command of troops. Therefore, the appointment of General Pedro P. Ramírez as minister of war on November 17 represented a tremendous windfall for the GOU.

The chain-of-command mentality impressed upon every officer from his first day as a cadet at the military academy predisposed the twenty members of the GOU's directorate to find some generals behind whom they could operate. Equally essential was penetration of the Ministry of War, which controlled the army establishment. Ramírez served the GOU on both counts. A veteran of the 1930 Revolution, General Ramírez was President Castillo's choice to replace a pro-Justo minister of war as part of Castillo's plan to consolidate his political hold on the government. The nickname Palito ("Little Stick") aptly described the stiff, slender general, whose puritanical lifestyle reflected a narrow outlook that he did not mind imposing upon others. Ramírez immediately appointed a pair of GOU activists as his private secretary and secretary-aide. The latter, Lieutenant Colonel Enrique P. González, soon rivaled Perón for GOU leadership.

On January 11, 1943, General Justo died unexpectedly of a cerebral hemorrhage. His passing left both the political landscape and the armed forces bereft of a dominant figure. The GOU reaped a double benefit from this vacuum. Its opponents within the army were now leaderless and susceptible to calls for institutional unity. Moreover, President Castillo now felt powerful enough to assert his ambition to continue the tradition of the Concordancia and perpetuate its "democratic fraud." He resolved to handpick his own successor and thereby provoked the GOU to rouse the army from its barracks. On February 17, the president let it be known that the government would promote the candidacy of Robustiano Patrón Costas.

Castillo's choice, a sugar magnate who owned much of the northern province of Salta, was a stereotypical character. In the words of one observer, he "stood for all that was hateful in the sugar monopoly: the traffic in Bolivian Indians, the shipping of peons in cattle cars, the company stores that kept laborers perpetually in debt, the poverty, the filth, the disease that were the price of great individual fortunes."[19] Moreover, as a Conservative leader quite at home with the institutionalized fraud of the Infamous Decade, Patrón Costas was a living symbol of the worst in Argentine politics. While president of the Senate, he had used his influence to secure Castillo's nomination as vice-president. Now Castillo was about to repay the debt.

News of the administration's anointment of a "crown prince" galvanized the GOU's organizing efforts, since Patrón Costas was anathema to all the various factions within the army. The lodge intensified its search for new members, with Perón assuming a prominent role. He was able to play upon one of his favorite themes, unity, and make his pitch to all officers, regardless of their feelings about the war in Europe.

At the same time, the political opposition began to make overtures to various military leaders in an attempt to head off what looked like certain defeat at the polls. While identifying themselves as "pro-democratic" on the basis of their sympathy with the Allied cause, many of these politicians made it clear that they would support a military coup, if necessary, to stop

Patrón Costas. Members of the GOU participated in these discussions. In late May, representatives of a sector of the Radical party approached General Ramírez to inquire whether he might be available as a candidate in the September elections.

When President Castillo found out that his minister of war had been consorting with the opposition, the pace of events quickened. The president demanded a full explanation in writing. Ramírez hedged, producing a statement Castillo found excessively vague. Having lost the confidence of the chief executive, Ramírez was expected to resign, but he delayed. On June 3, Castillo drafted a decree removing Ramírez from the cabinet. At the same time, the nominating committee of the conservative National Democratic party, scheduled to meet in a Buenos Aires hotel on June 4, prepared to declare Patrón Costas its presidential candidate.

The GOU had not planned to take any action until shortly before the September elections, but the loss of its front man in the Ministry of War would have been disastrous. The moment for decisive action was at hand, but GOU strategists found themselves without a general. The obvious choice, General Ramírez, was unwilling, and even if he had changed his mind, he had no troops under his command. General Farrell also had no soldiers to lead and excused himself on the ground that he was in the process of attempting to untangle himself from serious marital difficulties. The GOU conspirators hastily cast about for someone behind whom they could march.

On Thursday, June 3, Lieutenant Colonel González made contact with a likely candidate. General Arturo Rawson had been involved in past military conspiracies and for some time had been working on his own plans for the overthrow of Castillo. His current position as commanding officer of cavalry at Campo de Mayo gave him access to troops. Moreover, though originally a nationalist with pro-Axis leanings, he now gave signs of sympathizing with the Allies, an ambiguity that made him palatable to both the pro-Axis and pro-Allied factions within the army. At a luncheon several blocks from the Ministry of War, he proved more than receptive to González' suggestions. But neither man spelled out his intentions in detail nor made definite commitments regarding the political leadership of the budding military movement.

Later that night in the office of the cavalry school at Campo de Mayo, Rawson and González met with a dozen unit commanders who shared their eagerness to topple the government. Most of the officers present were not associated with either the GOU or Rawson. Some had a strong sympathy for the Allied cause. Together they had decisive military strength at their disposal. The assembly agreed that Rawson should lead the next day's march on the Casa Rosada, and approved a manifesto that had been drafted earlier in the day. The parties dispersed with conflicting views as to who would head the new regime.[20]

When word reached Castillo that Rawson had left Campo de Mayo at the head of a column of 10,000 men and that none of the other military units in and around the capital would defend the government, the seventy-year-old president wearily boarded the naval minesweeper *Drummond* and headed across the river. He would eventually put ashore at La Plata and submit his resignation. Meanwhile, the insurgents, most of whom had no idea why they were marching, paid an unexpected price for leaving their barracks. As they passed the naval mechanics' school on the edge of the city, its director ordered his sailors to fire on the column. Rawson's men, in great confusion, at first shot at one another. They then surrounded the school and shelled it with artillery until a white flag appeared. The misunderstanding cost perhaps thirty lives and a hundred wounded. An army officer partially responsible, Colonel Eduardo J. Avalos, would not forget the incident two years later, when decisive but potentially risky action on his part might have altered the course of Argentine history.

General Rawson made his way to the Casa Rosada. When a sufficient crowd of onlookers, more curious than enthusiastic and somewhat confused by the sudden coup, had gathered in the Plaza de Mayo, he appeared on the balcony and announced that the army had acted to save the constitution and preserve law and order. The only response of note from the populace was the burning of several buses by unidentified individuals. By nightfall, Rawson had assumed the presidency and was choosing his cabinet.

In retrospect, the Revolution of 1943 irrevocably changed the political process in Argentina. Yet the person who eventually benefited most from Castillo's ouster played a minimal role. It is undisputed that Colonel Juan Perón did not attend the crucial meeting at the cavalry school on June 3, did not march with the Rawson column and did not surface in public until the next day, when the success of the operation had been assured.

Perón himself insisted that his contribution to the revolution was critical. On the other hand, several of the officers who participated in the events have downgraded his role and have provided grist for an accusation that was to follow Perón for the rest of his life: that he was a coward who always shrank from the slightest possibility of physical danger.

When the impending dismissal of General Ramírez and the nomination of Patrón Costas combined to produce a sudden crisis, Perón did not join in the negotiations with Rawson, but he did work on the document that became the official manifesto of the June 4 Revolution. According to the colonel, he personally wrote the entire text by hand at 10:00 P.M. on the third of June.[21] In addition, Mercante claimed that on the same day Perón had given him instructions to mount a commando operation for the purpose of arresting President Castillo, but countermanded the order at 9:00 P.M. because Castillo had learned of the coup plans and had taken security precautions.[22] What Perón did on the fourth is much less evident.

According to his own version,[23] he first went to an officers' club where
Farrell was spending the night. "General, there's a revolution," the colonel
announced, rousing his superior from a deep sleep. "What revolution?"
responded Farrell with his customary acuity. Perón also claimed to have
visited several infantry units to dissuade them from resisting the advance
of the Rawson column and to have helped put an end to the shooting at
the mechanics' school.

The testimony of various participants in the coup contradicts that of
Perón. At dawn on the fourth two of them "passed by Pcrón's apartment
and phoned him without result. They had the impression he was in hiding."[24] According to Colonel Avalos, when Rawson led his column toward
the Casa Rosada, Perón was nowhere to be seen. "He appeared in the
morning, at Farrell's side. Isn't it curious? Perón always was next to Farrell. He knew how to choose. He knew precisely where and with whom
to position himself."[25] Farrell at that point was given command of the
First Army Division, and Perón, remaining in his shadow, became his
chief aide.

General Rawson lasted only two days as head of state. Perón, González
and other GOU members viewed his assumption of the presidency as a
usurpation. "Rawson became president by a fluke," Perón told an interviewer in 1960. He "was able to proclaim himself president because of the
hesitancy of Ramírez."[26]

The new chief executive alienated important military leaders with his
choice of cabinet members. Although he made some noncontroversial appointments, such as General Ramírez for minister of war, his list included
a couple of conservative politicians identified with the Castillo administration and several known German sympathizers. Thus with one stroke Rawson managed to anger officers who wanted a fresh, clean approach to
government as well as those who favored the Allies. His refusal to revise
the list united his opponents. According to Perón, they "forced him to
resign by threatening to chuck him out the window of the Casa Rosada if
he did not do so."[27] When Ramírez arrived, the officers who had sacked
Rawson curtly informed him that he was Argentina's new president.

The June 4 military coup took the great majority of Argentines by complete surprise. In the days that followed the ouster of Castillo, rumors
about the supposed political orientation of the new regime inundated
Buenos Aires. The Supreme Court, following the precedent it had set
thirteen years before, officially recognized the de facto government. Presidential decrees dissolved Congress, postponed the elections scheduled for
September and deleted the adjective provisional from the official title of
the administration.

But what plans did the new rulers have for the future? From the available evidence it seems clear that neither Ramírez nor the GOU officers
behind him had any coherent notion of what they wanted to do. Both

Rawson and Ramírez had made public statements affirming their faith in the constitution. Yet the actions of the de facto regime did not point to a restoration of constitutional government. According to one close observer, the officers who engineered the coup did not begin to think about what to do with the government until after they had seized it.[28] Perón, however, had plans of his own.

Lieutenant Colonel Domingo A. Mercante recalled that "Long before June 4, 1943, Perón had very clear ideas about the social revolution that had to happen in the country."[29] Indeed, according to Mercante, on May 15, 1943, Perón interjected a call for revolution into a talk he gave at a GOU meeting, and was informed on the following day that an order for his arrest had been issued. (Lieutenant Colonel González later told Perón the order had been rescinded.[30]) Perón also made contact with labor leaders shortly after June 4. This search for working-class support implied an awareness on his part that a radical shift in labor policies by the new regime might give revolutionary substance to the events of June 4.

Castillo's ouster not only confused the Argentine public but also provoked considerable head-scratching in the United States. North American observers used a single criterion in judging what had happened. Overlooking the domestic context in which the coup took place, they focused solely on whether the officers behind the new regime were pro-Axis or pro-Allied, a dichotomy that easily translated into "pro-totalitarian" or "pro-democratic."*

The United States quickly recognized the Ramírez regime. But any doubts Washington had about the new administration soon vanished when the State Department received a copy of an alleged GOU document purporting to reveal the true intentions of the military rulers of Argentina. Supposedly distributed on May 13, 1943, the manifesto called upon the army to emulate German expansionism in Europe and create, by means of a dictatorship, a powerful Argentina that would gain control over the entire continent: "With Germany's example, the right spirit will be instilled into the people by the radio, by the controlled press, by literature, by the church, and by publication, and so they will venture upon the heroic road they will be made to travel. Only in this way will they forgo the easy life they now enjoy."[31]

Although the document has gained wide acceptance as proof of the GOU's agenda for Argentina,[32] it must be viewed with great skepticism. Professor Potash has convincingly argued that it did not represent the collegial thinking of the GOU and is probably not authentic.[33] Dispatches

---

* An FBI report prepared shortly after the coup quoted a reliable source describing Rawson as "definitely pro-Nazi in the past." It depicted Ramírez as "pro-Nazi," "a devout Hispanist," and "admirer of Germany," "a neutralist," and (last but not least) a "friendly Argentine nationalist." Hoover to Berle, 835.00/1548, June 10, 1943.

sent to Washington by the U.S. embassy in Buenos Aires early in 1946 suggest that the document originated in a small group of ultra-nationalist army officers not connected with the original GOU.[34]

Thus the main piece of evidence used to establish the GOU's Nazi orientation collapses under careful scrutiny. In this regard, the observation of the Argentine historian Félix Luna is particularly apt. He posits that many officers may have been pro-German because of their training, professional admiration for a formidable army and distaste for democracy in Argentina, but this surely did not make them Nazis.[35] His distinction is both valid and important.

An even more serious charge against the Revolution of June 4 was that it was not just pro-Nazi but an integral part of a German plot. According to one interpretation along these lines,

> Argentine Fascists remained in [the] shade so long as [the] victory of Nazi Germany appeared possible since that victory would have automatically placed them in power without risk or effort. So soon as [a] German defeat appeared certain, they and their German Nazi advisors realized that Argentine Fascism had to seize power openly and positively, in order to preserve the country as a base for winning the ideological war which would follow the ending of armed conflict in Europe and thus to insure Fascism's survival. . . .[36]

A similar view of the Castillo overthrow postulated that

> The coup d'etat of June 4 was prepared in minute detail by Nazi agents . . . whose objective was to create in Argentina a Nazi-type regime and at the same time one that would serve as a point of support to contribute to a Nazi victory in Europe and Asia and second, to spread Fascist regimes to South America . . . and third, in case of a Nazi-Fascist defeat on the battlefield, to preserve a bridgehead in America. . . .[37]

There is no objective evidence to support these claims. Indeed, the June coup took the German embassy in Buenos Aires by surprise.[38] The accusation that the Revolution of June 4 bore a made-in-Berlin tag tells more about the accusers than about what really happened. The first of the above-quoted paragraphs appeared in a telegram sent to the State Department by U.S. Ambassador Spruille Braden in 1945. The latter quote came from the head of the Communist party in Argentina.

General Ramírez' assumption of the presidency opened the door for the GOU. Lieutenant González, who had nurtured a close relationship with Ramírez, moved into the key post of presidential secretary. Other GOU operatives became interior minister and police chief of the federal capital. González then influenced Ramírez to name as minister of war General Farrell, who to the surprise of no one brought with him Colonel Perón as his chief aide. Perón was finally in a position to fulfill his dictum that "in revolutions men impose their will from the second row, and not from the first, where they invariably fail and are removed."[39]

The stage was now set for Perón's drive for power. It was a two-pronged thrust, aimed at the institution that had just demonstrated its ultimate authority over the political process, and at a group that could become his political base among the citizenry. His efforts to master the army and to gain the support of Argentina's workers occurred simultaneously, a feat that reflected his genius and energy.

6

Wooing the Military

Projecting vigor, good looks, meticulous grooming and charm, Juan Perón cut a dashing figure in the military garb of the day. A shade over six feet and solidly built, he stood out in a crowd. The blotchy veins that webbed and reddened his face, the effects of psoriasis, were the only flaws in his youthful appearance and were easily offset by the dazzle of his smile.[1]

An FBI report forwarded by J. Edgar Hoover to the State Department on December 28, 1943, describes Perón's way of relating to his military colleagues in the following terms:

> He speaks with vivacity and energy, with no care as to style or words. Sometimes he's violent, but then calms himself and laughs loudly. He gives the impression of possession of a permanent sense of humor, and gives the feeling that he does not take things seriously.
>
> He improvises. He says, without warning, all that he wants to say. . . . He does not boast about his physical power, but he shows it. He takes off his jacket and walks up and down with his regulation Kahki [sic] shirt, exhibiting the pistol in his belt. He bangs the table and does not hesitate when referring to other chiefs and officers, or in stating that he will fix that situation "by blows." But he does all this laughing. If he becomes flustered over a discussion, it only lasts a second.[2]

Perón watchers, both domestic and foreign, multiplied like Patagonian hares. The spectacle of an obscure colonel emerging from nowhere and making what many were convinced was a run at the presidency became the topic of conversation from the Confitería (sweet shop) del Molino next to the Congress to the swank Richmond Café on Florida Street. The benevolence with which Perón viewed Fascism and his willingness to depart from the time-honored rules of the political game worried politicians hoping for a return to normalcy.

In an interview recorded in the early 1960s, Perón gave an important clue to his thinking at the time. "I returned [from Europe] at a moment when the [political] battles, as usual, were being rigged. I asked myself, 'What would happen if someone began to fight for real and announced I'm going to play to win?' "[3] He emphasized his determination to bring about a revolution rather than participate in a gentlemanly game of musical chairs, but the clear impression emerges that any structural change he sought to produce in Argentine society was a means rather than an end. He did not follow any ideology, but instead set a strategy that had as its aim the capture of political power.

His position in the Ministry of War provided access to levers that controlled the army. The manipulation of assignments, for example, was a most potent weapon, and the pliant Farrell gave his top aide free rein over this and other functions of the ministry. Perón, on his part, carefully cultivated the fiction that General Farrell was in charge.

The initial strategy adopted by the colonel focused upon the need to expand the GOU. In the weeks following the coup, Perón sought new members by claiming for the lodge all credit for Castillo's ouster. He conveniently forgot the critical role played by non-GOU officers and created the impression that he had personally led the revolution.[4] One of his early maneuvers was to circulate a document spelling out the current objectives of the organization.[5] Unity and loyalty were the GOU's watchwords. "For a military man there ought to be nothing better than another military man, and the defense of all is the obligation of each individual. . . . The members of the GOU do not have personal ambitions. Their only ambition is the good of the army and the homeland." Although the document insisted that the GOU "has no chief and is a collegial body," it contradictorily stressed not only the chain-of-command doctrine but also the principle that when the time for action arrived, "the chief of the army [General Farrell] decides and we execute."

During the next few months, non-GOU officers made several unsuccessful attempts to oust Farrell and Perón. At the same time Perón enlisted into the GOU Colonel Eduardo Avalos, now commanding officer of the Campo de Mayo garrison, and installed several of his followers as aides to Ramírez. The president could not seem to make up his mind about Perón and constantly backed down from decisions to remove him. As one writer noted: "These reversals were so consistent that the President's wife, who often thought she had convinced him at home to act against Perón, wondered whether he was not being drugged through his coffee at the Casa Rosada."[6]

Meanwhile, the Ramírez administration found itself face to face with serious international problems. Statements made shortly after the coup by the president and his foreign minister, Admiral Segundo Storni, gave the impression that the new regime was about to break off relations with the Axis and perhaps even declare war on the side of the Allies. But pro-Allied members of the government, such as Storni, could not overcome the resistance of avowed Axis sympathizers like Lieutenant Colonel González and the bona fide neutralists.

On August 5, in a letter to U.S. Secretary of State Cordell Hull,[7] Admiral Storni insisted that both the Argentine people and their government rejected totalitarian ideologies and sympathized with the Allied cause; however, internal conditions made it impossible to bring about an abrupt change in the country's neutrality policy, especially at a time when the Axis powers were on the brink of defeat ("[An] unexpected rupture would . . . put Argentine chivalry to a hard test"). The letter closed with a plea for a "gesture of genuine friendship," in the form of military aid that would "restore Argentina to the position of equilibrium . . . with respect to other South American countries." Under the circumstances, the text represented naiveté in the extreme. It originated with Storni, but underwent revision at the hands of other members of the government.[8]

Hull's response,[9] delivered at the end of the month, has been deemed one of the most severe diplomatic censures ever directed by the State Department at a Latin American government.[10] In the bluntest of terms Hull scorned Argentina's failure to live up to her inter-American obligations and flatly rejected the request for arms.

When the Argentine government released both letters, an uproar ensued. The GOU decided on the need for a sacrificial lamb, and Admiral Storni was chosen. He resigned, taking full responsibility for the contretemps and insisting (falsely) that Ramírez knew nothing about his letter.[11] General Alberto Gilbert replaced him. The hard line taken by Hull thus succeeded in removing from a key government post a man who strongly identified with the Allies.

In mid-October, the regime took a sharp turn to the right,[12] a move that reflected not any ideological commitment on the president's part but rather his pendular approach to governance and the pressures of military factions committed to conflicting objectives. He removed several politically moderate members of his cabinet and replaced them with notorious reactionaries. An ultra-conservative who had written anti-Semitic novels became minister of justice and public instruction, while General Luis Perlinger, a notorious Nazi-phile, took over the Ministry of the Interior, which had charge of internal security. The regime suspended publication of several Jewish newspapers and drew a reproach from President Roosevelt.[13] In the weeks that followed, the educational system shuddered from a series of restrictive measures culminating in a decree making religious classes compulsory in the public schools.[14] Meanwhile, Perlinger repressed Communists and liberals alike. On December 31, all political parties were banned and the regime tightened its grip on the mass media.

Perón handled himself prudently during this period. While Ramírez revamped his cabinet, the colonel helped secure the selection of General Farrell to fill the office of vice-president, made vacant by the death of the incumbent in July. Farrell also remained minister of war. Thus Perón kept control over the army while his compliant superior moved to within one step of the presidency.

Perón also began to make contacts with the political parties. The Radicals did not take kindly to the new regime's designation of September 6 as a holiday in commemoration of the overthrow of Yrigoyen in 1930. Perón promised to abolish the observance.[15] The fishing expedition in Radical party waters did not net any front-line leaders,[16] so the colonel and his inner circle showered attention on some minor figures within the party. A few of them proved susceptible to blandishment.

In addition to his recruitment of traditional politicians, Perón was able to attract an entire sector that had already broken off from the main body of the Radical party. FORJA found in Perón the leader for whom it had long been searching.[17] The nationalistic, anti-imperialist line the group had developed seemed embodied in the philosophy Perón was beginning to espouse. Members of FORJA furnished the colonel with the intellectual element his increasingly heterogeneous movement lacked.

The extent to which Perón's influence within the administration had expanded came into public view on November 12, 1943, when the Buenos Aires daily, *La Prensa,* reprinted an interview he had given to a Chilean journalist. "The Argentine army," declared the colonel, "has about 3,600 combat officers on active service. Well, all of us, with the exception of maybe 300 who don't interest us, are united and bound together by an oath; we have all signed and submitted to the Ministry of War requests for retirement [i.e., resignations]. I have them all in my files. The officers who are not with us don't interest us because they are not elements we need for the work to which we have pledged ourselves."

The reporter's conclusion was eerily prophetic: "If the tide keeps on as it is going and there aren't any complications on the international scene, Colonel Juan Perón can in a short while be the chief caudillo of the Argentine Republic, who knows for how long."

On the next day, Perón issued a clarification, insisting that "Ramírez commands and we obey."[18] His declaration that "I myself know that I prefer to be the ultimate collaborator in a good cause rather than appear to have personal ambitions I have never entertained and have always rejected" drew congratulations from the president.[19] If Ramírez believed Perón, he truly deserved what later befell him.

As Perón's power grew, the president's problems intensified. Cordell Hull was now firmly convinced that only international pressure could turn the Argentine government from its neutralist course. His rigid, moralistic approach to diplomacy descended with full force upon the military regime. Ironically, this occurred at a time when reverses on the battlefield had removed any physical threat the Axis might have posed to the South American continent. The Ramírez administration soon obliged Hull by furnishing an ample excuse for some vigorous twisting of the screws.

The weapons buildup in Brazil continued to alarm the Argentine army. Once again the regime approached the Third Reich for help. Lieutenant Colonel González utilized his Nazi contacts to arrange that an Argentine official be sent to Berlin to negotiate an arms deal with the Germans.[20] Ramírez and the rest of his cabinet knew about the scheme. Unbeknownst to the Argentines, their representative also happened to be a spy for the Nazis. Under diplomatic cover, he set sail for Europe, but when his ship docked in early November at the British port of Trinidad in the Caribbean, he disembarked and was promptly arrested by British authorities (no doubt tipped off by Allied spies operating in Argentina).

Then, in late 1943, a coup shook nearby Bolivia. The insurgents had the support of a secret Bolivian military lodge and the Nationalist Revolutionary Movement led by an economics professor named Victor Paz Estensoro. The overthrown government had been participating fully in the inter-American collective-security program. The State Department immediately raised the specter of Nazi involvement. One of the key pieces of evidence to support this charge was a letter allegedly sent by a Bolivian officer to a German diplomat. (In fact a British intelligence agent forged the epistle.[21]) When Washington learned that Paz Estensoro and some of his associates had conferred with Perón in Buenos Aires shortly before the coup and that Argentina had promised aid to the new rulers of Bolivia, this was considered sufficient proof to convict Perón of implementing the alleged GOU manifesto advocating Argentine hegemony over South America.[22]

In retrospect, the charge seems ludicrous. Internal conditions in Bolivia provided reason enough for the coup.[23] The prior regime had promoted U.S. war needs by keeping tin production up and the price of tin so low that the miners had to live in appalling misery. (On December 21, 1942, hundreds of them were machine-gunned to death by soldiers during a peaceful protest.) One of the goals of the 1943 coup was to place Bolivian needs ahead of those of foreign nations (e.g., the United States).

In January 1944, the State Department had received from the British evidence that the Argentine "official" detained in Trinidad was a German spy. With its "proof" of Argentine involvement in the Bolivian coup, Washington was able to alarm other South American nations with the bogey of Argentine expansionism and convince every Latin government except Argentina to withhold diplomatic recognition from the new regime in Bolivia. U.S. naval units anchored off the coast of Uruguay in a show of force, and the Treasury Department prepared to freeze Argentine funds in U.S. banks.[24]

In Argentina, meanwhile, the San Juan earthquake and ensuing relief efforts dominated public attention. But behind the scenes the regime was making desperate efforts to cope with a rapidly deteriorating situation. On January 24, Foreign Minister Gilbert informed the U.S. ambassador in Buenos Aires that the revelations stemming from the arrest of the German spy in Trinidad proved Nazi interference in Argentine affairs and furnished sufficient grounds for a break in relations with the Axis. But in a face-preserving gesture designed to blunt domestic opposition, he urged Washington not to take any public steps that might be construed as external pressure until Argentina made a formal announcement of the diplomatic rupture.[25]

At a special meeting of the GOU on the evening of January 25, an announcement of the intended rupture produced a stunned reaction. González and Avalos supported the regime in the face of strenuous dissent. Perón took masterly advantage of the situation. He backed neither side but instead played the role of the good soldier, willing to obey orders.[26] On the next day, a decree signed by the president and General Gilbert severed diplomatic relations with Germany and Japan* on the ground that a Nazi spy ring had been uncovered in Argentina. The ultra-nationalists who had enthusiastically supported the Ramírez regime responded in predictable fashion. Several government officials resigned in protest, and the federal interventor of the province of Tucumán ordered all flags to fly at half mast.

To justify the diplomatic break and secure the backing of pro-Allied Argentines, Ramírez would have had to make a clean, public sweep of all German agents operating in Argentina. But this would have required the cooperation of his own internal-security people, who had been responsible for letting these agents go about their business.[27]

Nearly three weeks after the rupture, angry GOU officers demanded the ouster of both González and Gilbert. It is quite likely that Perón both fueled and directed this outburst of indignation.[28] According to a dispatch from the U.S. embassy to Washington,[29] Perón had obtained a copy of a State Department message indicating that the British would have refused to join in any sanctions against the Ramírez regime because of their dependence on Argentine beef. He argued that the Yankees had bluffed Gilbert into breaking with the Axis. Ramírez caved in to the pressure and eliminated not only Gilbert but also González. But by doing so he put himself in line for the next sweep of the broom.

---

* Italy, under Allied invasion and German occupation, no longer counted as an independent Axis power.

Perón gave various explanations for what befell Ramírez. In a 1945 interview with a Spanish journalist, he declared that the president "was thrown out because he had named a nationalist general [Perlinger] minister of the interior and had appointed nationalist governments, that is, Nazi governments, in the fourteen provinces."[30] In taped memoirs, he alleged that Ramírez had begun to promote the interests of the oligarchy.[31] Of course neither of these fanciful justifications even approximates the truth. The continuing crisis caused by the break with Germany spawned rumors, no doubt encouraged by Perón,[32] that Argentina was about to declare war on the Axis, decree a general mobilization and even send troops to fight the Japanese in Asia. Ramírez met with top military officials in a desperate attempt to deny the rumors, but was unable to allay their fears.

Matters rapidly reached a breaking point. On February 23, perhaps in response to threats from Ramírez,[33] the GOU dissolved itself. Its members were now freed from solemn oaths they had taken to support the regime. The next day, an emboldened Ramírez put his head on the block by ordering Farrell's dismissal. At a meeting of ex-GOU officers at the War Ministry, Perón announced that "the time has come to put things in their place."[34] The group then voted to remove Ramírez.

At 9:00 P.M. on the fourteenth a military delegation drove to the summer presidential residence in the nearby suburb of Olivos and confronted Ramírez with the news. He fumed but had no recourse but to submit. He tried to play one last card. His letter of resignation concluded: "I yield to the imposition of force and present my resignation from the post of president of the nation."[35] One of the civilian members of the cabinet was quick to point out that such a patently irregular transfer of power would be regarded abroad as the equivalent to a coup and would open up the issue of diplomatic recognition of the next regime.[36] So on the following day General Farrell and a group of officers visited Ramírez and persuaded him to write a second letter, delegating his mandate to vice-president Farrell because he was "fatigued by the intense work of governing."[37]

With Farrell moving to the Casa Rosada, the crucial War Ministry became acephalous. Perón aspired to the job but met with resistance from his pro-Axis colleagues, who interpreted his refusal to oppose the break with Germany as sympathy for the Allied cause. The colonel called a meeting of ex-GOU leaders to marshal support for his candidacy. Only seven attended. Meanwhile ten of his former GOU comrades gathered elsewhere and resolved that someone else be appointed.

Though beaten in a GOU head count, Perón unleashed his ultimate weapon.[38] He realized that the loss of the War Ministry would terminate his ambitions. General Farrell, never able to refuse the smiling colonel, ignored the mandate of the majority and named Perón to the post on an interim basis.

On February 29, the day after Perón took office, a lieutenant colonel and long-time GOU member led a revolt of an infantry regiment in a suburb northeast of Buenos Aires. He demanded the reinstatement of Ramírez, a civilian cabinet and a general election. No other units joined in, and the uprising collapsed in the face of a threat by Perón to bomb the rebels.[39]

The aborted countercoup must have impressed upon Perón the need to strengthen his grip on the officer corps. He dispatched General Orlando Peluffo on a week-long tour of every major military garrison. The object of the mission was to obtain as many signatures as possible on a loyalty oath recognizing Farrell as the new "chief of the revolution," and promised obedience to the orders of the interim minister of war. Hundreds of officers signed the document.[40]

Perón could now turn his attention to General Perlinger and the pro-Axis faction that backed him. The U.S. intelligence apparatus in Buenos Aires kept a close watch on the ensuing power struggle. A March 2 background paper prepared by the Office of Strategic Services described Perlinger as a person of "long-standing and thoroughgoing pro-Nazi views," in close contact with the German embassy and once in debt to a German bank in Buenos Aires. Perón, on the other hand, was the most able member of the new cabinet, not a cultured person but possessed of an affable personality, decision-making ability and a capacity for violence. "His ambition is to become the leader-president of Argentina, appointed to the office by managed elections which would give him prestige and the stability of legality."[41] The report depicted Farrell as pro-Nazi but completely dominated by Perón, with a reputation for stupidity and womanizing.[42]*

The decisive confrontations between Perón and Perlinger occurred in early July 1944, when an assembly of army officers met to fill the vacant vice-presidency.[43] Perón won by the narrow margin of six votes. With help from Admiral Alberto Teisaire, the new navy minister and a staunch ally, Perón quickly demanded and received Perlinger's resignation. Teisaire replaced him and Perón's control of the armed forces reached its apogee.

His domination, however, was not complete. Perón might have removed from contention his major rivals, but this merely rendered his military

---

* The pathetic figure of Farrell was rapidly becoming the object of porteño scorn. A report by the U.S. military attaché in Buenos Aires described a rumor making the rounds in April: "Farrell is afraid that the Nationalists or Perlinger will try to kill him. He fears Perón but can't get along without him. He has found that being president places a restraint on the activities he likes most—going to night clubs and prize fights. He would like to get back to being a minister or just a general." 800, weekly stability report, John W. Lang, brigadier general, U.S. military attaché, Buenos Aires, April 11, 1944 (Suitland).

opponents leaderless and quiescent for the moment. Perón still had to handle the armed forces with care. A series of reforms he promoted within the military establishment during the latter part of 1944 constituted his principal efforts to remain in good standing with his supporters in the officer corps, or at least to neutralize any rallying points for the opposition.

During the thirteen months it took Perón to achieve this advantage, he was waging a parallel campaign to win the backing of Argentina's labor movement. That he could operate effectively on two such disparate fronts attests to a breadth of vision and limitless energy that set him apart from military as well as civilian competitors. Argentina's working class would never be the same again.

7

Wooing the Workers

On October 27, 1943, President Ramírez named Perón as head of the National Labor Department. In tribute to its moribundity, workers referred to the modest-sized agency as the "elephants' graveyard."[1] Yet to Perón it would soon yield a treasure more precious than ivory—the key to control of the Argentine labor movement.

A simple ceremony marked his assumption of the post, which he would hold in addition to his duties at the Ministry of War. The significance of the occasion escaped contemporary notice. Perón made a short speech and then went right to work. Calling together the chiefs of the various divisions and sections of the department, he told them: "I come here with seven buckets of paint in seven different colors. We have to make a work of art, and you are the artists."[2]

Argentine workers had first attempted to organize in the latter half of the nineteenth century.[3] The earliest trade unions were spontaneous outgrowths of benevolent societies formed by immigrants struggling for survival in a new and at times hostile environment. Somewhat later, ideologies taking root among workers in Europe crossed the Atlantic and found eager converts among the exploited victims of an unfettered, free-market capitalism. However, the new movements promoted their own exclusive panaceas. The anarchists, for example, tried to develop a network of unions and federations that could confront the government at every turn with weapons such as the general strike. Socialists advocated working-class conquest of political power through the electoral process. Syndicalists joined the competition with a call for bread-and-butter, nonpolitical unionism. The resulting ideological and factional squabbles enfeebled a labor movement facing long odds in a fight against unyielding employers backed by the full resources of the government.

A Socialist party founded in 1896 mobilized middle-class porteño intellectuals and professionals concerned about the plight of labor. Pursuing
reform within the system, the Socialists saw themselves as a democratic,
political arm of the trade-union movement. But the entrenched rulers of
Argentina were not about to surrender power so long as they controlled
the electoral machinery. Socialist deputies in Congress provided the first
representation enjoyed by the working class. Although several were accomplished parliamentarians who fought heroically for protective labor laws,
the Socialists were doomed to institutionalized impotence by their inability
to attract mass support from the workers for whom they claimed to speak.

The Radical party, though basically middle-class, made some gestures
toward labor during the first Yrigoyen administration. The government
protected the workers' right to organize and strike and tried to remain
neutral in labor disputes, instead of prosecuting labor leaders under repressive laws enacted by prior administrations. This new policy permitted
the unionization of a number of new industries. But the Radicals governed during two horrendous outbursts of anti-labor violence that Argentine workers have never forgotten. In January 1919, a metalworkers' strike
in Buenos Aires occasioned bloody attacks on workers by both the police
and private vigilante groups. Three years later, the equally sanguinary
crushing of protests by rural laborers in Patagonia demonstrated vividly
to the workers which side the Radicals were on when a serious labor-
management confrontation developed. The Radical party proved an adequate vehicle for smoothing the road for middle-class participation in
Argentina's political life, but labor still awaited the representation of its
interests.

The Bolshevik Revolution made itself felt in Argentina with the formation of a Communist party that stood for an international working-class
movement under Soviet leadership.[4] During the 1920s it remained relatively small and beset by factionalism. The reactionary Uriburu regime
unleashed a vicious persecution of Communists, many of whom were sent
to concentration camps set up in the remote reaches of Patagonia.

In the critical period from 1930 to 1943, the Argentine labor movement
underwent a profound transformation. The Depression and the outbreak
of World War II spurred industrialization, as the country could no longer
rely upon the purchase of manufactured goods from abroad. Meanwhile,
because the flow of immigration had come to a halt in 1930, the demand
for manpower in the new industries, which sprang up in thick batches in
and around Buenos Aires, had to be met by workers from the interior.
Native-born Argentines rather than transplanted Europeans, they formed
a distinctive subgroup within the working class—darker-skinned, lacking
political consciousness, cut off from their paternalistic relationship with an
estanciero, scorned by race-conscious upper- and middle-class porteños,

and demeaningly characterized by the nickname *cabecitas negras*, "little black heads."[5]

During those same years, vigorous efforts were made to set up a central organization to represent the interests of trade unions on a national level. In 1930, the Confederación General del Trabajo (General Labor Confederation), or CGT, came into being. Dominated by syndicalists, it was originally conceived as independent of all political parties and ideologies. But the anti-labor measures adopted by the Uriburu regime and the governments of the Concordancia made it impossible for labor to remain indifferent to politics. In 1935 the Socialists displaced the syndicalist leaders of the CGT, but had little success in reversing the policies of the administration. In addition, they had to fight off constant challenges from the displaced syndicalists and an expanding Communist party for control of the confederation.

The flames that engulfed Europe in the latter part of the decade singed organized labor in Argentina. The Socialists were quick to enlist in the fight against Fascism and used the resources of the CGT to support Republican Spain. Later they identified with the cause of the Allies. The Communists became entangled in the tergiversations of the Kremlin's foreign policy, and for the duration of the Hitler-Stalin pact had to defend Hitler and Mussolini as innocent victims of British imperialism. Only when the Germans invaded Russia did the Communists rediscover their devotion to anti-Fascism, a switch the Socialists took great delight in underscoring as they competed with the Communist party for leadership in the labor movement.

Meanwhile, the average worker had to endure worsening conditions that made the fuss over World War II seem quite irrelevant. In 1938, Archibald MacLeish wrote that "any visitor [to Buenos Aires] who will leave the boosters behind and cross the creek to the industrial suburb of Avellaneda can see enough hen coop housing and smell enough rancid squalor to last him as long as he can remember."[6] Ysabel Rennie, writing six years later, noted: "In the last normal year before the outbreak of war brought the inflation of living costs, the National Labor Department calculated that the average porteño family of five needed 147 pesos a month to live decently. As against this figure, the average white-collar worker made 128 pesos, and the average laborer, 78."[7] In April 1943, a report prepared by the National Labor Department concluded that "in general, the situation of the worker in Argentina has deteriorated, in spite of the upswing of industry. Whereas huge profits are being made daily, the majority of the population is forced to reduce their standard of living. . . . The gap between wages and cost of living is continuously increasing."[8]

The Socialist-run CGT, with its passionate interest in international causes and a bureaucracy isolated from the concerns of the rank and file, seemed helpless to stop the downslide. Its prestige reached a nadir in March 1943 when the confederation split in two as a result of a dispute between Socialist factions, one of which had strong backing from the Communists. Thus when the military seized power in 1943, it had to deal with what were called the CGT No. 1 and the CGT No. 2.

At that moment, CGT membership included about 331,000 out of a total of 547,000 unionized workers.[9] But fewer than a third of all industrial laborers and about one-tenth of the total work force in Argentina were organized. It was Perón's genius to recognize the political potential offered by the labor movement's disarray and its changing composition.

Perón initiated contact with labor leaders in his office at the War Ministry shortly after the June 4 coup. Exactly when he made the decision to woo the working class is unclear. However, a crucial factor in this decision was his concept of leadership as an end in itself, a phenomenon that fascinated his military mind. He was convinced that he was a born leader and could translate into action the theories he had studied during his army career. The first step was to form a mass of followers and prepare them to be led. (The homey analogy he used in his revealing book *Conducción política* [Political Leadership] explains the point perfectly: "to make a rabbit stew, the first thing you have to have is the rabbit."[10]) He went on to disclose that he took advantage of his position in the National Labor Department to go after his "rabbits," the workers of Argentina.

Perón's observation of organized labor in Mussolini's Italy may have inspired in him an appreciation of the potential power of the movement in Argentina. He correctly sensed that no military regime in Argentina could long survive without popular backing—a lesson he claimed to have learned from the Revolution of 1930. The working class constituted a ready reservoir of such support.

Perón was well aware of the disarray that had always plagued the labor movement. The Communist party had been making considerable gains among workers in the new industries blooming in and around Buenos Aires. Influenced by his anticommunist outlook, Perón saw this as a serious threat.

As a military man, Perón knew that Argentina had to extend the process of industrialization to include the manufacture of armaments. In this way Argentina could free herself from dependence upon foreign governments for the purchase of weapons and strategic equipment. A disciplined labor force would be vital to this process.

Organized labor's initial reaction to the June 4 Revolution was cautiously optimistic. But on June 9, the head of the National Labor Department told labor leaders that the government would collaborate only with those unions that met the following conditions: "complete abstinence from political affairs, both domestic and international; limiting of union programs to strictly union activities; complete inter-union peace . . . and the clear representation of the true human and social interests of the labor half of our economy."[11]

This clear message was soon implemented. In July the regime decreed a "law of professional associations" requiring the unions to stay out of politics and subjecting their activities to minute government control. The next step was the closing of CGT No. 2 on the ground that it was dominated by Communists. The regime then took over several of the largest trade unions. The anti-labor ideology that had suffused the Uriburu administration had returned with a vengeance. However, some unusual occurrences on the fifth floor at the Ministry of War seemed to contradict the reactionary policies of the Casa Rosada and caused many workers to suspend judgment.

Several days after the coup, Perón told some of his collaborators that "we need to get the unions to come here right away."[12] His suggestion was carried out by Mercante, who would become his indispensable link to the labor movement. The son of a railroad engineer who was an active member of La Fraternidad (the union of firemen and engineers founded in 1887), Domingo Mercante grew up on stories of strikes and repression.[13] His brother belonged to the Unión Ferroviaria, the syndicate representing railroad workers other than firemen and engineers. Mercante was personally acquainted with many union members and used these connections to spread the word that union leaders would be welcome at the War Ministry.

These initial contacts took the form of meetings at which labor officials were encouraged to discuss the concerns of their constituents.[14] They conferred with Mercante alone, or they were brought directly to Perón. The impression they took away with them was that despite the anti-labor policies of the regime, there was someone in high office who was willing to lend them a sympathetic and courteous ear. A perspicacious railroad worker drew two conclusions from his first encounters with Perón. "First I observed that [he] had the virtue of leaving his audience satisfied without promising them anything. . . . Second, I had no doubt that Colonel Perón was the leading brain of the revolutionary movement."[15]

These sessions enabled Perón to acquire some grasp of the perceived needs of organized labor. He also developed ties with men like Juan A. Bramuglia, an attorney for the Unión Ferroviaria, and Angel G. Borlenghi, an official of the Confederation of Commercial Employees. They would subsequently form the hard core of his coterie of union supporters.

A promising opportunity soon presented itself. In response to a work stoppage at the large meatpacking plants near Buenos Aires, the police arrested the leaders of the strike and shipped them off to Neuquén in northern Patagonia. When repressive measures failed to intimidate the workers, Perón arranged for the War Ministry to deal with the situation. He had a military plane fetch José Peter, a Communist who ran one of the striking unions, and negotiated a deal whereby the companies agreed to sign the industry's first collective-bargaining contract, the workers received a slight pay increase and the government released the imprisoned labor leaders.

On October 3, six thousand workers jammed a soccer stadium to cheer the arrival of Peter, who made several triumphal turns around the playing field. Joining in the applause was a military officer, whose presence underscored the government's role in ending the strike. "I walked among them dressed in my uniform," recalled Domingo Mercante, "and nobody bothered me, although they looked at me with hatred in their eyes."[16]

The National Labor Department, in existence for nearly forty years, had never been more than a statistics-gathering agency with limited authority. An army officer had been placed in charge of the department on July 2. He made some efforts to improve its performance, to the extent that Perón may have regarded him as a competitor.[17] President Ramírez had mixed feelings about the colonel's contacts with union leaders. He favored any initiatives that might head off what he saw as Communist subversion of the labor movement, but was uneasy about Perón's methods. In the end, the prospect that Perón would become so occupied with labor problems that he would cease to be a threat to him probably convinced Ramírez to grant his request to become the chief of the department.[18]

Perón immediately pressed to have the National Labor Department converted into the Secretariat of Labor and Social Welfare.[19] The Argentine constitution limited the number of ministries within the executive branch, and the full quota had already been filled. The creation of a secretariat, by presidential decree, circumvented this legal barrier and also took jurisdiction of labor matters out of the Ministry of the Interior, to which the National Labor Department had belonged. The new entity was virtually independent, and its writ went beyond not only the gathering of statistics but also the confines of the working class. Broadly stated, the major responsibility of the secretariat was to secure greater social and distributive justice. Perón took Mercante with him to the secretariat and made him head of its social-action division.

The Secretariat of Labor and Social Welfare occupied what was once the deliberative council of the municipality of Buenos Aires, one block from the Plaza de Mayo. Perón's arrival transformed it into a beehive, much to the delight of some of the holdover staff, highly trained technicians who had grown frustrated with the impotence of the old National Labor Department.

In the forefront of this ready-for-action band was an austere Catalán who would soon become a key figure in Perón's first brain trust. José Miguel Francisco Luis Figuerola y Tresols, a native of Barcelona, had been a specialist in the study of the social and legal problems of the Spanish worker.[20] He had helped organize the Spanish Ministry of Labor in 1920 and served as its secretary-general four years later. In 1930, Figuerola emigrated to Argentina. Within a short time he was publishing scholarly articles on labor law, which led to his nomination as chief of statistics at the National Labor Department.

For ten years he investigated labor problems in Argentina. Amassing statistics, grinding out technical analyses and honing his skills, Figuerola was the quintessential Hispanic, Catholic intellectual. Serious and disciplined, he reserved several hours each day for the study of Greek and Roman classics, music and meditation. His private library housed ten thousand volumes.

Polar opposites in many ways, Perón and Figuerola were drawn together by the magnetism of reciprocal needs. The colonel recognized that Figuerola was a walking encyclopedia of data and ideas. The dour émigré saw in Perón the vehicle for translating into action his own social theories.

Perón's philosophy received its first airing in a radio speech he delivered on December 2, 1944. Every social problem, he explained, involves three interested parties: employers, workers and the state. The unity of this trio should form the basis not only for the solution of these problems but also for the struggle against Argentina's real enemies: bad internal politics, foreign ideologies, false apostles who betray the masses, and the "occult forces of perturbation in the field of international politics." In rather dramatic terms, he pledged himself to an all-out effort on the workers' behalf. "I am not a man of sophisms or of halfway solutions," he declared. His choice of words bespoke a flair for demagoguery that would mark his public utterances. The main point of the discourse was that the creation of the Secretariat of Labor and Public Welfare marked the dawn of a new era in which the government would assume full responsibility for the regulation of labor-management relations.[21]

How the secretariat could dull or eliminate the conflicting claims of employers and employees while its chief bore into the fray the banner of the working class remained without explication. Indeed, the apparent contradictions in Perón's concept of the "new era" illustrate nicely the man's incredible talent for both having and eating his cake. He could hold himself out as a "humble soldier to whom the honor has befallen to protect the working masses of Argentina,"[22] without slacking his advocacy of a harmonization of the forces of capital and labor. He could even make Marxist noises ("the secretariat . . . will go down in history as the magnificent bridge in the evolution of the bourgeoisie toward domination by the masses"[23]), which would worry business and military leaders and helped prepare the way for his subsequent "adoption" by the left many years later. Of course the interests of labor did require enhancement to correct the imbalance caused by past injustices, yet the position to which Perón aspired was that of leader of the workers' crusade for equality and ultimate arbiter of labor-management disputes.

His passion for unity impelled him to seek converts in the business community, or at the very least to try to neutralize its opposition to him. In late 1943 he met with leading U.S. businessmen and assured them that if they treated their Argentine workers fairly they could always count on his cooperation in whatever labor problems they might encounter.[24] On July 28, 1944, he created a new Secretariat of Industry and Commerce to promote business interests.

His major effort to sell himself to employers was a speech delivered at the Buenos Aires Stock Exchange on August 25, 1944. The occasion demonstrated his somewhat ingenuous candor. After reiterating his dedication to social justice and to a perfect balance between labor and capital, he urged the acceptance of government measures potentially costly to employers. "It is necessary to know how to give up 30 percent," he postulated, "rather than lose everything." The Communist menace provided his justification for seeking the unionization of as many workers as possible. "Modern experience shows that the better organized masses of workers without doubt are those who can be best directed and led in a completely orderly way," he added, displaying his tendency to think in paternalistic terms.[25]

This speech contained some of the most Fascist-like utterances ever put on the public record by Perón, but he continued to elude easy classification. For example, one of the first formal steps he took as head of the secretariat was to secure the repeal of the law of professional associations, singled out as perhaps the most reactionary of the decrees issued by Ramírez.

Perón's labor strategy at the secretariat followed a two-pronged approach.[26] He directed the agency to prepare new laws and intervene in labor-management disputes on the side of the workers. He also set about the long-range task of reshaping organized labor.

The new secretariat drafted statutes affecting social security, housing, vacations and rural labor. They were immediately signed into law by the president. While this in no way amounted to a revolution,[27] the secretariat had undoubtedly taken a quantum leap forward. Perón also brought about the creation of labor courts throughout the country as a means of carrying out his directive that all protective labor legislation was now to be enforced. Further, the secretariat took an active part in bringing to an end controversies between labor and management. The unspoken assumption behind all of this activity was that the scales of justice had been tipped so long in favor of business that a proper adjustment could not be reached without a period of decision-making that openly favored workers. A second guiding principle was practicality: in examining the difficulties faced by various syndicates, the technicians at the secretariat were careful to look for and deal with problems that could be solved.[28]

The organizational phase of Perón's strategy involved the encouragement of unionization in trades and industries where the workers had not yet formed syndicates. His door at the secretariat was always open to groups of workers, but the one condition he placed upon entry was that his visitors come in a representational rather than individual capacity. Thus in order to share in the advantages the secretariat could offer, unorganized workers had to form unions.[29] Dependent upon the government for leverage in disputes with employers, these new syndicates were born with ties to Perón.

With the established unions Perón had to follow different tactics. He utilized the secretariat to provide them with benefits and favorable settlements in disputes.[30] Some of their leaders received government positions. (Juan Bramuglia of the Unión Ferroviaria, for example, was named as federal interventor of the province of Buenos Aires.) Where feasible and necessary, such as in the textile industry, he fostered the creation of parallel unions, which eventually displaced the existing unions.[31] One of his favorite tactics was to encourage ambitious second-line officials to break away from their unions and form new syndicates, which they would lead, with the help of rapid recognition and preferential treatment by the secretariat.

Perón's handling of the packinghouse workers aptly illustrates his political skills in manipulating labor unrest.[32] It also brought to the front ranks of his movement a man who was to flash and then sputter like a Roman candle in a few brief moments on or near the center stage of Argentine history.

The release of the Communist union official José Peter demonstrated to the packinghouse workers that the government could intervene on their behalf. The next step involved the elimination of Peter, who had formed a federation of factory-based unions in the meatpacking industry in 1932 and had been struggling without success to improve salary levels and working conditions, both of which were deplorable. The colonel's instrument would be Cipriano Reyes, a remarkable worker who was already locked in battle with Peter and the Communists.[33]

The son of a circus performer, Reyes had entered the work force at an early age and had quickly thrown himself into some bitter labor-management disputes during the twenties and thirties. On more than one occasion his efforts resulted in arrest and confinement. A self-educated man who found his anarchist coworkers as attractive as he found the Communists repellent, he developed his own distinct brand of militancy, at times hot-tempered and prone to violence. In 1944 he put together a federation of meatpackers' unions to compete against Peter's group. He led a series of strikes, some against U.S.-owned plants, and provoked the government to intervene. Perón invariably secured settlements favorable to the workers. On the first of these occasions, he visited Berisso, a meatpacking center, and in a dramatic gesture walked arm in arm with Reyes through the city streets.

In September 1945 there would be more labor trouble, this time erupting into violence and taking the life of one of Reyes' brothers. Both Perón and Mercante attended the funeral. Within weeks the various gestures that the colonel had made to Reyes and the packinghouse workers would pay him big dividends.

Perón's campaign for labor support was aimed not only at individual unions and leaders but also at the CGT.[34] A pro-Perón bloc of CGT officials outvoted their anti-government opponents and secured the confederation's participation in the regime's independence-day celebration on May 25, 1944. Three months later the same bloc succeeded in reversing the CGT's pro-Allied posture and put the organization on record as favoring the government's neutrality policy.

At this point Perón in no way controlled the CGT or the labor movement. The colonel had no punitive mechanisms at his disposal and could not enforce the loyalties of organized labor.[35] But what he could and did do was bind labor's recently acquired privileges to his tenure in office. Union leaders understood perfectly well that if Perón lost power, the progress they had been making would swiftly deteriorate.

Material benefits were not all that was at stake. For the first time a government was treating workers with respect instead of repression. They were beginning to feel like citizens who mattered, and they owed this psychic gratification to the colonel.[36]

Perón later referred to this stage of his career as the charismatic period.[37] He began to appear before labor unions throughout the country and carry his message of hope. The workers responded with enthusiasm. A tone was set at a meeting of railroad workers in the city of Rosario in December 1943, when a labor leader introduced Perón as "Argentina's Number One Worker."[38] The colonel's mystique was taking shape.

8

Problems with Washington

Fifty-five kilometers (thirty-five miles) southeast of Buenos Aires along the yawning estuary of the Río de la Plata, the municipality of La Plata stands as a tribute to urban planning and civic pride. Buenos Aires' double role as capital of the nation and of the province of Buenos Aires had enabled provincial interests to exercise a disproportionate influence over the national government. Federalization of Buenos Aires and the transfer of the provincial capital to La Plata in 1880 solved the problem. Honored by the switch, the inhabitants of La Plata decided to build within the bounds of a perfect five-kilometer (three-mile) square a city worthy of their new status. As befit the capital of Argentina's richest province, La Plata grew into a thriving metropolis, enriched by the presence of a first-rate university, the construction of modern port facilities, and rapid industrial development.

On June 10, 1944, a scant four days after the Allies had landed on the beaches of Normandy, Minister of War Juan Perón journeyed to the University of La Plata to inaugurate a new professorship of national defense. Before an audience of civilian, military and ecclesiastical dignitaries he delivered a lengthy, learned discourse on "The Significance of National Defense from a Military Point of View."[1] When a text of the speech arrived in Washington, it set off a burst of indignation.

The incident provides illuminating insights into North American attitudes toward Perón at a time when relations between the two countries were rapidly deteriorating. The colonel later claimed that he had been misquoted and misinterpreted.[2] An examination of the speech and the U.S. reaction to it belies the former charge but supports the latter.

The lecture updated and elaborated upon the nation-in-arms concept Perón had found appealing twelve years earlier. Postulating that "war is an inevitable social phenomenon," he explained that although Argentina wanted peace and had no aggressive designs on her neighbors, she could not ignore the possibility of attack from without. He then spelled out in some detail the type of defense system Argentina should adopt.

But for North American observers, Perón had cut his discourse from the same cloth that produced the bogus GOU manifesto of May 13, 1943. They found in the speech nothing less than the blueprint for the creation of a totalitarian state. Although Perón's domestic opponents saw no need to panic—indeed, the newspaper *La Prensa*, a consistent critic of the colonel, had praise for his words[3]—Washington chose to interpret the lecture in the worst possible light.

Part of this reaction may be attributable to pique at the way Perón phrased some of his ideas. For example, he explained that his concept of national defense would be relevant no matter which side won World War II. Coming close on the heels of one of the war's pivotal events, this statement struck Washington as insulting at best.[4]

A report prepared by the Office of Strategic Services (OSS) began with the observation that "Colonel Perón's distinctly unlearned background suggests that the speech is the work of a far more erudite and literate person, or persons." Perón's stint as a professor and his prior publication of a book expressing some of the very same ideas found in the speech had apparently escaped the writer's notice. The report went on to take out of context a paragraph about the need to "make the coming war popular," which Perón meant as a measure to be taken when war was imminent. For the OSS this was part of a plan for psychological and political preparation the military regime intended to put into immediate effect as part of its expansionist policy.

Finally, the report attributed sinister significance to a passage that merits reproduction:

> In effect, someone will have to show, beyond the shadow of a doubt, that the United States, England, Russia, and China—supposing that they win the war, and the same applies if Germany and Japan win—will never in the future have interests which might lead to a new conflagration among themselves, and that the winners might not try to establish a hateful imperialism in the world which would drive the oppressed to rebellion, and finally give credence to the belief that the word "war" has been discarded from all dictionaries.[5]

The OSS analyst found this forecast cynical. Time has proved these words to be uncannily prophetic.

The U.S. response to the La Plata speech followed naturally from the picture of Perón that had been taking shape in embassy reports. A biographical report compiled from intelligence sources in early 1944 presumed his unfriendliness to the United States in the admitted absence of concrete evidence.[6] John F. Griffiths, a Foreign Service auxiliary officer supposedly covering cultural matters but in fact a political specialist deeply involved with Perón's opponents, supplied the ambassador with a steady flow of reportage unflaggingly hostile to the colonel, and always minimized his popular support.[7] Perón's activities at the secretariat disturbed labor attaché John Fishburn. Though admitting the colonel's programs were not much different in substance from those of his immediate predecessor, he disliked the politicization process Perón had initiated and seemed unhappy that secretariat officials had not made any contact with the embassy until February 1944.[8] Brigadier General John W. Lang, the U.S. military attaché, kept in close contact with anti-Perón military plotters.[9]

The sour taste Perón stimulated in embassy officials derived from a combination of sources. His background and public utterances fostered suspicion that he had Fascist, or at least authoritarian, tendencies. He was careful to keep a certain distance between himself and the embassy, avoiding the reach of U.S. influence but encouraging U.S. officials to convert their frustration into dislike. The anti-Perón mood of the embassy meshed in symbiotic fashion with the attitude of the State Department toward Argentina.

British ambassador to Argentina Sir David Kelly noted in his autobiography: "When I arrived as ambassador in June, 1941, a sullen resentment had set in in Washington which was manifested in turn against each succeeding regime in Argentina and became more and more violent after each disappointment."[10] Out of what Kelly called a "he who is not with us is against us" mentality arose thinly veiled hostility on the part of State Department officials handling Latin American affairs. Setting the tone was Secretary of State Cordell Hull, whose personal resentment toward the Argentines as a result of their performance at the Rio Conference in 1942 had grown increasingly bitter.[11]

Thus when Argentina broke off diplomatic relations with the Axis in early 1944, instead of appeasing Washington, the move seemed to whet the State Department's appetite, especially after Farrell replaced Ramírez. Despite assurance to the contrary by the Farrell regime, Hull took the position that the removal of Ramírez was the work of pro-Axis elements angered by the rupture with Germany and bent upon hindering the collective-security efforts of the other American nations. He decided to treat the change in administrations as a coup engineered by groups threatening continental solidarity and asked for a consultation among the American republics prior to their recognition of the new regime.

Hull's plan was to convince the Latin American community to withhold diplomatic recognition in order to bring pressure upon Farrell. Convinced that he had the support of a majority of Argentines and the rest of the continent as well, the secretary hoped for nothing less than the ouster of the military government. The U.S. policy, however, looked very much like intervention in the domestic affairs of Argentina. Welles, for example, branded it as the use of "overwhelming power to dictate to the people of a sovereign American state what they should and should not do about their internal concerns."[12] Chile, Paraguay and Bolivia immediately recognized the Farrell regime and thereby shattered Hull's hope for a united front against Argentina.

Perón made a number of efforts to secure U.S. recognition. In early March he sent an emissary to convey to embassy officials his intent to restore constitutional rule in the near future.[13] At the same time he attempted to arrange a secret meeting with Norman Armour, the U.S. ambassador, but was rebuffed.[14] It was ironic that the United States pursued an antagonistic policy toward Perón at the very moment he found himself in a power struggle with the ultra-nationalist, pro-Nazi faction led by Perlinger.[15] The exigencies of the situation required him to seek a quiet rapprochement with Washington. But the faintest whiff of subservience to State Department pressure would have undermined him.[16]

Ambassador Armour had the difficult task of implementing the non-recognition policy. He remained in Argentina but had no official contact with the regime. On June 2, he attended a secret meeting with Perón.[17] As a price for recognition, Armour suggested that the government supply him with a list of specific actions it had taken and proposed to take in order to implement the break in relations with Germany. Perón's reply was that to do so would create the impression that Washington was dictating to Argentina. An impasse had been reached.

Eight days later, Perón delivered his La Plata lecture. The State Department chose to regard it as a provocation and on June 22 recalled Armour to Washington "for consultation," a euphemism indicating the two countries were on the brink of a rupture in diplomatic relations. A skeleton crew remained in the U.S. embassy and continued to abstain from direct contact with the regime. On July 26, the State Department issued a document, similar in tone to Hull's letter to Storni, attempting to justify its policy toward the Farrell government.[18] It provoked the recall of Argentina's ambassador in Washington.

A number of other Latin nations also withdrew their ambassadors. At first Great Britain refrained from following suit, but Hull convinced Roosevelt to appeal to Churchill, who yielded and summoned Ambassador Kelly home. However, just prior to his departure Kelly met clandestinely with Perón and Farrell, to whom he made it clear that U.S. pressure had necessitated his withdrawal.[19] This effectively undercut Hull.[20]

Diplomatic measures alone, as the secretary realized from the start, were not going to bring Argentina to heel. It would be necessary to tighten some economic screws. But without wholehearted cooperation from the British, this strategy was likewise doomed to fail.

The British were determined not to jeopardize shipments of meat from Argentina. In addition, they were quite conscious of the vulnerability of their substantial investments in Argentina to retaliatory seizure if the dispute were carried to extremes. They hoped to maintain their trade position with Argentina in the postwar period and recognized the North Americans as commercial competitors. On July 14, Prime Minister Churchill reminded President Roosevelt of his country's dependence upon Argentina: "The stamina of the [British] workman cannot be maintained on a lesser diet in meat."[21] By late August, the British were negotiating with the Argentines to renew the contracts which would guarantee an uninterrupted flow of meat across the Atlantic.

The economic sanctions that the United States applied on its own account were ineffective. In August the Treasury Department froze Argentine gold deposits in the United States, and in September Argentine ports were declared off limits to North American ships. At the same time the State Department severely restricted U.S. exports to Argentina. The result, predicted ahead of time by the U.S. embassy when it attempted to dissuade Washington from its declaration of economic warfare against the Farrell regime,[22] was that Great Britain, South Africa and other Latin nations increased their trade with Argentina. The sole victims of Hull's policy were U.S. firms, who complained bitterly to the State Department.[23]

The only weapons left were verbal. At a press conference on September 7, Hull affirmed his belief that Argentina was going to become an asylum for Nazi war criminals.[24] Later that month, President Roosevelt made a public statement expressing his support for Hull's Argentine policy and taking note of the "growth of Nazi-Fascist influence and the increasing application of Nazi-Fascist methods in a country of this hemisphere."[25]

After much huffing and puffing, the house refused to fall. The assumption that a majority of Argentines wanted to join the Allied camp and would respond to U.S. encouragement by somehow forcing the Farrell regime out of office turned out to be wishful thinking. Hull merely enabled Perón to wave the banner of Argentine nationalism and gain great popularity by standing up to the "Yankee colossus."

Hull's resignation on November 27, the result of ill health, paved the way for an eventual face-saving resolution of the controversy. The balance of power within the State Department shifted in favor of those who felt U.S. policy toward Argentina was not accomplishing any positive results and was straining relations with the rest of Latin America. At the same time, the Farrell regime was fearful lest it be excluded from forthcoming international conferences, especially one which would establish a United Nations organization for the postwar era.

Hull's replacement, Edward R. Stettinius, and his assistant secretary for Latin America, Nelson A. Rockefeller, were willing to terminate the feud with Argentina to further hemispheric solidarity. During an inter-American conference held at Chapultepec in Mexico City in February 1945, the delegates worked out the conditions under which Argentina might regain the good graces of the American community of nations. She would have to declare war on the Axis, repress residual Axis activity within her borders and sign whatever agreements the conference might reach. (The United States had also been pressuring the Farrell regime to transfer the government to the Supreme Court and schedule national elections—the procedure required by Argentine law in the event the country was without a legitimate head—but Perón made it clear that this condition was totally unacceptable.[26]) The North American delegation to the conference committed the United States to recognize the Farrell government and favor Argentina's admission to the soon-to-be-formed United Nations.

The Argentine government subscribed to these terms. On March 27, with nary a blush at the lateness of the hour, Argentina declared war on Germany and Japan. On April 9, the United States formally resumed diplomatic relations with Argentina. At the UN Conference in San Francisco several weeks later, Argentina gained admission to the United Nations, with the help of the U.S. delegation and over the loud objections of the Soviets.

Juan Perón would always react with skepticism to moralizing from Washington and exhibit confidence in his ability to handle the Yankees. The U.S. accommodation to the Farrell regime may have given birth or nourishment to these attitudes.

The United States and Argentina seemed to be on the verge of a new era of normalized relations. But anti-Argentine elements both inside and outside the State Department were not about to acquiesce. The sudden death of Franklin D. Roosevelt on April 12 made it easy for them to hint that Rockefeller had taken advantage of the sick president to bring about a change in the North American posture toward the Farrell regime. Unfavorable publicity criticizing U.S. support of Argentina at the San Francisco conference added to the pressures. Therefore, a disconcerting instability underlay U.S. policy at this juncture, and a zig that had become a zag was about to zig again.

9

The Emergence
of Evita

In 1944, Juan Perón outmaneuvered his opponents within the armed forces, embraced the labor movement and survived a diplomatic onslaught by the United States. He also entered into an intimate personal relationship that would define an entire phase of his political career and would hover over his shoulder, a spectral reminder of a golden past, until the day he died. Eva Duarte became first his lover and then a junior partner and spouse, arrangements that violated social norms binding mistresses and wives to the roles tradition assigned to them.

Perón's liaisons with women provide much more than picturesque footnotes to his public life. They throw light upon aspects of his character that bore upon his capabilities as a leader and statesman. Moreover, the impact some of these relationships had not only upon his career but also upon the course of Argentine history was substantial.

An impressive volume of rumor has burgeoned, most of it the work of his political enemies, ascribing to him a panoply of sexual aberrations that supposedly provide clues to his behavior. As he took his first steps in the political arena, the colonel profited immensely from the sex appeal he projected. His virility attracted women and also drew admiration from macho-minded men. Yet he never fathered any children, a circumstance that fostered claims that he was sterile. According to a political theorist who worked with him during this period, earlier in Perón's military career when fellow officers used to sit around in the barracks and exchange tales of their amatory exploits, Perón confessed he had nothing to contribute because he had known no women except his wife.[1] This inspired whispers charging him with impotency. Yet at the same time there were reports that during his stay in Italy he had had a German mistress.[2] Various deviations ranging from voyeurism to pedophilia have also been ascribed to him.

As might be expected, there have been Peronist counterclaims, equally suspect. For example, Perón himself is said to have asserted that while delayed in Spain in 1940 he spent a number of months in Barcelona, where he met, moved in with and possibly impregnated a Catalán schoolteacher.[3] During his exile in Spain, nearly two decades later he supposedly dispatched a friend on a search that led to Rome, Milan and finally a hospital in Florence, where the woman had died. No trace of any child was found. The problem with this story is that the available evidence indicates that Perón passed briefly through Barcelona on his visit to Spain in 1940.[4]

When Perón became a public figure in late 1943, several of the magazine articles profiling him mentioned that he was living in a Buenos Aires apartment with his daughter. *Time*, for example, told its readers: "A widower, he has a pretty seventeen-year-old daughter, María Inez."[5] According to the *Inter-American Monthly*, Perón was "devoted to his lovely eighteen-year-old daughter, Isabelita."[6] A radio fan magazine in late 1943 even published a photograph of the grinning colonel with his "daughter."[7] But as Perón's power increased and his association with Eva Duarte grew more notorious, the mists of oblivion enveloped María Inez/Isabelita.

The truth of the matter is that a teenage girl was sharing Perón's drab apartment on the corner of Arenales and Coronel Díaz, just across the street from a large brewery. She came from Mendoza, where she met him during his tour of duty at the mountain-warfare school. Her nickname, coined by the colonel and inspired by her overbite, was Piranha. He took her to boxing matches at Luna Park and introduced her as *m'hija*, "my daughter."[8]

Perón's dalliance with Piranha evidenced a disregard for convention that pushed beyond indifference into the realm of defiance. It also was an early indication of a weakness for young girls. Although not many details about the affair are known, one thing is certain: when Evita moved in with Perón, Piranha moved out and, according to one source, returned to Mendoza.[9]

Evita's entrance also nipped another budding relationship. Perón had remained close to the Tizón family after Aurelia's death and had developed an attachment to one of his sisters-in-law, a schoolteacher. According to Julián Sancerni Jiménez, a Radical politician and friend of the Tizóns, the colonel had actually announced he was going to marry her, but Evita changed his mind.[10] The notable feature about this episode is that the sister-in-law was nearly Perón's age. Thus it stands as an exception to Perón's weakness for women many years his junior.

Evita too departed from the pattern. Far from being a docile, nest-keeping companion, she was a strong personality in her own right. Her story, even scraped of its incrustation of myth, richly deserves epic status.[11]

On May 9, 1919, at a ranch near the tiny town of Los Toldos about 200 kilometers (120 miles) from Buenos Aires, an Indian midwife helped deliver a daughter to Juana Ibarguren. The infant's father, Juan Duarte, had political contacts enabling him to enjoy the social status of an estanciero, even though he merely rented his ranch from its owner. Thus he could indulge in the perfectly acceptable social luxury of maintaining two families. His legal wife and three legitimate children lived in the pampa town of Chivilcoy. Juana Ibarguren, his concubine, worked as a servant on the ranch and kept her brood, now numbering five, in a house in Los Toldos. He had given these children his name and a modest amount of financial support. When his fifth child was born, he apparently balked at acknowledging his paternity, and the child's birth and baptismal certificates did not bear his name. However, she was called Eva María Duarte.

Descended from Basque immigrants, Juana Ibarguren had never been able to escape her lower-class background, although one of her brothers managed to become a railroad stationmaster. Her relationship with Juan Duarte gave her a recognized, but not respected, position on the fringe of local society. Whenever Duarte's wife and legitimate offspring came on one of their frequent visits to the ranch, Juana and her children had to remain out of view, a situation that was remedied in 1922 by the decision of Duarte to leave the ranch and live with his legal family in Chivilcoy.

Evita, as Eva María came to be called, experienced poverty and social ostracism during her early years in Los Toldos. On January 8, 1926, her father was killed in an automobile accident. Juana Ibarguren loaded her children into a sulky and journeyed to Chivilcoy for the wake. It was Evita's first trip away from home, and one that would fester in her memory for the rest of her life. Duarte's wife refused to permit the six visitors to enter the mortuary where the body lay. They had to remain outside, peering in, until the mayor, Duarte's brother-in-law, took pity on them and decided they could make a quick pass by the flower-bedecked corpse. He also let them join the tail end of the funeral procession, but only as far as the cemetery gate.

Returning to Los Toldos, Juana Ibarguren now had to struggle to make ends meet. Elisa, the second eldest of her daughters, found work in the local post office (as a result of the intervention of one of Juana's lovers, according to one version). Juan, the only male in the family, clerked in a grocery store. Juana herself took in sewing. Blanca, the firstborn, continued her studies at the provincial normal school en route to a teaching career. Erminda and Evita made their way through elementary school.

By early 1931, Juana had had more than enough of Los Toldos and decided to seek a better life in Junín, a larger town not far away. Helped by friends who had political leverage, she arranged for Elisa to be transferred to the post office in Junín. Juan, a personable youth called Juancito by his family and friends, bounced from job to job until he found steady employment as a traveling soap salesman. Evita, by now approaching adolescence, remained in school.

Juana at first resumed her sewing. But the economic situation of the family soon improved when Blanca received her first teaching job and Juana began to cook meals for various bachelor military men and professionals. (This led to the canard, palpably false yet a persistent component of the Evita myth, that Juana ran a bordello.[12]) Within a short time Blanca married a lawyer who had taken meals at her home, and Elisa became the wife of an army major stationed nearby.

The same path to security and respectability lay open to Evita, but she chose not to follow it. Instead, she devoured the fan magazines that chronicled the lives of movie, stage and radio celebrities and began to see herself in the bright lights of Corrientes Street, at the heart of the theater district in Buenos Aires. "She sang all the time," recalled a neighbor. "When she was eight years old she was already saying she was going to be an actress."[13] Her formal stage debut on October 20, 1933, in a school play, might not have electrified Junín, but it convinced her that she had seen the future.

As she entered her teens she was an attractive youngster, petite and brunette, with a pale complexion and large brown eyes. Yet she was neither stunning nor vocally gifted.

The most widely accepted account of Evita's departure from Junín holds that she attached herself to Agustín Magaldi, a popular tango singer known as the sentimental voice of Buenos Aires, on tour through the province of Buenos Aires, as he completed an engagement in Junín. According to one version, Magaldi's wife accompanied him on the trip, and Evita went with the couple to Buenos Aires, where she lived for a short time in their apartment. The inevitable derogatory variation depicts Evita seducing Magaldi and serving as his mistress until shortly after they returned to the capital. She did in fact arrive in Buenos Aires in early 1935, at the tender age of fifteen. Her brother, Juancito, fulfilling his obligatory military service nearby, was on hand to welcome her and cast himself as her protector, a role she would someday reciprocate.

Evita's migration to the big city in search of work paralleled the migration of rural workers who were leaving the countryside to provide the manpower for the shops and factories that were sprouting around the edges of the capital. Although a decade would pass before she realized it, her formative years had given her an intuitive grasp of the social and political alienation they felt.

The struggle for survival in Buenos Aires tested the aspiring actress from Junín. She would endure hunger and illness. Within three months of her arrival in the Argentine Big Apple, and nearly six weeks before her sixteenth birthday, Evita had a bit part in a play. Someone, perhaps Magaldi, had opened a door for her.

Several more minor roles, a tour of the provinces and the publication of her photo in a few magazines followed in rapid succession. Though earning barely enough to survive (one witness has declared that her mother made her send money back to Junín[14]), she managed to find friends willing to give her career an occasional boost. In 1937 she appeared in her first motion picture and participated in her first radio drama. The latter was of particular importance because it exposed her to a mass audience. The parts she played were still secondary, but they were coming with increasing frequency. Her brother, meanwhile, hovered in the background, going back to work for the soap company (Radical Soap was the trade name of the product) and even doing a turn as a radio announcer.

In April 1939, opportunity beckoned in the guise of a co-starring role in a radio melodrama. As a recent biography notes, "Eva was good at conveying suffering. When she found the soaps she found her acting career."[15] Promotion for the program included more fan-magazine exposure and the publication of stories about her various "romantic" interests.

Her new stature as a radio starlet led to several movie roles and a contract to do radio shows sponsored by the firm that produced Radical Soap. She was still a member of supporting casts, but her appearances now were much more substantial than the walk-on parts she'd had to play on the legitimate stage. Indeed, she would never again appear before the footlights.

Evita's detractors have reiterated that during this period she advanced her career by engaging in a series of meretricious relationships with men in positions to help her.* This is a portrayal that emerged from malicious gossip spread by political opponents after she became First Lady. It is as hyperbolic as the vision of Evita that would later inspire her followers to petition the Vatican that she be canonized. While she undoubtedly gave up her virginity during these difficult years,[16] she did not sleep her way to success.

She was ambitious, restless and insecure. She had by now begun to acquire a bit of polish but the rough edges still came through in her speech and behavior. Publicity shots show her as a typical 1930s starlet, youthful, alabaster-skinned, hair often swept back, a coy expression often on her face.

These were the days when she sat for the photos that would provide the grist for a puerile campaign to discredit her. The June 18, 1940, issue of *Cine Argentino* published the most famous of these under the headline "Eva Duarte Surprised by the Camera." They displayed the winsome brunette in various pinup poses, baring her legs (not her best feature), shoulders and a bit of breast. By the standards of the day the photos might have been daring, but they did not go beyond existing limits. How-

---

* Rabid Evita-haters, exemplified by author Jorge Luis Borges, to this day insist that she was a "common prostitute." See P. Theroux, *The Old Patagonian Express*, pp. 373–74. There is not the slightest shred of evidence to support this charge.

ever, the idea that their first lady had posed in this way was apparently too much for many straitlaced Argentines. Evita's enemies later on reproduced one of the poses in postcard form and widely distributed it.

For the first nine months of 1943, Evita dropped out of public view. One explanation was that she was suffering from some serious illness. But by springtime she returned to work with a flourish, signing a contract on September 21 to play the lead roles in a radio series entitled *Heroines of History*. She would interpret the Tsarina Alexandra, Sarah Bernhardt, the Empress Josephine of France, Isadora Duncan, Queen Elizabeth of England, and Madame Chiang Kai-shek. For Evita, life would soon imitate art.

A military regime was now ruling Argentina, and Eva Duarte, ever mindful of the need to cultivate useful contacts, turned her attention to the men in the braided uniforms. She had a well-placed friend in Oscar Nicolini, who served as secretary to the head of the Post and Telegraph Offices, a federal department also charged with regulation of the broadcast industry. He introduced her to his boss, Lieutenant Colonel Aníbal F. Imbert. It was Imbert who accompanied her to the January 22 Luna Park extravaganza on behalf of San Juan earthquake victims and presented her to Colonel Perón.

Given what is known about their personalities, Evita probably took the initiative in rapidly cementing the relationship. She found new quarters for them in a building on Posadas Street, behind the posh Alvear Palace Hotel and not far from Radio Belgrano, where she worked, although for the sake of appearances the couple rented adjoining apartments. Perón must have been fascinated by the uninhibited aggressiveness of his new companion. He did nothing to conceal their liaison. Indeed, on February 3, both he and Mercante allowed themselves to be photographed with her on a visit to the radio station.

In 1944, Evita's artistic career lurched forward at a frenetic pace, undoubtedly propelled by her association with Perón. She continued the *Heroines of History* series while at the same time participating in thrice-weekly propaganda broadcasts sponsored by the Secretariat of Labor and Public Welfare. Entitled *Toward a Better Future*, these programs filled the airwaves with praise for the progress of the Revolution of June 4 and for the military officers at its helm.

In the midst of all these radio broadcasts, Evita maneuvered into the best movie role of her career. The film, called *Circus Cavalcade*, featured well-known Argentine stars Libertad Lamarque, Hugo del Carril and Armando Bo.[17] During production, Evita was rumored to have engaged in a bitter quarrel with Lamarque, whose subsequent disappearance from Argentine movies has been attributed to Evita's custom of rewarding friends and punishing enemies. Of more significance was a change in Evita's appearance during the shooting of the film. She bleached her hair for the part she played, and decided to remain a blond.

In addition to these professional activities, Evita found time to share her compañero's interests.[18] She sat in on meetings Perón held in the apartment with military and civilian associates. The colonel must have approved of her presence. The contributions she made at these sessions might not have always been substantive, but they were occasionally memorable. One witness present at a gathering of nationalists at the apartment described her impact. "We were discussing a pending government appointment when Evita burst in. Perón introduced her. 'Hi, boys,' was the way she greeted us. She seemed very high-strung, and her words came out in torrents. Nor did she hesitate to voice her opinions in very direct language. 'Why do you want to appoint that *negro* [a term used for dark-haired people]?' she said of the person we were considering. 'He's a shit.' We were all quite astonished."[19]

Perón's handling of his relationship with Evita bordered upon provocation. He appeared in public with her, and she comported herself in an uninhibited, often crude way. Many of his fellow officers were shocked. They felt Perón was setting a bad example for the army.[20] If the colonel's personal style and direct way of speaking distinguished him as a breath of fresh air to many who encountered him for the first time, his flaunting of Evita went a bit too far. It was in response to criticism by his army colleagues that Perón made his classic riposte: "They reproach me for going with an actress. What do they want me to do? Go with an actor?"[21] On September 6, the U.S. embassy reported a decline in his personal prestige, in part because of the "Eva Duarte situation."[22]

By the end of 1944, Perón was still endeavoring to consolidate his position vis-à-vis the armed forces. He had for the moment successfully defused the threat posed by nationalist elements within the army, yet there were still military conspirators waiting for him to stumble. His affair with Evita gave them cause for hope.

In the closing months of World War II, it was evident to Perón that the de facto government in power since June 4, 1943, could not continue indefinitely. The pressures for a return to the constitution were mounting from both within and without Argentina. Since the colonel had no intention of returning to the barracks himself, he would have to work out a strategy to provide an orderly method for the military government to retire with the honor of the armed forces intact and a political platform of his own to present to the people of Argentina. But he had a major hurdle to surmount in the conviction held by many that he was a committed Fascist, or even worse, an agent of Nazi Germany.

10

The Nazi-Fascist
Taint

Mar del Plata, 400 kilometers (250 miles) south and slightly east of the federal capital, sits on the outer edge of the province of Buenos Aires where the latter distends into the South Atlantic. In summer the city's beaches groan under the weight of porteños in flight from the heavy heat of the capital; a palatial casino panders to the gambling instincts of sporting Argentines. During the winter months the city shrivels to a modest size and the pace of life becomes more relaxed.

The winter of 1945 was different. On July 10, a German submarine, the U-530, steamed into Mar del Plata and surrendered to the Argentine navy.[1] Thirty-eight days later the U-977 followed suit. The appearance of the two vessels, months after the fall of Berlin, gave rise to rumors of every hue. The most imaginative was that one of these submarines had transported Adolf Hitler and Eva Braun, alive and well, to some unspecified spot along the coast of Patagonia before heading for Mar del Plata. According to another version, the U-boats had deposited a vast treasure somewhere in southern Argentina.

The latter rumor became a key link in the forging of an accusatory chain that directly connected not only Juan Perón but also Eva Duarte to the Third Reich. In addition, the publicity generated by the incidents helped fuel what persisted as a central issue in Argentine domestic politics: Perón's supposed Nazi, or Fascist, philosophy.

The basis for the charge that Perón and Evita were involved with the Nazis derived from German documents discovered after the war. An Argentine politician, Silvano Santander, marshaled the evidence in a book written to prove that the couple served as Nazi agents in Argentina.[2] In the 1970s other writers revived the accusation.[3] The facts upon which the indictment rests contain gaping holes. As so often occurs, the conclusions of Perón's critics have gone far beyond what the evidence warrants. At the same time one may legitimately doubt Perón's total innocence in the matter.

The gist of the case against the colonel and his lady is that they were in close contact with the German embassy early in the war and aided Nazi espionage activities. Moreover, when the defeat of the Axis was inevitable, Perón is said to have facilitated the escape of many leading Nazis by selling them Argentine passports. German submarines, of which the U-530 and the U-977 were the last in a stream, were supposed to have smuggled ashore gold and other valuables as payment for these documents. Ludwig Freude, a German businessman living in Argentina, allegedly coordinated the transfers, and the payments somehow found their way into bank accounts in the name of Eva Duarte.

Santander's documentation seems clearly false. For example, he put Perón in the German embassy at a poker game with Nazi and Argentine army officials at a time when the colonel was still in Europe.[4] The linchpins to his proof of Evita's involvement are letters written by a German naval captain and dated in 1941 and 1943. They refer to Perón's liaison with the actress.[5] Yet by all accounts this relationship did not begin until 1944.

The surrender of the German U-boats at Mar del Plata attracted the sustained and meticulous scrutiny of U.S. intelligence operatives, who received substantial cooperation from the Argentine government. The box of documents detailing the investigation of the matter and available at the National Archives in Washington fails to confirm in any way that a treasure had been landed. Nor do any of the diplomatic or intelligence reports in the archives provide any factual support for the charge that Perón and Evita were Nazi agents.*

In mid-1944, Perón did send a representative to Spain to attempt once again to negotiate an arms deal with the Germans.[6] By this late date the fortunes of war made it certain that Berlin would never have been able to deliver on any agreement, so Argentine motives for engaging in these discussions (which were discontinued in September) remain unclear. Since U.S. antagonism foreclosed the possibility of procuring North American weapons, the negotiations could have reflected bona fide concerns about the defense capabilities of the Argentine army and did not necessarily carry with them any pro-Nazi commitment.

On the inevitable other hand, Perón did enjoy close contacts with various Germans in Argentina. Ludwig Freude was a particularly intimate friend. Accused of handling Nazi financial interests in Argentina after the

* An FBI document entitled "German Espionage in Latin America" (June 1946, copy on file with author) links Perón with the Nazi arrested in Trinidad on October 20, 1943, en route to Berlin to arrange a weapons deal. It also mentions Perón's support of Bolivians instrumental in the 1943 coup in Bolivia and of extreme right-wing elements in Brazil. However, these activities do not make the colonel an agent of the Third Reich, since his perception of Argentine national interests might have motivated him in each of these instances.

break in relations with Germany, Freude became the target of U.S. demands that the Farrell regime clean up all vestiges of Nazism within the country. Perón made strenuous, and ultimately successful, efforts to protect him.

In addition, Perón's own testimony establishes the type of relationship he had with members of the German community. When the time came for Argentina to declare war on the Axis, the colonel felt the need to explain, almost apologetically, the government's action to his German friends.[7]

Another criticism centered upon the regime's reluctance to act decisively against German spy networks operating in Argentina. There is no credible evidence to establish that Perón himself was actively cooperating with Axis agents. He maintained an appearance of impartiality, even after the diplomatic rupture, at a time when both German and Allied spies continued their espionage and counterespionage. The colonel was mainly concerned about finding out what each side was doing. In October 1944 he told a foreigner he rightly suspected of spying for the Allies: "What I'm doing now is like rolling a coin on its edge. A push from either side will topple it, and I'm not going to let anyone give it that push."[8]

Cordell Hull's prediction that Argentina would become a haven for Nazi war criminals after the war mirrored a growing concern about the German migration to Argentina in the final stages of the conflict, a flow that continued during the immediate postwar era. Perón justified this open-door policy on humanitarian grounds (although his humanitarian instincts never led him to denounce Nazi wartime atrocities) and on the basis of his great distaste for the Nuremberg trials, which rubbed against his military sensibilities. (He called the trials "an infamy, unworthy of the conquerors."[9]) He also had more practical reasons: the scientists and technicians who found refuge in Argentina would help in the industrialization of the nation. Whether he received (or extorted) any compensation for the help he provided these refugees cannot be determined. Rumors about the so-called Perón fortune trace the beginnings of the colonel's accumulation of wealth to the money he and Evita supposedly made selling passports.[10]*

Perón's open admiration of Mussolini fortified allegations that he aided and abetted the Nazi cause. He believed that Mussolini was a great man.[11] When he heard that S.S. troops had rescued Il Duce on September 12, 1943, from the mountain fortress where he was being held prisoner, the colonel offered a toast to celebrate the feat.[12]

---

* A recent scholarly article reports that the stories of high Nazi officials converting their property into gold and fleeing Europe by submarine in the waning months of World War II originated with a British "black propaganda" operation designed to convince German soldiers and civilians that their leaders were deserting them. See R. Newton, "Indifferent Sanctuary: German-Speaking Refugees and Exiles in Argentina, 1933–1945," *Journal of Inter-American Studies and World Affairs*, Vol. 24, November 1982, p. 395.

Of course, he always denied in his public statements that he was either a Fascist or a Nazi. The most to which he would admit was a willingness to cling to an idea even though it might have been shared by Mussolini or Hitler.[13]

A fundamental premise guiding Perón held that Mussolini's Italy and Hitler's Germany were developing an alternative to capitalism and communism. World War II, in his view, was no more than a concerted effort by these dominant systems to crush their budding competitors. The alternative emerging from the Italian and German experiments was a third ideology or position that took a middle ground between free-market capitalism, in which big business called the tune, and the dictatorship of the proletariat.[14] In speeches during 1944, he reiterated the proposition that the state should harmonize the interests of employers and employees and thereby achieve true social justice.

This approach obviously carried with it a predisposition toward authoritarian rule. The corporate states established by Franco in Spain and Salazar in Portugal were relatively benign versions of the brutal systems imposed by Mussolini and Hitler. Perón likewise betrayed a predilection for authoritarianism. In his August 1944 speech at the Buenos Aires Stock Exchange, he told his audience of businessmen that the Secretariat of Labor and Public Welfare would "channel the Argentine labor movement in one direction . . . so that it would proceed rationally, in accordance with the directives of the State."[15]

However, the notion that social justice can be reached by a balancing of the interests of capital and labor is rooted in papal encyclicals of the late nineteenth and early twentieth centuries. An intellectual tradition that emerged from these documents produced in Latin America supporters of the Hispanic-style corporate state, but they eventually tempered their enthusiasm for authoritarian government. The same young Catholics who embraced the Franco solution during the 1930s became Christian Democrats who won free elections and governed Chile and Venezuela in parliamentary fashion three decades later.

In addition, expediency always enjoyed first priority in Perón's scheme of things. He would never sacrifice practicality on the altar of ideological coherence. Moreover, his admiration for the German and Italian experiments burned most brightly when the Wehrmacht was enjoying its spectacular successes on the battlefields of Europe. Recognition of the excesses committed by the Nazis was not forthcoming until the Allied victory had been assured.

His perception of the shortcomings of Italian Fascism provides useful insights into his thinking. On April 10, 1945, a scant nineteen days before the bullet-riddled bodies of Mussolini and his mistress dangled from garage rafters in Milan's Piazza Loreto, Perón told the second secretary of the U.S. embassy that Il Duce committed two major errors: his political party indoctrinated only a bit more than half of the Italian population; and the Fascist militia did not replace the regular army, which was at heart anti-Fascist.[16] In a taped interview twenty-three years later, he expanded upon this theme, declaring that Mussolini's failure to crush the Socialist and Communist parties, to replace the army with his Fascist militia and to win over the monarchy led to his downfall.[17]

Perón's critical analysis of Fascism betrayed a startling degree of ignorance. The disastrous mistakes Mussolini made in setting foreign policy were blithely overlooked. How Il Duce's expansionist aims in Africa and Albania could have been satisfied without a professional army Perón never explained. The bankruptcy of Italian Fascist doctrine, the spreading rot of corruption that afflicted the Fascist party, Mussolini's ultimate madness in plunging Italy into a calamitous war for which she was unprepared—all seemed to escape Perón's notice. Even more remarkable is the fact that he was personally present in Italy (not for the purpose of looking at the Leaning Tower of Pisa, he often boasted[18]) at a time when many of these signs of weakness were surfacing.

A point at which Perón openly parted company with Nazism was the latter's emphasis on racial purity. Despite charges that he was anti-Semitic,* he criticized anti-Semitism and took some steps to discourage his ultra-nationalist supporters from persecuting the large Jewish community in Buenos Aires.[19] He did so, however, on practical rather than moral grounds. In taped memoirs, he recorded his response to a German who, having escaped to Argentina after the war, urged Perón to do something about the Jewish problem: if Hitler couldn't solve it with 100 million Germans, how could he, Perón, accomplish anything with only 20 million Argentines, the colonel asked. Moreover, he pointed out that it was impossible to kill them or deport them. Therefore, the best way to deal with them was to incorporate them into Argentine society as much as possible.[20]

Another marked difference between Perón and those who would have reproduced a true Nazi or Fascist regime in Argentina was the colonel's visceral distaste for violence. It is true that he would often close his eyes to brutalities committed by others in his name, and that from time to time he would indulge in inflammatory rhetoric. But he never had the slightest inclination to make violent action a centerpiece of his political philosophy in the manner of Mussolini or Hitler.

---

* He was reported to have made an anti-Semitic speech in which he referred scornfully to the "Jewry of Roosevelt and Stettinius," to officers at Campo de Mayo on March 27, 1944. State Department Report, October 1944. However, the author of a subsequent biographical sketch doubted the authenticity of the speech (State Department, Division of Biographic Information, August 23, 1946; copies on file with author), which appears to have been an invention of his political enemies.

Finally, Perón's military background set him apart from Mussolini, Hitler and the Fascist ideologues of Argentina. The esteem in which he held the army as an institution made him ever reluctant to transform it totally into an instrument of the state.

Whether or not Perón was really a Fascist was far from academic in 1945. His enemies insisted upon making it the central issue facing Argentina. They defined the confrontation of the day as a struggle between democracy and Nazi-Fascism. Yet the "democratic" side included the Communist party as well as politicians intimately involved in the perversion of the democratic process in Argentina during the 1930s. For Perón's opponents, the domestic concerns of various sectors of Argentine society, including the working class, were of secondary importance. This was to prove a mistake from which they have yet to recover.

11

Spruille Braden

The opposition confronting Perón in 1945 seemed formidable. The Radical, Conservative, Socialist and Communist parties all singled out the colonel as their prime target and began to work out a common program of action. Large numbers of university students agitated vociferously against the regime.[1] Wealthy estancieros and industrialists looked with growing alarm at the "revolutionary" aspects of the government's domestic policies. Moreover, the contempt in which the upper-class families now held Perón would be surpassed only by their visceral distaste for Evita later.

The ban on political parties and the sporadic repression imposed by General Perlinger during his tour as minister of the interior impeded the coordination of a political assault upon Perón. Internal divisions, especially among the Radicals, played into the colonel's hand. But by the autumn of 1945, there were signs that the tide might begin to turn. In late April, anticipating the possibility that the impending fall of Berlin would set off large popular demonstrations, the military regime made sweeping arrests of both military officers and civilians, and later accused them of plotting against the government.[2] The scant evidence produced to justify the detentions marks them as both overreactive and badly timed. They occurred at a moment when U.S.-Argentine relations were warming and provoked much criticism in the North American press.

At 2:00 A.M. on April 23, Perón took the unusual step of issuing a written statement denying that he would be a presidential candidate in any future election.[3] This reflected his own unease at military disapproval of the use he was making of the various offices he held to promote his political ambitions. These measures failed to suppress pent-up emotions on the part of pro-Allied sectors of the populace. In May the surrender of Germany triggered three days of celebration in the capital and other large cities. It did not take much to convert these festivities into anti-government street demonstrations. At the end of the month, the regime decreed a law, to become effective in August, permitting the organization of political parties and electoral courts.[4]

The universities had been hobbled by restrictive measures taken by the Ramírez regime in late 1943.[5] Professors who protested against the government had lost their jobs as the military took control of the major universities. Most of the students followed the instincts of young people everywhere under similar circumstances and manifested their disapproval of the regime at every turn. Their protests even went to the extreme of reflecting class bias. "Books, yes! *Alpargatas* [hemp-and-cloth shoes], no!" they would shout at pro-Perón workers, in a reference to the traditional footwear of the common laborer, and workers would respond with the converse.

By early 1945 the government was trying to normalize the situation. The dismissed professors regained their positions, and university autonomy was restored. These measures succeeded only in encouraging student opposition to the regime.

The forces opposing Perón suffered from one basic disadvantage as they faced off against the colonel's coalition. The latter had a leader around whom to rally. The opposition lacked a personality who could galvanize and direct the fight against Perón. The solution turned out to be simpler than anyone might have dreamt. If the colonel's opponents needed a leader, the U.S. State Department would send them one.

On April 9, 1945, the United States and Argentina resumed diplomatic relations. While this signaled North American acceptance of a regime previously characterized as Nazi-Fascist and seemed to indicate that Washington would seek to work out a modus vivendi with Buenos Aires, the belief that Farrell, Perón and their associates were a pack of Nazis had not died. A number of public officials, the press and a large segment of the public still held firmly to this view. These seeds of contradiction received a heavy dose of fertilization with the nomination of Spruille Braden as the new U.S. envoy to Buenos Aires.

It was a puzzling choice, since Stettinius and Rockefeller,[6] who were directing Latin American policy at the State Department, favored a normalization of relations with Argentina within the framework of the conditions worked out at Chapultepec, while Braden was a hard-liner in the Cordell Hull mold. Indeed, the ambassador-designate suspected that President Roosevelt himself had personally chosen him.[7] However, the nomination seems to have been Rockefeller's idea[8] and was undoubtedly inspired by a desire to placate the lingering ill will at State and in the public at large toward the Buenos Aires regime. But Rockefeller could not have it both ways. Braden would judge compliance with the Chapultepec accords on a much stricter basis than would his superiors; indeed, his predisposition appears to have been that good-faith compliance was a priori impossible.

Roosevelt died on April 12. His successor, Harry S. Truman, entered the White House with no understanding of Latin America and at a critical juncture in world affairs. He decided to rely upon the advice of Cordell Hull, still a very sick man but as rancorous as ever toward the Argentines. At this point Stettinius and Rockefeller dispatched a special mission to Argentina for the purpose of setting in motion the new policy of friendly relations.[9] Braden was never consulted. The delegation, headed by State Department official Avra Warren, included economic and military representatives. It spent several days in Buenos Aires and enjoyed red-carpet treatment from Perón, who was especially eager to reach agreements for the purchase of military equipment. The Warren mission left the impression that a weapons deal would be negotiated and that U.S. and Argentine military personnel would soon consult on questions of continental security. However, Braden, about to depart for Buenos Aires, made it clear to the State Department that no arrangements of any kind would be made with Argentina without his approval.[10]

Spruille Braden was a perfect foil for the colonel. The new ambassador fit the Yankee image many Latins embraced.[11] Perón readily admitted that "if he didn't exist, we would have had to invent him."[12] At the same time he was far from a novice at dealing with Latin America.

Spruille Braden's life began in a log cabin in a Montana mining camp, where Mary Kimball Braden gave birth to her only child.[13] Her husband, William, was an engineer who specialized in the location and development of new mining properties. At first a consultant to various mining companies, he soon decided to set out on his own. An opportunity to purchase part ownership in an apparently exhausted Chilean copper mine called El Teniente enabled him to put into action an innovative technique for extracting low-grade ore on a mass-production basis. El Teniente became a fabulously successful operation and the cornerstone of the newly formed Braden Copper Company. Young Spruille spent his childhood in Chile, returning to the United States for his secondary and college education. He took a degree in mine engineering at Yale, where he played on a water-polo team captained by Archibald MacLeish and earned All-American honors in his junior and senior years.

After graduation, Braden rejoined his parents in Chile and worked on various mining projects with his father. There he met, courted and wed an upper-class Chilean. Soon other occupational challenges beckoned him and he engaged in a variety of business ventures relating to Latin America. His fluency in Spanish and experience in Chile proved invaluable assets.

The stock-market crash and ensuing depression sorely depleted the Braden family fortune, but did not discourage Spruille from his entrepreneurial interests. When the Roosevelt administration took office in 1933, he found he had political contacts that made it feasible for him to seek the ambassadorship to Chile. But he failed to secure the nomination. Instead, he was appointed delegate to an inter-American conference in Montevideo. His diplomatic career would span fourteen years.

From 1935 to 1939 he headed the U.S. delegation to the Chaco Peace Conference in Buenos Aires and helped negotiate an end to the bloody war between Bolivia and Paraguay. In the process he developed a distaste for certain Argentine officials who he believed were obstructing the conference. Ambassadorial assignments to Colombia (1939–1942) and Cuba (1942–1945) followed in succession.

As a diplomat, Spruille Braden adopted a muscular style that set him apart from most of his colleagues. Bluntly outspoken, consummately self-confident and aggressive, he eschewed the niceties of his new profession and, in the words of one contemporary, "would go into any situation with both fists."[14] His physical appearance complemented his personality. Jowly, barrel-chested, massive, he was the prototypical buffalo in a porcelain bazaar[15]—the Argentine equivalent of the bull in a china shop. His behavior at times matched the image. Given his role as ambassador of the Yankee colossus in countries that fell within the U.S. sphere of interest (or, to use a metaphor popular with many Latins, representative of the shark in the lake of sardines), Braden's approach was unabashedly proconsular. He defended U.S. business interests with vigor, although he did not hesitate to take a tough line with them when he thought they were in the wrong. For example, in Colombia he pressured a recalcitrant Pan American Airways to eliminate German pilots from an airline owned by Pan Am and operating close to the Panama Canal.

By the time he took charge of the embassy in Havana his activities were becoming more open. As Arthur Schlesinger, Jr., wrote in *Fortune* magazine, "Cuba marked a new phase. Braden began to throw his weight around and he began to taste the delights of popular acclaim. He was already developing the disposition toward itinerant speech making that Colonel Perón was later to know so well."[16]

The new U.S. envoy to Argentina brought with him an ideological outlook appropriate to his background. A staunch promoter of the free-enterprise system, he fervently believed that U.S. capital had a positive, expanding role to play in the economic development of Latin America, a conviction that made him an uncompromising foe of both Fascism and Communism. At the same time, certain prejudices accompanied him to Buenos Aires. His stay during the Chaco Peace Conference had given him a generally sour opinion of certain Argentines. Moreover, his many years in Chile probably infected him with an anti-Argentine bias not uncommon on the Pacific side of the Andes.

Whatever Braden's instructions from the State Department might have been, the new ambassador went to his post with a specific goal in mind. A cable he sent to Washington in July made his intentions clear.

Perón as the one outstanding leader now on [the] Argentine scene is [the] embodiment of [the] present Fascist military control, but he is only an individual, whereas the movement consists of many, was bred by the Nazis and furnishes the latter with [the] foundation on which they hope to build the "victory of the post war." Indeed, while [the] elimination of Perón and the military would be a big step forward, U.S., and consequently British security will not be assured until [the] last vestings of the evil principles and methods [the] existing Gov't represents and practices have been extirpated and a reasonably effective democracy exists in Argentina.[17]

Sir David Kelly summed it up nicely: "Mr. Braden . . . came to Buenos Aires with the fixed idea that he had been elected by Providence to overthrow the Farrell-Perón regime."[18] The U.S. ambassador apparently wanted to do for the Argentines what General Douglas MacArthur was doing for the Japanese.

Ambassador Braden arrived in Buenos Aires on the afternoon of May 19. He wasted no time in making his presence felt. Having been previously informed that an old friend of his was in jail for political reasons, he made a point of loudly inquiring about him during his reception by Argentine military and civilian officials at the airport. In a matter of hours the friend was released. Braden's "campaign" had begun auspiciously.

By tradition, the presentation of credentials by a new ambassador begins with a carriage ride to the Casa Rosada. A mounted escort of grenadier guards, resplendent in ceremonial costumes that dated back to the colonial era, accompanied Spruille Braden to the Government House on the afternoon of May 21. In formal attire, the new ambassador cut an imposing figure in the Salon Blanco (White Room). After an exchange of pleasantries, he emerged to find a small gathering of onlookers, attracted by the profusion of U.S. and Argentine flags decorating the entrance to the Casa Rosada. They applauded him.

The next morning he met with North American correspondents. His forthright answers to their questions included a declaration that although the United States was committed to the principle of nonintervention in the affairs of other nations, it was State Department policy to promote representative government and freedom of the press, speech and assembly throughout the Americas. The United States was not shedding the lives of its young merely to give lip service to democracy, he told them. The ambassador immediately won over the reporters, most of whom followed the lead of Arnaldo Cortesi of the *New York Times* and, as one diplomat put it, "foamed at the mouth when they heard Perón's name."[19] The North American press would lionize Braden during his tour of duty in Argentina.

On that afternoon, at a reception given by General Farrell for newly accredited diplomats, the president went out of his way to be cordial to Braden, but succeeded only in making a negative impression. "He was pitiful in self-belittlement," the ambassador wired Washington, "and except for [his] previous theme of frankness [our] only conversation was his reiterated invitation for me to polish off with him a particularly good bottle of Scotch he possesses."[20]

At the same affair, Braden for the first time met his soon-to-be antagonist, Colonel Perón.[21] The vice-president buttonholed the ambassador and explained in detail Argentina's pressing need for U.S. military equipment. He wanted very much to maintain what he saw as the progress achieved by the Warren mission. Braden replied that "you have an extremely bad press and public opinion abroad and you will first have to do things,"[22] an obvious reference to the Chapultepec accords. Perón assured him there would be no problem.

One week later, Braden pulled the plug on any expectation of military aid Perón might have entertained. The State Department announced that no U.S. military mission would be sent to Argentina until the Farrell regime fulfilled all its obligations as defined by the Chapultepec conference. This was a serious setback for Perón, who was counting upon arms purchases from the United States to fortify his hold upon Argentina's armed forces. He chose to treat the move as a broken promise (although no formal commitments had been made by the Warren mission).

The State Department decision was the first of a volley of blows to be aimed at the government. Perón's careful campaign to build a political power base suddenly became a life-and-death struggle for survival. Braden's goal of eliminating the military regime greatly encouraged the domestic opposition. The colonel was fully aware of the threat emanating from the U.S. embassy. The stage was now set for a series of head-to-head encounters between the two men.*

Ambassador Braden paid an official call on the vice-president at the Casa Rosada on June 1,[23] the same day the *New York Times* published a front-page article denouncing press censorship in Argentina. Perón embraced his visitor, in the Latin style of greeting, and turned on the charm. He explained at some length the Revolution of 1943, the evolution of Argentine policy toward the United States, his program for labor and commitment to cooperation with Washington. Braden was not impressed.

---

* Because of Braden's fluency in Spanish, he could speak in private with Perón. The only sources for what went on during these meetings are the participants themselves. Immediately after each interview, Braden sent to the State Department cables detailing his version of what had occurred. He also published his memoirs in 1971. Perón left no contemporary written records. He gave verbal accounts of one of the encounters to various associates, and secondhand versions of his descriptions have survived. He also talked about his meetings with Braden in the course of interviews during the 1960s.

For him, it was a replay of his prior talk with the colonel, "like a stalled phonograph record."[24] He pointed out that under the Chapultepec accords Argentina had promised to give the Allied powers access to German diplomatic archives and take over properties controlled by German interests. In addition, all Nazi agents in Argentina were to be arrested and turned over to the United States. Perón insisted that Argentina would comply.

Braden then proceeded to speak to the colonel, as he put it, not as ambassador to vice-president but as friend to friend. He pointed out that the incarceration of political prisoners, as well as the increasing censorship of the press, had a very negative effect upon North American public opinion. As he later noted, his comments were a "lecture on freedom of the press American style."[25] While agreeing that the situation would have to be improved, Perón requested in turn that steps be taken to control criticism of Argentina in the U.S. press. Braden replied that he could do nothing about it. The meeting concluded with the usual mutual pledges of cooperation.

Despite Braden's opinion of Perón as a "great promiser but a poor performer,"[26] the vice-president did lessen restrictions on the press and secure the release of almost all political prisoners within a short time after the interview.[27] The *New York Herald-Tribune* was quick to publicize the ambassador's role in forcing these measures.[28] Moreover, on June 13, Braden received a visit from Oscar Lomuto, an official from the government press office.[29] Speaking on Perón's behalf, Lomuto assured Braden that U.S. correspondents in Argentina would not be subject to any restrictions or obstacles. On that same day, claiming he was acting pursuant to Lomuto's request,[30] Braden issued to the North American reporters a statement conveying the vice-president's assurance. The local press publicized the statement and created the impression that the U.S. ambassador was defending freedom of the press in Argentina. Perón was unhappy about this, and Lomuto weakly insisted that Braden had promised to keep the details of their meeting secret.[31]

On June 15, three hundred of the nation's business firms and commercial institutions published a manifesto declaring that "a long series of measures, attitudes, resolutions and speeches have converted social agitation into the gravest question this government must face." Singled out for special criticism was "the creation of a climate of jealousy, provocation and rebellion, in which resentment and a permanent feeling of hostility and demands are stimulated."[32] A few days later, the Sociedad Rural (Rural Society), representing the big ranching and farm interests, issued a similar pronouncement. The oligarchy had now declared open war on the regime. To Perón it all seemed part of a grand scheme hatched and directed by the U.S. ambassador.

It was during these frigid mid-winter days that Spruille Braden himself took to the stump. As ambassador, he received numerous invitations to speak, and he took advantage of them to pour gasoline on the fire. Braden always insisted that he never abused his position by making public attacks upon or criticism of the Argentine government.[33] While it is true that the ambassador never specifically targeted the military regime in his discourses, he reiterated the urgent necessity of rooting out the last vestiges of Fascism from wherever they might still exist. Given the fact that he never attempted to hide his conviction that Perón and his associates were Nazi-Fascists, his audiences must have interpreted the speeches as he intended them, clarion calls for the overthrow of the Argentine government.

On the last day of June, Perón summoned the ambassador to his office in the Casa Rosada for a confrontation. Perón left no account of the meeting. According to Braden,[34] the vice-president complained about a campaign by "economic interests" against the government, and added: "I have the army with me to a man and more than 4 million laborers who recognize me as their leader and sole benefactor. If these [economic interests] try anything we will fight in the streets and blood will flow." Braden innocently inquired what all this had to do with him. Perón replied that the U.S. correspondents were part of the movement against him.[35] Braden denied this, and for a moment the two men engaged in an angry shouting match. Perón then intimated that if the "liars and troublemakers" did not stop their attacks on the government, they might become targets for retaliation by the fanatical elements among his followers. Objecting to what he perceived as a thinly veiled threat, Braden expressed his grave concern at the possibility that any correspondents might be physically harmed and rejected Perón's suggestion that the U.S. press be controlled in any way. In a cable dispatched to the State Department at midnight of the same day, the ambassador reported that "Perón's astonishing outburst . . . confirms he is dangerous" and in a rather boastful tone attributed the colonel's behavior to his realization that Braden was putting him in a position that, if maintained, would lead to his downfall.[36]

Two days later, the embassy received a phone call from someone purporting to be from the War Ministry. The caller threatened any U.S. journalist who continued to "confuse the situation."[37] The *Herald-Tribune* correspondent received a more specific threat and took refuge in the embassy residence. Braden was jubilant. He claimed a number of his ambassadorial colleagues agreed with him that he was "forcing Perón into a corner, [and] that in his insane ambition he will fight like a cornered wild animal and is capable of anything (repeat anything)."[38]

On that same day, Perón made his most militant public reference to the storm swirling around him. In a speech to insurance-company employees,[39] he declared: "A few days ago [referring to the June 14 businessmen's manifesto] they called me an agitator of the Argentine masses. I do not reject that title, and if one day the needs of justice or the country require me to be a real agitator of the masses of workers, I shall not hesitate one second to put myself out front." He then threw out a challenge similar to the one he had issued to Braden. Referring to efforts to create a climate of rebellion in Argentina, he told his audience: "We are waiting for this insurrection, and we do not fear it. We have the necessary force to repress it with our army, which is firm and united, and at the army's side we have that other courageous army, labor, united in solidarity with our secretariat."

Perón obviously felt threatened by what he saw as a well-orchestrated campaign against him. He was convinced that the U.S. correspondents were participating in it. Hence in his mind the press was fair game for retaliation. The government forbade domestic newspapers to reprint news or commentary published abroad about Argentina. In addition, the Secretariat of the Press and Information attempted to pressure local editors to publish the contents of leaflets viciously attacking North American correspondents stationed in Buenos Aires.[40]

The State Department instructed Braden to call on Perón and impress upon him the seriousness with which Washington viewed these developments. On July 5, the ambassador met with the vice-president in an encounter that has become immortalized in Peronist mythology. The two men have given conflicting versions of what happened. There were no witnesses to their conversation.

According to Braden,[41] they discussed the threats directed at the North American correspondents and the regime's efforts at censorship. The vice-president deplored the worsening of U.S.-Argentine relations, which had been on the mend as a result of the Warren mission, and inferred that Braden's speech-making constituted interference in Argentina's domestic affairs. Braden claimed he responded by informing Perón about the "general popular regard" Argentines felt for the U.S. ambassador. Perón told him, "You must not count on that. I too receive great applause wherever I go, and yet I know that there are others who would like to beat me. You must realize that our people are two-faced." Braden's version had the session concluding on a satisfactory note, with Perón guaranteeing that the correspondents would be safeguarded.

Perón's account bore no resemblance to Braden's. In the weeks and months that followed, he told associates that Braden had raised the problem of disposition of Axis property in Argentina and the concessions desired by U.S. airline companies in the postwar era. The ambassador made it clear that if Perón acceded to North American wishes, Washington would put no obstacles in the way of his presidential candidacy; whereupon Perón replied, "In our country we call people who sell out the fatherland to foreigners sons of bitches." Enraged, Braden stormed away, leaving behind his hat. On the following day Perón found some Casa Rosada employees playing soccer with the hat; he rescued it and had an orderly return it to the U.S. embassy.[42]

It is possible that both men were telling the truth, and each saw fit to omit that portion of the dialogue the other reported. However, the likelihood that Perón fabricated his version is overwhelming. From what is known about Braden's attitude toward the colonel before their encounter, it is totally inconceivable that he would have offered any kind of a deal that might have resulted in a Perón presidency. The ambassador's self-designed mission was to destroy Perón, not compromise with him. The "offer" made by Braden, Perón's "classic" rejoinder and the anecdote of the hat satisfied the colonel's needs so snugly that they compel the conclusion he invented the story as part of his tactic of playing upon the nationalist emotions of people whose support he needed during this crucial period. Finally, his credibility is badly damaged by a detailed account he gave of what he claimed was his final meeting with Braden, after his inauguration as president, when he told his antagonist to leave Argentina or be unceremoniously expelled. The anecdote, which he repeated on a number of occasions,[43] is pure fantasy, because Braden had left Argentina in September 1945, and the inauguration took place in June 1946.

The attacks upon the regime were now beginning to reach the sensibilities of officers reluctant to expose the armed forces to the inevitable damage that would result from an unseemly collapse of the military government. On July 6, President Farrell announced that elections would soon be held, that the military would guarantee there would be no fraud, and that the people's choice would succeed to the presidency.

Perón, meanwhile, decided that his best defense would be a vigorous offense. On July 9, pamphlets distributed by the CGT called on workers to demonstrate on Perón's behalf in front of the secretariat.[44] Union members from the nearby industrial suburbs, some carrying placards that proclaimed "Perón for President," gathered in downtown Buenos Aires to listen to speeches and chant slogans such as "We're not Nazis or Fascists. We're Peronists."[45] It was the CGT's first public manifestation of political support for the colonel, a significant step on the part of organized labor. Braden, by now totally consumed by his feud with Perón, cabled Washington that the demonstration was "a serious setback" and left the vice-president with "so little prestige as to make his position untenable if [the] forces of potential opposition were in [a] condition and of a disposition to take positive action."[46] Accurate, dispassionate reporting from the field had given way to partisan boasts and unrestrained optimism.

The Perón offensive also took aim at the ambassador himself. On July 18, in the wake of an unfortunate disaster that had recently cost the lives of hundreds of Chilean miners at the Braden Copper Company (in which Braden no longer held any interest), a phantom organization called the American Trade Union Committee sponsored a rally in a Buenos Aires theater to blame Perón's adversary for the accident.[47] The audience of seven hundred heard a spirited harangue by Blanca Luz Brun, an attractive Uruguayan poet who was to cavort on the fringes of the Peronist movement for several decades. At the same time a flood of handbills ridiculing "Cowboy Braden" and the "Al Capone in Buenos Aires" inundated the downtown section of the capital,[48] and a piglet whose flanks bore the legend "I'm Braden" ran loose on Florida Street.[49]

Perón liked to boast of his skill at provoking the ambassador.[50] The leaflets irritated Braden, but did not slow him down in the slightest. On the day of the theater rally he departed on a lecture tour that would take him to the important cities of Rosario and Santa Fe, where he continued his indirect but unmistakable assault on the Farrell regime. Returning to Buenos Aires he was greeted by an impressive, well-dressed crowd of five thousand Argentines, who massed in front of the Retiro Station, waved hats and handkerchiefs and shouted his name in a rhythmic chant.[51] At this point there could be no doubt who was the leader of the political opposition.

In August, Perón made public the results of his poaching on Radical party ranks by naming a trio of veteran but second-line Radicals to important positions in the cabinet. However, this unexpected gambit had no braking effect on the momentum the opposition was beginning to gather.

Caught up in the euphoria of the waning days of World War II and encouraged by Ambassador Braden's speeches, the political opponents of the military regime began to feel optimistic. But they fell prey to a lack of restraint and the eschewal of compromise, unfortunate characteristics that have long plagued Argentines. The taste of victory made them oblivious to the blunders they were committing.[52]

Their identification of the political struggle in Argentina with the global conflict now drawing to a close caused them to seek the same ultimate goal the Allied powers were demanding: unconditional surrender. The facile assumption that the Argentine military government was Nazi-Fascist led them to conclude that it deserved the fate being inflicted upon the Axis nations. But this put them on a collision course with the armed forces. A majority of the officer corps was truly determined that their colleagues in government return to the barracks, but to them it was absolutely crucial that in the process military honor remain intact.

The opposition refused to understand this. They were delighted when a French tribunal condemned Laval and Pétain to death, and when the Nuremberg trials were convoked. The chilling impact these events had upon the Argentine armed forces should have been readily apparent. The officer corps was not going to hand over political power to any group that might use that power to inflict retribution upon the military establishment.

Although some members of the opposition were in contact with military leaders, the forces seeking to oust Farrell and Perón were not disposed to work out any kind of face-saving deal with the men in uniform. Early in 1945 the Socialists began to urge that the government be handed over to the Supreme Court, which would serve as caretaker until elections could be held.[53] This proposed solution was in accord with an 1858 law providing for the transfer of power when neither the president nor the vice-president was able to continue in office. It would have badly damaged military prestige and was clearly unacceptable to the army. Yet "The Government to the Court" became a principal rallying cry for the opposition.

The second blunder was the creation of an impression that the anti-regime movement opposed the social and economic gains Perón's labor policy had bestowed upon the working class. The conservative, business-oriented elements of the coalition openly attacked this policy, while the Socialist and Communist parties allowed themselves to be drawn into apparent conflict with their supposed constituency. Some would later complain that Perón had hoodwinked the labor movement, an excuse that overlooks the fact that the colonel was providing Argentine workers with what they really wanted. Perón's rivals never advocated positive programs of their own that spoke to the real needs of the workers. When the Supreme Court began to declare some of Perón's labor decrees unconstitutional, the slogan "The Government to the Court" took on the aspect of a serious threat to the gains recently won by the rank and file.

Finally, the status of Spruille Braden as the preeminent figure of the opposition could not have been more counterproductive. The U.S. ambassador truly relished the adulation he was receiving and acted as though destiny had ordained him to lead Argentina back to the path of righteousness. The idea that Perón's opponents would permit themselves even to appear to be following the lead of a foreign ambassador testifies to an awesome ignorance of political realities in Argentina. Brigadier General Arthur B. Harris, the new U.S. military attaché in Buenos Aires, was one observer who understood what was happening. Displaying remarkable prescience, he reported in late August: "There can be little doubt that one of [Perón's] campaign slogans will be along the lines that the electorate will have to choose between Perón and Braden when they cast their votes."[54]

Indeed, Perón needed the ambassador as his main antagonist. He knew the advantages that would accrue from such a match. He insisted that the opposition was Braden's creation and that the ambassador provided both the brains and the muscle behind the effort to unseat him. As a matter of historical record, the opposition existed long before Braden's arrival. The diplomatic records now available for inspection reveal no evidence the ambassador was actually directing the anti-regime coalition. Indeed, he often complained about its timidity. However, his constant contacts with the political opposition testified to his up-to-the-elbows involvement. Perón was quick to exploit this to the fullest.

On August 5, as a mushroom cloud over Hiroshima gave birth to the atomic age, the government lifted the state of siege that had been in effect since the Castillo era. But the opposition would not be placated. During the rest of the month demonstrations against the government became almost daily occurrences in downtown Buenos Aires, and violence often flared when groups of ultra-nationalists attempted to disrupt them. At a rally to welcome back politicians who had fled to Montevideo, a Socialist leader ominously hailed the advent of an era of civil disobedience.[55]

Argentina's university students took to the streets almost every day, and clashed with the police and ultra-nationalists. The casualties they sustained merely spurred them to greater heights of frenzy. Perón's tentative efforts to win academic support met with little success. At the end of the month he decided to appeal to the students directly in a radio address. But his attempt at "pacification" merely drew hostile reactions from student leaders.[56]

August was a very bad month for Perón. The only news that might possibly be viewed as positive was the unexpected announcement that Ambassador Braden had been named to replace Rockefeller as assistant secretary of state for Latin America. The opposition would now lose the benefits of Braden's physical presence and speech-making, while Perón could still use him as a symbolic target for verbal abuse. However, Braden would take charge of the State Department's Latin American policy.

On August 28, the ambassador delivered his farewell address at a luncheon given in his honor at the elegant Plaza Hotel. An overflow crowd of friends and admirers jammed the main dining room and several adjoining salons to hear him launch what the *New York Times* called "the most acerbic denunciation against the present Argentine government that had ever been heard from a person with an official position inside or outside Argentina."[57] (So much for Braden's insistence that "never, while in Argentina, did I criticize the government or any Argentine official."[58]) With his sure grasp of Spanish, the ambassador rose to the occasion.

> We would not be loyal to our native land and the principles we profess to defend if as soon as certain activities are discovered we did not denounce them openly and were not prepared to eliminate them from the roots. The war that has just ended was not fought only against the major wrongdoers, but also against their followers, accomplices and procurers. . . .
>
> Let nobody think that my removal to Washington means the abandonment of the job I have begun. The voice of liberty has been raised in this country, and I believe that nobody can strangle it. I shall hear it from Washington with the same clarity with which I have heard it here in Buenos Aires.[59]

The audience, which had constantly interrupted his ringing phrases with applause and shouts of encouragement, gave him a prolonged standing ovation at the finish. A U.S. diplomat described the scene: "By the time the speech was over, you couldn't hear yourself think. People jumped up on tables and cheered. A mob followed Braden to his automobile and kept screaming 'Liberty! Liberty!' "[60] The ambassador might be going home soon, but his spirit would remain behind. The opposition was convinced that it now had the momentum to carry the day.

12

The Opposition
Mobilizes

The twin-engine transport plane bearing air force markings began its descent toward an airfield near Córdoba, the most important city in Argentina's interior.[1] A heavy cloud cover soon smothered the DC-3 in a gray embrace. The downward glide produced bumps and wobbles as the plane dipped as low as 150 meters (under 500 feet) from the earth in search of visibility.

The transport had left Buenos Aires that September morning with an escort of three fighter planes. It carried military visitors from several Latin countries en route to the aviation factory in Córdoba, where the first Argentine-made gliders were to roll off an assembly line. The decision had been made to fly because War Minister Juan Perón, the ranking Argentine official on the trip, was pressed for time by political exigencies.

Unable to find any breaks in the billowy clouds, the pilot of the DC-3 opted to change course toward an airfield north of the city, and radioed instructions to the fighters. Gaining altitude, he noticed one of the fighters on his tail and tried desperately to communicate with it, but the escort's radio did not seem to be functioning. The smaller craft was following the DC-3 in an attempt to find a way out of the clouds but had to maintain a speed much greater than that of the transport and was closing in rapidly. A frantic veer was not enough to avert disaster. The planes brushed against each other.

One of the DC-3's propellers shattered the tail of the fighter and caused it to plunge earthward. The transport sustained heavy damage to its right engine and began to lose altitude rapidly. The clouds suddenly parted, to reveal reddish earth approaching with a rush. The pilot coaxed a last-second surge of power from his failing engines and vaulted the plane over the rivulet into a plowed field. Skidding for more than a kilometer, it left a great whirl of dust and yawning ditch in its wake before slowing to a halt.

Though outwardly calm, Perón suffered psychological aftereffects from the experience. He would never shake his fear of flying. The suspicion lingered that the fighter pilot might have been an Argentine kamikaze out to put an end to the strong man behind the Farrell regime. Although no evidence was ever adduced to support this supposition, the tough tactics to which the opposition was now resorting put assassination within the realm of possibility.

The politics of confrontation adopted by Perón's enemies continued to gain momentum during early September.[2] The proposal that the government be handed over to the Supreme Court became an insistent demand, and more calls for civil disobedience were raised. In addition, steps were taken to unite the opposition. The idea of forming a coalition of parties was not new, nor did it originate with Ambassador Braden. The Communists had advocated a Popular Front during the late 1930s. The Socialists had pushed for a coalition in the months before the 1943 Revolution. The Radicals, though still split between the anti-personalists and Yrigoyenists and traditionally cool to electoral coalitions, were now amenable to a multi-party effort. In July a democratic coordinating board was formed to give substance to the concept.

Due to distrust and perhaps to overconfidence, the opposition heeded neither President Farrell's promise of elections nor the decrees promulgated by the regime to normalize the political and electoral processes. The first priority of the board was to force Farrell and Perón out of office. Since it would have been impossible to do this without military aid, board members began making clandestine contacts with officers who might be willing to turn against the regime. Sympathy was especially strong in the navy, by tradition pro-British and more reflective of upper-class economic interests. In the front ranks of the officers eager to march on the Casa Rosada, however, was the familiar figure of General Arturo Rawson.

Following his removal from the presidency on June 6, 1943, Rawson had been sent out of the country to serve as ambassador to Brazil. When Argentina broke off relations with the Axis in early 1944, he issued a public statement hailing the move in such extravagant terms that the regime immediately recalled him to Buenos Aires.[3] He received no further military assignment and had to endure a period of inactivity.

The military plotters hesitated to take any overt action without evidence of massive civilian support. Therefore, plans were drawn up for an anti-government demonstration, the occasion for which would be a march for the constitution and liberty through the streets of Buenos Aires on Wednesday, September 19. What historian Félix Luna was to call "history's hurricane"[4] was about to sweep across Argentina.

Well-placed intelligence sources kept the Ministry of War apprised of the opposition's strategy. Perón understood perfectly the link between the march and the military uprising planned in its wake. On the evening of September 13 he drafted a general order for all army commands.[5] It warned of the impending attempt to overthrow the regime and appealed for institutional loyalty to repulse efforts to restore the old system of electoral fraud, political corruption nad economic exploitation.

The government might easily have denied permission for the march, but that remedy might have been worse than the disease, given the climate of excitement in Buenos Aires at the time. Therefore, even though some of Perón's labor supporters urged him to ban the demonstration, the minister of the interior, Dr. Hortensio Quijano (one of the Radicals Perón had recently brought into the cabinet), authorized the march after lengthy negotiations with its organizers. He was doubtless acting under instructions from the colonel.

On the evening of the big event, Perón moved to protect the working class from any infection that might spread from the agitation of his opponents. In a lengthy radio address, he invoked what was to become one of his favorite slogans: "From home to work, and from work to home." He urged the workers to remain vigilant but calm in the face of what he saw as a real possibility of "disorders and perhaps fighting." For the instigators of the march he reserved some choice epithets: "obscure forces of regression"; "certain political figures of a past that does not permit them a future"; "foreign elements, reactionary spirits, politicians with terminal illnesses and egotistical plutocrats."[6]

The march for the constitution and liberty assembled in the Plaza del Congreso, ten blocks due west of the Plaza de Mayo. Huge posters of General San Martín and other figures from Argentine history, as well as banners bearing anti-government slogans, festooned the fringes of the plaza as it filled to capacity with exuberant demonstrators. A suspiciously timed strike of trolley-car workers did not deter the marchers, who came in automobiles, buses, and even sulkies. The police underestimated the crowd at 65,000, while the organizers claimed 500,000, just as certainly an exaggeration. Whatever the exact total, attendance exceeded the turnout for Yrigoyen's funeral and comprised the largest gathering ever seen on the streets of Buenos Aires.

The organizers of the march had prepared well for every contingency. Marshals lined each intersection to control the flow and prevent incidents, which never materialized. The demonstrators sang the Argentine national hymn and "The Marseillaise." At 3:00 P.M. a brief proclamation calling for the transfer of power to the Supreme Court and immediate elections with no military involvement was read over the loudspeakers set up in front of the Congress building. Then, under a sky cloudless except for a single billowy formation that suggested to onlookers the shape of a V (for victory, the symbol of the Allies and the political opposition in Argentina), the march for the constitution and liberty began.

It was a glorious procession, pouring out of the plaza past the Confitería del Molino, whose grilled balconies and tapered tower stood guard at the entrance to the Avenida Callao. Except for the modest participation of workers from several Communist-controlled unions, the marchers were from the middle and upper classes and were fashionably dressed. In its front ranks were the leaders of the opposition—notables from the various parties, former government officials, retired military officers and student leaders.

The demonstrators aimed whistles and catcalls at the Ministry of War as they passed the corner of Callao and Viamonte. From the fourth floor Perón and a circle of intimates kept a close watch on the proceedings. The colonel remained outwardly calm and even took his customary afternoon nap in the small apartment that adjoined his office.

Several blocks further along the route, an unexpected incident nearly caused a disruption. A uniformed military officer stepped out on a balcony and began to harangue the demonstrators. People began to hiss and shout him down until word spread that the orator was General Rawson, taking advantage of the opportunity to say a few words about the bond between the Argentine people and its army. Jeers turned to cheers, despite the inappropriateness of puerile posturing by the leader of a supposedly clandestine conspiracy against the regime. Another uniformed figure watched silently from his apartment window. When recognized, General Pedro Ramírez drew a resounding chorus of boos and quickly drew his curtain.

The march ended two and a half hours after it had left the staging area with the reading of another proclamation at the Plaza Francia. The multitude pledged in unison to fight for the constitution, liberty, progress and justice and then peacefully dispersed.

In perpetration of the myth that the opposition to Perón was created and controlled by Spruille Braden, Argentine writers have placed the U.S. ambassador among the marchers.[7] However, no photos or eyewitness accounts have ever been adduced to support this claim. In a recent interview, the ambassador flatly denied that he participated and stated that while the demonstration was taking place, he was lunching with officials from the Argentine chancery at the Plaza Hotel.[8] Although representatives from the U.S. embassy did observe the event, Braden was surely astute and diplomatic enough to avoid the obvious error of appearing as a participant in a public rally against the regime to which he was accredited.

The march for the constitution and liberty was a stinging slap in the face at the Farrell government and revealed the extent and nature of popular dissatisfaction with military rule. The political opposition was euphoric, convinced that the political careers of Farrell and Perón were over. Perón's initial post-march reaction, according to one witness, was blind rage.[9] He talked of reimposing the state of siege and bringing criminal charges against the politicians responsible for the demonstration. Once his emotions had cooled, he decided to ignore the civilian participants, but to haul General Rawson before a military tribunal.

The general went ahead with his plans for a coup in the city of Córdoba on September 24. But the Ministry of War learned about the details of the plot in time to take precautionary measures. Artillery units surrounded the conspirators and put a quick, bloodless end to the adventure.[10]

The regime's reaction to the putative putsch was sudden and harsh. On Wednesday the twenty-sixth, Farrell reinstituted the state of siege, which suspended a number of important constitutional guarantees. The police in turn made mass arrests and filled the jails with opponents of the regime. Because the press was forbidden to report what was happening, a plethora of alarmist rumors coursed the city.[11] Though the president reiterated his promise of free elections and gave assurances that the state of siege would be lifted once the opposition ceased its seditious activity, the pervasive unrest that had gripped the country since August intensified.

What role did the U.S. embassy play in creating or nurturing this climate of destabilization? The political opposition clearly had a life of its own, but drew much encouragement from Braden while he remained in Buenos Aires. He was in close touch with many of its leaders and after his departure left word for the embassy to pursue these contacts. A top-secret cable sent to him on September 30 by embassy official John Griffiths details the nature of the U.S. involvement:

> In line with your verbal instructions and wishes I have continued maintaining limited, carefully selected contacts with opposition elements well known to me, including dissident members of the armed forces and especially two civilian friends and spokesmen for high-ranking naval officers. Was kept constantly informed of plans for local action, principally civilian and naval, in doubtful case Rawson should succeed in Córdoba venture.[12]

The type of aid the United States was contemplating came to light in another top-secret telegram, dispatched on that same day to the State Department by the chargé in Buenos Aires. The cable discussed the option of a diplomatic breakdown between the United States and Argentina "as a signal to the dissident forces in the navy and elsewhere," as well as an accompanying statement explaining that the break was intended "to free our hand to help the Argentine people free themselves, i.e., openly to furnish material help to revolutionaries who started anything with any chance of success." The chargé recommended against a rupture, however, because the only dissident group left within the armed forces, the navy, would not be able to carry off the coup by itself.[13]

The repression of the opposition in late September did not snuff out the embers of discontent. Most of those arrested gained their freedom within a few days because the government had no evidence to link them to the Córdoba conspiracy nor the stomach to keep so many leading citizens behind bars.

In early October the students took the initiative in the struggle against Farrell and Perón and occupied universities throughout the country.[14] The buildings they held became gaudy displays of anti-government propaganda, obvious symbols of rebellion that the regime could not tolerate. The police quickly recaptured the buildings and the freshly emptied jails filled once again, this time with young people. In a street fight between students and ultra-nationalists, a ten-year-old boy was shot to death and the opposition gained a martyr.

The officer corps had been growing increasingly restive as Argentina headed toward what seemed to be an abyss. The majority had viewed Rawson's antics with disfavor, but now preferred a solution that would permit them to retire from politics with their honor intact. To many, the continued presence of Perón and his cohorts was the major obstacle to a graceful exit. By the time the police had finally occupied the universities, enough officers were ready to sacrifice Perón that it would take the slightest spark to ignite them. Eva Duarte would unwittingly furnish that spark.

13

Ouster

Arturo Jauretche, an Argentine historian and one of the few intellectuals who supported Perón during this period, once described the relationship between the colonel and Evita as a union of "two wills, two passions for power."[1] Evita's ambition, at first confined to artistic and financial matters, matched her compañero's relentless political drive. She now enjoyed opportunities to influence the entire spectrum of the communications media and did not hesitate to use them. In May 1945 a U.S. military attaché reported that Evita was virtually running the government agency charged with censorship.[2] A U.S. embassy memorandum concluded that "the person who has the greatest influence in the Government Press Office, next to Colonel Perón himself, is his well-known companion Señorita Eva Duarte. She has become extremely interested in publicity and is in close daily contact with the work of the office."[3]

How much money Evita made from these activities cannot be determined. Given the way businesses traditionally dealt with government regulation in Argentina and in light of Evita's insecure, impoverished background, it would be reasonable to assume that she extracted pecuniary rewards in exchange for the benefit of her influence upon the federal bureaucracy.

Perón's liaison with Evita stuck in the craw of many of his military colleagues, whose displeasure grew as the political situation deteriorated. As one officer testified, "The impudence of that woman at times reached intolerable heights. For example, one day she stood next to Perón at the swearing-in of a minister and let her arm drape across the back of [President Farrell's] chair."[4] Another military man criticized Perón to his face for bringing Evita to his (Perón's) residence at the Campo de Mayo.[5] But the objections to Señorita Duarte went beyond disgust at Perón's public appearances with his mistress and Evita's crude behavior. There were also complaints that Evita and her brother Juan were trafficking in gasoline rationing stamps.[6] Thus the Nicolini affair proved to be the last straw.

Oscar Nicolini, Evita's initial contact in the Post and Telegraph Offices, was a close friend of her mother, who had originally made his acquaintance during a postal inspection tour of Junín.[7] He had also introduced the actress to his superior, Colonel Imbert. Now, in late 1945, he was to receive his reward for services rendered to the Duarte family. On October 1, Perón had Minister of the Interior Quijano designate Nicolini to replace Imbert as director of the department.

The news was a double slap at the officer corps at Campo de Mayo. One of their number had been actively seeking the post and enjoyed the support of his peers. Moreover, the officers had recently complained to Perón about corrupt practices in which Nicolini was allegedly involved, and Perón had promised to do something about it. A promotion for Nicolini was not what Campo de Mayo had in mind.

Responsibility for conveying their outrage fell to General Eduardo Avalos, the commander of the garrison. A key figure in the march of the Rawson column of June 4, 1943, General Avalos became Perón's friend and ally during the difficult infighting that preceded the colonel's consolidation of military support. At a Casa Rosada meeting of garrison commanders in late July 1945, three months after Perón's public disavowal of presidential ambitions, Avalos had actually urged that his colleague stand as the revolution's candidate for the presidency.[8]

Yet the bespectacled, cigar-chomping general began to loom as a potential competitor for Perón. He had earned the loyalty of most of his subordinates at Campo de Mayo. Despite his suggestion that the colonel enter politics, he actually resented Perón's political machinations. The affair with Evita deeply disturbed the general.[9] The growing unrest in August and September may have further disillusioned him. Therefore, when the Nicolini affair erupted, he was disposed to take a tough stand.

On Saturday, October 6, one day after the news of Nicolini's appointment became public, General Avalos met with Perón in the War Ministry and made clear to the colonel the depth of feeling at Campo de Mayo against Nicolini.[10] Perón initially feigned disinterest and put responsibility for the appointment, which he termed irreversible, on the interior minister. Not satisfied, Avalos stormed off to see General Farrell. The figurehead president meekly suggested that the two men settle matters between themselves. That afternoon, while a crowd accompanied the coffin of the martyred student to the nearby Recoleta Cemetery, Avalos and Perón met again in the latter's apartment. Eva Duarte was the only witness. Avalos repeated his demand that the Nicolini nomination be revoked, and Perón replied that he was fed up with Campo de Mayo interference in nonmilitary matters. Evita interrupted twice, urging her compañero to stand firm and intensifying the deep distaste Avalos felt toward her. Finally the general suggested that Perón listen in person to the complaints of his officers. The colonel agreed, on the condition that the meeting be held at the Ministry of War.

In retrospect, Argentines convinced of Perón's tactical infallibility speculate that he appointed Nicolini in order to provoke a decisive confrontation with his enemies. The evidence points elsewhere. On Sunday, October 7, he was still angry at the demands made by Avalos. The Nicolini appointment was clearly a blunder forced upon him by the Duartes. Inability to say no at this crucial juncture and miscalculation of his military support were the key factors that pushed Perón to the brink.

In the meantime, feelings at Campo de Mayo continued to run high. At an officers' meeting on Sunday, the decision was reached to put the garrison troops on a state of alert, ready to march on Buenos Aires. General Avalos assured everyone that the affair would quickly be brought to a satisfactory conclusion.

By coincidence, Monday October 8 was Perón's fiftieth birthday. It was also marked by the beginning of what might aptly be called "The Ten Days That Shook Argentina."

At 11:00 A.M. General Avalos and ten other Campo de Mayo officers arrived at the War Ministry. They found Perón and more than forty of his army supporters waiting for them. The colonel opened the meeting with a defense of Nicolini as an able public servant with twenty-five years of meritorious service behind him. Denouncing Campo de Mayo intervention in the business of the revolutionary government, he demanded a vote of confidence from the group, and added that the choice was between Avalos and himself.

Avalos took the bait and accepted Perón's terms. The colonel then left to attend a birthday luncheon in his honor while his backers voiced their approval of his leadership. Having lost the rigged vote, Avalos' contingent returned to the garrison, where the general announced that, having given his word, he would now apply for retirement.

The officers at Campo de Mayo resolved not to accept a defeat so artfully imposed upon them. Some urged Avalos to delay his retirement decision for a few days. Others wanted to march on the Casa Rosada that very night. Avalos concluded that no action should be taken until the following day and returned to his quarters. His subordinates, however, resolved to demand that the government remove Perón from office, call immediate elections and guarantee that the voting take place under conditions of "immaculate purity." The process had developed a momentum of its own. Perón, not Oscar Nicolini, was now the issue.

In the meantime, reports of unrest at Campo de Mayo were reaching Perón. Several junior officers came to his apartment that very afternoon to advise him that their unit had turned against him. "Don't worry," he told them. "Things will turn out the way I want them to."[11] He dispatched

Colonel Franklin Lucero, a War Ministry official, to the garrison. Avalos assured the visiting colonel that everything was normal. At Lucero's bidding, the general phoned Perón and told him not to worry.[12]

On Tuesday morning the young officers at Campo de Mayo presented Avalos with their demands. But the general was loath to order troops out of their barracks, at least before one last attempt at a peaceful settlement. He persuaded his emotionally charged subordinates to let him invite President Farrell to listen to them in person.

By now it was clear to Perón that things were far from normal at Campo de Mayo. Colonel Lucero, realizing that he had been duped, drew up military plans for quelling the incipient revolt. This sudden turn of events kept Perón from a scheduled appearance at the war academy. Waiting for him there were a colonel and thirty-five captains, pistols in hand, determined to assassinate him. Not connected in any way with the Campo de Mayo dissidents, they formed the vanguard of a conspiracy other officers had launched during the latter part of September.[13] The lack of coordination between the two groups saved Perón's life.

Lucero gave his plans for the use of troops and planes against Campo de Mayo to Perón's adjutant, for delivery to the colonel at the Posadas Street apartment. But when he received the documents, Perón hesitated, insisting that he did not want to cause bloodshed. The adjutant explained that the papers requiring his signature were merely contingency plans.

At this point Evita, who was listening to the conversation, could no longer control herself. "Let's get out of here, Juancito," she interjected in near-hysterical tones. "Let's go to Uruguay and leave all this behind."

Perón turned on her abruptly. "Look, stop bothering me," he snapped, gesturing toward the door. "Be quiet."[14] It was one of the very few times he would ever act harshly toward her in front of a third person. She left the room, and he signed the plans.

Caught between warring factions, General Farrell agreed to meet with the Campo de Mayo officers at 1:00 P.M. Later in the morning Lucero visited the president and sought his approval of the contingency plans Perón had signed. Farrell, in a jovial mood and apparently enjoying his new role as mediator, put Lucero off, telling him he was about to leave for Campo de Mayo. Twenty-four bombers loaded for action sat ready at a nearby airfield as Farrell departed.

In his capacity as minister of war, Perón might easily have given the order to attack Campo de Mayo, yet he was as determined as Avalos to avoid violence.[15] A clash at this juncture might have seriously weakened one of the two institutions upon which his political strategy rested. Therefore, he had to rely upon the president to negotiate a way out of the crisis. But Farrell had a backbone of marshmallow—the very quality that had led to his selection as president.

At Campo de Mayo excitement mounted as Farrell failed to arrive at the appointed hour. At 2:00 P.M. he finally appeared and confronted a crowd of about a hundred officers assembled in the main dining room.

Avalos opened the meeting by informing Farrell of the decision taken by his subordinates and asked for an immediate response. A glance at the faces of the men around him brought home to the president the gravity of the situation. With measured phrases charged with emotion, he urged the officers to rethink what they were doing, since the ouster of Perón might trigger a massive revolt by the workers. He suggested that the colonel be permitted to retire voluntarily from the War Ministry after a decent interval but made clear his reluctance to cut Perón off from all his government posts. Avalos insisted that Perón resign immediately from every public office he held. Farrell turned to the officers, who shouted in unison their support for Avalos' demand. Farrell shrugged his shoulders. The meeting began to disperse.

The president requested that the generals present remain with him to work out the details. They decided to form a committee to convey their decision to Perón. One further condition was set: if the delegation did not return by 8:00 P.M., Perón's resignation in hand, Campo de Mayo troops would march on Buenos Aires.

That afternoon, as Perón awaited word of his fate, his militant supporters gathered at his War Ministry office. Many of them urged him to fight, but he held fast to the conviction that armed resistance to Campo de Mayo would not serve his purposes.

When the delegation arrived in Buenos Aires, one of its members, General Juan Pistarini, volunteered to carry the news to Perón. Since Pistarini and Perón were close personal friends, the group decided to let him do the unpleasant job.

Shortly after 5:00 P.M., Pistarini entered Perón's office. Their conversation was brief. Perón's version was that he asked the general whether Farrell had agreed he ought to resign. When Pistarini answered in the affirmative, the colonel instructed one of his aides to cancel all plans for action against Campo de Mayo and asked for a piece of paper. He scribbled a one-sentence resignation and gave it to the general. "I give this to you so they'll see that my hand didn't shake when I wrote it," he said,[16] and after a tearful farewell to his staff, he withdrew to his apartment.

The scene at Posadas Street resembled a wake. Wearing a stained red smoking jacket and his uniform pants, Perón moved restlessly about a table laden with cold chicken and wine. Evita could not hold back the tears. A gloomy pall of cigarette smoke enveloped the apartment.[17]

At Campo de Mayo, the delegation returned and announced that it had fulfilled its mission. General Farrell, who had remained at the garrison, left with his escort. Avalos told his officers what had happened and they responded with cheers.

But their euphoria was myopic. With power in their grasp, the general and his men had little idea how to exercise it. Avalos had agreed with Farrell that the latter should remain in office, and that the chief of police, a Perón intimate, should be replaced, but the rebels had formulated no other plans. They were underestimating their adversary.

At 6:00 P.M. Interior Minister Quijano stunned journalists by announcing that in honor of the forthcoming Day of the Hispanic Race (the name Latins have given to the celebration of Columbus' discovery of America on October 12), the government was decreeing elections for the following April; moreover, in accord with a promise to himself that amounted to a promise to the Argentine people, Colonel Perón was resigning all his public duties. The statement, which Félix Luna termed a "skillful deformation of the truth,"[18] was broadcast to the nation within minutes of its release.

The next morning General Avalos began to hear complaints from his men. A group of officers told him they thought Quijano's statement was grotesque and a brazen mockery of their efforts. Moreover, they had heard a Spanish-language radio broadcast from New York calling Perón's resignation a clumsy maneuver by the colonel and his "Nazi-Fascist" ally, General Avalos. Finally, the appointment of Colonel Aristóbulo E. Mittelbach, a Perón intimate, as the new police chief was disturbing. The ingenuous general reassured the men and promised to meet with them every morning before he departed for the city.

News of Perón's resignation stunned labor leaders who had committed themselves to his cause.[19] The consensus at a meeting of union representatives in Quilmes, a suburb of Buenos Aires, was that Perón had received unjust treatment and that labor should express its solidarity with him. The next morning a delegation of union officials headed by telephone worker Luis Gay went looking for the colonel. They found him, along with Mercante and other intimates, at the Posadas Street apartment. Cipriano Reyes, the dynamic meatpacker from Berisso, soon joined the impromptu conclave.

Gay and his associates urged Perón not to abandon his leadership of the trade-union movement and suggested that he ask for permission to give a farewell address to the workers as a way to cement the nexus between Perón and the gains recently achieved by the working class. Their pledges of support pumped new life into the colonel, and he realized that he had a high trump card yet to play.

Meanwhile, President Farrell received visits from key military figures pressuring him to appoint Avalos as minister of war. Though he would have preferred someone else, he was unable to refuse. In the early afternoon he took a call from Perón, who asked permission to bid good-bye to the personnel at the secretariat and perhaps also use the state radio network to make one final speech to the workers. Farrell agreed.

Whether traceable to stupidity or covert sympathy with Perón's intentions, Farrell's acquiescence brought fresh hope to the colonel's supporters. The labor leaders left to organize a rally in front of the secretariat at 7:00 P.M. Perón himself felt confident enough to tell a journalist he had plans for a comeback and to deny that the army had forced him to resign.

As the evening rush hour began to clog the downtown streets, workmen hastily nailed together a platform in front of the main entrance to the secretariat and aimed a battery of loudspeakers at Perú Street, where workers had begun to gather in the late afternoon. Placards bearing the colonel's likeness and slogans such as "Perón for President" bobbed up and down to the rhythm of songs whose improvised verses hailed "Argentina's Number One Worker." When Perón emerged from the secretariat, he was greeted by an enthusiastic roar from the crowd.

The speech Perón then delivered was one of the most effective of his entire political career.[20] He recounted in some detail the accomplishments of the secretariat and placed them in the context of a continuing social, political and economic struggle. "We shall win in one year or we shall win in ten, but we shall win," he promised. Pledging to devote all his energy to the cause of the working class, he stressed the need for calm ("You don't win with violence, you win with intelligence and organization"), but also issued the veiled threat that if necessary "one day I will ask for war." The conclusion of the speech was aptly sentimental. "I'm not going to say farewell to you. I'm going to say 'Hasta siempre' [literally, "Until forever"], because from now on I shall be with you, closer than ever."[21] The unstated message was clear: the elimination of Perón would nullify the gains realized by workers over the past two years. The colonel had issued an implied invitation for his supporters in the labor movement to seek ways to help him regain power.[22]

The speech enraged the Campo de Mayo dissidents. Now joined by the would-be assassins from the war academy, they vented their rage upon General Avalos, who again counseled patience and assured them that Perón's influence was a thing of the past.

On Thursday, October 11, Avalos took command of the War Ministry and named Admiral Héctor A. Vernengo Lima as new minister of the navy. He also announced to reporters that a "new era" in Argentine history had dawned. But he disclosed no further details. That evening several hundred officers debated what form the new era should take. In a stormy session, they argued over whether to leave Farrell in office and what role the political parties should play in the provisional regime. It was also suggested that Colonel Perón be removed from the scene.

At that very moment the democratic coordinating board was meeting to decide what the political opposition should do. A consensus was reached to stick to the slogan that the government be delivered to the Supreme Court. As Félix Luna has cogently reasoned, this was a tactical disaster.[23] With Perón on the sidelines and a political vacuum rapidly developing, the opposition should have cooperated with Avalos, helped form an interim coalition cabinet, reassured the workers that their gains would be respected, and proceeded to elections under the recently established ground rules, which were perfectly adequate and fair. Instead, they pressed for a solution that would have humiliated the army, and thereby alienated a majority of the officers now in a position to determine the fate of the nation.

While his military and political adversaries were fumbling opportunities, Perón was worrying that his speech to the workers might provoke an extreme reaction from his enemies. Indeed, rumors about planned attempts on his life began to reach him. He decided that the time had come to leave the Posadas Street apartment. In response to a suggestion from Mercante, he wrote a note to General Avalos asking for a leave of absence from his military duties and informing the war minister that he would be staying at the ranch of one of his political allies in the town of San Nicolás. At midnight he slipped behind the wheel of an automobile and said good-bye to Mercante.

"You're not going to leave the country, are you?" his faithful Achates asked. "We're going to keep on playing the game, right?"

"You bet we are," Perón reassured him.[24] Evita, her face a mask of worry, joined him in the car, as did a young friend. Rodolfo (Rudi) Freude, son of suspected Nazi agent Ludwig Freude, had been told by his father to give Perón whatever help he needed. The colonel drove not to the ranch but to a friend's house just outside the city. On Friday he motored to Tigre, a resort on the delta of the Paraná River just north of Buenos Aires, and took a launch through a web of waterways to the well-stocked summer home of Ludwig Freude. Attended by a servant named Otto who spoke virtually no Spanish, the couple enjoyed an idyllic day together as Rudi returned to the city.

14

Arrest

Friday, October 12, was a national holiday, the Day of the Hispanic Race. Soccer-mad porteños breathlessly awaited the afternoon match for the coveted British Cup. Racing, a team from the working-class suburb of Avellaneda whose mastery of the intricacies of the game had earned for it the nickname Academia, was to face everybody's favorite, the beloved Boca Juniors. (Technique would prevail over sentiment, 4 to 1.)

Meanwhile, on one flank of the elegant Plaza San Martín, where bull-fights were staged in colonial times, a stately mansion once belonging to one of the nation's wealthiest families and now housing the Círculo Militar (officers' club) found itself temporarily transformed into the seat of a deliberative body exercising governmental functions. The meeting of military men who had gathered the previous day at the Círculo Militar was assuming the characteristics of a permanent session. No decisions had been reached, and the existence of a power vacuum was becoming painfully obvious to all.

By mid-morning people were converging upon the Plaza and gathering under the budding shade trees. It was an elegant crowd, men with jackets, ties and hats, women in the latest fashions. They came from the Barrio Norte, the downtown neighborhood of the upper and upper-middle classes. Some brought sandwiches and wine. Others enjoyed caviar and champagne as they reclined on blankets. In Peronist folklore, the affair would become known as the Picnic in the Plaza San Martín.

Inside the Círculo Militar, naval officers were urging that the government be transferred to the Supreme Court, while their army colleagues remained adamantly opposed to the idea. Outside, the picnic turned into a political rally. Students and politicians had joined the crowd, now concentrating in front of the Círculo. Argentine flags unfurled; people sang the national hymn and "The Marseillaise." A radio announcement that the holdover cabinet members from the Farrell administration had resigned encouraged the chanting of "The Government to the Court!"

The assembly of officers grew increasingly chaotic as shoving matches among the participants enlivened the proceedings. Demonstrators completely surrounded the building. Whenever a uniformed figure appeared on a Círculo balcony, he was greeted with cries of "Go away!" "Votes yes, boots no!" and "Back to the barracks!" At about 3:00 P.M., Admiral Vernengo Lima, long a bitter enemy of Perón, attempted to address the throng.

"I've just been with the president," he began.

"He's not our president," the crowd responded.

Fighting to make himself heard, Vernengo Lima urged that the military be given the chance to restore representative government to Argentina. "Today it is indispensable that the army bring back to the country its democratic institutions. We in the army and navy are today wholeheartedly committed to this proposition."

"You've said this to us so many times before" was the response from the crowd.

The admiral's rejoinder: "I am not Perón!"[1]

No heed was paid to his declaration. Someone posted a "For Rent" sign on the walls of the Círculo. When an officer tried to take it down, the crowd attacked him. That night an exchange of gunfire between the police and some of the demonstrators emptied the plaza. A forty-six-year-old physician lay dead on the sidewalk. More than thirty civilians and policemen were wounded.

As events in the Plaza San Martín unfolded, Domingo Mercante met with union leaders at the Secretariat of Labor and Welfare, the first step in an effort to organize working-class support for Perón. The possibility of calling a general strike was raised. The labor representatives promised to consult with their membership and to consider ways to utilize the CGT. A group of newly appointed secretariat functionaries, accompanied by the police, burst into the room and terminated the conference.[2]

Although Avalos and Farrell were able to resist pressure to hand the government over to the Supreme Court, they found it prudent to remove Perón from circulation. Fear that an attempt might be made on his life contributed to their decision. Colonel Mittelbach, the new police chief and a Perón sympathizer, drew the assignment and set out in search of the colonel. He had both Juan Duarte and Rudi Freude arrested. It was not until he made contact with Mercante that he learned of Perón's whereabouts. Mercante took him to the Freude house that evening. When they arrived, the police chief informed the colonel that Farrell had ordered his detention, and that he probably would be interned on a naval vessel or on the island of Martín García. The thought of being placed in the custody of the navy greatly distressed Perón. He requested an opportunity to talk with Farrell. Mittelbach accompanied him back to his apartment and agreed to convey his appeal to the president.

The police chief could not convince Farrell to meet with his ex-vice-president and was reluctant to tell Perón the bad news. He asked Major Héctor D'Andrea, his assistant and a long-time Perón opponent, to relay the message. D'Andrea first visited Farrell in order to receive instructions in person from the president. Showing unusual spine, Farrell told D'Andrea to reject any request by Perón that he be detained at an army installation.

A spring rain was falling when the major reached Posadas Street in the early hours of Saturday morning, the thirteenth. He found Perón freshly shaven and dressed in civilian clothes. As Farrell had predicted, when informed that he was to be taken to the island of Martín García, the colonel pleaded that he not be delivered into the hands of the navy. D'Andrea stood firm.

A totally distraught Evita emerged from the bedroom. "What's happening? Why has he come?"[3] Her voice was shrill, bordering on hoarseness. She grabbed Perón's arm and held on tightly as the major and the colonel, joined by Mercante, filed out the door. Perón had to tear himself, literally, from her frantic embrace. The elevator gate clicked shut and the trio dropped out of sight, leaving Evita alone, sobbing, in the hallway.

The car bearing Perón, Mercante and D'Andrea sped toward the port, now heavily guarded by navy personnel. Not a word was uttered during the trip. When they emerged from the car, Mercante embraced Perón and whispered "Confidence! Have confidence!"[4] Perón's only response was to implore his friend to take care of Evita. The collar of his raincoat upturned, he disappeared aboard the gunboat *Independencia*.

Saturday dawned with an invigorating briskness bestirring many porteños to stroll to the Plaza San Martín and visit the previous day's battleground. Farrell and Avalos were still struggling to form a government. They named a new head of the Secretariat of Labor and Public Welfare and an anti-Perón officer to replace Mittelbach as police chief, yet Argentina continued to be without a cabinet. Finally the two generals hit upon a solution approximating the opposition's key demand. They offered Dr. Juan Alvarez, the attorney general, the task of picking a cabinet of distinguished civilians to administer the government on a caretaker basis until the election of a new administration. (The attorney general was not a cabinet member, but rather an appointee of the Supreme Court.) At the same time, the army would remain in power behind the scenes, would guarantee the "purity" of the coming elections, and could then retire with its honor intact.

Mercante, meanwhile, kept contacting labor leaders and raised with them the possibility of a strike. During the day he roamed about Greater Buenos Aires and spread the word of Perón's arrest. Late in the afternoon he learned that his presence was requested at the War Ministry. When he arrived at his former workplace, he was arrested and confined to Campo de Mayo.

That night the new secretary of labor and public welfare delivered a national radio address in which he assured workers that their gains would be respected. However, he made it clear that the government would no longer act as advocate for labor, but would adopt a neutral attitude in conflicts between employers and employees. When they received their paychecks for that week, many workers would discover they had not been paid for October 12, despite a decree issued not long before by the secretariat requiring compensation for holidays.[5]

In 1930 the tiny, wooded island of Martín García gained notoriety as the prison without walls that housed deposed President Yrigoyen. Fifteen years later, it again welcomed a distinguished involuntary visitor. Juan Perón found himself confined to a small though comfortable house under the watchful eye of two guards. He took advantage of his enforced idleness to begin work on his version of the events leading to his downfall, a self-serving memoir to be published pseudonymously in pamphlet form.[6] He also penned five letters, four of which have survived and provide priceless insights into his actual frame of mind during this nadir of his political career.

To Mercante he sent a long, disjointed note tinged with self-pity and righteous indignation. He disclosed that he was suffering from jangled nerves that kept him from sleeping and was very preoccupied about Evita's health. "As soon as they give me my retirement, I'm getting married and to hell with everything else," he vowed. He also boasted that "I am content not to have caused the death of a single person on my behalf and to have avoided all violence."[7] Though serious consequences might yet follow, he insisted he had a clear conscience.

He complained that despite promises to the contrary he had been placed incommunicado on the island. "When I arrived here, I knew what man's word of honor is worth. Yet I have what they lack: a faithful friend and a woman who loves me and whom I adore." The epistle concluded with denunciations of ingratitude ("the luxuriant flower of our time") and perfidy. Significantly, though the note was to be hand-delivered and hence secure, it made no mention of any expectation that the workers would be mobilized to effectuate his release.

Perón wrote two letters to Evita. One of them, sent by regular mail shortly after his arrival on Martín García, has never been published. The other, delivered to Evita by hand, was a tender expression of his love for her. "My adorable treasure," it began. "Only when we are apart from our loved ones can we measure affection. From the day I left you, with the greatest grief imaginable, I have not been able to calm my anguished heart. Today I know how much I love you and that I cannot live without you." He promised to marry her as soon as his retirement from the army was finalized and to take her away with him to Patagonia (hardly, one would imagine, a spot where she would have chosen to live). "My treasure, be calm and learn to wait. All this will end and life will be ours." He also indicated he would try to return to Buenos Aires by any means possible.[8]

Perón also sent Avalos a formal, legalistic letter[9] complaining of his treatment and demanding that he be transferred to the jurisdiction of the army. He asked that his retirement be expedited and that he be informed of the specific charges against him.

The importance of these letters lies in the fact that they confirm neither the anti-Peronist smear that Perón in his hour of crisis was a coward, nor the Peronist article of faith that he held fast to the cause of the working class even during his confinement. The truth of the matter was that Perón, as was his wont, played it both ways. He was prepared to retire from the arena, should circumstances suggest that his political career had aborted, but he also left open the possibility of a return to the fray in the event his fortunes revived. He hid in the protective mist of ambiguity (which some have mistaken for indecision) and preserved his options. At a time when the rest of Argentina was passionately dividing into pro- and anti-Perón factions, the subject of the controversy remained singularly uncommitted.

While Perón was writing letters, Evita scoured the city in search of an attorney who would file a writ of habeas corpus on her lover's behalf. Labor lawyer Juan Bramuglia turned down her plea. He feared that if a judge granted the writ, the actress and her compañero would flee the country and leave the working class to its own devices. Evita was furious with him and would never forget his "disloyalty." She met with similar rejections from other lawyers.

Though he complained about being held incommunicado, as early as Sunday, October 14, Perón received a visit from Captain Miguel Mazza, a physician who had served with him in Mendoza. Captain Mazza brought news from Lucero about the military backing upon which Perón could still count and took with him the various letters the colonel had written. More importantly, the doctor and Perón hit upon a ploy that would return the latter to the mainland. Dr. Mazza would discover that Martín García was bad for Perón's health.

On Monday, October 15, a U.S. embassy official wired Washington that "Perón is out politically speaking with no known army support and little among collaborationist labor."[10] The local political opposition was of the same view and continued to withhold cooperation from a government that was making every effort to conciliate the traditional interest groups. But while Avalos and Farrell awaited the attorney general's cabinet selections, tensions began to build in the working-class districts of Greater Buenos Aires and the interior.

Word of Perón's arrest disturbed politically unsophisticated peasants who had developed a strong emotional attachment to the colonel. In Tucumán the sugar-workers' union called a strike and dispatched representatives to Buenos Aires. In the industrial city of Rosario and in several of the suburbs near the capital, there were small demonstrations for Perón's release. Reyes and his meatpackers' union were particularly active in agitating on behalf of Perón and Mercante. Except for *La Epoca*, the only newspaper to support Perón, the press virtually ignored these rumblings and thereby contributed to the illusion that calm had settled over the country.

The CGT found itself pressured by protests against Perón's confinement and the change in policy suggested by the speech of the new head of the secretariat. The confederation had recently suffered internal disputes over the extent to which it should support the Farrell-Perón government, and in early September several important unions had withdrawn in protest at the "collaborationist" (i.e., pro-Perón) line the CGT was following.

On Tuesday, October 16, the central committee of the CGT met to decide what response, if any, the confederation should make to the arrest of Perón and the labor policy of the new administration.[11] The members of the committee were well aware of the demonstrations that were taking place all over the country, but were split as to whether the CGT should invoke its ultimate weapon by calling a general strike and over the wisdom of demanding Perón's release. Some of those who favored a strike did not, as a matter of principle, want to put the CGT on record as demanding freedom for Perón, since this in their view did not relate directly to working-class interests, while a few of those who thought a general strike call premature or otherwise inappropriate wanted to take action to bring back Perón. The end result of some obvious compromising was a vote of 16 to 11 in favor of a twenty-four-hour general strike, to begin at midnight on Thursday the eighteenth, but with no mention of the colonel's imprisonment as one of the causes. The committee demanded free elections, a lifting of the state of siege, freedom for all political prisoners and the retention of all social gains realized by workers.

While the committee debated, Reyes and his meatpackers were taking to the streets.[12] On the sixteenth, after a rally in Berisso, they split up and visited a number of large factories near Buenos Aires, in order to try to persuade as many workers as possible to join them for a march on the capital. Their rallying cry was "Free Perón." The police blocked them at one of the bridges leading to Buenos Aires, but a number of participants managed to cross police lines and stage some hit-and-run demonstrations in the downtown area. It was a useful dress rehearsal for things to come. The CGT strike vote and the militance of the meatpackers provoked a few union leaders who opposed Perón into public denunciations of the threatened work stoppage and the activities of Cipriano Reyes and his associates. But their protests were straws in the wind.

On Monday and Tuesday when several delegations of union representatives called on Avalos to express their concern at the new regime's labor policy, the general assured them that the government would respect worker gains. Inevitably, the visitors expressed solicitude for the plight of Colonel Perón. The general insisted that threats to Perón's life had necessitated his removal to Martín García and that he was not a prisoner.[13] Even as Avalos spoke to the labor leaders, rumors that Perón had fallen ill and was about to be transferred to the military hospital in Buenos Aires began to circulate.

Immediately upon his return from Martín García on Sunday, Captain Mazza had gone directly to Farrell and had pointed out that the humid weather on the island could adversely affect Perón's health. With an X-ray ostensibly revealing that Perón was suffering from a lung condition, the doctor persisted in his appeals to Farrell and visited Vernengo Lima as well. Farrell fell for the ruse and pressed the admiral to transfer Perón to the military hospital. Avalos, as gullible as ever, readily concurred. Only Vernengo Lima expressed skepticism. He insisted that an independent medical commission examine Perón.[14]

On the evening of Tuesday the sixteenth, a pair of civilian doctors accompanied Captain Mazza to Martín García on a torpedo launch. They found Perón, dressed in a blue bathrobe, waiting for them in his chalet. To the naval captain who was supervising the visit, the colonel seemed "hale and hearty."[15] At first he did not object to the examination. But after a whispered exchange with Mazza, he withdrew his consent. Since technically he was not a prisoner, the visiting doctors had to respect his wishes. Matters having reached an impasse, the naval captain radioed Vernengo Lima and asked for instructions. The admiral threw up his hands and gave the order that Perón be taken to the military hospital.[16]

15

The Seventeenth of October

On Wednesday, October 17, 1945, United Mineworkers' President John L. Lewis unexpectedly called off a twenty-six-day strike of U.S. soft-coal miners; the British rushed troops to quell an insurrection in the Dutch colony of Java in Indonesia; General Charles de Gaulle pledged to hand over to elected representatives the emergency powers he had exercised during the war; twenty-one-year-old actress Ava Gardner (whose path would cross Perón's nearly two decades later) married bandleader Artie Shaw; and in Washington, the Senate Foreign Relations Committee, after lengthy debate, unanimously approved President Truman's nomination of Spruille Braden as assistant secretary of state for Latin America.

But in Argentina, the seventeenth of October was to reshape the political landscape of the country and mark the onset of an era that has yet to pass. An entire social class would shed its invisibility, and at the same time Argentine society, ever prone to divisiveness, would find for itself a new dichotomy, defined by one's attitude toward Juan Domingo Perón.

The events of October 17 have been respectively mythologized and deprecated by Peronists and by those who view Perón as a national disaster. The main distortion that has crept into Peronist folklore puts Evita on the cutting edge of efforts to rescue Perón. The accepted version for true believers holds that she roamed the factories and workshops of Buenos Aires and its suburbs, rallying workers behind Perón's banner. Curiously, this version is also current among anti-Peronists, who like to paint Perón as a whimpering coward, snatched by a woman from ignominious defeat. There is no truth to this description of her role. On the other hand, many anti-Peronists look upon the seventeenth of October as the handiwork of a few labor leaders who forced their recalcitrant followers to march on

Buenos Aires, and of police who transported workers to the Plaza de Mayo.

What in fact occurred was a natural consequence of developments on Monday and Tuesday. Concern for Perón's safety had aroused large segments of the working class, and militant leaders such as Cipriano Reyes supplied sparks. The CGT strike vote also contributed to the atmosphere by setting in motion preparations that were accelerated on the day the rank and file began to march. Thus it is an academic exercise to argue whether the seventeenth of October was a spontaneous eruption or the result of manipulation. Without a mass of workers thoroughly aroused by the loss of a man who symbolized their aspirations *and* a group of energetic leaders eager to trigger a crisis, events would not have unfolded exactly as they did. Given these two conditions, some kind of explosion could hardly have been avoided.

Things began to stir early in the morning in the grimy suburbs that link La Plata and Buenos Aires.[1] In Berisso and Ensenada, the followers of Cipriano Reyes set out again, chanting "We want Perón," their women and children marching with them. In Avellaneda and Lanús, closer to Buenos Aires, the metalworkers also took to the streets. Factories and workshops closed down or never opened. The railroad workers declared a strike and cut off rail traffic in and out of the federal capital.

The Riachuelo River, virtually an open sewer even in 1945, fringes the southern flank of Buenos Aires. The first groups of demonstrators easily traversed the four drawbridges that led into the city, but by mid-morning the police had raised them in an effort to stem the tide. It proved a Canute-like gesture. The eager army crossed on small boats and wooden pilings. The hardiest among them plunged into the fetid waters and swam to the other side. Police and military units made feeble attempts to divert the marchers as they headed toward the Plaza de Mayo.

The futility of these defensive measures has given rise to accusations that the police actively conspired to free Perón. Yet neither Farrell nor Avalos gave orders that the marchers were to be turned back or dispersed. Individual police officers sympathized with Perón and made no effort to conceal their feelings. The discovery that the police were with them heartened the demonstrators: one of the more touching photos taken on October 17 shows an old woman, plainly a cabecita negra, reaching up to shake the hand of a policeman on horseback.[2]

The officers at Campo de Mayo were not happy with reports they were receiving about unrest in Buenos Aires and the suburbs. They dispatched a colonel to confer with Avalos at the War Ministry and to urge that army troops be used to seal off the downtown area. Avalos told him not to worry, and that nothing was going to happen. "There are women and children among the demonstrators," he added, "and I'm not going to let the uniforms of our soldiers be stained with blood. All they want is to see Perón and be sure that he's well. After that they'll leave the way they came."[3] The specter of the June 1943 shooting at the mechanics' school might still have weighed heavily on his mind.

While Avalos procrastinated and workers streamed toward the city, Perón sat quietly in his blue pajamas on the twelfth floor of the military hospital. He had signed in at 6:30 A.M., after a bumpy four-hour boat ride from Martín García, and had been given the chaplain's apartment, with its bedroom, living room and telephone, as his temporary quarters. By mid-morning, a number of his collaborators had gathered there, and perhaps a thousand workers, having discovered his whereabouts, were demonstrating in front of the hospital. Apparently he could have left at any time, but he chose to remain and await developments.

At the Casa Rosada, President Farrell surveyed the Plaza de Mayo from an upstairs window. One of his aides asked him what measures should be taken. "Not a one," he replied. "Why bother? If the people are calm and quiet, don't mess with them." Admiral Vernengo Lima urged him to order the police to move against the demonstration. "No, no" was his measured response. "The police aren't going to disturb anyone."[4] When word reached him that the bridges over the Riachuelo had been raised, he reached for the telephone and passed the word that they should be lowered immediately.

In downtown Buenos Aires, well-dressed porteños stood on the sidewalks and gaped at the invasion. Dark-haired, dark-skinned marchers wore coveralls or other types of factory garb. One of them, a woman worker who had come all the way from Rosario, costumed herself as the Argentine Republic, complete with ankle-length dress and a sky-blue-and-white sash.[5] They carried improvised banners and placards, some with Perón's picture attached; they sang popular tunes with new verses composed for the occasion; they chanted for their colonel. Though it was a warm, very humid spring day and by noon a few drops of rain fluttered from overcast skies, they kept arriving.

Meanwhile, in a courthouse some twenty blocks from the Plaza de Mayo, Attorney General Juan Alvarez was still laboring to put together a new cabinet. Drawing from the traditional elite groups, he had come up with a list of names that pleased him. Now he was ironing out the final details, blissfully unaware of the human tide engulfing the city.

Though still confident that matters were under control, General Avalos had to decide how to placate the swelling crowds and make them disperse peacefully. To this end he attempted to summon Mercante from the Campo de Mayo, where he was still under house arrest, but the lieutenant colonel, upon his release, had gone immediately to the military hospital to consult with Perón.

Columns of workers continued to assemble without pause, and it was becoming evident that Avalos had no real plan to meet the crisis. A surrealistic atmosphere had developed at the Casa Rosada, with confusion and indecision reigning hand in hand. The only person untouched by the excitement was General Farrell, who seemed to float about it, not really caring and relishing his spectator's role.

The scene was also chaotic at the military hospital, where labor leaders, military officers and civilian politicians clustered around Perón and offered conflicting advice. Phone calls began to arrive from the Casa Rosada, and self-appointed representatives of the colonel were traveling back and forth between the Government House and the hospital. Through it all, Perón remained calm and cautious, still in his pajamas, looking for the right moment.

By 4:30 P.M. the heat was so oppressive that many men in front of the Casa Rosada began to strip to the waist. The fountains in the plaza became wading pools, especially for the children. It was at this point that Mercante finally made his way to the Government House.

Avalos still clung to the hope that reassuring words from the man recognized by all as Perón's right arm would disperse the crowd. He ordered Mercante to go out on the balcony, where a microphone had been installed, and tell the people that Perón was safe. Mercante, aware that still more workers were on their way to the plaza, adopted delaying tactics. He reached for the microphone and began his speech by uttering the words "General Avalos . . ." The ploy had its intended effect. The crowd whistled him down and would not let him continue. Mercante shrugged his shoulders. Avalos seethed. Vernengo Lima directed a captain to disperse the crowd with machine-gun fire from the roof of the Casa Rosada. The captain asked for a written order, which Avalos refused to give.

The farce continued as Eduardo Colom suddenly appeared on the balcony. Editor of *La Epoca*, the only newspaper that was supporting Perón, he waved a copy of the latest edition and requested permission to speak to the crowd. As Avalos hesitated, the mercurial Colom grabbed the microphone. "Fellow citizens," he began, "I have been assured by General Avalos that Perón is free." "We don't believe it" was the choral response. "I don't either," continued the journalist, "but I'm going to the military hospital, and within fifteen minutes, I'll bring him here. Stay where you are until I return."[6] The military aides standing at the doorway to the balcony stared at one another in disbelief. Avalos had by now reached catatonia. Colom took advantage of the paralysis that seemed to have seized everyone on the balcony and quickly disappeared. He hurried to the military hospital and offered to take Perón back to the Casa Rosada because, as he put it, the crowd in the plaza had just proclaimed him president. Perón politely refused.

In the meantime, at the British embassy Ambassador Kelly was receiving reports that workers had spontaneously shut down the British-owned railways. He decided to pay a call on the naval minister (still the only cabinet minister in addition to Avalos). The ambassador approached the Plaza de Mayo in his chauffeur-driven limousine. "There was a cordon of mounted police immediately around the Casa Rosada, but they were making no effort to enable anyone to get through the crowd or interfere with the latter in any way. . . . The crowd made way readily on seeing the flag, contenting themselves with shouting through the window in a friendly fashion: 'Long live Perón!' and 'Down with Braden!' "[7] Admiral Vernengo Lima assured Sir David that everything possible would be done to protect the railways, and the ambassador departed. Shortly afterward the admiral gave up all hope of persuading Avalos to take energetic countermeasures and headed for the Naval Ministry to organize a revolt of his own.

By late afternoon the disorder in the Casa Rosada had attained its apogee. Military authorities summoned to Avalos' presence a nineteen-year-old student who had been exhorting the crowd from the flatbed of a truck festooned with loudspeakers.[8] The boy was escorted past heavily armed soldiers crouching behind sandbags stacked up against doors and windows facing the plaza. He entered a room and found himself face to face with the war minister, who requested him to address the demonstrators from the balcony and try to quiet them. The boy, one of Perón's followers, complied with the directive, but had no effect upon his listeners.

It was now plain that the only person who could calm the crowd was Perón, but he refused to answer Farrell's phone calls. The colonel was playing for time. He wanted the crowd at the Casa Rosada to reach its maximum size, and he had yet to decide the terms he would set before making an appearance at the plaza. He finally chose a delegation from among his friends to negotiate on his behalf with the military men in the Government House. The delegates reached a consensus that he should insist on speaking from the Casa Rosada balcony (Avalos had proposed that he talk to the crowd from a hotel facing the plaza), and that he should demand the resignations of both Avalos and Vernengo Lima. Furthermore, Farrell would have to appoint Perón supporters as minister of war, police chief and head of the Secretariat of Labor and Public Welfare.

While his negotiators worked out the details, at Mercante's urging General Avalos visited Perón at the hospital. The meeting took place, without witnesses, at 8:00 P.M. Neither man ever disclosed what transpired. Their encounter marked the end of the general's career.

At that very moment a distinguished-looking gentleman entered the Casa Rosada and asked to see Farrell. Attorney General Juan Alvarez had finalized his cabinet choices and wanted to present the list to the president. As oblivious to the events of the day as the oligarchy he represented had been to the changes Argentina had been undergoing for the past several years, he had to be told bluntly that his services were no longer needed. He took his list, donned his hat, and went home.

By 9:00 P.M. an agreement had been reached whereby Perón would speak from the Casa Rosada balcony and over the government radio network. Farrell left for the presidential residence, where he was to confer with Perón. The colonel finally dressed himself in civilian clothing and emerged from the hospital. Mercante, afflicted with stomach pains from a bleeding ulcer, was unable to accompany him. After an examination by Dr. Mazza, he remained in the hospital and thus could not be at Perón's side during these critical moments.

At 9:45 Farrell and Perón had their conversation at the residence. The president agreed to all the terms set by his former vice-president. Shortly after 10:30, they returned to the Casa Rosada, and thirty minutes later, both men stepped out on the balcony.

Perón's appearance touched off a fifteen-minute ovation from the crowd, which now numbered nearly 300,000, according to the most reasonable estimates. Many of them waved handkerchiefs at him, while others held aloft ignited newspapers rolled to serve as torches. They chanted slogans and seemed to galvanize him with their enthusiasm. Palms outstretched, he gestured at them with the choppy movements that would become one of his trademarks.

Farrell took the microphone first. He announced a new cabinet, composed entirely of Perón's confederates, and touched off a delirious cheer by declaring that under no circumstances would the government be handed over to the Supreme Court. He thereupon introduced Perón as "the man who has won everybody's devotion."[9] Deeply moved and finding himself in need of a few moments of calm to gather his thoughts, the colonel asked that the crowd sing the national hymn.[10] He then improvised a speech that delighted the mass of humanity before him.[11]

"Workers," he intoned, and another unbridled outburst delayed him for a few minutes more. "Almost two years ago, from this same balcony, I said I had three honors in my life: to be a soldier, to be a patriot, and to be Argentina's number one worker. Today, this afternoon, the president has signed my request for retirement from active service in the army. With it I have given up voluntarily the highest achievement to which a soldier can aspire: to wear the palms and laurels of a general."

Calling the demonstration a "fiesta of democracy" and a "rebirth of worker self-awareness," he expressed a desire "to press all of you against my heart, as I would do with my mother." Curiously, this was the first (and would be the last) reference he would make to his mother in a public forum.

The fervid crowd participated by shouting words of encouragement (like "Hoorah for Perón's old lady [mother]") and even asked questions ("Where were you?"), converting the speech into a dialogue.

He concluded by urging the demonstrators to return home peacefully and to "spend the strike day celebrating the story of this assembly of workingmen of good will."

"Tomorrow is Saint Perón's day" was the jubilant response. "Let the bosses work!"

Perón brought his speech to an end by asking his listeners to remain in the plaza for fifteen minutes more so that he might "feast his eyes" on the magnificent spectacle before him. Another tumultuous ovation followed, enabling him to savor his moment of triumph. He raised his arms aloft and clasped his hands like a victorious boxer, breaking out of the pose only to embrace each of the men on the balcony with him. At last he disappeared into the Casa Rosada, and the great crowd began to disperse in all directions. The events in the plaza were now history, soon to be transformed into myth, but there remained a two-scene epilogue to the drama.

A column of demonstrators, led by young militants from the right-wing Alianza Libertadora Nacionalista, or ALN (Nationalist Liberation Alliance) marched up the Avenida de Mayo to the building where the newspaper *Crítica* was published. The daily had infuriated Perón supporters with its deprecatory coverage of the events leading to the colonel's restoration. The demonstrators hurled first angry words and then stones at the edifice. Suddenly gunfire erupted from within the building. ALN members ducked behind parked cars and unsheathed the pistols they customarily carried. A full-scale battle ensued. The police, unable to bring the situation under control, had to summon army troops in order to force the defenders of *Crítica* to surrender. A seventeen-year-old member of the ALN died from a bullet wound, and nonfatal casualties numbered from forty to fifty. The incident provided an inappropriate ending to a day remarkable for its festive, peaceful atmosphere. It would not be the last time that violence would mar a celebration involving Perón.

During the final hours of October 17, Admiral Vernengo Lima made a last desperate attempt to stem the Peronist tide. As he left the Casa Rosada, he conversed briefly with General Avalos and took with him the impression that the latter intended to order troops from Campo de Mayo to prevent Perón from regaining control of the government. The admiral resolved to lead a naval revolt that would complement the army's march on Buenos Aires. He sent telegrams to important navy installations ordering the fleet to converge upon the Río de la Plata. But his colleagues were reluctant to commit themselves until assured that Campo de Mayo would in fact revolt, and it soon became apparent that General Avalos had no desire to lead a revolt. Vernengo Lima had no alternative but to surrender. On the eighteenth he presented himself at the Naval Ministry, where he was detained. He subsequently retired from the service.[12]

When Perón finally departed from the Casa Rosada, Captain Santiago Menéndez, his adjutant, drove him to Posadas Street. But a crowd of well-wishers had already gathered in front of the apartment, and he was in no mood to deal with them. Menéndez suggested a return to the military hospital.[13]

When they arrived back at the chaplain's apartment, Menéndez gave orders to the sentry to bar all visitors. Perón, exhausted, flopped on the bed, but nervous excitement still gripped him. When the door to the apartment opened and a uniformed officer entered, he instinctively reached for a knife he had placed beneath the pillow. The man in the doorway was one of his close associates who had come to help keep watch over him. It was at this point that Perón directed Menéndez to telephone Evita, inform her of his whereabouts, and ask that she come to the hospital in the morning.

What Evita actually did on the seventeenth of October has never been established with certainty or in detail.[14] When Perón arrived from Martín García that morning, she and her brother appeared at the hospital. She spoke with him from the lobby by telephone, but did not go up to the chaplain's quarters. Since a host of his friends and collaborators did visit him there, it is safe to assume that Perón for reasons of his own did not want her around him during the crucial period. Though some labor leaders later claimed that she spent the seventeenth (as well as the two previous days) helping to mobilize the demonstration,[15] their after-the-fact testimony smacks of myth-making. There is evidence that at some point during the day she suffered physical abuse during a taxi ride,[16] although the exact circumstances have never been clarified. She eventually returned to the Posadas Street apartment, where she spoke with Perón at least once by telephone and listened to the radio broadcast of his balcony speech. On the morning of the eighteenth she met him at the hospital, and they motored to the ranch in San Nicolás, where they had originally planned to go on the night of October 12.

Argentina would never be the same after the seventeenth of October. The working class had for the first time marched its way onto the political scene and achieved an enduring degree of self-awareness. The collective experience of that day would raise Argentine workers above their counterparts in the rest of Latin America. This distinction still endures and is perhaps Perón's most notable legacy.

Juan Perón emerged as both cause and effect of October 17. His labor policies gave workers something to lose if they did not mobilize in his defense. At the same time, the mass demonstration brought him back from the brink of oblivion and enabled him to continue his quest for the presidency.

Perón's actual performance on the seventeenth and the days leading up to it illuminate his peculiar brand of leadership. For the most part, he remained passive and did not exercise firm direction over the forces at his disposal. He eschewed the strong-man role, as he would throughout his career, yet an aura of decisiveness surrounded him.

The dramatic events of October 17 gave birth to twin myths. The Peronist version, in which Evita played the lead in Perón's rescue, did not take shape for several years. The political opposition, however, lost no time in developing a fantasy of its own: Perón's henchmen created and manipulated an unruly mob that forced the weak-kneed Avalos to permit Perón to return. An oft-quoted passage from the Socialist weekly, *La Vanguardia*, typifies this interpretation.

> In the depths and hidden recesses of society, there lies accumulated misery, grief, ignorance, poverty more mental than physical, unhappiness and suffering. When a social upheaval or stimulation by the police mobilizes the latent forces of resentment, they cut every moral restraint, unleash uncontrollable forces, and the part of the population that lives this resentment, and perhaps for this resentment, spills into the streets, threatens, shouts, tramples, attacks newspapers and pursues in a demonic fury its own permanent allies.[17]

The Communist party of Argentina disassociated itself from the worker mobilization of October 17. The party newspaper called the demonstrators "armed bands . . . obeying a plan of action directed by the colonel and his Nazi advisors."[18] Put off by Perón's anticommunism, the party hewed to a line that separated them from their supposed working-class constituency. To the present day, the Communists have yet to recover from this tactical blunder.

The American reaction to the seventeenth of October evidenced both bewilderment and a reluctance to face facts. The U.S. embassy, which had consistently downplayed popular support for Perón, was at first stunned. At noon on the eighteenth, Chargé John Moors Cabot cabled Washington that "practically no one with whom I have talked has even to his own mind [a] satisfactory explanation for [the] events of [the] last 24 hours. There is [a] general consensus that [the] Perón forces [are] very much stronger than anyone realized, that anti-Perón forces were caught unawares and there is evidence that popular sentiments suddenly reacted in favor of Perón."[19] By 6:00 P.M. the chargé had recovered his anti-Perón perspective and cabled that popular feeling was "skilfully taken advantage of and organized by desperate members of Perón's clique."[20] He also downplayed the size of the Plaza de Mayo crowd. In a cable dispatched on the following day, he referred to the "excellent organization of hoodlums on Fascist line like Brown Shirts and Black Shirts."[21]

Coverage in the *New York Times* was similarly uncomprehending. Correspondent Arnaldo Cortesi, who had suffered various unpleasant experiences at the hands of the regime, attributed the popular mobilization to efforts by the police and called the crowd in the plaza "mostly very young, many boys . . . undoubtedly for the most part recruited from the working classes."[22] Although he did note that Perón's following among workers was greater than "most people" believed, he added that "intimidation and actual violence" contributed to the success of the pro-Perón forces. It is instructive to compare the New York Times coverage of October 17 with that of the London Times. The correspondent for the latter was obviously present in the plaza and captured the spirit of the event. "All the personalism peculiar to Argentine politics and the mystic fervor of the Argentine people reached a frenzied climax of enthusiasm last night. . . . The crowd was not preoccupied with ideologies or doctrines, or propaganda, but wanted only Colonel Perón. . . . It felt an almost religious emotion for [him]."[23]

What most perplexed North American observers was the support Perón received from workers. Accounts of the seventeenth of October could not obscure this allegiance, although efforts were made to minimize it. The State Department was not satisfied and worriedly informed the embassy in Buenos Aires that the American public was beginning to believe the majority of Argentine workers backed Perón. Since this was at variance with the truth as Washington imagined it, the embassy was urged to convince the press corps to provide the American people with "accurate information" about Perón's popularity.[24]

In time the standard North American interpretation of October 17 merged with that of the political opposition in Argentina. By December, Serafino Romualdi, an official of the American Federation of Labor, was quoting with evident approval a description of the Plaza de Mayo crowd as "in addition to a few misguided workers . . . policemen in civilian clothes, fanatic nationalists, Nazis and Fascists, Perón government employees, military men and underworld characters of both sexes."[25]

Argentine reaction to the events of October 17 had social overtones. The fact that many in the crowd had cooled themselves in the fountains in the Plaza de Mayo seemed to bother some of the newspapers almost as much as Perón's return to power. A deprecatory term attached to the colonel's motley supporters: descamisados, or shirtless ones* (proper por-

---

* Who first used the term to describe the October 17 crowd is not known. On October 18 La Epoca, Eduardo Colom's rabidly pro-Perón afternoon paper, referred to the demonstrators as "shirtless" (p. 5). On the nineteenth La Epoca compared them to the sans-culottes of the French Revolution (p. 1) and in a separate article criticized certain unnamed papers for using the expression as an insult to Perón's supporters. Colom's recollection thirty-six years later was that Crítica was the "guilty" newspaper. Interview with Eduardo Colom, Buenos Aires, July 24, 1980. However, the October 17 issue of Crítica called the demonstrators muchachones ("young toughs"). It has been impossible to locate a copy of Crítica for October 18, a day on which it might not have been published. Therefore, Colom himself may have coined the expression.

teños would not be caught dead without a jacket and tie, even on the warmest of summer days). Perón seized the word like a gift from heaven, and it became a standard to which he rallied the workers of Argentina. Henceforth his followers would proudly proclaim themselves descamisados as they marched into battle against the oligarchy and other enemies, both domestic and foreign.

16

The Presidential Campaign

On October 22, after several days of rest at the farm in San Nicolás, Perón returned to Buenos Aires. It was at this point that he decided to fulfill his promise to Evita and formalize their relationship. The brief civil ceremony was secret and the public record of it contained a number of falsifications.[1] A notary from Junín prepared the official document, which stated that the marriage had taken place in Junín. The document also subtracted three years from Evita's age, stated that her name was Eva Duarte,[2] characterized Perón as "single" rather than "widower," and certified a prenuptial medical examination that was never given. The actual tying of the knot occurred in the Posadas Street apartment. Domingo Mercante and Juan Duarte served as witnesses. Evita's mother substituted for her son at the religious ceremonies in the Church of St. Francis in La Plata on December 10.

On November 13, the government decreed that elections would be held on February 24, 1946. This advanced the voting date by two months. The opposition raised no objections, since the existing parties were already well organized. Perón was starting from scratch, and a quick election appeared to be to his disadvantage.

However, the fledgling political forces that would comprise the Peronist coalition were already stirring.[3] On October 24, a group of union leaders met to launch the Labor party, modeled after the similarly named party that had recently taken power in Great Britain. The platform they adopted was progressive, democratic and statist, advocating increased industrialization, economic planning, women's suffrage, full employment, profit-sharing, agrarian reform and the nationalization of public services and essential mineral sources. Luis Gay was chosen to head the party, with Cipriano Reyes as his first vice-president. The new entity declared itself ready to support the candidate who subscribed to its principles. No one could doubt that this meant Perón.

The Labor party came into being without an independent constituency of its own and emphasized principle above loyalty to a leader. A clash with the retired colonel was inevitable, but for the coming elections the party needed Perón as much as he needed the party.

As the Laborites were assembling their political machine, the ex-Radicals who had defected to Perón formed their own party, called the Unión Cívica Radical Junta Renovadora, or UCRJR (the Radical Civil Union, Renovating Board). The Junta Renovadora (JR), as it was popularly called, responded to the leadership of Dr. Quijano and claimed the mantle of Yrigoyen. In late November, the party offered its presidential nomination to Perón. The JR, unlike the Labor party, had no platform of its own. Its raison d'être was to provide Perón with organizational support and to present a slate of candidates for the concurrent congressional and gubernatorial elections.

A miscellaneous assortment of conservatives and nationalists comprised the rest of the Peronist coalition. FORJA, the organization of young Radical intellectuals, voluntarily dissolved, and its members joined the Peronist ranks. The ultra-right-wingers who had quarreled with Perón over Argentina's diplomatic break with the Axis rejoined the fold. The ALN, whose young militants had functioned as civilian shock troops for the regime since August, enrolled in the crusade with great zeal, despite their disdain for elections. In a ceremony befitting the seriousness with which the group held itself, the ALN solemnly installed Perón its leader. One of the organization's officials then tried to lecture him in the art of running a campaign. "I'm your leader now," Perón reminded him. "I give the orders and you follow them."[4] But despite his admonition, ALN members continued to set off outbursts of violence and engage in occasional acts of anti-Semitism. Perón deplored these excesses, but would not disassociate himself from the ALN.

The opposition wasted little time in shaping its strategy, which rested upon the pivotal concept of the united front.[5] The Socialists, Communists and Progressive Democrats all agreed to line up behind candidates nominated by the Radical party for president and vice-president. The coalition adopted the name Unión Democrática (UD), or Democratic Union. Its campaign slogan: "For Liberty, Against Nazism." The parties chose their own candidates for federal deputies, provincial governors and provincial legislatures.*

Although still bedeviled by internal divisions, the Radical party agreed

---

* As in the United States before passage of the Seventeenth Amendment, federal senators in Argentina were elected by their respective provincial legislatures.

to join the UD and supply its standard-bearers. At a convention in December, the party nominated José P. Tamborini and Enrique N. Mosca for the top slots.

Though no surprise in light of his position in the party hierarchy, the selection of Tamborini was devoid of inspiration, a shortcoming that matched the candidate's most salient characteristic. A fifty-nine-year-old surgeon from Buenos Aires, Dr. Tamborini had earned his political spurs as a federal deputy, minister of the interior and federal senator. Noting his "humble origin," a U.S. military intelligence report on him concluded: "He is not brilliant, either as a statesman or orator, and his personality is not striking."[6] Félix Luna, after listing his positive qualities, observed that "He would have been a great president, twenty years before. . . . If his name didn't arouse resistance, neither did it evoke enthusiasm. And to confront Perón, they needed a man who could convey emotion and fervor."[7] Mosca qualified as a ticket-balancer, having served as governor of the populous province of Santa Fe, which was also the political center of gravity for the Progressive Democrats.

UD partisans were not worried about their candidates' lack of luster. The view current among the political opposition was that Perón could not win free elections. All but two daily newspapers of Buenos Aires supported the UD and slanted their campaign coverage accordingly. The UD candidates had access to the radio. The political-experience factor weighed heavily in favor of the Tamborini-Mosca ticket.

One other key element seemed at first blush to be working on the side of the UD. Spruille Braden had assumed responsibility for U.S. policy toward Argentina. The Senate confirmed his appointment as assistant secretary of state on October 22. Braden continued to speak out against the "Nazi regime" in Argentina and the "threat" posed by Perón.[8] He set in motion what he hoped would be his master stroke even before he took office. On October 3, he quietly directed the State Department to examine captured German documents and compile a comprehensive record of both Nazi infiltration in Argentina and Argentine complicity with Axis powers.[9] Later that month Secretary of State Byrnes requested the FBI and the Departments of Justice, War, the Navy and the Treasury to cooperate in the project.[10]

Perón's opponents were so confident of victory that many of them entertained the firm conviction that the government would either cancel or corrupt the election. Therefore, from the very outset of the campaign, UD members began to conspire actively to overthrow the regime by force. They kept in close touch with the U.S. embassy and other North American contacts. Although there is no evidence that they received money or arms from the United States, available documents provide illuminating details of plots being hatched by an opposition that proclaimed itself "democratic."

By early November, a stream of individuals had solicited advice from embassy officials regarding methods of contacting arms dealers in the United States and elsewhere.[11] Later that month, an Argentine businessman visited Spruille Braden in Washington and asked whether the State Department would furnish submachine guns and bazookas to "anti-Perón" elements for whom money was no problem. Braden refused to involve the U.S. government.[12]

A U.S. military intelligence report originating from Uruguay in mid-December gave details about what was called the "Argentine Resistance Movement."[13] The civilian branch of its central committee included José Tamborini and other representatives from political parties in the UD. Three generals formed a military committee. Brazilians were supplying weapons—rifles, machine guns, grenades, revolvers—which were being stored in southern Brazil. A fleet of yachts stood ready to transport these weapons to Argentina. The uprising was scheduled to occur before the elections. On January 21, U.S. Chargé Cabot informed Secretary of State Byrnes in a top-secret cable that the "revolution" would begin on January 22 or 29.[14] Four days later he assured the secretary that the "possibility of [an] early revolutionary movement appears steadily increasing."[15]

Perón was aware of the plots. In an interview published in the *New York Times* on January 31, he accused his opponents of smuggling arms into Argentina from Uruguay and the U.S. embassy of participating in the conspiracy. He offered no proof and probably had none, save for his knowledge of the contacts between the plotters and embassy officials.

The armed rebellion failed to go beyond preparations. A U.S. military intelligence report pointed to continuing dissension within the movement as the principal barrier to action.[16] In addition, as the campaign swung into high gear, it became increasingly likely that the elections would be held, and that the armed forces would in fact assure an honest vote. To opposition pundits, this meant victory for the UD at the polls.

The nonconspiratorial side of the UD campaign began on December 8 with a rally at the Plaza del Congreso, the launching site for the march for the constitution and liberty. The meeting was an obvious effort to recapture the political momentum of the march and to turn the calendar back to the pre-seventeenth of October era. The demonstration was well attended and disciplined, but did not replicate the euphoria of September 19. Tamborini gave a dull speech, and the rally concluded on a tragic note when ALN toughs clashed with UD marshals. Gunfire eventually erupted and took four lives. It was a shocking occurrence, to be repeated several times during the next months, and was indicative of the passions sparked by the campaign.

A major problem for UD was its platform. The coalition had taken a firm stand against Nazism, but the "Nazi threat" was not readily apparent to most Argentines. The UD came out in favor of liberty and democracy in the abstract, with shopworn rhetoric the Radicals had used at the turn of the century. On bread-and-butter issues, Perón had preempted the field, and the UD was finding it difficult to stake out a corner of its own.

One response to this dilemma was to pound away at Perón on a number of peripheral points. *La Vanguardia,* the Socialist party weekly, accused him of having been expelled from Chile for espionage,[17] and gave prominent play to the charge that his candidacy violated the constitutional proscription against reelection. Though the argument was tenuous at best,* it afforded a pretext for dubbing Perón the "Impossible Candidate."

Another opportunity to snipe at Perón materialized as a result of the first rally sponsored by the Labor party. Before a crowd of at least 200,000, Perón made his initial public use of the term *descamisado* (shirtless) when he declared, "We shall march through our peaceful streets, enthusiastic for our cause, without calling anybody 'rabble' or '*descamisado.*' "[18] At the conclusion of the speech, he doffed his jacket and rolled up his sleeves in a gesture that would become a standard Peronist symbol. A young man in the crowd passed up to him an Argentine flag attached to a staff. Nailed below the banner was a man's shirt. For several minutes Perón waved the "flags" to an enthusiastic roar from the audience. *La Vanguardia* demanded that a military court of honor consider whether the retired colonel had committed an offense against the Argentine flag.[19]

These pinpricks did not concern Perón nearly so much as the constant infighting among his followers. The Laborites, sparked by such independent spirits as Cipriano Reyes, fought with the experienced politicians of the JR. In several provinces (including Buenos Aires), each party presented its own slate of candidates for offices other than the presidency and vice-presidency. In other provinces and the federal capital, they combined forces and then battled over the composition of the joint list of candidates. When the Labor party nominated Mercante to run for vice-president on the ticket with Perón, the latter was forced to let it be known that he preferred Dr. Quijano, the choice of the JR. This reflected a cold political judgment, since it made no sense to present two military men to head the ticket. Quijano also added geographical balance. The Labor party yielded to Perón's wishes, but tapped Mercante to run for governor of Buenos Aires Province.

Quijano served his purpose well. With his white hair, mustache, potbelly and string tie, he projected an aura of old-fashioned respectability.[20] His behavior was always correct and he obeyed Perón faithfully. Crowds

* Article 77 of the Argentine constitution stated that "the president and vice-president . . . may not be reelected except with an interval of one term." Perón had served as vice-president. The contention that he was now running for "reelection" seems to stretch the word beyond its meaning.

would respond to his campaign oratory by shouting "Give it to them, grandpa!"[21]

Financial difficulties apparently beset Perón, at least at the onset of the campaign.[22] Reliable data are unavailable to show how the Peronists and the UD financed their efforts. The UD clearly had ample backing, since it could count upon big business. Perón, on the other hand, had to utilize modest contributions from his labor-union followers and more substantial offerings from wealthy friends like Ludwig Freude. Later in the campaign, some business firms seeking to hedge their bets provided Perón with funds that helped him defray the expenses of several provincial tours.

The government, securely in the hands of his supporters, had an asset more valuable than money at its disposal: control over labor policies. Mercante took over the secretariat shortly after October 17, and in his first meeting with union representatives, he made it clear that his number-one priority was securing Perón's election. This meant that the bread-and-butter demands many of the labor leaders wanted to press had to be set aside until after February 24. Worker unrest was the last thing Perón needed during the campaign. He did not want individual unions to create situations that might lead to strikes.

In December the regime decreed a salary increase, paid vacations and a year-end bonus for all workers. This not only pleased its immediate beneficiaries but also placed the UD in a political bind. The Chamber of Commerce, the Argentine Industrial Union and other groups representing business complained about the financial burdens imposed by the decree. The Communist party actually went on record *against* the salary and benefit increases bestowed upon workers. In mid-January commercial and manufacturing interests staged a three-day nationwide lockout in protest. But both the government and organized labor held firm, and industry soon capitulated.

In early February, Perón's campaign received an unintended boost from the Supreme Court, which invalidated as unconstitutional a decree creating regional delegates of the Secretariat of Labor and giving them authority to fine employers who violated the law. This ruling, when combined with a prior decision abolishing the labor courts, brought home to workers how fragile their gains would be in the hands of an unfriendly regime.

As in the United States, an electoral college made up of electors chosen by a majority of voters in the various provinces and the federal capital selected the president. Since the remote reaches of Patagonia and the far northeast were territories rather than provinces, their inhabitants did not vote in presidential elections. This substantially reduced the amount of traveling candidates had to do.

Both Perón and his UD adversaries made several tours of the interior in the course of the campaign. These trips generated both enthusiasm and violence. The UD candidates journeyed on what was called the "Victory Train." It attracted both gunfire and rocks during the first of two odysseys, and returned to Buenos Aires in a badly battered state.[23] As Perón departed on his second tour (on a train dubbed La Descamisada and draped with banners, one of which proclaimed him king), the crowd that bade him farewell turned into an uncontrollable mob, running amok through the downtown, destroying UD posters, roughing up suspected "oligarchs," stoning buildings where anti-Perón newspapers were published and setting off exchanges of gunfire that produced several casualties.[24] In the course of Perón's trip, he narrowly avoided disaster when police discovered dynamite on the tracks. Unidentified gunmen fired on a group of his supporters as they waited for the train to pass on its way through Buenos Aires Province and wounded six persons.[25]

The tours were grueling tests of physical endurance, but Perón thrived on them. He virtually lived on the train and spent every available moment between stops in preparation for his next speech. His personal appearances in the politically unsophisticated hinterland produced memorable vignettes illustrating the emotion he stirred. For Raúl Bustos Fierro, a JR politician who served as one of five regular speech-makers, the tours evoked a montage of sentimental images. "In Tucumán," he recalled, "a little old man and his grandson rode on horseback all night and all day to present a bouquet of mountain flowers to Perón. In Salta two hundred horsemen encircled the train and serenaded us with their guitars. A delegation of Indians visited the train in Jujuy. The only words they said in Spanish were 'Perón, Indian leader.' "[26]

Evita joined Perón on several of his trips. It was the first time a candidate's wife had ever campaigned in the interior. She remained discreetly in the background, yet she did not hesitate to inject herself into behind-the-scenes deliberations. Her first significant public exposure occurred on February 9 at a Luna Park rally for women and students. It proved a rather trying experience: when she announced that her husband could not attend on account of illness and tried to read a message from him, the crowd drowned her out with cries of "We want Perón."[27]

The establishment Buenos Aires newspapers did not conceal their political sympathies in their coverage of the campaign. They gave detailed attention to the UD and scant heed to Perón. La Prensa exercised its freedom of the press by providing remarkably unbalanced reporting during this period. Reflecting clear class biases, it depicted with ill-concealed disdain the unbridled exuberance of Perón's descamisados. An article describing the arrival of Perón by train at the Plaza Once station on February 20 reached a giddy pinnacle of snobbery. It quoted Perón's followers, as they entered the station, exclaiming with surprise: "Look how big the wall is!" In the waiting room "they turned the fans on and 'to be comfortable' took off their jackets and even their pants. Some of them went so far as to take off all their clothes and do popular dances of exotic origin. All this drew applause. In the intervals, others dedicated themselves to making speeches, the sentiments of which it is not possible to transcribe."[28]

Press coverage in the United States aimed directly at Perón and reached a crescendo in February. Arnaldo Cortesi set off another blast, this time in the *New York Times Magazine*. Entitled "Portrait of a Rabble-Rouser," the article compounded Cortesi's previously skewed version of the seventeenth of October by claiming that Perón's balcony speech that night was filled with ungrammatical sentences and two-syllable words.[29]

Life sent a photographer on one of Perón's campaign tours through the interior.[30] To the delight of the U.S. embassy,[31] he managed to snap a picture of the candidate sitting next to Rudi Freude. It appeared in a February 25 *Life* photo story smearing Perón. Captions used in the article referred to him as "the son of a rich rancher," called his private life "scandalous," and reported that "Evita occupies much the same position in the Perón regime that Goering's actress wife did in Nazi Germany."

If *Life* took the low road, *Look* traveled by sewer. It published a photo story entitled "Tomorrow's Hitler," titillating readers with the unmistakable impression that Perón was a sexual pervert. "At [the] military academy," one caption read, "pinups [a female nude and a foppish officer] show Juan's interests. . . . [A] camera fan, Perón took numerous nudes of Indian girls in Patagonia, keeps them in a drawer of his desk."[32]

While the U.S. press jabbed at Perón, the project that Spruille Braden had begun on October 3 was rapidly approaching completion. State Department officials had been feverishly at work on a massive indictment of the Castillo, Ramírez and Farrell-Perón regimes. Drawing upon Nazi records discovered in Germany, the Braden-directed team spared neither effort nor expense to make its case against Argentina. By early February the explosive document had been assembled.

The explanation most frequently offered for the decision to release the State Department report before the elections was that Washington had begun to realize that Perón had broader public support than had been attributed to him, and that a last-minute attack was necessary to insure his defeat. Braden himself subsequently insisted that he felt from the start that Perón would win. [33]

However, State Department documents placed a different gloss on the decision. On February 2, U.S. Chargé Cabot informed the secretary of state that recent events (which he did not specify) indicated that Perón had lost considerable ground, that he was running short of money, that the elections would be honest, and that the UD would win.[34] Six days later, Byrnes informed him that the Braden report was about to be made public.[35] On that same day Cabot wired back urging that it not be released. "To throw [an] atomic bomb directly at [the] Argentine government in [the] present supercharged atmosphere is to court incalculable results," he warned.[36] Publication should follow from an extreme turn of events, he counseled, such as a Perón coup or fraudulent elections, or in the event the United States should decide to cut off relations with Argentina in the wake of a Perón victory at the polls. Cabot suggested in a subsequent cable that the State Department pressure the Argentine government by threatening to publish the report. He also opined that the document probably would not harm the "democratic cause" in Argentina.[37] In an immediate reply, Byrnes told him that the "department feels this is [the] right course of action and the one least vulnerable to criticism from [the] points of view of principle and long-range policy and objectives."[38]

And so on February 11, 1946, the State Department made public a 131-page memorandum pretentiously entitled "Consultation Among the American Republics with Respect to the Argentine Situation." It immediately became known as the Blue Book.

The "consultation" the State Department claimed it had initiated on October 3 was a transparent sham. Officials from other Latin nations first saw the Blue Book several days before its release. Much of the report's content rehashed previously published charges, such as those dealing with Argentina's supposed involvement in the 1943 coup in Bolivia. The authors treated the Castillo, Ramírez and Farrell governments interchangeably and ignored the internal dynamics of Argentine politics. Part III, a brief against the "Nazi-Fascist" character of the Farrell regime, could have been UD campaign literature.

As the *New York Times* pointed out in a front-page story, "the document's issue was obviously timed for its possible effect on the Argentine elections of February 24."[39] As such, it ranked as heavy-handed interference in the internal affairs of another nation. The timing of the release made adequate rebuttal before the balloting virtually impossible (although Perón did rush a reply into print[40]). Fairness did not enter into the State Department's calculations.

The Blue Book attracted extensive publicity in Argentina. *La Prensa* and *La Nación* reprinted the entire document in several installments. If the "democratic" forces had any misgivings about help from Spruille Braden, they repressed them. The UD embraced the report, while many individuals named as Nazi sympathizers by the Blue Book hastened to publish newspaper advertisements denying the charge. On February 21, Cabot reported to Washington that the "great majority of people with whom [the] embassy comes into contact are pleased at [the] publication [of the Blue Book]."[41] This was more indicative of the type of people who had contact with the U.S. embassy than of the mood of the Argentine electorate.

In contrast to the State Department's eleventh-hour interference with the electoral process, the Roman Catholic church made its effort to influence voters at the very outset of the campaign.[42] In mid-November the Catholic bishops, pursuant to a long-standing custom, issued a pastoral letter to be read from every pulpit, one that spelled out moral guidelines for the Catholic electorate. Couching their directions in theological, non-partisan terms, the bishops reminded their flock that no Catholic could in good conscience cast a ballot in favor of a candidate who advocated the separation of church and state, the abolition of religious teaching in the public schools or legalization of divorce. The UD subsequently included in its platform a plank advocating the second of these propositions, while Perón opportunistically defended the teaching of Catholic doctrine in the public-school curriculum.

Throughout the campaign Perón stressed his Catholicism and the inspiration his social doctrines derived from papal encyclicals. He enjoyed unofficial support from certain clerics and several days before the balloting made a highly publicized visit to the shrine of the Virgin at Luján. On the other hand, some priests criticized him openly, and Catholic journals called attention to the doctrine of the lesser evil (the UD being less evil than the "totalitarian" Perón).

How many votes the bishops actually cost the UD is uncertain. The women of Argentina, who would be most susceptible to clerical dictates, did not enjoy the right to vote. The bishops issued their letter well in advance of the election, at a time when it would have minimum impact. Most Argentine men probably discounted it and made their decision on the basis of other factors, although Perón probably gained some small advantage from the document.

In Argentine political campaigns, candidates are officially nominated shortly before the election, rather than at the very beginning of the campaign. On Friday, February 9, from an enormous stage set up at the intersection of the Avenidas de Mayo and 9 de Julio, the UD presented its Tamborini-Mosca ticket to a large crowd. The rally that was to formalize the nominations of Perón and Quijano was scheduled for Tuesday, February 12, one day after the release of the Blue Book.

The culminating public event of Perón's campaign attracted several hundred thousand enthusiasts to the broad expanse of the Avenida 9 de Julio where it crosses Corrientes Street, in the shadow of the white marble obelisk, one of the city's most notable landmarks. A podium was improvised on the second-floor balcony of a corner building that faced the obelisk, from which loudspeakers radiated in all directions.

February 12 was an oppressively hot midsummer day, and intermittent showers sent even the most diehard Perón enthusiasts scurrying for cover. Yet the mood of the crowd remained jubilant. Youths in shirt-sleeves shouted "We are the descamisados" and covered the nearby walls with slogans. A troop of costumed gauchos on horseback provided color.

The candidate himself spent the afternoon resting and making last-minute revisions to his speech. He was trying to fight off a bad cold and felt rather nervous about the rally. Evita radiated optimism. Reviewing his attire, she secured to his lapel a button with his likeness on it (a "little Perón," she called it) and gave him a kiss for good luck.[43]

When he stepped out on the balcony, he expressed concern about the size of the crowd. A cloudburst had just cleared the area, and people were just beginning to filter back into the streets. Ever mindful of the descamisado mystique, an announcer informed the audience that because of his cold Perón would not doff his jacket. The candidate stepped before the microphones and began with his familiar salutation: "Compañeros."

The charismatic attraction that Perón possessed now made its presence felt. It reached the thousands of people who were still seeking shelter under awnings, in doorways and against building walls. They scurried like ants to fill the empty spaces in the streets and sidewalks below the podium. A forest of poles from which shirt-banners defiantly fluttered began to bob and sway. Some of those in attendance, as La Prensa could not resist noting, carried burlap bags to ward off the rain.[44]

Perón usually improvised his campaign speeches. On this occasion, however, he donned his eyeglasses and read from a lengthy text. The constant interruptions from the crowd interfered with the radio transmission of his message, so he retired to a microphone set up in a room adjacent to the balcony in order to concentrate on his radio broadcast. He returned to the podium only for his stem-winding conclusion.

The speech was an effective piece of campaign oratory, the major portion of which focused on his promise of political, social and economic justice for all Argentines. He attacked his opponents as defenders of class privilege. Underscoring the incongruity of a "Democratic Union" that included the Communist party, he denied that either he or the workers of Argentina were in any way totalitarian, and claimed he was much more democratic than his adversaries. At several points he cited Franklin D. Roosevelt as a model and an example of a great popular leader obstructed by the vested interests.

He saved his strongest point for last. Without mentioning the Blue Book by name, he responded to it, on his own terms. He accused Spruille Braden of being the "inspiration, creator, organizer and virtual chief of the Democratic Union." The ex-ambassador, according to Perón, had interfered unabashedly with the internal politics of Argentina. He subordinated the local press and joined forces with the old politicians in an effort to impose a regime of quislings. He even concocted the march for the constitution and liberty so that "his little army of traitors" might pass in review. Of course, the ex-colonel added, the ambassador did not engage in these activities with the support of the North American people or the U.S. government. His conclusion: "Let those who vote on the twenty-fourth for the unholy oligarchy-communist alliance know that by doing so they are simply delivering their vote to Mr. Braden. The choice at this crucial hour is this: Braden or Perón."[45]

It was a classic exercise of political judo, setting the Blue Book on its head and bringing Spruille Braden back to center stage. Tamborini and the UD became irrelevant. Walls everywhere would suddenly sprout the scrawled disjunctive "Braden or Perón."

The publication of the Blue Book and Perón's riposte did not alter the mood of confidence that suffused both camps. Perón felt from the start that he would win. To his close associate, Dr. Ricardo Guardo, the outcome appeared uncertain until an incident not long before the election at a Mar del Plata beach frequented by upper-class families. "I had just been nominated for federal deputy on the Peronist slate and the newspapers had carried my name. When we arrived at the beach and settled down at our tent, a group of young people—students—came by and began to heckle me. The situation became ugly, and the police had to rescue us. As we reached the parking lot, all the chauffeurs who were standing watch over the limousines that belonged to the families of the youths who had reviled us came over to me and said 'Don't worry, Dr. Guardo, we're going to win.' At that moment I knew we would."[46]

To the very end, the UD stalwarts maintained their optimism. The Communist party newspaper, La Orientación, cautioned its readers: "Once the elections have passed we will be in the second phase of the great democratic task. We don't agree with those who ingenuously believe that Peronism will disappear because of a simple defeat at the polls. This defeat, of course, will affect its thinned-out ranks and will subject its leadership to an even greater decomposition."[47]

On February 24, a hot summer Sunday that would normally occasion an exodus from the cities to beaches or mountains, Argentines stayed home and went to the polls. It marked the first election since before the 1943 Revolution. Fifteen thousand troops guarded the polling places, as the armed forces fulfilled their pledge to the nation.

When the polls closed, leaders of the Democratic Union voiced their satisfaction with the way the election had been administered. The violence, coercion and fraud that had stained past elections were not repeated. As U.S. Chargé Cabot reported to Secretary Byrnes in response to a cable that virtually begged for evidence of irregularities,[48] "[The] voting procedure and counting of ballots have unquestionably been [the] fairest in Argentine history."[49]

Days passed as the slow process of tabulation by hand ran its course. It was not until early April that the final results become known. Perón had won a clear-cut victory, beyond all expectations, with a 304–72 margin in the electoral college. The Tamborini-Mosca ticket carried only the provinces of Córdoba, Corrientes, San Juan and San Luis. The popular-vote tally gave Perón nearly 1.5 million votes, as against 1.2 million for the UD, a percentage edge of 52.4 percent to 42.5 percent.[50] In the federal Chamber of Deputies, where a system of proportional representation allocated to the majority party in each province and the federal capital two-thirds of the seats, with one-third going to the party placing second, the Labor party and the JR combined to win a two-thirds majority. The big loser in the congressional elections was the Socialist party, which failed to win a seat for the first time since 1912. In the provincial elections the Peronists won the gubernatorial races and legislative majorities everywhere except in Corrientes. This meant that all but two Senate seats went to supporters of Perón.

When the dimensions of their defeat became apparent, the UD parties greeted the news with stunned silence. There were no congratulatory telegrams to Perón, nor any thoughtful inquiries into the reasons for the debacle. *La Prensa* was silent.[51] From Washington, Spruille Braden confined his reaction to an announcement that the United States would soon send a new ambassador to Argentina.[52] The Blue Book became a historical relic a scant two months after its publication.

The 1946 elections provided an accurate gauge to the temper of the Argentine people, despite the claim that the government rigged the results by tolerating violence against the opposition.[53] The fact remains that the UD enjoyed unfettered access to the press and radio. Virtually all the big newspapers backed the Tamborini-Mosca ticket. Though violent incidents did occur with some degree of frequency, they reflected the bitter divisions provoked by the campaign as well as an unfortunate and customary Argentine tendency to resort to impulsive violence, rather than neo-Nazism. Balloting was secret and scrupulously clean, affording the citizenry ample opportunity to reject the bullying tactics used by certain pro-Perón elements. The results—a majority supporting Perón and a strong minority rejecting him—spoke for themselves.

Perón won because the issues he stressed touched the concerns of most Argentines. His advocacy of political, social and economic justice attracted the support of the middle class as well as labor. Moreover, his brand of nationalism carried with it broad-based appeal. Small businessmen and industrialists opposed to the economic dominance of farming and livestock interests and to foreign competition found Perón a beguiling alternative.[54] In addition, there were some conservatives who hated the Radicals so passionately that they could not bring themselves to support Tamborini. Finally, Perón was an attractive, dynamic candidate, heading a political coalition driven by youthful enthusiasm.

The opposition, on the other hand, symbolized the past. Its leaders, supposedly seasoned politicians, were out of touch with the electorate. The presence of the Moscow-line Communist party in the ranks of the UD and the movement's links to the United States gave it a foreign taint to which the Blue Book provided a finishing touch. Tamborini was, in a word, dull, and easily yielded to Braden as Perón's primary target.

For the United States, Perón's victory was a bitter pill, underscoring the limits of Washington's ability to control events in Latin America. Historian Hubert Herring drew the proper conclusion: "We got an Argentina obstinately out of hand—that is, an Argentina that would not permit us to name her president."[55] Braden-style diplomacy, in the form of direct political interference, had failed. More subtle methods, based upon the economic relationship between the two countries, would yield Washington more satisfying results.

Perón, long a force behind the throne, emerged as a constitutionally elected leader with a working-class power base and solid military backing. Before him lay a six-year term which he would begin with a secure majority in both chambers of Congress, an economy that had prospered during the war and an opportunity for creative statesmanship. He embarked upon the presidency not as a politician with parliamentary experience and a commitment to the democratic process, but rather as a military man schooled in the military traditions of his country and shaped by military values. His particular genius was in transferring the essence of military leadership to the game of Argentine politics and in comprehending his fellow citizens far better than any of his contemporaries. He would exercise this genius, for better and for worse, for the next twenty-eight years.

Part IV

The
First
Presidency

(1946–1952)

17

A New Beginning

On the third anniversary of the Revolution of June 4, 1943, Juan D. Perón took office as Argentina's twenty-ninth chief executive. He was the nation's first elected president since Roberto Ortiz and the first cleanly elected president to enter the Casa Rosada since Hipólito Yrigoyen in 1928.

The glittering uniform and insignia he wore to the inaugural festivities attested to a resolution passed on May 29 by the Peronist majority in Congress, urging that the president-elect be restored to his rightful rank in the army. Farrell then reinstated Perón retroactively to October 17 (a gesture that preserved his pension) and promoted him to brigadier general as of December 31, 1945. Although he had ostentatiously cast aside the opportunity to become a general in his October 17 speech, he did not turn his back on the reinstatement and promotion. Given his affection for military life and its accoutrements, there can be little doubt that he asked for both, under circumstances that elevated his wishes to command status.

By tradition, Argentine inaugurations unfold in two steps. Perón and Quijano first took their oaths before a joint session of Congress. A boycott on the part of all but one opposition deputy marred the occasion. Although the British influenced many aspects of Argentine life, the Anglo-Saxon notion of the good loser had never taken root. Perón's adversaries transformed the antagonisms of the campaign into intransigent resistance to the new administration, without even the courtesy of a honeymoon period. The members of the minority bloc failed to provide any pretext for the disdain they were expressing for the voters' decision. It was all the more deplorable in light of the attendance by Radical deputies at the inaugurations of presidents Justo and Ortiz, whose elections had resulted from blatant electoral fraud.

Perón's inaugural address was both statesmanlike and generous.[1] He promised a quest for social justice and national reconciliation within bounds set by the constitution and the laws. Rejecting any desire for vengeance, he declared himself "president of all the Argentines, friend and foe alike" and claimed he was closing the book on the injustices and insults he had suffered.

After a ceremonial parade down the troop-lined Avenida de Mayo to the Casa Rosada, a throng of dignitaries filled the White Room of the Government House, where Farrell was awaiting his onetime protégé. The two men entwined in the obligatory embrace, and then the outgoing chief executive handed over to his successor the symbolic sash and baton. But Farrell's political career ended on a slightly sour note. Emerging from the Casa Rosada, he discovered that no one had provided a limousine to carry him home. He had to walk the entire length of Florida Street to his apartment.[2]

It was not until the next day that Perón and Evita roamed through the palatial mansion that would be their official residence. In a burst of boyish irreverence, the general slid down the banister and made one of his associates race him to the bottom of the grand staircase.[3]

The first challenge for the new president was to put together a team of competent administrators who could execute the ambitious plans he had in mind for what would be called the "New Argentina." Because the coalition that had promoted his candidacy had not attracted many experienced politicians, he had a limited pool of talent upon which to draw. Nonetheless, he did manage to find some capable individuals and to make some imaginative appointments that gave the early years of his presidency a progressive aura.

From the ranks of labor he tapped Juan A. Bramuglia as minister of foreign relations.[4] A bright young lawyer, Bramuglia brought to his new job intelligence, energy, freshness, and a heavy cross to bear—the undying enmity of Evita, who would never forget his refusal to help release Perón from Martín García.

Though he did not appoint him to a cabinet post, Perón made it clear that his chief economic advisor would be Miguel Miranda.[5] The son of impoverished Spanish immigrants, Miranda elbowed his way into the business world and became a tin-ware magnate during the wave of industrialization of the 1930s and early 1940s. Though initially opposed to Perón, this prototypical self-made man quickly succumbed to the colonel's charms. They discovered they shared many ideas about economic policy. Perón, holding the somewhat simplistic notion that a person who had successfully managed his private business affairs was best suited to handle the economic affairs of the nation, made Miranda a virtual czar over the economy.

José Figuerola became secretary for technical matters. As the government's chief planner, he would provide invaluable assistance in shaping the economic and administrative reforms Perón would launch.

Other noteworthy choices included labor leader Angel Borlenghi as minister of the interior, Oscar Nicolini (of the Nicolini affair) to head the postal and telegraph services, Evita's brother Juan as private secretary to the president, Rudolfo (Rudi) Freude as a member of the president's secretariat, and José María Freire, an obscure official of the glassmakers' union, to head what would now be the Ministry of Labor and Public Welfare.[6] Domingo Mercante, who had won a smashing victory as the Labor party's candidate for governor of Buenos Aires Province, had no official position in the national government but continued to be regarded as Perón's closest associate and heir apparent.

Reference to Perón's initial appointments would be incomplete without a mention of the most picturesque. The president's brother, Mario, still ranching in Patagonia but eager to share in the spoils of victory, made known his desire for a government job. Perón, fully aware of his brother's capabilities, was at a loss for a response. Dr. Ricardo Guardo, a close associate who had just been named president of the federal Chamber of Deputies, suggested the perfect slot for Mario: director of the Buenos Aires zoo. The position carried with it a free residence on the zoo grounds and access to the animals' food. Thus, Mario could house and feed his wife and six children, and would be safely out of Perón's hair.[7]*

Though Perón took care of his brother, he did nothing for his mother. Indeed, she did not even attend his inauguration. This has nourished all kinds of speculation about the relations between the president and his mother. Her remarriage to a Chilean farmer supposedly displeased Perón. (According to one version making the rounds in Buenos Aires, the couple had been living together out of wedlock, and the military forced them to marry when Perón attained the vice-presidency.[8]) After he took office, she and her husband appeared in the capital and tried to obtain a taxi license. The president was not happy about this and did nothing to help them.[9]

Even to the present day the myth persists among anti-Peronists and Peronists alike that Perón did not even bother to attend his mother's funeral when she died in 1953, and that he was trying out a new speed-

---

* Perón gave a different version of the appointment. He claimed he pressed Mario to take a government position, and the only job humble Mario would take was that of head zookeeper. "I like animals; what I don't like are people" was Mario's epigrammatic explanation. "Documentos: Las memorias de Juan Perón (1895–1945)," *Panorama*, April 14, 1970, p. 22. In a giddy flight of fantasy Perón ascribed astonishing zoological achievements to his brother: Mario could enter the gorilla's cage and slap it around; he treated the animals so well that a number of them—lions, tigers, and even the hippopotamuses—had offspring in captivity; and he let a sick orangutan sleep in a bed next to his. T. Luca de Tena, *Yo, Juan Domingo Perón*, pp. 21–22.

boat on the Río de la Plata at the moment of her burial. The easily ascertainable facts that Perón accompanied his mother's body to the cemetery from the Buenos Aires military airport, to which an air force plane had brought it from the city in southern Argentina where she died, and was present at the funeral mass and burial—all of which newspaper photos amply documented[10]—have not discouraged repetition of the canard. This is but another example of the distortion of a valid observation about Perón's character or career—in this case the unusual behavior he manifested toward his mother—with inexcusable misstatements of fact.

June 4 marked not only the inauguration of a new president but also the debut of a new first lady. María Eva Duarte de Perón, as she would formally be known, assumed the most important role in her career. Eva Duarte the actress officially disappeared. (Her last film, *The Prodigal*, never had a public showing. The director gave the master print to Perón after the elections.)

As first lady of Argentina, Evita was required to make various appearances at state functions. From the very beginning it was obvious that she brought to her new position a disarming freshness and uncommon style (which upper-class Argentines would find tasteless). At an inaugural banquet, she raised eyebrows by wearing a gown that left one of her shoulders bare. Protocol dictated that she sit next to the cardinal of Buenos Aires. A published photo recording the event for posterity provided a delectable feast for the gossip mongers of the Barrio Norte, as well as grist for a satirical revue at a downtown theater.[11]

At the dawn of Perón's first presidency one could find signs that his wife would engage in more than ceremonial activities. During the campaign she had freely voiced her opinions in private debates over the choice of candidates for various offices. Even before the inauguration, when the election results became known, she made a speech thanking the women's organizations that had helped in the campaign and urging passage of legislation that would give women the right to vote.[12] Shortly after Perón took his oath, Evita moved into an office on the fifth floor of the Central Post Office (Oscar Nicolini's domain) and began to busy herself in a host of minor governmental matters. Perón did not discourage her. To the contrary, he had no interest in the day-to-day problems of administration and was happy to leave them to Evita. But he never set any specific limits on her work, and before long she was telling cabinet ministers what to do. The minister of labor, whose pliant personality apparently secured the job for him, quickly became a virtual errand boy for the first lady, and she moved her office to his ministry.

As he set his presidency in motion, the tasks confronting Perón were formidable. He had to fuse the ungainly, often boisterous elements of his political coalition into a disciplined organization that could effectively counter a hostile opposition. The promises he had made to bring social justice to Argentina required some degree of fulfillment, but within the limits set by economic realities. It no longer suited the national interest to remain the bad boy of the inter-American family, and therefore Argentine foreign policy had to achieve reintegration into both the hemispheric and worldwide communities.

Yet the new president could count upon several key advantages, such as control of both houses of Congress and almost all the provincial governments. The solid victory he had won at the polls presented him with a mandate to carry out the ambitious goals he had set for his administration. Argentina's neutrality during virtually all of World War II and the weakened economies of the ravaged nations of Europe also created distinct opportunities for the new regime in Buenos Aires.

In 1946 he saw a challenge, he wanted to win, and he coveted the fruits of victory. Hence he plunged ahead with verve and determination. For many, this would become a golden era of progress toward the dream of a New Argentina.

18

Political Consolidation

Two months after the elections, U.S. Chargé Cabot reported to Washington that the Peronist camp was not exactly a paragon of harmony. "Some Laborista leaders even claim they have [a] whip-hand over Perón," he observed.[1] The squabbles between the Labor party and Junta Renovadora (JR) factions during the campaign now paled in the acrimony over the division of the spoils.

The election of federal senators for the capital touched off an ugly row.[2] Since Buenos Aires had no equivalent of a provincial legislature, voters chose a slate of electors committed to a particular party and pair of senatorial candidates. The Labor party and the JR presented a joint set of electors evenly divided between the two groups. The Laborites wanted Luis Gay designated as one of the two senatorial candidates, but at the eleventh hour, as a result of an artful maneuver by the JR (supported, if not instigated, by Perón), Admiral Teisaire's name was substituted for Gay's. The Peronist slate won in the capital. On February 26, when the senatorial electors for Buenos Aires met to make their formal choice of two senators, the Labor party decided to turn what should have been a ratification ceremony into a bitter struggle to select Gay instead of Teisaire. Since the electors were evenly split, an impasse appeared likely. However, the JR bloc managed to attract one Laborite elector to their side, and the admiral prevailed.

The episode was typical of the way the more experienced JR politicians outfoxed their Laborite competitors. Nonetheless, Perón was unhappy at the headaches the Labor party was giving him. Its leaders continued to insist upon their independence (indeed, they had even rejected Perón's choice for president of the party) and to clamor for recognition as principal architects of the electoral landslide.

Moreover, Cipriano Reyes posed special problems for the new president. He was mercurial, unpredictable and violence-prone. Elected to the Chamber of Deputies from Buenos Aires Province, he refused Perón's offer of the presidency of the lower house. He also parried attempts to drive a wedge between himself and Luis Gay. At Mercante's inauguration, Reyes' followers chanted his name and forced Mercante to invite him to share the balcony with the governor and his special guests, Perón and Evita.

This might have been the last straw, for on May 23, without any advance notice, Perón ordered the dissolution of all the parties that had supported his campaign and the formation of a new entity, which a short time later received the clumsy, unimaginative appellation Partido Unico de la Revolución (Single Party of the Revolution). The JR obediently voted itself out of existence. Reyes, on the other hand, defied the order and attempted to rally behind him the eighty-two other Laborites who had won seats in the Chamber of Deputies. His was a lost cause, however. All but one of his co-partisans went over to the Partido Unico. Gay resigned the presidency of the Labor party and later became the secretary-general of CGT. The lack of popular backing behind the party became painfully apparent, as the rank and file did not lift a finger to save the organization that claimed to represent their interests. Reyes, ever indomitable, continued the struggle and for a while kept the party alive. But as a viable political force, "laborism" was finished, and the days of its caretakers numbered.

As a military officer Perón had always placed the highest premium upon organization. As a politician he had reiterated the need to organize his followers and denounced the evils of personalism. He even insisted upon his own dispensability.[3] But when the time came to select a permanent name for the organization (everyone agreed that Partido Unico was inappropriate), Perón permitted the adoption of the term Peronist party.[4] The press for some time had been calling his followers Peronists, in accord with the common practice in Argentina to refer to a group by the name of its leader. This was the first time, however, that a major political party assumed as its formal title the name of an individual. Moreover, this political party considered itself more than a party; it was a movement.

Despite his sermons on the value of organization, in reality Perón cultivated contention and disarray. This was especially true with respect to the Peronist party. He set the labor wing against the political wing, and later when a women's branch came into being, the inevitable tricornered squabbles that erupted gave him endless delight. "I manage things best in a *quilombo*"[5] was one of his favorite sayings.*

* The word *quilombo* is difficult to translate. Of Brazilian origin, it was a slang expression for a whorehouse, but in the context in which Perón used the word, it connoted perpetual uproar and confusion.

The restructuring of the Peronist party would take nearly a year. However, the business of the Congress could not wait for the majority party to organize, and so the Peronists had to plunge into the maelstrom of legislative activity on April 29, 1946, when the new Chamber of Deputies met for the first time.

The voters of Argentina had given Perón a greater-than-two-thirds majority in the lower house. The exact split was 109 to 49. The Radical party had taken 44 of the minority seats. Of the 109 majority, 64 came from the Labor party, 22 from the JR, 19 from slates with combined Labor-JR participation, and 4 miscellaneous Peronists. All but 2 of the 30 elected senators owed their allegiance to the president.

Though it has been fashionable to condemn Perón and the Peronists for their repressive treatment of the opposition deputies and to elevate the latter to martyr status for what they suffered during Perón's first two terms, a closer look at the legislative process reveals some shading of gray rather than stark black and white. The Argentine government had always been strongly presidential, with Congress relegated to a subsidiary role.[6] The powers given to the chief executive made it clear that his function was to govern the nation. The concept of checks and balances never found more than token acceptance because of the Spanish tradition of a strong central authority and the reluctance, if not refusal, of Argentines to engage in the flexible give-and-take essential to a system based on a true separation of powers. The electoral laws increased the possibility that one party would gain a two-thirds majority in the Chamber of Deputies. These laws dated back to 1912, when they were viewed as democratic innovation for ensuring minority representation.

Ironically, the inability to compromise—a national trait that undoubtedly contributed to the enactment of the laws of which the Peronists took full advantage—set the opposition deputies on a course that had to end in disaster for them. Indeed, they seemed to race like lemmings toward their own political destruction. The election, in their view, settled nothing. They continued to see themselves in a struggle against Nazism. In the Chamber of Deputies they might have been a minority, but they were a veritable who's who of Argentine politics. Moreover, they were confronting a majority composed of men with little or no political experience, lacking in finesse, bumble-prone and heterogeneous in philosophical outlook. It was a mismatch by any standard except the one that mattered—the head count.

The strategy of the Radicals from the very beginning may be described as opposition, obstruction and provocation.[7] At the very first session, Radical-bloc leader Ricardo Balbín disrupted the traditional formalities by insisting that the choice of a temporary president of the chamber be put to a vote, although the position was ceremonial and customarily went to the oldest deputy (who in this case happened to be a Peronist). The issue resolved itself along party lines, a harbinger of things to come. On May 28 a joint session of Congress convened to accept the results of the vote by the presidential electors. Again the Radicals converted what should have been a ceremonial occasion into a heated debate and touched off a series of pungent exchanges with the Peronists. The position of the Radicals, that Perón could not legally assume the presidency because his candidacy was illegal, seemed untenable in view of their full participation in the campaign against him, but they persisted to the point of boycotting the inauguration. It was becoming clear that the minority would give no quarter and were turning the Chamber floor into a cockpit.

The events of June 28 are illustrative.[8] The Radicals objected to being seated on the right-hand side of the Chamber. They charged that the government's economic policy was totalitarian, and that the regime was destroying both trade-union liberties and freedom of the press. The Peronists replied in kind and dragged into the debate not only Spruille Braden but also Patrón Costas. Personal insults bounced back and forth like tennis balls. A U.S. embassy official who attended the session reported that "the Radicals seemed to take considerable pleasure in this political debate which came as a complete surprise to the Peronists. . . . This deliberate attempt to provoke the Peronists during the first ordinary session of the lower house may be a forerunner of obstructionism."[9] When the deputies tired of the seating issue, they began to propose tributes. Among the persons honored were Franklin D. Roosevelt and Ramón Castillo.

The behavior of the Radical deputies compounded principled opposition with intractability, frustration and intellectual snobbery. Their skill at scoring clever debater's points and at coining elegant insults might have reinforced their own egos, but did not advance their cause. Perhaps the Radicals would have suffered even if they had comported themselves with decorum and moderation. But they did not, thereby providing ample pretext for repression in the form of punishment for breaking rules. The fact that the severity of the retribution far exceeded anything the pretexts might have justified should not obscure the Radicals' own contribution to the fate they endured.

The 109 Peronist deputies who squared off against the Radical minority could count upon but a few of their number for resourceful, intelligent leadership. Perón's choice for president of the Chamber was Ricardo Guardo. A medical doctor, dentist and professor, Dr. Guardo was one of the first members of the academic community to declare his support for Perón. His brother-in-law was minister of industry and commerce, while his wife was fast becoming one of Evita's intimate friends. His imposing height and piercing blue eyes set him apart from his colleagues in the Congress. Easygoing and blessed with a hearty sense of humor, he ran the Chamber with a tolerance that would vanish when he lost favor with the president and had to step down from the post. Also notable were newspaper editor Eduardo Colom and Raúl Bustos Fierro, who had the sharpest tongues within the Peronist bloc and could hold their own in debate with the Radicals, and John William Cooke, a twenty-five-year-old overweight law student who appeared to have a bright political future.

But the Peronist bloc had more than its share of incompetents. A U.S. embassy observer reported that from time to time voice votes came out favorably for the opposition on the first call because Peronist deputies did not understand how they were supposed to vote. The leadership would have to request a second vote and make every effort to pass the word to their troops.

Dr. Guardo tells an anecdote about a Peronist deputy from Buenos Aires Province who wanted to introduce a bill calling for the intervention of the provincial government and the removal of Governor Mercante. "Why do you want to do that?" asked the incredulous Chamber president. "He's one of our men." "Because every day for the past month I have been trying to see him and he refuses to receive me" was the indignant reply. Guardo suggested that there were better ways to deal with the problem.[10] The clumsiness of the Peronist majority from time to time became heavy-handed, but at this early stage more often through ignorance than a conscious desire to repress. The Radicals could not refrain from unleashing verbal barbs that reached an apogee when Ernesto Sammartino, one of the sharpest tongues on the minority side of the aisle, referred to his Peronist colleagues as a "zoological inundation." The insult earned him a three-day suspension.

Perón, of course, did not much care about the quality of his legislators. He kept a close watch over what went on in the Chamber. Every morning Dr. Guardo and the president of the Senate met with him in the Casa Rosada to discuss the day's legislative agenda. The president would make known his views about bills to be introduced, pending legislation and tactics to be utilized. Dr. Guardo had responsibility for transmitting the president's wishes. Once Perón made clear what he wanted, debate within the Peronist bloc came to an end. There were rare occasions, such as the ratification of the Treaty of Chapultepec[11] and the passage of a law making religious education obligatory in the public schools,[12] when Peronist legislators were permitted to follow their consciences and either vote in opposition or abstain from supporting the president. But appeals to party unity and respect for Perón's desires soon elicited unquestioning obedience on the part of the legislators.

With the Congress securely in Peronist hands, one branch of government remained beyond the president's control. The judiciary loomed as an obstacle to efforts to construct a New Argentina. The Supreme Court of Argentina had already demonstrated its willingness to make independent judgments counter to the wishes of the Casa Rosada. Moreover, it had become involuntarily entangled in politics when the opposition insisted that it take over the government. Though the court did nothing to encourage this demand, neither Perón nor his followers could easily forget the slogan "The Government to the Court." Finally, according to an eyewitness to the incident, when Perón visited the court in mid-1945, its president called him a "Fascist."[13]

By law the Argentine Supreme Court was composed of five justices, one of whom had recently retired. Three of the remaining four had been appointed long before the 1943 Revolution and had ideological views and values at variance with the new rulers of Argentina. The one jurist who had been picked by the post-1943 military government was militantly Catholic, Hispanophile and generally supportive of the regime.[14]

Many Peronists could not resist invoking the analogy of President Roosevelt's struggle with the U.S. Supreme Court during the 1930s. However, Roosevelt's plan to pack the court with additional members provoked furious opposition, some of it nonpartisan, from the legal profession and other segments of society. Resistance to Perón's attack on the Supreme Court developed along partisan lines only. The problem in the United States eventually disappeared when several justices retired and the court as a whole adjusted its views (or "followed" the 1936 election returns). With a politically oriented appointment Perón could have reduced to 3–2 the potential split against him. Further retirements might have followed. It was not inconceivable that the Argentine court, if given the chance, might have chosen to march in step with public sentiment. Moreover, if the president had followed Roosevelt's example and had asked Congress to create two additional seats on the court, such legislation would not have run afoul of the Argentine constitution and would have been quickly enacted. Thus, solutions existed that could have insulated Peronist legislation from constitutional invalidation without wreaking institutional havoc upon the court. Perón, however, recognized no value in preserving the integrity of the judicial system, and opted for an approach that would totally "Peronize" the courts.[15]

Article 45 of the Argentine constitution listed as grounds for the impeachment of Supreme Court justices "malfeasance, or . . . criminal offenses committed in the discharge of their functions, . . . or common crimes." The inclusion of malfeasance as a ground provided open-ended possibilities, of which the Peronists would take maximum advantage. The procedures for impeachment required a two-thirds vote in the Chamber of Deputies. Conviction necessitated a two-thirds vote of the Senate.

The proposal to impeach the three supposedly anti-Peronist members of the court, a document of some 6,500 words, set forth two counts and supporting arguments worthy of Lewis Carroll. The court's recognition of the de facto governments in 1930 and 1943 violated the constitution and hence amounted to malfeasance. The second charge was an attack upon decisions the court had rendered in the 1943–46 period.[16]

The two accusations were contradictory. On the one hand, the petition took a narrow, legalistic approach that might have been defensible on strictly technical grounds. Nowhere in the 1853 Argentine constitution was there any suggestion that a coup d'état might carry with it any legal validity. As an OSS report in early 1945 pointed out with respect to the 1943 Revolution, "under the circumstances, the correct thing would have been for the members [of the Supreme Court] to resign. They did not do so, but continued to function and pretend that the national constitution was still in force."[17] Thus, an argument could have been made that judicial recognition of the de facto regimes had been improper. Whether this reached the level of impeachable malfeasance was a separate issue, untouched by either proponents or opponents of the petition.

To support their second charge, the Peronists contended that a number of court decisions hindering the work of the de facto regime were illegal. Upon close inspection, it becomes obvious that the crux of the allegation was that these judgments were erroneous, although the arguments to support this conclusion were not persuasive. Stripped of rhetoric, the charge carried with it the notion that Supreme Court justices might be removed if two-thirds of the Congress disagreed with their decisions.

At the trial in the Senate, a slight problem for the government developed when one of the accused justices engaged Dr. Alfredo I. Palacios to defend him. Perhaps the most colorful politician Argentina has produced, Palacios was the first Socialist party candidate ever to win a seat in Congress and had drafted much of the social legislation for which Perón later secured enactment. A waxed mustache and a fondness for dashing capes imparted to his appearance an eccentricity befitting his quixotic nature. He practiced law, taught at the law school and fought occasional duels with political adversaries. The students adored him. What the Peronists feared most about Palacios at this juncture was his formidable eloquence. The solution they devised was to amend the Senate rules for impeachment trials.[18] Under the new procedure, the prosecution would present in writing the charges and supporting arguments, while the defense would likewise offer its answers and argumentation in written form. The secretary of the Senate would read both documents aloud in the Senate chamber, with an interval of twenty days separating the prosecution and defense recitations. The objective of these amendments was to eliminate the possibility of oratorical pyrotechnics by the defense. Though Palacios did his best to interject oral argument into the proceedings, his efforts foundered against the overwhelming majority the Peronists enjoyed in the Senate. On April 30, 1947, each accused was found guilty as charged and removed from office.

The impeachment of the Supreme Court signaled the end of an independent judiciary in Argentina. In a number of the provinces, Peronist-controlled legislators engaged in similar attacks upon jurists whose views did not conform to the new orthodoxy. Under the precedent now established, any judge whose interpretations of the law displeased the majority party risked summary dismissal. In practice, this tended to occur only when political issues were at stake.

For Perón, the process of impeachment represented no more than another step in his single-minded quest for unity (or "institutional lockstep," as one North American commentator has put it[19]). Many of the Peronist legislators, especially those without legal training, in all probability did not understand what they were doing, but the lawyers in the majority bloc deserved reprobation. They readily cast aside their constitutional obligations and surrendered to the demands of party unity. The appropriate analogy is not to the Roosevelt court-packing plan, but to the impeachment of President Andrew Johnson, whose alleged crime was differing with the majority party in Congress. By the narrowest of margins he escaped conviction when several senators belonging to the party that was seeking to remove him chose to follow their consciences.[20] The Supreme Court of Argentina found no such principled support.

With control over Congress, Perón could secure the enactment of any legislation he sponsored. The ouster of the three Supreme Court justices eliminated any possibility that his legislative programs might be declared unconstitutional. Virtually limitless power was now within his grasp.

19

The Quest for Economic Independence

Perón brought to the presidency two campaign promises that would become pillars of the ideology that was to bear his name. Social justice and economic independence had been his constant themes. Although they were broad and flexible enough to justify almost anything in the hands of a pragmatist like Perón, the new president felt the need to launch his term with some concrete measures that would prove he was not simply mouthing slogans.

The call for social justice was central to his commitment to the working class. The government would integrate workers into the political process on a par with employers and take steps to "humanize" capital, and would also distribute to workers a larger share of the gross national product, in the form of income, health care, education and housing. To Argentine nationalists, economic independence meant ending foreign domination over important sectors of the economy, such as public services and transportation, and over the terms of trade with the rest of the world. Perón hoped to achieve the bread-and-butter aspects of social justice through the expansion rather than the redistribution of existing wealth. To grow and yet remain economically independent in Peronist terms, therefore, meant reliance upon internally financed development instead of foreign investment.

The fulfillment of these goals depended upon the performance of the Argentine economy, Perón's economic policies and a third component over which the government had no control—external economic factors. The intertwining of these elements would produce complexities unforeseen by Perón as he plunged ahead on the economic front with boundless optimism.[1]

In his constant effort to rewrite history, Perón later insisted that the country was in dire economic straits when his first term began.[2] Anti-Peronists asserted that he took over a nation poised at the take-off point of development.[3] In fact the Peronist government came to power under circumstances that presented both unique advantages and difficulties. World War II had spurred industrial growth, since the country could no longer import many consumer goods. At the same time, the export of Argentine products, mainly from the agricultural and livestock sectors, had created a favorable balance of trade and had produced foreign exchange and gold in excess of $1.6 billion. Moreover, in the immediate postwar period the depleted nations of Europe would require cereals and meat.

On the other hand, the forced moratorium on imports had produced an impressive backlog of needs. Capital equipment and raw materials obtainable only from abroad had to be purchased in the near future, and this could quickly gnaw away at the accumulated reserves. Moreover, Great Britain held a substantial portion of these reserves in sterling owed to Argentina as a result of wartime purchases. A financial crisis had forced Britain to declare these funds inconvertible into any other forms of currency. This meant the funds could be spent only in Britain, which at the moment could not supply Argentina with the goods she needed. The U.S. economy, having switched to peacetime production, did have the capacity to fill that need, but political disputes between Washington and Buenos Aires had provoked North American restrictions on trade with Argentina.

It soon became evident that Perón's vision of a New Argentina was a far cry from that of an agricultural society, destined to supply grain and meat to the industrialized nations in return for manufactured goods. The president intended a radical transformation and firmly believed he could succeed.

One of his early presidential directives instructed José Figuerola to draw up an economic program for his administration. The secretary for technical matters prepared an elaborate document detailing priorities for a range of government activities. He suggested to Perón that it be called a "five-year plan," and the president concurred.

On Monday afternoon, October 21, at a joint session of Congress boycotted by the opposition because of the irregularity of the proceedings, President Perón unveiled the plan.[4] Legislators found neatly bound copies, in two volumes, on their desks as they took their seats. After some introductory comments, the president and Figuerola, who sat next to him, presented the plan. For four hours they read alternately, with the monotony relieved only by the shifts between Perón's Argentine accent and Figuerola's Catalán inflections. The senators and deputies listened like schoolboys. They were not expected to debate the proposal, which would vest broad authority in the chief executive.

Ambitious would be a mild descriptive to bestow upon the plan. It proposed to achieve full employment, enrich the lives of workers, increase the national income and divide it more equitably, maintain price stability, develop and decentralize industry, and build up the nation's infrastructure through massive investments in transportation, communications facilities and energy production. The price tag initially attached to this epic venture was the equivalent of about $1.5 billion.

In the last weeks of the Farrell regime, the president-elect secured the issuance of several decrees designed to improve Argentina's international financial and commercial positions. The government nationalized the Central Bank, which had previously operated under the influence if not control of representatives of foreign banks doing business in Argentina. In addition, Farrell decreed into existence an entity known as IAPI, or Instituto Argentino de Promoción del Intercambio (Argentine Institute for Trade Promotion), described by Brazilian economist Celso Furtado as "the most comprehensive attempt yet made in Latin America to bring exports under the control of the State."[5] IAPI monopolized the export of agricultural goods and livestock by purchasing them from local producers at one price and selling them abroad at another, in order to strengthen Argentina's bargaining position and divert to industrial development earnings created by the price differential. Miguel Miranda, in whom Perón had the utmost confidence, was named to head the Central Bank and IAPI, as well as the National Economic Council. The former tin magnate had no patience for the cautious counsel of economists or the doubts of bureaucrats.

The first two years of the Perón administration produced a heady mix of growth and prosperity. The five-year plan gave Argentines a sense that at long last their country was surging forward. On the home front, projects such as the natural gas pipeline from the oil fields of Comodoro Rivadavia to Buenos Aires were nearing completion.[6] Argentina was acquiring its own merchant fleet and improving its system of air transportation. Industrial production was in high gear, and workers were earning salaries that gave them more purchasing power than they had ever enjoyed.

A series of dramatic measures heralded what was publicized as a new era of economic independence. Argentina used its foreign exchange reserves to pay off its foreign debt and to purchase from International Telegraph and Telephone the River Plate Telephone Company, serving Greater Buenos Aires. (The price: $95 million.) In November 1946, Argentina bought three French railroads. Ever adept at symbolism, Perón journeyed to Tucumán on July 9, 1947, the anniversary of the 1816 declaration of political independence from Spain, and announced that Argentina was now economically independent.

"I have always thought," the president told a gathering of provincial officials on November 29, 1947, "that we were going to live without any economic crises during the six years of my administration. Today, as a result of new studies that have been made, I believe we are going to have sixty years without crises."[7] In reality, within six months, unmistakable signs would point to the development of serious economic problems that would turn boom to bust and force drastic changes in government policy.

A number of factors conspired to dim the bright hopes ignited during the early years of Perón's first term. Perhaps the most important was a failure to escape the dilemma created by Argentina's triangular trade relationship with the United States and Great Britain. To achieve industrial development, the Argentines would need raw materials, capital goods and other manufactured products from the United States, but they could offer in return only agricultural goods and livestock, for which the United States had no need. England required meat and cereal exports from Argentina but could not furnish the machinery and raw materials essential to the industrialization program upon which the Argentines had embarked. If Argentina could have converted into dollars the pounds earned from exports to Great Britain, the problem would have been solved.

Shortly after Perón's inauguration, an official mission from London arrived in Buenos Aires to begin complex discussions on three matters of vital interest to both countries. The disposal of Argentina's sterling balance in England, the future of Anglo-Argentine trade and the fate of the British-owned railways in Argentina were the items on the agenda for Miguel Miranda and Sir Wilfred Eady, who headed the negotiating teams for their respective nations. During weeks of tough bargaining, Miranda held to the position that Argentina ought not purchase the railways ("We do not propose to use our blocked funds in order to buy out-of-date equipment," the president reportedly commented[8]). In early September, an impasse having been reached, the British announced they would return to London.[9] However, a last-second intervention by Perón saved the day.[10] The negotiators agreed that Argentina would not collect the balance of the sterling owned by Great Britain but blocked in London, and would use it only to cover any deficits Argentina might incur in trade within the sterling area; Britain would purchase most of Argentina's exportable meat for the next four years; and a mixed Argentine-British corporation would take over the railroads, which were now in a state of disrepair and required extensive modernization.

The Miranda-Eady agreement immediately came under heavy fire from the Radicals, who accused Perón of selling out the fatherland. *La Prensa* and *La Nación* complained that the British had gained the advantage over the Argentines.[11] Nationalists who normally supported Peronist policies were also critical. Perón, who had acted in a reasonable, moderate and pragmatic way, found himself accused of perpetuating economic colonialism.

Ironically, it took U.S. intervention to save him from what promised to be substantial political embarrassment. The accord conflicted with the terms of a $4 billion loan the United States had granted Great Britain in late 1945. The purpose of the loan was to help Britain pay off its debts and to establish the convertibility of the pound into dollars. Washington opposed the Anglo-Argentine agreement, and as a result the British had to scrap it.

At this point, Perón decided to use the sterling balances to purchase the railroads outright. Three factors underlay his decision. Further delay in utilizing these funds meant risking loss from postwar inflation. Moreover, there was speculation (apparently unfounded) that the United States might take the railways as collateral for its loan to Britain. Finally, nationalization under these circumstances would bring a huge political dividend. ("Now they're ours," proclaimed gigantic posters at the rally celebrating the acquisition.)

However, the railroads were obsolete and in a state of disrepair. They would require substantial new investment, but funds that might have been used for this purpose had been spent on their purchase. On balance, the deal brought Argentina more psychic gratification than economic gain.

One of the terms of the 1945 U.S. loan was that Britain pay her creditors in freely convertible pounds (which meant pounds convertible into dollars). This led to such a dollar drain that on August 20, 1947, Britain was forced to declare the inconvertibility of the pound. In the preceding ten months, Argentina had been able to convert 59 million pounds into dollars as a result of her favorable trade balance with Britain. But once the flow of dollars from Britain dried up, the consequences of Argentina's one-sided trading relationship with the United States soon became painfully apparent. Only the gold and dollars accumulated during the war were available as payment for U.S. imports, and the brisk trade sparked by Perón's push for industrial development caused these reserves to dwindle more rapidly than anyone had anticipated. By mid-1948, a foreign-exchange crisis had arrived. The gold and dollars were gone, and Argentina could not even pay off the backlog of her commercial commitments. North American companies in Argentina were prohibited from remitting dollars back to the United States, and the expanding Argentine debt to the United States remained unpaid.

Trade with the nations of Western Europe did not provide a satisfactory alternative. These countries desperately needed cereals and meat, but could pay neither in dollars nor in the machinery and raw materials required by Argentine industry. IAPI, which monopolized the overseas sale of Argentine exports, drew heavy criticism, especially from the United States, for the allegedly high prices it charged for agricultural products and livestock. However, manufactured goods available in return from Western Europe were higher priced than similar products made in the United States, and Argentina was receiving only partial payment for exports, since she had to extend credits to some of these countries to stimulate trade.

The Marshall Plan drove a final nail into the coffin that bore Perón's ambitions to transform Argentina into an industrial power. When the U.S. program to revive the economies of Western Europe was first announced, Argentines looked upon it as a solution to their currency problem. Early statements from Washington made it appear likely that the United States would purchase Argentine farm products with dollars and then ship them to Europe.[12] But in fact the Marshall Plan was detrimental to Argentina. Anti-Argentine sentiment in Congress and among officials in the aid program (one of whom once noted that "maybe the present was a good time to beat the Argentine to its knees"[13]), plus the availability of U.S. agricultural surpluses, severely limited the amount of Marshall Plan money that reached Argentina. Indeed, in the execution of the plan there was outright discrimination against the Perón government. Canada received more favorable treatment, and the agency administering the plan intervened in trade negotiations between Western European nations and Argentina to the disadvantage of the latter. The restrictions Buenos Aires had to put upon the outflow of dollars as a result of the 1948 balance-of-payments crisis provoked problems with Washington, because the measure prevented North American companies from remitting profits and was viewed as proof of Argentina's hostility to U.S. capital. Therefore, the dollars the Argentines did succeed in obtaining had to be used to pay Argentine debts to the United States. Finally, the Marshall Plan reduced the demand for Argentine agricultural products in Western Europe and undercut the modest trade relationships Buenos Aires had been developing with various European nations.

The policies initially adopted by the Perón administration toward the agricultural sector of the Argentine economy have drawn criticism from those who charge Perón with having crippled farm production at a time when he should have stimulated it.[14] They point to a reduction in the area under cultivation, a decrease in production of various crops and farmers' complaints about the pricing practices of IAPI. The latter, according to the critics, destroyed incentives. Moreover, the emphasis upon industry led to a neglect of the needs of agriculture at a time when a shift in population from the countryside to urban centers made farm mechanization imperative. A shortage of farm tractors is cited as support for this charge.[15]

On the other hand, private exporters might not have been able to command the prices IAPI charged for Argentine farm products and surely could not have extended credit. If Argentina had produced more cereals and livestock during the 1946–1948 period, there was no guarantee that these goods could have been sold abroad or could have brought convertible currency in return. The exchange problems afflicting Western Europe combined with competition from the Marshall Plan to make increased Argentine exports unprofitable or unlikely.

The policies Perón pursued reflected his own political priorities and lack of sophistication in economic matters. His industrialization program depended upon earnings from the agricultural and livestock sectors but created disincentives for farm production. The president was clearly reluctant to make difficult choices involving the allocation of limited resources.

Perón's political commitment to social justice exacerbated the economic situation. The unions, with support from the government, pressed for higher wages, which in turn gave workers more purchasing power. But they used a substantial part of this power to consume greater quantities of meat, thereby reducing the amount available for export. Moreover, salary raises far outpaced increases in productivity. This redistributed wealth that might otherwise have been used for investment. When added to the government's easy credit policies and continuous expansion of the money supply, the high wage scales fed an inflationary spiral. Perón could not refuse worker demands, at least during these early years, nor was he ready or willing to counter nationalist sentiment hostile to foreign capital. This made it extremely difficult to achieve the capital investment necessary for sustained industrial growth.

As the Argentine economy sputtered, Perón was compelled to act. In late 1948 he asked some of his advisors to prepare a report on the situation. Submitted early the next year, the secret document outlined the extent of the crisis and recommended stopgap measures such as curtailment of nonessential imports.[16]

Though refusing to concede publicly that an economic crisis existed, the president followed the suggestions in the report and in addition made one dramatic move. He fired Miguel Miranda. Though rumors abounded that Perón had discovered his involvement in "dirty business" and that he had incurred Evita's displeasure,[17] the economy czar had in fact outlived his usefulness. The freewheeling style he had perfected was no longer producing results, and the time had come for a new strategy. Perón turned to Alfredo Gómez Morales, a career civil servant and trained economist. "Miranda led an assault team," the president told him. "Now we need a consolidation team."[18] The great experiment was over. Argentina would now resort to more traditional economic policies in an attempt to regain her forward motion.

Though Perón and the Peronists were quick to lay blame on the United States and external factors for the snags the Argentine economy encountered in 1948, the fact remains that domestic mistakes and miscalculations contributed to the reversal of fortune. Central to the approach initially adopted by the Perón administration was a quantum leap in the degree of state intervention in the economy. Yet Argentina did not have a sufficient number of trained, competent technicians who could administer the programs launched in 1946, and an unavoidable amount of bureaucratic bungling occurred. Unfortunately, in this crucial period Argentina did not enjoy much of a margin for error. Moreover, Perón may have underestimated the intensity and extent of U.S. opposition to him. During his struggle with Braden, he was quoted as advising a colleague to "stay with me and don't worry. You will see that when the smoke all clears away the Americans will be down here with satchels trying to get [commercial] orders from us."[19] Although U.S. entrepreneurs eventually did considerable business with the Argentines, Washington's economic policy toward Perón did not include assistance that would facilitate large-scale imports from the United States. Finally, Perón's reading of international politics led him to conclude that war between the United States and the Soviet Union was both inevitable and imminent. This contributed to decisions such as IAPI's hasty purchase of a large quantity of World War II surplus trucks from the United States. Much of this material ended up rusting on the docks of Buenos Aires and Rosario.[20]

External factors contributed heavily to the failure of the Argentine economy to meet the ambitious goals set by Perón at the beginning of his first term in office. This did not deter him from taking action to realize his vision of social justice. The labor movement would enjoy substantial gains, but at a price that would prove costly both to the movement itself and to certain individuals within it.

20

Nationalizing
Organized Labor

Though the social justice to which Perón aspired was meant to benefit the poor in general, it was the workers who made truly spectacular progress during the early phase of the Perón era. The tangible gains that had won Colonel Perón the allegiance of the majority of Argentina's workers continued to mount and strengthened President Perón's image as benefactor of the proletariat. By 1948, for example, the real wages of skilled industrial workers had increased by 27 percent over the 1943 level, while unskilled factory hands were earning 37 percent more than in 1943.[1] Fringe benefits showed steady improvements, as did social security coverage. Moreover, workers received genuine psychological boosts from the appointments of men (and later women) from their ranks to high posts in the administration and from the government's program of nationalizations.[2]

The price labor paid for these benefits was a loss of independence. Perón's fetish for organization was to shape the labor movement into a monolithic, hierarchical, bureaucratized, and totally stultified structure. A key step in this process by which Perón gained complete control of labor was the presidential promulgation of a new law of professional associations on October 2, 1945, just prior to his forced resignation from the Secretariat of Labor. Under this decree, which Congress later ratified, only those worker organizations to which the secretariat (later the Ministry of Labor) granted union status could bargain with employers, represent the interests of employees before governmental bodies and participate in political activities. The ministry could grant this status to only one union per industry.

The government now had a powerful weapon with which it could eliminate anti-Peronist unions.[3] However, some unions and union leaders who supported Perón and his administration also wanted to preserve a degree of independence. Labor party officials who obeyed Perón's directive and joined the Peronist party were among those who resisted the inexorable march toward state control. They found themselves caught between the demands of the rank and file, who wanted to share in the benefits workers were receiving from the government, and their own desire to maintain as much freedom of action as possible.[4] It was to prove an insoluble dilemma, and eventually they would capitulate.

The CGT, perched at the apex of the trade-union movement, did not fall easily into Perón's hands. On the critical eve of October 17, it had not rallied vigorously to his defense, and throughout 1946 there were indications that despite its support for the government's labor policies, the confederation was preserving the independent spirit of the all-but-defunct Labor party. In November the CGT's central committee met to choose a new secretary-general. Perón's candidate finished a poor third in the voting, as the CGT's governing body elected Luis Gay to run the organization.[5]

Gay, the bespectacled ex-president of the Labor party, resolved to keep the CGT free from government control. When the president called him to the Casa Rosada to congratulate him on his victory, Perón offered him a team of experts to advise him and even write his speeches. "Look, Mr. President," Gay replied, "you have many problems to deal with. Let us, men with twenty, twenty-five years' experience in the labor movement, run the CGT." "Then I will manipulate the unaffiliated unions" was Perón's airy response. "That's your business, Mr. President. Ours will be to take care of the CGT."[6] An attempt to overextend the new secretary-general by giving him other jobs did not sufficiently distract him from his trade-union duties. More decisive action had to be taken. The appearance of a delegation of North American labor officials in Buenos Aires in January 1947 supplied a convenient pretext.[7]

Just as Cordell Hull's letter to Admiral Storni in 1943 had had the opposite effect from its intended thrust, and just as Braden's interference in Argentine politics had helped Perón, the visit of the U.S. labor leaders proved similarly counterproductive. They hoped to assure themselves that the CGT was independent of state control and to encourage those among their Argentine counterparts who wanted to maintain the confederation's freedom of action. But they unwittingly sparked Gay's ouster and pushed the organization much deeper into the stifling embrace of the regime.

The genesis of the affair was an invitation issued to the American Federation of Labor in August 1946 by the Argentine ambassador, who suggested that AFL representatives visit his country to obtain a true picture of the trade-union movement and the extent of worker support behind Perón. For the AFL, the invitation came at an opportune moment. During a meeting of the International Labor Organization in Mexico City in April, a delegation from the Argentine CGT had sought recognition as representatives of their country's labor movement, over objections that their organization was in fact an instrument of the regime. AFL leaders had been uncertain as to what position to take on the issue. Moreover, at this very moment they were in the process of plunging into the politics of the nascent cold war. The U.S. unionists were putting together an inter-American labor group to rival the Communist-controlled Latin American Workers' Confederation, and had to decide whether to invite Argentina's CGT to join them. On the condition that the CGT also extend an invitation, the AFL accepted the offer and put together a delegation. But the inclusion of Serafino Romualdi assured both complications and controversy.

Romualdi, a dedicated anti-Fascist and anti-Communist who fled Mussolini's Italy in 1923, had spent World War II courting Latin American labor leaders sympathetic to the Allied cause. He had also worked for Nelson Rockefeller in the State Department's Office of Inter-American Affairs, and served a stint with the OSS in Italy in 1944 and 1945.[8]

His credentials as a dispassionate observer were highly suspect. In an article he published in an AFL magazine in December 1945, he had called the Argentine CGT "fake," and added that "only the obtuse [workers] fail to recognize that economic advantages—temporary and illusory at best—can never compensate for loss of liberty and democratic rights."[9] He had close ties to the "democratic" union people, now isolated and without any rank-and-file support. Yet despite the suspicions that Romualdi justifiably engendered among Peronists, his Latin American experience and fluency in Spanish permitted him to exert considerable influence over the AFL contingent and to shape the course of the visit.

The delegation arrived on January 19, oblivious to the delicate situation confronting Gay and those of his colleagues trying to keep the CGT independent. Neither the State Department nor embassy personnel in Buenos Aires gave any indication that they were aware of Gay's plight. The AFL delegates soon found themselves awash in confusion and controversy as the conflict between Gay and Perón came to a head. The common strand was the president's use of the AFL visitors in his assault upon the CGT's secretary-general.

The Argentine government gave a warm welcome to the U.S. labor representatives. But a committee from the Ministry of Labor monopolized the airport reception and relegated Gay and his CGT associates to the sidelines—a deliberate snub the Americans immediately noticed. Then the government officials proposed to take the visitors directly to Perón. The AFL delegates, fatigued from the long trip, insisted they needed time for rest. Romualdi, already behaving abrasively, negotiated a postponement of their meeting with the president. That night at the City Hotel just off the Plaza de Mayo, the AFL group met with Gay and presumably discussed the proposed new inter-American labor organization.

On the next day, the delegates trooped to the Casa Rosada. After a formal exchange of pleasantries, Perón asked to speak with them privately. He objected to a phrase, included in a press release distributed by the delegation and published in local newspapers, to the effect that the North Americans had come to conduct their "own investigations" into the Argentine labor movement.[10] Much ado was made over the word "investigate," which the Argentines took to suggest some wrongdoing upon which foreigners wished to pass judgment. Romualdi jumped into the fray and began a verbal slugging match with the president. Their argument reached its apogee when Perón shouted "I know what you are up to, Mr. Romualdi," and added in Italian "*A bravo intenditore poche parole*"[11] (the equivalent of "A word to the wise is sufficient").

The debate must have bewildered the rest of the AFL representatives. The flap over the word "investigate" made no sense to them, since the invitation and all subsequent correspondence had made it clear they would be in Argentina not as tourists but as observers charged with reporting back to the AFL their impressions of the local labor movement.

What they did not realize was that circumstances had changed. Gay had taken charge of the CGT, and Perón wanted him removed. It is also conceivable that the AFL presence in Buenos Aires at this particular moment bestirred in Perón the apprehension that independent-minded elements in the CGT might make some overt move toward greater autonomy. Given his tendency to improvise, it is likely that he made the decision to provoke a showdown with Gay after the arrival of the AFL group. In his taped memoirs he claimed to have recorded a conversation between Romualdi and Gay that proved the latter was about to sell out the CGT to the North Americans.[12] Since Romualdi reported to the embassy that Gay had promised to "work for independence" from government control, the president may have received intelligence about Gay's pledge and resolved to make certain it would never be kept. Moreover, Romualdi himself later admitted that he was in contact with a porteño friend who was organizing an underground movement against Perón.[13] If the president's security agents had informed him of this, he would have viewed Gay's contacts with the AFL spokesman as subversive.

The man whom Perón would later call "a traitor to his country [Italy] and a traitor to the workers," a "bandit" and a "boor"[14] was bent upon sowing disruption. The embassy cabled Washington that Romualdi was "not averse to stirring up trouble with and for the delegation."[15] His opinions about the CGT and Argentine labor seemed to have ossified long before the visit. Though he would tell embassy people that there was still a spirit of independence worth supporting within the confederation,[16] nothing he did during the trip brought anything but harm to Gay and his friends.

The unpleasant experience with Perón convinced the AFL delegation that they should return home. This option became even more attractive on the following day when a pro-government newspaper attacked Romualdi. However, that afternoon Foreign Minister Bramuglia spoke with several of the North American visitors and told them that Perón wanted to talk with the chairman and vice-chairman of the delegation. Over Romualdi's strenuous dissent, the entire group voted to accept the president's offer.

On the next day, despite more press criticism of Romualdi (who was now being linked to Braden), the two leaders of the AFL group visited Perón and had a long, friendly conversation resulting in agreement that the North Americans should remain and confer with anyone they wished to see. The president did not object to the delegates' reiterated desire to work primarily with the CGT. As a result, the entire contingent (except for Romualdi, who left on a private trip to Montevideo) met with Perón again to reorganize their visit, and then went freely about their business. Romualdi eventually rejoined the group and continued to draw press fire. But by now he was a secondary target, because the storm over Luis Gay had burst into public view.

Shortly after the Perón-Romualdi clash, the president summoned to the Casa Rosada a group of CGT officials (minus Gay) and accused the secretary-general of betraying the Argentine labor movement. When a representative from the metalworkers' union asked for proof, Perón hinted that intelligence operatives had recorded conversations between Gay and the North Americans at the City Hotel, but would not produce the evidence.[17] The CGT leadership was not about to toss Gay into the dustbin on the basis of an unsupported accusation by Perón. But the president resorted to the tactic of transforming the issue into one of loyalty to him, to the Peronist movement, and to Argentina.[18] Dissent would thereby become tantamount to treason. To save Gay one would have to attack the president, which not even Gay himself wanted to attempt.

When the two protagonists met briefly in private not long afterward, Gay realized he had no choice but to resign. But Perón wanted to make an example of him. On January 24, at the CGT rally on behalf of the five-year plan, he began his speech by warning workers to be on guard against enemies from within. Two days later, La Epoca broke the story of a conspiracy, involving Gay, Romualdi and everybody's favorite bête noire, Spruille Braden, to steal the CGT from Perón.

The rest of the pro-government press followed suit and intensified the assault on Gay, whose fate was now sealed. He refused to defend himself before the CGT's central committee, even though some of his friends were willing to stand by him. On January 29, the issue before the committee was whether to accept his resignation or expel him. Interior Minister Borlenghi (at Perón's bidding) argued for the moderate alternative. The committee voted to permit him to resign.[19]

The AFL delegation departed on February 9. Two of its members made press statements expressing satisfaction with the visit and hoping for increased friendship between the United States and Argentina.[20] However, the detailed report the delegation submitted to the AFL two months later was pure Romualdi.[21] It condemned the CGT for its close ties to the government and dismissed what it called the "overdue economic reforms" carried out by Perón as politically motivated (a conclusion cynics might equally have drawn about the New Deal).

Meanwhile, the actual status of the confederation evolved closer to the characterization made by the AFL document. Under Gay the organization had advocated worker interests before the government. It would soon be advocating the interests of the state before the working class.[22] Aurelio Hernández, a journeyman bureaucrat who led the fight to expel Gay, was chosen as the new secretary-general. He tried unsuccessfully to be more responsive to his perception of Perón's wishes and lasted less than a year in the job. Though he accepted the close ties now linking the CGT to the government, he at least had had some experience in union leadership and had stepped forward on his own to run for the top post. The same could not be said of his replacement, José Espejo, an obscure truck driver from San Juan, and Evita's choice for the job. Most members of the CGT's central committee did not know who he was, but they dutifully elected him secretary-general.[23] At this point the confederation clearly revealed itself as an arm of the government.

In the first two years of his initial term, Perón consolidated working-class support. He saw to it that workers received a greater share of the national income and increased their levels of consumption. At the same time, he moved to secure their unconditional backing through the unions and the CGT. Organized labor had become the backbone of the Peronist movement and continues to serve in that capacity to the present day. Perón reserved for himself the role of head. Evita would rapidly assume the function of the vital nerves linking brain and spinal cord.

21

The Third
Position

The U.S. representative at Perón's inauguration was the new ambassador, George S. Messersmith. Ordered to arrive on time for the ceremony, Messersmith survived a flight buffeted by storms that delayed the arrival of his luggage. He reached Buenos Aires several days before the inauguration and had to present his credentials immediately. A frantic search by embassy officials turned up a local waiter Messersmith's size and build. With a bright brown overcoat covering his borrowed formal attire, the ambassador took the traditional carriage ride to the Casa Rosada to open what he hoped would be a new era in U.S.-Argentine relations.[1] Little did he realize that he would soon be chafing in the straitjacket of another man's notion of how Washington should treat the incoming administration.

Though Perón's triumph at the polls should have called for a rethinking of U.S. policy toward Argentina, Assistant Secretary of State Braden remained as antagonistic as ever toward his adversary in Buenos Aires. With bulldog tenacity, he seized upon the shibboleth of compliance with the Chapultepec agreements, and especially those conditions calling for the elimination of residual Nazi influence, as justification for his intransigence.

But the times were changing. Braden's approach to Argentina ran counter to the rising tide of the cold war. In March, Winston Churchill had delivered his famous Iron Curtain speech, and the spirit of wartime cooperation between the United States and the Soviet Union was rapidly turning sour. U.S. policymakers were becoming preoccupied with securing the hemisphere against Soviet penetration and were eager to obtain Argentina's cooperation.

Braden had no love for the U.S.S.R., but he saw great danger in what he insisted were Argentine designs to form a "southern bloc" of nations hostile to the United States and under Perón's control. Moreover, he viewed the programs of the Perón government as a serious threat to North American investment in Argentina.[2]

The battle that the assistant secretary continued to wage was a losing one. The specter of Argentine expansionism never did materialize as a credible peril to U.S. or Latin interests. North American investors, though often unhappy with economic policies adopted by the Peronists, were not at all reluctant to deal with Argentines.[3] Perón himself was clever enough to undercut Braden by stressing his friendship toward the United States and Argentina's need for private capital. In addition, as time passed, Braden's charge that the Perón administration was not rooting out the remnants of Nazism in Argentina began to sound like the carping of a scold. Perhaps he should have resigned at a decent interval after the Argentine elections. Instead, he chose to stand his ground and keep fighting, a decision that led to an unseemly squabble with his successor in Buenos Aires.

Messersmith was a career diplomat who had been serving as ambassador to Mexico. On February 16, 1946, he had sent a letter to Braden from Mexico City, declaring that "the Blue Book is a convincing and tremendously important document. It is a splendid job."[4] But he had been in Buenos Aires for fewer than three months when Braden complained to Secretary of Commerce Henry A. Wallace that the new ambassador was trying to protect Nazis in Argentina in order to reach an understanding with Perón.[5]

One of the ironies of the Braden-Messersmith feud was the assistant secretary's complaint that the ambassador not only refused to follow his instructions but was actively insubordinate.[6] Braden clearly did not want Messersmith to be another Braden. Indeed, he was determined to consign Messersmith to the role of errand boy.

The dispute surfaced by the end of June 1946. Messersmith wanted to make his own judgments about Argentine compliance with the Chapultepec accords, while Braden considered himself the final arbiter and clung to criteria that seemed harsh and inflexible. Moreover, the assistant secretary was constantly feeding his point of view to his friends in the press corps.[7] Messersmith deeply resented the insinuation that he was selling out to Perón and felt that the assistant secretary was undercutting him at every turn. He did not hesitate to hit back at Braden, and in one memo to Dean Acheson complained that a serious problem confronting him was the aftermath of the ex-ambassador's improper intervention in the domestic politics of Argentina.[8]

The controversy over Ludwig Freude was a case in point.[9] For Braden, Freude symbolized the Nazi connection still tainting the Argentine government. Relying on captured German documents, the assistant secretary alleged that Freude had masterminded the Nazi espionage effort in Argentina after the Farrell regime had cut diplomatic ties with Germany.[10] He wanted to make the declaration of Freude as an undesirable alien and his deportation a condition of Argentine compliance with her inter-American commitments. Messersmith considered this to be not only unjust but also absurd. He was not convinced, on the basis of the evidence available to him (including records from both the U.S. and British embassies), that the charges against Freude had been substantiated.[11]

Messersmith also discounted the idea that Argentina had aggressive designs on her neighbors and wanted to form a southern bloc. As he pointed out in a cable to Washington, "one of the principal difficulties which President Perón has is with extreme nationalists who have removed their support from him because they know he considers this southern bloc idea politically and economically unwise and infeasible."[12]

Having failed to achieve either the overthrow of Perón in 1945 or his defeat at the polls in 1946, Spruille Braden now fought a rearguard action to impose diplomatic isolation upon his old antagonist. But the feud with Messersmith took its toll, and in the end pressures from the Pentagon to integrate Argentina into a hemispheric-defense alignment overcame the tenacious resistance of the assistant secretary. In June 1947, both Braden and Messersmith resigned, marking the end of Bradenism in the State Department and the beginning of a policy of conciliation toward Argentina.*

Juan Perón had his own reasons for wanting to improve Argentina's relations with the United States. He realized it would be difficult, if not impossible, to carry out the five-year plan without North American imports. His armed forces needed new equipment that the United States might be willing to supply. Moreover, it was in Argentina's interest not to provoke Washington into any confrontation that would prejudice her international standing.

At the same time Perón could not ignore considerations militating against too close a relationship with the United States. The banner of nationalism raised aloft by the Peronists contained deeply woven anti-Yankee strands. Perón's past experiences with Washington had not been positive. His personal style as well as philosophy of government predicated independence from the North Americans. His solution to the problem was a masterpiece of creative opportunism. Unveiled in the first year of his first term, Perón's policy would sally forth under the pretentious title of the Third Position.

The new policy first came to light one day after the inauguration, when Argentina unexpectedly resumed diplomatic relations (broken off since 1917) with the Soviet Union and sought trade talks with the Russians.

---

* Spruille Braden became a consultant for U.S. companies doing business in Latin America. His political views veered sharply to the right, and in the 1960s he was listed as a member of the national council of the John Birch Society. He died on January 10, 1978, at the age of eighty-three. *Washington Post,* January 12, 1978, p. C-11.

As East-West tensions heightened, these jarring developments gave rise to speculation about Soviet designs for a foothold in the southern cone of the hemisphere. But Perón was quick to reassure Washington that Argentina remained firmly committed to the defense of the continent and would stand by the United States in the event of war with the U.S.S.R.[13] Indeed, it was in the cold war context alone that Perón manifested a shrewd grasp of realities in the United States. He immediately detected the rising mood of North American anticommunism and played to it with repeated reminders of the value of Peronism as a barrier to Soviet penetration. The president threw all his weight behind congressional ratification of the Treaty of Chapultepec, despite violent street protests by shock troops from the ALN.[14] At the same time, not-so-subtly working both sides of the street,[15] he continued to denounce the evils of capitalist imperialism.

The Third Position became the cornerstone of Argentina's foreign policy.[16] Its aim was to steer a middle ground between the contending big-power ideologies, communism and capitalism, in much the same manner as the economic philosophy Perón had been espousing from his earliest days in public life.

In typically freewheeling fashion, Perón did not content himself with developing a foreign policy for Argentina. He claimed that his was a solution for all those nations unwilling to enroll themselves in the blocs dominated by the United States and the Soviet Union. On July 6, in a global radio address he called for the adoption of the Third Position as a means to put an end to the cold war. In a follow-up note to other Latin American governments, he invited them to join together for peace and make contact through the good offices of the Vatican.[17]

The most charitable comment that can be made about this venture into world politics is that it nicely reflected the pervasive sense of unreality, perhaps the result of geographic isolation, that has often characterized Argentine self-perceptions. Except for some wispy hint of Argentine economic aid to postwar Europe, the address was so ethereal that its intended audience had great difficulty discerning just what concrete proposals Perón was offering. While foreigners struggled to elicit meaning from the discourse, Peronist organizations in Argentina immediately launched a campaign to promote the president for a Nobel peace prize.

After his downfall, both he and some of his followers would credit the Third Position as the intellectual progenitor of the nonalignment policy adopted by many nations of the Third World.[18] Yet as critics have noted, Argentina's voting record at the United Nations during the heyday of the Third Position was totally inconsistent with the doctrine's anti-imperialist rhetoric.[19] Argentina did not, for example, lend principled support to colonial peoples in their struggles for independence. In reality, the Third Position turned out to be little more than a slogan.

The opportunistic thrust of the Third Position rested upon a fundamental assumption that influenced many of Perón's foreign-policy decisions during the immediate postwar era, his view of World War III as both unavoidable and imminent. Perhaps this reading of events was a logical corollary of his theories of the "nation in arms" and "war as an inevitable social phenomenon." Whatever the source, he wanted Argentina to be in the best possible position not only to survive but also to take maximum advantage of the impending holocaust.

Though Yankee-baiting and denunciations of dollar imperialism remained standard weapons in Perón's arsenal of rhetoric, the Argentine president took care not to engage in any serious sabotage of the grand designs the United States was developing for hemispheric security and unity. At inter-American conferences in Rio de Janeiro in August 1947 and Bogotá in early 1948, the Argentine delegations generally cooperated with the North Americans. The Bogotá meeting set up the Organization of American States (OAS). The Argentines successfully fought against the vesting of military functions in the OAS and argued for limitations on the organization's political powers—a reaction consistent with the traditional Argentine insistence upon the prerogatives of national sovereignty.

Meanwhile, in line with its strategy for hemispheric security, the State Department had decided to try a new approach to Argentina. President Truman felt that the United States should try to do business with Perón, and that the best way to implement this policy was to put businessmen in charge of the embassy in Buenos Aires.[20] The first of these, dairy executive James Bruce, set out to improve commercial relations between the two nations. Although mounting difficulties caused by Argentina's dollar shortage and harmful competition from the Marshall Plan complicated his task, he developed a good rapport with Perón and performed creditably, as did his successor, Stanton Griffis. A partner in an investment firm, with an interest in various entertainment operations (such as Madison Square Garden in New York City), Griffis carried on the policy of promoting U.S.-Argentine trade.

Both Bruce and Griffis had to deal with Perón's periodic anti-Yankee outbursts, clearly intended for internal consumption but nonetheless disrupting efforts at rapprochement. The president sought to have it both ways, reserving the right to blame Uncle Sam for real or imagined ills while preserving Yankee good will for other purposes. His periodic tirades did not pass unnoticed in Washington.

The North American news media publicized these occasions and also stressed the authoritarian aspects of Peronist rule. Attempts to restrict freedom of the press invariably arouse U.S. journalists, and the Argentine case was no exception. Ambassadors Bruce and Griffis tried to improve Perón's image in the United States, but it was a losing proposition.

Although the Argentine president projected a negative impression upon the North American public, he often succeeded in charming individual visitors from the United States. To cite but one example, he developed a warm friendship with Archie Moore, the black light-heavyweight boxer who made a number of successful ring appearances in Argentina. (As Moore explained it, Perón and Evita "treated me like a man—which is more than I can say for a lot of people."[21]) The president spoke some English and occasionally surprised Americans with his ability to understand what they were saying.*

The successes Argentina's foreign policy achieved during the first half of Perón's first term must be credited in large part to the work of Foreign Minister Juan Bramuglia, one of the most capable members of the administration. He reached the zenith of his career in September 1948, when he presided over the UN Security Council during the tense weeks of the Berlin Blockade and earned worldwide acclaim for a diplomatic performance that gave an immeasurable boost to Argentina's prestige.

But Bramuglia could never shake loose from the shadow of Evita, implacable in her determination to destroy him. As the first lady's influence expanded, her allies turned against him in their zeal to curry favor with her. The Peronist press ignored him during his moments of international triumph. (Indeed, on at least one occasion his likeness was blanked out of a published photo![22]) A whisper campaign intimated that he had ambitions to succeed Perón as president in 1952. The pressures finally took their toll in August 1949, and Bramuglia resigned.[23]

Although Evita has usually received full credit for Bramuglia's demise, the removal of the foreign minister in fact suited Perón's needs. The original appointment reflected the president's urge to consolidate his labor-union base, but by 1949 the working class was securely under his control. Bramuglia was clearly expendable and could serve as a useful scapegoat at a time when the economic situation was rapidly deteriorating. In addition, Perón may well have heard rumors about his minister's supposed political ambitions. Bramuglia's ouster was one of a series that would claim as victims most of the truly capable people in the administration as Perón replaced the best and the brightest of his associates with individuals of dubious ability or character.

---

* At least once the element of surprise came from his visitors. Ambassador Griffis' memoirs contain a charming description of a meeting between the president and a delegation from the Association of Women's Clubs in Texas. "Through it all Perón was very polite—until the leader of the group suddenly said in English to her fellow visitors, 'All right, girls, let's go,' and without warning the entire delegation closed around Perón and burst into the strains of 'The Eyes of Texas Are upon You.' I had never seen the dictator look frightened before, but he was quite uncertain what it was all about and looked anxiously at his guards lurking behind the screens. Nevertheless he sat it out and finally bowed out the delegation with a translated assurance that the eyes of Texas would be fully satisfied in watching his administration befriend the descamisados." S. Griffis, *Lying in State*, p. 263.

22

The "Rainbow Tour"

In the meteoric trajectory of the political career of Eva Perón, 1947 was the year of the star-shell burst. For twelve months she had been serving a difficult apprenticeship in the twin roles of wife of the president and his surrogate contact with the common people of Argentina. Now a momentous opportunity presented itself, in the form of an invitation from *Generalísimo* Francisco Franco to visit Spain. Similar bids from Italy and France followed, and Evita prepared to launch herself into the arena of international diplomacy.

At this point her performance as first lady lacked polish. From the beginning of Perón's presidency she had struggled to master the niceties of her new position. But as wine tastes of its own grape, Evita remained the product of her formative years, unable to shed her culturally disadvantaged past. The rough edges would not vanish overnight. When she spoke extemporaneously, her tone and choice of words were from the heart, by way of Avellaneda or La Boca. Her taste for ostentation in dress for ceremonial occasions seemed to increase, and she developed a childlike fixation on jewelry. These were flaws that invited cultivation. Shipping magnate Alberto Dodero, an intimate of the Peróns during these years, showered her with gifts of precious gems, and others followed suit.

If Evita's goals as first lady had been merely to please her husband and maintain the admiration of the Peronist masses, she would have unquestionably attained them. But she also sought social success, which meant acceptance by the elite, and benign tolerance had never been a virtue of the Barrio Norte oligarchs. They refused to recognize the ex-actress of dubious origins, despite her position as the president's wife. The Sociedad de Beneficencia (Charitable Society), a foundation created and administered by the patrician families of Buenos Aires, had customarily conferred upon each first lady the title of honorary president. The nomination was denied to Eva Perón because of her "youth." (Evita's classic rejoinder: "If they can't accept me, let them name my mother."[1])

Her other role, that of Perón's political helpmate, was still in the formative stage. She had never concealed her intent to participate fully in the creation of a New Argentina, and Perón encouraged her. But in this early period she moved gingerly in public and remained far from the center stage she would later occupy. From the very beginning the opposition viewed her activity with alarm. On July 22, 1946, Radical Deputy Ernesto Sammartino introduced a bill that would have prevented wives of public officials from enjoying any governmental prerogatives and from representing their husbands at public functions.[2] These efforts proved futile.

The first lady's overt political involvement began when she campaigned for the passage of a women's suffrage law. It was during a radio address on the subject that she presented herself in terms that linked her to an important segment of her audience. "I speak as compañera (comrade) Evita," she declared. "The women of my country know well that they are listening to the heart of a girl from the provinces, educated in the rude virtue of work."[3] It was an image she would refine to perfection.

She also began to make appearances at factories and before labor groups. In July 1946, she made a symbolic gesture—the presentation of a workers' petition to Perón—foreshadowing her assumption of the role of intermediary between the proletariat and the president.[4] Additionally, her interest in social welfare blossomed. On September 7, 1946, the government took over the Sociedad de Beneficencia and Evita set up an office in the same building. Her door at the old Secretariat of Labor was always open to poor people seeking help, and she soon earned the title "Lady of Hope."[5]

In December 1946, she made her first solo trip to the interior, a visit to the city of Tucumán. She was now representing Perón at an increasing number of ceremonial functions and was speaking out on public issues. During the first five months of 1947, she delivered some twenty political speeches. Her voice tended to be shrill, her delivery somewhat stilted, but she was gaining valuable experience in the art of platform oratory.

Evita's political beliefs reflected those of her husband, and she did not presume to question or attempt to influence them. But she had no inhibitions about thrusting herself into the full range of administrative matters that comprised the grist of routine governmental activity. On this level she relied upon emotion and intuition, qualities she possessed in abundance.

Personal loyalty was the virtue she valued most highly. In this respect she set herself apart from her husband, who never felt constrained by bonds of allegiance. As she once told a prominent Peronist, "It's worth your while to be in good with me politically. I'll defend you, I'm a good friend of my friends, and this you won't get from Perón."[6] The premium she

placed upon loyalty invited exploitation, especially on the part of opportunists who had little else to offer except lapdog fidelity.

To understand what made Evita tick, it is necessary to keep in mind
the duality of her roles as first lady and political figure. One anti-Peronist
interpretation of her behavior makes bitter resentment, deriving from the
rejections she suffered during childhood as well as those inflicted by the
porteño elite, as motivating her ambition. Her goal, according to this view,
was vindication, in the form of proving to her social superiors that she
could beat them at their own game. Thus, since trips to Europe had long
been part and parcel of the upper-class curriculum vitae, Evita seized
upon the invitation from Spain as an opportunity to demonstrate that she
too could tour the continent in style.

While containing some element of truth, this explanation overlooks the
political Evita. The first lady not only saw herself as an essential contribu-
tor to the Peronist revolution but also as an embryonic historical personage.
"I struggled much during my life with the ambition to be someone," she
once wrote to her husband.[7] As she later admitted to a friend, she felt a
desire to "cut a figure in history."[8] As a radio actress she had played a
number of great women. Now she would join their ranks. The European
trip would put her on center stage and help her achieve a place in the
history books, social acceptance or rejection by the oligarchy notwith-
standing.

Franco had his own motives for extending the invitation, which he had
first tendered to Perón himself. The Allied powers had excluded Spain
from the United Nations, and in the immediate postwar period the Franco
regime faced diplomatic isolation. Argentina alone had stood by her
mother country and opposed the application of sanctions against Spain.
In addition, the Marshall Plan did not include Spain, which was suffering
from the same shortages as the rest of Western Europe. Argentina was a
potential source of economic aid.

For the Argentines, however, certain risks attached to friendly relations with Spain. It was in Perón's interest at this juncture to cultivate good
relations with the Yankee colossus. North American cooperation could
facilitate the progress of the five-year plan. A trip to Spain by Evita might
raise hackles in Washington and even provoke retaliation by the State
Department. Foreign Minister Bramuglia vigorously opposed the idea.
But Perón, perhaps incapable of taking U.S. hostility toward Franco seriously because it derived from principle (indeed, history eventually proved
him correct on this score), decided to let his wife go.

Evita on her part cared nothing for North American sensibilities. Unlike
her husband, who could Yankee-bait and praise Uncle Sam almost in the
same breath, the first lady was viscerally anti-American. "As far as I'm
concerned," she told the Spanish ambassador to Argentina just before her
trip, "the gringos don't matter."[9] She even requested that Franco meet

her at the airport and be photographed with her. "Won't gringo Truman be furious to see us together!" she added with relish.[10]*

As preparations for the first lady's odyssey intensified, the usual spate of rumors began making the rounds in Buenos Aires. From Washington, Drew Pearson contributed a report that Evita had planned to borrow an Argentine battleship for her Atlantic crossing, but the list of traveling companions she had invited had grown so large that not even the *Queen Elizabeth* could accommodate them.[11] In fact, Evita would travel by air. Her entourage included several military attachés, a hairdresser, two wardrobe mistresses, a speechwriter, a photographer, brother Juan Duarte, Father Hernán Benítez (Evita's confessor), Alberto Dodero (who had offered to cover expenses not defrayed by the inviting countries) and the person with the most difficult assignment of all, Lilián Lagomarsino de Guardo, who was to be Evita's companion and advisor in matters of protocol.

Departure week proceeded at a hectic pace. At a farewell party Labor Minister Freire toasted the first lady with extravagant praise. Her down-to-earth reaction: "Thanks, *che*. Now, what do you want me to bring you from Europe?"[12] On the day before her plane was to leave, a demonstration at the Plaza Italia enabled the descamisados to bid Evita good-bye. A voice interrupted the radio transmission of Perón's speech and directed several uncomplimentary epithets at the president.[13]

At airport ceremonies attended by a large throng of government officials, foreign diplomats and cheering well-wishers, Evita kissed her husband and climbed aboard an Iberia DC-4. At 4:20 P.M. on June 6, 1947, the four-engine plane left Argentine soil.

Eva Perón fully appreciated the political significance of her foray into international diplomacy. As the aircraft reached cruising altitude, she called her companions together and urged them to be on their best behavior. "All over the world they're watching us, and some people are hoping we fall on our faces so they can come down on us. So don't screw up."[14]

Evita's impending separation from Perón and her homeland had aroused in her tremendous anxieties. On the day of her departure she penned to her husband a touching note in which she expressed her fear of an accident

---

* U.S. Ambassador Messersmith seemed oblivious to her true feelings about the United States. At an April 15 luncheon, the first lady told him about plans for her trip. Messersmith urged her not to go because the tour would harm Argentina. Evita listened intently and then informed her host that he had persuaded her to change her mind. "Don't be worried about my going to Spain," she assured him, apparently with a straight face, "because that is out now." Messersmith believed her and immediately fired off to the State Department a top-secret memo announcing his diplomatic triumph. On the very next day the Buenos Aires newspapers headlined that the Casa Rosada had finalized arrangements for Evita's trip. See Messersmith to Acheson, 735.52/4-1847, April 18, 1947.

and spelled out instructions to be followed in the event of her death.[15] She advised him to be wary of Rudi (presumably Freude) because of his fondness for business deals, and to keep the faithful Mercante forever at his side. In earthy language that was pure Evita, she concluded by urging him not to believe rumors about her childhood in Junín. The letter reflects the state of mind of a girl from the provinces about to plunge bravely into the great unknown, aware of her limitations yet fired by an ambition to be someone.

A transatlantic plane trip originating in Buenos Aires was a stern test of endurance. After a two-day flight with stops in northern Brazil and the Canary Islands, the Iberia DC-4 and the Argentine transport that accompanied it approached the Barajas Airport outside Madrid. Franco spared no effort in welcoming his guest. Several squadrons of Spanish air force fighter planes escorted the visitors. The *generalísimo* himself led the official greeting party. The roads from the airport to the center of Madrid were lined with soldiers holding back large, flag-waving crowds eager to catch a glimpse of the Argentine first lady. After years of civil war, deprivations and diplomatic isolation, the Spaniards regarded Evita as a young and beautiful queen who had come to brighten their lives. There were shouts of "Franco, Perón, *un solo corazón*" ("Franco, Perón, one single heart").

On the following day, June 9, a uniformed Franco bestowed upon Evita the Grand Cross of Isabel the Catholic and eulogized her before an enormous throng that overflowed the Plaza de Oriente. The first lady's response touched upon political themes. Wearing the gem-studded decoration with obvious pride, she declared: "Argentina is marching forward because she is just with her people, and because in the crusade of her battle for bread and wages, she knew how to choose between false, deceitful democracy and true, distributive democracy, where great ideas are called by names as simple as these: better pay, better housing, better food, a better life."[16]

During the eighteen days she spent in Spain, Evita toured the length and breadth of the Iberian peninsula. "I come as a rainbow between our two countries," she declared,[17] using a metaphor that would attach to her trip and convert it into a "Rainbow Tour."

The Spanish people showered her with gifts, and she absorbed adoration like a sponge. At one point, the receptions so overwhelmed her that she asked Father Benítez what an illegitimate child like her had done to deserve them.[18]

She stayed in palace rooms decorated with gold brocade and furnished with museum pieces. In Seville she rode in a coach for twenty blocks lined with children who tossed flowers and released doves. In Granada she dined by artificial moonlight.[19]

Her performance was virtually flawless except for habitual tardiness, which at one point delayed the start of a bullfight by thirty minutes, an unheard-of occurrence. The public utterances she made were suitably circumspect, though she raised eyebrows when she told a throng of sixty thousand in Vigo: "In Argentina we are trying to reduce the number of poor people and the number of rich people. You should do the same thing."[20]

Her final stop was Barcelona. Franco paid her the ultimate tribute by flying from Madrid to the Mediterranean port in order to be on hand for her departure. It was the first time he had traveled by plane since 1937, when General Emilio Mola, his rival for command of the Loyalist forces, died in a crash.

The U.S. embassy in Madrid summed up the visit begrudgingly: "Personally, the Señora may have had something of a triumph. It is recognized that she carried out a difficult task with poise and intelligence, and that she is a force of importance in her country."[21]

At 5:00 P.M. on June 26, the Rainbow Tour hit Rome. Italy presented a more challenging environment for the first lady, who now found herself for the first time (except for her brief stopover in Brazil) in a non-Spanish-speaking country, and in a political atmosphere in which hostile groups would be free to ventilate their feelings toward her. On the other hand, she would have the opportunity to meet the Pope.

The latter occasion topped her agenda. On the day after her arrival, clad in a black dress and matching mantilla, the Grand Cross of Isabel the Catholic around her neck, Evita appeared (on time) at the Vatican for a private audience with Pius XII. The encounter took place in the Pope's library, lasted for nearly thirty minutes and produced the major disappointment of the trip. She expected to receive the Rose of Gold, the highest papal decoration bestowed upon women, and perhaps even a marquisate, an honor that had previously been bestowed upon only two Argentine women, both members of the oligarchy. Though the Pope received her with all the pomp due the wife of a chief of state, he presented her with only a rosary, the customary gift for such a visit. The following day, a Vatican messenger delivered to the Argentine embassy a papal decoration for President Perón.

Evita's arrival in Rome set off a round of protests, mainly by the large and well-organized Italian Communist party. One night a crowd of demonstrators swarmed around the Argentine embassy, where the first lady was staying, and shouted "Perón, Fascist! No to Perón and no to Mussolini." Though the experience did not seem to throw Evita off-stride, the threat of more extensive disturbances in the industrialized north of Italy no doubt contributed to changes that were made in her itinerary.

It was in Italy that the physical strain of the tour took its first toll. Exhaustion and ill health were given as reasons for the cancellation of a number of previously announced appearances by Evita, as the first lady spent much of her three-week stay in Italy either at rest or on tourist excursions. During this same period, Perón was pressing forward with various initiatives, such as his declaration of economic independence in Tucumán and his worldwide radio appeal for peace.*

The Rainbow Tour suffered a major setback in mid-July when a formal invitation to visit Great Britain failed to materialize. Prior to Evita's departure from Argentina, several of the first lady's intimates had spoken to the British ambassador in Buenos Aires about the possibility of including London on her itinerary. The suggestion aroused much dismay in the British Foreign Office. The need to import Argentine beef required the cultivation of good relations with the Perón government, but a visit by Evita could jeopardize those ties. The British ambassador in Buenos Aires was instructed to reply that if the first lady came to England, His Majesty's government would be pleased and would accord her all the courtesies due a distinguished visitor of her station.[22] No immediate response to the ambassador's statement was forthcoming, and Evita departed for Spain without firm arrangements for a stopover in England.

A conventional interpretation of the negotiations that followed holds that Evita's sole motivation for wanting to go to London was to crown her journey with a stay at Buckingham Palace as the guest of King George VI and Queen Elizabeth. Thus if the Rainbow Tour was a quest for social respectability, a reception by the British royal family would demonstrate more than anything else to the Argentine upper classes that the poor girl from Junín had outdone them. Perhaps there was some truth in this, but another plausible explanation merits mention. From the outset the British press grabbed hold of the story of Evita's proposed trip to London and made much of the symbolism that would attach to any contact the ex-actress would have with the royal family. Preliminary arrangements, which called for an invitation to tea with the queen at Buckingham Palace, were unfavorably compared to a prewar visit by the wife of an ex-president of France and a 1942 visit by Eleanor Roosevelt, both of whom were lodged at the palace during their sojourns.[23] Publicity of this sort must have reached Evita. Given her sensitivities, she could hardly have ignored the social implications of a visit to England, once Fleet Street trumpeted them to the world.

Near the end of her stay in Spain, the British Foreign Office confirmed that she would arrive in England on July 15 for a four-day unofficial visit.[24] But the king and queen were scheduled to be in Scotland during that period, and Evita was not about to subject herself to what she reasonably viewed as a snub. In early July, the Argentine ambassador in London

---

* His activities belied a CBS News documentary film which conveyed the impression that while Evita was in Europe, he devoted himself to ceremonial appearances at sporting events. "Perón and Evita," *The Twentieth Century,* narrated by Walter Cronkite, on file at the Georgetown University Library.

called upon Labor party prime minister Aneurin Bevin and informed him that Evita would come only on an official visit. Bevin replied that there had been no official state visits to England since 1939, and that because of the current postwar austerity, the British government was not disposed to arrange one.[25] As a result of this impasse, the Rainbow Tour never touched down on British soil.

The low key to which the Rainbow Tour had shifted during the latter phase of the visit to Italy was sustained as the señora journeyed to Lisbon for a sightseeing interlude in Portugal. On July 21, she flew to Paris. The initial impression she produced at the Orly Airport was favorable. French Foreign Minister Georges Bidault, upon seeing her for the first time, was heard to murmur: "How young and pretty she is!"[26]

Evita spent five days in Paris. She lunched with President Auriol and his wife at their summer home, dined at the Quai d'Orsay with the foreign minister and his wife, attended the signing of a Franco-Argentine trade agreement and went shopping with Madame Bidault. The first lady again handled herself well, except for some minor misunderstandings such as her annoyance when one of two nightclub performers dressed as a camel presented her with a bouquet of flowers from the "animal's" rear end.

Much of the French press devoted exhaustive coverage to her activities. As the U.S. embassy reported, "Her visit . . . provided a welcome journalistic relief during a protracted heat wave from the long stories of national and international political, financial and agricultural difficulties."[27] The left-wing newspapers, led by the Communist *L'Humanité*, tried to ignore her, except for occasional cutting references to the Argentine brand of "Fascism" she represented. *France Dimanche* enlightened readers by publishing one of the pictures of "Eva Duarte Surprised by the Camera," as well as a photo of army officer Juan Perón posing with a bare-breasted Patagonian Indian woman.[28]

The last leg of the tour took Evita to Switzerland. Rumor had it that she traveled to the alpine republic in order to deposit in a Swiss bank account large sums of money acquired as a result of business deals in Argentina. A variation on this theme holds that she somehow carried with her gold obtained from Nazis admitted to Argentina after the war and valued at $800 million, and deposited this fortune in numbered accounts in Swiss banks.[29] The problem with this interpretation was that the decision to visit that country was not made until shortly before she arrived. According to an Argentine diplomatic official, he met with Evita in Paris and suggested the visit; he went to Berne to make the arrangements; then he rejoined her in southern France and accompanied her on the train trip across the Alps.[30] Thus the Swiss visit was a last-minute addition, a fact that contradicts the notion that she had planned to engage in financial transactions during her stay.

The most memorable aspect of Evita's brief stopover occurred when she stepped into a waiting automobile at the train station in Berne. A volley of ripened tomatoes sailed from the crowd and splattered the Swiss minister of foreign relations, who was on hand to greet her. On the following day, a stone shattered the windshield of the car in which she was riding. Both incidents were the handiwork of individuals, rather than political groups, and Evita took them in stride.

By now the first lady had been absent from Argentina for a month and a half. The Rainbow Tour had exacted a physical toll from her, but she was not quite ready to return to her descamisados. On August 9 she flew to Lisbon, where she boarded a steamship (at the request of her husband, who was not yet convinced that the new Argentine airline was sufficiently safe). An Atlantic crossing brought her to the northeast Brazilian port of Recife, and from there she took a flight to Rio de Janeiro, in order to put in an appearance at an inter-American conference of foreign ministers. Though she had nothing of substance to contribute, her glamorous presence enlivened the proceedings.

On the morning of August 23, President Perón, his entire cabinet, the officers of the CGT, cadets from the military academy and representatives from youth and women's organizations formed the vanguard of a huge throng lining a dock in Buenos Aires to await the *Ciudad de Montevideo.* An earsplitting cacophony of sirens, horns and whistles drowned the roar of the crowd as the figure of the first lady, leaning against a rail and waving a handkerchief, came into view. Tears were streaming down her cheeks. She could scarcely wait for the plank to be lowered before she dashed from the ship to embrace her smiling husband.

The Rainbow Tour had come to a glorious end. Evita had demonstrated that she was a political figure in her own right. The trip had generated an enormous amount of publicity, even a cover story in *Time*,[31] and although much of the reporting was sensationalistic, trivial or negative, it did her no harm at home. She had kept Argentina in the spotlight with her, an accomplishment highly regarded in a country where an inordinate premium attaches to international notice.

The trip proved costly for one member of Perón's inner circle. Ricardo Guardo, president of the Chamber of Deputies and one of Perón's more sensible advisors, fell abruptly from political grace under circumstances strongly suggesting that the strain of traveling together over an extended period of time had produced a falling out between the first lady and Señora Guardo. A Peronist official who rode in the car that took Perón and Evita home from the dockside welcome claims that Evita told her husband "Watch out for Guardo. He's a traitor."[32] Although Perón belittled the accusation, Guardo lost his position as Chamber president, and he did not stand for reelection in 1948.

During Evita's absence, rumors that she would "retire" from politics provided a counterpoint to the heavy media coverage of the Rainbow

Tour. A segment of the officer corps was said to be disenchanted with her intrusions into politics and disgusted by reports of financial irregularities on the part of the first lady and those around her.[33] The whispers intensified when a bout with the grippe confined her to bed shortly after her return. But before long she resumed the frenetic pace characteristic of everything she did.[34]

At the top of her agenda at this point was the enactment of a women's suffrage law, which had passed the Senate but was now stalled in the Chamber of Deputies. On September 9, in the first lady's conspicuous presence, the Chamber approved the bill after the usual tumultuous debate. Two weeks later, at a rally in the Plaza de Mayo, Perón signed the bill into law and then presented it to his wife as representative of those it enfranchised.

The first proposal to extend voting rights to women had been presented to the Congress in 1919. Progressive legislators (mostly Socialists), encouraged by Argentina's tiny feminist movement, fought for similar bills during the 1920s and 1930s. The Peronists could now boast that they had made women's suffrage a reality, and that Evita had been instrumental in the process.

It is important to keep in mind that the Peronist concept of feminism differed markedly from the basic beliefs that have long animated the movement for equal rights for women in the United States and Europe. Indeed, old-line Argentine feminists (virtually all of whom were anti-Peronist) were accused of trying to import foreign ideas that denied women their domestic role and put them in competition with men.[35] The new Peronist feminism accepted woman's traditional responsibilities. As Evita declared in her ghostwritten autobiography, "We were born to make homes. Not for the street."[36] She also expressed the view that "no woman's movement will be glorious and lasting in the world if it does not give itself to the cause of a man."[37] Shortly after the enactment of the new law, efforts were begun to organize what would become the politically potent women's branch of the Peronist party.

Evita also continued her labor and social-welfare activities. In March 1948 the official press credited her with settling a work dispute involving bank employees—the first recorded instance of her intervention in a labor conflict.[38] In mid-1948, the government granted legal recognition to a corporate entity called the María Eva Duarte de Perón Social Aid Foundation, which became the engine of her social-welfare endeavors.

The first lady was equally active backstage at the Casa Rosada. Her first priority was to take care of the members of her immediate family. Her brother Juan had been serving as the president's private secretary from the beginning of the term. Of three brothers-in-law, one became a senator from the province of Buenos Aires; another was named to the Supreme Court to replace one of the impeached justices; the third rose to the post of director of customs for the port of Buenos Aires. Sisters Blanca and Elisa obtained government jobs. In addition, Evita secured appointments at all levels of government for those she considered loyal friends.

The relationship between Juan and Eva Perón formed the bedrock upon which rested the latter's reputation as the most powerful woman in the contemporary world. The president trusted her. He regarded human nature with great cynicism and felt a particular unease toward any Peronist with leadership capabilities. But Evita was in a category of her own. Her influence derived totally from him, to such an extent that she could never threaten his authority nor compete with him. He may have been oversimplifying when he stated that "Eva Perón is a product of mine,"[39] but it was this attitude that permitted him to view with equanimity the political heights to which she scaled.

The first lady readily accepted the role Perón had fashioned for her. She never tired of heaping extravagant praise upon him. As she chirped in her autobiography, "I was not, nor am I, anything more than a humble woman . . . a sparrow in an immense flock of sparrows. . . . But Perón was and is a gigantic condor that flies high and sure among the summits and near to God."[40]

No doubt this reflected, at least in part, her own insecurity. But at the same time, her adaptation to the role of political first lady unleashed her relentless ambition to be someone.

In countless ways Perón and Evita complemented each other. Their disparate characteristics meshed together neatly to make them a formidable team. Perón was the master of the Machiavellian maneuver. Evita acted impulsively. Perón's temperament made him prefer statesmanlike posturing. Evita relished striking out against the oligarchy and other enemies, real and imagined. Responsibility was something Perón avoided like the plague, especially in matters such as the elimination of important members of his political entourage. Evita's passionate likes and dislikes provided both a sword for his political executions and the shield behind which he could hide.

On the public platform they were a formidable pair. According to a North American observer who witnessed one of their performances,

> Evita was beautiful and wore a tailored suit. She took off her jacket and began a denunciation of the oligarchs. Hers was the voice of a fishwife: raw and raspy, guttural, comfortable with slang and bad Spanish. She made clear what the Peronists would do to the Barrio Norte if any harm befell her husband.
>
> Perón came next, doffing his jacket and rolling up his sleeves. He had a big, perfectly controlled voice, a rolling tone and a remarkable presence. He reminded me of Governor Dewey. He could range from a whisper to a roar. His enunciation was perfect, as was his Spanish.[41]

Perón had an aversion to spontaneous physical contact.[42] He was superb at haranguing crowds from a balcony, but would not mingle with them and expose himself to adulation at close range. Evita, on the other hand, was totally uninhibited about mingling with her public. When she held open house in her office for any individuals who wanted to bring their problems to her, she customarily kissed women visitors when they departed. Once, a poet who was present in the office attempted to interpose himself between the first lady and a supplicant with a syphilitic sore on her mouth. She brushed him aside and pressed her lips against those of the unfortunate woman. "Never do that again," she told him later. "It's the price I have to pay."[43]

Having emerged from poverty and degradation, Evita could symbolize Perón's followers, the working class and the dispossessed. As she developed this role, the Peronist masses saw her as their advocate, representing them before her husband and articulating their needs. Proximity to the president made her the perfect intermediary, from the points of view both of those who believed in her and of Perón, who could now control the demands of his followers.

For Perón, the ideals he espoused were tactics, disposable or adjustable as circumstances dictated. His wife, a professional actress accustomed to playing parts, came to believe the words she was mouthing. She *became* Evita with a fervor that made her more Peronist than Perón.[44]

Perón occasionally felt the lash of Evita's stormy temperament. Once, according to an eyewitness, she angrily pulled his sword from its scabbard and threw it out the window of the residence as they dressed for a gala.[45] A friend of U.S. Ambassador Bruce reported that during a fox hunt they argued bitterly about Miguel Miranda, and Evita declared: "If you feel that way about me, why don't you get a divorce?"[46]

Of the various myths about Eva Perón, perhaps the most distorted pictures her as the dominant partner, the real macho of the couple, the de facto ruler of Argentina. However, it would be equally erroneous to resort to the other extreme and regard Evita as no more than Perón's mindless instrument. Perón did nudge Evita into her political role, but she was predisposed to assume it and carried it off with great gusto. He did manipulate her to a certain extent and benefited from her promotion of him. However, it was always in her interest to aggrandize him. She in turn accumulated political power and did not shrink from exercising it, often capriciously. But in every instance it was power that he delegated to her, or that he did not wish to wield.

Totally committed to Perón, Evita contributed a passion and an energy that lent a singular touch to the Peronist movement. Yet there would be times when the lack of formal limits on her activity and the zealousness that marked her style created problems for the president. The very qualities that were the essence of Evita carried with them a potential for excess that could embarrass her husband.

23

"Peronizing" the Constitution

On May 1, 1948, President Juan D. Perón inaugurated a new session of the Argentine Congress. His followers had repeated their 1946 triumph in elections held earlier that year. They now controlled every seat in the Senate and held a better than two-thirds majority in the Chamber of Deputies. With two years of parliamentary experience behind them, the Peronist deputies displayed a mood of confidence that matched the buoyant optimism pervading the nation as a whole.

In his three-and-a-half-hour address to the legislature, Perón included one item of major import. He gave a nod to constitutional reform, a project some of his supporters had been urging since the 1946 campaign. To opponents of the regime and many foreign observers as well, any attempt to tamper with the 1853 constitution had but one real purpose, the elimination of Article 77, which provided that "the president and vice-president . . . may not be reelected except with an interval of one term." They listened skeptically as Perón told the Congress: "My opinion is against such a change [in Article 77]. . . . In my view, reelection would be an enormous danger for the political future of the republic."[1] As one North American scholar noted, "his followers had come to know that when Perón said 'no' he occasionally meant 'yes.' And this was one of those occasions."[2]

Under Article 30 of the 1853 constitution, "Either the whole or any part of the constitution may be amended. The necessity for such amendment must be declared by Congress by a vote of at least two-thirds of its members; but the amendment shall not be made except by a convention summoned for that purpose." In compliance with the supreme law of the land, Peronist deputy Eduardo Colom introduced a bill calling for a congressional declaration of necessity.[3] Shortly afterward Perón assigned to José Figuerola the task of preparing a new constitution.

The Radical deputies vigorously opposed the reform, although in the course of the past half century, Radical politicians, as well as Socialists and Conservatives, had advocated changes in the constitution. The Radicals also objected to the form of the declaration of necessity, on the ground that it did not specify which provisions of the constitution were to be amended. They argued that the proposed bill presented a blank check to the convention, and that it would enable the Peronists to institutionalize a totalitarian or Fascist form of government.[4] But Article 30 clearly permitted the convention to rewrite the constitution as it pleased.

After the Chamber of Deputies enacted a bill convoking a constitutional convention, the government scheduled a national election to choose delegates. The opposition parties could not agree on a common stand. The Socialists ordered their people to cast blank votes, while the Communists presented candidates advocating the nationalization of various industries, a minimum wage and worker control over production. The Radical party held a national convention that voted to contest the Peronists at the polls, over the objections of a strong minority favoring a boycott of the entire process.

Meanwhile, the Peronists geared up for another appeal to the electorate. Despite the president's avowed opposition to a removal of the bar to reelection, his followers left no doubt about their intentions. The new president of the Chamber of Deputies, Héctor Cámpora, declared: "We can hardly consider our republic to be democratic when the fundamental law still contains an article which, while ostensibly sustaining the principle of protecting the people, nevertheless legally constitutes an obstacle to the free expression of the people's will."[5]

The campaign itself was clean, but only in a formalistic sense. The government severely restricted the opposition's access to the mass media and reduced anti-Peronist efforts to token resistance.[6]

While the opposition could not effectively compete with Perón's followers, the campaign did furnish a spirited popularity contest among prominent Peronists. Domingo Mercante, governor of Buenos Aires Province and widely recognized as Perón's most likely successor, topped the field and won the post of presiding officer at the convention. But it also created for him a conflict of interest on the issue of presidential reelection.

The Peronists, as expected, won a smashing victory in the December elections and could count on slightly more than two-thirds of the delegates. The Radical party took forty-eight of the forty-nine seats allocated to the opposition.

As the convention approached, political bickering among the Peronists intensified. An early casualty was José Figuerola, whose work as Perón's intimate advisor over the years had attracted the enmity of others in the president's inner circle. According to some accounts, Evita disliked him intensely. During the latter months of 1948 he had performed Herculean labors in preparing a draft of a new constitution, as well as supporting documents that reflected his consistently meticulous research. But a number of Perón's associates criticized his work, and the president himself was not entirely satisfied with it. The Figuerola draft was put aside and Perón turned to a commission set up by the Peronist bloc in Congress to study proposals for constitutional reform. The head of the commission, Arturo E. Sampay, was a law professor whose views mirrored the social and economic teachings of the Catholic church and were slightly more progressive than those of Figuerola.

Sampay assumed the role of leading intellectual luminary at the convention, which began on January 24, 1949, in the Chamber of Deputies. The man he replaced faded even further into the background. Just before the convention ended, the Peronist majority added to the new constitution a clause requiring that only native Argentines could attain ministerial status within the government. This eliminated the Barcelona-born Figuerola from his ministerial post.

The Catalán, one of the most capable individuals in the inner circle of the Casa Rosada, had served Perón well for nearly six years. Yet when he was set upon by his enemies, Perón refused to lift a finger to save him. The chief executive was content to remain a voyeur and worried only about avoiding responsibility. This produced a reverse type of quality control that removed the best people from his entourage and attracted mediocrity or worse in their stead. Perhaps it was true, as one Peronist who knew him well put it, that at heart he was an admirer of second-raters and scoundrels.[7] Or perhaps he was beginning to take seriously the adulation being showered upon him and could not tolerate any associates whose intellectual or leadership capacities might in any way detract from his own preeminence. Whatever the cause, the casualty list would mount.

The pre-convention jostle for political position also suggested that the first lady's position within the government had not yet achieved its apex. Though she helped in the campaign to elect delegates, she played no role in the preparation of the new constitution, nor did she address the convention.

The low profile to which Evita had been consigned did not, however, discourage the claque of Peronist officials who had hitched their careers to the first lady's star. They took a longer view of things and spun dreams of an Evita presidency in 1952. They reasoned that if Perón meant what he had said and the convention heeded his words, Evita would be his natural successor. This group found itself silently sympathizing with the opposition, which fought to preserve the ban. But at the same time, they were trapped by a principal article of their faith—unswerving allegiance to Perón. Therefore, not only could Evita's supporters not move a muscle in defense of Article 77, but they also had to beg Perón to change his mind about reelection.

Domingo Mercante figured prominently in the convention. The governor enjoyed a unique position in the Peronist firmament. Long and faithful service at Perón's side, plus his critical contribution on the seventeenth of October, made Mercante the number-two man in the movement. Evita herself was genuinely fond of the retired colonel and viewed him as the embodiment of fidelity. It was not uncommon for crowds at Peronist rallies to chant "Perón! Evita! Mercante!"

Moreover, as governor of the wealthiest, most populous province in Argentina, Mercante had achieved remarkable success.[8] The opposition controlled the provincial senate and a number of municipalities. Instead of attempting to purge anti-Peronists, he worked with them and in many instances won their support. He also permitted a much greater degree of press freedom than the national government. This tolerant attitude and the progressive image earned by his administration gave an immense boost to his popularity. Although he could not approximate Perón's charisma or intellectual breadth, he remained the most credible successor to the president.

Mercante's handling of the convention demonstrated both his personal style and leadership qualities. A U.S. embassy document noted his "commendable ability and judiciousness."[9] The governor maintained a cordial relationship with Moisés Lebensohn, the leader of the Radical delegates. Lebensohn frequently met in private with him during preliminary sessions and throughout the convention. The two men maintained their political distance, but Mercante promised to respect the Radicals' right to argue their points within the parliamentary limits adopted by the assembly, and he kept his word. Whenever Peronists tried to interrupt or shout down a Radical speaker, Mercante intervened to permit the minority delegate to continue.

A more difficult problem for the governor was the unresolved fate of Article 77. One week after the formal opening of the convention, Mercante and a group of Peronist leaders met with the president in Olivos. The latter told them in no uncertain terms that the reelection ban must not be changed. The visitors took this to be his final word on the subject and prepared to convey the decision to the convention. But when the moment arrived to make a formal announcement on the subject, a proposal to amend the article to read "The president and the vice-president shall continue in office for six years and can be reelected" came forward for consideration.

What happened to produce this 180-degree turn remains something of a mystery. According to Eduardo Colom, who claims Evita for a source, Perón expected Mercante and the others in the group to refuse to take no for an answer. He was very upset when they left and could not sleep that night. "Mercante is more interested in working to succeed me than in interpreting my wishes," he complained to the first lady.[10] Taking her cue, Evita contacted the Peronist leadership at the convention and instructed them to introduce the reelection amendment.

The Radical party, divided on the question of whether to cooperate at all in the constitutional reform, stood in monolithic solidarity against any proposal that might prolong Perón's mandate. When the time came to debate the motion to amend Article 77, the Radical delegates set off a burst of verbal pyrotechnics, after which they marched out of the room.

The constitutional convention was much more than just a pretext to change Article 77. The proceedings also gave expression to social and economic ideas that had been crystallizing around the Peronist movement since 1943 and brought into being political reforms, in addition to presidential reelection, that would strengthen the already powerful hand of the chief executive.

A simple addition to the preamble signaled this thrust. The original language remained virtually intact, except for the acknowledgment of a commitment to achieve a "socially just, economically free and politically sovereign" nation. These were the watchwords of the Peronist movement.

Article 37 spelled out the parameters of social justice. It listed the rights of the worker, of the family and of the aged, and guaranteed to all citizens equal access to education and culture. The enumeration of worker rights came verbatim from a 1947 speech by Perón.[11] It covered working conditions, wages and social security, but not strikes—an omission made much of by critics. However, the last of the listed guarantees spoke to the right to defend professional interests, and the strike might reasonably be construed as a permissible means of defense.

A section entitled "The Social Function of Property, Capital and Economic Activity" incorporated the economic nationalism advocated by the Peronists. A fundamental change was achieved by the declaration that "private property has a social function," which replaced the clause stating that "property is inviolable" in the 1853 constitution. The new Magna Carta placed capital "at the service of the national economy."[12] Article 40 gave the legislature broad authority to intervene in the economic life of the nation. It also reserved to the government control of all subsoil resources and natural sources of energy.

The language of the revised articles 38, 39 and 40, drafted and promoted by Sampay, symbolized a fundamental shift away from the liberal capitalism underlying the 1853 constitution and toward Perón's Third Position. The laissez-faire philosophy of the former would now yield to a recognition of the state's authority to intervene for what it deemed to be the common good.

Perón himself subscribed in principle to these theories of economic nationalism and statism. But he also espoused a flexible pragmatism that permitted him maximum freedom of movement (and that offered an easy mark for the criticism that Peronism was whatever Perón said it was at any given moment). The circumstances leading to the adoption of Article 40 illustrate how pragmatic he could be and suggest that he did not exercise an iron-fisted control over the convention.[13]

The 1853 constitution provided that "expropriation on a ground of public utility must be provided by law and compensation [must be] previously made." This did not sit well with Sampay and other nationalists, in part because of dissatisfaction with the machinations of certain foreign-owned utilities during the Infamous Decade, and also as a result of their unhappiness with the price Perón had paid for the British railroads. They wanted the constitution not only to require expropriation of all public utilities but also to insure the government would not pay out excessive compensation for them. So Sampay drafted provisions that declared public services to be the inalienable property of the state, calling for expropriation according to law, and setting as the formula for indemnification original cost minus amortization *and* minus any excess profits realized during the period of private ownership.

When this proposal was made public, Perón found himself besieged by representatives of foreign companies operating utilities in Argentina. Diplomats from the Swedish, Belgian, Dutch and U.S. embassies expressed their grave concern. The indemnification formula, according to those who opposed it, might produce expropriations that would leave private companies in debt to the government.[14]

Instead of declaring his views on this important issue, the president wavered, telling the U.S. embassy he would eliminate the indemnification provision[15] and ordering Sampay to do so; when the law professor and Mercante in turn called upon him at Olivos and urged him to stand firm, Perón smiled his famous smile and appeared to agree. But on the next day, when the convention was scheduled to vote on Article 40, Juan Duarte brought orders from Perón that the controversial provision be dropped. Sampay and Mercante managed to stall him until the delegates had already approved the entire article as drafted by Sampay.

Perón subsequently informed the U.S. embassy that it was too late to undo the convention's adoption of Article 40.[16] He solemnly promised he would never invoke the authority given him by the new constitution to expropriate any North American properties. This satisfied neither the embassy nor the State Department, much to Perón's surprise—another example of his inability to understand the North American mentality. U.S. officials asserted it was a violation of international law and would work as a disincentive to private investment from abroad at a time when Argentina needed and was seeking foreign capital. The embassy pressed Perón for further assurances, which the economic exigencies of the moment forced him to give.[17]

The 1949 constitution made several significant changes in the political structure. It not only permitted the reelection of a president but also did away with the system of electors copied from the United States. There would henceforth be direct presidential election by popular vote. The date of the presidential election was advanced to November 11, 1951. The voters of each province, rather than the provincial legislators, would choose national senators. The number of ministers was raised from eight to twenty.

Although the constitution to a certain extent guaranteed civil liberties, it also included provisions that alarmed the political opposition. Article 15 declared that "the state does not recognize the right to violate freedom," and proscribed "national or international organizations, whatever their purpose, which support principles opposed to the individual freedom recognized in this constitution, [and] those that threaten the democratic system by which it is inspired." Despite the implication that this language was aimed only at the Communist party (which was legal in Argentina at the time and remained so throughout Perón's two terms), its thrust might also affect any political group the regime wished to suppress.

The provisions of the 1853 constitution authorizing the declaration of a state of siege in cases of foreign attack or domestic disturbance remained intact, but the new document also permitted the president to declare a "state of precaution and alarm" without congressional approval, an amendment that carried with it an obvious potential for abuse.[18]

The delegates unanimously adopted the Peronist constitution on March 11, 1949. All public officials were then required to swear allegiance to the new supreme law of the land. The Radical minority in Congress, faced with an unpleasant choice between resignation and submission, opted for what they saw as the lesser evil and took the oath. The president attended a joint session of the Congress on March 15 and formally swore to uphold the revised constitution. The oath was administered to him by Domingo Mercante, whose political career peaked at the convention. The governor of Buenos Aires Province would remain for a while longer the heir apparent to Perón, but relations between the two men would never be the same.

24

Stifling Dissent

The opposition . . . has been demonstrating but one thing: that they are bad losers. . . . They use the public platform and the benches of Congress not to offer criticism or responsible opposition, but to . . . destroy other men's prestige. . . . When the opposition is not conscientious, altruistic, fair-minded, calm, objective and impersonal, but rather intractable, sterile, negative, gross and contumacious, there can exist neither democracy nor the minimum conditions for living together in a civilized way. . . .

All these abuses must come to an end. To accomplish this, the normal measures the law gives us are enough. I have said we would be tolerant even with intolerance, but that we would not tolerate misdeeds or infamy. . . . Against their obfuscation, their hatred, their pettiness, we have preferred to use serenity and disdain. But our response must be governed by the need to defend the collective welfare and tranquility.[1]

In a radio address on August 21, 1947, shortly before his wife's return from Europe, Perón fulminated against what he termed efforts to defame the country abroad, provoke a coup by the armed forces, sabotage the economy and infiltrate the trade unions. He also angrily and categorically denied the charge that freedom of the press no longer existed in Argentina.

At first blush it is hard to imagine why Perón paid such heed to his enemies. Weak and divided, they posed no real threat to his grip upon the nation, particularly at a time when Peronist social and economic policies were exhilarating a large sector of the populace. Nonetheless, periodic denunciations of the opposition remained part of his platform repertoire. The charismatic leader needs to prove himself against apparently fitting adversaries,[2] as Perón had done during the 1946 election campaign "against" Spruille Braden. Anti-Peronist politicians had inherited Braden's adversarial relationship with the president. It was very much in his interest to keep the public aware of their existence and their challenge to him. The eventual decimation suffered by the anti-Peronists does not necessarily establish his ignorance of their usefulness. Lack of restraint may have had much to do with what happened.

For example, Perón's military mentality assigned the same strategic objectives to warfare and politics alike: the defeat or neutralization of the enemy. In the context of an election, this made perfect sense. Once the reins of government were securely in Peronist hands, however, the strategy of conquest was antithetical to the need to preserve the appearance of competition. Opponents too often or too decisively beaten could hardly be taken seriously. The concentration of power at the state's disposal, a basic tenet of Peronism, made it impossible for the opposition to survive. The temptation to use and abuse authority to suppress dissent became irresistible.

The tactics adopted by the opposition also contributed to the breakdown of democracy. In the Chamber of Deputies the Radicals continued their strategy of intransigent nay-saying. Though the majority bloc in the Chamber made it impossible for the minority to participate effectively in the lawmaking process, it was obvious that in any case the latter would not have opted to cooperate. They did not make even the slightest good-faith effort to work out some kind of modus vivendi with the Peronists. Whatever faint opportunity for accommodation may have existed during that first year quickly evaporated.

A band of eloquent Radicals in the Chamber of Deputies formed the cutting edge of the opposition to Perón.[3] They tried in vain to block virtually every piece of Peronist legislation, even measures that the Radical party platform included. Badly outnumbered, they could do no more than use the floor of Congress to air facts and arguments embarrassing to the government. The few newspapers not under Peronist control would reprint or summarize their speeches, which provided the only political criticism to reach a mass audience. Restriction upon press freedom slowly congealed this last channel of information.

The Radical deputies did not limit themselves to debate on the merits of proposed legislation. Driven by frustration, temperamental impulse, or a combination of both, they spiced their utterances with invective and insult aimed at the president, the first lady, members of the administration and their colleagues on the other side of the aisle. The cloak of congressional immunity protected them from criminal prosecution as long as they spoke from the floor of the Chamber, but did not always save them from reprisals, as the fate of Ernesto Sammartino demonstrates.

Perhaps the most acid-tongued of the Radical deputies, Sammartino exemplified an exaggerated fusion of Latin machismo and political combativeness. He seemed to hold a special grudge against Evita, for reasons rumored to stem from a relationship between them before she met Perón. On August 8, 1946, he accused the Peronist majority of knowing "like Panurge [a character from Rabelais] the forty forms of theft."[4] Not amused by this elegant literary allusion, the targets of his jibe voted to suspend him for three days. Two months later, a beefy stranger invaded his law office and attempted to "settle accounts" with him for his verbal abuse of Perón and Evita. Quick with his fists, Sammartino pummeled and routed the intruder.[5] There were suspicions, never confirmed, that the bumbling assailant was acting on orders from the first lady or some government official. On June 26, 1947, Sammartino made his reference to the Peronist majority as a "zoological inundation." It provoked a near-riot in the Chamber and a subsequent duel—pistols at twenty paces—with Eduardo Colom. Each participant took a single shot and missed. Finally, on August 5, 1948, the Peronists decided that Sammartino's behavior had become intolerable and voted to expel him. This deprived him of immunity from criminal prosecution, and he immediately went into hiding. Several weeks later, he escaped across the river to Uruguay.

By 1948, the mood of the Chamber of Deputies had changed perceptibly from the quasi-innocent freewheeling that characterized the early period to knee-jerk subservience to the Casa Rosada.[6] Discussion of the merits of proposed bills grew less frequent; time spent paying tribute to Perón and Evita increased. Héctor Cámpora's assumption of the presidency of the Chamber accelerated this deterioration. The dentist-politician was the first Peronist legislator to proclaim that he considered it an honor to admit to being "obsequious to General Perón."[7]

Commencing in 1948, the Congress enacted a series of bills designed to restrict dissent and hobble the opposition.[8] The most serious and least justifiable was the so-called law of disrespect, which made it a crime to offend the dignity of a public official in matters relating to the exercise of public functions. A disrespect law had been on the books for decades and evidenced the degree to which the cultural value attached to personal dignity outweighed Argentine society's commitment to free speech. The Peronists decided to strengthen the law by eliminating the legal defense of truth. The penalty was a prison sentence of up to three years. The new law offered no precise definition of disrespect, but instead vested enormous discretionary authority in Peronist prosecutors and judges.

The law of disrespect proved to be an effective weapon against opposition politicians who could not restrain their rhetoric when they delivered speeches outside the Congress. Several Radical deputies in addition to Sammartino lost their seats. Leaders from the parties not represented in the Congress suffered similar fates. The first to seek asylum in Montevideo was conservative Vicente Solano Lima, who fled in late 1947.[9] A stream of politicians followed him into exile, as it became increasingly unhealthy to engage in aggressive partisan activity.

On the other hand, the Peronists were surprisingly tolerant of the Communist party. In his relations with the United States, Perón often found it convenient to boast about his success in countering the threat of Communism.[10] His political philosophy, he claimed, provided a thoroughly effective vaccine. At the same time, he needed to be able to invoke the menace of Communism whenever it suited his purposes, and to stress that Peronism was the only viable alternative to international socialism. The Communists remained in opposition to Perón, but abandoned the line that he was no more than a Nazi-Fascist, and argued instead that his reforms did not go far enough.[11]

The economic elite managed to survive. Wealthy Argentines groaned under the burdens of heavy taxation, worker demands for salary increases and government controls, but did not lose their property. There were very few expropriations. The oligarchs served as convenient targets for denunciation by Perón and Evita. The Peronists preferred to engage in subtle forms of harassment, best exemplified by the setting up of a smelly fish market on the steps of the exclusive Jockey Club on Florida Street. The president's strategy never called for the economic destruction of the oligarchs. Peronist doctrine assigned an important role to private capital. Perón could live without anti-Peronist politicians, but he needed the captains of industry and agriculture.

The most effective strategy Perón utilized to debilitate his political opponents was to deny them any means of communicating with the electorate. This he accomplished by closing their access to the radio and newspapers. Direct intervention by the government and coerced acquisitions by individuals with close ties to him created a monopoly that eventually strangled the possibility of a free exchange of ideas and information in Argentina. The police thwarted attempts to publish underground newspapers and pamphlets. Restrictions on public meetings, the use of loudspeakers and placement of posters were enforced only against the opposition parties. These various measures, combined with the law of disrespect, silenced political debate.

Peronist control of the airwaves deprived the opposition of a nationwide audience. Radio had achieved a high degree of popularity among the common people of Argentina, and the president had no intention of permitting his adversaries to compete with him for this crucial constituency. Since the government already had considerable authority to regulate broadcasting, it was an easy matter to take over the entire industry. On the pretext of promoting national defense and the spiritual needs of the country, IAPI purchased the major networks. Argentine listeners soon consumed a steady diet of propaganda extolling the president, his wife and their philosophy of government.

The 1853 constitution guaranteed freedom of the press in two separate articles, one of which protected the right of individuals "to publish their ideas through the press without prior censorship," while the other prohibited the Congress from enacting "laws restricting the freedom of the press or placing it under federal jurisdiction." The 1949 constitution left these provisions intact, but the protection they furnished proved eggshell thin.

Perón grew more categorical regarding freedom of the press as the fourth estate moved closer to becoming an arm of the government. His early statements carried qualifications that reflected his true convictions: he believed in "liberty without licentiousness" and opposed the "arbitrary invocation of freedom of expression that concealed campaigns meant to confuse and disorient public opinion." He would not let the press serve as "weapons of economic disturbance and social divisiveness, nor vehicles of foreign ideas or political ambitions."[12] Thus, he read what he wanted into the constitution, and once the Supreme Court had been "Peronized," his interpretation became the law of the land.

A series of business deals concentrated ownership of a substantial segment of the press in the hands of people close to the government.[13] This process began in 1947, when Evita purchased the daily newspaper *Democracia* with funds furnished by Alberto Dodero and others. *Democracia* became an unofficial organ of the Peronist movement and resorted to wide coverage of sports and crime to attract popular readership.

The next step was a quantum leap toward monopoly. A publishing company owned by British capital and controlling not only newspapers and magazines but also a radio network was acquired by a new corporate entity whose shareholders were anonymous but in all likelihood included Evita. The organization, called Alea S.A. (Inc.), subsequently purchased the Buenos Aires newspapers *Crítica, La Razón, Noticias Gráficas* and *La Epoca*.[14] Only *La Prensa* and *La Nación*, the best known and most prestigious of the porteño dailies, and the afternoon paper, *Clarín*, remained free from Alea's clutches. The press empire created by Alea comprised not only newspapers and magazines but also printing presses and real estate. The showplace of the corporation was a new forty-three-story skyscraper, the tallest building in Buenos Aires, near the waterfront.

Alea's newspapers all faithfully echoed the Peronist line, although from time to time they served as factional instruments of intra-party squabbles. Ostensibly they were independent of the administration, but one simple fact demonstrated the absolute control that Perón and Evita maintained over the entire enterprise: the director of the publishing conglomerate was Carlos V. Aloé, the administrative secretary of the president.

Aloé's military career began in 1922, when he was a member of Perón's company at the army school for noncommissioned officers.[15] Before joining Perón's inner circle, he had risen to the rank of major. Especially devoted to Evita, he offered blind loyalty unleavened by any discernible intelligence. (Anti-Peronists made him the butt of jokes and drew upon his gaucho pretensions by dubbing him El Caballo, "The Horse.") He took charge of Alea without relinquishing his top-level posts, and brought with him a total lack of journalistic experience.

It was, of course, true that the Perón government could not have hoped to bring about far-reaching economic and social change without media access enabling the regime to publicize its programs and plans. The free press in 1946 was almost entirely in the hands of opponents of the new regime. More importantly, the tradition of freedom of the press in Argentina did not encompass a sense of responsibility to provide an outlet for competing views (as, for example, *La Prensa* demonstrated in its coverage of the election campaign).

Therefore, the securing of some publishing operations that would be sympathetic to Perón was an understandable priority. However, the effort to develop a Peronist press went further and proceeded not merely to compete with anti-Peronist publishers but to destroy them.

Alea's acquisitions occurred at a time when government-imposed restraints were causing publishers to despair.[16] Confiscation of existing stocks of newsprint, quotas on newsprint imports, limitations on the number of pages per newspaper edition and officially decreed wage increases for newspaper employees supposedly served national economic needs, which the Peronists interpreted as overriding the constitutional guarantees of freedom of the press. Yet under the circumstances no one could doubt that these measures were actually aimed at stifling voices that refused to join the pro-Perón chorus.

The symbol and anchor of the opposition press, *La Prensa*, bore the brunt of the "legal" onslaught. Founded in 1869, the newspaper had always been under the ownership and control of the wealthy Paz family. Already famous throughout Latin America, the venerable daily attracted worldwide attention with its stubborn resistance to Perón.

La Prensa identified with the interests of the agricultural and cattle-raising sectors of the economy and did not sympathize with the aspirations of the working class. Pro-British, anti-Yrigoyen, pro-Allied, anti-Fascist, and pro-Braden, the paper shared no common ground with Perón. Its first editorial set as the new daily's purpose the expression of "true public opinion,"[17] a professed goal that has remained constant throughout the paper's history. However, the publisher traditionally exercised firm and sole control over editorial policy.[18] In the mind of the member of the Paz family running the paper, "true public opinion" and the opinion of the publisher generally coincided. Since Perón believed that he alone was the authentic interpreter of the will of the people, a collision was inevitable.

As liberals in the United States embraced *La Prensa*, the newspaper became a symbol of democracy, an ironic twist in view of the paper's tolerance of electoral fraud during the Infamous Decade. Of course, most *La Prensa* supporters in the United States had never read the paper (no easy task because of its poor layout and turgid style). They acted as though it were a paradigm of responsible journalism, whereas in reality, at least in its political coverage, it was more like a stuffy version of a contemporary Hearst newspaper or the *Chicago Tribune*.

The opinion that *La Prensa* was a bad newspaper, of course, cannot excuse efforts to destroy it. From the very beginning of his presidency Perón made the daily a target of invective. Unlike opposition politicians, who could limit their public appearances, the newspaper became an inviting target of mob violence. It occupied a stately building on the Avenida de Mayo, a scant block from the Plaza de Mayo. On January 24, 1947, after a Perón speech on the five-year plan from the Casa Rosada balcony, a crowd apparently led by right-wing shock troops gathered outside *La Prensa*, shouted epithets ("Yankee-lovers! Traitors!"), and then launched an attack upon the bolted doors with stones conveniently heaped at a nearby construction site.[19] Tables from a cafeteria and iron grates supplemented their arsenal. They also tried to set fire to the building. The police were in no hurry to lift the siege.

The Peronists constantly accused *La Prensa* of being a tool of foreign interests but never produced any concrete evidence. The newspaper did in fact benefit from its overseas connections. For example, documents from the U.S. Office of Coordinator of Inter-American Affairs show that the wartime agency arranged for U.S. merchant marine vessels to carry scarce newsprint to Argentina for *La Prensa*'s use during the war.[20] But this does not prove that Washington had any control over the content of the paper. Peronists who have condemned *La Prensa* as being anti-national yet have found nothing objectionable in subsidies the Nazi German embassy paid to certain so-called nationalist newspapers elevate hypocrisy to giddy heights.

La Prensa's foreign friends did not always use prudence in defending the paper. U.S. embassy records show that in 1947 the United Press solicited congratulatory telegrams, on the occasion of the daily's seventy-eighth anniversary, from various U.S. cabinet members, as well as from the foreign offices of Great Britain, Sweden, Belgium, Brazil and Perú.[21] Letters from the Buenos Aires UP representative asking foreign governments to praise *La Prensa* fell into Perón's hands. His knowledge of the fact that the UP was then receiving from *La Prensa* a $10,000 monthly fee,[22] thought to be the highest sum paid by any newspaper to a news service, undoubtedly fortified his conviction that the overseas press had other interests besides the dissemination of news and was hardly objective about Argentina.

In 1949 the assault on *La Prensa* intensified.[23] Perhaps the decline of the Argentine economy inspired government efforts to choke off independent sources of information. A congressional committee formed to investigate reports that the police were torturing students and workers arrested for political reasons decided instead to scrutinize the financial operations of *La Prensa* and *La Nación*. The aim of this fishing expedition was to substantiate the accusation that the newspaper had illegally failed to pay duties on imports.

In early 1951, the noose tightened around *La Prensa*. A series of labor disputes beset the paper, and outbreaks of violence made it difficult to meet publication deadlines.[24] A *La Prensa* employee was shot and killed as he tried to enter the building. Congress "investigated" the matter, and on April 11, 1951, approved a bill expropriating the paper. By setting off against its present value the amount of past import duties the government claimed *La Prensa* owed, the Congress determined that Alberto Gainza Paz, the publisher, actually owed Argentina a substantial sum. He escaped to Uruguay, and then to the United States, where he poured fuel on a widespread outrage many North Americans felt about the incident. Meanwhile, Congress handed over the newspaper to the CGT, which resumed publication in November. At this point, only *La Nación* and *Clarín* among the Buenos Aires papers remained in non-Peronist hands. They survived by exercising great discretion. Nothing remotely critical of the administration appeared on their pages.

While Perón and his followers were "purifying" the political panorama, the labor movement was undergoing a similar process.[25] The government's authority to grant legal status to unions and its control over collective bargaining made it easy for the Ministry of Labor and CGT to stifle opposition elements within organized labor. The prosperity of the first several years of Peron's administration and the favorable treatment it afforded workers helped the regime to impose conformity upon the trade unions. There was no need to resort to naked repression. Of course, exceptions could be found, the most notorious involving the man who had become the symbol of labor opposition to Perón.

Cipriano Reyes clung stubbornly to the original ideals of the Labor party, even after virtually all its leaders and rank and file had defected to the new Peronist party. In the Congress, of the eighty-three deputies elected on the Labor slate, only Reyes and one colleague refused to join the Peronist ranks. Reyes soon found himself aligned with the Radical opposition on an increasing number of issues, but by this time he had lost his following in the meatpacking plants and was reduced to the role of gadfly.

He met with a member of the Soviet diplomatic mission in October at a time when, according to an FBI report, he was under surveillance by the Buenos Aires police.[26] Six weeks later, escorted by two bodyguards and armed with a revolver, he conferred with a U.S. embassy official, who described him as "a man of considerable native shrewdness," "certainly ambitious as well as opportunistic and probably fairly unscrupulous."[27]

The writer added that Reyes recognized the fight he faced, but seemed to accept it willingly, almost eagerly. If he wanted trouble, it soon came.

On July 4, 1947, as he left his home in La Plata to ride by taxi to Buenos Aires, an automobile pulled up alongside and a burst of machine-gun fire riddled his cab. The driver took a fatal hit. Reyes escaped with head wounds. He subsequently made a dramatic appearance in Congress, his head bandaged, to denounce the attempt. His assailants were never identified. It was suspected that a government official, responding to a vague suggestion by Perón that something be done about Reyes, arranged the ambush.[28] The incident foreshadowed a dark streak of violence that would plague the Argentine labor movement.

Though Reyes and his movement had been reduced to impotence, their mere existence bothered Perón. On January 30, 1948, the government stripped the Labor party of its legal status. This meant the Laborites could not participate in the March congressional elections. Thus Reyes lost his seat in the Chamber, as well as the privileges and immunities that went with it. Nonetheless, he refused to fold his tent. In the latter part of the year, as the first harbingers of a slump in the economy appeared, Perón decided that Cipriano Reyes was a luxury he could no longer afford. But the process of eliminating him developed some bizarre twists, involving such unlikely figures as John Griffiths, J. Edgar Hoover, U.S. Supreme Court Justice Robert Jackson, and the ubiquitous Nazi Martin Bormann.

The mood was set on September 8 when President Perón addressed a gathering of workers in Santa Fe, on the Paraná River north and slightly west of Buenos Aires. The speech reverberated with violent language uncharacteristic of Perón. The professional politicians, he intoned, "are beginning to engage in secret propaganda. . . . Once before they actually spoke of hanging us; my reply to that was the order to every descamisado to buy three meters of rope, without threatening anyone." But now "they are again talking of hanging us. We shall not buy rope again, but let it be understood that the Argentine people are beginning to feel tired of lies and threats." He added ominously: "I, who have asked for peace and order, shall not allow my voice to tremble the day when I order that they all be hanged."[29]

When the axe fell two weeks later, the victims of his wrath turned out to be the ragtag remnants of the Labor party. In the early morning hours of September 24, the Buenos Aires police chief summoned representatives of the press to disclose details of a frustrated plot on the lives of the president and first lady.[30] The assassination, the chief reported, had been planned for October 12. The authorities had just arrested the individuals who were planning the dastardly deed—Cipriano Reyes and eleven cohorts, most of whom belonged to the Labor party. A trio of priests were among those accused. (Two of them were released when it was confirmed that they had been merely visiting the third, an active member of the cabal, at the inopportune moment of his capture.) The police also implicated John Griffiths, formerly with the U.S. embassy in Argentina and at the time living in Uruguay.

With the first rays of dawn, people began to arrive in the Plaza de Mayo. By late afternoon, more than 200,000 had gathered, some carrying rope, others bearing scaffolds. A dummy dangled in the spring breezes from a noose attached to the frame of a building under construction next to the plaza. Perón's speech, singling out Griffiths for special mention, blamed the United States for instigating the plot. Ignoring his standard closing exhortation that the audience disperse peacefully, a portion of the crowd menaced the Banco de Boston building, which housed the U.S. embassy, but the police repulsed them.

The fact of the matter was that Reyes and his luckless colleagues had been entrapped by military officers who solicited from them political support for a phony coup.[31] The Laborites engaged in conversations with the fake conspirators, and this gave the government a pretext for the arrests.

Why Perón decided to throw an "assassination party," as U.S. embassy cables referred to the rally, was difficult to divine. He may have felt the need to stage a circus in order to take people's minds off the budding economic crisis or to whip up popular support for programs such as the proposed constitutional reform. An attack on the United States seemed peculiarly inopportune, since at the very moment Perón was denouncing the "Yankee imperialists," Ambassador Bruce was in the United States to promote U.S.-Argentine trade. The Peronist press toned down its attacks on the contrived North American involvement almost immediately. Moreover, the chief of police later confessed to Ambassador Bruce that the events arose from the need to "maintain for the government the strong support of the working class."[32]

The Griffiths connection was likewise difficult to fathom. Perón had been fully cognizant of his sympathies and activities when, in the guise of a cultural attaché, he served as a vital contact person with anti-Peronist elements during the Braden days. Upon his retirement from government service he had relocated in Montevideo, Uruguay, where he opened an export-import business. Yet the siren song of Argentine politics proved irresistible to him.

The Uruguayan capital attracted a growing number of anti-Peronist exiles, with whom Griffiths kept in close touch.[33] He was apparently on his own, as bitterly opposed to Perón as ever, partaking of the gossip that forms the lifeblood of any expatriate community. A cable to the State Department from the embassy in Buenos Aires discounted the possibility of his active involvement in any efforts to create labor unrest in Argentina or to instigate a coup. But it described him as a "chronic agitator" who "to say [the] least was indiscreet. [He w]as bitter in voicing criticism of Perón and Evita without any apparent thought as to who might be listening."[34] Thus he presented the Peronists with an inviting target.

Griffiths resolutely maintained his innocence. In the course of investigating the case, the embassy learned for the first time that its former "cultural attaché" had been engaged in a cloak-and-dagger caper worthy of a Grade-B Hollywood movie.[35] During his tour of duty in Buenos Aires, he had been gathering information, based upon the testimony of an Argentine friend, concerning Nazi activities in Argentina. This friend claimed to have actually lunched with Martin Bormann, the notorious Nazi war criminal, in Uruguay. In early 1948, Griffiths traveled to Washington and arranged an interview with Supreme Court Justice Robert H. Jackson, who had been the chief U.S. prosecutor at the Nuremberg war-criminal trials. He succeeded in convincing the justice that he had important new evidence of Bormann's whereabouts. Jackson contacted President Truman, who concluded that the matter merited at least some preliminary investigation, and requested that J. Edgar Hoover conduct an FBI check of Griffiths' story. Hoover dispatched an agent, who spent seven weeks in Uruguay and Argentina but could not substantiate the claim. Indeed, the agent began to develop a suspicion that Griffiths, whom he judged as unreliable, had spun his report out of whole cloth in an attempt to embarrass Perón.[36] Bormann's escape to Argentina remains to this day an unproven hypothesis.[37]

Meanwhile, the ill-starred Cipriano Reyes fell into the hands of members of the notorious "special section" of the police.[38] They used electric-shock torture in an effort to loosen his tongue and link him with Griffiths. The most they could wring from Reyes was the fact that he had once dined with the North American. They then shipped him off to prison. In April 1948 the judge who had ordered the confinement of the Laborite "plotters" decreed their release. A few days later the police rearrested them. Cipriano Reyes remained behind bars until Perón's overthrow in 1955. Of all those who suffered political persecution during this era, he seems to have been singled out for the harshest treatment. According to Eduardo Colom, it was because he had sworn to kill the president, and Perón knew he was capable of making good on his oath.[39]

In mid-1948 a correspondent for the *New Yorker* penned the following description of Argentina's political climate:

One does not encounter in Buenos Aires today the orthodox trapping of a dictatorship. Lurid and sensational reports to the contrary, a visitor feels no cold breath of terror, no weight of secret police. There are no restrictions on travel; people move about freely. Opponents of the regime have no fear of speaking to foreigners, meeting them at their hotels, or inviting them to their homes. There are no concentration camps, and, as far as a stranger can make out, no political prisoners.[40]

This was perhaps the best that might have been said about civil liberties in Argentina. The repressive aspects of Peronism could not help but appear relatively benign to the foreign observer measuring coercion against norms set by Nazi Germany or the Soviet Union. The Peronists would never approximate these depths, although the situation in Argentina would worsen five years later.

25

The Conductor

On April 9, 1949, the final day of a National Congress of Philosophy, a distinguished gathering of thinkers from nineteen nations listened to a lengthy disquisition by a speaker whose speculations on the human condition may have surprised many in the audience. President Juan D. Perón, still very much a lecturer at heart, took advantage of the conference to expound upon the philosophical roots of the Peronist movement. His discourse, later published in book form,[1] sought to place the Third Position in a historical perspective and justify the claim that it was an ideology.

Perón and his followers were apparently troubled by criticisms from those who found vagueness in the slogan calling for a "socially just, economically free, politically independent" Argentina and who pressed for a clear definition of Peronism. The president had essayed an explanation the previous year when he declared: "Peronism is humanism in action . . . a doctrine of social economy under which the distribution of our wealth . . . may be shared out fairly among all those who have contributed by their efforts to amass it. . . . Peronism is not learned, nor just talked about: one feels it or else disagrees. Peronism is a question of the heart rather than of the head."[2] He also stressed that the doctrine he preached was profoundly Christian and had papal encyclicals as its source. But these aphoristic pronouncements did not satisfy the need for a more serious, systematic explication of Peronism, which he sought to present in his 1949 ghostwritten lecture.

After sketching the history of philosophical thought in its quest for a delineation of human values, Perón rejected the collectivism of Hegel and Marx, the latter producing what he termed the "insectification" of the individual. In constant struggle with collectivism was a force Perón called individualism or egoism, easily recognizable as the wellspring of liberal capitalism and likewise denounced by the president.

The model advocated by Perón was a balance between collectivism and individualism, a search for communal well-being that would satisfy both earthly and spiritual needs. He labeled his goal an "organized community," the attainment of a perfect harmony between conflicting forces, "a state of justice, where each class exercises its functions for the benefit of all."[3] The Peronists would baptize their political philosophy *justicialismo*, a word that does not translate easily into English.[4]

For Perón, *justicialismo* synthesized ideas he had been espousing since his entry into politics. The new doctrine contained two elements that particularly appealed to his military outlook. The principle of unity, at the core of *justicialismo*, required a delicate balance of social classes and interest groups. As a prescription for the success of his political party it made excellent sense, since the Peronist movement was a coalition of workers, the army, portions of the middle class and certain entrepreneurs. But once Perón became president, an effort to impose unity upon a bitterly divided society inevitably led to repression.

In addition, because of the dynamic nature of the forces at play, the achievement of equilibrium required a considerable flexibility. This dovetailed with Perón's tendency to view politics in military terms and to utilize situational tactics to reach strategic goals. It also exposed him to barbs such as the observation that his "tactical contradictions are as natural to him as the twists and turns of his intestines."[5] Yet the flexibility in *justicialismo*, as manipulated by Perón, enabled it to survive and appear relevant to the changing world of the 1960s and 1970s. The tactical freedom it gave Perón brought astonishing results in these later years.

Unity and flexibility required verticality (or chain of command), a basic tenet of Peronism that provided a threadbare cloak for its authoritarian essence. Given the fractious, uncompromising nature of Argentines, there could be no balance of competing social forces without the intervention of an arbiter of last resort. Nor could a movement that accommodated a heterogeneous membership function without a leader, or, to use a term preferred by Perón, a *conductor*. Tactical flexibility in the military could be efficacious only if exercised by one person. Perón would apply this same principle to civilian politics.

Although *justicialismo* shared certain features with Fascism, attracted individuals with Fascist inclinations and relied upon a leader who was once an admirer of Mussolini, Peronism was not a criollo variant of Italian-style totalitarianism.[6] Perón exercised power and achieved stability by building a popular base of support among workers and others, and then by giving his people what they wanted. He did not demobilize the working class, as Mussolini had done, but rather politicized it. He never attempted to create institutions, such as associations representing economic sectors and subject to government control, which characterize the Fascist corporate state.[7] The ideology of Peronism did not take shape until several years after Perón came to power and reflected an effort to rationalize an alliance of forces he had already put together en route to political domination, as well as a political style he had adopted from a military model. *Justicialismo* was a form of populism reflecting Argentine reality, an amalgam of elements containing traces of authoritarianism, social democracy as embodied in the British Labor Party, and Roman Catholic social doctrine.

The attempt to systematize *justicialismo* as a doctrine foundered upon the shoals created by Perón's flexibility fetish. He insisted not only upon cultivating vagueness but also glorifying it as a virtue. This led to flights of nonsensical obscurantism such as the following passage from a speech on September 5, 1950:

> Peronism is not sectarian. Some say it is a centrist party: grave error. The centrist party, like that of the left and the right, is sectarian, and we are totally anti-sectarian. . . . Our Third Position is not a centrist position. It is an ideological position that is in the center, on the left or on the right, according to the circumstances. We obey circumstances. We believe we are not a cause, but rather a consequence, of those circumstances.[8]

On October 17, 1950, at the Plaza de Mayo celebration of what was now called "Loyalty Day," President Perón proclaimed to a large gathering the Twenty Truths of *justicialismo*,[9] a pithy distillation of the sum and substance of his new doctrine. "True democracy is the system where the government carries out the will of the people defending a single objective: the interests of the people," postulated truth number one, leaving open the question of how the will of the people was to be ascertained. According to truth number four, "There is only one class of men for the Peronist cause: the workers." The discrepancy between this maxim and truth number eleven—"Peronism desires the establishment of national unity"—would never cease to cause bedevilment, since one cannot claim to be a working-class movement and a multi-class alliance without eventually tripping over the contradiction. Aphorisms such as "the best of this land of ours is its people" encapsulated the political, social and economic goals of *justicialismo* in appropriately mushy terms. All in all, the Twenty Truths were not likely to rival the Ten Commandments or the Sermon on the Mount, but the Peronist faithful treated them as divinely inspired dogma.

In stark contrast to the ghostwritten 1949 speech that limned a theoretical, doctrinal framework for his movement, a series of lectures Perón delivered to a group of union officials in 1951 explored a subject to which he was able to bring his own personal ideas and judgments. *Conducción política (Political Leadership)*, the title given both to his talks and the book that reprinted them, provides a singular glimpse into the thought processes and values that guided Perón throughout his political career. Of the plethora of written materials which he himself produced or which appeared under his name, this collection is by far the most valuable, as it demonstrates clearly the extent to which he borrowed from military concepts to construct an approach to civilian leadership.

A base element of Perón's notion of leadership was the proposition that the leader* is born, not made. One can teach the techniques of leadership, but the art itself springs from within the gifted individual.

For Perón, politics, like warfare, meant conflict. Its goal was to impose one's will upon the "enemy." His definition of leadership applied equally to the military and political spheres. The leader is to be judged by results alone.[10] The corollary that ends justified means, though not made explicit, lurked in the shadows.

Another idea Perón borrowed from the military model was the need for centralized control in the hands of the *conductor*. This required him to explain what set the leader apart from the tyrant or dictator. His distinction was that political doctrine alone imposed restraints upon the leader.[11] Thus *justicialismo* was the sole rein that kept him from exercising absolute rule. But a close reading of his lectures points out how illusory a harness his political philosophy actually was. At various points he praised the elasticity of *justicialismo* and the need to make people not only understand it but feel it.[12] Doctrine must transcend abstraction, he urged, and convert into action. Moreover, he even made the startling admission that the choice of a slogan calling for an Argentina socially just, economically free and politically independent derived not from overriding doctrinal considerations but rather from strategic necessity.[13] So much for *justicialismo* as a constraint.

In politics as well as in the military, an essential component of leadership is the availability of a group of people capable of being led. In Perón's words, "to make a rabbit stew, the first thing you have to have is the rabbit."[14] A prerequisite for political leadership is the formation of what he called the mass, the civilian equivalent of the general's army, a citizenry not merely willing but ready and able to be led.[15]

The relationship between *conductor* and mass was of critical importance. The leader's first task is to locate his mass. (This, Perón confessed, explained his decision to take charge of the Secretariat of Labor and Public Welfare.[16]) Next, he must train his mass by inculcating them with doctrine, so that—here he injected a soccer metaphor—"everybody kicks toward the same goal."[17] He must organize his followers in a simple structure, yet one cohesive enough to ensure stability. An indoctrinated,

---

* Throughout the lectures, Perón used the word *conductor* rather than *líder*, an indication of his view that the leader coordinates and guides people toward a common goal, in the manner of an orchestra conductor. The translation of *conductor* as leader should not obscure this nuance of meaning.

organized mass then becomes transformed into a people or community conscious of its rights and duties.

No one who ever watched Perón perform in front of a mass audience could miss the symbiotic relationship between them. According to Arturo E. Sampay, who wrote many of his speeches,

> Perón seemed in a trance in front of a crowd. He could divine what they were feeling and what they wanted. Once, during an anti-Yankee campaign, he had to give a speech and wanted to shift to a more positive line. Two hours beforehand, he asked me to give him some ideas on improving U.S.-Argentine relations. But when he went before the microphones, he delivered a completely opposite speech, attacking the United States. Afterward he walked over to me, shrugged his shoulders, and said: "Sorry, but it just came out differently. We'll have to wait for another opportunity." He was like a medium.[18]

It is important to grasp what Perón meant when he stressed that the civilian leader must convince his followers before he can lead them. This requirement of persuasion related only to the acceptance of leadership, and not to every order issued by the leader. "How could I lead a great movement," he asked, "if each time I made a decision I had to ask the Peronists whether they agreed with what I intended to do?"[19]

Conducción política exposes the amorality underlying Perón's approach to politics. What succeeds is good, and success justifies the mantle of leadership. But strategic goals, as elaborated by *justicialismo*, must remain elastic and loosely defined, not because of any intrinsic value in vagueness, but to assure they can be reached. Since achievement of this changeable goal is the measure of success, doctrinal flexibility primarily benefits not the mass but the leader—i.e., Perón.

Perón's lifestyle, shaped by a long army career, remained unchanged by his new station. He kept his desk neat, his pencil sharpened, his hair cut and his shoes shined.[20] He was ostentatious only in his fondness for military garb. When the occasion demanded, he could bedeck himself in any number of splendid uniforms. He entertained a particular weakness for dashing capes.

His culinary preferences remained underdeveloped. Shortly after the inauguration, he proudly confided to some close friends that he had engaged an excellent new cook and invited them to dinner. Hopes for a gourmet feast were dashed when the president disclosed to his assembled guests that the chef had previously supervised the preparation of food at a local hospital. Then they all sat down to a predictably institutional meal.[21]

It was an inside joke among Peronists that when the *conductor* asked you to eat with him, you would be well advised to arrange for supplementary food either beforehand or afterward. He was perfectly content to dine on stew or a simple steak and salad, washed down with ordinary table wine. Nor was he averse to helping prepare food when the occasion permitted. At a farm he owned in San Vicente, it was not an uncommon sight to find him mixing ingredients for a homemade mayonnaise.[22]

Though he lived in a huge mansion on the Avenida Alvear on the edge of the Barrio Norte, he took little interest in the comfort or elegance of his home environment. The sole concession to his tastes were contributions from brother Mario. A pair of royal deer and gazelles graced the grounds of the downtown residence. Ostriches, storks, guanacos, flamingos and llamas roamed about the premises at San Vicente. A blackbird named Negro lived in the mansion and liked to perch on a presidential shoulder.[23]

The work schedule he followed was a direct carryover from his military days. He rose at six and arrived at the Casa Rosada by seven. He returned to the residence for lunch with Evita in the early afternoon and then was chauffeured back to his office, where he worked until ten or eleven in the evening.

For diversion, Perón enjoyed the company of his poodles, of whom he was inordinately fond. He spent most weekends with Evita on the farm in San Vicente, where they rode horses together and watched cowboy movies. The president maintained his keen interest in boxing and was a frequent ringside spectator at Luna Park matches. He also had a passion for riding motorcycles, speedboats and racing cars.

Perón's love for sports became an instrument of national policy.[24] Social programs began to emphasize athletics as a means of promoting public health and popular culture. The government constructed recreational facilities and encouraged widespread participation in sports, especially on the part of young people.

There were, of course, other dividends to be gained from sports. Perón made every effort to identify himself with successful athletes and share in their glory. He understood the bread-and-circus aspect of mass psychology, whereby fanatical dedication to a team or individual athlete could serve to absorb energies that might otherwise be directed to politics, and to deflect attention from economic problems that were beginning to buffet the nation. He also recognized the domestic propaganda value flowing from triumphs in international competitions. The president readily accepted the title "First Sportsman of Argentina" and secured maximum advantage from the victories won by Argentine athletes during his presidency. These included three gold medals in the 1948 London Olympic Games—one of them for Delfo Cabrera's triumph in the prestigious marathon—along with the stunning successes of race-driver Juan Fangio and fine performances by golfer Roberto DeVicenzo.

Any list of Juan Perón's imperfections would have to include a peculiar gullibility that made him susceptible to bizarre ideas. Two incidents that occurred during his first presidency illustrate this weakness: the sagas of the Bolivian pseudo-dentist and the Austrian atomic scientist.

Of all Perón's physical attributes, his famous smile may have been the most precious. Therefore, when the president developed problems with his teeth, it was a matter of grave concern.[25] Dr. Guardo advised removal of the diseased teeth and constructed a model prosthesis that would restore the presidential grin to its pristine luster. Miguel Miranda, however, told Perón about a Bolivian dentist who had recently arrived in Buenos Aires and utilized novel techniques to save rotting teeth. The president consulted the Bolivian, who convinced him to undergo the new treatment. The dentist from La Paz gave him intramuscular injections and then applied a coat of cementlike substance to the four or five loose teeth that were bothering him. Meanwhile, Guardo, having discovered that his patient had abandoned him, complained to Evita, who berated her husband for permitting himself to be treated by the Bolivian. Perón agreed to seek further consultation.

Dr. Stanley D. Tylman, a prominent U.S. dentist, happened to be in Buenos Aires at a conference and was summoned to the residence. In the presence of the Bolivian and Dr. Oscar Ivanissevich, the Argentine ambassador to the United States, Dr. Tylman looked at Perón's teeth. His reaction, in the form of an exclamatory comment in English, caused the Bolivian to attempt to usher him hastily out of the room. Ivanissevich, who understood what the North American had said, insisted upon a further examination. Dr. Tylman then explained the extent of the dental malpractice that had been perpetrated.*

Perón's teeth had to be pulled. The Bolivian had his license to practice in Argentina revoked. An investigation into his background revealed that he had purchased his dental degree from a Bolivian university in the chaotic days following the end of the Chaco War.

The cement-in-the-mouth caper was an in-house sideshow when compared with the nuclear-energy spectacular Perón directed in 1951. Unfortunately for the president, the performance attracted an international audience and turned out to be pure farce, with Perón in one of the comic leads.[26]

Argentina and the rest of the world first learned of a sensational new discovery in the field of nuclear science on March 24, 1951, when the president summoned reporters to the Casa Rosada to announce that "controlled thermonuclear reactions on a technical scale" had been produced at an experimental station on Huemul Island in western Argentina.[27] Neither uranium, plutonium nor tritium had been used to achieve this

---

* In a speech to the Michigan State Dental Association in 1952, Dr. Tylman declared: "I examined President Perón's mouth and found conditions calling for extensive treatment. The conditions of infection had not been recognized by the dentist who treated Perón, but I felt that if untended they might have caused his death in a matter of weeks from systematic poisoning. Already the president was a very sick man." *Detroit Times*, April 23, 1952, p. C-35.

result. He stressed that the process was entirely new and would be utilized to harness nuclear power for peaceful purposes only. He then introduced to the journalists the man responsible for the breakthrough: Ronald Richter.

Richter had credentials that lent some substance to his claim. Born in a district of Austria that later became part of Czechoslovakia, he obtained his doctorate in natural sciences from a university in Prague and during World War II worked on improving the design of high-speed airplanes for the Luftwaffe. This brought him into contact with Professor Kurt Tank, one of the top Nazi experts in aerodynamics.

Near the end of the war, Richter encountered problems with the Gestapo, who suspected him of being a British spy and restricted his activities. Professor Tank had better luck. He was one of a number of German scientists and technicians who managed to flee from the Third Reich to Argentina. He and some of his former colleagues installed themselves in a military-aviation factory in Córdoba, where they developed facilities for the design and production of planes for the Argentine air force.

At the war's end, Richter wandered from country to country in Europe. By now he had become interested in nuclear physics, but was unable to find work that suited him. In 1948, at Tank's suggestion, an Argentine official contacted him in Paris and invited him to fly to Buenos Aires. The thirty-nine-year-old scientist readily agreed and arrived on August 16. Eight days later, he went to the Casa Rosada for an interview with the president.

Perón listened intently to the Spanish translation of Richter's earnest exposition of what he claimed were novel theories about nuclear technology. No doubt still enthralled by German efficiency, the *conductor* agreed to support Richter's experiments. No investigation was conducted to determine whether any scientific basis underlay the grandiose scheme the Austrian was proposing. For Perón it seemed like a golden opportunity to bring Argentina into the atomic age.

Richter began his work in Córdoba, but soon demanded his own laboratory. On July 21, 1949, the decision was made to build a new research center on Huemul Island, near the picturesque Andean resort of Bariloche. A team of scientists headed by Richter then went to work in search of ways to harness the power of the atom.

On March 22, 1950, a somewhat reluctant Richter had Argentine citizenship thrust upon him. He had not yet completed the two-year residency required by law, but the government waived this condition in its haste to number him among the citizenry.

The crash program on which Richter had embarked bore its first fruits on February 16, 1951, when the scientist informed Perón that he had produced and controlled nuclear energy through a process of fusion. The president jubilantly seized upon the news as proof that Argentina had reached the forefront of the race to control the atom. Although there is some evidence that the President had doubts about Richter's claim,* Perón could not resist the temptation to make the news public in the most politically opportune way. The moment he chose for the announcement coincided with the opening of an OAS conference of foreign ministers, and with a rising chorus of foreign criticism of Peronist repression of *La Prensa*. Both the president's own statement and newspaper accounts were careful to refer to Richter as an Argentine citizen. (One headline even called him a gaucho.[28]) Several days later, the "wizard of Huemul" received an honorary degree from the University of Buenos Aires.

In late June both Richter and Perón were promising the completion of an atomic plant in six to eight months.[29] Their grand scheme involved the use of nuclear energy to fuel Argentina's heavy industry, which suffered from a scarcity of coal. The president sharply denounced rumors denigrating his atomic project, and in a burst of bombast warned that Argentina was capable of repelling any foreign aggression aimed at stealing or destroying her nuclear capability.

But by early 1952, the wizard's promises had produced no results, and Perón found himself under pressure to subject Richter's work to impartial evaluation. After several investigations by Argentine scientists, it became painfully apparent that the project was semblance without substance. On November 22, 1952, the government closed down the facility at Huemul and tried to forget about the whole affair.†[30]

Anecdotal evidence suggests that Perón also may have had a weakness for spiritism. A U.S. embassy official reported rumors that Evita's mother organized spiritist sessions and that "President Perón believes himself to be in direct contact with the Liberator General San Martín through current seances."[31] An anti-Peronist accused Perón of inviting a Brazilian medium to practice his arts in the Casa Rosada.[32] Perón later denied that the medium had influenced him in any way but admitted receiving him for the purpose of humoring the Brazilian government, which he said contained many spiritists. He called the medium a "serious man" and his performance "nothing to laugh at, far from it."[33] His open-mindedness toward spiritism would cause problems in 1950 and disaster in his twilight years.

---

* Perón was reported to have told Prince Bernhard of the Netherlands that he was suspicious of Richter, and to have requested Dutch assistance. He added that he would not seek help from the North Americans or the British because they would keep Richter's findings for themselves. Chapin (The Hague) to secretary of state, 735.5611/6-751, June 7, 1951.

† Despite its absurdity, the Richter episode demonstrates Perón's amazing luck in achieving historical vindication. The creation of a National Commission on Atomic Energy at this early date provided an institutional framework that stimulated research and gave Argentina a preeminence she still enjoys among Latin nations in the nuclear field.

26

At the Pinnacle

In many ways 1950 turned out to be a pivotal year for the government, the *conductor* himself and his first lady. Perón's political mastery had eliminated all genuine challengers to him. His competent associates and advisors had almost all fallen by the wayside. His inner circle offered nothing but escalating adulation. The five-year plan had accomplished as much as it could within the constraints of available resources. Growing economic difficulties had converted a brave new idea into a salvage operation. Organized labor, virtually incorporated into the government, formed a pillar of support for Perón, but its leaders were losing touch with the rank and file as wage restraints imposed in the fight against inflation made workers realize that their interests might not necessarily coincide with those of the state. Finally, Evita's political career was reaching its zenith, yet clouds were gathering on the horizon.

The March gubernatorial elections in four provinces gave Perón occasion for reasserting his popularity among the voters. He toured the country and made a number of appearances in Buenos Aires Province, where Domingo Mercante was seeking reelection.[1] Mercante was highly popular and would win in a landslide. Aware of the governor's stature not only as crown prince but also as a potential competitor, Perón may have wanted to make certain that the results in Buenos Aires Province could also be read as a vote of confidence in him.

What invested the campaign with even more significance was the nomination of Ricardo Balbín as the Radical party candidate. El Chino, a nickname his Oriental features had earned for him, was the acknowledged leader of his party and its probable standard-bearer in the next presidential election. In late 1949, the Peronist majority had expelled him from the Chamber of Deputies because of disrespectful language he had supposedly used in a speech in Rosario,[2] and for several months he had to keep one step ahead of the police, an impediment to his ability to campaign in the province, although he did manage to appear at rallies, speak and then elude his pursuers. On election day, he turned up at the polls to vote and was arrested as he departed. He remained behind bars until Perón pardoned him on January 2, 1951.

The new economic team the president installed in 1949 struggled in vain on a slope made even more slippery by inflation, unfavorable terms of international trade, and a drop in industrial and agricultural output. The coming election prevented resort to measures that might have reversed the downward trend, because they would also have alienated the Peronist constituency. Therefore, government economists had to confine themselves to a holding operation that could at best merely decelerate the slide.[3] The last thing Perón needed at this moment was a drought, but in early 1950 the fertile topsoil of the countryside began to parch.

Argentina's economic posture vis-à-vis the United States was also in a state of crisis. What had become a chronic dollar shortage prevented the importation of critical materials from the United States. Restrictions on the outflow of dollars in private hands and government policies such as the maintenance of wages at high levels made life difficult for North American companies doing business in Argentina. This in turn discouraged additional foreign investment at a time when Perón needed capital from abroad in order to stimulate the growth essential to the success of the five-year plan.

The solution Washington deemed most appropriate for Perón's economic ills was a loan from the U.S. Export-Import Bank to a consortium of Argentine banks to enable the country to pay off financial obligations to North American exporters. The State Department supported the proposed loan on both economic and political grounds.[4] Moreover, in the course of working out the details, the North Americans were able to wring from Perón a satisfying solution to a number of outstanding problems, including various complaints against the government by U.S.-owned meatpacking plants, Argentine approval of a Braniff Airlines request to extend its routes to Buenos Aires, the granting of import permits on favorable terms to U.S. motion-picture distributors, and finally, the big prize, Argentine ratification of the 1947 Treaty of Rio de Janeiro, which had formalized a system of mutual defense in the Americas.

Perón on his part recognized Argentina's desperate need for dollars, but also knew he had to protect his image as a nationalist. As late as May 1, with rumors of the negotiations flying thickly, he was reiterating to the Congress a solemn pledge he had previously made: "I will cut off my hands before signing anything that amounts to a loan to my country."[5] When news of the $125 million agreement finally broke, Perón took refuge in semantics and called it a "credit." His enemies gleefully dubbed him Venus de Milo.[6]

As the ink was still drying on the deal with the Export-Import Bank, North Korean troops poured across the 38th parallel into South Korea. The United States announced it would go to the defense of the beleaguered South Koreans, and the UN Security Council voted to intervene militarily. Both the Third Position and Perón's statesmanship would now be put to the test.

The president's initial response was to notify the Security Council that he supported its decision, and to instruct his ambassador in Washington to convey to the State Department his approval of the prompt U.S. action.[7] The latter message was consistent with his oft-repeated commitment to stand by the United States in any armed conflict with the Communist bloc.

However, this raised the issue of the extent of Argentina's support. In response Perón exhibited what most charitably might be called creative indecision. At the annual comradeship dinner of the armed forces in July, he again expressed solidarity with the United Nations, whose officials interpreted this to mean that Argentina would send military aid to South Korea. Then reporters at a press conference heard Perón praise Washington for sending troops into battle and proclaim that his government would make a worthy contribution to the UN cause. When asked to elaborate, he trotted out one of his pet aphorisms: *"Mejor que decir es hacer"* (the equivalent of "Actions speak louder than words").[8]

At this point he seemed on the verge of departing from the traditional Argentine policy of neutrality. Rumors heightened a growing atmosphere of tension, especially within organized labor. Street demonstrations in Buenos Aires and Rosario protested the sending of Argentine troops to Asia. Whether they were inspired by ultra-nationalists, Communists, or Peronist union leaders, or whether the actions were spontaneous outbursts by the rank and file, it seems clear that the government did not instigate them and that they gave expression to widely held popular sentiment. Perón, the self-proclaimed interpreter of the Argentine people, had no other recourse than to give public assurance that the Argentine armed forces would remain at home. "I will do what the people want," he meekly explained.[9]

The thaw in U.S.-Argentine relations during the first half of 1950 was merely a swing in the pendulum. By August, Perón was again criticizing the United States and described the Korean War as a conflict between Communists and capitalists.[10] But 1950 also witnessed a more significant, longer-range shift in Argentina's relationship with the United States. For the first time the value of U.S. imports from Argentina exceeded those of Great Britain. In addition, the value of North American investments in Argentina surpassed Britain's total.[11] Finally, the United States stood poised on the verge of regaining its prewar position as Argentina's primary supplier of goods. The Peronist crusade for economic independence had clearly failed to prevent a greater-than-ever dependence upon the Yankees.

Though the new Peronist constitution permitted presidential reelection, Perón repeatedly insisted that he would not be a candidate. This merely inspired his loyal followers to redouble their pleas that he run for a second term. In April 1950, the CGT called a special congress "to manifest its vehement desire that General Perón be reelected president of the Argentine nation in order to assure the prosecution of his historic work in favor of the country and of its laboring masses."[12]

Despite constant affirmations of loyalty, the CGT still could not count upon the monolithic backing of the entire proletariat. Strikes, often encouraged by the government in the early stages of the Perón era as a means of achieving the higher salary levels that "social justice" demanded, continued to break out, even though official policy now frowned upon them.[13] Bank employees, printers, sugar workers and meatpackers stopped work in defiance of the Ministry of Labor. These were by no means political actions. The striking unions professed their undying devotion to Perón, but found it necessary to respond to pressure from workers who had resolved to defend their economic interests against the ravages of inflation.

In late 1949, the most serious of the strikes erupted. Railroad workers, frustrated by delays in negotiations over salaries and fringe benefits, began to interrupt rail service. The Unión Ferroviaria, representing all railway employees except engineers, denounced the stoppage as an "attack [on] the homeland, *justicialismo*, and General Perón."[14] The government, declaring the strike illegal, called it part of an international Communist conspiracy to shut down transportation systems in the West. Perón fired his minister of transportation. Evita made personal appearances to urge the workers to return to their jobs, all to no avail.

Perón finally broke the strike in January by decreeing a military mobilization that in effect drafted the railroad workers into the army and subjected them to military law. Undoubtedly Socialist and Communist labor leaders could be found within the leadership of the strikers. There was also some evidence that Governor Mercante, through whose province most of the railroad lines ran, may have tried to utilize the conflict for his own purposes.[15] But these factors did not make the strike political. It was in the government's interest to politicize the conflict and to portray it as an attack upon Perón. An admission that economic considerations motivated the workers would undercut the basic Peronist premise that the interests of the working class coincided with those of the state.

Though Eva Perón once described herself as a sparrow,[16] by 1950 the heights to which she was soaring suggested that her metaphor was far too modest. The first lady had consolidated her roles within the Peronist movement and was pressing forward with all the energy and enthusiasm she could muster.

Her hand was most visible in the work of the María Eva Duarte de

Perón Social Aid Foundation, which had grown into a gigantic enterprise embracing virtually all public as well as private welfare activity and extending into the fields of health and education.[17] Launched in 1948, the foundation quickly attracted an outpouring of voluntary contributions reflecting bona fide generosity augmented by the euphoric pulse of the evanescent economic boom, as well as the self-interest of individuals and groups eager to ingratiate themselves with the first lady. In order to carry out the many projects she had in mind, Evita became persuaded of the need to stabilize the foundation's income. This she achieved when the CGT agreed to contribute two days' pay per year from every worker's salary (May 1 and October 12, both paid holidays), and every worker's annual salary increase for one month, beginning in 1949. A year later, with the foundation operating at flank speed, a government decree transferred to it 20 percent of the annual income from the national lottery.

Although the María Eva Duarte de Perón Foundation maintained the façade of a private organization, in substance it could hardly be distinguished from a government entity and gave every indication of becoming a state within a state. Evita served as president, with Perón's treasury minister as its administrator. Its headquarters were located in a government building. A federal law exempted the foundation from taxation. State support clearly augmented its ability to raise money, although Perón did draw the line at direct government subsidy and vetoed a bill that would have appropriated funds to the foundation from the public fisc. The private nature of the foundation also made it easy to justify one of its distinctive characteristics—the absence of any strict accounting of income and expenses. This encouraged rumors that Evita and her intimates were enriching themselves in the process, a charge that has never been proven.

The foundation's actual record was impressive. The organization built homes for orphans, unwed mothers and the elderly; shelters for working women; lunch facilities for schoolchildren; children's hospitals; vacation colonies for workers; low-cost housing; schools for nurses. Many of these projects were located far from the capital and brought social welfare to the interior for the first time. On several highly publicized occasions, the foundation dispatched foreign aid, such as provisions for Ecuadorian earthquake victims, toys for Italian children, and even clothing for needy children in Washington.

An undertaking especially dear to Evita's heart was the Children's Village, constructed on the outskirts of Buenos Aires. In the words of U.S. Ambassador James Bruce,

It has tiny houses, shops, banks, a school, a church and jail, luxurious dormitories, dining rooms and playrooms. In theory, two hundred poor children aged from two to five years live there, and eight hundred more come in by the day. After a two-hour tour a visiting diplomat's wife commented: "This is the wish fulfillment of a little girl who had never had a doll's house of her own."[18]

Fleur Cowles, author of a harshly critical book about Evita, found the village empty and lifeless, a theatrical set kept in readiness for a play that would never be performed.[19] On the basis of her single cursory visit, she intimated that children scarcely if ever used its facilities, and that its sole function was to impress gullible tourists.

The suggestion that insincerity lurked behind the first lady's preoccupation with children is nonsensical. Unable to have children of her own, Evita compensated by attempting to spread her protective wings over the young people of the entire nation, and especially the less fortunate, with whom she could readily identify. She bore with great pride the honorary title "Spiritual Mother of All Argentine Children." Moreover, Perón himself had always felt a special affinity for youth. "In the New Argentina the only privileged ones are the children," proclaimed one of the Twenty Truths of *justicialismo*. It was not an empty slogan.

The annual Argentine Children's Soccer Championship, inaugurated in 1949 and reaching full stride the following year, typified Evita's genuine concern for the young. The foundation underwrote a soccer tournament for boys thirteen years of age or younger, organized in squads representing the various professional teams throughout the country. The participants wore the team uniforms and played before cheering crowds in their stadiums. A series of elimination matches determined a national champion. The tournament not only made childhood dreams come true but also provided a first opportunity for many youngsters, especially those from the interior, to have a physical examination and to experience supervised athletic training.

The María Eva Duarte de Perón Foundation translated into action the Peronist philosophy of social justice. In her ghostwritten autobiography, Evita labored to differentiate the foundation's work from traditional programs to aid the less fortunate. "It is not philanthropy, nor is it charity, nor is it alms nor is it social solidarity, nor it is benevolence. It is not even social welfare," she insisted. "To me it is strict justice." She went on to explain that "alms and benevolence, to me, are an ostentation of riches, and power to humiliate the humble . . . what I give belongs to those who receive it. I do nothing but return to the poor what the rest of us owe them, because we had [*sic*] taken it away from them unjustly."[20]

This rather ingenuous distinction overlooked the simple fact that if the poor were being unfairly milked, the Peronist government should have tried to eliminate this injustice at the roots rather than dispense palliatives. But Perón was never of a mind to bring about a truly radical redistribution of wealth in Argentina. Evita's Robin Hood approach served him better. It did not disturb the status quo, but did bring tangible political dividends. Every structure built or used by the foundation bore its name prominently, and every foundation activity drew accolades from the Peronist press. Perón could enjoy the benefits, but could also disclaim responsibility when the foundation came under criticism for activities such as extorting funds from private businesses[21] and intervening against workers in labor disputes.[22]

Across the Paseo Colón from the Union Bar, where tango singers voiced melodic complaints about cruel fate and heartless women, Evita's foundation took over a parcel of land owned by the University of Buenos Aires and raised upon it a neo-Grecian temple to serve as its headquarters. Statues of the first lady in various poses lined the edge of the roof above each of the Doric columns; this gave the façade of the building a severe aspect hardly appropriate to the style or substance of the great charitable enterprise.

On September 29, 1950, the institution underwent an official name change and became the Eva Perón Foundation. This corresponded to a transformation of the first lady's image that had begun earlier and reflected her new identity.[23] The official press now referred to her as Eva Perón, a much less awkward designation and more suitable to a political figure of substance.

By 1950 there remained not the slightest doubt that she wielded enormous power within the Peronist movement. Her archenemy, Juan Bramuglia, had been forced to resign from the Ministry of Foreign Affairs, José Figuerola had been replaced by Raúl Mendé, a onetime Jesuit seminarian who enjoyed her confidence, and Dr. Armando Méndez San Martín, appointed minister of education in 1950, was reputed to owe his nomination to Evita. Her influence continued to be decisive, as it had been from the beginning of the term, in the staffing of lower positions in the federal bureaucracy.

The extent of her influence upon organized labor at this point is less certain. José Espejo, the CGT's secretary-general, was one of her most slavish followers. It is likely that through him she was able to affect appointments to jobs within the various union bureaucracies. She was also participating in the settlement of labor disputes. During the 1950–1951 railway strike she made a dramatic visit to rebellious workers in an effort to persuade them to return to their jobs.

She also stood at the forefront of a constituency that was becoming a significant element of the Peronist movement. On July 26, 1949, the women's branch of the Peronist party sprouted into existence, and shortly afterward Evita was chosen as its first president. The new organization launched a massive membership drive and would soon compete for positions on the Peronist slates of candidates in federal, provincial and local elections. In late 1950, the first rumors that Evita would be the party's nominee for vice-president on a Perón-Perón ticket suggested how far and in what direction this process had carried.

Although her political power kept expanding, Evita remained as dependent as ever upon her husband. In a three-hour speech to women delegates at a Peronist convention on July 25, 1949, the first lady postulated that "for women, to be a Peronist means, above all, loyalty to Perón, subordination to Perón and blind trust in Perón."[24] As she gained political momentum, the praise she heaped upon Perón became more extravagant, and the exhortations to total subservience more insistent.

On June 14, 1950, Eva Perón addressed a national conference of governors in Buenos Aires. To her usual expressions of fidelity to the *conductor*, she added a new note: "I think the best tribute I can give each day to General Perón is to burn my life on the altar of happiness for the lowly. . . . The best tribute I can render to him is to try to interpret his ideas of love of country and collaborate modestly but feverishly, until death if necessary, to safeguard the cause of Perón. . . ."[25] For the audience, by now no doubt inured to her hyperbole, these morbid phrases may have meant nothing special. In retrospect, however, they were grimly prophetic.

On the morning of Monday, January 9, 1950, as temperatures in the center of Buenos Aires soared toward the day's high of 38 degrees C. (100 degrees F.), Eva Perón accompanied a group of government dignitaries to the inauguration of a new headquarters of the Taxi Drivers' Union. In the middle of the customary invocation by a priest, a stabbing inguinal pain convulsed her. She managed to mask her discomfort and weather the ceremony, after which she complained to Dr. Oscar Ivanissevich, the current minister of education. He wanted to examine her as soon as possible, but she insisted it was nothing serious. Several days later, she called him to say that the pain had worsened. Ivanissevich gave her a complete checkup and diagnosed her condition as acute appendicitis. On January 12 he performed surgery on her.

Official bulletins assured the descamisados that the operation had been successful. However, if Dr. Ivanissevich is to be believed, a stark drama was unfolding behind the scenes. According to statements he made many years later, while the first lady was hospitalized she underwent tests that revealed she was suffering from uterine cancer; he proposed a hysterectomy, but she angrily refused, maintaining that there was nothing wrong with her and that the diagnosis was the work of her enemies, who sought to eliminate her from politics.[26] Four months later, Ivanissevich resigned from Perón's cabinet, apparently under pressure from Evita. The surgeon pointed out that Evita's mother had had a similar cancer, but submitted to a hysterectomy and lived to a ripe old age (seventy-seven) before succumbing to the disease.

Verifiable information about the deterioration of Evita's health does not exist. However, the legend of Eva Perón the Martyr has taken a prominent spot in Peronist mythology, to the effect that Evita's love for the poor caused her to sacrifice her energy, her health, and in the end, her life.[27]

Health problems had haunted Eva Perón throughout her adult life. The frailty of her constitution served only to inflame her determination to reach as quickly as possible the goals she had set for herself. During the early years of Perón's first term, she occasionally succumbed to sickness or exhaustion. According to Raúl Salinas, an official of the municipality of Buenos Aires who accompanied her on a political trip to Tucumán in early December 1946, she fainted in the midsummer heat yet struggled to complete her scheduled appearances.[28] Physical difficulties beset her during the Rainbow Tour. In September 1947, when a U.S. diplomat suggested that she slow down her pace, she replied that she couldn't because the descamisados needed her.[29] In the Peronist newspaper *Democracia,* a eulogistic account of her daily activities in mid-1948 contained the following passage:

> Her health is not what could be desired. An acute bronchitis makes her cough often. She asks for aspirin and tea. The rings under her eyes are even more pronounced because of the paleness of her face. She is cold, and they put an overcoat over her shoulders.[30]

In August 1949, a U.S. military attaché quoted her as admitting she had shed ten kilos (twenty-two pounds) during the past year.[31] Whether this weight loss resulted from illness or dieting (in which she indulged to keep a slender figure) or some combination of both, she did not say.

There are indications that Evita was known for some time to be suffering from a chronic ailment. The Spanish ambassador to Buenos Aires noted that the color of her skin had become "suspicious,"[32] an observation confirmed by Raúl Salinas, who has described her coloring as amber, emitting an insalubrious though attractive glow.[33] He added that her condition was originally diagnosed as anemic, and that she began to receive injections long before her 1950 operation. Nini Montiam, a Spanish actress who enjoyed a close friendship with the first lady, claims to have witnessed the administration of blood transfusions during this same period.[34] In a book published during his exile, Perón declared that the first symptoms of Evita's illness became apparent in late 1949, and he called it "a strong anemia."[35] Others believed she was suffering from leukemia.[36]

Dr. Pedro Ara, a Spanish physician who served as a cultural attaché at the Franco regime's embassy in Buenos Aires, and who would later embalm Evita's body, has given some illuminating testimony about her physical condition and capacity to transcend it. He had never examined her professionally but had heard reports that she was suffering from anemia.

At an October 17 celebration, probably in 1948,* Dr. Ara had the opportunity to stand next to Evita as she delivered a thirty-minute speech from the Casa Rosada balcony. He watched her very carefully for signs of fatigue or heavy breathing that an anemic person would display under great emotional and physical stress. At the finish of a stem-winding performance she was as fresh as when she began. Accepting her anemia as fact, he concluded that he had witnessed "a case of inexplicable biological and physical resistance; a case of a colossal victory of willpower over bodily weakness."[37]

Anemia was not her only health problem. An authoritative book about the first lady asserts, without citing sources, that her afflictions included constant vaginal discharges which from 1949 on made it impossible for her to have sexual relations.[38] This symptom seems related to the cancer Ivanissevich claims to have detected in January 1950.

For Evita to have escaped the immediate consequences of serious illness, her condition would have had to be discovered in time, and she would have had to receive proper treatment. If Dr. Ivanissevich had in fact made an accurate diagnosis during her hospitalization for appendicitis, it is quite possible that a hysterectomy would have removed or arrested the malignancy. What we do not know is exactly what he told her, whether he also revealed these facts to Perón, and how the president reacted.

One possible interpretation is that the first lady could not bring herself to permit the removal of her womb. For psychological and even cultural reasons, the "Spiritual Mother of All Argentine Children" perhaps could not cope with the symbolism inherent in a hysterectomy. Rather than face the crisis in a rational manner, she may have seized upon the paranoid suspicion that the diagnosis was somehow the work of enemies who wanted not merely to force her into a prolonged convalescence but also to destroy her last physical link to motherhood. Her subsequent drive for the vice-presidential nomination could have represented an effort to sublimate the knowledge that she had cancer.

It is also possible that she did not really understand how sick she was. Delia Parodi, one of Eva's intimate friends, has opined that "in the beginning she did not have a true appreciation of her malady."[39] Her ignorance might have resulted from an inadequate explanation by the doctor, or from the fact that her uterine cancer was not really diagnosed in January 1950.

---

* He did not specify the year. However, he described what he called the first performance of the march *"Los muchachos peronistas"* ("The Peronist Boys") in front of Perón. Dr. Ivanissevich composed the lyrics to the song, an old tune originally borrowed by the printers' union and converted into a march called "The Peronist Printers." Its initial performance was in 1948. *El Cronista Comercial,* April 19, 1974 (obituary of Dr. Ivanissevich). If the events depicted by Dr. Ara did occur in 1948, then Perón's statement that the first symptoms of Evita's anemia appeared in late 1949 was in error.

From the facts presently available, it is impossible to assess the quality of the treatment she was receiving. The only evidence of malpractice comes from testimony of Atilio Renzi, the superintendent of the residence, who described an incident occurring after her condition had worsened considerably: "One day a blunderer gave her radiotherapy so carelessly and incompetently that he burned her to the point of charring her skin. It caused her more pain than the cancer."[40] If this story is true, one wonders whether it represented the norm or the exception.

No evidence has come to light about Perón's role. However, he did have a peculiar attitude toward doctors and medicine. Perón always fancied himself an expert in the healing arts. He insisted again and again that if he had not entered military service, he would have followed in the footsteps of his physician-grandfather. He fondly recalled his mother's work as a lay practitioner of medicine. His taped memoirs contain an anecdote that captures his pretensions. Alberto Dodero, his good friend, returned from a trip to the United States and informed the president that a North American doctor had told him he had cancer. Perón assured him that Yankee doctors were never right about these matters and offered to cure him. "I had him two months on grapefruit. Grapefruit and water. And he got better."[41]

A joke Perón told on many occasions further illustrates his attitude. "When I'm sick," he would say, "I go to the doctor so that he may live well. Then I go to the pharmacist so that he may live well. Then I take the doctor's advice and the pharmacist's pills and I throw them out with the garbage, so that I may live well."[42]

It is not unreasonable to suppose that Perón the *curandero* (healer) may also have practiced his "skills" upon Evita. His own boundless self-confidence in these matters, plus the low opinion in which he held the medical profession, make it entirely plausible that he may have encouraged his wife in her avoidance of proper physical examinations or her refusal to accept the advice of physicians.

The first lady's health crisis was not the only ominous event of 1950. On October 15, the Escuela Científica Basilio (Basilio Scientific School) obtained an official permit to hold a rally in Luna Park.[43] The organization, to which the government had recently given legal recognition, promoted the cause of spiritism. The theme of the meeting was "Jesus Christ is not God," a proposition not warmly received in Roman Catholic circles. Perón himself sent a message of greeting. All this so outraged the clergy and more militant faithful that they attempted to disrupt the proceedings. Several weeks later, the president again demonstrated disrespect for the church by absenting himself from Buenos Aires just as a papal legate was arriving from Rome to attend a national eucharistic congress.[44] The incidents betrayed a careless attitude on Perón's part toward a powerful institution that remained independent of Peronist control. Though he and

Evita made a fence-mending appearance at the final ceremony of the congress in Rosario, the chief executive seemed oblivious to the fact that he was playing with fire.

As 1950 came to an end, Juan Perón could shed Alexandrian tears, for there were no worthy enemies left for him to conquer. He had consolidated into a monolithic support structure the various elements of the Peronist movement and had reshaped the political, economic and social systems to reflect his ideology. Though sober analysts could find indicators pointing to an end to the prosperity which buoyed the first years of the Perón era, the president betrayed no loss of confidence in his ability to weather storms. The chorus of the popular marching song *"Los muchachos peronistas"* proclaimed: "Perón, Perón, how great you are!" There were signs that the *conductor* was beginning to believe it.

Evita's emergence as a political figure galvanized the entire Peronist movement, from Perón and his acolytes to the lowliest descamisado. She supplied the magnetic current that linked the leader to his mass, that infused Peronism with soul, that lent a unique quality to the charismatic glow of the *conductor*. She complemented him exquisitely, her violent rhetoric enabling him to play the unifier, her contact with people freeing him for more elevated matters of state, her manipulation of the bureaucracy shielding him from the unpleasantness of imposing discipline. In executing his directions, responding to his subtle suggestions and exercising her own discretion, she served his needs perfectly.

Yet the moment was approaching when she would succumb to desires to exceed the bounds he placed upon her political role. At the same time, she would also seek to deny the physical constraints of the disease that was silently devouring her from within. On these two fronts, she would meet with failure, but in a way that would assure her immortalization in the consciousness of the Peronist faithful.

27

Evita and the
Vice-Presidency

In mid-August of 1951, a deafening din of publicity heralded an event that would become one of the great moments in the history of Peronism. The CGT had designated the twenty-second of the month as the day of the *cabildo abierto* (open meeting), at which the working class was to offer the vice-presidential nomination to Eva Perón.[1]

By now the Peronists had ritualized the mass meeting in celebrations of October 17 and other special occasions, but the *cabildo abierto* was meant to be something truly extraordinary. Instead of the familiar Plaza de Mayo setting, the vast expanse of the Avenida 9 de Julio was chosen as the site. Workmen raised a large platform against the Ministry of Public Works facing north at Moreno Street, with giant photos of the proposed nominees flanking the stage. Block letters spelling PERÓN—EVA PERÓN traced an arc over the Peronist shield, which formed a backdrop, and the slogan "The Ticket for the Fatherland" decorated the frontal restraining barrier.

The CGT declared a general strike for August 22 and made preparations to transport people to the rally. From as far away as Patagonia and the arid mountains of the northwest, the descamisados, the cabecitas negras, the forgotten Argentines in whose name Juan Perón ruled, were to participate in a spectacle meant to formalize Eva Perón's de facto position as second in command within the government.

Yet the *cabildo abierto*, like most other milestones in Perón's career, was not at all what it seemed to be. Perón could not have welcomed the idea, but he let events run their course, only to lose control of the situation in a moment of high drama. In the immediate wake of the *cabildo abierto*, perceptions of what had in fact taken place were as confused within Argentina as they were distorted by the media abroad. It took nearly two weeks for the ultimate resolution to unfold.

The political gavotte began with a decision to advance the date of the elections from February 1952 to November 1951. The Peronists then implored an unconvincingly reluctant president to run for reelection. At the same time his wife marshaled forces behind the scenes in an effort to create irresistible pressures which would propel her to the vice-presidency.[2] Evita's authority and prestige derived solely from her status as Perón's wife. In the end, he alone would decide whether to put her on the ticket. Evita's hope was that he would find himself unable to ignore the public clamor her followers would bestir. But although he generally disliked saying no to people, Perón always managed to impose his will, one way or another, in matters of substance.

The women's branch of the Peronist party and the CGT pushed hard for the first lady's candidacy. Far from being puppets on the strings of Evita's ambition, both groups realized how much they had to gain from her success. She would not only continue to represent their interests but would also be able to operate from an institutional base. The constituent elements of the Peronist movement were constantly competing with one another, encouraged to do so by Perón, who carefully imposed a sense of insecurity upon them as a control mechanism. The drive to put Evita in the vice-presidency was in large part a reaction by the CGT and the women's branch against the adversary roles Perón had assigned to them.

The rising tide of support for the first lady easily swept Domingo Mercante aside. No longer was the name of the governor of Buenos Aires Province linked with Perón's. "Perón Keeps His Word, Evita Dignifies It" appeared again and again as a partisan slogan. The charter of the high executive council of the Peronist party declared that the only national leaders recognized by the movement were the president and his wife.[3] Congress, in enacting legislation that made provinces out of the territories of La Pampa and Chaco, renamed them Eva Perón and General Perón.

While the bandwagon gathered momentum during the first six months of 1951, Juan Perón seemed content to tolerate the campaign. Other matters, such as the confiscation of *La Prensa* and his dramatic disclosures regarding Argentina's arrival into the atomic age, were distracting him. The repression of political dissidents was intensifying and brought him considerable embarrassment when a Communist student arrested by the police was revealed to have been brutally tortured.

In early August, the CGT's governing body approved a formal resolution calling for a Perón-Perón ticket and presented it to Perón. The president graciously accepted the document, but would commit neither himself nor his wife. On August 4, the confederation announced plans for the *cabildo abierto*.

Though Evita's path to the vice-presidency seemed unobstructed, ominous rumors of military discontent were gathering like storm clouds over the pampa. The anti-Evita revulsion that had motivated many of the uniformed conspirators against Colonel Perón in 1945 was again simmering, according to reports circulating in the capital. The armed forces were now bridling against the possibility that a woman—especially *that* woman— might be in line to become their commander in chief.[4]

According to one interpretation of the events that followed, military leaders pressured the president into vetoing the nomination of Evita.[5] It seems more likely, as others have maintained, that Perón used the military's distaste for his wife as an excuse for aborting her candidacy. This enabled him to stop the pro-Evita campaign and blame her bad fortune on the military.[6]

Perón's political strategy may also have been shaped by his awareness of several military conspiracies brewing against him. He quelled one of them in April, with the arrest of its leader, a colonel in the infantry. A second was led by retired general Benjamín Menéndez, an inveterate plotter whose career as an instigator of unsuccessful coups began in 1941 with a botched attempt to oust President Castillo.* Menéndez, however, was a political reactionary not highly esteemed within the armed forces. General Eduardo Lonardi, a potentially more charismatic officer, led the third group of conspirators. Perhaps still smarting from Perón's contribution to his expulsion from Chile in 1936, he was attempting to organize fellow artillery officers against the regime.

On the evening of July 30, General Menéndez met secretly with leaders of the political opposition.[7] The group responded positively to his plans. The presence of Arturo Frondizi, the number-two man in the Radical party, and his enthusiasm for the coup greatly encouraged the general, who now felt he could count upon a degree of popular approval. Exactly when Perón first detected the existence of the Menéndez and Lonardi plots is uncertain. General Lucero, his army minister, knew enough to admonish Lonardi in August.[8] Lucero must have informed the president, who may well have obtained earlier information from other intelligence sources.

Hence it is likely that Perón's political decision regarding Evita took into account the seeds of discontent sprouting within the one institution powerful enough to displace him. At this point a coup had no chance of success. The plotters lacked organization, a sufficiently broad base within the armed forces and the requisite civilian support. Evita's nomination would not have affected the conspiracies, but might in the long run have strengthened anti-Peronist sentiments within the officer corps and improved the chances for a successful coup.

More importantly, the elevation of Evita to the vice-presidency would produce nothing of political value to Perón. Her usefulness did not depend

---

* His grandnephew, General Mario Benjamín Menéndez, would serve as governor of the Malvinas (Falklands) and commander of Argentine troops during the brief occupation of the islands by Argentina in 1982.

Juan Perón at the age of three.

Juan and brother Mario, ages nine and thir-
teen respectively.

Colonel Perón, army ski instructor, in western Argentina in 1942.

A rare photograph of Colonel Perón and his adversary, U.S. Ambassador Spruille Braden (third from right), *lunching together in July 1945.*

*Perón accepting the symbols of the
presidency from General Farrell
on June 4, 1946. To the left of
Perón and in the background is his
brother-in-law, Juan Duarte.*

Perón and Evita.

President Perón addressing the nation. To his right are Evita and Domingo Mercante, governor of Buenos Aires. To his left, Vice-President Hortensio Quijano.

President Perón addressing a rally in the Plaza de Mayo from a balcony of the Casa Rosada. To his left is Governor Mercante. To the right of his outstretched right hand is Héctor Cámpora, president of the Chamber of Deputies.

A typical Peronist crowd in the Plaza de Mayo.

Evita's last public appearance with Perón on the inauguration day of his second presidency, June 4, 1952. A prop hidden by her fur coat permits her to stand in the open car.

President Perón riding Mancha, the horse he used on ceremonial occasions.

Courtesy Diario *La Nación*

President Perón greeting members of a girls' basketball team.

Perón disembarking in Rio de Janeiro, as Brazilian authorities frustrate his attempted return to Argentina from exile in Madrid, December 2, 1964. In front of him is Augusto Vandor, behind him Delia Parodi.

Right-wing Peronists brandish weapons during the bloody shootout that marred Perón's return to Argentina on June 20, 1973. Note photo of Evita on scaffolding.

The Peronist Party Congress nominates Perón for president in a Buenos Aires theater on August 4, 1973.

Perón reviews a parade in his honor from a balcony of the CGT headquarters on August 31, 1973. To his right is José López Rega, his left, Isabel and CGT general secretary José Rucci, who would be assassinated four weeks later.

Isabel Perón mourns her dead husband. José López Rega stands at her right.

upon any official position she held, but rather upon her status as wife of the *conductor*. It was in the interest of the CGT and the women's branch to advocate Evita's cause in order to strengthen their positions within the movement. Surely Perón understood their motives.

The effect of her illness upon the vice-presidential selection is unclear. There is no evidence to suggest that Perón used it as an argument for withholding the nomination from her, but if the gravity of her condition had been understood, whether or not she ran with her husband would have seemed irrelevant, since her days were numbered. One explanation is that Perón still did not accept the fact that she was beyond cure. Another is that he was not certain how much longer she had to live, yet resolved not to open the way for even the short-term problems her election to the vice-presidency might spawn.

From every province and territory of Argentina, loyal Peronists surged toward the capital as the day of the *cabildo abierto* drew near. They came in trains, buses, taxis, trucks and automobiles, responding to the CGT's urgent call. This was not the spontaneous convergence of the fabled October 17, 1945, but rather a national peregrination carefully orchestrated by the confederation. The mood was one of celebration, not anxiety. Instead of raised drawbridges, special sporting events, entertainment and free food greeted the visitors. The *cabildo abierto* breathed a festival atmosphere. "PERÓN–PERÓN, 1952–1958" proclaimed hand-painted slogans on walls of buildings everywhere. Few in the crowds that roamed the downtown streets had any doubts about the outcome of the rally or the composition of the ticket.

At 2:00 P.M. on the twenty-second, the broad Avenida 9 de Julio groaned under the largest crowd ever to assemble in the capital. The human sea extended back as far as the obelisk at Corrientes Street, eight blocks away. The government estimated the audience at 2 million. It was the dead of winter, yet fate produced one of those balmy afternoons that so often attended rallies during the Perón era that the term "Peronist day" became part of the popular lexicon.

The formal proceedings did not begin until 5:20, when Perón appeared on the platform. The earsplitting roar his presence touched off eventually subsided, and the CGT's José Espejo stepped to the microphone. In the name of the Peronist faithful, he pronounced what had become a standard watchword when the mass greeted its leader: "We're here, General!" An orchestrated chorus of calls for Evita roared to a crescendo.

"My general," Espejo continued, "we note the absence of your wife, Eva Perón, she who is without equal in the world, in history, in the love and veneration of the Argentine people. Comrades, we can't go on without the presence of Eva Perón."[9] He directed a squad of CGT officials to fetch her and escort her to the stage. Fifteen minutes later, an automobile bearing Eva made its way toward the platform.

The woman who mounted the steps and looked out upon the frenzied crowd was a far cry from the fledgling first lady of 1946, or the glamour queen of the Rainbow Tour. The blond curls and gaudy attire had long since given way to what one scholar has called "the streamlined, eternally classic style which was to be hers—and uniquely hers at that time—until her death."[10] Her hair was pulled back severely, accentuating the growing gauntness of her features. Tears flooded her eyes. She raised her arms in response to the delirium, and a look of uncertainty clouded her expression.

Espejo read the CGT resolution urging Perón and Evita to run together as candidates and implored the couple to accede to the confederation's wishes. "You, señora, . . . must accept this new sacrifice which your people ask of you, and the fatherland demands."[11]

Now it was Evita's turn, her moment at center stage, alone in the political spotlight. But instead of responding to the offer Espejo had pressed upon her, she launched into a brief, explosive oration, a curious discourse that both revealed Eva Perón at her rhetorical best and at the same time was totally inappropriate to the occasion. The speech is a classic in its rhythmic cadences, violent imagery and naked passion. The ravages of illness may have taken their toll upon her body, but they also hoarsened her voice to a lower, more dramatic pitch. The fires within her invested that voice with a chilling power. She said nothing new—extravagant praise of her husband, tribute to the workers, revilement of the oligarchy, reference to herself as a "humble woman" with a desire to be only a "bridge of peace between General Perón and the descamisados"—but she never said it better. Her hyperbole reached its zenith in the peroration, when she invoked her "spiritual authority" to proclaim Perón the victor in the coming elections.[12]

Juan Perón followed his wife to the microphone and delivered a brief address that paled in comparison to the electric speech Evita had given. At one point, as he paused for applause, someone in the audience shouted "Let Comrade Evita speak!" When he concluded, José Espejo told the crowd what they already knew, that Evita had not given an answer (in truth, neither had Perón), and announced that the *cabildo abierto* would recess until the next day, when the CGT would again ask her to accept the nomination. But this was hardly satisfactory. The descamisados saw no need for delay and demanded an immediate answer.

Organization, that most highly prized of Peronist virtues, had characterized every mass meeting staged in Argentina since Perón's inauguration. From conception to dispersal, every aspect of a rally was meticulously controlled. But at this moment, before the largest gathering ever assembled by the Peronists, for the first time ever, things began to get out of hand.

The protests overwhelmed Espejo, who had to call upon a reluctant Evita to talk to the crowd. This touched off an incredible dialogue between thousands of Argentines, who insisted upon an affirmative answer, and an emotion-rent first lady, who knew she could not tell them what they demanded to hear. She tried desperately to extricate herself.

"I ask you . . . for a decision so transcendental in the life of this humble woman, give me four days to think about it."

"No! No! No!"

"Comrades . . . Comrades . . . I do not renounce my post in the struggle. I renounce the honors."

"No! No! No!"

"Comrades . . . Comrades . . . I will do what the people say."

"Answer! Answer!" Her voice was beginning to break, and she seemed on the brink of losing her composure.

Now Perón and others on the platform were buzzing around her, giving frantic advice about what to say. Concern etched itself on their faces. A sense of helplessness hovered.

Evita then launched into a rambling paean on the virtues of their president, but the crowd would have none of it and interrupted. Perón snarled an order that the rally be brought to a close, a vain gesture under the circumstances. He argued with CGT officials on the stage.

"Comrades . . . Comrades . . . Tonight at nine-thirty, on the radio."

"No! No! No! Now! Now!"

The protest drowned her words. Finally Espejo returned to the microphone. "Comrades, Comrade Evita has asked us to wait two hours. We are going to remain right here. We shall not move until she has given an answer responsive to the wishes of the working people."

Espejo's directive went unheeded as the great crowd slowly dissolved into turgid streams wending among empty buildings awash in artificial light. Most of the spectators left with the impression that the first lady had accepted. Those who turned on the radio at nine-thirty heard neither the promised message from Comrade Evita nor any official explanations.

The next day's newspaper compounded the confusion. "The President and His Wife Accept the Mandate" announced a subheadline on the front page of *La Razón*. On August 27, members of the high council of the Peronist party formally named Perón and Evita as candidates and on the following day presented their decision to the president at the Casa Rosada. The movement to nominate Evita had now reached the point at which a decision could be put off no longer.

On the evening of August 31, the people of Argentina listened as Eva Perón put an end to the suspense. In a short speech taped earlier in the day and broadcast at eight-thirty, the first lady announced her "irrevocable and definite decision" to decline the nomination. In measured, somber tones, she stressed that it was her own free choice to remain off the ticket, and that it was consistent with the only great ambition that she had ever had:

that it will be said of me, when they write the marvelous chapter that history will surely dedicate to Perón, that there was at his side a woman who dedicated herself to bring to the president the hopes of the people, and that the people lovingly called the woman "Evita."[13]

On the next day, the leaders of the CGT solemnly announced that August 31 would henceforth be known as the "day of the renunciation."

The rumors came like locusts: the military had presented an ultimatum to Perón; Evita was gravely ill; etc., etc. The foreign press developed the fanciful but baseless theory that it was the descamisados who had failed Evita; so many of them had stayed away from Buenos Aires on August 22 that Perón read the size of the crowd as a vote of no confidence in Evita and therefore withheld the nomination from her.[14] The most plausible explanation, that her candidacy was not in Perón's interest, was ignored.

With the elimination of Evita, it was necessary to find another nominee. At this date, there was but one recourse, to call upon Hortensio Quijano to stand for reelection. The sixty-eight-year-old vice-president had performed loyally and unobtrusively as a figurehead, and was now in even worse health than Evita. The first lady herself had to call upon the aged politician and implore him to accept. He reluctantly agreed to join the ticket.

28

Reelection

With elections only two months away, Perón was just beginning to formulate a strategy when two occurrences strengthened the stacked deck he already held. The physical collapse of his wife marked the onset of the final throes of her struggle against cancer, a prolonged agony that could no longer be kept secret. As the Peronist movement began to heap honors on the first lady for her "selfless abnegation," she finally succumbed to the debilitating effects of disease. No doubt the emotional toll of August 22 and 31 accelerated her collapse. She was confined to bed on Monday, September 24.[1] By a grim coincidence, on that same day the First Argentine Congress on Cancer opened in Buenos Aires.

The last week in September also marked the culmination of General Menéndez' effort to oust Perón.[2] Attempts to coordinate his conspiracy with that of General Lonardi foundered. On September 22, the latter decided to withdraw from the lists and told his followers they were free to join Menéndez. Meanwhile, convinced that he had to act before the coming elections, Menéndez set Friday the twenty-eighth as his target date, which coincided with Perón's attendance at a ceremony at Campo de Mayo. Moreover, he determined that a Friday coup would prevent the president and the "thieves" around him from making off with their ill-gotten gains, since the banks would be closed for the weekend.

The military forces upon which the conspirators counted were remarkably scant. The plan was to move a detachment of tanks from Campo de Mayo to the air base at El Palomar. Naval warplanes would then join the rebels at the base and support them in an attack upon Buenos Aires. Sympathizers from the nearby military academy would also participate in the assault.

The plan depended upon surprise, speed of execution and the achievement of early successes, which would convince other units to join the uprising rather than execute orders to repress it. In early September the minister of the air force had ordered all his planes disarmed; the element of surprise was already an illusion. Any mistakes or unforeseeable mishaps would eliminate the speed factor. Yet the incredibly long odds against him did not deter General Menéndez in the slightest. On the afternoon of Thursday, September 27, he composed a pompous manifesto, without which no self-respecting military coup could proceed, and sent it to a print shop. All was in readiness.

The first phases of the operation went smoothly. Menéndez arrived at Campo de Mayo at 5:45 on Friday morning. Soldiers committed to the conspiracy and led by Captain Alejandro Lanusse (whose path would cross Perón's more directly at a later date) had already occupied gate number 8. Menéndez met with a group of his followers at the cavalry school, where he made a brief inspirational speech. At the same time, reconnaissance planes prepared to take off from a nearby base in order to drop copies of the manifesto upon Buenos Aires.

But when the conspirators hurriedly made their way to the tank regiment that was to invest the coup with firepower, their revolution became a comedy of errors. The 180 tanks in the unit were still in the fueling process. The delay exposed the rebels to harassment by a handful of loyalists who had discovered what was happening. Ensuing gunfire produced several casualties. The sounds of battle created the impression (quite accurate, as events unfolded) that all was not proceeding as planned by the plotters, and this discouraged others from making common cause with them. Moreover, by now Army Minister Lucero had received word of the uprising and had begun to take countermeasures.

Realizing that time was of the essence, General Menéndez gave the order to move out of Campo de Mayo and led his contingent through gate number 8. Behind him were three tanks and almost three hundred men. A military writer described the general's plight at this moment with classic understatement: *"A la revolución le faltaba volumen"* ("The revolution lacked volume").[3]

On the way to El Palomar, Menéndez passed by the military academy, from which he hoped to draw the same support General Uriburu had attracted in 1930. The commanding officer, once a member of the GOU, was unimpressed by the size of the rebel force. "No more revolutions, General!" he informed Menéndez.[4] The column proceeded to El Palomar, which insurgent troops had already occupied. But a mechanized column en route from a nearby army installation could not link up with Menéndez, as loyalist units intercepted it and forced it to surrender.

This left the general in a hopeless position. Pro-Perón soldiers began to arrive at the air base and surrounded it. Recognizing defeat, Menéndez made his way to the military academy, where he turned himself over to the commanding officer. The naval aviators who were to land at El Palomar flew instead to Uruguay, where they sought political asylum. By midday the Menéndez rebellion was history.

Meanwhile, utilizing authority created by the 1949 constitution, Perón declared a state of internal war throughout the entire country, a measure that enabled him to place severe restrictions upon civil liberties. At the same time the CGT called a general strike and summoned the descamisados once more to the Plaza de Mayo. Some workers, hearing of the coup, set up blockades on the principal highways between Campo de Mayo and Buenos Aires. Perón, preferring to use military force to suffocate the rebellion, probably tolerated these efforts as expressions of political faith, once it became clear that the rebels would not even begin to march on the capital.

At 3:30 P.M., the president addressed a cheering multitude from a Casa Rosada balcony. As the crowd chanted "My life for Perón!" and demanded punishment for the insurgents, Perón bestowed lavish praise upon the great majority of military men who had remained faithful to the government. He blamed the coup on the "dark forces of capitalism and imperialism."[5] For those who had taken up arms against him, he had nothing but contempt:

> The leaders of this mutiny, dishonest men without a sense of honor, have done what all cowards do, abandoning their troops and leaving them to their own fate. Not a one of them was capable of fighting and dying at his post. Comrades, we soldiers know we have but one duty: to die for our honor; and the soldier who is not capable of dying for his honor is not worthy to be a military man, nor an Argentine.[6]

These words would take on a hollow ring four years later when General Perón himself would forgo the privilege of risking death for his honor.

News of the attempted coup was kept from Evita as long as possible. By early afternoon she could tell something was afoot, and Perón had to let her know the details. At the same time, the presidential press office released the first bulletin informing the public that she was seriously ill. It described her condition as "an anemia of regular intensity that is being treated with transfusions, absolute rest and general medication."[7] The announcement was timed to produce maximum political impact in a moment of crisis.

That evening Evita once more took to the airwaves, this time to thank the people of Argentina for their loyalty to Perón. In low tones thick with emotion, the first lady spoke "in the name of the humble and the descamisados, for whom I have gladly left behind me the shreds of my health." She almost broke down completely when she begged her listeners to "pray to God to restore me to the health I have lost, not for my sake, but for Perón and for you, my descamisados."[8]

On the following day, an official medical bulletin declared:

> The general state of Señora Eva Perón is one of great weakness, intensified as a consequence of the profound emotions she had to endure yesterday afternoon. This morning she will undergo another blood transfusion. The illness of Señora Eva Perón will require a relatively prolonged period of treatment and total rest.[9]

Despite her condition, the first lady still managed on September 29 to summon José Espejo, two other CGT officials and the minister of war to her bedside and arrange for the procurement of weapons to be distributed to workers' militias that were to be formed for the defense of Perón.[10] Money from the foundation would be diverted to buy 5,000 automatic pistols and 1,500 machine guns from Prince Bernhard of the Netherlands, who had visited Buenos Aires earlier that year. For those who would one day want to believe in a revolutionary Peronism, Evita's gestures symbolized a class-conscious realization that the future of the movement lay not in a balance of forces precariously maintained by the *conductor*, but rather in total identification with the needs and aspirations of the workers. Evita intuitively sensed that when push came to shove, they alone could be trusted to fight for Perón.

The president, on the other hand, had no intention of permitting the formation of workers' militias. The idea was totally foreign to his vision of the "organized community." Moreover, as a military man he could never bring himself to take a step that might one day lead to the destruction of the institution that had nurtured him. In all likelihood, he appreciated the intensity of his wife's protective instincts and therefore tolerated the deal. He did not have to veto it because he knew there were other ways to keep weapons out of the hands of the descamisados.

While Evita reacted emotionally to the coup, which she saw as evidence of a continuing threat to Peronist rule, Perón's attitude was characteristically pragmatic. He looked at the uprising in terms of opportunity for both short- and long-term political gain. Menéndez' folly made it easy to stir his partisans to a fever pitch just before the elections. The rebellion also provided an excuse to jail opposition leaders. Finally, the declaration of a state of internal war quashed the opposition's faint hopes for a minimally open campaign.

A military tribunal dealt severely with the disloyal officers, General Menéndez receiving a fifteen-year sentence; his subordinates were given lesser terms. Captain Lanusse, for example, was condemned to four years in prison.

The Menéndez coup marked a turning point in the politicization of the military. In July, Perón had declared that "no member of the armed forces who is worthy of his rank believes that it is the mission of the armed forces to form the basic support of a government."[11] But after the uprising, the Peronists would insist that the primary task of the military was to defend not the nation, but the president.[12]

Coming hard on the heels of both the Menéndez coup and the public disclosure of Evita's ill health, Loyalty Day 1951 was the perfect occasion to whip the Peronist faithful into a frenzy that would culminate on election day. All the ingredients of an emotional orgy were at hand, and Perón could be counted upon to play the chef. He decided to dedicate this October 17 to his stricken wife and to call upon the descamisados to pay tribute to her service to the cause—with special emphasis upon the sacrificial renunciation of August 31.

In the fortnight preceding the sixth anniversary of Perón's restoration, the rank and file offered masses for Evita's speedy recovery. Vehicular traffic on the road between Buenos Aires and the Shrine of the Virgin in Luján slowed to a crawl to accommodate pious pilgrims making the long trek on foot to ask the Mother of God to cure the "Mother of All Argentine Children."

An unusually large crowd overflowed the Plaza de Mayo at the appointed hour of the appointed day. By now a thoroughly stylized annual celebration, Loyalty Day this year would be different: in the minds of many on the balcony as well as in front of it, the apprehension persisted that this might turn out to be the first lady's last October 17.

Evita, under heavy medication and on her feet for the first time since her confinement to bed in September, feebly acknowledged the cheers that greeted her. Pale, emaciated, a wisp of her former self, she needed physical support from Perón. The swiftness of her decline startled those who had last seen her at the *cabildo abierto*.

José Espejo began the ceremony by bestowing upon her the CGT's "Recognition of Distinction of the First Category." Then Carlos Aloé, in the name of the president, honored Evita with the Grand Peronist Medal, Extraordinary Class. Perón placed the emerald-studded pendant around his wife's neck and embraced her. It was a moment frozen in eternity for those who witnessed it. Perón the cynic could not suppress the emotion that overwhelmed his customary platform demeanor.

When Evita took the microphone, she was speechless for the first time in her life. Perón had to intervene and give her time to compose herself. In a voice that betrayed the intensity of his feelings, he expressed his "public gratitude and profound thanks to this incomparable woman for all seasons." His panegyric peaked with the assertion that Eva Perón was "one of the greatest women humanity has produced."[13]

The crowd hushed as Evita finally began her speech, which had the unmistakable ring of a political last will and testament. In a barely audible voice, she told her beloved descamisados that nothing could have kept her away from them on this glorious day:

> The enemies of the people, of Perón, and of the fatherland have known for a long time that Perón and Eva Perón are willing to die for the people. Now they also know that the people are willing to die for Perón.
>
> I ask you today, comrades, only one thing: that we all swear publicly to defend Perón and fight to the death. And our oath will be to shout for a minute, so that our cry will reach the furthest corner of the globe: "My life for Perón!"[14]

The faithful responded with ear-shattering zeal. There were undoubtedly many who saw this as a symbol, a hyperbolic pledge of partisan allegiance. For Evita, for the less sophisticated descamisados, and for others yet unborn or at that moment too young to appreciate it, those words embodied a total commitment that would one day produce grave consequences. When the echoes subsided, Evita continued:

> I know that God is with us, because he is with the lowly and he has a low opinion of the oligarchy's pride. For this reason, victory will be ours. We will have to win, sooner or later, whatever the costs, whoever may fall.
>
> My descamisados, I would like to say more to you, but the doctors have forbidden it. . . . I ask you one thing: I am sure I shall be with you soon, but if this does not come to pass because of my health, take care of the general, be loyal to Perón as you are now, because to be loyal to Perón is to be loyal to the fatherland and to yourselves.

As John Barnes has written, "The passion, the love, the hatred, it was all there as before. But there was a difference. The crowd knew it. There were many men as well as women weeping openly in the plaza."[15] By-passing the normal procedures for canonization, the government declared October 18 to be Saint Evita's Day.

The 1946 election achieved renown as the cleanest in Argentine history. The 1951 election did not come close to challenging this distinction.[16] Though Peronists still claim fairness for the process by which Perón gained a second term, what they really mean is that people were permitted to cast their secret ballots without coercion and that the final count was honest. However, in the crucial areas of mass-media access and the ability to campaign without physical intimidation, the opposition faced such formidable obstacles that their creditable performance was little short of miraculous.[17]

The new election law enacted by the Peronists made coalitions impossible, since failure to run a presidential candidate would cause a party to lose its legal status. Thus Perón faced an array of opponents rather than a revived Unión Democrática. The Radicals, seeking to tap public sympathy generated by his persecution by the government, nominated Ricardo Balbín for president. Arturo Frondizi, Balbín's lawyer, joined him on the ticket. Despite his obvious courage, Balbín was but a slight improvement over Tamborini. The platform upon which the Radicals ran promised domestic programs indistinguishable from those offered by the Peronists and took an extremely anti-imperialist, isolationist line toward foreign policy.[18] As a result, the more conservative wing of the party withdrew from the campaign.

The nation's radio networks, all under government control, refused to sell air time to the Radicals. Within the fourth estate, only *La Nación* gave even minimal coverage of the opposition's campaign. Balbín's appearances in the interior were disrupted by the police or Peronist mobs. The candidate himself managed to survive unhurt, but a number of his supporters did not share his good fortune. At a rally on November 8 in the Plaza Constitución, Balbín had hardly begun his speech when police charged at the spectators. In the melee that followed, a score of civilians suffered wounds requiring medical treatment.*

The Peronists waltzed through the campaign.[19] "Let Perón continue" was their main slogan. The *conductor* took a temporary leave of absence from office and made Rear Admiral Alberto Teisaire, who was president of the Senate, the nation's acting president. Because of Evita's illness, Perón planned no campaign trips and limited himself to four radio addresses.

On October 28, Argentina's Juan Fangio won the world championship in auto racing in Barcelona. For his fellow countrymen, whose driving habits aped his devil-may-care style, it was cause for national celebration. Fangio dedicated his victory to Perón. Within a short time, a news item with even greater impact monopolized newspaper headlines: Evita underwent major surgery.

On Saturday evening, November 3, Perón brought his wife to a hospital built by the Eva Perón Foundation in Avellaneda and placed her under the care of Dr. Ricardo Finochietto, one of the nation's most respected physicians, who determined that surgical intervention was necessary. The government sent for Dr. George Pack, a cancer specialist from New York. Dr. Pack had attended the Congress on Cancer in Buenos Aires in September and had secretly examined Evita at that time. In the midst of a political campaign in which the Peronists were dipping into their stock arsenal of anti-Yankee rhetoric, Dr. Pack's involvement was not announced. On November 6 he performed the operation.

---

* The other parties fared even worse. Gunfire broke up a Communist rally in Paraná. Among the casualties (which included two deaths) was the party's presidential candidate. A bullet in the back put him into the hospital and out of the campaign. Alfredo Palacios, the Socialist standard-bearer, was jailed in the wake of the Menéndez uprising.

Before submitting to the knife, Evita taped a short message to her compatriots. On Friday, November 9, the nation's airwaves carried her feeble
voice declaring that "not to vote for Perón is, for an Argentine—I say it
because I feel it—to betray the fatherland."[20] Congress met that same day
and enacted a bill creating a special exception to the election laws and
permitting the first lady to vote from the hospital.

Spring rains soaked Buenos Aires on election Sunday. Perón voted early
in the morning. Several hours later, an official delegation composed of
representatives from the Peronist and Radical parties arrived at the hospital with a ballot box for Evita. It was a vivid experience for David Viñas,
a young Radical later to distinguish himself as an author.

Made nauseous by the toadying of those I found around Eva Perón, I was
moved by the image of the women outside who, on their knees, praying on
the sidewalk, kept touching the box that held Evita's vote and kept kissing
it. A fascinating scene, worthy of a book by Tolstoy.[21]

The Peronists won handily. Perón garnered 4.7 million votes, as against
2.4 million for Balbín. However, the Radicals almost matched the Peronist
total in the city of Buenos Aires. In the Chamber of Deputies, the Peronists
captured all but twelve seats. The Senate remained completely Peronist.
Domingo Mercante having retired from politics, the newly elected governor of Buenos Aires was Carlos Aloé, who would impose a repressive
grip upon the province. For the first time in the nation's history, a number
of women assumed elective offices.

"The first election I won with the men," Perón had declared before the
election. "This one I shall win with the women."[22] If he had stopped
there, his statement would have qualified as the prediction of an astute
politician. But he added, "and the third I shall win with the children"—
an uncannily accurate long-range prophecy that would be fulfilled, but in
ways Perón could not have imagined.

29

The Death of Evita

On November 3, 1951, before the first light had dawned on the day Evita would enter the hospital in Avellaneda, a bomb shattered the showcase window of Peuser's, a publishing house in Buenos Aires. The target of the attack was a display of a new book, *La razón de mi vida* (translated into English as *My Mission in Life*), the autobiography of Eva Perón.

The inspiration for Evita's literary endeavor came from Manuel Penella de Silva, a Spanish journalist of intriguing antecedents.[1] The son of a famous musician, he spent much of World War II as a correspondent in Germany. Eventually expelled as unsympathetic to the Nazi cause, he took refuge in Switzerland and soon became acquainted with Benito Llambí, Perón's ambassador in Berne. Penella's political views were somewhat unorthodox. He believed that women could be the salvation of humanity, not by competing with men for political power and adopting masculine characteristics, as he felt had occurred in the Anglo-Saxon countries, but rather by bringing feminine virtues to bear upon policy formulation. He advocated the creation of consultative "legislatures," composed entirely of women. As he expressed his thoughts to Llambí, the ambassador told him that the future he envisioned was becoming a reality in Argentina (though perhaps not in the precise form the Spaniard had in mind), and pointed to Eva Perón as the woman most closely embodying his ideals.

Yielding to the irresistible urge to see for himself, Penella made the long trek to Buenos Aires. With the aid of an introduction from the ambassador, he managed to win the first lady's confidence. Concluding that she shared his views about women, he besought her to let him ghostwrite her autobiography. The project appealed to her, and she obtained Perón's approval.

The diminutive, chain-smoking Spaniard shadowed Evita in her daily round of activities and drew from her the story of her life as she wished it to be told. His access to her aroused the enmity of her sycophants, who ceaselessly conspired to oust him from their midst. Despite these obstacles, he managed to produce a manuscript.

Though Evita seemed pleased with the draft, Perón's reaction was negative. The Spaniard's vision of women in politics did not accord with the *conductor*'s notions on the subject. As one writer put it, in the area of political theory, Perón "had his own homemade laboratory, and would not permit anyone else to mix in his acids."[2] He turned the manuscript over to several of Evita's intimates, who proceeded to rewrite it and purge most of the distinctive features Penella had inserted. The chief culprit was probably Raúl Mendé, Perón's minister for technical matters, whose literary pretensions dwarfed his actual talents. The final product, which appeared in the bookstores shortly before October 17, 1951, trivialized its subject.

My Mission in Life blends adulation of Perón in its most extreme form ("I think that Perón resembles more another class of geniuses, those who create new philosophies and new religions"[3]); autobiographical insight ("I recollect that as a child, I always wanted to recite"[4]); sentiment ("Perhaps someday when I am gone for good, someone will say of me what so many children of the people are wont to say when their mothers are gone, also for good: only now do we realize that she loved us so much"[5]); resentment ("Nothing belonging to the oligarchy can be good!"[6]); genuinely feminist perceptions ("the world today suffer[s] from a great absence: that of women. . . . We are absent from all the great centers constituting a power in the world"[7]); antifeminist perceptions ("The number of young women who look down upon the occupation of homemaking increases every day. And yet that is what we were born for"[8]); sense ("The oligarchy never has been hostile to anyone who could be useful to it"[9]); and nonsense ("General Perón has said that *justicialismo* would not be possible without syndicalism. . . . This is true, first, because General Perón has said so, and second, because it is actually the truth"[10]).

The Peronist propaganda machine immediately hailed the book as a masterpiece. Critics extolled its literary merits. A group of writers petitioned the Ministry of Education to award to the author a "Grand Prize of Honor." Copies of the book—paperbacks for the masses, deluxe editions for the Peronist elite—flowed from the printing presses. It became a required text in the schools. The refusal of U.S. publishers to bring out an English translation provoked heated denunciations[11] and a bomb explosion at the U.S.-operated Lincoln Library in Buenos Aires.*

* Vantage Press, a subsidy house in New York, finally undertook to enlighten North American readers. See E. Perón, *My Mission in Life*. Editions in Portuguese and Arabic, as well as braille, also appeared.

In the months following the elections, the first lady's condition remained the central concern of the Peronist faithful. Nothing else seemed to matter much, not even the government's frustration of another military coup in the making (a feeble aftershock of the Menéndez fiasco) on February 2, nor the death of Vice-President Quijano in early April.

Evita's agony cast a pall over what should have been a happy interlude, a time for Perón to savor his triumph and to look ahead to the second term. But these luxuries would have escaped him even if his wife had been healthy because the economic crisis bearing down upon Argentina could no longer be ignored.

A pair of confidential reports prepared by his economic advisors in June and November 1951 spelled out the seriousness of the balance-of-payments bind.[12] The rising cost of imports due to the Korean War and a disastrous drop in farm production caused by droughts were identified as causes. The stopgap measures adopted before the elections had not improved the situation. Now that the voters had renewed Perón's mandate, he felt politically able to take more drastic measures.

Summoning Alfredo Gómez Morales to the residence, he queried his finance minister as to the available options. Gómez Morales replied that the government would either have to seek credits from abroad or embark upon an austerity program at home. The president resolved upon the latter course.[13]

In a somber speech to the nation on February 18, Perón unfolded his 1952 economic plan, an emergency package designed to attack the inflation spiral, stimulate agricultural output and improve the balance of trade. "Consume less and produce more" was the new slogan of the day. A reduction in public expenditures and a two-year freeze on wages and prices anchored the president's anti-inflation strategy. On a more tangible, immediate level, the requirement that restaurants and hotels observe one meatless day each week and the startling appearance of black bread in stores and markets drove home the government's determination to reduce internal consumption of beef and wheat in order to expand exports.

Widespread preoccupation with the state of Evita's health no doubt distracted public attention from the economic crisis and thereby made Perón's task easier. She did not recuperate well from her surgery. On March 6, 1952, when U.S. Ambassador Bunker made a farewell call at the Casa Rosada on the occasion of his departure from Argentina, Perón discussed his wife's condition at some length. He told Bunker that an anemia accompanied by a persistent low fever was complicating her recovery; her weight had fallen from 58 kilos (128 pounds) to 51 (112); she was also experiencing kidney problems, which Dr. Finochietto said were a common aftereffect of the type of operation she had undergone. Evita, the president noted, had a constitution with little resistance to illness.[14] In April a cabinet minister was reported as commenting that

"Evita is unable to sleep at all well, and arises at odd hours—from four o'clock on; she is holding early morning audiences. . . . The general described her as being bone-thin and 'as green as spinach.' "[15]

On May Day, Evita gave what was to be her farewell performance before her descamisados. Again, Perón had to support her. He looked as though he were holding a doll in his hands.[16] Wearing her Grand Peronist Medal proudly, she made a short speech laden with violent images.

> The people will follow Perón against the pressure of traitors from within and without; who in the darkness of night want to leave their viper's venom in the soul and body of Perón. And I ask God not to let these stupid people lift a hand against Perón because . . . Woe be that day! Woe be that day! That day, my general, I will go forth with the women of the country, dead or alive I will go forth with the descamisados of the fatherland, and we won't leave standing a single brick that is not Peronist. . . . I want my people to know we are willing to die for Perón; and I want the traitors to know we will not come here to say "We're here" to Perón as we did on September 28, but we will go out and take justice into our own hands.[17]

In her peroration, she claimed that her role was to be a "rainbow arc of love between the people and Perón," a metaphor oddly misplaced amidst the dark threats. Perhaps it conveyed nostalgia for happier days— the European tour, and those glorious, frenzied hours at the Ministry of Labor.

On May 7, Evita's thirty-third birthday, the Congress bestowed upon her the title "Spiritual Chief of the Nation," an honor conjured up by Héctor Cámpora, who specialized in such matters. It was a busy day for her, as a steady stream of visitors passed through the residence to convey their salutations. Everyone wanted to pose for photographs with her. The unstated suspicion was that this might be the last chance. According to one reliable account her weight had shrunk to 37 kilos (81 pounds).[18]

Inauguration Day, June 4, was brisk, clear and cold, a typical "Peronist day." Evita insisted upon attending the ceremonies. This required injections of a painkilling drug and the fashioning of a brace that would fit her long fur coat and enable her to stand during an open-car ride.[19] Critics have cited this as evidence of Perón's heartless exploitation of his wife in the final months of her life. They have charged that he squeezed the last gram of profit from her pathetic presence.[20] This interpretation underestimates Evita. Although a cancer was destroying her from within, her willpower had not been broken. The fierce determination that had carried her to the summit would not permit her to die quietly and out of view. Total physical prostration might have kept her away from the inauguration, but she had not yet reached that point.

It was to be her last public appearance. At the traditional joint session of Congress, she sat in the seat that would have been occupied by the vice-president (the deceased Quijano not yet having been replaced).[21] Tributes to her work and her courage were the central themes of the proceedings. Propped up next to her uniformed husband in the Packard convertible that took them down the Avenida de Mayo to the Government House, she endured the afternoon chill and saluted the crowd. Her skeletal frame seemed barely able to support the glistening emeralds of the Grand Peronist Medal that hung from her neck.

Late that night, a pair of German equilibrists taunted death by traversing a wire that stretched from the top of the obelisk to the roof of one of the buildings fronting the Avenida 9 de Julio. A resplendent audience of government officials and diplomats savored an evening of music and ballet at the Teatro Colón. Neither Perón nor the first lady attended. Evita, exhausted and in agony, retired to her bed. She would not leave her sickroom alive.

Youth, glamour, adulation, agony and early death—Evita's lot fed Argentina's lust for sentimentality like nothing else in the country's history. As the end approached, a mass psychosis seemed to grip the country.

Because death was in no hurry to take her, Evita herself could participate in the delirium. For example, there was the matter of the monument. The idea seems to have originated in early 1951, when the first lady urged Perón to approve the construction of a fitting memorial to the seventeenth of October. The original plan called for a statue of a worker rising above a mausoleum that would house the remains of a descamisado. As Evita began to sense that her own days were numbered, she expressed the wish that she too be put to rest in the monument's crypt. The concept then changed from that of a tomb of an unknown descamisado to that of an Argentine Taj Mahal.

Leon Tomassi, an Italian sculptor who at the time was working on the figures that would decorate the roof of the new Eva Perón Foundation headquarters, drew the task of preparing a model, which he presented to Evita late in 1951. She instructed him to make the interior more like Napoleon's tomb, which she recalled from her visit to Paris on the Rainbow Tour.[22]

On June 26, 1952, the Chamber of Deputies passed a law authorizing the erection of the memorial, now known as the monument to Eva Perón. Instead of a statue of a descamisado, a likeness of the first lady would tower above the edifice. On July 7, the Senate approved the law, which created a monument commission charged with executing the plan.

Evita embraced the project with all the enthusiasm she could muster. She insisted that the structure be colossal in size and be located in the Plaza de Mayo. This created serious problems, since the modest size of the plaza would not permit the proportions upon which the first lady had set her heart. Architectural harmony did not concern her, and the commission had to confront the impracticality of her desires.[23]

Implicit in any planning for the first lady's last resting place was the question of the form in which she would be laid to rest. During the final months of her life, rumors began to circulate that Perón intended to have her body preserved. Lending sustenance to the speculations was the presence of Dr. Pedro Ara, the Spanish cultural attaché in Buenos Aires and an anatomy professor who specialized in the preservation of the human body.[24]

On July 18, one of the physicians who had been attending Evita appeared at Dr. Ara's home close to midnight and informed him that the president wanted to embalm the first lady's body. The reason for the arrangement with Dr. Ara was a sudden crisis: Evita had lapsed into a coma and her death was expected momentarily. However, it turned out to be a false alarm. The first lady recovered consciousness as abruptly as she had lost it. Nonetheless, these sudden turns jarred Perón and the inner circle into taking action to provide for her demise, which now seemed more imminent than ever.

That Sunday, before a giant altar set up at the foot of the obelisk, a mass was offered for the dying Evita. A steady downpour failed to keep the faithful away (although it did prevent an orchestra from performing Schubert's Mass). Father Hernán Benítez, the first lady's confessor, delivered a sermon at the request of the president, who suggested that he prepare the populace for Evita's passing. The Jesuit's words were broadcast to the nation. They were so much like a funeral oration that Atilio Renzi, the superintendent at the residence, cut the wires of Evita's radio set. This greatly disappointed Eva, who had been looking forward to the sermon.

In a country where popular religion has a firmer grip than orthodox Catholicism upon the hearts of the lower classes, the death throes of Eva Perón touched off a predictable outpouring of gifts believed to have curative powers. Charms, holy water, sacred bones and objects of every description arrived daily at the residence and were carefully stored. At the same time hundreds of people gathered near the building in round-the-clock prayer vigils.

On Saturday, July 26, Eva Perón again lapsed into a coma, from which she would not recover. Father Benítez administered the sacrament of extreme unction. The immediate family and her intimate associates stood by and waited for the chapter to close. In the late afternoon, Dr. Ara received a call and set out for the residence.* Radio bulletins informed the nation that the first lady's condition was worsening.

---

* *Time* magazine, eager as always to print negative rumors about the first lady, would state that "Ara was on hand at Evita's deathbed, reportedly to make sure that the doctors gave her no drugs that would affect the embalming." November 28, 1955, p. 25. Dr. Ara called this "false and grotesque." P. Ara, *El caso Eva Perón*, p. 67. Since he did not reach the residence until after she died, there is good reason to believe him.

At 8:23 P.M. one of the doctors in attendance turned to Perón and said, "She has no pulse."[25] It was over. Juan Duarte lost control. "There is no God! There is no God!" he screamed, rushing from the bedroom.[26] Perón remained impassive. Raúl Apold, director of the government press office, composed an announcement to be broadcast at 9:30 P.M. He "adjusted" the time of death to 8:25.

Shortly afterward Dr. Ara arrived. His instructions were to prepare the body for immediate public display at the Ministry of Labor. After the funeral, he was to embalm the remains, which would eventually be placed in the monument. Perón gave him complete authority to do the job as he saw fit. However, when the owlish professor objected to plans to use CGT headquarters as Evita's temporary resting place, the president told him that this was his wife's wish. He assured Ara that proper facilities would be provided, and that security would be adequate.* The labor leaders, who had struggled mightily if in vain to make Evita vice-president because they believed she would guarantee their interests, now perceived a symbolic value to be gained from possession of her corpse.

The doctor worked feverishly through the night, nervous with the knowledge that the outcome of the entire project hung on the quality of the preliminary work he was now doing. Early the next morning, the first lady's coiffeur spent more than an hour arranging the corpse's hair. Juan Duarte, at last composed, came in and removed a few locks for his mother. One of Evita's attendants, pursuant to an instruction given by the first lady on the day of her death, removed her red fingernail polish and replaced it with a natural color. Perón himself dropped by and asked some technical questions about the preservation process. The blue pajamas Evita had been wearing were removed and the corpse was wrapped in a white shroud. An Argentine flag covered the lower part of her body. The rosary Pius XII had given the first lady was carefully positioned among the fingers of her clasped hands. An Eva Perón Foundation ambulance delivered the cedar coffin, which was airtight and topped by a glass panel to permit public viewing.

It was nine-thirty when the funeral procession left the residence en route to the Ministry of Labor. The ambulance carried the coffin, while Perón, members of the family and the inner circle followed in automobiles.

Thus began what one anti-Peronist writer has called a "bacchanal of necrophilia."[27] The government encouraged the flow of emotion (and even commissioned Twentieth Century-Fox to film the spectacle), but it

* The original plan had been to inter the body temporarily at the downtown Church of San Francisco. However, a delegation from the CGT visited the residence in the early morning hours of the twenty-seventh and urged Perón to allow the body to rest at the confederation's headquarters. He acceded to their request (how willingly is not clear), much to the displeasure of Evita's mother. See O. Borroni and R. Vacca, *La vida de Eva Perón*, pp. 317–18; "Historia del Peronismo: La segunda presidencia —III," *Primera Plana*, May 21, 1968, p. 50.

would be a serious mistake to attribute the spectacle to Peronist manipulation. What happened was in fact a genuine expression of unrestrained grief.[28]

Normally a ten-minute drive, the trip from the residence to the Ministry of Labor took nearly two hours. As the procession neared its destination, the crowds thickened, undaunted by a steady rain. Streetlights adorned with black crepe looked down upon a sea of humanity straining for a glimpse of the improvised hearse. Extravagant floral wreaths had already begun to accumulate against the outer walls of the building where Perón had nourished his first contacts with organized labor and where his wife had later presided over her "Court of Miracles." The flowers would mount like snowdrifts, threatening to blanket the entire edifice.

A double file of three hundred and fifty uniformed nurses from the Eva Perón Foundation nursing school formed an honor guard through which the cortege passed on its way to the entrance of the ministry. The main hall on the second floor had been converted into a chapel. The coffin was placed on a catafalque and raised slightly at one end. Cadets from the military academy and a delegation of workers stood watch next to the casket. The archbishop of Buenos Aires, Monsignor Manuel Tato, and Father Benítez celebrated mass. It was now time to open the doors to Evita's adoring public.

Perón had promised that every Argentine who wanted to visit the body would be given the opportunity to do so, no matter how long it took. Perhaps he did not realize the emotional intensity Evita's death had unleashed. As he viewed the endless line snaking from curb to curb and extending for block after block, he muttered to his press secretary, "I never knew they loved her so much."[29] They stood in the rain under umbrellas or folded newspapers, silently, patiently. "Even Heaven Weeps," a headline informed them. Only when they passed the bier did some lose control. The first-aid stations were kept busy attending to those who collapsed. Several people died from heart attacks. According to an official estimate, 65,000 mourners visited the corpse each day.

On Monday and Tuesday, all activity in Buenos Aires ceased, in deference to the wake. When stores and shops reopened, their windows housed displays honoring the deceased. In the poorer neighborhoods, homemade altars decorated with candles, flowers and Evita's photo sprouted on street corners and empty lots.

As the mourning gave no signs of abatement, Dr. Ara grew restive. He wanted to get on with his work as soon as possible and dreaded the risk of an accident that might spoil the corpse. His concerns were well-founded. Peronist officials insisted on opening the casket to wipe clean the underside of the viewing glass, and once they even pumped a current of fresh air into the interior of the coffin. This meddling so upset the professor that on August 6 he persuaded Perón to prohibit anyone from touching the casket and to limit the duration of the wake.

The death of Evita profoundly shook Juan Perón. Throughout the public viewing he stood by the coffin for hours at a time, his face frozen in a glazed expression.

The hands of the clock on the tower of the Ministry of Labor remained permanently fixed at 8:25. The regular 8:30 P.M. radio newscasts were advanced by five minutes in order to facilitate a daily commemoration of the moment of Eva's death. Each morning Argentines observed a fifteen-minute period of silence during which passages from *My Mission in Life* were reverently recited over loudspeakers. Both houses of the legislature of Buenos Aires Province enacted a bill changing the name of the city of La Plata, the provincial capital, to Eva Perón.* A trade union cabled the Vatican to request the immediate initiation of proceedings to canonize the late "spiritual chief of the Argentine nation."

On Friday evening, August 8, the public viewing of the body abruptly terminated. Word that the wake would continue the next day at the Congress sent people scurrying up the Avenida de Mayo to form a new line. After a special mass on Saturday morning in the chapel at the Ministry of Labor, Evita's remains were transported atop a special gun carriage to the Congress building, where public viewing resumed for one more day.

In some miraculous way, Evita's funeral procession avoided the giddy excesses that had marred much of the official and public reaction to her illness and death. Dignity, stubbornly resisted during the long ordeal, was maintained throughout the ceremonial transit between the Congress and CGT headquarters. It was an impressive yet muted spectacle, perhaps yielding to a collective weariness that pervaded the nation.

At 3:00 P.M. on Sunday the tenth, after the last of seven eulogies heaping hyperbole upon hyperbole, the flag-draped casket was taken from the Congress and positioned upon the gun carriage. As a military band struck up Chopin's Funeral March, thirty-nine white-shirted trade-union officials (twenty-nine men, ten women) took hold of a network of ropes and began to pull the heavy vehicle slowly down Rivadavia Street, between lines of military cadets, nurses and young workers. A pair of armored cars flanked the casket and escorted it along a passage that separated the spectators from the honor guard. The president, his cabinet and Evita's family followed the carriage. A squadron of air force planes passed overhead.

Two million Argentines filled the Plaza del Congreso and lined the route. As the cortege passed, flowers descended like snowflakes from the

---

* This inspired the cruel anti-Peronist joke, most recently repeated by Jorge Borges: "Why so much discussion between La Plata and Eva Perón? Why don't they call it 'La Pluta'? [a play on words combining La Plata with *puta* (whore)]." *Cambio 16,* August 30, 1976, p. 42.

balconies of nearby buildings. The crowd broke the police lines and followed the procession as it turned into the Avenida de Mayo, skirted the Casa Rosada and veered right at the Paseo Colón. It took nearly three hours to reach Evita's temporary resting place, where the crack regiment of grenadiers, resplendent in their red-and-white costumes, stood watch. Flowers covered every balcony of the confederation headquarters. After a twenty-one-gun salute and the playing of taps, the coffin was lifted from the gun carriage and taken into a salon of the CGT edifice. It would remain there only one day. On the third floor, Dr. Ara had prepared his laboratory and would begin the serious work of preserving Evita's remains.

The death of the first lady left a vacuum both for Perón and the Peronist movement. Until he met her, Juan Perón had never experienced an intimate relationship that affected his professional or public life. The loss of Eva was like an amputation. There was no one who could really replace her, except Perón himself. Ten days after she died, he announced that he would man her desk at the Ministry of Labor several days a week and receive the public. In addition, he assumed the presidency of the women's branch of the Peronist party. But these were roles to which he was ill-suited.

The adjustment he would have to make to her absence was a challenge every bit as formidable as his struggle for the presidency. Indeed, his ability to continue governing to a large extent depended upon how well he would rise to the occasion.

Part V

The Second Presidency

(1952–1955)

30

A Taste of Terror

In the bedroom of a fashionable apartment not far from the building where Perón and Evita once lived, a shirt, jacket and trousers lay neatly folded on a chair near a night table. A man on his knees leaned against the bed as if in prayer, one arm tucked under his bent head. He was clad in underwear and socks. A pool of blood smeared the sheets on which he rested and the rug beneath him. On the floor next to his left leg was a .38-caliber revolver.[1]

A handwritten note on the night table contained the following message:

My dear General Perón:
   The evil of certain betrayers of Perón and of the working people . . . and the enemies of the fatherland wanted to separate me from you; angry because they knew how much you love me and how loyal I am; for that reason they kept defaming me and they succeeded; they filled me with shame. . . .
   I have been honest, and no one could prove otherwise. . . . I say one more time that the greatest man I know is Perón. . . .
   I ask you to take care of my beloved mother and my relatives. . . . I came with Eva, I leave with her, shouting long live Perón, long live the fatherland, and may God and your people be with you always. My last embrace is for my mother and for you.

> Juan R. Duarte
> Forgive me for the
> handwriting, forgive
> me for everything.[2]

Juan Duarte's body was discovered on the morning of April 9, 1953, three days after he had resigned under a cloud of suspicion from his post as Perón's private secretary. Even before his remains had reached their resting place in the Recoleta Cemetery, people were beginning to whisper. In the Barrio Norte, where cynicism was one of the few pleasures the

Peronists had not been able to suppress, the favorite joke was: "Everybody knows he committed suicide, but nobody knows who did it."

Juan Duarte had always been Evita's favorite. Her death deeply depressed him, no doubt because he realized how vulnerable she had left him. He had been living well, far beyond his salary. A bachelor, he had grown accustomed to the easy pleasures of the flesh. Everything he had and was he owed to his sister. Now he found himself totally dependent upon Perón.

In the aftermath of Evita's passing, one long loose end remained, and Juan Perón needed his brother-in-law to help fashion what the president hoped would be a neat knot. A considerable amount of property belonged to the first lady at the time of her demise. The exact contents and worth of her estate continue to be both a mystery and a subject of controversy even to the present day. The machinations to gain control of it began soon after the funeral.

On October 17, 1952, the first Loyalty Day observance without Evita, an announcer read aloud a document dated June 29 of that year and purporting to be Evita's last will and testament. After the usual worshipful praise of the general (e.g., "Perón is my sun and my sky"), the text stated:

> I want all my property to be at the disposal of Perón as sole sovereign representative of the people. I consider that my property is the patrimony of the people of the Peronist movement, which likewise belongs to the people. . . .
>
> While Perón lives, he can do what he wants with all my property: sell it, give it away, even burn it. . . . But after Perón, the heir to my property must be the people. . . .[3]

Perón then announced the creation of the Evita Foundation (an entity separate from the Eva Perón Foundation), which would see to the execution of the will. Congress in turn voted to exempt Evita's estate from taxation.

There was one slight hitch in the grand scheme to carry out the instructions left by Evita: the June 29 document did not comply with the legal requirements for a will (for example, there were no witnesses to her signature) and was therefore null and void. This meant that the first lady died intestate and that her property was subject to distribution under the law, which provided that it devolve in equal shares to the husband (Perón) and the decedent's mother.

Perón was well aware of his legal quandary. According to allegations made by Juana Ibarguren de Duarte in a lawsuit brought against him after his downfall, he sent emissaries to attempt to persuade her to sign her rights over to him and she refused; finally the president used Juancito; the private secretary went to his mother and begged her to give up her interest in Evita's estate; he told her that if she did not sign, his life would be in danger and he would have to leave the country, whereupon Juana signed.[4]

Juan Duarte may have performed another important service for his employer. On October 1, he and Héctor Cámpora left Buenos Aires on a trip to Europe. There was immediate speculation that their mission was to arrange for the transfer of Evita's Swiss bank accounts to Juan Perón's name. According to a U.S. embassy cable, they were carrying a letter from the president of the Argentine Supreme Court stating that all other heirs had waived their claims, and that the president was now entitled to all his wife's property.[5]

In reality, Juana did not surrender her claims until after her son had departed.[6] Moreover, as subsequent events would disclose, Perón never did come into possession of any fortune hidden away in Swiss banks. Therefore, one may surmise that no such fortune existed, or if it did exist, Perón was never able to touch it.

It strains credibility almost to the breaking point that Perón did not arrange that any Swiss accounts be smoothly and silently transferred to his name at Evita's death. The notion that Juan Duarte would have to go to Switzerland to do the job, and that he would bring with him a legally useless letter containing a false statement, is absurd. But the possibility of massive bungling cannot totally be discounted.

Once Juana had signed the release, her son's usefulness to the president evaporated. In addition, for the first time during the Perón era, accusations of corruption within the government received official recognition. In a September 13 speech to the Peronist bloc in Congress, Perón himself railed against the dishonesty of certain public officials and promised that the judicial system would deal with them. Whether this was an attempt to find scapegoats for the economic pinch Argentines were feeling, or an indication that graft had reached such a high level that it could no longer be safely ignored, Juan Duarte was now a sitting duck, inasmuch as he was apparently deeply involved in shady business deals.

In early April 1953, speculators were blamed for a serious meat shortage that had hit Buenos Aires. Juan Duarte's name was prominently mentioned.[7] The CGT called for an investigation, and Perón announced it was time to put an end to corruption in government. He appointed a team of military officers to look into the matter, and they began with the office of the President's private secretary.*

---

* According to one account, in late March an actress complained to Perón that Juan Duarte had defrauded her, and in the process of checking out the accusation the president discovered that his brother-in-law was engaged in a number of questionable money-making ventures. República Argentina, *Libro negro de la segunda tiranía,* pp. 221–22.

By April 6, Juan Duarte had resigned his job in the Casa Rosada. For two nights he roamed the Buenos Aires theater district with friends. On Thursday morning, April 9, the day of his death, he was scheduled to meet with the military investigators.

The Duarte family refused to believe he had taken his own life. At the wake his mother and sisters kept repeating that he had been murdered. Rumors began to circulate, one of which had him killed at the airport as he attempted to flee the country.[8] The authorities certified suicide as the cause of death. The body was interred without an autopsy.

Perón terminated the investigation of his brother-in-law and none of its findings were ever made public. He later claimed that Duarte had contracted syphilis as a result of frequent visits to houses of prostitution, and that it was the disease, along with Duarte's knowledge of its incurability, that drove him to take his own life.[9]*

Controversy over Duarte's death flared into public view after Perón's overthrow, when a police commission reopened the case.[10] The chief investigator, Navy Captain Aldo L. Molinari, concluded that he had been assassinated. In a book presenting the case for murder, Captain Molinari cited testimony by neighbors that they saw several men carrying a blood-stained Juan Duarte to his apartment on the night of his death. He also referred to the results of an autopsy performed in 1956 and revealing not only that Duarte's head was bruised but also that the fatal bullet had been .45 caliber rather than .38.[11]

Judge Raúl A. Pizarro Miguens, who had certified the death as suicide in 1953, then took up the cudgel. He published a book challenging Molinari's assertions and brought a lawsuit against the captain to clear his name.[12]

Taken together—the charges and countercharges, the facts and innuendoes, and the incompleteness and irregularities of the proceedings in 1953 and 1956—the sum and substance of the Duarte case is that whether he committed suicide or was murdered remains a mystery. What is more significant, however, is that it would not be the last instance in which unexplained circumstances would shroud the violent death of a person whose elimination served Perón's interests.

Juan Duarte was not the only member of Eva Perón's inner circle to fall from favor after her death. The faithful José Espejo lost his job after the crowd hissed and whistled at him as he began his speech at the 1952 Loyalty Day observance. Coming on the heels of a similar reception at a soccer match, it was in the nature of a vote of no confidence by the rank and file. He resigned shortly afterward.

---

* Support for this version may be found in a cable Ambassador Nufer sent to Washington on the eve of Duarte's trip to Europe. The ambassador noted that "sources report Duarte seriously ill, presumably cancer." Nufer to secretary of state, 735.11/10-152, October 1, 1952.

Héctor Cámpora was replaced as president of the Chamber of Deputies. Perón made him a special ambassador and sent him on several innocuous goodwill missions overseas. Armando Méndez San Martín was on the verge of being dumped as minister of education when he saved his job by dreaming up the idea of creating a union of secondary students, which would channel teenagers into athletic and cultural activities consonant with Peronist ideals.

Finally, the supreme council of the Peronist party dealt a harsh blow to any comeback hopes Domingo Mercante may have entertained. The ex-governor's public appearances with Evita during the last year of her life fed speculation that he might return to politics.[13] But on April 30, 1953, the governing body of the party expelled him for obstructionism, disloyalty, lack of ethics, sowing confusion and encouraging the circulation of false rumors.[14] It was a bitter pill for the onetime "heart of Perón," who faded quietly into retirement.

Harsher misfortunes awaited anti-Peronists. On the afternoon of April 15, the CGT called a strike and summoned its hosts to the Plaza de Mayo. The gathering was clearly meant to bolster the president in the face of the economic difficulties that were now besetting the working class. The crowd was large but not uniformly enthusiastic. Many in attendance came only because their union delegates took attendance in the plaza.

José Espejo's successor, Eduardo Vuletich, gave Perón an extravagantly obsequious introduction: "We want to say to you that you do what seems best to you. We the workers exist only to ratify, only to obey you consciously and willingly."[15]

Perón then launched an exhortation aimed at blaming speculators for the crisis and fortifying popular support for his anti-inflation program. A muffled explosion cut him off in mid-sentence. Smoke poured from the ground floor of the hotel facing the plaza.

"Comrades, comrades," he kept repeating. "Comrades, those people, the same ones who circulated rumors every day, today it seems as though they are noisier than ever. They want to bomb us. . . ." Another explosion, this one closer to the speaker's platform, sent a dense cloud of smoke in eruption from a nearby subway entrance.

"Comrades, comrades!" The president was now trying to hold the crowd's attention and prevent a panic. "I think we're going to have to go back to the days when we went around with garrotes in our pockets." The last phrase seemed to excite those who had not begun to disperse. "Perón! Perón!" they roared. "Punish them! Punish them!"

Now the *conductor* and his mass were on the same wavelength and were exchanging strong signals that produced a reciprocal charge. "This thing about punishment you are telling me to do," the president replied. "Why don't you do it?"[16]

Though Perón concluded by telling his listeners to go home, his violent improvisation had found receptive ears. The shock troops of the ultra-right were present in the Plaza de Mayo and were quick to seize upon the president's call for rough justice. His words sent them off on a rampage that would give Buenos Aires its first taste of genuine terror under the Peronist regime.

One group headed for the Casa del Pueblo (People's House), head-quarters of the Socialist party and its now-silenced newspaper, *La Van-guardia.* "Jews! Go back to Moscow!" they screamed, throwing stones at the building.[17] There were sixty people inside. The response they received when they phoned the police for help was that no units were available due to the events in the Plaza de Mayo. Soon pieces of burning paper began to float through holes in the windows. The besieged Socialists barely managed to escape before a truck battered down the steel entrance and the edifice was put to the torch. Gasoline-fed flames destroyed the Juan B. Justo Workers' Library, which housed a priceless collection of books, newspapers and pamphlets dealing with the labor movement in Argentina. The firemen who arrived belatedly on the scene merely kept the blaze from spreading.

As smoke poured from the Casa del Pueblo, other groups attacked the Casa Radical (Radical House) and the headquarters of the conservative Democratic National party. Again, police and fire-fighting units remained impassive. The damage inflicted was not so extensive as that sustained by the Socialists. One reason was that the arsonists had hit upon an idea that diverted them away from these buildings. They decided to strike at the heart of the oligarchy: the Jockey Club on Florida Street.

A foreign resident of Buenos Aires and member of the exclusive social club described the atmosphere there as tense in the early hours. The place was virtually deserted. Then the first contingent of shock troops arrived. Three jeeps came to the Tucumán Street entrance. The majordomo tried to keep them out, but they forced their way by him. Several men with hatchets went upstairs to the main hall and hacked original paintings by Goya and Velásquez out of their frames. They piled them on the floor and started a bonfire. They also smashed to pieces a statue of Diana the Huntress. The majordomo called the fire department. The answer he received was "We have no instructions to put out a fire at the Jockey Club."[18] The burning of the Jockey Club amounted to one of the worst instances of art vandalism ever perpetrated. But the rioters demonstrated they were not totally ignorant of the finer things in life. They plundered the club's well-stocked wine cellar.

When the foreign eyewitness returned in the early hours of the morning for a second look at the wreckage, he discovered that "in front of the club there were three or four fire hoses strung out on the street. Holes had been punched in them, and water was spurting straight up in the air."[19] Fire had completely gutted the building.

It was a costly day in many ways. The bombs killed five people and wounded ninety-three. The Justo Library and the paintings and tapestries in the Jockey Club could never be replaced. The bombing in the Plaza de Mayo and the nocturnal rampage represented a serious escalation in the struggle between Peronists and anti-Peronists. Those who planted the explosives must have known that innocent bystanders would be victimized. Only good fortune prevented loss of life during the evening disorders. Yet the Peronist newspaper *Democracia* wrote approvingly of the "flames of purification."[20] The hardening of attitudes was even more evident in a congressional debate several weeks later, when Peronist deputies rose to defend the arsonists.

Although Perón did not specifically pass the word to set the fires, the government obviously tolerated the arson to the point of ratification and even kept it within limits. Perón always abhorred disorganized violence, but on this occasion it suited his purposes and was easy to contain. The ultra-rightists were his first terrorists. Later the left would have its turn.

Having promised repression, Perón quickly delivered. The investigation of the incident assumed a decidedly political coloration, and prominent members of the opposition filled the jails.[21] Many of the political prisoners regained their freedom by August, when Perón was seeking better relations with the United States and found it useful to make some mild conciliatory gestures. In addition, Perón still needed his opposition, if for no other reason than to permit contested elections which the Peronists could win. He sorely needed the legitimacy that elections alone could provide.

Therefore, even though the April violence had poisoned what was left of the political atmosphere, elections had to proceed on schedule. The president decided to wait until 1954 to fill the vacancy left by Quijano's death. The Peronist nomination went to Admiral Teisaire, who had been serving as president of the Senate. The Radical party candidate suffered the usual constraints that made it impossible for him to reach a mass audience. Nonetheless, when the votes were counted after the April 25 balloting, he had captured a creditable 2.5 million, as compared to Teisaire's tally of nearly 5 million.[22]

The gap between Peronists and anti-Peronists had long been wide. The overt opposition went through the motions, but as a political force it had given way to a hard-core band of covert operatives committed to Perón's overthrow. Their goal was to destabilize the regime. Perón's task was to deny them the opportunity to do so. His performance in the Plaza de Mayo on April 15, 1953, demonstrated that he was capable of making the kind of careless mistake that could accomplish for his foes what they seemed incapable of doing for themselves.

31

Making Friends Abroad

On February 20, 1953, a presidential train carried Juan D. Perón into an Andean tunnel linking Argentina with Chile on his first visit to a foreign country since he entered the Casa Rosada. He arrived under circumstances far different from those that shrouded his departure from Chile in 1937.

In the first year of his second term, the Argentine president was assigning a higher priority to foreign policy. Efforts to forge new bonds with the rest of Latin America and even to mend relations with the United States had become major preoccupations. He may have been looking for new challenges, since his domestic opponents had long been reduced to impotence. Moreover, foreign-policy initiatives could serve only to strengthen his position at home. Control over the mass media would enable him to conceal any failures he might suffer and to convert modest successes into major triumphs.

Perón would frequently tell Latin Americans that "the year 2000 will find us either united or enslaved."[1] Rooted in Simón Bolívar's unsuccessful effort to unify the continent after the Spanish yoke had been cast aside, the notion derived contemporary inspiration from the nascent European Common Market. Perón advocated as a first step economic union with Brazil and Chile. He saw a confederation of Latin states as the only road to development free from domination by capitalist or Communist imperialism.

In the abstract, this idea was visionary. Perón was the only Latin leader willing to promote union vigorously, and he did so until the day he died. However, once he began to do more than talk about union, it could no longer remain an abstraction, and political reality intruded. For example, the Perón regime had long been engaged in attempts to sow the seeds of *justicialismo* abroad,[2] a practice as normal to Peronists as the export of Communism by Russians or free enterprise on the part of North Americans.

But Latins viewed what they saw as Argentine imperialism with great apprehension and distaste. The fact that Perón sought to encourage Latin political movements with goals similar to his made him vulnerable to the charge that his talk of continental union cloaked a grand scheme to extend Argentine hegemony over the rest of South America.

In addition, it was necessary to implement the concept of unity by means of specific policies and programs. In this regard, the Argentine performance merited low marks. Perón was not disposed to take on the task personally and work out a consistent, patient, intelligent strategy but preferred instead to rely upon instinct, which did not serve him well, for he displayed a remarkable proneness to blunder. His genius for political leadership seemed to desert him when he dealt with Latin American policy. This was especially evident during his trip to Santiago, which was hardly a model of diplomatic finesse.

Perón's visit came about as a consequence of the election of General Carlos Ibáñez del Campo as president of Chile in late 1952.[3] Ibáñez had first won that office in 1927, but four years later his inability to deal with the Depression and resistance to his authoritarian methods provoked a civilian uprising that forced his resignation. During the next two decades he spent a considerable amount of time in exile in Buenos Aires. He and Perón eventually formed a close personal friendship. Although Ibáñez' political philosophy was rather vague, it shared with *justicialismo* elements such as nationalism, anti-oligarchy rhetoric, concentration of authority in the presidency and a foreign policy independent of the United States. However, the working class did not support him, and the dour Chilean lacked Perón's charisma.

The Argentine *conductor* rejoiced at Ibáñez' victory. Shortly after assuming office, the new Chilean president formally invited his friend in the Casa Rosada to cross the Andes.

The Peronist press made much of the impending journey and its announced goal of achieving economic union with Chile. The delegation that was to accompany the president grew larger by the day. It comprised government, labor and Peronist party officials, military officers, journalists, a large group of security agents, and sports celebrities led by racing driver Juan Fangio. On the Pacific side of the mountains, Senator María de la Cruz, Perón's most open and ardent Chilean admirer—who delighted in being called the "Eva Perón of Chile"—made extravagant speeches to herald the coming of the *conductor*.

But shortly before his departure Perón committed an inexcusable gaffe that almost aborted the trip. In an interview with the editor of a newspaper owned by the Chilean government, he suggested, in a careless, offhand way:

I believe that Chilean-Argentine unity, a complete unity and not a halfway one, should be made total and immediate. Simple economic unity will not be sufficiently strong. . . . In this situation, one must be bold. Create unity, and then solve problems as they arise. Just as when you take a cold shower, if you stick a finger in the water first, you hesitate. It's better to put yourself immediately under the shower and adjust afterward.[4]

He also said, with a wink, that Argentina would give Chile all the meat and wheat she needed, and allowed that he would be disposed to accept the annexation of Chile by Argentina.

When all this appeared in print, the Chilean reaction ranged from disbelief to indignation. Ibáñez' spokesman took pains to insist that the discussions between the two presidents would touch only upon economic union. The political opposition (which included unsuccessful Socialist party presidential candidate Salvador Allende) hammered away relentlessly at the Argentine leader and his Chilean supporters. Perón disavowed the interview, but his excuses failed to convince anyone. For a brief moment, it looked as if the trip might be in jeopardy, but he weathered the storm.

The Argentine president and his large entourage arrived in the Chilean capital at 6:00 P.M. on February 20. The next day Perón and Ibáñez signed an agreement subscribing to the principle of economic union. The rest of the six-day visit was purely ceremonial. Perón gave several speeches and turned on the full force of his personal charm. The Chilean public, especially the lower classes, seemed receptive to him.

At the same time, however, he committed two more blunders. Claiming a sore throat, he let his minister of technical matters, Raúl Mendé, deliver a speech for him in the city of Concepción. With Perón and Ibáñez on the platform, Mendé made the tactless assertion that all past presidents of Argentina and Chile had sold out their countries.[5] This provoked a barrage of criticism in the press.

An even worse mistake was Perón's blatant intervention in a particularly volatile area of Chilean politics. The 1952 contest had been the first national election in which women had been permitted to cast ballots, and Ibáñez had done well among the newly enfranchised voters. Drawing upon his own experience, Perón decided that a women's movement could be very useful to his Chilean friend. But lacking both an Eva Perón and a strong sense of verticality, feminist politics in Chile had become mired in personality squabbles. The Argentine president, therefore, thought it appropriate to use his magnetic presence in an effort to unify Chile's women. One day before his departure he met with several women leaders, including the mercurial María de la Cruz, and promised a large sum of money to help them organize. The next day, the Chileans met with Perón's representatives, who handed over a suitcase stuffed with Argentine pesos.[6]

It was naive to think that the equivalent of about $50,000 could put an end to the feuding. Not only did it persist, but a week after Perón left, a Chilean magazine published details of the Argentine meddling. In the ensuing uproar, María de la Cruz claimed the money had been donated for the construction of a medical clinic and day-care center. She also announced she was returning the pesos to the Eva Perón Foundation in Buenos Aires (an intriguing admission regarding the source of the funds). The scandal badly damaged the political careers of the women involved, especially María de la Cruz, whom the Chilean Senate subsequently expelled.

Perón's trip to Chile was a great success at home. As a cable from the U.S. embassy in Buenos Aires noted, he proved he could travel confidently abroad and be well received, facts that much impressed not only his followers but also the opposition. "Argentine ego does not easily condemn the Argentine who makes a big international splash."[7] It mattered little that economic union remained a distant goal.

Shortly afterward Ibáñez reciprocated the visit. The Chilean president flew to Buenos Aires on the afternoon of July 6. Perón staged a rally in his honor and then brought him before a joint session of Congress for some oratorical tributes by the members. The trip culminated in the signing of a treaty that called for a reduction in customs duties, increased trade and the creation of a joint council that would devise further ways to implement economic union.[8]

Later that year Paraguay, Ecuador and Nicaragua signed similar agreements, the latter on the occasion of a visit to Buenos Aires by President Anastasio Somoza.[9] Bolivia followed suit in late 1954. As with Chile, the treaties were preliminary in nature. Confederation was still very much in the distance. Moreover, an indispensable element in any South American union was Brazil, and Perón was having great difficulty attracting the continent's largest country.

It would have taken a Herculean effort to overcome the deep-rooted antagonism between Argentina and Brazil, a reality first exploited by Great Britain and then by the United States as cornerstones of diplomatic policy toward South America. However, the upset electoral victory of Getúlio Vargas in 1950 brought to the Brazilian presidency the one politician who might have been able to work out an arrangement with the Argentines. A populist leader who took power in 1930 as a result of a coup and ruled until his overthrow by the armed forces in 1945, Vargas was sympathetic to Perón and open to the idea of continental unity. According to Perón, when Vargas took office again, the latter promised they would meet in Rio de Janeiro or Buenos Aires to sign the sort of agreement Perón later made with Ibáñez.[10]

But Vargas was beset by political opponents who loudly branded overtures to Perón as efforts to create an anti-U.S. bloc in the southern cone of the continent, or worse yet, evidence that Vargas had in mind the formation of a workers' organization similar to the Argentine CGT and designed to help him secure the same monopoly of power the Argentine leader exercised.[11] Vargas' young minister of labor, João Goulart, knew

Perón personally and made a number of trips to Buenos Aires. This provoked the accusation (later proven false) that Goulart was purchasing weapons with which Brazilian worker militias would be armed.[12] In 1954, Vargas cracked under the pressure and committed suicide. Goulart's association with Perón would later haunt him. He became president of Brazil in 1961, and three years later fell victim to a military coup. One of the justifications U.S. officials put forward for supporting his overthrow was the charge that he was about to attempt a Peronist solution to the crisis confronting his nation at that time.[13]

The only other foreign trips Perón made during his second term took him north to Paraguay. The first, in October 1953, was a ceremonial affair preliminary to the signing of an accord that called for closer economic ties between the two countries. During the visit, Perón conceived the idea of making a grand gesture that would endear Argentina to her landlocked neighbor. He resolved to return within the year and bring back with him trophies (weapons, banners, etc.) the Argentines had won from Paraguay in the nineteenth-century War of the Triple Alliance, in which little Paraguay rashly took on Argentina, Brazil and Uruguay.

Originally scheduled for May 1954, his departure had to be postponed because of a coup that brought General Alfredo Stroessner to the Paraguayan presidency. Three months later, Perón and the trophies made a dramatic appearance in Asunción, the capital. Stroessner and his fellow citizens were so touched that not only did they make Perón an honorary citizen but the army decreed him an honorary general.[14] These tributes would one day prove extraordinarily useful to him.

While embarked upon a more aggressive Latin American policy, Juan Perón rather suddenly warmed up to Uncle Sam. He saw no inconsistency between this new tack and initiatives that seemed to compete with U.S. interests in the continent. Nor, apparently, did the North Americans, because they did not reject his courtship.

Two events in 1952 helped prepare the way. Shortly before Evita's death, Albert F. Nufer was named U.S. ambassador to Argentina. A career diplomat who had recently chaired a joint Argentine-U.S. Committee on Commercial Studies, Nufer quickly developed a close working relationship with Perón. The election of Dwight D. Eisenhower in November opened up the possibility that a business-oriented Republican administration would be amenable to a strengthening of commercial ties with Argentina.

By 1953, the state of his nation's economy had convinced Perón that he needed an infusion of foreign capital. In March he unveiled draft legislation designed to make investment in Argentina more attractive. President Eisenhower's announcement one month later that he was sending his brother Milton on a fact-finding tour of Latin America created an opportunity for Perón to demonstrate his new mood.

The State Department at this time was reluctant to create the impression it wanted better relations with Perón. On the other hand, Milton Eisenhower could not ignore Argentina. Therefore, his itinerary called for a stay of only two days in Buenos Aires, as compared with four in Venezuela, four in Colombia, three in Bolivia and six in Brazil. Moreover, the State Department arranged for the two-day sojourn to fall on a weekend, in the wistful hope that Perón would be out of town.[15] Finally, the visitor took with him photographs of his brother as gifts for the various chief executives upon whom he would call. All but the one to be presented to Perón bore Ike's personal autograph.[16]

These efforts to slight Perón went for naught. The *conductor* had his own agenda and shaped the Eisenhower visit to his own purposes. In the words of John Moors Cabot, assistant secretary of state for Latin America and a member of Eisenhower's delegation, "to our openmouthed astonishment, when we stepped from the plane, we got the red-carpet treatment."[17] Perón was at his best, radiating charm from the moment he greeted his visitors at the airport. That evening he and Eisenhower attended the boxing matches at Luna Park. On Sunday, as a special treat Perón took his guest to "The Game" in Argentine soccer, the match between traditional rivals Boca Juniors and River Plate.[18]

Shortly before leaving for the airport, Eisenhower expressed to Perón his concern about restrictions his government had placed on the circulation of U.S. magazines and newspapers in Argentina. The president assured him all obstacles would quickly be removed, and in fact they were.[19] As Eisenhower was departing, Perón gave him a box full of books about Evita and a large album containing photographs of the two-day visit. If the Argentine was upset at not receiving Ike's autograph, he certainly did not show it.

Milton Eisenhower later wrote that Perón "was at once the most attractive and the most ruthless man I ever met."[20] This observation, however, did not lead to any suggestion of new ways to deal with the *conductor*. The Republican administration seemed content to react to Perón's gestures positively, but without enthusiasm. Assistant Secretary Cabot denied rumors that Perón was asking for U.S. loans in return for improved relations.[21] The State Department did decide, apparently in response to a request by Perón, to keep Ambassador Nufer in Buenos Aires, despite a prior announcement that he would be transferred. North American businessmen soon began to arrive in the Argentine capital.

Perón on his part secured congressional approval of the new foreign investment law, making it easier for overseas investors to take home profits and repatriate capital. He also made conciliatory public statements, such as his declaration during his first trip to Paraguay: "Thank God there is an Eisenhower."[22]

The implications of the warm welcome he was now extending to North American capitalists did not bother Perón. In his own mind he was being flexible, adjusting to new conditions. But given the anti-imperialist rhetoric that had long been a part of Peronism's warp and woof, many of his followers must have been perplexed. Moreover, his pro-U.S. gestures furnished ammunition to opponents begging for issues.

32

In Search of
Foreign Capital

The crisis of 1952 disrupted the long-range economic planning the Perón administration had launched in 1946. The five-year plan came to an end in 1951, amidst problems requiring short-term emergency measures. It was not until November 28, 1952, that the president unveiled his second five-year plan, in an effort to set the nation back on a course toward prosperity.

As was now standard practice in Peronist Argentina, the role of the Congress was merely to ratify whatever legislation the executive branch presented. During the first five days of December, Perón and Raúl Mendé read the plan to the assembled legislators.[1] After perfunctory debate, the Senate and Chamber of Deputies enacted it into law, to become effective on January 1, 1953.

The second five-year plan differed both in thrust and scope from its predecessor. The 1953–1957 program attempted to fashion a far-reaching, integrated blueprint for economic and social development, and to maintain a generally balanced approach to all aspects of the economy. Much more attention was devoted to agriculture. The need to improve grain and cattle production was now clearly a priority. In addition, there was explicit recognition of the role private initiative would have to play if the goals of the plan were to be met. Both incentives and ground rules for investors were clarified.[2]

The anti-inflation measures adopted during the 1952 emergency remained in effect. Needing to hold down prices and wages in order to preserve the stability essential to orderly growth, Perón had to keep organized labor in check and to utilize his powers of persuasion to defuse worker discontent.

Perón's attitude toward the private sector during his second term may have dismayed those of his followers whose political leanings were left of center, but it was not out of character. Argentina's first worker had always admired successful businessmen, especially of the self-made variety. He never considered them part of the despised oligarchy. Indeed, he sought their counsel in matters of state and was at ease among them. His economic philosophy, calling for protectionism and the expansion of private enterprise under guidelines set by the state, was congenial to them. Under the second five-year plan, he openly relied upon increased investment by Argentine entrepreneurs. It was at this point that a newcomer to the world of high finance appeared at Perón's side and began an association that would last until the latter's death.

Born in 1917 of Syrian stock, Jorge Antonio went with his parents from their home in Buenos Aires to Uruguay, where he grew up in modest circumstances. At the age of seventeen he returned to the city of his birth and found work as a meatpacker and trucker. During compulsory military service he trained to be a male nurse. While in the army he attended night classes and earned the Argentine equivalent of a high school diploma.[3]

After a brief stint in several minor government jobs, he decided to go into business for himself. His timing was perfect. This was the boom period of the Perón era, and Jorge Antonio rode the crest. Investing in an auto dealership, he soon purchased a radio station and a television channel, and then turned to the importation of TV sets from abroad. Within a short time his financial position had vastly improved.

In 1950, after failing to convince General Motors to set up a plant in Argentina, the energetic Antonio flew to Frankfurt and put the same proposition to officials of Mercedes-Benz.[4] The German auto industry was still struggling to emerge from the devastation wreaked by World War II, and the South American market offered attractive possibilities for the future. The Germans promised to build a truck factory in Argentina. In the meantime they arranged through Antonio to export five hundred buses and a new model passenger car, which became very popular with taxi drivers.

Jorge Antonio was now Mercedes-Benz' man in Buenos Aires and was becoming a key contact for other German companies. His reputation was growing steadily. One element alone was missing, and it fell into place in 1952, when he accompanied one of his German associates to the Casa Rosada to negotiate for a permit to set up the truck factory. He met Juan Perón.

The *conductor* took an immediate liking to Antonio and agreed to facilitate the venture with Mercedes-Benz. "He was my friend," the president said later. "A businessman. He was not a czar in Argentina, as people said. No such thing. He was a man who made good deals, and we helped him, just as we helped everybody."[5] Despite Perón's bland assertion, it soon became clear that Antonio had a special status that he did not shrink from using. Some indication of his modus operandi has come to light in conjunction with his attempt to participate in North American investment in Argentina during Perón's second term. When the *conductor* began to woo the Yankee dollar in earnest, Jorge Antonio was quick to try to snatch a piece of the action.

In an interview with *U.S. News & World Report* published on July 10, 1953, Perón downplayed his nation's need for foreign investment. However, the passage of a new law easing restrictions on foreign capital and his eagerness to meet with representatives of U.S. firms suggest that he was actually quite eager to welcome fresh capital from abroad. His attitude was based upon economic considerations and long antedated the Milton Eisenhower visit. But in spite of the interest displayed by a number of North American companies, the only real success Perón enjoyed came from negotiations with industrialist Henry J. Kaiser and Standard Oil of California.

Kaiser visited Buenos Aires in August 1954 during a South American tour organized by the mayor of New Orleans, DeLesseps Morrison. Ambitious to convert his city into the major commercial gateway to Latin America, Morrison was an enthusiastic promoter of U.S. trade with the rest of the hemisphere. During his stay in Argentina, Kaiser conceived an idea that went far beyond importing and exporting.

In the aftermath of World War II, the famed shipbuilder had expanded into the production of motor vehicles, including the Kaiser-Fraser passenger car and the jeep. But once supply caught up with demand, the economies of scale favored the large auto manufacturers. By 1954, Kaiser was ready to abandon the automobile business. It occurred to him that he might profitably relocate his operation in South America. Kaiser had always been an effective salesman, and Perón did not require much convincing. Delighted by the prospect of a Kaiser automobile factory in Argentina, he immediately entered into preliminary talks with his distinguished visitor. It was at this point that Antonio made his initial intrusion.

According to Morrison, "As the discussion [with Perón at the Casa Rosada] went on, I noted with interest each time a figure or estimate was brought up, Perón hesitated, glanced at a dark, silent man at the end of the table, then made his decision. This mysterious consultant had been introduced to us as Jorge Antonio."[6] Morrison concluded that Antonio opposed the Kaiser deal unless he could participate in it. He told this to Henry J., who strenuously objected to any sort of tie-in arrangement. Kaiser conveyed his feelings to Perón and threatened to terminate the talks, whereupon Antonio withdrew.

This testimony alone does not establish any impropriety on the part of Antonio, who may merely have been keeping a close watch on his competitors. However, like a fly after honey, he could not keep away from the Kaiser project, and soon he made his intentions unmistakably clear.

Responsibility for negotiating with the Argentines fell to Edgar Kaiser, Henry J.'s son. Aided by a team of lawyers including the well-known

Washington attorney Lloyd N. Cutler, Edgar put together an agreement whereby a company called Kaiser Industries of Argentina would be created to manufacture automotive vehicles. Kaiser would contribute the capital equipment and ship it from the United States, in return for a 40 percent interest in the undertaking. The remainder of the necessary capital would be provided by a state enterprise under the control of the Argentine air force and by the sale of shares to the general public.

Jorge Antonio now reappeared. He turned up at a meeting between Kaiser representatives and Perón and later asked to see the North Americans at their hotel. According to Cutler, Antonio created the impression that he was speaking on Perón's behalf and made the following proposition: instead of forming a single Argentine company, they would create two, one of them to manufacture vehicles, the other to distribute them; Kaiser and what Antonio called "our group" would jointly own the second company, which would sell the Kaiser vehicles. The composition of "our group" was never spelled out, but Antonio strongly implied that it included Perón. Since automobiles were in short supply in Argentina and could be sold at very high prices, the second company could cull tidy profits from the Kaiser operation.

Afterward, the Kaiser delegation wrestled with its new problem: they didn't want to lose the deal with Perón, but wanted no part of Jorge Antonio. Under Argentine law there was nothing illegal about the latter's proposal, but if the *conductor* himself was involved, the connection might prove embarrassing in a post-Perón Argentina.

An ingenious maneuver extricated them. Edgar Kaiser and one of his attorneys went directly to Perón and put the matter in his lap. They suggested that the proposal would not be fair to the Argentine shareholders and asked bluntly whether Antonio was speaking for the president. Perón of course denied this. He replied that it was up to the Kaiser officials to decide what partners they wanted and to do what they thought was right. The impression Perón left was that Antonio had been bluffing, and that the Kaiser people, like good poker players, had called his hand. Antonio did not hold the ace, and when Edgar Kaiser said no to him, the project went ahead as originally planned.[7]

Although Antonio came away empty-handed, his standing with the president was no way diminished. That Perón would tolerate this attempt to profit from an intimate relationship with him lends support to the suspicion that others were doing the same thing. In 1976, for example, an investigation into scandals involving Prince Bernhard of the Netherlands and the Lockheed Aircraft Corporation brought to light the fact that during the Perón era Argentine officials were collecting a 10 percent commission on commercial contracts arranged by the prince between Dutch companies and Argentina.[8]

As Juan Perón surveyed his nation's economy at the outset of his second term, one fact was painfully obvious. Argentina was facing an energy crisis which threatened to grow, due primarily to a shortage of petroleum. Domestic consumption was steadily increasing and would continue to rise if the president's plans for industrialization were fulfilled. Yet production by the government-owned enterprise, Yacimientos Petrolíferos Fiscales, or YPF, and the foreign companies to whom concessions had been granted lagged far behind. Argentina was now using precious foreign exchange to import about 60 percent of her petroleum needs. Recent explorations suggested the existence of untapped reserves so vast that the country might one day become an exporter of petroleum. But the national budget could not support the allocation of substantial sums to YPF for the development of these oil fields.

Ever the pragmatist, Perón decided to solve the economic problem by dealing out new concessions to foreign companies. This in turn spawned political problems, but at the outset he felt confident he could surmount them.

Petroleum had always been an emotional issue in Latin America. México, Venezuela and Brazil had struggled with the dilemma of how to balance the need for capital and technology to achieve large-scale oil production against the disadvantages of allowing foreigners to exploit, and hence control, the vital resource. Argentina now faced the issue.

In his eagerness to preempt the nationalist position on the domestic political spectrum, Perón had long clung to the banner of anti-imperialism, and in particular had made strong statements against yielding an ounce of Argentine sovereignty in the matter of oil production.[9] In addition, Article 40 of the Peronist constitution of 1949 stated that oil wells "are irrevocable and inalienable properties of the nation, with the corresponding right to share in their production. . . ."

Despite these potential obstacles, Perón began to consider granting new concessions to foreign oil companies in 1953.[10] Any contracts he secured would require legislation, either in the form of a law covering all agreements for the production of petroleum by foreigners, or congressional approval of individual accords. Perón opted for the latter approach, which he felt would be easier to "sell" to the Congress and public. In either event, he would have to prepare the country for a shift in petroleum policy. Thus the negotiations received newspaper coverage. The opposition immediately objected as strenuously as they could to what they called Perón's big sellout.

The *conductor* replied in detail and in kind on April 19, 1954, before a capacity crowd in Luna Park. Six days before elections to fill the vacant vice-presidency and half the seats in Congress, Perón defended his petroleum policy with a stinging attack on the Radicals. He offered several justifications for dealing with foreign interests. First, it was the only way to increase domestic production at a time of pressing domestic need. Self-sufficiency in petroleum, he pointed out, would save $300 million annually in foreign exchange. Next he trotted out the bogey of World War III and argued that oil imports from abroad would not be available if a general conflict erupted. Up to this point he was relying on logic, but then he predicted that in two decades nuclear energy would probably replace 80 percent of petroleum uses. Therefore, if Argentina failed to exploit her oil in a hurry, it would become a useless resource. Finally, he interpreted Article 40 to mean that the product of the oil wells, rather than the wells themselves, was the inalienable property of the state—a gloss that seemed to turn the constitutional provision on its head.[11]

Having committed himself to a new petroleum policy in the face of political opposition, the *conductor* now had to secure some kind of agreement with the foreign companies. This proved more difficult than he had expected. It was one thing to negotiate one on one with Henry J. Kaiser; dealing with the international oil trusts was another matter. They were powerful and experienced at driving hard bargains. Moreover, oil contracts raised inherently touchy questions of sovereignty.

By mid-1954, four groups were actively negotiating with the Argentines: Standard Oil of New Jersey, Standard Oil of California, Royal Dutch Shell, and a joint venture involving the Atlas Corporation and Dresser Industries.[12] Since several regions in southern Argentina offered possibilities for exploration, Perón was willing to work out pacts with more than one company.

Atlas-Dresser at first appeared closest to a deal. In September they proposed an ambitious scheme for oil exploration, the construction of a pipeline from their fields, and even uranium development.[13] Two months later, they entered into an agreement with the ubiquitous Jorge Antonio to form a joint U.S.-Argentine company to carry out the project.

If Atlas-Dresser thought that associating with Antonio would give them an inside track, they were mistaken. The president's friend brought nothing to the deal, which eventually fell apart. Within a short time, the international giants—particularly Standard of California—were monopolizing the government's attention.

As the negotiations intensified, differences on several key points persisted. There were problems about the price to be paid for oil produced by the companies and sold to the government (Perón's claim that once oil left the ground it became the property of the state was conveniently forgotten), the method of settling disputes between the government and the companies, and the location and size of the territory to be exploited.*

* To settle the last point, Perón actually told representatives of the foreign companies to work out a division of the available territory themselves! An official of Standard of New Jersey told him this would never work in practice and the idea was scrapped. Vaky to Department of State, 835.2553/2-255, February 2, 1955.

In mid-December, the talks with Standard of California suddenly stalled. The company raised additional demands that substantially changed its position.[14] Concurrent difficulties began to hamper discussions with the other groups as well.

Perón now found himself in trouble. He had gambled on a policy that would have permitted foreigners to develop Argentina's petroleum. If he could not produce at least one contract, his decision would appear ill-advised in retrospect, and the reputation he cultivated for getting things done would suffer. His frustration bestirred him to the extreme of requesting help from Henry F. Holland, assistant secretary of state for Latin American affairs. In a letter soaked in self-pity, the president complained about Standard's new attitude and the political use to which his opponents were putting the oil contract.[15] Holland had met Perón on several recent visits to Buenos Aires and had cultivated a warm relationship with him, but it was nonetheless extraordinary, and reflective of the *conductor*'s beleaguered state of mind, that such an epistle would be dispatched to the State Department.

Washington made inquiries into the matter but did not otherwise pressure the oil companies, and the negotiations eventually resumed. On April 25, 1955, the Argentine government and Standard of California signed a major agreement for the exploitation of a large tract of land in the Patagonian territory of Santa Cruz.[16] All that now remained was congressional ratification of the executive decree.

Under the terms of the pact, which was to last forty years, the company acquired exclusive rights to explore and develop a 50,000-square-kilometer area in southwest Santa Cruz. California would sell oil and gas produced there to YPF and could export excess petroleum once the nation's domestic needs were being met, with proceeds from foreign sales to be split evenly with the government. The company agreed to invest at least $13.5 million in exploration costs and acquired the option to build an oil refinery in Argentina.

Perón transmitted to Congress a bill approving the contract and a message defending his action as essential to economic growth and consistent with *justicialismo*. He hoped for speedy ratification, but for once his rubber-stamp legislature balked.[17] The small band of Radical deputies, led by Arturo Frondizi, tore into the contract and accused the Peronists of giving away the country's petroleum reserves. Frondizi wrote a book denouncing the pact. From outside the Congress, the Socialists joined the fray. Enough Peronists wavered that the Chamber of Deputies delayed its approval. The government then asked Standard to agree to some minor adjustments in the contract language.

The issue soon became a political football, and rational debate yielded to partisan rhetoric.[18] The controversy over the oil contract reached its height at a time when other events were loosening Perón's grip on Argentina. This undoubtedly added to the hesitancy of many Peronist legislators to follow the *conductor* without question as they had done so often in the past. Time expired on Perón before he could secure ratification of the pact. He always insisted the nation would have gained from the deal, but never had the chance to prove it.

The economic policies followed by Perón in his second term did slow inflation, increase real wages and improve Argentina's balance of payments.[19] At the same time, the droughts in the countryside ended and agricultural production improved. It is ironic that a political crisis overtook this upturn in the economy and left many Argentines uncertain whether it was a temporary deviation from a downward trend attributable to Peronist economics, or a vindication of the *conductor*'s genius. This irresolution would keep the lure of Peronism alive and help give Perón another turn at the helm.

33

The Lure of Sybaris

"In the Argentine government, there is no one, neither governors, nor deputies, nor judges, no one; there is one government only and it is Perón."[1] These words, uttered by Carlos Aloé in July 1954, captured the essence of the autocracy Peronism had become. Perón sat in splendid isolation atop an organizational structure keyed to the basic principle of verticality. Those below him in the chain of command were mindless sycophants, like Aloé, to whom the *conductor* was of quasi-divine origin. Party discipline had reached the point where a high-ranking official could declare: "No Peronist begins by analyzing situations. It is enough that General Perón wants something for all of us to be ready to carry it out immediately."[2]

Glorification of the president permeated all aspects of Argentine life. School texts sang his praises.

> Perón is the leader.
> Everybody loves Perón.
> Everybody sings "*Viva* Perón"!

proclaimed a first-grade reader, which also taught youngsters that Evita loved them and that they should follow Perón's directive to produce more.[3]

The death of Evita had removed a significant restraint upon Perón's freedom of action. Their relationship had been such that he always had to answer to her and risk her sharp tongue, despite the ultimate control he exercised over the government and their household. They lived together, worked together, relaxed together. Now he was free to follow his instincts.

In addition, much of the challenge was now gone from his work. The maneuvering that had guided him to the Casa Rosada and the manipulation of presidential power had exhilarated him. But by 1953 his domestic opponents were capable of minor irritation at best, and on the international scene there were no new Bradens in sight. Thus Juan Perón became vulnerable to an insidious enemy from within—a creeping, pervasive boredom.

His passion for sports consumed him more than ever. Motorcycle-riding became a particular addiction. He liked nothing better than to mount an expensive new model and roar off, full throttle, on a test run. He also enjoyed driving race cars and piloting speedboats on the river. Boxing remained his favorite spectator sport. Archie Moore returned to Buenos Aires and presented him with the gloves he had used in winning the light-heavyweight title. When Jack Dempsey turned up in Argentina, Perón delighted in escorting the ex-champion and his onetime Argentine challenger, Luis Firpo, to public functions.

But these diversions were not sufficient. Perón needed something more to spark his interest. It was at this juncture that Education Minister Méndez San Martín came up with the idea of creating the Unión de Estudiantes Secundarios, or UES (Union of Secondary [High School] Students).[4] Faced with the prospect of losing his job if the ministry did not soon show signs of life, he convinced the president to approve the creation of an organization that would "Peronize" Argentina's teenagers.

On the surface the notion made a modicum of political sense. Perón had already pronounced his famous dictum that he would win the next election with the children. The universities continued to nourish anti-Peronism. If the hearts and minds of young people could be won before they reached the universities, the regime could sponsor Peronist groups that would counterbalance, if not eliminate, the student organizations that stubbornly resisted the *conductor*.

Politicizing adolescents would not be easy, however, and would call for some degree of caution. Argentina was at heart still very traditional and very Catholic. Anything that smacked of interference with the family would invite strong opposition.

The new union set out to foster sports-oriented recreation. There would be boys' and girls' branches, with facilities for both provided by the government. Perón embraced the concept with great enthusiasm. He even offered to convert his summer home in Olivos into an athletic facility. According to one account, he suggested in a rather offhand way that the girls take over the Olivos estate; Méndez San Martín, hanging on his every word, took the utterance at face value and ordered construction to begin immediately.[5]

Perón at the time was still living in the official presidential residence. The summer house, on a gentle rise overlooking the river, was vacant most of the year. Even when Perón did use it, there was more than enough space for UES activities. So much for the most innocent gloss that can be put on the decision to convert the Olivan fields into a paradise for teenage girl athletes.

The constant presence of pubescent females in gym shorts at one of the president's homes set off the most lurid spate of rumors ever to beset Perón. He and his intimates were accused of engaging in sexual orgies with the girls. According to the standard gossip, the sole function of UES was to amuse the dictator and slake his perverse appetite for youthful bedmates.*

In the wake of Perón's downfall, an investigating commission could uncover evidence of but one incident that came even close to an orgy. Several of the UES girls testified they attended a Christmas party in 1953 at Olivos with the president and members of his entourage; they remained there for three days and received gifts of expensive jewelry; Perón then took them to his farm in San Vicente, where they kept him company for several more days.[6] The commission also found that Perón created in Olivos "an atmosphere saturated with erotic intent"; he showered the athletes with gifts, addressed them in familiar terms and arranged for a plastic surgeon to provide cosmetic treatments for girls who needed them.[7] The inference of wrongdoing here seems a bit strained.

A former UES member, now the wife of a military officer, gave the following account of life in the Olivos "playpen." Her description is credible because she was attempting to convince the listener that the talk of scandal was totally baseless.

> These were the happiest days of my life, a golden age gone by. Perón was always very correct in his behavior toward all the girls. He would greet the UES delegates when they arrived at 7:00 A.M. The rest of the girls would appear later. He would say to them, "This is your house," and ask them what they wanted for lunch. He would then personally give directions to the cook.
>
> He would instruct us in various sports, like fencing and swimming. He taught us to ride motorbikes. "Don't look at the ground," he'd say, "look ahead of you." And he'd ride around the facility with us.
>
> He'd eat lunch with us, and talk to us like a father. "Keep smiling and keep moving ahead," he'd say.
>
> At times he'd act like a boy, and run around in circles. But he was always careful with the girls. Everyone had to leave by 7:30 in the evening and had to be accompanied by a member of her family.
>
> He taught us the doctrine of a sound mind in a sound body. The idea was to keep teenagers active and learn through sports the importance of working together.[8]

Another view of life at Olivos has been provided by C. Virgil Gheorgiu, a famous Rumanian author who came to Buenos Aires in late August

---

* A booklet published shortly after Perón's ouster exemplifies this view of the goings-on at Olivos. Entitled *Mis amores con Perón (My Love Affair with Perón)*, it purports to be a first-person description of one teenager's sexual exploitation by the president. A fair reading leads to the conclusion it is pure fiction.

1955 to write a biography of the president. Perón invited him and his wife to stay at Olivos, where he had a firsthand look at what he estimated to be hundreds of girls dressed in shorts as they sunbathed and practiced fencing, tennis and motorbike-riding. "Perón would come almost every day to look at them," Gheorgiu reported. "It was a very lovely sight."[9] As the investigating commission put it more succinctly, the president had become the nation's number one spectator.[10]

One afternoon when the girls gathered around a table for a snack, the president declined to drink anything because of a problem he said he was having with his liver. Resolving to try out on their host the nickname they had heard was his during childhood, some mischievous students began to chant: "Pocho's not drinking his milk!" Perón let out a guffaw, and from then on the girls referred to him as Pocho.[11] (Turnabout being fair play, people began to call the UES girls "Pochonettes.")

The *conductor* was having a good time and did not care who knew it. He would don his cap and sporting outfit, mount one of his motorbikes and ride merrily through the downtown streets, a squadron of Pochonettes following him on their bikes, like children on the heels of the Pied Piper, laughing, shouting, delaying traffic. Glares of disgust shot out from behind closed shutters; at this point it was most unwise to manifest open disapproval of presidential behavior. Some considered it the license of a potentate flouting his omnipotence, but there were deeper roots to the open self-indulgence Argentina now witnessed.

Juan Perón held society's conventions in flagrant contempt, an attitude manifested by conduct that seemed designed to shock his compatriots. His long affair with and subsequent marriage to Eva Duarte was perhaps the most notorious instance. The interlude with Piranha also falls into this category. An adolescent-like rebelliousness simmered not far below the surface of his genial exterior. He did not care what "proper" people thought of him. This trait appears at first blush incongruous in a political figure. Yet in part it may have fortified the popularity he enjoyed among Argentina's have-nots, who resented the scorn directed at them by the oligarchs and their middle-class allies, and applauded when Perón thumbed his nose at them.

Evidence of the attention the president was devoting to the teenagers supports the criticism that he was neglecting affairs of state. Bored with duties as chief executive and head of the Peronist party, he turned to the simpler pleasures of coaching youngsters, romping with them and savoring the delights of voyeurism.[12] In one sense, he was returning to those happy days he spent at the school for noncommissioned officers.

The presidential preoccupation with teenagers coincided with a grave political crisis that bloomed in late 1954 and continued into 1955. Perón made serious mistakes dealing with the crisis. It is probable that he had grown mentally soft and that his willpower had eroded. His fascination with UES was a symptom of, if not a contributing factor to, a deterioration in his leadership capabilities.

The UES caper demonstrated bad judgment on Perón's part. Even worse was his choice of one of the teenage girls as a live-in companion. Nelly Rivas was hardly a rumor. Perón appeared with her in public and in photographs. She was a basketball player, the daughter of a janitor, a cute brunette and fourteen years old when she met the fifty-eight-year-old *conductor*. Before long she was living with him.

According to Nelly Rivas' own account, she began to visit the Olivos facility in October 1953, in her capacity as a UES delegate from her school. One of the customs at Olivos was for delegates to lunch with Perón. Nelly had her turn. Soon she was a regular at the president's table. One day she lunched with him at the downtown residence. They talked all afternoon and into the evening. Darkness fell. Though a presidential limousine might easily have taken her home, she spent the night in the mansion. A week later, Perón invited her to the Luna Park boxing matches. One of his military aides accompanied her. They sat two rows behind Perón. Again she remained overnight in the residence. When a heavy downpour provided a pretext for her third overnight stay, she simply moved in, and remained there until Perón's ouster.[13]

In the year after Evita's death, gossip had Perón courting an attractive young widow who was one of Argentina's best women tennis players, and also Mussolini's daughter, Edda Ciano. The range of potential companions available to him must have been unlimited. Why did he pick a fourteen-year-old who possessed neither great beauty nor keen intellect nor social standing nor useful connections?

"I like women," he once said. "I could never live without one. I have always needed a woman."[14] The implication here is that it made little difference *which* woman he had at his side. By way of explanation, he added that he did not think it was immoral for a man to like women. "What would be immoral is to like other men." This statement and derogatory references he often made about the sexual preferences of his enemies[15] suggest that Perón may have needed the constant presence of a woman to demonstrate his heterosexuality.

Nelly's description of the relationship is instructive. "What always comforted me was the nearness of the hour when the general arrived. He told me all his problems. I was kind of a rest for him. He confided his problems to me, and I tried to give him my opinions."[16]

Was Nelly Rivas his mistress, or merely an ornament? After his downfall, a military tribunal found that he had engaged in sexual relations with her.[17] The basis of its finding was testimony by Nelly herself and by several members of Perón's inner circle. When Nelly wed an ex-employee of the U.S. embassy in 1958, her husband was quoted as making the ingenuous admission that it was like marrying a divorced woman.[18] In March

1954, Perón brought her with him to a film festival in Mar del Plata, where a galaxy of international film stars had gathered,* and stayed with her in a hotel.

The paternal aspect of the relationship was apparent. The president fussed about Nelly's education and even secured a private tutor for her. He also urged her to read Plutarch. In a letter to her when he was no longer president, he referred to himself as "Daddy." The nickname he bestowed upon her, Tinolita, was an ultimate show of affection, for it was the name of one of his poodles.

Though the president was busy with new interests, his late wife had not been forgotten. Popular veneration continued at full throttle. Those Peronist officials who competed in servility to her while she lived now strained to outdo one another in exalting her memory. Meanwhile, Dr. Ara went quietly about his work in the special laboratory at CGT headquarters, and in a matter of months had completed the embalming. The final product contained all her organs in a state of perfect preservation and could withstand exposure to air. Evita's eyes were closed in an expression of tranquility. The masterpiece was now ready for exhibition, but progress on the monument was lagging badly.

On the first anniversary of Evita's death, newspapers announced the unveiling of the model of the long-awaited mausoleum.[19] Accounts stressed the planned dimensions of the structure. It would stand 137 meters above ground (as compared to the 91-meter height of the Statue of Liberty). The total weight of the monument would reach 43,000 tons. The structure would contain fourteen elevators. Sixteen marble theme statues, depicting subjects such as love, the colonel and the *conductor*, would line the circular base.

None of the stories commented on the changes that the project had undergone. Plans for a Plaza de Mayo site, as demanded by the dying Evita, had yielded to common sense. The new location would be a park on the Avenida Libertador, between the new law school and the presidential residence. The other alteration was more startling. Instead of a giant sculpture of the first lady, a sixty-meter statue of a descamisado would form the centerpiece. Fists clenched, legs in an open stance, shirt open and posture heroic, this figure possessed one remarkable attribute: its face resembled Juan Perón's.[20]

Evita's body would be laid out for public viewing in the crypt of the monument. Perón decided that until construction was completed it would

* The roster included Robert Cummings, Irene Dunne, Errol Flynn, Joan Fontaine, Jeanette MacDonald, Fred MacMurray, Ann Miller, Mary Pickford, Walter Pidgeon and Edward G. Robinson. Flynn borrowed a stack of chips and played the number five for an hour at the casino. It never came up, and he lost $2,000. Perón refused to accept his check. "La Segunda Presidencia—VIII," *Primera Plana*, June 25, 1968, pp. 48–50.

be wise to keep the body in the CGT building. He entrusted to Dr. Ara and a squad of guards under the Spaniard's direction responsibility for the safekeeping of the corpse. Evita's mother and sister were permitted to pray in front of the locked door to the lab, and occasionally Dr. Ara let them inside. Perón made a single visit, two days before the first anniversary of his wife's passing. He never returned.

As Juan Perón moved steadily toward his sixtieth birthday, his face seemed puffy and the skin condition that had always affected it required him to use makeup. He also suffered from a severe tic of the eye. Telltale traces of gray were still absent from his slick hair. Many suspected that he was using dye to maintain a relatively youthful mien.

In 1953 Perón nearly paid a dear price for his passion for motorcycles. On a road near the Olivos residence he swerved to avoid hitting a pedestrian and suffered facial injuries when he fell off the bike.[21] This was probably the source of rumors that he was afflicted with cerebral cancer.[22]

Though the cancer rumor had no basis in fact, Perón did incur health problems in 1955. The degree of seriousness was such that the government sought help from the United States. The Argentine military attaché in Washington visited a North American doctor and asked him to make a secret trip to Buenos Aires to examine Perón. The doctor flew to the Argentine capital in February 1955 and diagnosed the president's ailment as "an arterial condition, a type of spasm induced by excessive smoking." He ordered his patient to give up cigarettes. Perón's health greatly improved. If he had not recovered, he would have required an arterial decortication, the excision of sympathetic nerve fibers to free the obstructed blood vessel.[23]

By the Argentine spring of 1954, the economic crisis had eased, Peronist political control seemed as secure as it had ever been, and the president's international prestige had never been higher. Relations with the United States were improving. The oil negotiations were proceeding apace, and the Argentine government was on the verge of securing from the Export-Import Bank in Washington a $60 million loan to finance the purchase of machinery for a steel mill. With Nelly Rivas in his nest and the UES nymphettes constantly on view, the *conductor* could spend his leisure time in the idyllic setting of Olivos or in pursuit of his avocation as active sportsman and devoted sports fan.

It seemed the best of times, but on the surface only. Bureaucratization, the triumph of mediocrity and the fetish of verticality had weakened the Peronist movement. Too much now depended upon Perón. It would take only one major misstep by the *conductor* to reveal the vulnerability of Peronism, and an opportunity for blunder would soon be at hand.

34

At War with the Church

The live audience at Olivos and radio listeners throughout the country could sense that something out of the ordinary was in the wind. Perón's tone was harsh, his words were blunt, and the structural unity that had become a hallmark of his speeches was missing. The president was issuing a comprehensive indictment against a new enemy. On November 10, 1954, Juan Perón crossed the Rubicon in his war with the Roman Catholic church.

"Some think this is a question of the church, or a question of the students, or some other kind of question," he declared. "No such thing! What I'm talking about is a question of politics."

He blamed the political opposition for playing the matador, using the church as a red cape. But they would not fool the general. "We're not going after the cape," he announced. "We're going straight for the bull-fighter."[1] Yet as one astute observer noted, "The rest of the speech was magnetically devoted to the cape,"[2] as Perón unleashed a cloud of invective against "some bishops," "some priests" and "some Catholics" who were engaging in conspiracies to undermine his regime. He even named three bishops, twenty priests and several Catholic organizations. "The church has nothing to do with this," he insisted. But his scattershot assault could hardly avoid hitting the only major institution not under his control.

Whatever their true feelings, Juan Perón and the Argentine hierarchy had preserved an atmosphere of reciprocal benevolence. The pre-election pastoral directives issued by the bishops had helped the Peronists. Moreover, the church kept its silence in the face of the deterioration of civil liberties in Argentina. The regime on its part respected the privileged position of the church, especially in the area of education.

Though hardly a religious person, Perón had always labored to nurture in the minds of his followers the impression that he was devoted to his church and his faith. On numerous occasions he made public manifestations of his Catholicism, one of the most recent and most dramatic on November 15, 1953, when he knelt in the Plaza de Mayo to deliver a prayer he had personally composed to the Virgin of Luján.[3] His speeches often stressed the similarities between *justicialismo* and the social teaching of the church. The November 10 outburst signaled a radical change. It was bound to have a disruptive effect upon many rank-and-file Peronists, who would face a conflict between their faith and the demands of their secular leader.

Perón's speech shattered the peaceful coexistence between Peronism and the church that had been coming apart for some time.[4] For example, by executive decree Perón had eliminated from the list of government holidays certain Catholic holy days as well as widely celebrated feast days such as March 19 (Saint Joseph) and June 29 (Saints Peter and Paul). The Congress was considering bills to legalize prostitution and divorce, the latter advocated by several deputies from the women's branch of the Peronist party. The hierarchy did not resist the loss of the holidays, but made clear its firm opposition to the proposed legislation.

In 1954 the breach widened. The incident involving the Basilio Scientific School repeated itself in a slightly different form when an obscure North American faith healer held a series of well-attended revival meetings in Buenos Aires in May and June. Theodore Hicks, also known as Brother Tommy, visited Perón and made several appearances at the Casa Rosada during the run of his performances. According to one source, Eva Perón Foundation ambulances brought sick people to the services.[5] Although Catholics complained that Hicks' public evangelical meetings violated both the constitution and federal laws, the authorities made no effort to stop him.

On July 11, a group of lay Catholics met in the city of Rosario to found a Christian Democratic party. There were no political luminaries of note among them, nor did they represent any organizations with large memberships. Yet the president viewed this development with considerable alarm.

In September the pace of events quickened. The Casa Rosada received reports that priests were using their pulpits to advise parents against sending their daughters to "student clubs of doubtful morality."[6] The youth branch of Catholic Action, a lay society sponsored by the church, began to compete openly with the UES. On September 21, denominated as Student Day by the government, a Catholic Action youth celebration in Córdoba outdrew a program organized by the UES. On the same day, a gala UES party staged at the Olivos residence turned into a "bacchanal," according to rumors circulating widely in the capital.

On September 9, Peronist deputies introduced a bill granting illegitimate children the same legal rights as offspring from legitimate marriages. The hierarchy denounced this as an assault on the sanctity of the family. (It would also have had important income-redistribution effects, since the bastard offspring of upper-class fathers would have had the same inheritance rights as legitimate children.) The bill was withdrawn, but the Peronist press thereupon launched an anticlerical campaign. More importantly, at the end of the month the president himself made some biting complaints about Catholic interference with the trade-union movement.[7]

People on both sides of the dispute kept alive the hope of finding some way to avoid a collision. On October 22, a solution seemed at hand as Perón suddenly switched to his favorite role of mediator and hosted a meeting between representatives of his movement and the hierarchy.[8] Sixteen bishops, two cardinals, the apostolic delegate and officials from the CGT and the UES attended. The conference went smoothly. Cardinal Antonio Caggiano denied that the church was hostile to the regime and promised that if any subversive activity was going on within his institution, it would be put to a halt. Three weeks later, Perón loosed his verbal blast.

The decision to confront the church was a colossal blunder, the worst of Perón's public career. It united his political enemies. Indeed, it gave them a magic slogan that would be as effective, if not more so, than the phrase from which the *conductor* had secured seemingly endless mileage. Instead of "Braden or Perón," the choice would now be "Christ or Perón."

The conflict succeeded in paralyzing many Peronists who were also devout Catholics. The fact that at this very moment Perón was also radically shifting his position toward foreign capital and the oil companies compounded the confusion in the minds of the faithful. The flexibility he viewed as essential to leadership was now beginning to boomerang.

Why did Perón commit himself to a war with the church?[9] An anti-Peronist explanation held that the inevitable dynamic of a totalitarian system compels the ultimate subjugation of all organizations and institutions not under the complete control of the state; thus he could not refrain from attempting to bring the church to heel. This theory falls far short of the mark. Though authoritarian, Peronism never qualified as a form of totalitarianism. Opposition political parties, for example, continued to exist. More to the point, Perón was pragmatic to the core and never acted for ideological reasons. He could easily have avoided his clash with the clergy.

The explanation most commonly offered by Peronists is that members of the inner circle deceived Perón and caused him to make the mistake. Méndez San Martín is the most popular villain of the piece. According to this version the education minister convinced Perón to attack the church in order to create a smoke screen for the mess he had made with the UES. The presence of Masons within the government—Vice-President Teisaire being the most highly placed—was also said to have influenced Perón to engage in cassock-baiting. This theory is also weak. Peronists have always, as an article of faith, held their leader innocent of any errors in judgment and rationalized disaster by putting responsibility elsewhere. But Perón had access to information from his intelligence services, had near him a number of practicing Catholics who argued against the course of action he took, and made the final decisions. No amount of whitewash can cover up these facts.

A final theory, which seems most plausible, is that Perón actually thought that church-related activity in the political, trade-union and youth spheres threatened the Peronist movement. His analysis of the gravity of the danger was erroneous, as was his choice of a tactical response. A new Christian Democratic party could only have helped Perón because it would have further factionalized the opposition. (Indeed, the embryonic party would itself soon split into factions.[10]) How it could have made significant inroads upon the Peronist constituency is difficult to imagine. Indeed, none of the Latin American Christian Democratic parties have ever developed followings anywhere near the size of Perón's. But when Perón looked at Western Europe and saw Catholic political parties gaining power in Italy and Germany, he became convinced that this was part of the Vatican's worldwide strategy and that Argentina was on the Pope's list. The Catholic threat to the CGT was likewise an illusion. One can find no evidence that any church-connected groups were "subverting" the Peronist unions. But Perón had become nervous, perhaps overreacting to the creation of a Latin American branch of an international association of Catholic syndicates. The challenge to the UES, however, may have had some substance, since the union was in fact quite vulnerable to Catholic resistance.

At this crucial juncture, the *conductor* was on his down cycle, still bored, more interested in sports and his Pochonettes. He did not exercise firm or creative leadership, but instead let the conflict escalate. In so doing, he badly underestimated the strength of Catholicism in Argentina.

In the wake of the November 10 speech, the police arrested some of the priests Perón had called subversives.[11] The hierarchy sent Perón a letter conveying "astonishment and stupor" at his accusations.[12] In a pastoral letter the bishops drew the line between God and Caesar. "No priest can or should take part in partisan political struggles. . . . [But] in the face of atheistic, materialistic communism, in the face of absolute divorce, in the face of compulsory lay education, as in other questions of doctrine, no priest can remain indifferent."[13]

The *conductor* having spoken, his loyal lieutenants could do no less than stampede in the direction he had pointed. The CGT and the Peronist party scheduled a rally in Luna Park on November 25. The banners and placards read "Perón, yes! Priests, no!" "Divorce!" and "Neither Clerics

Nor Communists!" The speeches bristled. Vice-President Teisaire, representing the party, Delia Parodi for the women's branch and CGT General Secretary Vuletich tore into the new opposition. Parodi, a darkly handsome woman with an incendiary platform style, told the crowd that "we know that many roads lead to Rome, but *every* road leads to Perón."[14] Vuletich made one declaration that would endure: "Now they say we are going to burn the churches, and they are liars."[15]

Perón, when his turn came, played his favorite role of peacemaker. His words, coming after the angry rhetoric of the trio that preceded him, were the essence of moderation. He told the assembly that the clerical infiltration had been nipped in the bud, that there was no more to worry about and that the affair was now closed. Those among his listeners whose passions had been roused felt let down. They left the building and hanged a priest in effigy.

"Problem Brought to an End," a headline in the Peronist daily *Democracia* informed readers on November 26. The pronouncement was premature. A week later, an executive decree abolished the federal department that administered compulsory religious education in the public schools.

December 8 was a Catholic holiday, the Feast of the Immaculate Conception, and also marked the official end of the church's Marian Year. The Catholics applied for a permit to stage a public procession. The government granted the request, but then began to worry that the parade might turn into a political demonstration. Church authorities were cautioned to maintain the religious atmosphere of the event, and the procession's route was altered to keep it away from the heavily populated sections of the city. Despite these measures, Perón and his advisors could not leave well enough alone. On the same day, boxing idol Pasqual ("Pasqualito") Pérez, who had just won the flyweight championship in a fight in Tokyo, was scheduled to land at the downtown airport. The president decided to be on hand to greet him. The Peronist propaganda machine covered the city with news of Pasqualito's arrival. At the same time, the authorities reduced the number of buses that might carry people to the Catholic celebration, and ordered taxi drivers to keep away from the route of the procession.

A crowd in the neighborhood of 4,000 joined Perón at the airport. The religious event attracted about 100,000. In the symbolic struggle to "win the street," the Catholics had clearly prevailed. A Catholic daily dared to publish an aerial photograph of the procession. The government immediately closed down the newspaper and banned all public religious acts.[16]

Throughout December, a series of blows shattered what was left of the fragile modus vivendi between church and state. The regime banned the use of religious symbols in public during the Christmas season. During congressional consideration of a general reform of family law, a Peronist deputy introduced, without prior notice and late at night, an amendment making divorce legal. It passed, and the president signed the bill.* The Congress also enacted laws legalizing prostitution and granting rights to illegitimate children.

In the abstract, the Peronists could have justified these three pieces of legislation on their merits. Under the circumstances, the new laws could hardly be seen as other than part of the anti-Catholic campaign. Despite protestations to the contrary by Perón and others, the regime had gone far beyond the parameters of the conflict as originally defined. The new laws had nothing to do with the political activities of "some priests," but instead aimed directly at an area the church had marked out as of vital import to its spiritual mission.

Within the Peronist movement itself, individuals known for their ties to the church lost political appointments. One member of the cabinet, Antonio Cafiero, submitted his resignation on grounds of conscience.[17]

Midsummer brought a lull to the conflict. Perón's brother, Mario, died of peritonitis on January 12 at the age of sixty-two. Argentines deserted the cities for the cool breezes of the ocean or the mountains. Those who remained in Buenos Aires had the opportunity to witness the opening of a striptease club on Florida Street.

"The relations between the church and the state are cordial," the *conductor* told a conference of governors on February 11.[18] The truth was quite the reverse. A series of steps taken by the Ministry of Education made life increasingly difficult for Catholic schools. An executive decree reduced the number of national holidays by eliminating more Catholic feast days. There was talk of a constitutional separation of church and state, and of taxing church-owned property. Perón made a great show of cordiality toward non-Catholic religious leaders.[19] The controversy, moreover, coincided with the political uproar generated by the proposed contract with Standard Oil of California and with agitation resulting from a nationwide university strike.[20]

The hierarchy defended itself with great caution and even reluctance. A pastoral letter deplored the new divorce law. Yet at the same time the archdiocese of Buenos Aires forbade Catholics to participate in any meeting of a religious nature unless approved by ecclesiastic authorities.[21] Hesitation to confront the president head-on and a determination not to be drawn into any overtly political opposition to the regime characterized these early measures taken by the bishops. The same could not be said of anti-Peronist lay Catholics, who jumped into battle with relish. The weap-

---

* The law provided that one year after a legal separation, either spouse might request an annulment with permission to remarry. A statement that a reconciliation was impossible would suffice. Grounds for divorce were not specified, nor was there any mention of alimony. *Hispanic American Report,* Vol. 7, No. 12, January 1955.

on they developed and refined to a remarkable level of efficacy was a simple and time-honored method of communication and harassment— the pamphlet.[22]

Denied access to the mass media, Catholics utilized clandestine printing presses to churn out pamphlets in response to Perón's first attacks on the priests. The UES girls, Nelly, Jorge Antonio, the nickname Pocho, the morphology of Perón's features and skull as evidence of his innate criminality[23]—nothing was too sacred to escape comment by the pamphleteers, except perhaps the memory of Evita, who was invoked only to show how far the Peronists had strayed from the ideals she represented. The leaflets provided information that did not appear in the government-controlled press, such as an editorial in *L'Osservatore Romano*, the Vatican newspaper, denouncing religious persecution in Argentina. If one of Perón's objectives was to confuse Catholics by his insistence that church-state relations were cordial, the pamphlets sought to dispel the illusion by reporting the facts about the anti-Catholic campaign.

Perón's war on the church constituted an open invitation for the renewal of conspiracies against him. In February 1955 Catholic plotters began a series of clandestine meetings to explore the possibilities of insurrection.[24] The most prominent participant, Mario Amadeo, was a staunch Catholic and fervid nationalist who had supported Colonel Perón in the early stages of the military regime. But the Catholic conspirators suffered from disunity and had no prestigious leader capable of marshaling broad popular support. The Radicals, who had taken a pro-church position despite their anticlerical tradition, were not yet involved. The Christian Democrats, displaying a sense of self-importance out of proportion to reality, did not want to compromise themselves by backing a military revolt. Nationalists like Amadeo had no such qualms. Some began to make personal contacts with friends in the officer corps. Others explored the possibility of encouraging a naval revolt, since the navy was anti-Peronist to the core, in the hope that the army, when confronted with a choice between using force to defend Perón or ousting him, would opt for the latter.

In his message to Congress on May 1, Perón presented his view of the philosophical aspect of the dispute. He asserted that the state had a legitimate interest in the spiritual well-being of its citizens. "The souls of individuals taken together constitute the common soul of our people," he intoned.[25] At a Plaza de Mayo demonstration, Vuletich demanded the separation of church and state and the termination of compulsory religious education. Perón in his speech made no specific mention of the problem with the church, but stated merely that he would follow the wishes of the people. The rally concluded with the now-customary coronation of a beauty-contest winner, dubbed "Queen of the Workers."

The month of May saw the conflict escalate. The stream of pamphlets became a flood tide. The government made frantic efforts to suppress them, but arrests and confiscations merely increased the flow. On May 6, Catholic Action staged a street march that turned into a political demonstration provoking clashes with the police. On the next day a Peronist trade union denounced the "oligarcho-clerical reaction."[26] The Congress quickly passed laws abolishing religious teaching in the public schools, removing tax exemptions from church property, and calling for a constitutional convention to disestablish Roman Catholicism.

On the first Sunday in June, a letter from the priests of the archdiocese of Buenos Aires, read at all masses, informed the faithful that Rome still had at its disposal the ultimate weapon of excommunication, by which it could expel from the fold Catholics found guilty of certain serious offenses against the church.[27] In a nation whose constitution required the president to be Roman Catholic, this could have devastating consequences.

Thursday, June 9, was the Feast of Corpus Christi, traditionally the occasion for a religious procession around the Plaza de Mayo. The archdiocese applied for permission to observe the celebration on Saturday, ostensibly to avoid disrupting traffic, but in fact to secure a larger crowd on the weekend. The government granted a permit for the ninth and forbade a Saturday march. The organizers ignored the prohibition and went ahead with their plans. Half a million leaflets announcing the event were distributed at churches in the capital and its suburbs. On Friday the archdiocese announced that the procession would take place as scheduled, but inside the cathedral.[28]

That night Perón made a speech that sounded like a general's orders for combat readiness. He cautioned Peronists not to act without orders from above and declared that he would be responsible for issuing commands. "For every person our enemy can bring out, we shall bring out ten," he boasted.[29]

In the Argentine political context, to win the street was an important goal in the struggle for public opinion.[30] The sense of power it conveyed, both symbolic and real, could galvanize the victors and paralyze the losers. October 17, 1945, stood in bold relief as the classic example of what gaining control of the streets could accomplish.

The best the Peronists could offer on Saturday, June 11, was a rerun of the Pasqual Pérez welcome. Pasqualito had successfully defended his crown in Tokyo on May 30, and a tribute to him was scheduled for Luna Park. Once again, in a crucial test of mobilization, the Peronists came out very much on the short end.

By 3:00 P.M. the cathedral could not accommodate another body and the throng spilled out into the adjacent Plaza de Mayo. Estimates of the crowd ranged from 100,000 to 250,000. The demonstrators were well-dressed, respectable folk, to such an extent that the Peronists tried to draw a historical link between them and the multitude at the "picnic" in the Plaza San Martín on October 12, 1945. But the analogy did not hold, for the circumstances were dramatically dissimilar.

When the mass inside the cathedral came to an end, the Corpus Christi celebration became overtly political and a large column took off up the Avenida de Mayo toward the Congress. White handkerchiefs aloft, the protestors issued chants such as "We are the people!" "The police are Catholic! "The army is Catholic!" and "We have had enough of fear! Let Perón ask now, what do the people want?" Several participants carried the yellow flag of the Vatican. Members of Catholic Action led the march and controlled traffic. The police remained out of sight, under orders to avoid confrontation. The procession paused to demonstrate in front of the Congress building, where someone painted "Christ the King" on a wall, then headed back to the center of town and disbanded, apparently without incident. However, newspaper headlines on the following day trumpeted the news that an incident had indeed occurred.

"Traitors to the Fatherland and to God, They Burned the Argentine Flag" was the way *La Epoca* put it. "Deeds of Vandalism against Nationality," declared *La Prensa*. According to the press, demonstrators had hauled down the Argentine flag from its mast in front of the Congress, set fire to it and replaced it with a Vatican banner. Interior Minister Borlenghi had made the accusations at a midnight press conference and had displayed to reporters the charred remains of an Argentine flag.

Pamphlets contesting these claims appeared on the streets within a very short time. The Catholics countercharged that the police, acting under orders from Borlenghi, had burned a flag for the sole purpose of creating a scandal to offset the impression made by the Corpus Christi march.[31]

In recent years, a high Peronist official has given a description that has a certain ring of credibility. Federal deputy Oscar Albrieu, who was soon to join Perón's cabinet, avers that the truth rests somewhere in the middle. According to Albrieu, some of the young people in the front line of the march were carrying banners painted sky-blue and white, the colors of the Argentine flag. When they arrived at the Congress, they attempted to douse the perpetual flame installed in Evita's memory on the portico of the building, using the blue-and-white banners, which burned. They did not haul down the Argentine flag, which they could not possibly have reached on its high mast atop the roof of the edifice. However, someone mistakenly reported to the Ministry of the Interior that a flag had been burned, and everyone assumed it was the official flag of the Congress. Perón, hearing the report, telephoned the chief of police, who knew nothing about it and promised to investigate. The president told him he wanted the banner. But the chief could not find it, for the Catholics had taken with them the charred cloth. Since Perón was on his way and had given the impression he wanted to see a burnt banner, the chief ordered his men to burn something that looked like a flag. They lit fire to a shirt and presented it to Perón and Borlenghi.[32]

Albrieu concludes that both sides were wrong because neither Perón nor the Catholics burned a flag. But his version locates the truth much closer to the opposition's claim. The charges leveled at the demonstrators were based upon fabricated evidence.[33]

The government now felt impelled to retake the initiative. On Sunday, Peronists surrounded the cathedral and trapped several hundred people inside. When the police finally responded to calls for help, they put most of the Catholics under protective arrest.

The flag-burning incident, however, provided the pretext for the regime's most vigorous response to the Corpus Christi procession. The Congress met in special session and the CGT held a rally. In addition to posturing, the Casa Rosada issued an executive decree removing from their archdiocesan position Monsignors Manuel Tato and Ramón Nova, considered responsible for the subversive march.[34] Although they were Argentine citizens, both priests were thereupon "deported" from the country and put on a plane to Rome.

The response from the Vatican came swiftly. On Thursday, June 16, a decree issued by the Sacred Consistorial Congregation excommunicated all those responsible for ordering and carrying out the expulsion of Bishop Tato.[35] The document named no names. Whether it in fact excommunicated Perón would become a matter of controversy. The dispute did not erupt forthwith, because as the message from Rome was arriving in Buenos Aires, the city would begin a soul-searing fourteen hours of terror that would heap discredit upon anti-Peronists and Peronists alike.

35

The Beginning of the End

On three sides of the Plaza de Mayo, narrow streets intersect to form a compact grid upon which an important part of the Buenos Aires banking and commercial districts cluster. On weekdays, vehicular and pedestrian traffic compete for limited space on sidewalks and roadways. The plaza, a pleasant clearing in this urban tangle, converts two city blocks into a haven for passersby who prefer to sit on benches, feed the pigeons and contemplate the Casa Rosada.

On the morning of June 16, the usual downtown crowd easily absorbed several hundred men scattered in small groups a few blocks from the edge of the plaza on the perimeter extending from the Paseo Colón west, north and east back to the Avenida Leandro Além. In somber business suits, they looked no different from the multitude of porteños scurrying to work or strolling in search of coffee and a mid-morning snack, except that they seemed rather edgy and kept looking first at their watches, then at the heavy cloud cover overhead.

Mario Amadeo and a companion sat by a window in a bar at the corner of Belgrano and Bolívar.[1] They conversed in low tones, a practice cultivated by many Argentines as the regime became more repressive. A man in an overcoat crossed the intersection and paused for a moment on the sidewalk. Amadeo exchanged glances with him, and he quickly vanished. A misty rain was now falling. They sipped coffee and smoked cigarette after cigarette as an hour passed. A second hour passed. At 12:10, Amadeo stood up, spread several pesos on the table and left. His companion remained for several minutes more, then slipped out the door and hurried away in a different direction.

The day began routinely for Perón. His first task was to sign several decrees. Then came an appointment with Ambassador Nufer, who was to present him with a gift from a U.S. military official who had recently visited

Buenos Aires. Various meetings were to fill the rest of the morning. At noon, as part of the ongoing melodrama of the burnt flag, a squadron of air force fighter planes would fly over the cathedral to honor General San Martín, whose body lay in the church and whose memory the Corpus Christi march had supposedly profaned. But inclement weather threatened to force a postponement.

At nine Army Minister Lucero arrived with news of a rumored insurrection by the navy.[2] The general had been awake most of the night to investigate a report from one of his officers that a navy captain had invited him to join a "revolutionary movement" scheduled to break out on the sixteenth. During this tense period stories about impending coups by the notoriously anti-Peronist navy hardly qualified as news. The captain in question denied having made the offer. Lucero was satisfied that it was one more false alarm, but thought it prudent to inform Perón.

At 10:50 A.M. Nufer began an hour-long audience with Perón, whom he described as "not only cool and collected, but if anything more affable than ever." The president assured him that the controversy with the church was actually increasing his popularity.[3] As Perón conversed with Nufer, the Casa Rosada received word that the naval mechanics' school had revolted and that something out of the ordinary was happening at the Ezeiza Airport. The coincidence of these reports with the presumed false alarm convinced Lucero that this time a genuine coup had begun. He urged Perón to go to the War Ministry. The president agreed and gave General Lucero full authority to deal with any armed rebellion. A car drove him the short distance to Lucero's office in the massive edifice overlooking Dry Dock Number 3. At the same time a mounted detachment of grenadiers arrived at the Casa Rosada and assumed defensive positions.

The decision to take precautionary measures proved eminently sound. Elements within the navy had indeed set in motion an attempt to kill Perón and overthrow his regime. The plan was for naval aircraft to bomb the Casa Rosada. Marines supported by civilians stationed at strategic points around the Plaza de Mayo would then attack the Government House, while warships would steam up the Río de la Plata and airborne army troops would land at the municipal airport. Although the insurrection followed hard on the heels of the Corpus Christi procession, there was no causal relationship between the two occurrences.[4] The conspirators had been preparing for several months and were aware that Perón's intelligence services had picked up the scent. On June 14, Amadeo learned that the government had films of the house that was serving as headquarters for the cabal.[5] Fearful that the army was about to crack down on them, the organizers of the uprising resolved to strike first and set June 16 as the date for the coup.

It was a gamble, not so totally hopeless as the Menéndez fiasco of 1951, in that at least a decisive stroke would be aimed directly at the Casa

Rosada, but the lack of substantial army support lent an air of desperation to the endeavor. The haste with which final arrangements were made did nothing to improve the chances of success.

The first bombs were supposed to drop at 10:00 A.M., but the weather refused to cooperate. The general who was to take command of the rebel army troops was unable to fly out of the city and join the unit. Although a detachment of armed marines had quietly assembled at the Naval Ministry and the civilians had taken their positions, loyalist soldiers were surrounding the naval mechanics' school.

A makeshift squadron of navy planes had taken off from the base at Punta Indio on the mouth of the Río de la Plata early that morning. Using an airport in the suburb of Quilmes as a staging area, they had launched their foray at 9:30, as planned, but had to circle overhead because of the clouds. Six Beechcraft light bombers and three Catalina flying boats armed for bombing, accompanied by twenty trainers, waited in vain for a break in the weather. At 12:40, they decided to proceed with the attack. The pilot of one of the Catalinas swooped down along the Avenida Leandro Além and approached the Casa Rosada. He barked an order to his crew, and for the first time in history bombs fell on Buenos Aires.[6]

The original hope had been that Perón himself would be on the roof of the Casa Rosada to watch the aerial tribute to San Martín. Yet the rebels must have known that the Peronists would have assembled a crowd in the plaza as part of the ceremony. Both the formulation of the plan and its execution by the pilots evidenced a reckless disregard for obvious consequences.

An employee at the nearby British embassy looked out of the window in time to see "an old seaplane gliding in at a low altitude from the north. It released a trail of bombs that fell in a lazy curve. The whole thing seemed to happen in slow motion. There were explosions, and a plume of brownish yellow smoke rose skyward from the direction of the Casa Rosada."[7]

The first strike produced a direct hit on the greenhouse on the roof of the Casa Rosada. The blast shattered windows in the Treasury Ministry across the street and caused the first civilian casualties. People in the plaza scurried for shelter, and swarms of pigeons flew madly in every direction. The other bombers followed the flight path of the Catalina, but their aim was far from pinpoint. A crowded trackless trolley proceeding along the Paseo Colón caught a bomb and burst into flames. No one escaped alive from it. As the rain of destruction intensified, the toll of bystander deaths and injuries mounted.

Once the bombing had begun, the marines at the Naval Ministry launched thrusts at the Casa Rosada and the War Ministry. Already prepared for battle, they interpreted the air raid as the casting of the die. Scores of porteños huddled fearfully under the arcade along the Avenida Leandro Além and watched the rebel troops advance.

Juan Perón was in General Lucero's office on the sixth floor of the War Ministry. He did not remain there long. At the sound of a falling bomb, one of his aides rushed him into a corner next to a filing cabinet.[8] The explosive landed several hundred meters away and destroyed the windows of the office. Perón immediately retired to the basement.

An employee of the press secretary described the president's appearance as he entered the improvised shelter: "The arrival of Perón, dressed in flannel trousers and a sport jacket, was a surprise. Beads of sweat stood out on his forehead, his mouth was fixed in an expression of bitterness and disappointment, the lines on his face were more pronounced than ever. He behaved with openness, smoked a black Argentine cigarette that a sergeant offered him, and drank *mate*."[9] He was impatient for news of the coming of loyal air force fighter planes and gave orders against the bombing of the expensive new facilities at Ezeiza, which the rebels had captured.

The only time he showed emotion was when he received word that the CGT was calling upon the workers to assemble in the Plaza de Mayo. "Go back to the CGT," he directed the messenger who had brought him the news, "and tell the CGT that not one worker should go to the plaza."[10] But it was too late. Groups of workers conditioned to chant "My life for Perón" had already set out for the plaza, where they would serve as easy targets for the insurgent airmen.[11]

The battle continued for several hours. Navy planes from Ezeiza and the air base at Morón, which had also fallen to the rebels, made more strikes against the Casa Rosada, hit the central police headquarters, attacked the presidential residence and strafed the Avenida de Mayo and the Congress. They succeeded only in killing and wounding helpless civilians.*

The marines managed to reach a service station diagonally across the street from the Casa Rosada, where they engaged in a fierce exchange of gunfire with its defenders. Other rebel units en route to the War Ministry met superior forces and had to turn back. The arrival of armored vehicles manned by army troops doomed the insurgency. The marines had to retreat to the Navy Ministry, where they dug in and repulsed an ill-considered assault by a crowd of angry workers.

By late afternoon the revolt had collapsed. The pilots flew their planes across the river to Uruguay. The Navy Ministry surrendered to the army. One of the admirals who had led the rebellion committed suicide. The civilian participants, some of whom had seized a radio station momentarily during the uprising, either fled the country or went into hiding. Picking

---

* According to a U.S. embassy report, "The Argentines themselves behaved in a most peculiar way. Instead of fleeing the area, hundreds, perhaps thousands, were circulating around during the whole period of attack and even going into the Plaza de Mayo when a lull occurred, racing again for cover when fighting resumed or when a strafing attack was made." Siracusa to Department of State, 735.00/6-2255, June 22, 1955.

their way through streets blocked by burnt-out automobiles and sidewalks littered with rubble, the police collected dead bodies and helped secure first aid for the injured. An official announcement set the toll at 355 killed and more than 600 wounded.[12]

At 6:00 P.M. Perón spoke by radio from the War Ministry. He assured the nation that the insurrection had been suppressed and that the situation was now completely under control. For the army generals and the troops who had remained loyal to the regime, he had words of extravagant praise. He urged the workers to remain calm. But a scant few blocks away, under heavy rain, a crowd had already set fire to the headquarters of the archdiocese and was wrecking the interior of the cathedral next door. The horror of the bombing of the Plaza de Mayo had yielded to the shame of the burning of the churches.[13]

Groups of young men in raincoats smashed through the main portals, pillaged the altars and sacristies, and then ignited Molotov cocktails or other incendiary devices. Some donned vestments and performed sacrilegious parodies outside as flames licked at smashed stained-glass windows and cast flickering light upon the grotesque proceedings. Parishioners who arrived with the hope of defending their places of worship stood helplessly at a distance. One priest who was inside when the incendiaries burst through the door attempted to dissuade them. Escorting him to the sidewalk, they said they were avenging their fallen comrades and had no interest in harming him. The eighty-year-old parish priest at another of the churches was not so fortunate. When he implored the marauders to desist, one of them hit him on the head. He later died from the blow.

Even the Basilica of St. Francis, which had enjoyed special favors from Perón and Evita, fell victim to the frenzy. A dozen churches were put to the torch. Most of them were in the vicinity of the Plaza de Mayo, and all were in the downtown area of the city. Neither the fire department nor the police nor the army made the slightest effort to intervene.

The ashes were still smoldering when the pamphleteers printed a leaflet quoting from a speech Perón had delivered on May 1, 1953, shortly after the destruction of the Jockey Club: "When the time comes to burn, I'm going to be out front of you; but then, if it should be necessary, history will record the biggest bonfire that mankind has ever set."[14] Subsequent pamphlets placed full responsibility in the president's lap.[15] From the other side of the Atlantic, Sir Winston Churchill pronounced his devastating dictum: "Perón is the first soldier to burn his flag, and the first Catholic to burn his churches."[16]

Perón's initial reaction was to single out for blame a favorite scapegoat, the Communists.[17] In the book he wrote shortly after going into exile, he mentioned briefly the fact that several churches had been burned, but did not disclose who was responsible.[18] A book subsequently published under his name (apparently based upon a series of interviews he gave) refers to "certain groups of rascals" as the guilty parties.[19] Finally, in his taped memoirs, he first pointed out (inaccurately) that only four churches were burned—indeed, he seemed to take some credit for the fact that the rest of the churches were spared—and then accused the Catholics of setting fire to their own houses of worship. "The churches had been burned from within," he claimed. "It was an act of provocation. They burned the churches so that afterward they could make campaigns against me."[20]

Under pressure from the army, Perón directed his intelligence agencies to look into the burnings. They discovered that some of the incendiaries had come from the Peronist party and others from the Ministry of Public Health, but then drew the curious conclusion, which lacked any factual basis, that the whole incident was the work of a Masonic lodge.[21] A commission that investigated the matter after Perón's fall confirmed the prior findings with respect to the party and the Public Health Ministry and also traced participants to the CGT, the government petroleum company (YPF), the right-wing ALN and the federal police.[22]

A separate question concerns responsibility for the failure to make any attempt to extinguish the flames. During the Revolution of 1930, Captain Perón had led security patrols through the streets of Buenos Aires, squelched mob outbursts and protected buildings from fire. But as president, when faced with a similar situation, he did nothing. One of the generals in the War Ministry, when he heard churches were burning, asked Perón's permission to telephone the chief of police and order him into action. The chief replied that under extraordinary powers the president had delegated to the army, it was the latter's job to fight fires.[23] Perón, in constant contact with the chief throughout the day, could easily have given him orders to stop the conflagrations.

The verbal attacks upon the clergy by Perón and those who took their cues from him heaped dry tinder against the ramparts of the Argentine church. The fate of the Jockey Club had demonstrated that among Perón's followers were individuals capable of wielding torches. The fact that the inexcusable carnage in the plaza provided the spark could not justify the senseless acts that ensued. The psychological impact of the charred churches was devastating to Catholics with memories of the atrocities of the Spanish Civil War. By permitting the holocaust, Perón forfeited the political gain to be made from popular reaction to the casualties of the navy bombing. Despite the virtual blackout in the Peronist press, the government could not hide the physical evidence, and the spectacle of the ruined churches was as repulsive as the bomb damage.

The church itself was not reluctant to exploit the tragedy. The government's offer to reconstruct the buildings met with a cold rejection.[24] It was, of course, to Perón's advantage to clean up the mess as quickly as possible. But the Catholics preferred to let the ruins remain intact as a reminder of the persecution the president had instigated.

The events of June 16 shook Juan Perón to the marrow. In order to remain in power, he would have to choose between annihilating his enemies and accommodating them. The former option would call for ruthless measures to which Perón was not inclined to resort. He might have ordered or permitted the execution of the rebel leaders responsible for the Plaza de Mayo bloodshed, but he preferred instead to imprison them. To the Catholics he began to hold out the possibility of a reconciliation. In a speech on June 17, he repudiated the burning of the churches, guaranteed the safety of the clergy and promised to hold a plebiscite to settle the matter of church-state relations.[25]

But the opposition remained adamant. Taking the *conductor*'s blandishments as a sign of weakness, they encouraged a spate of rumors intended to destabilize the regime. The conferral of extraordinary powers upon General Lucero lent credibility to stories that Perón was about to resign or had agreed to share political power with the army or was a prisoner of the military, or that elements of the fleet were missing and in a state of rebellion.[26]

According to Lucero, several officers suggested to him that the army take over the government, but he rejected them.[27] In late June, the president revoked the authority he had delegated to Lucero, and the army returned to the barracks, its role in putting down the rebellion having officially terminated. Subsequent events fortified the supposition that the military may have imposed conditions on Perón.

Immediately after resuming full authority, Perón began to purge his cabinet and the CGT leadership. Angel Borlenghi, who had run the Interior Ministry from the beginning of the first term, resigned, as did CGT General Secretary Vuletich and Education Minister Méndez San Martín. The most important addition to Perón's team was the new minister of the interior, Oscar Albrieu, a Peronist deputy with a reputation for competence and moderation.

It was the latter's job to carry out a so-called pacification program developed by Perón and his advisors. According to Albrieu the basic features of the new policy embraced an accord with the hierarchy, the improvement of relations with the opposition parties and the democratization of the Peronist party.[28] Albrieu met quietly with the bishops and leaders of the opposition in an attempt to establish some kind of modus vivendi.

On July 5, Perón launched a personal initiative. He made a speech absolving the opposition parties of participation in the June 16 uprising and offered them a truce. The Radicals immediately asked permission to use the radio. Their petition was denied, on the ground that existing regulations did not allow political speeches on the government-controlled airwaves. Since Hugo de Pietro, Vuletich's replacement at the CGT, and Peronist party officials had recently used the radio for political appeals, the rejection had a hollow ring and hardly contributed to pacification.[29]

The regime also took steps to conciliate the church. The anticlerical press campaign came to an abrupt halt. Perón and Pius XII exchanged greetings on the Feasts of Saints Peter and Paul. A number of Catholics were released from jail. But on July 13, the bishops released a pastoral letter denouncing religious persecution in Argentina and enumerating the anti-Catholic measures taken by the government.[30] The hierarchy seemed disinclined to forget the past, especially since it lived on in laws at which the church took great umbrage.

If Perón was to gain his objective, it was soon clear that he would have to do more. On July 15, in a speech to Peronist legislators, he acknowledged that the revolutionary character of Peronism had required the curtailment of individual liberties. Then, to the surprise of his audience, he announced that "the Peronist revolution is over; there begins now a new stage, constitutional in character, without revolutions, because the permanent condition of a country cannot be revolution. . . . I have stopped being the chief of a revolution and have become president of all the Argentines, friends or foes."[31] He then renewed his pleas for peace.

Several days later, Ambassador Nufer had occasion to discuss with Perón some of the specific measures the latter had in mind to implement the promises he had made. The *conductor* indicated he would remove restrictions from the press and revise the electoral laws to give the opposition greater, albeit minority, representation in the Congress. Though he insisted he could still count upon the army's solid support, he stressed that if the armed forces deserted him he could paralyze the country with a general strike. He would not step down, he added, unless there were no other way to achieve peace. Nufer thought Perón was in good health, but

> definitely not as buoyant as on previous occasions, nor did he exude as much self-confidence. . . . I definitely found him a changed man, but cannot satisfy myself whether it is simply [the] result of shock of [the] revolt and its aftermath, or whether it means he is subdued because of outside influence.[32]

As *Primera Plana* put it, "Perón was wounded in one wing."[33] Rhetoric alone would not extricate him from the crisis. After his dramatic words on July 15, the opposition parties reiterated their request to use the radio. This time the Peronists did not refuse. Thus, for the first time since Perón became president, the nation's airwaves carried voices of dissent.[34]

Arturo Frondizi, now the head of the Radical party, had the initial opportunity, followed by conservative leader Vicente Solano Lima and then by a Progressive Democrat (also conservative). The tone of their speeches was moderate and surprisingly conciliatory. For once during the Perón era, rational political discourse seemed possible.

The truce endured for barely a month. So-called lightning demonstrations by anti-Peronists and attacks upon the police became more frequent. On August 15 the government announced the discovery of a plot to assassinate Perón. Two weeks later, the police found a cache of arms and explosives in the Barrio Norte. Meanwhile, the political climate made congressional approval of the contract with Standard Oil of California out of the question, and the bill languished in committee.

Many Peronists who look back upon this chaotic period lament Evita's absence. They maintain that she would have forced him to take whatever measures might be necessary to root out subversion. If Evita had not died, they argue, Perón would not have fallen.

Evita would never have tolerated Perón's dalliance with the UES. But she might have been neither able nor of a mind to prevent the conflict with the church. Her devoutness might not have offset the political judgments that led Perón to attack the clergy, or the excesses that followed. It is perfectly conceivable that she might have accepted the *conductor*'s insistence that his quarrel was merely with the "bad" priests and bishops.

What did make a difference was the fact that Evita in life played the unique role of providing the violent rhetoric of revolutionary Peronism. The *conductor* preferred to act as arbiter or peacemaker, remaining above the din of battle and maintaining the balance of forces within his movement. When Evita died, he could find no substitute for her. Therefore, when the situation demanded it, he had to supply the incendiary language. At that point he could no longer pose as moderator.

When peace overtures did not produce immediate results, more drastic measures had to be considered. The new head of the Peronist party in the capital, John William Cooke, wanted to organize street demonstrations.[35] Perón had a better idea. On the morning of August 31, newspapers and radio broadcasts disclosed the startling news that President Perón had resigned.

The incredulity that greeted the announcement was well-founded. Perón had submitted his resignation to the CGT and to the Peronist party, rather than to the Congress. Moreover, union and party leaders were convoking a Plaza de Mayo rally on that very day for the purpose of urging the president to reconsider. It was clearly a ploy to arouse popular emotions: the *conductor* was mobilizing the descamisados in the hope of stemming the tide that now ran against him.

The text of the written resignation contained a lengthy, somewhat repetitive description of the accomplishments of the Peronist revolution. His decision to step down derived from a commitment to achieve peace. He would become a "simple Peronist" willing to serve the movement.[36]

As Peronist leaders used the airwaves to implore the *conductor* to withdraw his resignation, crowds flocked to the plaza. Trucks from the Eva Perón Foundation distributed soup, bread and oranges to the faithful. Chants declaring "Perón must stay" and "We want Perón" reverberated through the city. Despite the cathedral's proximity, the throng ignored it. No anticlerical slogans were shouted. As a U.S. embassy observer noted, "it was as though the religious question had never existed."[37] At 6:30 P.M., Perón appeared on the balcony and set off a ten-minute ovation.

Of the countless public speeches Perón delivered in his long political career, the August 31 discourse ranks high on the list of most memorable. It is impossible to know for certain what he intended to say when he stepped before the microphones. One of his aides now claims that he planned to make further proposals in an effort to revive the truce.[38] Albrieu found the president's words "inexplicable."[39] The speech was violent, the sort of explosive harangue that Evita might have delivered yet more inflammatory than anything she ever said and infinitely more ominous because it came from the lips of the *conductor*. Whatever the cause, there could be little doubt that he lost control of himself on that gray afternoon and unloaded what would go down in history as the "five for one" speech, an outburst that sealed the fate of his second presidency.

He began by reviewing the bloody insurrection of June 16 and his efforts at reconciliation. "The political leaders have answered with speeches as superficial as they were insolvent; the instigators with their customary hypocrisy, rumors and pamphlets; and the executioners by shooting at the poor policemen on the streets." He was therefore giving the descamisados the same order he issued in 1945: "We must respond to violence with a greater violence." More specifically, he declared an open hunting season on rebels: "Anyone who anywhere tries to change the existing order in opposition to the constituted authorities or the laws or the constitution can be killed by any Argentine." He extended this permit to apply not only to those who took overt action against the regime, but also to those who conspired to incite rebellion against it. Then he issued the fateful pronouncement that "when one of our people falls, five of theirs will fall."[40] It was now a fight to the finish, with no quarter to be given, or so it seemed.

Almost as an afterthought he told the crowd he was withdrawing his resignation. His words did not include the usual request that they disperse peacefully. But despite Perón's open appeal for violence, the descamisados sang, chanted and shouted as they streamed off in all directions without incident. Their mood suggested that they believed they had just won a great victory.[41]

36

The Liberating Revolution

Amid the swirl of pamphlets that descended upon Buenos Aires in the weeks following the bombardment of the Plaza de Mayo were several recounting prophecies made by the Italian priest Don Luigi Orione during a visit to Argentina in 1934 in the company of Eugenio Cardinal Pacelli (later to become Pope Pius XII). The saintly Don Luigi foresaw a violent persecution of Argentine Roman Catholics, the destruction of churches, the murder of priests, and ultimate salvation that would come in a stream of blood from the interior of the country.[1] By September all but his final prediction had come to pass.

Conspiracies against the regime had lurked on the fringes of the political landscape throughout the Perón era. Opposition leaders still in Argentina or in exile from Montevideo, anti-Peronist trade unionists and many military officers shared a common hatred for Juan Perón and what he represented. But until the conflict with the church, disunity reduced their tentative efforts to the category of minor annoyance. The anticlerical campaign and the violence of June 16 submerged ideological differences and gave overriding priority to the elimination of Perón at any cost.

Yet only the army could rid Argentina of the *conductor*. If there had been any doubts, the failure of the navy revolt dissolved them. Nuclei of civilians drawn from Catholic ranks as well as from the political parties prepared themselves for insurrection, but only as support units for a military uprising. Naval conspirators were ready to try again but this time insisted upon army participation.[2]

Perón had been careful to entrust Campo de Mayo and other important garrisons in and around Buenos Aires to officers firmly committed to him. This meant that the best hope for a coup lay in units stationed in the interior and commanded by officers of dubious loyalty. In the period during which the president was attempting to promote "pacification," several loosely connected conspiracies were groping for the right opportunity to revolt.[3] At this stage the most likely leader of the dissidents was General Pedro E. Aramburu, the director of the education program for colonels and the highest-ranking officer among the plotters. Younger officers, particularly those in some of the army garrisons in the city of Córdoba, were eager to launch a coup.

Finally, the conspirators could count on the participation of General Eduardo Lonardi, now in retirement after his early withdrawal from the 1951 Menéndez fiasco. Lonardi stood ready to do whatever was necessary to oust Perón. Unlike many of the others, he was no newcomer to the fight against Perón. He had prestige and experience and was determined not to repeat the mistakes of the past.

Pressure on the conspirators mounted in early September. The "five for one" speech seemed to signal a resolve on Perón's part to crush all opposition with civilian violence if necessary. It provoked a general who had once earned a Peronist loyalty medal to launch a premature uprising at the headquarters of the Fourth Army Division in Río Cuarto, two hundred kilometers south of the city of Córdoba. The revolt aborted. In Córdoba itself, the officers of the artillery school had pledged themselves to Perón's overthrow and were on training exercises with their troops. When the maneuvers came to an end in mid-month, their weapons and ammunition would have to be turned in, so the decisive moment was rapidly approaching. Finally, naval air units ready to rebel were facing an imminent inspection that would expose their intentions. They sent word to the army conspirators that if a revolt did not begin before September 17, they would bombard the Casa Rosada again on that date.[4]

Weighing these various factors, Aramburu concluded that an armed rebellion at this time had no chance of success and decided to withdraw from active participation. But it was now impossible to postpone the coup. Into the breach strode General Lonardi. He knew the odds were against the conspirators, but also felt that delay would be fatal. On September 5, he assumed the leadership of the anti-Peronist revolution.

Meanwhile, the *conductor* was trying to cope with the fallout from his "five for one" speech. There were ardent Peronists who shook their heads in dismay after his call for violence. Interior Minister Albrieu went to Perón and submitted his resignation. The president took him by the arm and told him the reconciliation initiatives would continue. "All I meant to do was give a tonic to the people in the Plaza de Mayo," he explained.[5] As they were conversing, Congress was about to impose upon the city of Buenos Aires a state of siege, giving the chief executive extraordinary powers to deal with the threat of internal subversion.

On September 7, Perón received a delegation from several unions. His visitors made ritual pledges of unconditional support, to which he responded with some tough talk reminiscent of the August 31 speech. On that same day, Hugo de Pietro, on behalf of the CGT, formally made Argentina's workers available to serve in armed civilian militias. This was clearly a last-ditch effort by the labor wing of the Peronist movement to free the *conductor* from total dependence upon the army. But Argentina's number-one worker was still first and foremost a military man. He could not bring himself to do anything potentially destructive to the institution with which he identified. He also feared the possible consequences of arming workers. "It's easy to give guns to the unions," he is reported to have said. "What's hard is to take the guns away."[6] Therefore, on the next day General Lucero, speaking for the president, rejected the offer. But this was not enough to offset its harmful effects. The publicity it received heightened the sense of urgency galvanizing the conspirators. In addition, the pamphleteers charged that CGT's gesture was a first step in a Peronist scheme to dissolve the armed forces.[7]

General Lonardi had by now inherited the various insurgent groups that had previously responded to General Aramburu's leadership and had made contact with the navy.[8] On September 11, he unveiled his plan of action, which was to go into effect on Friday the sixteenth. It called for simultaneous revolts of army garrisons in Córdoba and elsewhere in the interior, the entire fleet, important shore installations and various air force units. The first and critical objective was Córdoba. Once that city fell, the rebels would head east to Santa Fe on the Paraná River, and then march south to Buenos Aires. Meanwhile, the fleet would blockade the Río de la Plata and support a final assault on the capital. It was an ambitious strategy, heavily dependent upon the correctness of Lonardi's conviction that if they could hold out for forty-eight hours, they would attract uncommitted officers to their side and pick up irreversible momentum.

On Wednesday, General Lucero went to Córdoba, ostensibly to be on hand for some training exercises by the army's Fourth Division. Albrieu had conveyed to Perón reports that a revolt was about to be launched by the younger officers in Córdoba, and the president summoned his military advisors. According to Albrieu, Lucero took the matter personally and interpreted it as a political move against him by the interior minister.[9] He flew to Córdoba to investigate for himself. The officers with whom he met assured him that nothing was brewing. Lucero, who put much stock in military honor, believed them.[10] Perón, in his taped memoirs, claimed that the general sent him a telegram declaring that "It can occur only to a crazy person that these people will revolt." The *conductor*'s opinion of his loyal associate's performance was less than generous: "When you count on guys like him, what can you do?"[11]

Lucero was apparently unaware that on that very Wednesday, General Lonardi had boarded a bus at Plaza Once in downtown Buenos Aires and made the overnight trip to Córdoba. As Lucero left the provincial capital on his way to make his erroneous report to Perón, Lonardi was arriving to take command of the insurrection. It was his fifty-ninth birthday.

On Thursday evening, Albrieu learned that Lonardi was in Córdoba. He checked with a local police contact, who assured him that all was well.[12] At midnight, the zero hour set by Lonardi, the green light flashed for what would become known as the Liberating Revolution.[13]

There was no more appropriate Argentine city than Córdoba to serve as the focal point for the uprising against Juan Perón. A thriving colonial metropolis when Buenos Aires was a struggling outpost, Córdoba had looked down with disdain upon the federal capital throughout its history. A cultural oasis with a distinguished university founded in 1613, an industrial and commercial center, a popular tourist attraction because of proximity to the rolling Córdoba hills, and a fortress of conservatism as well as devout Catholicism, Argentina's third-largest city furnished fertile soil for both civilians and military men opposed to Perón.

In the early morning hours, Lonardi assembled his followers at the artillery school and exhorted them to proceed "with maximum brutality."[14] Their first objective was to capture the infantry school. The battle raged for eight hours. The infantrymen finally surrendered. By afternoon, the insurgents had seized several radio stations and were ready to broadcast their proclamations to the nation.

Army uprisings in Mendoza and San Juan gained control of those western cities for the revolutionaries. In Curuzú Cuatía, near the border with Brazil and Uruguay, Aramburu changed his mind and assumed command of the rebel forces. However, loyalist troops managed to surround them, and he was forced to flee.

The naval phase of the revolution went smoothly in Puerto Madryn, Puerto Belgrano and Bahía Blanca, three major port cities on the South Atlantic. A fleet of warships began to rendezvous and steamed northward along the coast of Buenos Aires Province. The insurrection in Río Santiago, just outside the city of Eva Perón (formerly La Plata), ran into difficulty because of attacks from nearby army and air force units. An attempt by marines to capture Eva Perón met fierce resistance and failed. Admiral Isaac Rojas, the highest-ranking naval officer among the revolutionaries, had to leave Río Santiago aboard one of his ships because of air attacks on the city.

On the morning of the sixteenth, as reports of the various uprisings filtered into Buenos Aires, it was readily apparent that a serious, coordinated effort to overthrow the regime had begun. Scattered groups of armed civilian commandos took to the streets, pursuant to a plan to capture a radio station, but the police easily thwarted them. Antiaircraft guns were positioned near the Casa Rosada and along the waterfront. Yet an unruffled air still hung over the city.

Perón conferred with Lucero and the rest of his military high command at the War Ministry that morning to assess the situation. Once again, Lucero took charge of the defense of the government. The president seemed perfectly content to entrust his fate to his generals. At the Olivos residence, where Rumanian writer Virgil Gheorgiu was staying while he gathered material for his projected biography, Raúl Mendé assured the visitors, "It's nothing. Perón is stronger than ever."[15] Radio announcements over the Peronist-controlled radio stations downplayed the rebellion and maintained a tone of optimism.

On Saturday, a mood of relative calm continued in Buenos Aires, but housewives were now lining up at markets to stock up on provisions. All soccer games and horse races scheduled for that weekend were postponed. Porteños could listen to broadcasts from the navy in Puerto Belgrano, as well as from Uruguayan stations, to obtain different versions of how the revolution was progressing. The naval rebels announced that Admiral Rojas had taken command of the fleet aboard the cruiser *Seventeenth of October*. However, loyal army units were advancing by land toward Puerto Belgrano and Bahía Blanca.

But the nerve center of the rebellion, Lonardi's command post in Córdoba, attracted the most attention. Lucero and his associates worked out a careful plan, dubbed "Operation Cleanup," for the destruction of the rebel stronghold there. Loyalist troops began to close in on the provincial capital from all sides. Lonardi lacked foot soldiers who could be deployed to defend his positions. He had air support, as planes sent from Buenos Aires to participate in the siege of the city defected to his cause, but their efforts were not enough to turn back the troops gathering for a final thrust into Córdoba. The coup de grace was set for Monday the nineteenth.

In Buenos Aires a torrential rain poured from low-lying clouds as Monday dawned. A valet at the Olivos residence told Gheorgiu: "I'm forty-three years old, and I've never seen rain like this."[16] Mendé arrived early and informed the Rumanian that the revolt was in its death throes. "From today on," he asserted, "the president has decided to be energetic. We're going to exterminate our enemies and annihilate the opposition."[17] He waved a piece of paper, which he said contained a list of individuals who would immediately be sent into exile.

In Mendoza, where the rebels had set up a command post, a major arrived from Córdoba with a letter from Lonardi begging for reinforcements. Planes were available to transport troops to the beleaguered city, but compliance with the request meant risking loss of control in the western region, the only territory the rebels could legitimately claim. It was also the only place where they could set up a provisional government, a necessary step if the insurgency continued over an extended period of time. The major returned empty-handed to Lonardi.

The situation for the rebels in Córdoba grew increasingly desperate. Their troops, numbering 4,000, faced encirclement by loyalist army units with 10,000 soldiers to hurl into the attack. Lonardi made several attempts to persuade his adversaries to defect, but the generals in command of the siege refused. Córdoba was ripe for the taking.

Yet the order to advance never came. At 12:45 P.M., General Lucero sat before a radio microphone and in a shaky voice read a letter addressed by Juan Perón to the army and the Argentine people. Couched in the vaguest possible language (General Lonardi's son called it a "model of ambiguity"[18]), it sounded very much like a resignation, offered to the army for the purpose of enabling the generals to arrange a peaceful solution to the conflict. The announcement paralyzed most of the military units faithful to the regime.

This sudden turn of events was due to a threat by the navy to bombard an oil refinery in the city of Eva Perón and military targets within Buenos Aires. On Sunday, as the fleet approached the mouth of the Río de la Plata, the deterioration of Lonardi's position brought home to Admiral Rojas and his colleagues the urgent need for drastic action. They hit upon a plan to issue an ultimatum to the government: if it did not capitulate, warships would fire upon the Eva Perón refinery and the capital itself. To show they meant business, a cruiser shelled oil storage tanks in Mar del Plata.

When Perón heard about it, he voiced a deep dismay. According to Albrieu, he called the navy "barbarians," and complained of their willingness to destroy "the great work of my government, a project that cost $100 million."[19] He later wrote that he considered the refinery "like a son of mine."[20] The interior minister, who had accepted the fact that the regime was in a de facto civil war, found it curious that the president was so worried about property damage, and suggested that they could prevent the bombardment by putting family members of naval officers inside the refinery, an idea Perón rejected.[21]

At 5:30 A.M. on Monday, Perón told Lucero he had decided to announce that he was disposed to resign if that was necessary to ensure peace. It was a prototypical Perón gambit, an ill-defined gesture designed to preserve as much maneuverability as possible. The message Lucero was to read did not state directly that the president was offering his resignation. "For several days," it declared, "I have tried to leave the government, if that was a solution to the current political problems. Known public circumstances prevented me, although I keep thinking about it and insist upon my position of offering this solution."[22] The statement then put the army in charge of arranging a peaceful settlement. The justification given was the avoidance of the threat of a bombardment that would destroy invaluable property and take innocent lives.

As a resignation, the message was as irregular as the August 30 letters to the CGT and the Peronist party. Perón claimed that his purpose was to give his generals a document they could use in negotiations with the rebels (although there is no evidence that he ever explained to them exactly how they were to proceed), and that if he had really meant to step down, he would have complied with the law and sent his message to Congress.[23] Thus if we can believe his account, it came as a great surprise to him when the generals accepted his offer.

Perón initially explained his offer to resign as a means of avoiding a naval bombardment. The notion that he gave up the presidency to save an oil refinery seems ridiculous on its face. His apprehension of the navy's intention appears to have been highly exaggerated. Captain Hugo Guillamón, his naval aide-de-camp, relates that the president showed him how to reach the cellar of the downtown residence so that he might take refuge there if warships began to shell the mansion.[24] It did not occur to Perón that such an effort would surely destroy a substantial part of the Barrio Norte, an anti-Peronist stronghold.

While he overestimated the damage that might result from his refusal to step down, he made no recorded effort to calculate the harm Argentina might suffer at the hands of an anti-Peronist government. The elimination of gains made by the working class, the dismemberment of social welfare programs, the return to power of the oligarchy and the revival of exploitation by international capitalism were all foreseeable consequences of his demise, viewed through the prism of Peronist doctrine and rhetoric.

The reason for this lack of concern was Perón's perception of the goals of *justicialismo* as mere tactics for the purpose of achieving the "organized community." What was of the essence to him was not social justice or any of the other slogans, but the harmonious preservation of national unity. Once circumstances made the existence of this type of community impossible, Perón had no desire to plunge himself into what for him would be a senseless struggle for power.

A second explanation put full responsibility for his downfall on the generals to whom he entrusted the defense of the regime and who betrayed him. In a book he wrote shortly after going into exile, he singled out as the moment of betrayal their construction of his message as a resignation.[25] A few months later, he expanded the indictment to include charges that they vacillated in their effort to put down the rebellion and also persuaded him not to distribute weapons to the workers.[26]

In fact, it was Perón's own decision to leave everything to the generals. Given his military background and the leadership he supposedly exercised over his mass, not to have assumed personal command when the survival of the regime was at stake amounted to peculiar behavior by the man hailed as the *gran* (great) *conductor* in the Peronist anthem. Also, there is some evidence that even prior to the acceptance of his "resignation" he might have been thinking about leaving the country. His good friend Jorge Antonio approached the German embassy shortly *before* Lucero read his message to the army and the nation at midday on the nineteenth and inquired whether Perón might obtain asylum there.[27] Although Antonio may have made the request on his own, it is conceivable that Perón encouraged him, or knew about it and made no objection. The statement that his generals prevented him from arming the workers flatly contradicts other assertions he made opposing the move because it would result only in a slaughter of his followers. The context in which he made the claim is of great significance. He advanced it in a letter to John William Cooke, who would soon become the most prominent left-wing Peronist. This was a perfect example of Perón's habit of telling listeners what they wanted to hear.

A third rationale came to light in his taped memoirs, where he made the astonishing statement that

> our people, who had received enormous advantages and gains against the exploitation that had victimized them for a century, ought to have had a greater enthusiasm to defend what had been given them. But they didn't defend it because they were, as we say, "belly-ists." They thought with their bellies, and not with their heads and their hearts. . . . This ingratitude made me think that to give conquests and gains to a people incapable of defending them is a waste of time. . . . If all these things that make one puke had not existed, I would have taken charge of the defense and—I go out with a regiment, conclude the situation and the problem ends. . . .
> . . . The unions also disillusioned me. A general strike was prepared and they didn't go out. They tried to make deals with those on their way in. . . . Then I reached the conclusion that the Argentine people deserved a terrible punishment for having done this. . . .[28]

Thus the descamisados were at fault for not coming to the rescue. When they failed him, he decided to leave. The general who specialized in the study of military tactics refused to put his expertise to the test when his followers needed it most. The military man who excoriated fellow officers for not fighting to the death when they rebelled in 1951 fled for his life in 1955. The realist who refused to distribute guns to the workers because they would have faced certain death heaped criticism upon the workers for not taking to the streets without weapons. The *conductor* who wrote a book entitled *Political Leadership* refrained from putting his own theories into practice when mass mobilization might have tilted the balance in his favor in the critical days after the coup began. The president who systematically replaced strong, competent, intelligent associates with vapid sycophants complained when the weaklings in his entourage proved worthless to him in the crunch. The man responsible for creating a bureaucracy that ossified the Argentine labor movement could not understand why the unions did not produce another October 17 for him.

Why did Perón abandon his post without a fight? A military victory was within reach, especially in light of the imminent defeat of Lonardi in Córdoba. However, the total defection of the navy, the territorial control exercised by the rebels in the west and the dogged commitment of countless civilians to the overthrow of the regime suggest that the fall of Córdoba would not have ended the revolution and that a prolonged civil war would have resulted. Thus Perón may have concluded that he could not prevail if the conflict continued indefinitely. He may have recognized the debilitating effects of corruption, opportunism and mediocrity upon the Peronist movement. Although he would blame everyone but himself for this state of decay, he was well aware of its existence and guided his actions accordingly.

At the same time, even if he truly believed he could crush the rebellion, he may still have opted to leave. He referred on several occasions to the terrible tragedy in Spain, the results of which he had personally witnessed, as a compelling reason for avoiding a similar holocaust in Argentina. He knew well not only what it would have taken to beat the rebels in a long war, but also what he would have to do to govern the country afterward. An iron-fisted dictatorship would then be the only recourse. He could not play the moderator, the architect of national unity, the *conductor* of an "organized community." For him, that kind of victory was not worth winning, so he abdicated.

After broadcasting the message from Perón, Lucero transmitted to the insurgents an offer to meet at the War Ministry to discuss a settlement.[29] Lonardi would have none of it. He replied that the first condition for a truce was the immediate, unequivocal resignation of Perón. Lucero then designated a military junta of generals to carry out the task of ending the conflict, and submitted his own resignation to the president. The military junta proposed a meeting at the Cabildo in the Plaza de Mayo. The response from the navy was a demand for a twenty-four-hour truce and a conference aboard a warship. The junta meekly accepted.

On Tuesday the twentieth, a delegation from the junta made its way to the cruiser *Argentina* for a parley with Admiral Rojas. The outcome was an agreement that the president, vice-president and all cabinet members would resign, Lonardi would become president of a provisional government at noon on the twenty-second, and the military units fighting on Perón's side would return to their bases and await orders from the new regime. Shortly after the meeting adjourned, representatives from Lonardi reached the cruiser. They ratified the settlement, and also discussed the political aspects of the Liberating Revolution: a call for elections as soon as possible, a return to the 1853 constitution, the preservation of gains won by labor, and most important of all, "Neither Victors Nor Vanquished" as the theme for the process of reconstruction. On that same night, Lonardi declared himself provisional president of Argentina, on the ground that to do so immediately might help terminate the armed conflict.

While the junta was reaching an accord with the rebels, Perón made a final effort to salvage his presidency. On the evening of the nineteenth, he summoned Lucero and the junta to his residence and explained that he meant his statement not as a resignation, but rather as an offer to resign, a card to be held by the generals in their negotiations.[30] He may have merely been going through the motions. The generals, moreover, must have known by that time that an offer to resign on the part of the president was now worthless. Whatever the real motivations of the parties might have been, the outcome of the meeting was that the junta did not as a group accept the *conductor*'s interpretation. They retired to the War Ministry for further deliberations. Suddenly one of the generals thought to be loyal to Perón burst into the room. Several junior officers brandishing automatic weapons accompanied him. Resting his case upon the barrels of the guns at his side, he announced that Perón had resigned and directed the junta to get on with the business of dealing with the rebels.

In the early hours of the twentieth, word reached the residence that all was lost. "I'm leaving, Renzi," Perón told his majordomo. "I haven't slept for two nights, and I see there's nothing more I can do. I don't want more blood spilled, and I don't want those madmen to destroy the pipeline and refinery that cost so many pesos."[31]

He directed Renzi to pack a bag for him. "No suitcases, just a small bag where you can put some clothes and a little bit of money so I can keep moving in the days to come."[32] Renzi arranged a couple of shirts and a pair of socks. Exactly how much money went into the bag is a matter of speculation. According to one account, Perón took with him two million Argentine pesos and $70,000 (U.S.). He also packed a small portrait of Evita and a miniature of the Virgin of Luján.

At this critical juncture, the ex-president needed a Latin American embassy where he would be sure of a friendly reception. There was one obvious choice. At 8:00 A.M., Isaac Gilaberte, the presidential chauffeur, drove Perón and two aides through rain-drenched, deserted streets to the Paraguayan chancery, where the honorary citizen of Paraguay and honorary general in the Paraguayan army formally requested political asylum.[33]

Juan R. Chávez, the Paraguayan ambassador, was at his residence in the district of Palermo when he learned of Perón's arrival. He quickly drove his Cadillac to the chancery, where he found the fugitive seated in the kitchen, sipping mate and conversing amiably with some guards and the cook. He directed Perón and his aides to accompany him back to his home. While his famous guest sipped more mate in the drawing room, Chávez summoned his military attaché by phone. The ambassador's plan was to get Perón aboard the Paraguayan gunboat *Paraguay*, which had put into Buenos Aires for repairs and was tied up at a dock. It would be easier, in the ambassador's opinion, to protect Perón on the gunboat, in the event of an assassination attempt.

The clock on the Tower of the English in the Plaza Británica read 9:45 when the Cadillac passed by the President Perón railroad station (soon to regain its original name, Retiro). At the entrance to the port, a large puddle covered the roadway. The Cadillac tried to speed through it, but water gushed up into the engine and the vehicle stalled. Nearby, a driver slept behind the wheel of his empty bus. A familiar voice roused him from slumber; it was Juan Perón, asking for a push. For a brief moment, the driver gaped at the *conductor,* smiling, clad in a raincoat. He then hopped down from his seat, found heavy rope and towed the Cadillac almost two kilometers to the *Paraguay,* docked between a British and a Brazilian merchant ship.[34] The captain was on board to greet Perón and escort him on board. More than seventeen years would pass before he would again set foot on Argentine soil.

In those uncertain moments before the new provisional government took over, the possibility existed that the Argentine navy might attempt to remove him forcibly from his sanctuary, or that civilian anti-Peronists might attack the ship. One of his aides, convinced that Perón should leave the country immediately, arranged for an airplane to take him from the downtown airport directly to Asunción.[35] He also secured armed guards who would take Perón to the airport. But the ex-president refused to leave the gunboat without "guarantees" for his personal safety. The aide himself boarded the plane, took off and flew around in circles. His purpose was to make people think Perón had departed the country and thereby keep pressure off the gunboat.

As the *conductor* languished in the gunboat captain's cabin, other Peronists were left to their own devices. General Lucero appeared in civilian clothes at the U.S. embassy and asked for asylum.[36] Ambassador Nufer explained that his government did not recognize the legal right of asylum and urged him to take refuge at the nearest Latin American embassy, which happened to be that of Nicaragua.

Dr. Ara was in a state of great anxiety about the fate of his masterpiece. On Friday the sixteenth, he had been paid the final installment for his work, but he still felt a responsibility toward the cadaver. He visited the presidential residence on the nineteenth, but Perón was too busy to see him and promised to telephone. The call never came. The Duarte family feared that the body would be profaned. Evita's mother gave Ara a handwritten note authorizing him to take any precautions necessary for the safekeeping of the corpse. The doctor maintained a vigil over the remains of the first lady and all remained quiet, for the time being, at the CGT building.[37]

As evening settled over Buenos Aires on that wet, desolate Tuesday, the downtown streets remained strangely calm, empty of vehicular traffic and the usual bustle of pedestrians. At the intersection of Corrientes and San Martín, the staccato of small-arms fire punctuated the abnormal quiet. Members of the ultra-right-wing ALN had barricaded themselves in their downtown headquarters and had resolved to offer violent resistance to the Liberating Revolution. Two Sherman tanks lumbered up Corrientes, came to a halt near the intersection and trained their guns on the building. The Alianza defenders fled to adjoining offices as the bombardment began. Much of the edifice crumbled under the shelling. As the smoke began to clear, army troops captured Patricio Kelly, the colorful leader of the ALN.[38]

It was not until Tuesday that General Lonardi flew in from Córdoba and made his triumphal entry into the capital.[39] Delirious crowds lined the route from the downtown airport to the Casa Rosada and filled the Plaza de Mayo. Clouds of flowers descended upon him from windows and rooftops as he passed. At 2:00 P.M. he strode into the White Room of the Government House and accepted the presidential sash from cadets representing the three branches of the armed forces. After taking an improvised oath, he proceeded to a balcony to deliver his inaugural address. It was conciliatory, too much so for many hard-line anti-Peronists. Afterward a wild celebration gave vent to passions that had been kept in check for nine years.

In the city of Salta to the north, author Ernesto Sábato rejoiced at Perón's overthrow. Yet he had the sensitivity to understand that many of his fellow citizens were grieving:

> That September night in 1955, while we doctors, farm-owners and writers were noisily rejoicing in the living room over the fall of the tyrant, in a corner of the kitchen I saw how the two Indian women who worked there had their eyes drenched with tears. And although in all those years I had meditated upon the tragic duality that divided the Argentine people, at that moment it appeared to me in its most moving form. . . . Many millions of dispossessed people and workers were shedding tears at that instant, for them a hard and sober moment. Great multitudes of their humble compatriots were symbolized by those two Indian girls who wept in a kitchen in Salta.[40]

While working-class Peronists grieved, many opportunists who had flocked to the movement suddenly experienced dramatic conversions and joined the ranks of those who danced in the streets as the Liberating Revolution took power. The first important defection occurred one week after Lonardi's inauguration, when Admiral Teisaire presented himself at the Casa Rosada and met with the new chief executive.

In the meantime, Juan Perón sat down at a desk on board the *Paraguay* and penned the following note:

Dear Little Girl:

What I miss most is my little girl and the poodles, as I was just saying today to the Paraguayan fellows. The workers and the poor will now begin to appreciate who Perón is. Nonetheless, I'm not sorry I didn't start a civil war. Many would have died, and the country would have been destroyed.

Little girl, be calm. With what I have left you, you can live for a long time. As soon as I arrive [in Paraguay], I will send for you, and the two of us will have a quiet life. I am very tired and need a long rest. I think I have earned it. . . .

You are all I have, and the only beloved thing left for me. You can imagine I think of you all day long. Take care of the poodles for me, and when you come to Asunción, bring both of them to me. I love them a lot, those bandits. . . .

I forgot, but tell Ponce to bring to your home all the motorbikes that are at the residence. . . . They are for you, and when you come to Paraguay, bring them so that we can ride them together.

A big kiss from your daddy.

Juan Perón[41]

He dispatched the letter to Nelly Rivas, who was now at home with her parents, where she waited patiently for the signal to join her "daddy."

Part VI
Exile

(1955–1973)

37

Escape to Paraguay

Mario Amadeo clung to a railing on the torpedo launch as it knifed through the turbulent waves that agitated the muddy estuary. President Lonardi's foreign minister was heading toward a Paraguayan gunboat anchored eight kilometers offshore. His mission was to see to it that Juan Perón left Argentine waters safely.[1]

Threats of imminent attack from civilian commandos kept the crew of the *Paraguay* on constant alert. Rumors that the ex-president was planning to make a speech to the nation enraged anti-Peronists, while tales of mysterious women visiting the ship lent an erotic tinge to the unfolding drama.[2] On September 25, the provisional government issued a communiqué declaring that Perón's right to asylum would be respected. On that same day, for security reasons, the *Paraguay* left its moorings and steamed to an anchorage, where Argentine warships surrounded it.

Perón settled comfortably into the gunboat's routine. He ate with the crew and mixed easily with them. Just as he had done during his imprisonment on the island of Martín García in 1945, he devoted his days to the writing of an account of the events that led to his downfall.[3]

How Perón would get to Asunción remained a problem. President Stroessner of Paraguay had sent a DC-3 to Buenos Aires, but the risks of transporting Perón to an airport made this option unacceptable. The sister ship of the *Paraguay* had arrived from Asunción, but the Argentines did not want the ex-president to travel north by vessel. The journey would have taken him through the provinces of Santa Fe, Entre Ríos and Corrientes, past the large industrial city of Rosario, where pro-Peronist sentiments remained strong and army troops might have been persuaded to rally behind the *conductor*. With the fluvial exit foreclosed, there was now but one alternative left.

At 5:40 A.M. on Sunday, October 3, Captain Leo Nowak eased his twin-engine Catalina flying boat off the runway of an Asunción airport. Although conditions were far from favorable, President Stroessner's personal pilot had received orders to head for Buenos Aires.

Meanwhile, Mario Amadeo led an official delegation charged with supervising Perón's departure. They transferred from the torpedo launch to the *Paraguay*, where they went below to the wardroom and proceeded with the formalities. Perón, wearing gabardine trousers and ocher crocodile-hide shoes, remained silent while Amadeo and Ambassador Chávez exchanged diplomatic greetings.[4] By this time Captain Nowak had landed his seaplane in a trough of waves that were rocking even the cruiser *Nueve de Julio*, keeping watch at a discreet distance.

Photographs of these last moments aboard the *Paraguay* show a grim-faced Perón, his features betraying anxiety and perhaps lack of sleep.[5] He never liked to fly, even under the best of circumstances. Amadeo and several Paraguayan officials accompanied him into a small motor launch, which navigated the choppy waters to the flying boat. As Perón reached for the ladder to the seaplane, a rough wave caused the boat to lurch suddenly, and he had to grab Amadeo by the arm to avoid falling into the river.

Perón himself described the lift-off in these words:

> I positioned myself in the seaplane which was dancing restlessly on the ridge of the waves. Water was coming into the cabin, and rushed hard against the seats of the pilots. We hoped the wind would calm a bit. Suddenly I felt the motors roar furiously above my head. The pilot headed toward the open sea, but the plane fought against the current without being able to take off. It seemed as though we were stuck to the water. We kept afloat for two kilometers, after which the plane rose several meters but then fell suddenly and violently onto the rough river. The pilot refused to give up, tried again to take off, and shortly afterward we grazed against the masts of a ship and finally were on our way.[6]

Following close behind, two Argentine air force fighters provided an escort, which lasted until the slow-moving Catalina crossed the border. At that point a C-47 bearing Paraguayan markings met the flying boat and followed it to Asunción. In the cockpit of the escort plane was a distinguished co-pilot, President Stroessner himself. At 5:45 P.M., Juan Perón landed at the military airport outside Asunción.

Stroessner did not participate in the official welcome, which he left to a group of government functionaries. They put Perón in a limousine and drove him to the home of Ricardo Gayol, an Argentine businessman who had been residing in the Paraguayan capital for twenty-five years. Reporters eager to interview Perón had flocked to the international airport—which explained the decision to have him land elsewhere.

Perón's first stop on what would develop into a long meander was an impoverished yet charming "shoe-box of a country,"[7] a landlocked, subtropical smuggler's paradise. The population, mostly Guaraní Indians and people of mixed blood, engaged primarily in subsistence agriculture. The Guaraní language shared official status with Spanish.

On the morning of his first full day in Asunción, Perón distributed a brief written statement to impatient reporters. In it he declared that while he remained in Paraguay as a private citizen, he would abstain from political activity.[8] A few hours later he gave a long exclusive interview to the United Press (no doubt because its correspondent in Asunción happened to be the half brother of his good friend Ambassador Chávez). He attributed Peronism's overthrow to "oligarcho-clerical reaction" motivated by "ambition and money," and insisted that he had not really resigned from the presidency. His prediction of the fate of the de facto regime: "The government that comes to power with blood falls from power with blood." The Peronist party would survive because of its leadership and youth. "I have profound faith in its destiny and I want them to go on. They are grown up now. I left them a doctrine, a mystique and an organization. They will use these things when the time comes." As for his own plans, he stated he would remain in Paraguay and honor the conditions under which he was permitted to enter. He would not go to Europe "because it isn't necessary and I don't have the money to be a tourist, despite what my occasional detractors say about my wealth."[9]

This was the first of countless interviews Perón would give in the course of his seventeen-year exile, and it contained elements that would recur with regularity: self-justificatory explanations of the past, ambiguity regarding his own intentions, contradiction (he would respect conditions, one of which was not to make political declarations, and then blithely make a series of political declarations), phraseology crafted to irritate the occupants of the Casa Rosada, and afterward a denial of controversial statements attributed to him.

The publication of the U.P. interview coincided with the acceleration of the Argentine government's effort to denigrate Perón. The newspapers had already printed the text of two letters which he had sent from the gunboat to Nelly Rivas and which the police had intercepted. On the day Perón's declarations from Asunción were made public, the anti-Perón campaign hit full stride. Reporters were invited to a movie theater, where they were shown a film of Admiral Teisaire, Perón's vice-president, reading a statement which oozed acrimony. The admiral tagged the *conductor* with full responsibility for the decay and fall of the Peronist government. He denounced Perón's "cowardice and shamefulness in the face of the enemy"; reproached him for being the first deposed Argentine president to flee the country; attributed to him the idea of burning the flag; and asserted that "for a year he had practically abandoned affairs of state in order to dedicate himself to picturesque activities involving sports, the arts, etc."[10] The context left little doubt about the meaning of "etc."

In view of the direction the Liberating Revolution was beginning to take and the insecurities of the Lonardi regime in its second week of existence, Argentine reaction to the U.P. interview was no surprise. The Foreign Office in Buenos Aires requested that the Paraguayan government terminate Perón's exile because of his political declaration.[11] The Argentines were plainly dismayed at Perón's assertion that he had not really resigned, as this amounted to a claim that he was still constitutionally president. Since the magic seventeenth of October was close at hand, the possibility of a Peronist uprising could not be discounted.

Perón enjoyed his stay at Gayol's house. He was in high spirits, drank coffee constantly and resumed smoking. He spent his days chatting with visitors, dipping into his inexhaustible store of anecdotes and working on a book.[12] Although he said he could not make statements to the press because of the U.P. brouhaha, he conversed at length with a U.S. journalist, to whom he insisted that he had not remarried (the press was awash with rumors that he was about to join his third wife in Switzerland), his interest in Nelly Rivas was "parental" only, and he had not used his office to enrich himself.[13]

The first Argentine journalist who managed to penetrate the ring of police guards around the house represented a magazine that Perón's press secretary had permitted to appear in 1953, even though it was mildly critical of the government, in order to create the appearance that press freedom still existed in Argentina. Perón complimented his visitor on the high quality of the publication. When reminded that his regime had closed the magazine down, the ex-president exclaimed, "How barbaric! What a shameful thing!," and blamed the incident on the "bureaucracy."[14] The reaction typified his refusal to accept responsibility for any excesses committed under Peronist rule.

The Perón charm overwhelmed Gayol, who later declared:

> He was never in a bad mood, he always displayed smooth manners and was the perfect gentleman. . . . He kept a lighter in his hand to provide a light to anyone who pulled out a cigarette, but if anyone dropped a lighted match on the floor, he would pick it up with evident displeasure, but without holding up the conversation, and put it in the ashtray, making the person understand that this was the correct thing to do.[15]

Perón even went so far as to joke with Gayol about his teeth. "Everybody praises my smile," he told him, "without imagining that I can remove it with one hand."[16] And he startled his host by whipping out his dentures to prove the point.

Argentine pressures finally took their toll. On October 8, the *conductor*'s sixtieth birthday, the government of Paraguay announced it would intern Perón. October 17, the tenth anniversary of his triumph in the Plaza de Mayo, was the day chosen for the detention. The Paraguayan interior minister and several army officers accompanied Perón on a three-and-a-half-hour drive to the little town of Villarica, in a grape-growing region 160 kilometers east and slightly south of Asunción. He was now far from the Argentine border.

The internment was more like a holiday in the country. Perón resided in a small but comfortable house surrounded by green fields, three kilometers from Villarica. The townsfolk turned out en masse to greet him on the evening of his arrival. Local musicians serenaded him with Paraguayan songs, and later everybody sang "*Los muchachos peronistas.*" The Villaricans were delighted by the presence of the first international celebrity ever to visit them. Perón spent two weeks in this idyllic setting. He continued to work on his book and wandered freely, in the company of bodyguards, throughout the town. He even managed to do some touring on a motor scooter.[17]

Meanwhile, in Buenos Aires a military tribunal of honor composed of five generals (several of whom had served Perón faithfully) rendered a decision that attributed to Perón a wide range of misdeeds, including incitement to violence, attacks upon the Catholic religion, burning the flag and having sexual relations with a minor. It found him guilty of betraying the honor and tradition of the armed forces, and recommended that he be stripped of his rank and deprived of the use of the uniform.[18] Several weeks later, President Lonardi would sign a decree putting into effect these recommendations.

Two days after the tribunal handed down its judgment, Perón informed Stroessner that he wanted to accept the invitation of Nicaraguan President Anastasio Somoza for a visit. It is unclear whether his sudden desire to leave was motivated by the decision of the tribunal and the possibility of criminal proceedings against him—which might jeopardize his exile status—or by reports that assassination squads were on their way from Buenos Aires to Villarica.[19] Stroessner on his part neither pressured his guest to leave nor tried to persuade him to stay.

In the late evening of November 1, Perón made the long trip back to Asunción. After conferring with the Paraguayan president, he went to the airport, where Stroessner's personal DC-3 was waiting for him. An Argentine named Víctor Radeglia accompanied him on board the aircraft. (An obscure individual who had attached himself to Perón shortly after the latter's arrival in Asunción, Radeglia had assumed the role of private secretary to the ex-president and was the first in a string of mediocre intimates who would stand as living testaments to Perón's talent for welcoming the worst sort of people into his inner circle.) At 4:00 A.M. on the second, with Captain Nowak again at the throttle, the DC-3 took off on the next phase of Juan Perón's long journey in exile.

The normal air route between Paraguay and Central America hugs the west coast of the continent. Nowak, however, flew directly to Rio de Janeiro, causing renewed speculation as to Perón's real destination. Several days before his departure the Paraguayan government had requested overflight permissions for both the east- and west-coast routes.[20] Perón, apparently aware of his vulnerability aboard an unarmed plane during a long trip, decided to disguise his itinerary as a precautionary measure.

At 8:00 A.M. the DC-3 landed at the military section of the Galeão Airport on the outskirts of Rio de Janeiro. Perón remained with the aircraft as the crew serviced and refueled it. The extreme heat forced him to strip to his underpants during the wait.[21] The second leg of the trip took the DC-3 to Salvador, north of Rio de Janeiro, on the east coast of Brazil. The travelers spent the night on the plane at the airport. By now it was apparent that Perón feared flying in the dark as well as ambush.

Captain Nowak indicated his next stop would be Belém, on the mouth of the Amazon River, but the DC-3 continued further along the Brazilian coast to Macapá, an equatorial settlement on the northern edge of the Amazon delta in the manganese-rich territory of Amapá. In Macapá, Nowak reported that he was heading next for British Guiana, but instead put the plane on a course for Paramaribo in Surinam.*

After feinting toward the Dominican Republic, Captain Nowak changed his flight plan once again and headed for Venezuela. The DC-3 touched down at the Maiquetía Airport outside Caracas. For the first time since departing Asunción, Perón left the plane and the airport to spend the night at the luxurious Tamanaco Hotel, where he uttered to the press his famous dictum "Politics, war and women are not for old men."[22]

The last refueling stop was to be Panamá. Captain Nowak landed at the Tocumen Airport in Panamá City, where a crowd of journalists and curious onlookers awaited him. Carlos Pascali, the Argentine ambassador to Panamá under the Peronist regime, drove Perón to the deluxe Hotel El Panamá. On the next day, the exile paid a visit to Panamanian President Ricardo Arias. On his way out, he startled the press by expressing his desire to stay in Panamá. Somoza would have to wait. What was scheduled as a brief stopover turned into a nine-month sojourn.

Shortly after his arrival in Panamá, Perón told a Peruvian journalist that the Lonardi government would endure for only eighteen months.[23]

---

* The Paramaribo stopover produced one curious vignette. Upon his arrival, Perón learned that an acquaintance, Prince Bernhard of the Netherlands, was visiting the city. He sent greetings to the royal consort and asked to see him. According to Perón, although the prince was indebted to him for business favors he had bestowed during Bernhard's trips to Buenos Aires, the latter would not even deign to answer. In his taped memoirs, he heaped harsh invective upon the Dutch ("hybrids," was how he referred to them) and upon the prince, whom he called a "shit." T. Luca de Tena, *Yo, Juan Domingo Perón,* pp. 238–39.

His prediction was far off the mark. The anti-Peronist opposition had long been able to use hatred of a common enemy to paper over deep divisions. With the man who united them now thousands of kilometers away, the coalition burst its main seam much sooner than the *conductor* reckoned.

Although Lonardi had promised a policy of reconciliation, the task of meting out justice to imprisoned Peronist officials and of controlling the passions of those who had suffered at the hands of the Peronists taxed his capabilities beyond the breaking point. His first steps—the dissolution of the Congress, intervention in all the provincial governments and dismissal of all the justices of the Supreme Court—satisfied his supporters. But his treatment of organized labor produced signs of serious stress among the anti-Peronists.

Lonardi left the CGT intact. His minister of labor took a "soft" line toward the confederation and resolved to implement the president's pledge to respect the workers' gains. The unions reciprocated. The CGT leadership resigned, and the confederation reorganized itself. Textile worker Andrés Framini and Luis Natalini from the light and power union, both of whom were acceptable to the regime, were elected to direct the CGT.[24]

Lonardi's strategy was to create a climate in which labor leaders, even though Peronist, might collaborate with the government. But civilian commandos began to occupy various union headquarters, and leaders displaced by the Peronists ten years ago reappeared to claim the posts they once held. Moreover, pressures mounted to remove *La Prensa* from CGT control and return it to the Paz family.

Lonardi lacked a political base from which he might draw support for his "Neither Victors Nor Vanquished" philosophy. Admiral Rojas, whom Lonardi appointed as his vice-president, soon became the unofficial spokesman for those who wanted the administration to crack down on the Peronists and to follow a different economic policy. The president made several conciliatory gestures toward the hard-liners, such as the creation of a national commission of investigation, charged with the task of delving into accusations of malfeasance against officials of the deposed regime.[25]

But obdurate anti-Peronists were not appeased. On the evening of November 12, a delegation of high-ranking officers presented Lonardi with a series of demands, to which the president refused to accede. His three military ministers then gave him five minutes to write out his resignation. Thus ended the brief presidency of Eduardo Lonardi. In poor health during these crucial weeks, he died a scant four months later.[26]

A manifesto issued in the name of the armed forces on November 13 proclaimed General Pedro E. Aramburu as the new president, with Admiral Rojas remaining in the vice-presidency. Phase Two of the Liberating Revolution was about to begin. There would soon be no doubt who were the victors and who were the vanquished.

38

Panamá and Isabel

On November 8, 1955, Perón made the coast-to-coast jaunt across the isthmus from Panamá City to Colón in Carlos Pascali's Cadillac. His destination was the Hotel Washington, a stately, palm-fringed mansion built shortly after the opening of the Panamá Canal. Perón moved into a room that faced the Atlantic and intercepted cooling breezes. The ex-president could gaze out at ships entering and exiting the nearby canal. He was also within strolling distance of downtown Colón, a gamy rest-and-recreation center for North American sailors.

Perón's decision to live in Colón raised a number of eyebrows. The fact that the Hotel Washington was owned by the Canal Zone, an agency of the U.S. government, made his choice even more curious. In all likelihood Pascali convinced him it would be safer and more comfortable for him to reside next door to his ex-ambassador. Perón wanted to finish his book and needed a quiet place to work. Shortly afterward, Isaac Gilaberte, his former chauffeur, arrived in Panamá from Asunción, where he had gained asylum after taking refuge in the Paraguayan embassy in Buenos Aires. Gilaberte moved in with Víctor Radeglia, who was occupying a room adjoining Perón's.

Although he often complained privately about the heat,[1] Perón adapted well to Panamá. He dressed as a native in white trousers and *guayabera* shirts. A nearby beach resort owned by a Cuban and referred to as a "house of prostitution" by the U.S. consul in Colón[2] was made available to him. He was a frequent spectator at local boxing matches. The Panamanian government furnished him with bodyguards. Among his close friends were the mayor of Colón and a Jewish accountant who owned a print shop.[3]

The first order of business for the *conductor*-in-exile was to complete the manuscript he had begun aboard the *Paraguay*. Within weeks he concluded his literary endeavor, a poorly organized apologia for his decade in power and for his behavior during the events leading to his downfall. The title he chose, *Force Is the Law of Beasts*, was as self-righteous as the text.

Gwen Bagni, a North American author visiting Panamá in December, had the opportunity to meet Perón when a member of his entourage arranged an interview under the mistaken belief she was a journalist who might be persuaded to write some favorable stories about him. She found him relatively youthful in appearance. During lunch he kept telling her how impecunious he was, and displayed hands he claimed had sprouted calluses from typing his manuscript.[4]

Despite his age, Juan Perón still projected a physical presence many women found attractive. His fame and the residual aura of power still lingering about him no doubt were at the core of this magnetism. The sex appeal that had served him well a decade earlier had not totally lost its vitality. According to Bagni, who witnessed the phenomenon, whenever a woman caught his fancy, he would make his feelings known to one of his companions, and in a matter of moments she would be ushered into his presence. His tastes ranged indiscriminately from the sophisticated to the naive and unpolished.[5] To an Argentine journalist who queried him about it, he replied simply, "I like women."[6]

But there was a much more important element at play. Perón had always felt a strong need for female companions in order to demonstrate his masculinity and provide him with domestic services. He preferred continuity to variety. The interlude at the Hotel Washington found him in a particularly vulnerable mood, without a woman at his side and even freer of restraining influences than when he plucked Nelly Rivas from the ranks of the UES. It was at this juncture that he struck up a warm friendship with a pretty young brunette from Chicago.[7]

She was vacationing from her job with a restaurant chain when she met him. As a measure of his affection, he bestowed upon her the nickname La Gringuita (the "little gringa"). She worked at improving his English, he helped her with Spanish. An Argentine observer found her "feminine and cultured" and admired her prudence and discretion.[8] She appeared with him in public at a restaurant and a beach, where photographers captured their gleaming smiles.[9] Several times she postponed her return to Chicago, much to the dismay of her parents. A romantic attachment seemed in the making. It would have changed the history of Argentina.

Unlike the resolute Evita, La Gringuita wavered when opportunity knocked and returned to the Windy City instead of cementing her liaison with the *conductor*. She sent him letters and postcards almost every day, but theirs was the sort of relationship not meant to endure at long range. Events were about to unfold a turn that would seem farfetched in the context of pulp fiction.[10]

In mid-December a Cuban dancer with the pseudonym Joe Herald

brought to Panamá his troupe of seven young women. He had organized
the ensemble in Medellín, Colombia, and had then proceeded ahead of
them in search of bookings. Having found an opening at a nightclub in
Panamá City, he sent for the girls. Soon they were performing at a night-
spot called Happy Land. One member of the group was a twenty-four-year-
old Argentine named María Estela Martínez, who had been touring the
west coast of South America with a troupe that had come upon hard times
in Colombia and had dissolved. María Estela went by the stage name
Isabel.

She had the fresh-faced look of a teenager. Of medium height, her light-
brown hair pulled back, her body trim and erect, Isabel radiated a subdued
attractiveness that seemed incongruous on a nightclub stage. Peronist
propaganda would later describe her as a folk dancer. Photos of Joe
Herald and his troupe show the girls in skimpy costumes normally worn
in cabarets, where terpsichorean talent was not what attracted customers.[11]
A CIA report written nineteen months later and apparently referring to
the troupe called its Happy Land performance a "girlie show."[12]

Isabel first met Perón two days before Christmas when she joined several
of her associates from the Joe Herald ensemble in a trip to Colón to attend
a party with the *conductor* at the Hotel Washington. Isaac Gilaberte claims
to have arranged for the dancers to enliven the festivities. Perón found the
young Argentine much to his liking. By mid-January she was living with
him.

An associate who later fell out with Perón quotes a letter in which he
described her in glowing terms. "She plays the piano, dances, sings, cooks,
administers the household and makes life more pleasant for us. Not even
for pastry would we let her go" (a Spanish expression denoting high
regard).[13] Although she could not type, he made her his private secretary.

If Perón had now forgotten Nelly Rivas, young Nelly had not forgotten
her "daddy." On January 14, the police took her into custody as she
reached a town on the border between Argentina and Paraguay.[14] Accompanied by her parents, she had in her possession a camera, some jewelry,
cash and Perón's poodles. Their immediate destination was Asunción, en
route to Panamá. The authorities brought her back to Buenos Aires and
had her committed to a reform school, where she spent eight months.*

Perón's presence in a hotel owned by the U.S. government attracted
unfavorable notice. In mid-December the Argentine ambassador in Washington called upon Henry Holland, still assistant secretary of state for
Latin America, and requested U.S. help in persuading Panamá to oust
Perón.[15] The ambassador expressed displeasure at newspaper interviews
the ex-president was giving and complained that his statements amounted

* Several years later she married an Argentine employee at the U.S. embassy in
Buenos Aires, and went to live on a ranch in Uruguay. "La segunda presidencia—
VII," *Primera Plana,* June 18, 1968, p. 47.

to incitements to violence. Holland would not commit the United States to any action against Perón, but merely promised to study the matter. However, as time wore on, the impression gained currency in Argentina and elsewhere that because the hotel was U.S. property, the Yankees were protecting Perón and perhaps even "keeping him on ice" for a return to Buenos Aires in the event the Aramburu regime collapsed.[16]

The *conductor* exacerbated matters by using highly inflammatory language in an interview with a reporter from the *New York Herald-Tribune* in January. Perón was quoted as declaring:

> I made only one great mistake before. I spared bloodshed when I was in power and treated my opponents lightly. I shall not make the same mistake again. Many heads will roll when I return to Buenos Aires. It will be terrible but it cannot be helped.[17]*

By February the State Department was feeling the pressure to act, at least to the point of securing Perón's removal from the Hotel Washington. Contingency plans were formulated to close down the hotel in the event he refused a request to leave.[18] Resort to this extreme measure was avoided, however, when on February 27 he checked out of the hotel.

For the next two and a half months Perón and his small entourage stayed in a modest apartment in Panamá City, a scant block from the U.S. embassy. They then returned to Colón and rented a house. In the course of these moves, Carlos Pascali became an early casualty of the constant intrigues characteristic of life in the inner circle during the exile period. One version has it that Isabel and Gilaberte joined forces to drive a wedge between Perón and his ex-ambassador, an educated man who spoke frankly to the *conductor* and refused to flatter him.[19] A report from the U.S. consulate in Colón stated somewhat cryptically that Pascali's split with Perón was "due apparently to his age and his inability to keep up the pace with Perón's social and moral activities."[20]

From the moment of his arrival in Panamá, there was much speculation about the wealth at Perón's disposal. The assumption prevailed that he had extracted a fortune from Argentina during his decade in power and that he had carefully invested it abroad. He was also thought to have access to the enormous amount of money Evita supposedly shipped to Swiss banks. Perón steadfastly denied these stories. He told an Argentine journalist that he paid expenses out of his "savings" and what he earned from writing magazine and newspaper articles.[21] To the *Herald-Tribune*

---

* As was his career-long custom, he "clarified" these statements later, and said that it was the Aramburu regime that was provoking a civil war that would take a million lives. He insisted that he personally was opposed to bloodshed, and that the Newman story rested upon a mistaken translation of his words. *New York Herald-Tribune,* January 22, 1956. Thus he was now on record as both promising violence and deploring it.

reporter he declared that he survived financially only with help from his friends.[22] Later, in his taped memoirs, he complained that many Panamanians were interested only in the $700 million they thought he had brought with him.[23]

Nothing that Perón did while in Panamá suggested that he was a wealthy man. He lived frugally. Upon his return to Colón he acquired a small Opel sedan, which Gilaberte drove for him, but he made no other expenditures of substance. According to one source, he was receiving monthly checks from abroad in the amount of $500, which he claimed derived from an investment, and he took $70,000 with him when he left the country.[24] Thus, if he did have a vast fortune somewhere, it remained untapped.

Perón's Panamanian sojourn coincided with a dramatic turn of events in Argentina.[25] The government of General Aramburu launched a program of de-Peronization that delighted the most implacable of the *conductor*'s enemies. The regime set out to extirpate both the policies and the symbols of the New Argentina. What Perón had done through strict adherence to the forms of legality, the Liberating Revolution now sought to undo by executive decree and brute force. This in turn provoked resistance from Peronists and gave Perón the chance to agitate waters that were becoming increasingly troubled.

Two days after Lonardi's ouster, the CGT called a general strike. The confederation had planned a work stoppage for late September but had postponed it when the new regime took a conciliatory line toward organized labor. The November strike, ill conceived and badly timed, collapsed after one day. There were no specific, attainable goals that might enthuse the rank and file, and the action gave the government a pretext to seize control of the CGT. Aramburu also dissolved the Peronist party, and the repression that began somewhat haltingly after Perón's overthrow now reached full speed.

Within weeks every Peronist legislator, party official, top-level bureaucrat, labor leader and military officer who had escaped arrest in the first weeks after the coup and who did not flee into exile or take refuge in an embassy found himself behind bars. In many instances, the government seized the property of those arrested and began legal proceedings under which the burden of proof was on the individual to prove that he had acquired the property lawfully. The various commissions formed to investigate charges of wrongdoing tended to move slowly and inefficiently, operating under the presumption that the accused were guilty unless proven innocent. The Liberating Revolution permitted its system of justice to become a tool for vengeance and guaranteed the perpetration of the deep split between Peronists and anti-Peronists.

The Aramburu regime also intensified the process of blotting out all physical traces of Perón and Evita and of vilifying the exiled *conductor*.

Provinces, cities, plazas, streets, buildings, public works, monuments—
everything that had once borne the name of the ex-president and his first
lady—underwent a rechristening. Teachers crossed out references to them
in school texts. The statues atop the headquarters of the Eva Perón
Foundation were toppled to the street below and shattered into fragments.
The foundation itself was closed down and the building turned over to the
faculty of engineering of the University of Buenos Aires. The Children's
Village was dismantled. Aramburu brought this orgy of annihilation to a
grand climax when he ordered the downtown presidential residence razed,
treating it as though it were contaminated by some deadly communicable
disease.

The new rulers of Argentina convinced themselves that once people
looked at evidence of the dissolute lifestyles of their idols, they would
realize how badly they had been defrauded and would become permanently
disillusioned with Peronist rhetoric. The government made available for
public viewing Perón's extensive wardrobe, the fleet of motorcycles and
motor scooters at his disposal, and Evita's jewelry. These exhibits drew
large, curious crowds but did not change many minds. What the regime
had apparently forgotten was that neither Perón nor his first lady had ever
concealed their extravagance. Indeed, part of the essence of Evita's appeal
was the way she had flaunted her finery.

The effort to blacken Perón's image failed in large measure because of
the lack of competence and restraint on the part of those who set themselves
up in judgment over him. The final report of the commission formed to
investigate his conduct, entitled the *Black Book of the Second Tyranny*,
was an amalgam of fact, unsubstantiated allegation and argumentation that
fell far short of convicting Perón on every count. Instead of compiling an
exhaustive, dispassionate report on specific misdeeds committed by the
ex-president, the commission produced a tome that the Peronists could
easily dismiss as propaganda. The *Black Book* had as feeble an effect as
the display of Evita's jewels.

In a society where commemoration of the dead is a national fetish, the
embalmed body of Eva Perón was the most powerful symbol of the deposed
regime. The disposal of Dr. Ara's masterwork became one of the stickiest
issues confronting the Liberating Revolution. Wherever the government
might put the coffin to rest, the body would immediately attract Peronist
pilgrimages. Lonardi agonized over the problem but did nothing. However,
once Aramburu closed down the CGT, it was no longer possible to postpone a decision. In the context of the war on Peronism now being waged
by the regime, the possibility could not be discounted that the Peronists
might try to recapture the body and use it to rally the descamisados against
the government.

On the night of December 22, Lieutenant Colonel Carlos Eugenio Moore
Koenig, chief of the Army Information Service, led a squad of officers

armed with submachine guns into the CGT building, now under military control, and removed the cadaver.[26] For the remains of Evita, it was the beginning of a bizarre and covert journey. Moore Koenig and his men placed the body in a plain box, which they loaded onto the bed of an army truck. They drove the vehicle to a marine base in the city, where it remained for a day. When the base commanding officer learned what the truck contained, he wanted no part of its controversial cargo and ordered that the driver remove it from his jurisdiction. The vehicle was then parked unobtrusively in downtown Buenos Aires. The mysterious appearance of a candle and flowers next to the truck necessitated yet another move.*

Moore Koenig had the corpse transferred to a crate marked "Radio Equipment" and left it in his office. Meanwhile, the government still could not decide what to do with Evita. There was agreement that she should receive a Christian burial, but no one could suggest a suitable location secure from Peronist exploitation.

In June 1956, Colonel Mario Cabanillas replaced Moore Koenig at the Army Information Service. His predecessor neglected to inform him what was inside the "Radio Equipment" box, and he discovered Evita's presence one day by accident. When the shock subsided, he resolved to dispose of the body and set in motion a top-secret operation intended to erase all earthly traces of the first lady's cadaver.

The disappearance of the corpse set off a dizzying burst of rumors.[27] The body had been burned. It had been dumped in the river. It lay in an unmarked grave on the island of Martín García. It had been shipped to Europe. By shrouding in dark mystery the fate of Eva Perón's remains, the government avoided both the transformation of her grave site into hallowed ground to which the faithful would flock, and the ever-present risk that either Peronists or anti-Peronists would despoil the tomb. But the price to be paid was dear. Already Peronist women had demonstrated in the Plaza de Mayo under banners calling for their embalmed heroine. "Where's Evita?" would become a rallying cry, and the demand for the return of the body would be a constant problem for the occupants of the Casa Rosada.

On March 9, 1956, the regime decreed the nonexistence of Perón, Evita and Peronism. It would be illegal to display photos, paintings or sculptures of the deposed president or his wife, to use the words "Peronism," "Peronist," "*justicialismo*," "Third Position," or the abbreviation "PP" (for Peronist party), to publicize the dates commemorated by the prior regime,

---

* According to unconfirmed accounts, Major Antonio Arandia, one of Moore Koenig's squad, agreed to store the box in his apartment. Nervous lest the Peronists discover the body's whereabouts and attempt to recapture it, Arandia kept a loaded pistol under his pillow. One night he was aroused from his sleep by a noise and saw a moving shadow. He fired several shots at a dim figure in the doorway, only to discover that he had killed his pregnant wife, on her way to the bathroom. See O. Borroni and R. Vacca, *La vida de Eva Perón*, p. 340.

to fly the Peronist flag, or to sing or play the Peronist anthem "*Los muchachos peronistas.*" The newspapers could still write about Perón, but instead of using his name they referred to him by the code expression "fugitive tyrant."

The assault upon Perón, Evita, the Peronists and their trade unions did not derive solely from a thirst for vengeance. The Aramburu regime was about to essay a new economic policy that would redistribute income away from the working class and enrich the agricultural sector.[28] Lonardi's promise to respect the gains achieved by workers during the past decade vanished along with him in mid-November.

The attack upon the CGT and the entire Peronist labor movement put most of the old-line union bureaucrats behind bars. However, a new generation of leaders now emerged from the ranks. Though professing their loyalty to the *conductor*, these men earned their positions in the struggle against the regime and developed a degree of independence heretofore unknown within the Peronist movement. They would become a force to be reckoned with, not only by the rulers of Argentina but also by Perón.

In addition, as the government cracked down upon organized labor, sporadic acts of violence indicated that the descamisados were not going to surrender meekly. What came to be known as the Peronist Resistance arose from the ashes of defeat, as hard-line anti-Peronism encouraged Peronist militants to respond in kind.

The passage of time has given the Peronist Resistance the aura of legend. Close scrutiny reveals disorganized, sporadic outbursts of freelance sabotage rather than calculated efforts.[29] Perón encouraged violence in a letter he sent to Argentina shortly after the dissolution of the Peronist party. He urged that the Aramburu regime not be permitted to develop a political solution to the situation it was creating and that the Peronists organize "civil resistance."[30] In early December he dispatched Víctor Radeglia to Chile with handwritten directives to be smuggled across the border to Peronist leaders engaged in clandestine activity.*

The regime was well aware of the *conductor*'s exhortations. On December 16, in the course of his request for U.S. help in pressing Panamá to expel Perón, the Argentine ambassador in Washington accused the "fugitive tyrant" of making phonograph records and writing letters that incited his followers to resort to strikes, sabotage and even assassination.[31]

Thus a scant two months after his inglorious departure from Buenos

---

* Radeglia was arrested a month later as he crossed into Argentina from Uruguay. He was carrying Peronist propaganda material. Taken to Buenos Aires, he made a public statement that Perón was "mentally unbalanced." *Hispanic American Report*, Vol. 9, No. 1, February 1956. In a letter to the editor of the *Hispanic American Report*, Perón disavowed Radeglia, who he claimed was a Rumanian adventurer with a Communist past and was passing himself off as the *conductor*'s private secretary when in fact he had no connection with Perón. Ibid. In light of Radeglia's close association with the ex-president, Perón's assertions cannot be taken seriously.

Aires, Juan Perón was manipulating events in Argentina and reaffirming his
leadership over the Peronist faithful, who clung to the wisp of a dream
that their *conductor* would someday return to them. In these early months
of his exile, the fanciful expectation that he would descend from the sky
in a black airplane gained currency among his most ardent followers. He
kept these fantasies alive by reiterating his determination to remain a
factor in Argentine politics.

An associate who had occasion to observe Perón closely during this
period found him "full of hatred, rancor, resentment and desire for
vengeance."[32] The pursuit of power seemed to spur him to greater heights
than its exercise. The challenge of putting together a political movement in
the years from 1943 to 1946 had brought out the most creative aspects of
his genius. Now a much more arduous task loomed ahead. If boredom had
overtaken him during his second presidency, the difficulties of conducting
long-range political warfare on the men who had ousted him aroused him
from his lethargy. It is crucial to keep in mind that what consumed him
was the process of strategic and tactical maneuver, not any principled
commitment to substantive goals.

Perón fully realized that the situation in Argentina precluded any chance
of a countercoup that would restore him to power, and that the struggle
on which he had embarked was essentially political. However, there were
those among his more militant followers who believed they could overthrow
the Aramburu regime by force. Without Perón's approval, they resolved to
launch a conspiratorial movement which would have tragic consequences.[33]

The members of the military junta formed by General Lucero for the
purpose of negotiating a peace with the Lonardi-led rebels were among
the high-ranking military men who had been detained aboard naval trans-
ports in the weeks following the Liberating Revolution. It was not until
January 1956 that Aramburu signed a decree imposing involuntary retirement upon these officers and transferring them to incarceration centers on
land. Some of the prisoners were granted the option of remaining under
house arrest within a certain distance from Buenos Aires. Among them
were two generals, Juan José Valle and Raúl D. Tanco.

Neither Valle nor Tanco had ever engaged in political activity, nor were
they Perón intimates. Both had served on the short-lived military junta and
had voted to accept the president's "resignation." Within weeks of their
departure from the prison ship, they began to organize an effort to overthrow the government.

Valle took command of the operation. The manifesto outlining its goals
was somewhat vague, calling for free elections as soon as possible and the
preservation of the nation's patrimony, but saying nothing about Perón.
Although a number of individual Peronists joined the conspiracy and the
Peronist rank and file regarded it as an attempt to bring back the *conductor*,
the Peronist Resistance stayed on the sidelines and Perón himself kept

quiet. Thus the insurrection developed as a military "show," with minimal civilian support.

After several postponements, Valle set his zero hour for 11:00 P.M. on Saturday, June 9. The government was already aware of the conspiracy and of the identity of many of the participants when one of them fell into the hands of the police at midday on the ninth and disclosed the essential details of the planned uprising.

That night a small commando unit endeavored to take over a radio transmitter in Avellaneda so that Valle could broadcast a proclamation to the nation. The police were lying in wait and took the insurgents into custody. At the Campo de Mayo garrison, an effort to incite troops to revolt collapsed. In La Plata, rebels seized a military installation after an exchange of gunfire that took several lives on both sides, but could hold it for only a few hours. In the interior, several uprisings were quickly suffocated.

The Valle revolt lasted for no more than twelve hours. It would have gone down in modern history as merely another unsuccessful military putsch in Argentina, but for one chilling development. Instead of incarcerating the rebels, the Aramburu regime decided to shoot them. The government would ignore tradition and demonstrate how tough it really was.

Though Juan Perón had committed and tolerated many excesses in his day, one thing that could be said for him was that he never converted his jails into slaughterhouses. The same could not be said for General Pedro E. Aramburu.

At midnight on the ninth the regime imposed martial law and expressly authorized its security forces to execute summarily anyone caught disturbing the peace. Although the revolt clearly posed no possibility of success, an unprecedented bloodbath began. Almost immediately the men arrested in Avellaneda were led one by one in front of a firing squad and shot to death. In Campo de Mayo, La Boca[34] and elsewhere, the grisly scene was replayed. A group of workers who had no connection with Valle (they had been imprisoned before the revolt broke out) were transported from their cells in the town of José León Juárez and taken to a garbage dump, where they were riddled with bullets.[35] Unidentified armed civilians entered a Buenos Aires jail and took custody of Peronist leaders, including Oscar Albrieu and John William Cooke, confined since September 1955. The vigilantes delivered their captives to an army base for execution. However, the commanding officer would not act without orders from above, and his hesitation spared further bloodshed when word came that the Peronists were to be returned to the prison.[36]

General Tanco joined several other military rebels who had taken refuge in the Haitian embassy. An army squad, in flagrant violation of international law, broke into the embassy and dragged out the refugees. On the next day an embarrassed Aramburu ordered that the men be returned to the embassy.

Valle decided to surrender in the hope that this would put an end to the executions. In the early morning hours of Tuesday the twelfth, he told the police where they could find him and went quietly into custody. Later in the day he was transferred to the national penitentiary and informed he would be shot that night. Despite frantic efforts to save him by his teenage daughter, he faced a firing squad at 10:00 P.M.

The Aramburu regime put at least twenty-seven men to death in the aftermath of the Valle revolt. Anti-Peronists applauded the executions, while Peronists were horrified and adopted Valle as one of their martyrs. The gulf that separated the two Argentinas widened. The government no doubt reckoned that the benefits to be gleaned from a bloody repression would exceed the costs. In the short run this might have been an accurate assessment. But as Aramburu himself would ultimately discover, the total price turned out to be much higher than anyone had anticipated.

In a letter dispatched to John William Cooke on the day of Valle's execution, Perón manifested no trace of sympathy for the military rebels. The *conductor* criticized their haste and lack of prudence, and claimed that only their anger at having been involuntarily retired from the army had motivated their action. Making no effort to hide his resentment, he wrote that "If I . . . had remained in Buenos Aires, they would have killed me themselves, although it would have been only for the purpose of currying favor with the conquerors."[37] Later he would extol the patriotism of Valle and his followers.

In July the Panamanian government hosted a conference of Latin American heads of state, including President Aramburu. This made it necessary for Perón to leave the country temporarily, so he took advantage of the occasion to fly to Somoza's Nicaragua. But Perón and his good friend never did manage to exchange embraces, because as Perón flew to Managua, Somoza left for the conference. The *conductor* remained in Nicaragua for nine uneventful days[38] and then returned to Panamá.

Perón was now actively promoting the resistance, but he found it difficult to communicate with his people and decided to shift his base of operations. Venezuela, under the control of a military dictatorship, seemed a safe haven and a bit more accessible to Argentina. Its climate was more to his liking, and a number of Peronist exiles, including General Tanco, had gone there. On August 10, Perón said good-bye to his Panamanian friends and joined Isabel on a commercial Venezuelan airliner heading for Caracas.

39

Sojourn in Venezuela

The Venezuela to which Juan Perón repaired in 1956 suffered under the yoke of a dictator who shared little in common with his Argentine guest. Short, pudgy, moon-faced and repulsive, Marcos Pérez Jiménez relied upon military force and an efficient security apparatus to keep his fellow citizens in check.[1] Income from the sale of petroleum, Venezuela's subterranean treasure, enabled the man the North Americans nicknamed P.J. to indulge in monumental public works projects—such as the $70 million highway linking Caracas to the airport of Maiquetía, only twelve miles away but on the other side of a mountain range. Funds not squandered on hotels, stadiums and other grandiose confections found their way into the private bank accounts of P.J. and his associates, while urban poverty spread unchecked and the countryside stagnated. Washington found the Venezuelan despot congenial, however, since he mouthed a suitably militant brand of anticommunism and kept his hands off the substantial U.S. investments in his country.

It was nine in the evening of August 8, 1956, when the Venezuelan plane carrying Argentina's ex-president touched down at Maiquetía on a runway parallel to the Caribbean shore. As Perón and Isabel disembarked, a throng of several dozen Argentine exiles, led by General Tanco, surged forward to greet them. The air was hot and heavy with moisture, but Perón appeared fresh and buoyant. Isabel remained demurely in the background.

From the moment Perón set foot on Venezuelan soil, Rodolfo Martínez assumed the role of right-hand man, making statements to the press and sheltering Perón and Isabel in his apartment for several days.[2] Martincho, as his friends called him, had been an obscure political hanger-on but was the first Peronist to travel from Buenos Aires to Panamá for the express purpose of volunteering his services to Perón. He then settled in Caracas and helped make arrangements for Perón's arrival.

Nothing in Martincho's background qualified him to act as Perón's spokesman. Gilaberte, who soon arrived with the Opel, did not have the wit to do more than act as chauffeur and bodyguard. Isabel performed strictly decorative and domestic functions. Martínez (who was not related to Isabel) moved opportunistically into a vacuum and began to take care of the myriad details that complicated Perón's life.

It was no easy task. Dealing with the Argentine exiles in Caracas proved complicated, especially due to a coolness that congealed relations between Perón and General Tanco. Moreover, within the *conductor*'s inner circle, palace intrigues were in constant bloom.

Martínez' chief antagonist was Pablo Vicente, a handsome army major who had served as one of Perón's aides-de-camp in 1954 and 1955 and had participated in the Valle revolt. When Vicente made his way to Caracas, Perón invited him to become his assistant,[3] and Vicente immediately set out to oust Martínez.

Though outclassed by his rival, Martínez held his ground until March 1957, when he indiscreetly became involved in a brawl that resulted in his imprisonment. He claimed that an anti-Peronist Argentine had goaded him into a fight by insulting the *conductor*.[4] Perón later reported that the altercation occurred "in a place of dubious morality" and he had to pull strings to secure Martincho's release.[5] One of the conditions upon which he was set free was that he leave the country. Thus exited Rodolfo Martínez.*

A bacterial infection from contaminated drinking water felled both Perón and Isabel shortly after their arrival. It was only after they recovered from their illness that they could settle comfortably into a new life.[6] The couple moved to a modest two-bedroom house in a residential neighborhood. As much a creature of habit as ever, Perón followed a routine that included morning walks to the supermarket, work on his prodigious correspondence and another book, an afternoon siesta, and conferences with the many individuals who sought to gain his ear. On Friday evenings he watched boxing matches telecast from the United States on the *Gillette Cavalcade of Sports*. Weekends he relaxed at a nearby beach. Occasionally he visited a stud farm owned by Jorge Antonio.

Perón dressed simply, preferring cream-colored pants and short-sleeved sport shirts. His main meal of the day usually consisted of steak,

---

* Obscurity might have digested Rodolfo Martínez but for his habit of making copious notes of his experiences with Perón. In 1957 he wrote a book entitled *Grandezas y miserias de Perón (The Grandeur and Wretchedness of Perón)*. It contains a wealth of valuable detail on the Panamanian and Venezuelan phases of Perón's exile.

rice and a salad. He often prepared his own food. His three poodles, recently smuggled out of Argentina, were endless sources of diversion.

A Central Intelligence Agency report from this period relates that Perón "appears to be in perfect physical condition and could easily pass for a man in his forties."[7] The CIA operative, who had several encounters with the *conductor*, was impressed not only by his "overwhelming charm" but also by his excellent grasp of the political and economic problems of Panamá and by his ability to converse in English.

As was the case in Panamá, Perón's lifestyle exuded a frugality that did not square with published accounts of his great wealth. Martínez reported that Perón was involved in a business venture created with capital provided by Jorge Antonio. According to Martincho, Perón admitted that while in the Casa Rosada he had helped his friend, but with the understanding that Antonio would set aside part of the money he earned and place it at the disposal of the Peronist movement.[8] The *conductor* was in fact sending funds to his followers, but these appear to have been modest in amount.[9]

Although Perón had friends in high places within the Venezuelan government, the regime did not give him a free rein. The head of the secret police kept in close contact with the Argentine exiles and several Perón intimates, but made it clear that any sign of political activity on their part would result in serious problems for them. P.J. refused to see Perón.[10] On his part Perón privately criticized Pérez Jiménez for his failure to develop social programs for the benefit of Venezuelan workers.

Pérez Jiménez had once visited Perón in Buenos Aires, but their relationship was never warm. There is some evidence that what prompted P.J. to let Perón enter Venezuela was the snub he felt he had received from Aramburu during the Panamá meeting of Latin American heads of state.[11] The Argentines consistently played into the *conductor*'s hand. They pressured Venezuela to oust the "fugitive tyrant" so heavy-handedly that it became a matter of national pride for the Venezuelans to resist.

Meanwhile, the Aramburu regime was discovering that despite dogged efforts to exorcise Perón's ghost, the Peronist movement not only survived but even displayed a capacity for growth. This was especially true in the field of organized labor. When the Liberating Revolution ousted Lonardi and bared its fangs, the government undertook to eliminate Peronist labor leaders and encourage anti-Peronists who were trying to capture control of individual unions. A decree issuing from the Casa Rosada barred from union office anyone who had held a position of authority in the labor movement during the last three years of the Perón era. Democratic union elections were scheduled, in the hope that workers would turn their backs on those candidates who professed allegiance to the exiled leader.

However, the economic policies announced by the regime made it clear
to workers that the Liberating Revolution did not have their interests at
heart. A new breed of Peronist leader replaced imprisoned old-line bureaucrats, and these younger, more militant front-liners were quick to capitalize
on the anti-labor image projected by Argentina's rulers. As a result, although anti-Peronists made some progress, the Peronists kept their grip
on a majority of the syndicates, which gave them the leverage to mobilize
opposition to the government's austerity program. Work stoppages in
1956, 1957 and 1958 amounted to 5, 3.6 and 6 million days lost respectively in the city of Buenos Aires alone.[12] The regime tried to normalize
the CGT in 1957 by convoking a congress of union representatives, but
the split between Peronists and anti-Peronists caused the conclave to break
up in disarray. The sixty-two unions under Peronist control formed a
group called the Sixty-two Organizations, while the anti-Peronists brought
their syndicates together in a rival entity.[13]

The Peronist resistance virtually disappeared in the immediate wake of
the stern suppression of the Valle revolt. Perón urged his people to keep
fighting, but it was difficult for him to provide any tactical guidance from
a distance. The *conductor* therefore appointed John William Cooke not
only as his representative, with full authority to act in his name, but also
as his heir.[14] The portly ex-deputy, nicknamed Bebe, was well-suited,
though ill-positioned, to direct this phase of the struggle.[15] Tough, articulate and intellectually gifted, he nonetheless found it difficult to carry
out his assignment from behind prison bars. Yet several incidents of sabotage in early 1957 suggested that the resistance was reviving.[16]

Cooke's mandate also extended to the political sphere. But here the
movement was hurting badly. Peronist politicians had either escaped into
exile or were now enduring harsh confinements. Albrieu, Aloé, Cafiero,
Cámpora, Cooke, Gómez Morales, Mendé and Parodi were among those
who were paying a stiff price for their participation in the deposed government. The regime had some of them shipped to antiquated prisons in
Patagonia and Tierra del Fuego, where they barely survived the winter of
1956.

Several captive Peronists struck a major psychological blow for their
cause in early 1957. Río Gallegos, the port city in southern Patagonia
where Juan Perón had landed fifty-five years earlier en route to join his
father, provided a bleak setting for their caper. A penitentiary on the outskirts of town housed a group of well-known prisoners: Jorge Antonio,
Héctor Cámpora, John William Cooke, José Espejo and Patricio Kelly,
the notorious chief of the ALN. It was an unlikely mixture, demonstrating
that prisons, like politics, make strange bedfellows. Antonio the entrepreneur had little in common with Cooke the ideologue or Espejo the
union bureaucrat. Cámpora had taken a solemn oath to the Virgin of

Luján to abandon public life and spent his days in prayer. Kelly, a roguish tough guy, marched to his own drummer.

It was Jorge Antonio who hit upon the idea to attempt an escape. He concocted a scheme that brought one of his business associates, a man named Araujo, to Río Gallegos. Araujo made the necessary preparations on the outside. Antonio's wife and sister smuggled pistols into the prison during visits. The plan was to break out in the early hours of a Sunday morning, just after a change in guards. Araujo would have an automobile ready for a dash to the Chilean border, only seventy kilometers to the south.

The escape party was originally composed of Antonio, Cooke, Espejo and Kelly, the latter included because he would be useful in the event of trouble. At the last moment two men were added to the group: Héctor Cámpora, who found out about the plan and asked to join, and Pedro Gómiz, a brawny labor leader.

On the appointed night, March 17, 1957, when most of the guards were off celebrating pre-Lenten Carnival, Kelly put sleeping pills into the tea and mate taken by the other prisoners after dinner. At 2:10 A.M. the conspirators used their pistols to capture the only guard on duty at the moment and made their way silently out the front gate. Araujo and his automobile were nowhere in sight. A nervous Cámpora offered the suggestion that they return to their cells and try again on another day. A Ford traveling without lights approached in the darkness. It was Araujo. The fugitives clambered aboard and headed toward Chile. To avoid an Argentine border patrol post, they left the road and pushed the car through the countryside for several kilometers in a wide arc. At 6:00 A.M. they reached the Chilean border and requested political asylum. The Chilean guards permitted the car to pass. The fugitives then drove the road along the shore of the Straits of Magellan to the city of Punto Arenas, where they turned themselves over to the authorities.[17]

The escape created a sensation throughout Latin America. Highly embarrassed, the Aramburu regime demanded that the Chileans surrender the escapees, who were flown to Santiago and imprisoned. President Ibáñez was in the middle of domestic political difficulties and did not need the headache caused by the arrival of the Peronist fugitives. Nonetheless, the Chilean government determined that all except Kelly were bona fide political exiles and eventually released them. Kelly, considered to be a mere common criminal, remained in prison.

Patricio provided a farcical ending to the saga in late September. His presence in Santiago drew from the woodwork an exotic character from the past, the Uruguayan poetess Blanca Luz Brun, now living in the Chilean capital. Still an ardent Peronist, she collaborated with several of Kelly's associates from Argentina to pull off an even more picturesque jailbreak. She smuggled women's clothes to Kelly during a visit and Patricio calmly strolled out of the prison in drag. Now it was the Chilean government's turn to be embarrassed. Despite a full mobilization of security forces, Kelly had little trouble departing the country.[18]

Even before the Chilean authorities released him, John William Cooke set up what he called a forward command in Santiago. Its function was to coordinate the activities of the resistance inside Argentina and of the various Peronist exile groups throughout Latin America, in accordance with the *conductor*'s directives.

Cooke soon learned that this would be no easy task. Many Peronists were reluctant to accept his leadership. He was considered too radical, an advocate of the revolutionary brand of Peronism that saw itself as a working-class rather than multi-class movement.[19] Never a mainstream Peronist, Bebe lacked the sort of stature among his peers required to unify the movement.

What made matters worse was the *conductor*'s own peculiar style of leadership. Instead of using Cooke's forward command as his intermediary, he maintained his own direct communications with the various segments of the movement. This created countless difficulties for Cooke. The *conductor* wrote his own letters to leaders other than Bebe. Often, because of ambiguities in the text or self-serving distortions by the recipients of these precious epistles, the movement found itself subject to conflicting instructions.[20] At times a visitor would propose a course of action to Perón. As a standard practice the *conductor* would never say yes or no. He merely shrugged or winked. The visitor would take this as approval and carry out the suggestion, in the belief he was acting with Perón's approval. If the action succeeded, Perón took the credit. If it failed, the *conductor* disclaimed responsibility on the ground that his will had been misinterpreted.[21]

Disagreements over strategy and tactics as well as petty feuds kept the Peronist exile colonies in Chile, Uruguay, Brazil and elsewhere in disarray. Despite his constant lip service to the virtues of unity, Perón consciously stimulated this divisiveness and played upon it like a *maestro*. This was but another manifestation of *"me manejo bien en un quilombo."**

Meanwhile, within Argentina the political situation was beginning to clarify. The Aramburu regime remained committed to hold elections in the near future. The political parties, severely repressed under Peronist rule, began to reorganize. The Radicals had survived the Perón era in good order. Having sustained the burden of opposing the Peronists throughout a difficult decade, they now enjoyed great respect and were clearly the strongest of the legally sanctioned parties.

* See *supra* p. 161.

However, the ancient split between personalist and anti-personalist (or pro-Yrigoyen and anti-Yrigoyen) Radicals persisted. Arturo Frondizi led one faction, claiming Yrigoyen's mantle and maintaining a critical posture toward the government. His supporters gained control of the party machinery and were ready to nominate their leader to run for president. Ricardo Balbín headed the dissidents and fully supported the Liberating Revolution. In early 1957 the two wings decided they could no longer co-exist, and the party split. Frondizi's group took the name Unión Cívica Radical Intransigente, or UCRI (the Intransigent Radical Civil Union, or Intransigent Radicals), while Balbín became the leader of the Unión Cívica Radical del Pueblo, or UCRP (the People's Radical Civil Union, or People's Radicals).

The UCRP adopted both the virulent anti-Peronism and the economic policies of the Aramburu regime. The People's Radicals let themselves become identified with the provisional government, and thereby labored under all the disadvantages associated with incumbency without reaping any of the benefits. Frondizi, on the other hand, kept his distance from the Liberating Revolution and made conciliatory gestures toward the working class.

The impending restoration of constitutional democracy raised a fundamental dilemma: could millions of Peronists be incorporated into the system without permitting Perón's return to power? The government hoped that the ban on the Peronist party would fragment the Peronist mass, but it soon became apparent that this would be difficult to achieve.

The Socialist and Communist parties had long been cut off from their working-class constituencies and had been bitterly anti-Peronist for such a long time that they could find few Perón supporters willing to listen to them now. Emerging from his prison ordeal, Cipriano Reyes set out to revive the Labor party but failed in his attempt to set the calendar back a decade. Another figure from the past, Juan Bramuglia, organized a neo-Peronist party that promoted the idea of "Peronism without Perón." But the former foreign minister encountered debilitating opposition from the *conductor* in Caracas, old-line Peronist leaders and the Peronist militants.

While efforts to lure Peronists into new political alignments foundered, the possibility of establishing an alliance between Perón's movement and one of the other parties remained viable. Vicente Solano Lima, an early exile from Peronist repression, was one of the first to advocate such an arrangement and sought Peronist support for his Popular Conservative party in exchange for his promise that if elected president, he would legalize the Peronist party and then resign. Individuals close to Frondizi also began preliminary talks with Peronists about the possibility of a Perón-Frondizi deal.

With the ouster of Lonardi, the Liberating Revolution had identified itself as hostile to the self-perceived interests of workers, who remained solidly Peronist to defend themselves. The campaign to discredit Perón had failed to damage the mystique that enabled him to maintain leadership over organized labor and the other elements of his movement. How to deal with him was a continuing puzzle for the regime.

One option was to have him assassinated. The Peronists claimed that various killers hired by the regime had long been stalking Perón. It is difficult to know how much of this was concocted for propaganda purposes. The most colorful of these stories, often recounted by Perón himself, involved Jack, a Yugoslav assassin imported from Tangiers by an officer in the Argentine embassy in Caracas. When Jack learned the identity of his target, for some unknown reason he balked, and then decided to pay a visit to the *conductor*. "I remember him as being tall, blond, with a black shirt and, within the limits of his profession, a gentleman," Perón recalled later.[22] Jack told him about his assignment and then left the country.

While the hit man from Tangiers may have been a figment of the imagination, on the morning of May 25, 1957, an Argentine holiday celebrating the 1810 Revolution, a real bomb exploded in Perón's Opel. Fortunately for the *conductor*, his chauffeur was alone in the car, en route to purchase some meat and charcoal for a feast that afternoon. The blast shattered nearby windows, but Gilaberte escaped with minor injuries. The vehicle was completely demolished.[23]

Relations between Argentina and Venezuela rapidly deteriorated because of Perón. In July the Argentine government formally cut diplomatic ties with Venezuela. The Argentine ambassador in Washington asked the State Department to pressure Venezuelans to oust Perón.[24] This put Washington in an embarrassing position; at that very moment Rómulo Betancourt, a Venezuelan political leader bitterly opposed to Pérez Jiménez, was actively campaigning against P.J. from exile in the United States. A State Department request that Venezuela expel Perón would provoke a reciprocal request that the North Americans expel Betancourt.[25] Therefore, Washington had to turn down the Argentine bid.*

Events soon justified the Argentine government's preoccupation with Perón's political activity. On July 28, voters went to the polls to choose delegates to a convention that would reform the 1949 Peronist constitution. Perón directed his followers to cast blank votes. The count of ballots

---

* The United States did take steps to keep Perón from generating favorable publicity. In September the ex-president appeared on a Caracas television program that happened to be financed by the U.S. Information Service. The U.S. embassy made it clear to the program's host that any further appearances by Perón would cause U.S. sponsorship to be withdrawn. John Foster Dulles to U.S. embassy (Caracas), 735.00/9-1357, September 13, 1957; U.S. embassy (Caracas) to secretary of state, 735.00/10-957, October 9, 1957.

revealed: 2,119,147 blanks; 2,117,160 votes for the People's Radicals; and 1,821,459 for the Intransigent Radicals. The UCRP hailed the results. Frondizi's UCRI cast a covetous glance at the blanks.

On November 15 the provisional government officially scheduled general elections for February 23, 1958. Although a number of candidates would enter the presidential race, it was clear from the outset that there were only two serious contenders, Frondizi and Balbín. The latter could count on the endorsement of the regime and stood squarely behind the Liberating Revolution. Frondizi seized the banner of economic development and national unity, which would require him to reincorporate the Peronists into the political process without provoking the military and civilian hard-liners to whom Perón was anathema.

As the campaign began, both sides recognized the importance of the Peronist vote. If Frondizi could attract the *conductor's* followers to his side, he could easily win. If the Peronists cast blank votes or supported one or more of the minor candidates, Balbín would benefit.

Viewing the scene from Caracas, Juan Perón fully appreciated the leverage he now possessed. From his perspective a dispersion of the Peronist votes would demonstrate weakness on both his part and that of his movement. Solano Lima and his Popular Conservative party were too marginal to merit serious consideration. Nor was Perón about to boost Juan Bramuglia's neo-Peronist party, since "Peronism without Perón" was not a slogan that appealed to the *conductor*.

This left Perón with two alternatives, and he was in no hurry to make up his mind. His own followers were divided.[26] The revolutionary elements, with whom Cooke sympathized, urged their *conductor* not to play the electoral game and to remain adamantly opposed to any government that derived its legitimacy from the Liberating Revolution. A number of Peronist politicians, on the other hand, preferred to participate in the process. Perón encouraged both sides without committing himself.

Frondizi quietly courted those Peronists who were favorably disposed toward him.[27] Several of his supporters enjoyed friendly personal relations with key Peronists and explored the possibility of securing Perón's endorsement of their candidate. The most persuasive proponent of a deal with the Peronists was Rogelio Frigerio, an intellectual who edited a magazine called *Qué*. He and Frondizi had discovered that they shared basic beliefs about economic development and were in the process of forging a symbiotic relationship that would make Frigerio the Radical leader's most influential advisor and confidant.

On the Peronist side, Ramón Prieto was the chief advocate of a deal with Frondizi.[28] A journalist and adventurer who had fought with the Republicans in the Spanish Civil War and had marched with the legendary column of Luis Carlos Prestes in Brazil, the diminutive, energetic Prieto emphasized the convergence between the views expounded by Frigerio on the pages of *Qué* and the economic and social policies espoused by Peronism. He also felt that Frondizi's willingness to treat with the Peronists created an opportunity to breach the solid anti-Peronist front created by the Liberating Revolution. Conferring with Frondizi supporters in Buenos Aires, visiting Cooke in Santiago and making the long pilgrimage to Caracas, Prieto became a key figure in the delicate negotiations.

In weighing his options, Perón had to take into account the vast differences between a special election to choose delegates to a constitutional convention and a general election. It had been a simple matter to convert the July balloting into a referendum and to convince the Peronist faithful to cast blank votes in protest against the regime. But the selection of a president, Congress and provincial governors could have a substantial immediate impact on the life of every citizen. As the campaign progressed, Peronist voters could plainly distinguish between Frondizi, who offered them an olive branch, and Balbín, who offered them the back of his hand. Perón faced the risk that even if he ordered abstention, many of his followers might still vote for Frondizi.

Casting blank ballots also ran against the political grain of most Argentines. Any attempt by the *conductor* to keep Peronists on the sidelines might backfire and stimulate an interest in neo-Peronism. Bramuglia did not possess the charisma and prestige necessary to attract a large following. But in Montevideo a historical personage who still had at his disposal a reservoir of respect had risen from Peronist limbo and was active among the exiles. The name of Domingo Mercante still evoked memories of a glorious past. Anything Perón did to weaken his own control over the movement might boost Mercante's stock.

In his inimitable style, the *conductor* encouraged both the abstentionists and the pro-Frondizi faction. In his correspondence with Cooke, he gave every indication of opposing a political solution that would restore constitutional government.[29] Moreover, his references to Frondizi were often couched in derogatory terms.[30] Late in the year he consulted Jorge Antonio, who had flown to Caracas, and with a characteristic wink of the eye led his friend to believe he favored a blank vote.[31] At the same time he created in the minds of Frondizi supporters the impression that he was favorably disposed toward their candidate. "Frondizi can be an adversary," he was quoted as observing, "but never an enemy."[32]

Cooke, meanwhile, left Santiago in November. Making the long trek to Caracas, Bebe now had the opportunity to consult with Perón in person regarding the political decision that would soon have to be made.

In late December the *conductor* felt the time had come to confer directly with a Frondizi representative. He sent word to Prieto that he wanted Rogelio Frigerio to come to Venezuela. The editor of *Qué* arrived shortly after New Year's Day and engaged in a series of talks with Perón and Cooke.

At this juncture the regime of Pérez Jiménez suddenly and somewhat unexpectedly came crashing down, and Juan Perón found himself trapped in the rubble. On New Year's Eve the secret police discovered an incipient military revolt and arrested several officers. This did not deter the rest of the plotters from going ahead with their plans, and as 1958 dawned jet fighters attacked targets in Caracas.[33] The coup failed due to a lack of coordination. In response Pérez Jiménez ordered the detention of hundreds of officers and civilians. The Perón-Frigerio conversations took place during this period of extreme unrest, as it became evident that the pressures upon the regime were rapidly building and could not be contained much longer.

A series of strikes erupted on Monday and Tuesday, January 20 and 21. By Wednesday police were battling rebels armed with guns and Molotov cocktails. That night top army and navy officials conferred and agreed that the only way to avert a full-scale civil war was for Pérez Jiménez to leave the country. They informed P.J. of their decision, and in the early hours of the next morning the dictator, his family and several close associates boarded a plane at the small airport in downtown Caracas. Their destination was the Dominican Republic.

The fall of Pérez Jiménez unleashed passions that years of repression had nurtured. From the shanties on the hillsides around the city, angry mobs swept down upon the capital. Unchecked, they roamed Caracas in search of members of the secret police and other officials who symbolized the deposed regime.

The anarchy to which Caracas fell prey shattered the calm that had enabled Juan Perón to pursue his political goals without interference. A Venezuelan newspaper headlined the sensational (but fabricated) charge that "Perón Directed the Repression Against the Venezuelan People."[34] In addition, Patricio Kelly, who had journeyed to Venezuela and who was regarded as a Perón intimate, was accused of having helped Pérez Jiménez' secret police torture students. Thus Perón suddenly gained notoriety as an enemy of the "people," in whose name mobs were burning, looting and killing.

Physical danger more imminent than any he had previously faced now threatened Perón. He hid out in a friend's house while Roberto Galán, an Argentine friend who would later become a popular television and nightclub performer in Buenos Aires, drove to his home and packed his personal effects in suitcases.[35] There were nervous moments for Galán when a truckload of revolutionaries pulled up in front of the residence, before they decided Perón's home was empty and drove away. At the same time, efforts to find an embassy in which Perón might take refuge finally bore fruit when Rafael Bonelly, the Dominican ambassador, indicated that he would help the ex-president.

Late that afternoon Perón, Isabel, Cooke, Kelly, Gilaberte, Américo

Barrios (a journalist who was now Perón's private secretary) and several
other Peronists made their way to the residence that functioned as the
embassy of the Dominican Republic.[36] In cramped quarters, the Argentines
began a tense vigil. The house was unguarded and offered a tempting
target for mob violence. Perón and several of the others carried pistols.

The next morning the newspapers reported widespread looting throughout the city. Perón passed the time by telling anecdotes. Then one visitor
brought the news that everyone dreaded most: a mob was on its way.

A crowd numbering about a thousand soon materialized outside. Ambassador Bonelly went to talk to them. Perhaps their thirst for vengeance
was slaked, for they dispersed peacefully. Someone in the house blamed
Kelly for what had happened. The indomitable Patricio donned a hat and
pair of dark glasses, smiled enigmatically and walked out the door.

That afternoon a Venezuelan colonel phoned to inform Perón that
the new government had decided to permit him to leave the country. But
the condition imposed—that he travel alone—worried his companions,
who feared for his safety. After some negotiating, the Venezuelans agreed
to let Ambassador Bonelly accompany him. On Monday evening, January
27, a DC-3 took off from the downtown airport and carried Perón on the
next leg of his journey in exile, to the sunny Caribbean island ruled by
Generalísimo Rafael L. Trujillo.

40

Dominican
Interlude

Perón accepted the conditions set by the new Venezuelan government upon his departure, even though this meant leaving behind his poodles and Isabel. Roberto Galán took custody of the canines and promised to deliver them to the Dominican Republic as soon as possible. Isabel, along with Cooke and Barrios, remained inside the embassy for several days, until some semblance of order had been restored to the city and it was safe for them to book a commercial flight to Ciudad Trujillo.

When they reached their destination, Isabel and her two companions found Perón comfortably settled in the Hotel Jaragua, on the Avenida George Washington, facing the azure waters of the Caribbean. Isabel moved in with Perón, while Barrios and Cooke lodged at a more modest establishment not far away. In a short while, Roberto Galán arrived with the poodles. With his "family" now reunited and physically secure in a controlled environment, Juan Perón began the least active phase of his long exile.

"I breathed freely when I arrived in Ciudad Trujillo," Perón said later, "because I felt I was on friendly soil."[1] Trujillo made it clear from the beginning that the Argentine exile was welcome and would have a free hand to do whatever he pleased. The *generalísimo* assigned a military aide to accompany him and defrayed his living expenses. The two men often dined together.*

Rafael Trujillo did not merely rule the Dominican Republic; he owned most of it. The U.S. marines who occupied the country during the 1920s

---

* There was a slight irony underlying the admiration Trujillo felt toward Perón. In 1945 the president of Guatemala had purchased five hundred rifles from the Argentine army and had immediately turned them over to Dominican rebels seeking to overthrow the Trujillo dictatorship. Perón, who held the *benefactor* in the highest esteem, had been unaware of the intended use of the weapons and had even permitted them to be sold at a substantial discount. R. Crassweller, *Trujillo,* p. 236.

recognized his talents and helped him rise to the rank of colonel in the Dominican national guard. When the marines departed in 1930, Trujillo seized power. With help from the U.S. government and North American business interests, he established one of the most repressive, exploitative regimes ever to foul the Western Hemisphere.

Perón saw no evil around him in his two years in the Dominican Republic. He would occasionally offer Trujillo advice, which the *benefactor* graciously accepted (and then ignored). Once he urged his host to initiate more social-welfare projects. Trujillo replied that he could not emulate what Perón had done because the Argentine population was white, whereas 80 percent of the Dominicans were Negro. "The Negroes cannot be helped by social projects because they immediately destroy them," the *generalísimo* explained; he therefore had to be "paternal." Perón thought this racist rejoinder was "very wise."[2]

A spectacular parade through the streets of Ciudad Trujillo celebrated the twenty-fifth anniversary of Trujillo's assumption of the title *El Benefactor de la Patria* ("The Benefactor of the Fatherland"). Perón volunteered to march with a contingent of workers, but Trujillo summoned the Argentine ex-president to his side on the reviewing stand. The *generalísimo* was resplendent in his braided, decoration-laden uniform. Perón wore a white suit and sweated profusely in the tropical heat. By day's end he had lost two kilograms (4.4 pounds).[3]

Physical security was now no problem for Perón. Trujillo personally approved visa applications from Argentines, in some instances after checking with Américo Barrios.[4] Peronists moved freely in and out of the country. In mid-August 1958, a number of politicians and labor leaders met for several days with their *conductor*. To coincide with the conference and to honor Perón, Pasqual Pérez came to Ciudad Trujillo and fought a ten-round bout with an Italian boxer. The Argentines cheered loudly as Pasqualito won a unanimous decision.

Another visitor of note to the island was Hans-Ulrich Rudel, the World War II Luftwaffe ace, who arrived in Ciudad Trujillo with a proposal from the German construction firms he represented to build hospitals in the Dominican Republic. The legendary exploits of the ex-colonel included a return to the cockpit of his Stuka dive-bomber after the loss of a leg in combat on the Russian front. He had taken postwar refuge in Argentina and Perón had befriended him. He paid his respects to the exiled leader, who was delighted to see him.[5]

Perón's Dominican interlude partook of a restful quality that his long journey in exile had heretofore lacked. He and Isabel traveled freely around the country. He taught her how to ride a motor scooter and encouraged her to take fencing lessons, which he supplemented.[6] They moved to a less luxurious hotel and later took up residence in a small house.

The *conductor* had various opportunities to indulge his passion for playing doctor. He freely offered Trujillo medical advice. Once he tripped and fell in an effort to save a chicken that had been given as a gift to Isabel and was being pursued by neighborhood dogs. He thereupon taped his side with bandages. According to Barrios, X-rays subsequently revealed that he had broken a rib and that it was healing perfectly.[7]

To the outside observer, an atmosphere of unreality clung to Perón and his courtiers. A correspondent from the United Press once visited him and was treated to a three-day monologue by Perón. The reporter's impression was that isolation had taken its toll on the *conductor*:

> What he told me sounded absolutely outlandish. For example, he said the workers and students of Latin America would soon carry the banner of *justicialismo* to victory. At one point the people around him held a "kangaroo trial" of a driver accused of treating Perón with disrespect. At another, Isabel walked in with several poodles, each with a pink bow, on a leash. It was worthy of an Italian movie or a Tom Wolfe article, the contrast between Perón's fantasizing and the actual behavior of his entourage.[8]

Yet Perón was still very much a real factor in Argentine politics. His discussions with Frigerio in Caracas had produced the so-called Perón-Frondizi Pact, an agreement that would spawn a bitter dispute. According to the textual version of the pact later released by Perón, the *conductor* promised to order the withdrawal of all neo-Peronist candidates and to instruct Peronists to vote in whatever way would best repudiate the regime. In return, Frondizi pledged to reinstate the economic policies of the Perón era, terminate all legal proceedings based upon political charges, return all property taken from the Eva Perón Foundation and within two years not only reform the constitution but also convoke new general elections.[9] In early February, Prieto brought to the Dominican Republic a copy of the pact supposedly signed by Frondizi.[10] Frigerio claimed the document carried by Prieto did not contain any specific commitments.[11] Frondizi denied any involvement in the matter.[12]

The drafters of the pact must have realized that Frondizi could not live up to what was supposed to be his part of the bargain without provoking civilian resistance and military uprising. Frigerio may have been willing to promise anything to assure his candidate's election, perhaps in the belief that the powers of the presidency would enable Frondizi to deal effectively with Perón and the Peronists. Despite Frondizi's disavowals, he has admitted that during this period he was always apprised of what Frigerio was doing.[13]*

* Professor Potash, pointing to assertions by Prieto and Frigerio that the latter arrived in Caracas in early January and left during the outbreak of the coup that ousted Pérez Jiménez, argues that Frigerio must have traveled twice to the Venezuelan capital in January, perhaps returning after consultation with Frondizi. R. Potash, *The Army and Politics in Argentina, 1945–1962*, p. 266, fn. 120. Cooke attributed the apparent confusion in dates to the fact that Frigerio left Caracas during the first uprising against Pérez Jiménez. J. Cooke, *Peronismo e integración*, p. 54.

In early February Perón announced that he was directing his followers to vote against the status quo and left the impression that he had made some kind of deal with the UCRI candidate. Frondizi immediately denied he had ever sent representatives to negotiate with Perón, or had reached any secret agreement. Within the next two weeks Peronists within Argentina were distributing printed instructions signed by Perón endorsing Frondizi.[14]

When all the ballots were counted, the Intransigent Radicals had won a smashing victory. Frondizi garnered 4 million votes to Balbín's 2.4 million. The UCRI took all the provincial governorships, every seat in the Senate and 133 seats in the Chamber of Deputies. The UCRP elected only 52 deputies. The Peronists quickly assumed credit for the extent of Frondizi's victory and pointed to 690,000 blank votes, which they claimed were cast by militant members of their movement, as further evidence of their strength. The Intransigent Radicals insisted that their man would have won handily without Perón's blessing, on the merits of his own platform of reconciliation and development. Hard-liners within the military were unhappy with the results, and there were whispers of an impending coup.

In early March, Rogelio Frigerio, who would soon be named as Frondizi's secretary for economic and social relations, made another visit to Perón. His purpose was to stress the fragility of the president-elect's position and to urge Perón to discourage his followers from doing anything that might provoke military intervention. Perón responded favorably and prepared a directive instructing Peronists not to make any immediate demands upon the incoming government.[15] However, he still expected Frondizi to live up to the terms of the pact.

On May 1, 1958, at ceremonies attended by an array of international dignitaries (including U.S. Vice-President Richard M. Nixon), Arturo Frondizi took the oath of office.[16] The balding, bespectacled forty-nine-year-old attorney projected a no-nonsense image that reflected personal austerity in the Yrigoyen mold, keen intelligence and a confident vision of the direction in which the nation should be heading. A new era was about to dawn, or so it seemed.

In reality, Frondizi had set an impossible task for himself. His campaign appeal to the largely Peronist working class had raised expectations that could be met only after Argentina had achieved the economic development to which the new president had committed his administration. Yet his developmental policies and programs were long-range and not meant to achieve immediate results.[17] His failure to comply with the terms of the pact—which he steadfastly denied ever having signed—compounded the disillusionment of his constituency.

On the other hand, the armed forces made it clear they would not suffer the dismantling of the Liberating Revolution, and remained adamantly opposed to anything that suggested a revival of Peronism. Divided between those who wanted to retain control of the government and those in favor of a return to civilian rule, the military kept constant pressure on Frondizi, who lacked the massive popular support necessary to uphold his authority. His economic program and inability to appease the Peronists caused him to lose the momentum that had swept him into office. Moreover, the other political parties, true to Argentine tradition, adopted an uncompromisingly belligerent attitude toward the UCRI administration. Their aim was not to offer constructive opposition, but rather to force Frondizi out of office.

Finally, an economic crisis came to a head just as Frondizi assumed the presidency. Argentina's deteriorating balance of payments required the imposition of immediate measures that ran counter to Frondizi's overall strategy for industrial expansion.[18]

If Frondizi thought that tactical skills honed over a lifetime of political activity would enable him to surmount these obstacles, he had grossly overestimated his own capabilities. On May 7, he sent an amnesty law to Congress. The UCRP deputies immediately accused him of attempting to undo the Liberating Revolution. The Peronists grumbled that the bill did not go far enough. In July, Frondizi announced that the government had signed contracts with foreign companies to exploit the nation's petroleum resources. In view of his savage opposition to Perón's attempt to enter into the same type of contracts, this sudden reversal on Frondizi's part stunned supporters and opponents alike. By September the government had created another firestorm by proposing to legalize private education at the university level. This would open the way for institutions such as the Catholic church to compete with the state-controlled universities, which had previously enjoyed a monopoly in the field of higher education. On May 13, the government authorized a 60 percent salary increase for workers. As the economic situation worsened, Frondizi turned to the International Monetary Fund for help. In return, the fund required the president to impose a drastic stabilization program that called for wage restraints, the removal of price controls, a devaluation of the peso and a layoff of public employees.[19]

The problems that buffeted Frondizi during these tumultuous months encouraged army officers unhappy with his assumption of the presidency to agitate for his removal. He had to remain on guard against the possibility of a coup. One concession the military extracted from him was the dismissal of Frigerio from his government post. Frondizi's éminence grise, whom the army suspected of leftist sympathies, had become a lightning rod for attacks on the president. In mid-November, Frondizi's vice-president joined efforts to oust the president and was himself forced to resign.

Strikes by railroad and petroleum workers, the latter in opposition to the oil contracts, intensified the turmoil. Isolated incidents of sabotage appeared to be the work of Peronist militants. On November 10, Frondizi declared a state of siege. Cooke, who had taken advantage of the amnesty to return to Argentina, was arrested and jailed for a short time.[20] In January, workers occupied a state meatpacking plant to protest its imminent return to private ownership. Elements within the labor movement called a general strike that assumed insurrectional overtones and Cooke eagerly mounted the barricades. The government had to call out troops and tanks to dislodge the workers.[21]

Whether Perón issued the order responsible for these labor disturbances is not known. His letters to Cooke reflected a conviction that Frondizi would not comply with the pact unless the Peronists pushed him. As early as June 18, he called for "a violent campaign throughout the country" to force the government to amplify the amnesty it had decreed.[22] In mid-September he impressed upon Cooke the need for "action, action and more action."[23] In a letter dated December 20, he stressed the need "to begin passive resistance and civil disobedience, the same way we did against the dictatorship. I don't say that we are now going to begin throwing bombs," he added, "but that we ought to organize a pamphlet campaign, gossip, protests, disobedience, strikes, disorders, provocations, minor sabotage, etc."[24]

Labor unrest continued throughout 1959. By year's end, over 2.5 million workers had struck for a total of more than 11 million days in the city of Buenos Aires.[25] This display of militance, however, failed to achieve Perón's political goals, nor did it result in any tangible gains for the workers.

The labor offensive signaled the end of any possibility of a working relationship between Frondizi and the Peronists. In July 1959, Perón issued a public denunciation of Frondizi and released what he said was the text of the pact.[26] The statement provoked calls for Frondizi's resignation from the president's critics, but the embattled UCRI leader hung on, insisting that he had never signed the document.

During the first year of the Frondizi administration the star of Perón's heir began to fade and, coincidentally, a new Peronist leader emerged. As John William Cooke edged closer to the outer fringes of the movement, a metalworker named Augusto Vandor displayed signs of astuteness that would soon carry him to the front ranks of organized labor.

The liberalized political climate fostered by the new regime made a reorganization of the Peronist movement possible. The *conductor* decided to eliminate the tactical command, an amorphous body charged with the day-to-day operations of the movement within Argentina, and created in its stead a national delegation, made up of leaders drawn from the trade-union and political sectors. Cooke was to be the link between Perón and the national delegation.[27]

By now Bebe could no longer claim to be Perón's heir. His enemies circulated rumors that he had been "burned" in Ciudad Trujillo, an expression denoting a loss of favor with the *conductor*. He became enmeshed in petty intramural squabbles. Soon he was feuding with prominent members of the women's branch and several veteran Peronist politicians.[28]

Cooke's departure from center stage was hastened by his commitment to revolutionary Peronism. He warmly embraced the idea of a revolutionary strike in early 1959 and participated in the packing-plant seizure.[29] The uprising occurred several weeks after Fidel Castro's triumphal entry into Havana, an event which was to affect Cooke deeply.[30] But the moment for revolution was not yet at hand in Argentina. The government repressed the strike and adopted measures that eventually caused labor leaders to reconsider their militance. The failure of the strike further isolated Cooke from the Peronist mainstream.

In the desperate months following Perón's downfall, John William Cooke was an inspired choice to spearhead Peronism's struggle for survival. But now he had outlived his usefulness. In 1959, Perón removed Cooke as his delegate. Bebe moved further and further to the left as the model of the Cuban Revolution become increasingly attractive to him. By mid-1960, having been exiled to the margin of the Peronist movement, he went to live in Havana.*

There was no direct link between Cooke's demise and the emergence of Vandor as the most effective labor leader to rise from Peronist ranks. Unlike Cooke, Vandor made his own way to the top. Cooke's militancy would never flag. Vandor knew how to accommodate himself to political necessities. Cooke was a brilliant theorist. Vandor represented a flesh-and-blood constituency.

At the Philips factory in Buenos Aires where he worked Vandor used to flirt with a girl everybody called Little Red Riding Hood, so it was natural that his friends gave him the nickname El Lobo ("The Wolf"). It stuck with him for the rest of his life. Augusto Vandor quickly demonstrated that he was meant to lead the pack.

He had come to the federal capital in 1940, at the age of eighteen, from a small town in Entre Ríos Province, and enlisted in the marines. He returned to civilian life seven years later and took a job as a metalworker. Tall, fair-skinned and clear-eyed, he soon became active in the powerful UOM (Unión de Obreros Metalúrgicos), or Metalworkers' Union. One of his contemporaries has written admiringly of his "lively intelligence and extraordinary decisiveness."[31] His leadership derived from remarkable intuition and a capacity to inspire trust.[32] A passion for horse-racing was his only indulgence.

During the early days of the Liberating Revolution, El Lobo was ar-

---

* A biography of Che Guevara claims that Cooke and several other Peronists signed a pact with Che in 1960 for the violent overthrow of the Frondizi government. D. James, *Che Guevara*, pp. 182–83. In a letter to Cooke (one of only two he sent to his former heir in 1960), Perón denounced reports of the pact as "another Yankee 'cock-and-bull story.'" J. Perón, *Correspondencia Perón-Cooke*, Vol. II, p. 153.

rested and imprisoned. Upon his release he played an active role in the Peronist Resistance. He soon won the top position in the UOM and exercised substantial influence over the Sixty-two Organizations after the CGT had been dissolved. He supported the seizure of the meatpacking plant in January 1959 and once again saw the inside of a prison cell.

Vandor first met Perón in 1958 at a Peronist conference in Ciudad Trujillo. During lengthy discussions on the restructuring of the movement El Lobo listened intently but said very little. One night he sat with Perón and several others on the terrace of the Hotel Jaragua. They sipped whiskey and talked about Argentina. Vandor suddenly turned to Perón and said, "Look, General, I understand how sad it must be for you to be here, so far away from the fatherland." "My son," Perón replied, "I'm like an Indian fakir. Wherever I am at the moment, that is my country." As he returned to his hotel later, Vandor turned to a companion and blurted, "That son of a bitch! How could he say a thing like that?"[33]

Whatever Vandor may have felt toward the *conductor,* he was careful to keep his Peronist credentials in order. He recognized the source of his political power. Perón for his part treated Vandor with great respect, because he appreciated the strong ties binding El Lobo to his union and vice versa. The relationship between the two men would become one of the most intriguing aspects of Perón's struggle to remain in control of the movement that bore his name.

From the moment of his arrival in Ciudad Trujillo, there was speculation as to the *conductor's* next move.[34] The Dominican Republic seemed an unlikely permanent refuge, and much too provincial for his tastes. Moreover, the "friendly soil" on which he now trod turned out to have its drawbacks, as the stifling control Trujillo exercised inevitably subjected Perón and his visitors to tight surveillance. One Peronist described him as "a sad and lonely man."[35] After his break with Frondizi, the Argentine government renewed its efforts to oust him from the continent. The overthrow of dictatorships in Venezuela and Cuba put Trujillo under great pressure, and the *benefactor* had no need for the additional aggravation Perón's presence caused.

Fidel Castro's triumph in January 1959 destabilized the Caribbean. Relations between Havana and Ciudad Trujillo quickly worsened, in part because the deposed Cuban president Fulgencio Batista took refuge in the Dominican Republic. The new government of Venezuela pursued a policy of hostility toward Trujillo. Perón was astute enough to read the handwriting on the wall. Having barely survived the fall of Pérez Jiménez, he was not about to tempt fate a second time.

No other American nation was willing to grant him a visa. His only alternative was to seek asylum in Europe. Franco's Spain was the obvious choice, as the Spanish *caudillo* could hardly refuse the man who had stood by him in his hour of need. The Spaniards, however, were diplomatic enough to clear the matter first with the Argentine government, which proved eager to facilitate the "fugitive tyrant's" departure from the hemisphere. In late 1959, Perón secured permission to enter Spain.[36]

The Brazilian airline Varig furnished an eighty-five-seat Super Constellation for the transatlantic flight. Trujillo defrayed the cost of the charter, in the amount of $28,000. On the evening of January 25, 1960, Perón and the tiny group that was to accompany him gathered at the airport.[37] Isabel looked elegant in a flowery silk dress. Américo Barrios remained at the *conductor*'s side. Alberto Campos, an Argentine politician who would serve for a short time as Perón's delegate to his followers, and a North American friend of Barrios also boarded the plane. Both happened to be in Ciudad Trujillo and took advantage of a free trip to Spain. Perón's two poodles completed the entourage. (A third poodle had not survived the Dominican sojourn and lay buried under a tree in the garden of the house where Perón and Isabel had lived.) Later that night the Constellation raced down the runway and soared into the darkness, en route to intermediary stops in Bermuda and the Azores, with Madrid as its final destination.

Halfway to Hamilton, Perón's bad luck with air travel overtook him. One of the plane's four engines failed. Two U.S. coast guard aircraft escorted the Constellation back to Ciudad Trujillo. After a twenty-four-hour delay for repairs, the travelers returned to their seats and the journey began again.

The flight between Bermuda and the Azores took eleven hours. Upon arriving, Perón received a telephone message from the Spanish ambassador in Lisbon. The Franco government did not want him to land in Madrid and diverted his flight to Seville. This abrupt change of plans called into question the warmth of the reception awaiting him.

41

Spain

There were no military planes to escort Perón's Constellation as it approached Seville, nor did cheering crowds await him, nor was Francisco Franco on hand. An official from the Foreign Ministry and an air force general in mufti welcomed him as he stepped on Spanish soil for the first time in two decades.[1] The expatriate and his companions, along with their twenty pieces of luggage, made their way by limousine to the Alfonso XIII, the finest hotel in Seville, where they were to spend the night.

The next morning the man from the Foreign Ministry told Perón that a suite had been reserved for him at a hotel in Torremolinos, not far from the city of Málaga on the Mediterranean coast. The wording of this diplomatic invitation left no possibility of a negative response. The Argentines set out immediately in a rented car toward the picturesque town that would one day become a booming tourist center on the Costa del Sol.

The muted yet clear message in the selection of a place of residence for Perón was that the Spanish government wanted to minimize the international problems he might create and wanted him out of the way. Franco's treatment of the *conductor* was correct but cool. Perhaps his attitude reflected in part the strain in relations between the *caudillo* and Perón in the twilight years of the latter's second presidency, when Argentina and Spain squabbled over the terms of a commercial treaty. A Franco intimate has quoted the *generalísimo* as believing this to be a forerunner of the attack on the Catholic church, a turn of events Franco deplored and blamed on the nefarious influence of Masons. The *caudillo* called Perón "a weak man who first let himself be dominated by his wife, who was more intelligent than he, and now lets himself be dominated by the [Masonic] lodges."[2]

Perón remained for a few days at the hotel and then moved to a nearby house that was made available to him. The leisurely pace of life on the Costa del Sol allowed him to resume his copious correspondence, but he could not have cherished the isolation of his new surroundings. Having spent two years in a backwater, he longed to return to the mainstream.

The government may have preferred that he remain in Torremolinos but made no effort to stop him several weeks later when he journeyed to the capital. A Spanish friend offered him the use of a two-story, nine-room dwelling in El Plantío, a section of Madrid twelve kilometers from the center of the city on the highway to Galicia in the northwest. Perón, Isabel, Américo Barrios and the poodles moved in together.

In an interview with a North American professor on September 1, 1960, Perón emphatically denied that he had enriched himself while in office.[3] Some of his activities during this period shed a glimmer of light upon the wealth that he supposedly had at his disposal, but the existence of which has never been established to any degree of certainty.

Whatever assets he may have accumulated within Argentina either on his own account or as Evita's heir were beyond his reach as a result of a decree confiscating his property.[4] Allegations that he carried large quantities of cash with him in exile or had access to a fortune stashed for him in Swiss banks[5] have no apparent factual basis, although it is conceivable that one of his intimates took custody of funds belonging to him and held them in trust. In none of the countries where he took refuge did he display access to wealth.

The suspicion that he was unable to reach Evita's bank deposits in Switzerland adds to the puzzle.[6] According to one unsubstantiated account, because Evita had ordered the destruction of her birth certificate (in order to conceal her true age and her illegitimacy), Perón could not prove that a person named María Eva Duarte de Perón ever existed.[7] Another rumor holds that an Argentine industrialist whose property Perón had once expropriated and who had powerful Swiss banking connections prevented the *conductor* from reaching the funds.[8]

Evidence dating from the early exile period lends some support to the theory that he was trying to establish a claim to Evita's Swiss fortune. While Perón was languishing in the Dominican Republic, Américo Barrios made two trips to Switzerland in an effort to arrange for the ex-president's entry there. According to Barrios, Perón had a friend who was living in Switzerland and who had promised him financial help.[9] But the Swiss government would not issue a visa.

Even after landing in Spain, Perón could not get Switzerland out of his mind. A U.S. consul reporting on his arrival quoted a "well-informed source" as declaring that the ex-president had expressed an intention to travel to Switzerland at a later date.[10] At some point early in 1960, Isabel made a trip to Geneva.[11] Barrios had stated that she went to visit friends. Nini Montiam, a Spanish actress who had been close to Evita and who kept in contact with Perón during the years in Spain, claims that the *conductor* asked her to accompany Isabel and help her trace Evita's bank accounts; he assumed that Montiam knew where they were; the actress in fact knew nothing about the accounts, so Isabel went alone and came back empty-handed.[12]

There is no direct evidence to corroborate Montiam's testimony. However, Perón's taped memoirs (which he recorded during the early 1960s and presented to the actress as a gift) contain a curious passage denouncing Switzerland as a "hybrid" country and the Swiss as "bandits." He fulminated that "Switzerland is a place where they hide everything they rob from others."[13] The implication that he counted himself among the victims leaps from the page. There is a strong temptation to conclude that Perón believed Evita had deposited money in Swiss banks and that he was unable to lay his hands on it.

Further illumination of Perón's acquisitiveness comes from a decision by Evita's mother in 1961 to seek an annulment of the paper she had signed ceding to Perón her right to her daughter's estate. The government had taken the position that all property left by Evita (including several valuable pieces of real estate) had passed to the ex-president and therefore fell within the interdiction that had been placed upon Perón's possessions. Juana asserted that half of Evita's estate belonged to her. She secured the legal services of Eduardo Colom, who opined that she had a good chance of persuading the authorities to release half of Evita's property to her if she could establish a legitimate interest in it. He wrote to Perón and proposed a deal: if the *conductor* would admit to the validity of his mother-in-law's claim, she would give him half of whatever she recovered from the regime. According to Colom, Perón "reacted violently" and rejected the offer.[14]

The early phase of the exile in Madrid was difficult for Perón. He had hardly settled into his new home when President Frondizi made an official visit to the Spanish capital. The Franco government requested the *conductor* to absent himself from the city during Frondizi's stay. Perón left for a town in the region of Galicia in the northwest.

A new inner circle began to take shape around him. Emilio Romero, editor of the daily newspaper *Pueblo*, was a longtime Peronist sympathizer. Colonel Henrique Herrera Marín had led a Spanish military mission in the Dominican Republic, where he had struck up a friendship with the Argentine exile. Dr. Francisco Flores Tascón became Perón's personal physician. Jorge Antonio soon took up residence in Madrid and handled financial matters for the *conductor*.

Not many months passed before Américo Barrios disappeared from the scene. He appears to have been yet another casualty of the infighting that marked life in Perón's entourage. A veteran journalist, Barrios had brought a certain level of competence to the post of private secretary. The same could not be said of his successor, an ex-soccer player named José Manuel Algarbe.

Perón found the house in El Plantío pleasant enough and liked to putter in the small garden. But the location was inconvenient for him, and in late 1960 he shifted his base of operations to a comfortable apartment on Dr. Arce Street, one block from the Plaza de la República Argentina. The new address was highly appropriate. Dr. José Arce had been Perón's ambassador to the United Nations and had defended the Franco regime from efforts to ostracize it. The apartment rented for about $330 (U.S.) a month,[15] a tidy sum for Madrid in the early 1960s. By no means luxurious, the building was nonetheless fashionable enough to number Ava Gardner among its tenants.

The environment into which Perón now settled gave rise to a problem that had heretofore not bothered him during his odyssey. In conservative, Catholic Spain, open and notorious cohabitation was regarded with great disfavor. His relationship with Isabel was beginning to cause a scandal, and there were veiled hints that the Franco regime was uncomfortable with the arrangement. Dr. Flores Tascón's wife was particularly insistent that the ex-president marry his "secretary."[16]

On November 15, 1961, Perón finally yielded to the pressure. Señora Flores Tascón arranged all the details, which required her to secure the permission of a bishop with whom she was acquainted and the services of a priest. The ceremony took place later that night in the Flores Tascón home. The host and hostess stood as witnesses.

Still apparently yoked by the excommunication decree of June 16, 1955, Perón was technically ineligible to receive the sacraments, which include matrimony. Isabel, however, was a practicing Catholic. In order to lift from her the burden of sinful cohabitation, the bishop sanctioned a so-called marriage of convenience.[17]

At the time they formalized the bond between them, Juan Perón was sixty-six, while Isabel had turned thirty. Chabela, as her friends called her, had been with him for nearly six years. Seemingly content to look after household details, never once had she intruded upon the political discussions that consumed Perón. To the Peronist faithful, she was a woman of mystery about whom very little was known. Details of her background began slowly to emerge.[18]

Born on February 4, 1931, in the city of La Rioja, María Estela Martínez Cartas was the youngest of six children born to Carmelo Martínez, a bank clerk, and María Josefa Cartas. In 1934, the family moved to a modest middle-class neighborhood in Buenos Aires. Four years later, Carmelo died. María Estela completed six years of grade school. No record of any further formal education has come to light. As a teenager, she studied piano and dancing. A childhood friend recalled her as "on the quiet side and gentle."[19]

It was during this formative period that María Estela left home and went to live with José Cresto and his wife Isabel. Her brothers and sisters supposedly provoked the move by pestering her to find a job in order to help defray household expenses. The Crestos not only gave her meals and a place to sleep but also introduced her to spiritism. A practitioner of the occult arts, José had founded his own school in 1944. Isabel was a small-time Madre María, offering counsel and cures to those who sought her help. María Estela eagerly embraced the esoteric beliefs to which the Cresto household exposed her. Although she did not sever all ties with her family, she regarded the Crestos as surrogate parents. The death of Isabel in 1957 affected her deeply.

At the age of twenty, she enrolled in the National School of Dance, but after only one year she decided to strike out on her own and essay a career in show business. She took the name "Isabel" in tribute to the departed Señora Cresto and performed for several months with a Spanish troupe in Montevideo. For unknown reasons she joined another ensemble that was about to tour the west coast of South America. The decision was a fateful one, for it took her to Medellín, Colombia, and a rendezvous with Joe Herald.

Isabel ceased communicating with her family shortly after she met Perón. In 1965 during a visit to Argentina, she neither visited her mother as she lay terminally ill with cancer nor attended the funeral. She had no further contact with her siblings. José Cresto, however, subsequently spent time with her in Madrid.

One of the earliest articles profiling Isabel focused entirely upon her domesticity. She was depicted as an expert at preparing *empanadas* (meat pies) that were so irresistible that Ava Gardner often came downstairs to sample them. Her twin passions were said to be talking about medicine and eating honey.[20] These first published descriptions did not mention her continuing interest in the occult, which led her to the study of Zen Buddhism. Perón's reaction was one of benign amusement.

There is no evidence that Perón had strong feelings toward Isabel. He wanted a woman at his side, Isabel was there, and they could not remain together unless he married her. Warmth was not a factor in their relationship.

Although Perón had managed to circumvent the excommunication decree in marrying Isabel, he knew he would have to make his peace with the church if he ever hoped to return to power in Argentina. His strategy in this regard was to pursue two contradictory courses of action. He and many of his supporters denied that the June 16 decree applied to him. They argued that the Pope alone has authority to excommunicate a head of state; since the decree in question neither emanated personally from the Holy Father nor named Perón specifically, it could not have had any effect upon him.[21] (The relevant provisions of canon law support their contention.[22])

At the same time he made overtures to the Vatican to have the decree lifted. Jorge Antonio and Raúl Matera, a Peronist politician, traveled to Rome to deliver to Pope John XXIII a personal letter from Perón expressing repentance and pleading for absolution, in the event the decree had in fact excommunicated him.[23] On February 13, 1963, a bishop visited the Argentine exile with a copy of a Vatican decree lifting the excommunication. Perón knelt before the bishop and repeated what he had written in his letter. The bishop absolved him, and Juan Perón was once again constitutionally qualified to be president of Argentina.

News of Perón's departure from the hemisphere must have disconcerted his faithful followers and left them with a sense of abandonment. The Coordinating and Supervision Council, which had replaced the National Delegation as the *conductor*'s tactical arm within Argentina, issued a statement insisting that his stay in Europe would be "of brief duration" and that he had no intention of giving up the fight.[24] Yet the vast distance that now separated him from Buenos Aires would make his task exceedingly difficult.

At the dawn of the 1960s, the struggle being waged by the Peronists was growing in complexity. The militants had not abandoned the resistance and encouraged a brand of combative Peronism within the labor movement. At the same time, moderate Peronist union leaders were disposed to negotiate with the government rather than overthrow it. On the political front, although the Peronist party was proscribed, neo-Peronist parties were permitted to exist, mostly at the provincial level. Some responded faithfully to the *conductor*'s directives, others professed loyalty but more often than not acted independently, and a few openly advocated Peronism without Perón.[25]

Frondizi, meanwhile, clung to his goal of winning over a substantial segment of the working class and reconstructing the coalition that had swept him into office. But his economic program, calling for disproportionate sacrifices on the part of workers, doomed his political strategy. Even union officials willing to work out a modus vivendi with the government could not go along with him. Labor unrest, often marred by violence, forced him to declare a state of siege and resort to unpopular internal-security measures. This increased his reliance upon the military, which had never discarded its distrust of him. The president kept reminding labor leaders of the fate that would befall them if they pushed too hard and he fell from office. Although he would not yield to their economic demands, he did return the CGT to worker control early in 1961.

Thus in midterm Frondizi's presidency was a delicate balancing act that mesmerized onlookers. What made it even more spectacular was the intrusion of international factors. Frondizi's hopes for industrial development could not be fulfilled without investment from abroad. But when the Cuban Revolution turned sharply to the left and Washington sought collective inter-American action to isolate Castro, the Argentine president invoked his country's traditional postulates of nonintervention and respect for national sovereignty. Indeed, he volunteered to mediate between the Cubans and the North Americans, received Cuban Minister of Industry Ernesto Che Guevara (a fellow Argentine) at the Olivos residence and ordered Argentina's abstention on the vote expelling Cuba from the Organization of American States. Yet during this same period he reiterated his opposition to the spread of Communism, approved the Alliance for Progress and developed a warm personal relationship with the new U.S. President, John F. Kennedy, whom he greatly admired.[26]

Supporters of Frondizi's foreign policy saw it as consistent with the nationalistic impulses shared by a majority of Argentines. Critics claimed he was sympathetic to Castro in order to be able to invoke the Cuban alternative as inevitable if Washington refused to aid Latin America.[27] The Argentine military reacted in a much more simplistic fashion. A majority of the officer corps saw in the president's failure to back the North American crusade against Cuba proof that he was pro-Communist. They were already worried about the revitalization of left-wing radicalism within Argentina, since the appeal of Castroism had lent new life to the Communist party, student groups and even segments of the labor movement. They therefore demanded that the president immediately terminate relations with Havana, and on February 9, 1962, Argentina broke its ties with Cuba. Frondizi had temporarily averted a coup, but the crisis had not yet passed.

In March, Argentine voters would go to the polls to choose sixteen governors and nearly half the seats in the federal Chamber of Deputies. Although the Peronists were no longer supporting him, the president would not surrender his hope that the Intransigent Radicals could attract enough Peronist votes to keep their congressional majority and control of most of the provincial governments. He now took the calculated risk of permitting the Peronists to run their own candidates.

The proscription against the Peronist party remained in effect, but for the first time neo-Peronist parties could present openly Peronist nominees. Frondizi explained his fateful decision as a logical step in his attempt to integrate the Peronists back into the political process.[28] In his judgment their behavior had earned for them the right to participate in elections; to keep them outside the system might provoke them to turn to the left and perhaps even resort to violence.

It is difficult to fault Frondizi for his desire to lift the political ostracism of millions of his fellow citizens. As a long-range goal, healing the deep division between Peronists and anti-Peronists was indispensable to the restoration of a true democracy in Argentina. Whether this was the appropriate moment for the dramatic step the president now took, however, is subject to question. The military had long been as unhappy with his "softness" toward Peronism as with his policy toward Cuba. The break with Castro had only for the moment appeased the generals.

He must have reckoned that the UCRI would demonstrate enough popular support at the polls to discourage a military coup.[29] Victories scored by the Intransigent Radicals in pilot elections in December 1961 and January and February 1962 may have nourished his optimism. The critical projection he made was that more Peronists would vote for UCRI candidates if he allowed Peronists to run than if he continued to ban open Peronist participation.

Frondizi waited until several weeks before the election to finalize his decision. This complicated matters for the Peronists, who had to develop an electoral strategy without knowing whether they could present their own candidates. A stream of visitors to Madrid bombarded Perón with advice about the course he should chart. The *conductor* responded with vacillation, ambiguity and, in the end, weather-vane leadership.

The most pressing issue before him was whether the Peronists should contest the race for governorship of the province of Buenos Aires. This was a prize worth fighting for, since Buenos Aires was still the wealthiest, most populous of the nation's provinces, and remained as much a Peronist stronghold as it had been in the days of Governor Mercante.

Certain Peronist labor leaders were eager to enter the lists under the banner of Unión Popular (Popular Union), or UP, a neo-Peronist party. Textile worker Andrés Framini staked out an early claim to the gubernatorial nomination. Augusto Vandor strongly supported him, even though the two men were rivals.

On the other hand, a number of prominent Peronist politicians urged that the temptation to pluck Buenos Aires Province be resisted. They reasoned that a victory by the Popular Union would provoke a coup and wipe out the steady progress the Peronists had been making since the darkest days of the Liberating Revolution. The rivalry between the politicians and the labor leaders undoubtedly influenced those in the political wing who advocated caution. Framini's candidacy would greatly strengthen labor's hand in the jockeying for power within the Peronist movement.

Perón straddled the fence. He agreed with the politicians' analysis,[30] but refrained from ordering a blank vote either generally or in the Buenos Aires provincial election. When Vandor and Framini led a delegation of union leaders to Madrid, he let himself be swayed by their arguments and gave them a green light. But he added a wrinkle of his own.

On January 26, at a rally in Avellaneda, the Popular Union officially launched its campaign in Buenos Aires Province. For the faithful in attendance it was a return to the good old days as Peronist banners fluttered, bass drums supplied a rhythm for Peronist chants and a galaxy of notables from the Peronist past—Domingo Mercante, Juan Bramuglia, Delia Parodi, and others—delivered rousing speeches. But the high point of the proceedings was the announcement that the Popular Union candidates for governor and vice-governor of the province would be Andrés Framini and Juan Perón.[31]

It was a typical Perón gambit. Those who supported as well as those who opposed direct Peronist involvement in the Buenos Aires election considered the surprise move a master stroke. Everybody knew the government could not tolerate Perón's candidacy. The anti-participationists convinced themselves that Perón's goal was to force Frondizi to ban the entire UP slate. The pro-participationists interpreted the ploy as a means of making it absolutely clear to the Peronist electorate that Framini was Perón's candidate.

In a matter of days Frondizi's interior minister met secretly with the secretaries of the army, navy and air force. They signed an accord expressing resolute opposition to the return of Perón and the restoration of Peronism in any form. Two weeks later the election board of Buenos Aires Province refused to approve the nomination of Perón because of the criminal charges pending against him. But during the same period Frondizi reaffirmed his decision to keep the neo-Peronist parties, including the Popular Union, on the ballot. The Peronists selected a new running mate for Framini and the stage was set for the first reasonably free elections in the post-Perón era.

The campaign settled down to a three-way fight among the Intransigent Radicals, the People's Radicals and the Peronists in their various guises. There were no clear-cut substantive issues: the Peronists offered nostalgia; the People's Radicals wrapped themselves in the Argentine flag; the UCRI, appealing to Peronists and anti-Peronists alike, seemed to stand for opportunism. Most of the nation went to the polls on March 18. When all of the votes were tallied, nostalgia triumphed.

In the congressional elections the Peronists captured forty-one seats and 32 percent of the vote. The UCRI took thirty-eight seats with 24.5 percent of the vote and lost its majority in the Chamber of Deputies. Though Frondizi's party carried the federal capital, the Peronists walked off with nine governorships, including Buenos Aires Province.

At the Ministry of War, the Campo de Mayo garrison and other power centers of the military establishment, uniformed officers met to decide how to nullify the Peronist triumph. Hard-line elements urged an immediate coup. Cooler heads struggled to find a constitutional solution.

It is conceivable that Frondizi had reckoned that he stood to gain no matter how the Argentine people cast their votes: if the Peronists flopped at the polls, they would be discredited as a political force; if they won, he could annul the elections and thereby curry favor with the armed forces and civilian anti-Peronists alike.[32] He may have actually believed that the UCRI would triumph.

Responding to military pressures which he himself may have encouraged for political reasons,[33] Frondizi announced that the government was intervening in Buenos Aires and four other provinces won by the Peronists. This destroyed his claim to principled commitment to the democratic process, and even some leaders of his own party now abandoned him. Moreover, his decision failed to appease the hard-liners within the officer corps, especially in the navy, which was determined to oust him. The president tried to form a coalition cabinet, but Ricardo Balbín and the rest of the UCRP leadership turned their backs on him. General Aramburu made a tentative effort to mediate between the armed forces and the government, but to no avail.[34]

The curtain finally fell on March 29, when the military high command demanded Frondizi's resignation. When he refused, they took him into custody and flew him to the island of Martín García. The vice-presidency had remained vacant after the 1958 resignation of Frondizi's running mate. Thus a reluctant José María Guido, the president of the Senate and by law next in line for Frondizi's job, appeared before the Supreme Court to take the oath of office as provisional chief executive. His feeble claim to the presidency was not assured until after a stormy five-hour meeting of the generals and admirals, who were split over whether to seize the reins of power openly or to rule behind a constitutional façade. Officers from the Campo de Mayo garrison, led by General Juan Carlos Onganía, insisted upon legality and carried the day. The hard-liners, whom Argentines dubbed "gorillas," resolved to bide their time.

The individual who gained the richest dividend from the events of March 1962 was Augusto Vandor. Although Framini had been the victorious candidate, El Lobo had furnished the organizational skill and had pumped UOM money into the campaign. He was fast becoming the man to be reckoned with by the government, by his Peronist colleagues and by Perón himself. The *conductor* had set Framini up to counterbalance Vandor, but the latter carefully refrained from converting their rivalry into mutually destructive combat. Moreover, after the coup, when Perón offered to put him in charge of the Peronist movement in Argentina, Vandor declined.[35] At this point the top position would bring only trouble, whereas a lower profile gave him ample opportunity to maneuver. His astuteness marked him as a potentially formidable rival for Perón. He would not betray the promise he was now displaying.

42

"Operation Return"

On April 29, 1964, the Paraguayan consul in Madrid issued passport number 000940 to Juan P. Sosa, listed as a sixty-three-old professor from Asunción, and to his wife, Dalmira Remo de Sosa. The photographs attached to the document told a different story. They depicted Juan D. Perón and Delia Parodi.[1] The validation of the passport was an essential phase of a Peronist melodrama entitled "Operation Return."

In late 1963, Perón began hinting that he planned to terminate his exile within twelve months. At a December 31 party, he remarked that this was "the last New Year's Eve I shall celebrate away from my fatherland."[2] Peronists who visited their *conductor* in Madrid brought back reports that he intended to repatriate himself in 1964.[3] Soon walls throughout the country began to sprout the legend *"Perón Vuelve"* ("Perón's Coming Back").

The prospect delighted his followers as intensely as it nauseated those for whom his name was anathema, yet the whole affair had a distinctly unreal quality. The deep division between Peronists and anti-Peronists still rent the political landscape. The armed forces still opposed anything that threatened to undo the Liberating Revolution. There were even neo-Peronists who felt they could manage quite nicely without Perón. It seemed possible that the operation was no more than an elaborate bluff.

The two years separating the ouster of Frondizi from the start of Peronist agitation for "Operation Return" were marked by chaos and confusion. The main goal of the Guido regime and its military backers was to prepare for general elections that would permit a restoration of civilian rule. They were willing to tolerate a degree of Peronist participation but could not decide how much. Moreover, the conflict between the legalist and hard-line factions within the armed forces intensified.[4] The group that stood behind Guido became known as the *azules* ("blues"). Led by General Onganía, they advocated military professionalism and noninvolvement in politics. The *colorados* ("reds") were ultraconservative, implacably anti-Peronist and anticommunist. They preferred an outright military dictatorship.

What began as a political struggle exploded into a shooting war in September 1962, when red and blue units clashed in Buenos Aires and La Plata. Onganía's Sherman tanks, backed up by Campo de Mayo and air force fighters, carried the day. The *azules* then reaffirmed that free elections would be held, but also made it clear that they would not permit a revival of Peronism.[5] They did not disclose how they would resolve the contradiction embodied in their declaration.

The critical question was to what extent, if any, the Peronists could participate in the elections, scheduled for July. The situation remained extremely fluid, even more so because of the Peronist response to the Guido regime.

After Frondizi's unceremonious departure from the Casa Rosada, there were indications that the Peronist movement might turn sharply to the left. Andrés Framini, after a trip to Madrid, pronounced himself in favor of the class struggle and direct action against the forces of imperialism.[6] Radical elements within the Sixty-two Organizations called for the nationalization of key sectors of the economy, worker control over the means of production and confiscation of large landholdings.[7] Sporadic outbursts of violence conjured up the specter of the Cuban Revolution. Perón sent a personal emissary to Havana.

Yet while Framini made Marxist noises, other prominent Peronists projected a moderate image. Dr. Raúl Matera, a neurosurgeon who had assumed the post of secretary-general of the coordinating council of *justicialismo*, declared that Peronism was "a party of the true left, of the [papal encyclicals] *Rerum Novarum* and *Mater et Magister*, and the Alliance for Progress."[8] He set out to establish ties with the regime and with key members of the blue faction in an effort to secure the best deal possible for the Peronists in the coming elections.

The turn to the left was part of a complex game in which Perón pitted labor leader against politician, militant against moderate, left-winger against conservative, one personality against another. Any encouragement he gave Framini, for example, undercut Vandor as well as Matera. He was careful to nourish rivals to Matera within the political branch of the movement. Even in his swing to the left he meticulously avoided any gestures that might have revived Cooke's fortunes. Perón refused to utilize him as his Cuban connection. Instead, the *conductor* reached out to the fringes of his entourage in Madrid and appointed Héctor Villalón as his emissary.[9]*

---

* A newspaper reported that Villalón ingratiated himself with Castro, who put him in charge of the lucrative export of Cuban tobacco to Europe. *El Cronista*, August 10, 1964. Villalón's career as a wheeler-dealer has had remarkable longevity. In 1980 he turned up as an intermediary in secret negotiations involving the U.S., Iranian and

The leftward lean took on the aspect of a feint as it became increasingly evident that the Peronists were much better prepared to participate in an election than to start a revolution. The Unión Popular continued to serve as their main political vehicle. The regime decided to permit the UP to present candidates for all offices except president and vice-president. The UP then joined the Intransigent Radicals and several minor parties in a coalition, called the Frente Nacional y Popular (National and Popular Front), or FNP, for the purpose of running nominees for the two top posts.

The selection of the FNP candidates proved a major hurdle. Both the Peronists and the Intransigent Radicals felt the presidential nominee should come from their ranks. When the regime adopted a tougher line toward the Peronists in April 1963, it became clear that the FNP could not run Peronist candidates. The Intransigent Radicals indicated a preference for Oscar Alende, a former governor of Buenos Aires Province. But in May, Perón stunned the FNP by imposing upon it a "surprise" presidential candidate, Vicente Solano Lima.

A leader of the minuscule Popular Conservative party, Solano Lima had been making overtures toward the Peronists for the past five years. On his visits to the *conductor* in Spain the two men hit it off well.[10] The choice of Solano Lima was consistent with Perón's longstanding preference for surrogates who lacked political constituencies, independent judgment and the capacity to emerge from his shadow. It not only dismayed many Peronists but also split the UCRI. Alende's supporters abandoned the FNP and ran the ex-governor as the Intransigent Radical candidate. The Frondizi-Frigerio wing remained in the Front.

In the weeks preceding the election, the political outlook became even more blurred.[11] The regime disqualified Solano Lima. The Peronists reacted by releasing a letter from Perón directing his followers to cast blank votes.* Frondizi sent similar instructions to his supporters.

This left only three candidates of consequence in the race: Oscar Alende, representing one wing of the UCRI; General Pedro Aramburu, carrying the banner of a new party organized on his behalf; and Arturo Illia, a little-

---

Panamanian governments over the extradition of the Shah from Panamá and the release of the U.S. hostages. Randal, "Paris Lawyers Almost Upstaged Diplomats in Iran Crisis," *Washington Post*, April 16, 1980, p. A-12.

* Perón's role in the decision to order a blank vote gave rise to a dispute between the political and trade-union wings of the movement. According to one account, the *conductor* had provided letters containing contradictory instructions to be used as a situation demanded; Peronist labor leaders, who had never been keen about participating in the election, released the blank-vote epistle without actually consulting with Perón, to the dismay of the politicians. *Primera Plana*, July 30, 1964, p. 4; see also J. Rowe, "The Argentine Elections of 1963: An Analysis," Election Analysis Series No. 1, Institute for the Comparative Study of Politics (undated), p. 18.

known country doctor from Córdoba, nominated by the People's Radicals. When the votes were tabulated, Illia was the surprise winner, topping the list with 25.1 percent of the total. The blank vote reached 18.8 percent. If one adds the vote garnered by several provincial neo-Peronist parties allowed to present candidates, the Peronist vote came to about 24 percent. Alende took 16.4 percent, and Aramburu finished with only 13.9 percent.

On October 12, 1963, Arturo U. Illia became Argentina's fifth chief executive since Juan Perón left the country. He was a minority president confronting a Chamber of Deputies in which his party held but 72 of 192 seats, a working class still loyal to the memory of an exile in Madrid, and an officer corps not entirely happy about staying out of politics. He had no experience in national affairs and took office without any apparent strategy for dealing with the economy, which had plunged into a recession during the Guido interregnum.

What the president did have to offer was a refreshingly different political style. He was an honest, unassuming, tolerant man who governed softly and cautiously, without drama or guile. The snowy-haired sixty-three-year-old physician brought a reassuring bedside manner to the Casa Rosada. The contrast between this gentle man and his two elected predecessors could not have been starker.

Illia hoped to broaden his party's base among middle-class voters and attract some support from workers. The prescription he adopted was the pursuit of expansionary economic policies that would stimulate immediate short-term growth.[12] This approach called for an increase in state control of the economy in ways that recalled the Peronist era. Government expenditures were increased, the money supply was expanded and price controls were imposed. The agricultural sector and big business quickly became disenchanted with Illia. Moreover, economic gains were slow in reaching the middle and lower classes. Illia's inability to cultivate any sort of working relationship with organized labor sealed his fate.

The Guido regime had normalized the CGT in early 1963, only to have the confederation launch what it termed a "battle plan" to pressure the government into adopting economic measures more favorable to workers. The CGT's new secretary-general, veteran Peronist José Alonso, led a week of protests in May of that year to publicize labor's demands.

The unions suspended their program of agitation during the election campaign and the change in administrations. Despite Illia's adoption of economic policies incorporating certain of the CGT's own proposals, neither the confederation nor Perón adopted a conciliatory line toward the government. Labor leaders were more interested in power than in concessions, and were unwilling to abandon or curtail their political activities. They refused to jeopardize a role they had assumed at the start of the Perón era and to which they had tenaciously clung since his downfall.[13]

Perón gave Illia only until November 15 to lift all restrictions on Peronist political activity, a demand he must have known would be impossible to meet, and declared that his followers would otherwise take to the streets.[14] The CGT then resolved to resume the battle plan.

The next phase of the plan called for sudden work stoppages and seizures of factories.[15] During May and June of 1964, workers staged brief, nonviolent occupations of some 11,000 sites. Responding calmly and without resort to repressive measures, Illia treated the challenge as a matter to be left to the normal workings of the judicial system. But this did not work to his political advantage, and he was rapidly developing a reputation for ineffectiveness. Some critics faulted him for being too soft on the CGT. Peronist labor leaders were calling him The Turtle, and the nickname stuck.

This was the context out of which Operation Return emerged. The Peronists sought to take advantage of a weak government, but their own indecision and disunity hindered them.

Augusto Vandor remained in the forefront of those who were promoting Operation Return. His situation at this moment was peculiarly delicate. In late 1963 he had beaten back an attempt by Framini to wrest leadership of the Sixty-two Organizations from him.[16] About to face a similar challenge to his preeminence in the political wing of the movement, he had no choice but to throw himself wholeheartedly into preparations for the return. He would soon assume full responsibility for the entire affair.

Yet it was clear that if the *conductor* came home, Vandor's hopes to take over the movement would evaporate. This left him vulnerable to charges that he was trying to maneuver Perón into going back on his promise or into accepting government-imposed conditions so degrading they would assure Perón's demise as a political force.

Thus Operation Return took on the appearance of a chess game. Perón had originated the idea and now found himself under pressure from both the political and labor wings of his movement to go ahead with the plan. He could neither back down nor stumble without risking a fatal blow to his prestige.

What motivated him to create this dilemma for himself is unclear. The reasons he offered—that he wanted to unite the country and save Illia from a military coup[17]—merit dismissal out of hand. As he well knew, the mere hint of his return caused the bitterness between Peronists and anti-Peronists to reach new depths. If Illia had tolerated his return, the armed forces would have immediately ousted him.

A Peronist politician claims that the real reason for Perón's wish to return at this time was that he was suffering from an ailment he thought was cancer, and that he did not want to die on foreign soil.[18] On January 20, he underwent an operation performed by Barcelona surgeon Antonio Puigvert for the removal of a tumor of the prostate and growths on his bladder. The tumor turned out to be benign. If this was his reason for wanting to go home, it evaporated along with the cancer scare.

A factor suggesting he might make Madrid his permanent residence was the construction of a new home in a neighborhood called Puerta de Hierro on the outskirts of Madrid. He was paying a high rent for the apartment on Dr. Arce Street and needed quieter, more commodious quarters.* The lot was purchased in Isabel's name with funds Perón at one time claimed were given to him by Spanish friends,[19] and on another occasion hinted were sent by Rogelio Frigerio.[20] It took six months to complete the project, which the ex-president supervised during daily visits to the site.[21] His behavior did not square with the expectation of an imminent return to his homeland.

Thus Perón may not have been serious when he first floated the idea of a return, or he may have changed his mind and abandoned the idea in early 1964. But once his followers took him at his word, the project may have acquired a momentum of its own. It would not have been the first time in his career that he let himself be swept along by circumstances.

Perhaps he feared losing his grip over the Peronist movement and concluded that the only antidote was to launch the attempt, even though he knew the regime would not let him reenter Argentina. The return would thereby become a symbolic gesture designed to prove to the descamisados that he still cared for them and that his exile was involuntary. Perhaps he desired to counter the persistent accusation that he was a coward. An awareness that a last-minute cancellation would be interpreted by some as a failure of nerve on his part may have held him on course.

In mid-August a constellation of Peronist luminaries conferred with the *conductor* in Madrid. Among those present were Alberto Iturbe, now Perón's personal representative; Delia Parodi, who had replaced Matera as head of the coordinating council; and Augusto Vandor. On the evening of August 21, the visitors attempted to hold a press conference at a Madrid hotel. The police dispersed them, but they managed to distribute a communiqué declaring "General Perón has irrevocably ratified his decision to return to the fatherland this year as a determining factor for the unity and pacification of all Argentines."[22] When asked by journalists for a date, Perón's private secretary replied, "Not even we know."[23]

Illia, committed to a policy of reconciliation, was reluctant to make any public statements on the proposed return. Spokesmen for the Casa Rosada pointed out that Perón, like any Argentine citizen, was free to come home whenever he wished, but left the implication that he would have to face the criminal charges still pending against him.[24] The generals took the position that Perón was a problem for the civil authorities. How-

---

* According to one report, parties in Ava Gardner's apartment occasionally kept him awake. *Visión*, November 13, 1964.

ever, there was no doubt in anyone's mind how the officer corps felt about the ex-general.[25]

As the spring of 1964 arrived in the Southern Hemisphere, the issue of Perón's return rekindled old hopes and fears in Argentina. The Peronists launched a frenzied propaganda campaign under the aegis of a National Commission for the Return of Perón. Anti-Peronists cringed.

In early October, French President Charles de Gaulle arrived in Argentina on a tour of Latin America. Perón instructed his followers to greet the distinguished visitor as they would welcome their *conductor*.[26] It was an opportunistic gambit that succeeded.[27] Shouting slogans that linked the two men, the Peronists gave de Gaulle a warm reception.

In the weeks that followed, Operation Return created a giddy atmosphere that mesmerized not only Argentina but the rest of the continent. An ominous tone was set by Perón himself when he told a Mexican reporter: "Either I go back peacefully or I do it by means of a revolution."[28] Jorge Antonio, on the other hand, released a statement indicating that Perón would stay where he was "because objective conditions are missing."[29] Framini, Iturbe, Parodi and Vandor flew to Madrid in early November to settle on arrangements for the return. Other Peronists crossed the river to Montevideo and tried to persuade the Uruguayan authorities to admit their leader. The Argentine Foreign Ministry twisted arms in Paraguay to keep the Stroessner regime from opening its doors to Perón.[30] In mid-November officials in Buenos Aires betrayed their anxiety by reporting that Perón was on his way to Lima.[31] If the Peronists were waging psychological warfare, they were doing an excellent job.

Yet inside the Peronist camp at this moment there was rampant confusion. According to Iturbe, Operation Return was still up in the air when he made his November visit to Madrid.[32] He had no idea whether Perón still wanted to make the attempt and was stunned to find plans for the trip in a state of unreadiness.

At this point Perón put Jorge Antonio in charge of the details.[33] There was agreement that an attempt to land in Argentina involved too much risk. Therefore, the Peronist strategy called for a flight to either Uruguay or Paraguay.

The need to avoid the watchful eyes of not only the international press but also the intelligence services of several governments complicated matters for Antonio. He negotiated with Air France and Swissair for a charter, but officials of both companies told him they wanted no part of the deal if its purpose was to carry Perón back to the Western Hemisphere. He also approached other airlines and met with similar responses.[34]

On Monday evening, December 1, the U.S. embassy in Madrid informed Washington that a travel agency believed to be acting for the Peronists had reserved a block of seats on a regular Iberia flight departing at 1:00 A.M. on the second for Rio de Janeiro, Montevideo, Buenos Aires and

Santiago.[35] The booking specified Montevideo as the final destination. Similar reservations had been made on the same flight leaving on the sixth and the ninth. According to the reporting officer, the Argentine ambassador felt this was a smoke screen for Perón's true intention to take a chartered flight from Madrid to Asunción on the second.

Meanwhile, four of the five members of the National Commission for the Return of Perón—Framini, Iturbe, Vandor and Peronist politician Carlos Lascano—gathered at Antonio's apartment, which was under close surveillance by Argentine diplomats. The blare of recorded tango music and activity that appeared to be going on inside created a "fiesta of distraction," as Iturbe later put it.[36]

At 7:00 P.M., Jorge Antonio drove up to Peron's house in Puerta de Hierro.[37] A heavy police guard that had been posted several days earlier found nothing unusual in the arrival of Antonio, who had ostensibly come to fetch Delia Parodi, a guest of the Peróns. The ex-president, bedridden with the grippe, remained in his room, from which the sound of a television set reverberated. As Delia and Isabel exchanged hugs and kisses, Antonio's chauffeur had problems starting up the car engine. Isabel suggested that Antonio take Perón's gray Mercedes 220S, which was parked inside the garage. An employee brought the sleek sedan to the front steps and Antonio slid behind the wheel. Delia popped into the back seat and bade a final farewell to Isabel. They motored off. Perón was in the trunk.

It was not an easy position for a sixty-nine-year-old to assume, despite the pillow and blankets which cushioned the bumps. The grippe, the TV noise and the breakdown of Antonio's car were all parts of a carefully planned scenario that worked to perfection. Twenty blocks away a small, black SEAT 1500 sat empty in front of a billboard. Antonio pulled up behind it, released Perón from his hiding place ("Son of a bitch, what an uncomfortable way to travel!" were the *conductor's* first words when the trunk opened) and switched cars. The trio then set off toward the airport.

Meanwhile, at an inn not far from Barajas, the other members of the commission awaited their leader. They had managed to sneak unnoticed out of the city and had ordered a paella to celebrate the occasion. Perón, Parodi and Antonio arrived late because of an encounter with a motorcycle policeman who detained them momentarily because Antonio was driving with his headlight beams on high. Fortunately the officer did not recognize the celebrity in the front seat.

Later in the evening the commander-in-chief of the general staff of the Spanish army made his way to the inn and told the Argentines that boarding arrangements for Iberia flight 991 had been finalized. He accompanied them in an Iberia van that took them, via a back road, to the airport. The Franco regime seemed to be more than merely tolerating Operation Return.

There was one last obstacle to be cleared. The president of Iberia Airlines met the Perón party at the foot of the ramp of the DC-8 and announced that they could not board unless Jorge Antonio signed an agreement to indemnify the company for any losses it might incur as a result of the flight. At this stage of the game Antonio had little choice but to affix his signature, and the Peronists were permitted to enter the first-class section, which they had reserved in its entirety.

The Illia government reacted with characteristic indecisiveness to the news that Perón was approaching South America. Although the possibility of an attempted return had preoccupied administration officials for more than a month, the Casa Rosada had neglected to formulate contingency plans to deal with it. Public statements that Perón was as free as any Argentine citizen to reenter his homeland contradicted the regime's determined efforts to keep him in Spain. When word that Operation Return was in effect reached the president, he dumped the problem into the lap of his cabinet.[38] The military then took matters in hand and demanded that Perón be stopped in Brazil. Their insistence prevailed.

None of the first-class passengers aboard flight 991 slept during the journey. Perón, Antonio, the five members of the commission and two Spaniards who worked for Antonio had no idea what to expect on the other side of the Atlantic. The pistols that several of them were carrying attested to their anxiety that an unfriendly welcome might develop. The *conductor*, despite his aversion to flying, remained outwardly calm.

Galeão, the international airport of Rio de Janeiro, sits on the edge of the city adjacent to an industrial park that offers a dismal contrast to the scenic splendors that have made the former capital of Brazil South America's paramount tourist attraction. At 9:45 A.M. on December 2, in stifling heat which reminded the travelers that they had arrived in the tropics, Iberia flight 991 landed on a Galeão runway. As it taxied to a halt, Brazilian troops armed with submachine guns surrounded the plane.

The chief of protocol from the Ministry of Foreign Relations then entered the first-class section, and in suitably diplomatic language invited Perón to disembark. The *conductor* refused, citing international law. The Brazilian explained that his government was acceding to a request from the Argentine government and that the Peronists would be taken to a nearby air force base. Perón insisted that he was a passenger in transit on an airplane bearing the Spanish flag. The official left to consult with his superiors. In the meantime someone turned off the DC-8's air conditioner and the temperature in the first-class cabin began to soar. The Brazilian returned and informed the Argentines that if they did not leave the aircraft immediately, it would be towed to the air base. Perón and his party then departed from the plane under protest. They were relieved of their weapons before they set foot on Brazilian soil.

The Peronists with Perón later claimed that one of the military officers who escorted him to the base spoke Spanish with a North American accent,[39] a baseless concoction fortifying their leader's contention that North American imperialism was what kept him from returning to Argentina. In a letter written during his detention at Galeão, he accused Argentine officials of being "sepoys [a favorite Perón expression referring to natives of colonial India who served in the British army] in the service of the darkest interests of imperialism."[40]

The *conductor* and his friends remained under guard at an officer's club while the Brazilian government wondered what to do with them. The jet continued on its scheduled route. When it came back to Galeão later in the day on its return trip to Madrid, the Brazilians opted for a simple solution and put the Peronists back on the plane. Shortly before midnight, Argentina's most famous exile climbed up the ramp and plopped into a first-class seat. The DC-8 took off into the night and set its course toward Spain.

43

Vandor vs.
Perón

In the wake of Operation Return, there were some who could not resist
the temptation to conclude that the incident marked the end of Juan
Perón's political career. *Time* magazine reported that "in view of his
ludicrous humiliation, even Peronists now doubt he will ever again try to
return to Argentina; most agree that Perón has exploded the 'Perón myth'
once and for all."[1] An article in the *Christian Science Monitor* noted that
"Juan Domingo Perón's heyday appears to be over."[2]

But Juan Perón had no intention of retiring from the arena he had
dominated for two decades. Despite the restraints the Spanish government
imposed on him when he returned from Rio de Janeiro—he had to remain
in southern Spain for three weeks and reiterate his solemn (if tongue-in-
cheek) promise to refrain from political activity[3]—Perón soon demonstrated his unwillingness to step aside for a new generation of leaders. The
tactic he chose to reassert his authority proved remarkably effective. He
decided to use Isabel.

The results of the March 1965 elections persuaded Perón to play his
queen, for they created a context for Peronism without Perón. The government permitted full Peronist participation in the balloting for 99 seats in
the federal Chamber of Deputies. The Unión Popular continued to serve
as the major Peronist vehicle, while neo-Peronist parties in the provinces
also ran candidates. Under a new system of direct proportional representation, the UP won 36 seats with 31 percent of the vote. The neo-Peronist
parties added 8 seats and 7 percent of the total to the Peronist tally. The
UCRP trailed with 30 percent and 34 seats, although Illia's party maintained its plurality in the Chamber. A new party formed by Frondizi took
7 percent of the vote, and all the other parties dipped to new lows of
5 percent or less.[4]

Thus, Argentine politics seemed to be edging toward a two-party system.

The People's Radicals were in the process of absorbing large sectors of the old anti-Peronist coalition. The Peronists had held together their working-class constituency and were attracting support from people who in the past had enlisted in the small parties on the left. It was now conceivable that if the Peronists acted with restraint and were discreet in their relationship with Perón, they might aspire to a return to power via the 1967 gubernatorial and congressional elections.

At the same time Augusto Vandor had turned himself to the task of institutionalizing trade-union Peronism without Perón. It was a subtle game that he and Perón were now playing. Vandor continued to profess his loyalty to the man in Madrid. He knew he could not doff the Peronist colors without losing his followers. Perón understood Vandor's grass-roots strength and the importance of the metalworkers' union. He was reluctant to attack Vandor in public or to expel him from the movement.

In 1965 Peronist politicians were hoping to gain power through the ballot box. Union leaders who backed Vandor sought to reshape Peronism in ways that would establish the ascendancy of organized labor. Opposed to them were the so-called orthodox Peronists, advocating blind obedience to the *conductor*, and left-wing Peronists who viewed the integration of Peronism into the political system as counterrevolutionary.

Perón would later claim that he had prepared Isabel to play a political role,[5] but there is no indication that prior to 1965 he had taught her anything except how to ride a motor scooter and fence. Isabel had been conspicuously absent from political conferences held by the exiled Perón, and had taken no part in Operation Return. Nor did she display the slightest interest in the nuances of leadership as practiced by her husband. The domestic, decorative function had always seemed to suit her, especially as it permitted her to flatter her youthful appearance with the latest fashions in dress and hair styles.

What Isabel had to offer was the symbolism of her status as Perón's wife. Perón probably looked upon her as an empty vessel he could fill and manipulate at will. What he failed to realize was that others might exploit this same characteristic.

The ex-dancer's first foray into the political thicket attracted little notice. In May she flew to Asunción to see Jorge Antonio. The Franco regime had expelled him from Spain in the aftermath of Operation Return, whereupon he had taken refuge in the Paraguayan capital. He claims that the Illia government was seeking his extradition and that Perón dispatched Isabel with a letter to Stroessner on his behalf.[6]*

---

* One piece of evidence supporting the view that Antonio helped push Isabel into politics is a letter written by José Algarbe several weeks after Operation Return. Perón's private secretary had learned of Perón's departure from Madrid only after the DC-8 had left Barajas. He resigned from his post and in denouncing the deceit he attributed to friends of the *conductor* who promoted the ill-fated flight, he noted

In Asunción, Isabel stayed in a house rented by Antonio. When news of her arrival reached Argentina, a stream of Peronists began to converge upon the city. Most came in buses and trucks from the northern provinces. Vandor, Framini and other leaders made the trip from Buenos Aires. The pilgrims found Isabel to be shy and uncomfortable, her miniskirts accentuating an appearance that belied her age. Her stay lasted for about a month.

Although Perón paid his usual lip service to the goal of unity, his tactics during this critical period were more consistent with his traditional strategy of promoting disorder. It was now in the interest of those seeking a transition to Peronism without Perón to bring the movement together under the umbrella of a single political entity. The *conductor* knew that this would eventually relegate him to the ornamental role of elder statesman. The members of the return commission, known popularly as the Big Five, had been serving as a de facto executive committee. Perón ordered that the group be expanded to include leaders from other organizations, such as the provincial Peronist parties and the bloc of Peronist deputies.[7] The Big Five at first resisted and then carried out the *conductor*'s instructions selectively. Instead of fighting among themselves, they moved closer together. Moreover, Vandor was expanding his political influence. He had decided to support his own Peronist candidate in the Mendoza gubernatorial election scheduled for April 1966. A victory there would demonstrate the viability of Peronism without Perón.

In response, Perón dispatched Isabel to Buenos Aires. It was a clever stroke. The orthodox faction could use her to promote a loyalist candidate in Mendoza and to stem the tide of "Vandorism" on other fronts as well. The government made no effort to prevent her from entering the country.

In the middle of the Barrio Norte, not far from the empty lot where the presidential mansion once stood, the Hotel Alvear Palace evokes the elegance of pre-populist Argentina. In the second week of October, the tranquility characteristic of the hotel and its surroundings fell victim to street demonstrations and scuffles. To its chagrin, the management discovered that a guest who had registered in the name of María Estela Martínez was in reality the wife of Juan Perón.[8]

Word of Isabel's arrival unleashed passions that had barely begun to abate on the tenth anniversary of the Liberating Revolution. Militant members of Peronist youth organizations quickly assembled in the corridor leading to her room and appointed themselves her bodyguards. Anti-Peronists shouting "He shall not return!" and "Concubine, go home!" paraded outside. Fistfights developed, rocks sailed to and fro, a few gun-

---

that "Jorge Antonio and his inner circle played dirty from the beginning, fooling Perón's wife, making her think she could outshine Evita." *La Nación,* January 15, 1965.

shots were exchanged. Peronist leaders, including Vandor, trooped to the hotel to greet the visitor. At a press conference Isabel nervously insisted that she was a "messenger of peace" and twice repeated that "For a Peronist there can be nothing better than another Peronist," one of the hallowed Twenty Truths of *justicialismo*.[9]

The disturbances forced Isabel to switch hotels several times. The authorities deemed it prudent to cancel a permit for a Peronist rally on October 17.[10] This did not stop small groups of Peronists from taking to the streets and confronting the police. Isabel disappeared from view on the morning of the seventeenth.

Her presence in Argentina did nothing to heal the split between orthodox Peronists and those who favored Peronism without Perón. It might even have provoked the latter to the very brink of an open split at a conference held on October 21, when delegates adopted a resolution that was widely interpreted as an attack on Perón himself.[11] They also called for the immediate institutionalization of the movement and the formation of a new political party organized legally through democratic internal elections. Vandor made no public pronouncements at the conference. Whether he personally called the signals or, as one sympathetic observer has suggested, was pushed by his supporters into a confrontation with Perón,[12] the proceedings had all the overtones of a declaration of independence from Madrid.

The *conductor* reacted angrily. In a letter to Framini, who released it to the press, Perón called the Peronist dissidents "ingrates," "simpletons" and worse, and castigated them for washing the movement's dirty linen in public. Flashes of self-pity ("I am tired of all this because I see that my sacrifices have been useless") leavened the invective. There was even the hint of a threat: "They think I am dying and have already begun to fight over my clothes, but what they don't know is that death is going to take them up when they least expect it."[13]

Vandor, meanwhile, was tending to his trade-union flank. On November 18, the Sixty-two Organizations reelected him secretary-general for another two-year term. At the same time the federation of Peronist unions recognized Perón's appointment of Isabel as his personal delegate to replace Alberto Iturbe and solicited her permission to send a peace mission to Madrid.[14] In early December, Vandor traveled to La Rioja for a secret meeting with Isabel, who was touring the interior. She was quoted as announcing that "we have forged the definitive bases for the unity of Peronism."[15]

But the wrath of Jupiter, once aroused, is not easily placated. In private letters which found their way into print, Perón now lashed out at Vandor by name. An epistle he sent to a former comrade-in-arms referred to the latter as "an ambitious, incorrigible fellow who wants to reach where his capacity does not permit."[16] He also alluded to a maxim that was becoming one of his favorites, the need to use injections of antibodies to neutralize turncoats and traitors—an ominous doctrine that would one day haunt Argentine politics.[17]

There may have been another reason for Perón's decision to pull in the reins on his wayward disciples at this time. Stories were circulating that high-ranking military officers contemplating a coup against Illia had made contact with certain Peronist labor leaders. Any deals that might result from these meetings would seriously undercut the *conductor*. The reassertion of his authority evidently succeeded. One of the officers involved was reported to have asked his colleagues: "Why should we converse with the monkeys when we can talk to the owner of the circus?"[18]

In January the inevitable breach opened. José Alonso, a leading loyalist, created a new Peronist union federation called the Sixty-two Organizations Standing by Perón.[19] Vandor responded by ousting Alonso from his top post in the CGT. Both sides then concentrated on the battleground that would provide a critical test for the dissenting Peronists.

The Mendoza contest was now a struggle between Vandor and Perón. El Lobo had achieved what no one else had ever been able to do: he had gained recognition as a legitimate competitor for Perón, a worthy opponent who actually had a chance to unseat the aging *conductor*.

Perón more than anyone realized the nature of the challenge. A letter he sent to José Alonso in late January revealed the depth of his feeling: "In this fight . . . the principal enemy is Vandor and his clique. . . . It is necessary to go after them with everything and aim for the head, without truce or quarter. In politics you can't wound, you have to kill. . . . There has to be a definitive resolution. . . . That is my word and you know the saying that 'Perón keeps his word.' "[20] These were uncommonly violent metaphors, issued by one who numbered among his flock many zealots eager to execute his every whim.

Vandor kept quiet. He was confident of broad support among the rank and file, but knew he could not personally attack Perón, either in public or in private. In his view, Perón ought to remain head of the movement for life but should make decisions in consultation with the chief executive of a strong Peronist party in Argentina.[21]

In the weeks preceding the Mendoza election, there were ubiquitous portents of violence. A bomb exploded at the San Isidro racetrack near the table Vandor customarily occupied. Patricio Kelly, revolver in hand, took over the headquarters of a Peronist commission controlled by El Lobo.

In western Argentina, the Mendoza campaign offered dramatic proof that Perón had lost none of his magic. The cabecitas negras flocked to have a look at Isabel and lay hands upon her as though she were a touring saint. The veneration she inspired came solely from the fact that she was Perón's woman. They would always greet her by asking about him. Many gave her letters to take to Madrid. On one occasion a group of rural workers huddled together on the flatbed of a truck parked at night on the side of a highway just to watch Isabel's car pass by.[22]

The government hurt Vandor's candidate by permitting broadcasts of taped messages from Perón in support of his rival. Although the People's Radicals enjoyed the spectacle of a civil war among the Peronists, they were of no mind to facilitate the unification of the party under Vandor, whom they saw as an immediate threat.

In the match between the Vandorist and orthodox candidates, the latter finished clearly ahead. His backers hailed the result as proof that Perón's popularity had not waned and as a repudiation of Vandor. Their unrestrained glee made it seem irrelevant that another of the candidates in the field had actually captured the governorship.

It was a political setback for Vandor but his prestige within the labor movement remain intact. The loyalists had not yet dealt him the mortal blow for which their leader had called. Whether the inflammatory language in Perón's letter to Alonso encouraged violence is difficult to determine; bloody clashes were not new to organized labor. However, a scant month after the Mendoza election, Vandor's right-hand man died in a shoot-out at an Avellaneda pizzeria. The police never found out who fired the first shot and who actually killed Rosendo García, although an argument between friends of El Lobo and a group of pro-Perón union militants apparently set off the incident. Vandor himself barely escaped unharmed.[23]

Carrying out her husband's directives, Isabel had made a significant contribution to the defeat of those supporting Peronism without Perón. While she was still in Argentina, a final nail was placed in the coffin containing the hope that a reorganized Peronist party might gain power through the democratic process. On June 28, 1966, a military coup unseated Illia.[24]

It had been brewing for some time. The armed forces were unhappy with what they perceived as the government's chronic debility. The generals deplored the display of tolerance toward the Peronists, the handling of Operation Return and the presence of Isabel. Illia's failure to offer wholehearted support to the U.S. intervention in the Dominican Republic annoyed them. Moreover, the president proved inept at handling the high command. In November 1965 he provoked the resignation of General Onganía, the army commander-in-chief, long a backer of constitutional rule. This relieved Onganía of his sworn duty to uphold the government and made him susceptible to the blandishments of those who wished to unseat Illia.

The economic situation grew steadily worse. Inflation seemed out of control and the peso had to be repeatedly devalued. Argentine businessmen lost confidence and declined to make new investments. Yet Illia refused to ease up on restraints upon foreign capital.[25]

By 1966 every important interest group in the country was thoroughly disenchanted with the government. Political democracy had once again failed. There was widespread relief when the armed forces installed in Illia's place General Juan C. Onganía, nor was any concern expressed when it became clear that Onganía was not going to serve as an interim president but rather would be the chief executive of what was ambitiously baptized the Argentine Revolution.

During her extended visit, Isabel Perón had helped suppress a political revolt against her husband and had witnessed the restoration of military rule, developments of considerable import. Yet they paled before her meeting with José López Rega, an occurrence that was as inconsequential in its unfolding as it was pivotal in the history of Peronism.

44

López Rega

He was a forty-nine-year-old retired police corporal who had stood watch at the gate of the downtown residence during the Perón era. On several occasions he served among the many security guards who surrounded the president. A photo shows him clinging to the side of an open limousine, bending forward, tie flapping in the wind, as Perón in military uniform stood waving to the crowd.[1] He carried with him this and other snapshots depicting him in proximity to Perón. They were his only credentials.

Exactly how José López Rega first made contact with Isabel remains a mystery. One version which would later enjoy wide currency—that he worked as a bouncer at Happy Land in Panamá City—is apocryphal. The most plausible account puts the blame on Bernardo Alberte, a former military aide to Perón.[2] Alberte was making arrangements for Isabel's tour when López Rega walked up to him and introduced himself as the man who used to open the gate at the residence. Alberte vaguely remembered him. He asked for an introduction to Isabel, who happened to be nearby, and Alberte obliged.

The ex-corporal made the most of his opportunity. Before the year ended he was one of Isabel's attendants, carrying her luggage and performing other menial tasks as well as helping with security. He was persistent yet inobtrusive. On July 10, 1966, when Isabel at last returned to Madrid, she brought him with her.[3] Within a few months he had gained access to the house in Puerta de Hierro. Through Isabel's intercession he assumed the humble role of handyman and valet.

Neither Perón nor any member of his inner circle nor any of the Peronists who came to call upon their leader paid the new employee much heed. But there was something a bit different, a bit strange, about the man whose casual acquaintances called Lopecito and whose friends addressed as Daniel.

By eerie coincidence he was born on October 17 in the year 1916, the only child of lower-middle-class parents who had emigrated from Spain to Buenos Aires.[4] His mother died while he was still a young boy. A family-album photograph catches him at age five dressed in a Little Lord Fauntleroy outfit, one hand resting lightly on a chair, hair parted in the middle, eyes fixed in a distinctively riveting gaze.[5]

How much formal education he received is not known. He did complete primary school, and according to neighbors attended secondary school, although there are no records to confirm this.

His first ambition in life was to become a professional singer. At every opportunity he performed at local clubs. His repertoire ranged from popular songs to grand opera. In the late 1930s he supposedly went to the United States and sang in a New York restaurant for several years. Upon his return he had a brief radio engagement. Yet success eluded him, most probably because his voice was not really very good. So despite a reluctance to accept his limitations as a vocalist, he decided to settle into a more mundane existence. He married a librarian who lived nearby, fathered a daughter and took a job on the federal police force.

Routine police work is drab and unchallenging. López Rega patrolled a street corner and was later stationed in a courtroom. A propensity for odd behavior made it difficult for him to get along with his coworkers and to receive the appreciation he felt was his due. Loftier goals beckoned him.

He clung to his dream of achieving stardom as a singer. Performing again on the radio, he had his picture published in a popular magazine, which referred to him as an "international tenor."[6] His musical conceit produced signs that he and reality might be traveling on different tracks. According to an anecdote attributed to his wife, she had problems making ends meet on his meager policeman's salary because he liked to dress up in rented opera costumes, invite neighbors into the kitchen and entertain them with selected arias.[7] Many years later, when he had reached a pinnacle of power, he would tell the U.S. ambassador to Argentina about his stay in New York and then favor the diplomat with an impromptu rendition of "Rosemarie, I Love You."[8]

At some point López Rega must have realized he was not going to succeed in show business, because he turned all his energy in a different direction. What sparked his interest in the world of the spirits is unknown. A magazine article claims that once when he was on courtroom duty he witnessed the interrogation of a young Brazilian; the boy's relatives told him that they had made a promise to one of the spirit-cult deities they worshiped, to be fulfilled in the event the god saw fit to extricate the boy from his legal entanglement; what they said fascinated López Rega, and the Brazilians later put him in contact with some local practitioners of candomblé (also known as macumba), a cult originally brought to the Western Hemisphere by African slaves and widely practiced even today in

Brazil.[9] There is also some anecdotal evidence that he visited Brazil and made contact with cultists there.[10]

In early 1962 he retired from the police as a first corporal, only two grades up from that of raw recruit, and launched a new career. Purchasing a small press, he began to churn out his own writings on the subjects that had now become dear to him. Within a remarkably brief period of time he produced a body of literature that furnished a window into his psyche. Most Peronists ignored his published works when he appeared among them. The few who looked merely laughed. One day they would take him more seriously.

His major work, a thick volume entitled *Astrología esotérica: Secretos develados (Esoteric Astrology: Secrets Unveiled)*, promised to unlock the age-old mysteries of the universe and bestow divine wisdom upon the reader. It explained the various interrelationships linking colors, smells, sounds, planets, signs of the zodiac, parts of the human body and nations of the earth. His daughter Norma did some of the illustrations. The prose is simplistic; the ideas bewildering and apparently not very original.*

The author apparently felt capable of utilizing the mysterious forces about which he wrote to peer into the future and even alter reality. Indeed, he and an army officer inspired by the book subsequently opened a "beauty institute" to advise women on how to coordinate their dress, cosmetics and hairstyles with their zodiacal signs.[11]

In his preface to *Astrología esotérica,* the author disclosed that the secrets he was about to reveal did not originate with him but rather came from God the Father, who was disposed to share them with His children.[12] The notion of López Rega as intermediary comes into more dramatic focus in another of his works, *Alpha y omega: Un mensaje para la humanidad (Alpha and Omega: A Message for Humanity)*, coauthorship of which is attributed to the archangel Gabriel. López Rega describes how the re-nowned messenger of good news visited him as he slept and conveyed to him various teachings for the benefit of mankind. The archangel had some rather bizarre things to say: one night he waxed lyrical about the cow and humanity's debt to it. After listing the plethora of products obtained from the bovine family, he complained bitterly about the way we treat these precious creatures:

> Look at how cows live in our midst. You find them alone, in a state of gen-
> eral abandon, in meadows with scant natural pasture, in the midst of in-
> clement weather, suffering extreme heat. . . . Cows have to look for food,
> what their own devices can provide within the perimeter of their con-
> finement (concentration camps?) far from any sign of human endearment.
> It appears to be a place destined to shelter war criminals and not to nourish
> a food supply of the human race.[13]

* A magazine article that quotes extensively from the book includes deprecatory comments by rival astrologers, one of whom suggested that the subtitle should have been "Little Secrets Copied." *Así 2da,* March 2, 1973, p. 6.

López Rega gave no indication that he was writing with tongue in cheek. He was serious about the occult sciences and they absorbed him totally. Indeed, his pale skin, icy blue eyes and distinctive cheekbones gave him a physical appearance that could not have better suited the role he was now playing. The transformation must have bewildered his wife. According to another anecdote she is said to have related, he would occasionally vanish for a day or two; on his return she would ask where he had been and he would reply "in Egypt" or "on a trip to the stars."[14] When he left for Madrid, he in effect abandoned her.

One suspects that López Rega must have known of Isabel's appetite for spiritism before he approached her. Their common interest in the subject held them together. (There would inevitably be rumors of a sexual relationship, but there is no evidence to support this charge.) The fact that he sought her out attests to the degree of ambition motivating him.

Juan Perón's attitude toward his new employee ranged from benign tolerance to disdain. Occasionally he would express amusement at López Rega's outlandish comments, and thus "Daniel" came to be viewed as a kind of court jester. El Brujo ("The Warlock"), as his enemies would soon call him, did not hesitate to put his esoteric talents to work on behalf of the *conductor*. For example, he prepared astrological charts on all prominent military officers.[15] Perón did not reject this out of hand. The tolerance he had once displayed toward the Basilio School and the Brazilian spiritist reemerged.

López Rega's eagerness to exploit Perón became evident almost from the start. In late 1967 the ex-president learned that his majordomo was marketing in Brazil a drug advertised as having rejuvenating properties. On the label was a likeness of Perón and a claim that "he stays young because he drinks this medicine." Perón became furious and ordered López Rega from the house. It required a major effort by Isabel to cajole her husband into permitting Daniel to retain his job.[16]

Once his position became secure, his influence within the inner circle slowly expanded. Deplorable as this turned out to be, in retrospect one must admit that it took both seed and soil to produce the phenomenon of José López Rega. Perón's penchant for surrounding himself with mediocrities and his curiosity about occultism were not new. This time, however, the *conductor*'s foible would loose deadly side effects.

45

The Argentine Revolution

The coup that brought Onganía to the Casa Rosada enjoyed the tacit support of the Peronist leadership. Vandor and other union officials had been in contact with the military men planning the Argentine Revolution and had indicated that they would offer no resistance. Vandor's approval of the conspiracy marked a departure from his effort to restructure the Peronist party and a reaction to his defeat in Mendoza. Realizing he could not beat Perón at the ballot box, he decided to cast his lot with those who sought to eliminate elections. The type of military dictatorship on the drawing board would require constant behind-the-scenes negotiating between the regime and organized labor. This was his strong suit. Perón would have fewer cards to play.

There is uncorroborated evidence that the *conductor* had been aware of the impending overthrow of Illia well before it occurred and had indicated his approval of the military plan.[1] In the immediate aftermath of the coup, he offered what amounted to conditional approval of the Argentine Revolution. In a recorded message to the faithful he noted that the new military rulers had been making statements compatible with Peronist principles and that if they created a "popular government" he would be obliged to support it. He urged the regime to prepare the way for elections and warned against permitting "sepoys" and "sell-outs" to betray the "Revolution" to the forces of imperialism.[2] Instructions sent by the *conductor* directed the Alonso wing of the Peronist labor movement to keep its distance from the regime.[3] While Vandor made no public statements, his presence at Onganía's inauguration left no doubt about his attitude toward the incoming administration.

The optimism accompanying Juan C. Onganía to the Casa Rosada surged from an expectation well put by Perón himself several days after the coup: "I recognize Onganía's qualities as a military leader. . . . If [he] behaves as well in the political field as he has in the military, I believe the country can move forward."[4] Taciturn, serious and highly professional, the fifty-two-year-old general possessed the sort of leadership capabilities many Argentines felt were sorely needed in the Government House at this juncture.

Yet there was another side to Onganía, one that surfaced not long after he took office. He was an ultra-conservative Catholic, an implacable anti-communist and a rigid authoritarian, qualities that became evident when his administration plunged into an all-out war on immorality. The police cracked down on miniskirts, long hair worn by men and an opera that contained nudity.[5] These measures provoked ridicule, and porteños soon dubbed the mustachioed Onganía La Morsa ("The Walrus"). No one laughed, however, when the general ordered a heavy-handed purge of "subversive" elements from the universities. Political liberals as well as leftists lost their jobs, and a North American mathematics professor was among those beaten up by overzealous law-enforcement officials. The brain drain that soon decimated departments in the physical sciences gave a retrograde image to the Argentine Revolution.[6]

On the political front, Onganía took the simple approach of banning politics. He closed down the Congress and dissolved the political parties. Yet the government adopted a somewhat tolerant attitude toward the Peronists and treated organized labor gingerly. A determination to avoid past mistakes as well as Onganía's innate caution inspired these policies, which gave the president time to consolidate his power and develop an economic strategy.

It was not until April 1967 that the Argentine Revolution became more than a slogan. For several months Vandor had been spearheading talks between the unions and the regime in the hope of gaining wage concessions. Onganía refused to budge, so the CGT resorted to confrontation tactics. The regime not only crushed a general strike but also unveiled a new economic policy which put a firm lid on wages for the indefinite future.[7]

The goals of the plan were to fight inflation *and* stimulate industrial growth. The wage and voluntary price controls imposed by the regime were consistent with conventional stabilization programs, but the government also eased credit restrictions and increased the money supply as a spur to production. A 40 percent devaluation of the peso and a reduction in import tariffs were designed to attract foreign capital. The economic advisors who sold the plan to Onganía felt they had devised a balanced, imaginative strategy that would lift the country out of its stagnation. As long as the president could maintain political stability, they were confident their plan would succeed.[8] The tough, non-negotiable line he took on wage levels greatly encouraged them.

When he cracked the whip on labor, Onganía thwarted the ambitions of Augusto Vandor. Perhaps El Lobo should have realized that there was no way a straitlaced military man like Onganía could warm to a union leader who never wore a tie and liked to play the horses. Vandor had gambled on being able to establish a working relationship with the regime. In the eyes of the rank and file, he had lost his bet.

Evidence that Perón may have begun to accept his inability to affect the *pax onganiana* now descending upon Argentina came to light in late 1966 when Isabel embarked upon a business career. She was to help run an export-import firm that would ship foodstuffs to and from the Third World. Her partners were a trio of Spaniards and Perón's current private secretary, Rodolfo Valenzuela (a onetime soccer official whom Perón had appointed to the Argentine Supreme Court after its purge). The *conductor* gave visible encouragement to his wife's enterprise.[9] He also signed guarantees for some of its debts.[10]

Perón may have permitted his name and perhaps himself to be associated with a commercial venture because of a concern for his own financial security. The penury to which he had been exposed during his Latin American odyssey and the early years in Madrid had sensitized him to the value of money and to the undesirability of economic dependence. In addition, Isabel may have been eager to try her hand at business. It is quite conceivable that the trip to Argentina opened new horizons for her and made her reluctant to resume her domestic role. López Rega may have nudged her, although his influence at Puerta de Hierro was still in the embryonic stage and there is no evidence of his involvement in the formation of the new company. However, Valenzuela died in a plane crash several years later and Daniel thereafter become active in the business.

The export-import firm brought Perón nothing but trouble. Several creditors, alleging fraud, sued the company. The *conductor* feared a public scandal and sought help from Jorge Antonio, who negotiated a quiet settlement.[11] The company eventually folded.

The age factor conspired with the consolidation of the Argentine Revolution to decrease the possibility of a return by Perón. He was now seventy years old. His hair retained its dark color (either by nature's generosity or the magic of cosmetics), but the skin condition that had always afflicted his face had now produced extensive red blotches that betrayed his senescence.

He did his best to resist its encroachment. Every day he took a long walk through the streets of Madrid. He even attended yoga classes, conducted by a bibulous Englishman who would tipple during frequent recesses.[12] The extreme courtesy that had always been one of his hallmarks enabled him to demonstrate physical agility to visitors, as he would vault out of his chair to light their cigarettes and help them with their overcoats.[13]

His daily routine remained unchanged: up at seven; simple breakfast of tea and toast; morning walk; work on correspondence; frugal lunch (soup, meat and salad); siesta; reception of visitors; supper; TV watching or reading, with an occasional night at the cinema; to bed by midnight. Puerta de Hierro provided a pleasant, tranquil environment, its lofty pines sheltering luxurious homes tucked on one side of the highway leading to El Pardo, once the summer home of the royal family and now *Generalísimo* Franco's residence.

Perón's house had become a magnet for visiting Argentines. Although he complained of being treated like a tourist attraction,[14] holding court in his living room was an essential part of his day and he loved it. Still very much the lecturer at heart, he needed the steady stream of pilgrims who found their way to his doorstep. The opportunity to talk to Argentine students especially delighted him, and he mesmerized these young people, for whom he was a living legend. They in turn began to call him El Viejo ("The Old Man"), a term of endearment every Argentine uses to refer to his or her father. Yet these sessions almost always turned into rambling reminiscences, often characterized by outrageous distortions or misstatements of fact.[15]

It is difficult to assess his intellectual development during the long years of exile. He is said to have read extensively and to have kept in touch with contemporary ideas, although evidence of this is anecdotal and comes from followers who may be exaggerating the extent of his self-education. The theme of Latin American unity continued to engross him. Proximity to functioning democracies in Europe seems to have mellowed his attitude toward political opposition, and he began to nurture relations with non-Peronist Argentine leaders.

In 1967 he published a book that sought to substantiate his pretension to hemispheric statesmanship. Yet instead of developing fresh approaches to the problems of the 1960s, he offered shopworn Third Position rhetoric and a 1953 speech on Latin American integration. The slender volume is curiously eclectic, sandwiching a message he sent to a 1967 Peronist youth conference between explications on the meaning of *justicialismo* and commentary on international politics. Yet the text merits attention because it harbors passages that provide critical insights into the Perón mentality.

For example, in his epistle to the conference he blamed the plight of the Peronist movement upon the mistakes of its leaders (excluding himself, of course) and called for a "true revolution inside Peronism," to be carried out by the youth.[16] He termed this process a *trasvasamiento generacional*, indicating a generational transference of power from the old guard to the new through change that would be both natural and purifying. What he said appeared to signal a desire to infuse fresh blood into the top echelons of the movement, but there can be little doubt that his real intention was to create a new force he could manipulate to counter the growing influence of politicians and labor chieftains who were challenging him.

Several other illuminating concepts surfaced in the book. Perón's references to the "international synarchy" permit a glimpse at the dark side of his intellect. He professed a belief in the existence of a conspiracy among capitalists, Communists, Masons, Zionists and the Catholic church to impose a world order upon all nations. Thus there was only one kind of imperialism, which operated through the media of "dark forces," "sepoys," political and economic pressures, and, if necessary, armed conflict. World War II represented the successful destruction of outsiders (Germany, Italy and Japan) who had refused to submit to the system. The Yalta Conference divided the earth into spheres of influence under the control of the two major political components of the synarchy, the United States and the Soviet Union. The cold war was a sham. The Liberating Revolution merely executed the mandate of the "international synarchy" that Perón's Third Position government be eliminated.[17]

This fantastic confection belongs to a tradition of conspiracy theories dating back at least to the nineteenth-century view that the French Revolution was a Jewish-Masonic plot. Intelligent Peronists were (and still are) embarrassed by their leader's references to the synarchy and dismissed them as tactical pronouncements. However, Peronism's lunatic fringe harbored a number of individuals with paranoid tendencies which fed upon talk of shadowy worldwide conspiratorial movement.

Invocation of an international synarchy was of itself a harmless bit of nonsense. Another concept to which Perón adverted in the books would have far deeper implications. He used the expression "national socialism" to describe the political essence of *justicialismo*.[18] At first blush it seemed an unwise choice of words, conjuring up the image of the Third Reich and the charge that Perón was a "Nazi-Fascist." He attempted to circumnavigate this difficulty by insisting that he was using the term to distinguish his Third Position ideology from Soviet-style Communism in that he advocated socialism within one country—national, as opposed to international.

How his ideology amounted to socialism in the accepted meaning of the term he never explained. The transformations he brought to Argentina from 1946 to 1955 could hardly be deemed socialistic. However, he now liked to repeat the proposition that socialism (of the national brand) represented the wave of the future, especially among the nations of the Third World.

One suspects that Perón's characterization of *justicialismo* as "national socialism" during the 1960s had more to do with the rise of left-wing radicalism in Latin America, particularly among young people. He was very much aware of the popularity of Fidel Castro and Che Guevara, and of the appeal of the revolutionary option.[19] He knew he had to compete for the hearts and minds of Argentina's youth. Indeed, he had already betrayed his hand (and perhaps a touch of jealousy) by stating that "If in

1954 Russia had been as strong as it became later, I would have become the first Fidel Castro of America."[20] Of course, this flatly contradicted the international synarchy theory, which held that Russia was in league with the United States, but contradiction never bothered him.

Not many months passed before Perón was denouncing the Onganía regime. It was on trade-union terrain, however, that he made his most decisive move. Despite the hard line Onganía had taken toward the CGT, Vandor clung to the belief that negotiation with the government was still possible and served labor's best interests. Yet the regime's policies had provoked a spirit of worker unrest that provided grist for left-wing militants within the unions. "Collaboration" was fast becoming a dirty word. A CGT congress convened in mid-March 1968 for the purpose of normalizing the confederation after a year of turmoil gave Perón an opportunity to exploit this tension. He conveyed to Raimundo Ongaro, one of the combative labor leaders, his wish that the CGT toughen its attitude toward the regime. Ongaro then led an effort to seize control of the confederation, but succeeded only in splitting it.[21]

Now there were two CGTs, Vandor's and Ongaro's. The latter, called the CGT of the Argentines, proclaimed its loyalty to Perón and adopted a program calling for resistance to imperialist penetration (i.e., foreign takeovers of Argentine businesses), nationalization of key industries, worker participation in enterprise decision-making and agrarian reform.[22] Vandor and his followers retained their hold on the official CGT. They too professed their Peronist faith, but stuck closer to bread-and-butter issues. José Alonso, who had fought with Vandor in 1965, patched up his differences with El Lobo and joined forces with the moderates.

Though Perón had encouraged the scission, he kept in contact with both CGTs. In August he met quietly with Vandor in northern Spain and seemed willing to accept him back into the fold.[23] The *conductor* was now in a position to play one side against the other and to use either or both against the regime.

This was perfectly consistent with his vision of political leadership. He appointed Bernardo Alberte as his delegate and Jerónimo Remorino, formerly his ambassador to the United States and foreign minister, as personal representative. At the same time he put Pablo Vicente in charge of the so-called advance command in Montevideo.[24] He thus could give one type of instruction to one of these men; if problems arose, he could give a contradictory order to another. As might be expected, the troika soon began squabbling.

Perón had always viewed himself as a kind of secular pope. His concept of Holy Fatherhood required him to hold together the disparate elements of an unruly flock. He thought he should rarely, if ever, resort to infallible pronouncements, except in the vaguest of terms.[25] This self-image encouraged him to be all things to all visitors and appear to express agreement with almost anything his followers told him. Since Peronism embraced the entire political spectrum, it would call for extraordinary feats of leger-demain to keep everybody happy.

The emergence of groups committed to armed struggle against the regime and declaring themselves Peronist complicated his task. In 1963 and 1964, openly Castroite guerrillas had opened a front in the countryside of northern Argentina but had been crushed by the federal police.[26] Several years later, in response to Che Guevara's call for the creation of "many Vietnams" in Latin America, another small group of revolutionaries began to organize, but Guevara was killed in Bolivia before they could take to the field. They then underwent a conversion to Peronism, although they maintained their Marxist orientation. In early 1968, police surprised and captured some of them, now members of the self-styled Peronist armed forces, at a training camp in rural Tucumán.[27]

The evolution of a militant brand of left-wing Peronism would soon give birth to a dizzying array of discrete components. The scene became even more complicated when revolutionaries from the other end of the political spectrum converged upon Peronism. In the early 1960s, the ac-tivities of a right-wing youth group known as the Tacuara stirred fears of a resurgence of Fascism in Argentina.[28] Ultra-nationalist, anti-Semitic and anticommunist, the Tacuara harkened memories of Patricio Kelly's ALN. Led by an adventurer with the intriguingly un-Argentine name of Joe Baxter, they engaged in random acts of urban terrorism. The police crushed the Tacuara in 1964, but Joe Baxter escaped to become a legendary figure, supposedly fighting with the left-wing guerrillas in Uruguay and the Vietcong in Southeast Asia.[29]

Baxter's ideological passage would prove surprisingly typical, as other Argentine youths who began their political lives as right-wing Catholic nationalists moved toward acceptance of some form of Marxism. This process gained impetus from the concurrent radicalization of a number of clerics, who formed the Movement of Priests for the Third World on May 1, 1968.[30] Unlike Baxter but like some of their left-wing contem-poraries, many young Catholic students concluded that only Peronism could bring about a genuine Argentine revolution.

These subtle transformations occurred at a time when the Onganía re-gime seemed more firmly entrenched than ever. The government's eco-nomic policy succeeded in making inroads against inflation, reducing the budget deficit through an increase in public revenues and attracting new investments from domestic as well as foreign sources. The civilian sector apparently had resigned itself to an extended dose of authoritarianism.

Yet deeply subterranean rumblings suggested that this might be a fragile tranquility. The development stimulated by the new economic plan tended to be uneven and reached neither the mushrooming slums of Buenos Aires nor pockets of poverty such as the sugar-producing region of Tucumán Province. Worker resentment at the wage freeze heightened. Students were unhappy with the moralistic, anti-intellectual atmosphere that stifled the universities. The ferment intensified as a result of the global unrest of 1968, in the wake of riots in Washington following the murder of Martin Luther King, Jr., the Paris student rebellion of May, the short-lived relaxation of Communist rule in Czechoslovakia and antiwar demonstrations in the United States.

Although the polo-playing cavalry officer in the Casa Rosada felt confident that the Argentine Revolution was holding course and speed, what he failed to realize was that he sat perched upon a powder keg, and that it would take but one spark to set it off.

46

Bloody Upheaval

Nearly fourteen years after it had triggered the convulsions that toppled Juan Perón, the city of Córdoba once again brought an Argentine government to its knees. This time the outburst came not from traditionalists guarding the prerogatives of church, family and property, but from a coalition of radical students and workers.

The aviation industry that burgeoned in and around Córdoba during the 1940s and 1950s required a pool of trained employees whose presence in turn helped attract an automotive industry in the 1960s. By the end of the decade the city could boast a large concentration of skilled workers. Many enrolled in courses at the university, while large numbers of students took jobs in the auto plants. The process of radicalization affecting the university then spread to the factories.

The Córdoba unions, moreover, had remained independent of the CGT bureaucracy,[1] a circumstance facilitating the emergence of several important labor leaders who were highly capable, dedicated Marxists.[2] They tended to support Ongaro's CGT of the Argentines and advocated resistance to the regime.

The fuse that ignited Córdoba began to hiss on May 12, when a 16¢ price increase at a university cafeteria in the city of Resistencia provoked student protests that escalated in reaction to police brutality.[3] Several days later a medical student was shot to death by police trying to break up a demonstration. The unrest quickly spread. A clash between police and demonstrators in Rosario claimed the life of another student, and when a large crowd took to the streets in outrage, the army occupied the city.

The image of Onganía the strong man now seemed phantasmagoric. The army moved troops into Rosario first and then told the Casa Rosada.

The president hesitated to impose a state of siege, which would be tantamount to an admission that he had a serious problem on his hands. But then Córdoba exploded.

They called it the *cordobazo*, and it shook the country like no other event since October 17, 1945. Auto workers from a Renault factory marched into town and touched off a massive worker-student rally that soon became open insurrection. The rebels set up barricades and seized control of a hundred and fifty blocks. Buildings and automobiles burned as army paratroopers, supported by air force planes, tried to quell the uprising. With help from roof-top snipers the insurgents held out for two days. Superior military force finally recaptured the city. Official figures listed fourteen deaths and more than a hundred injured. The toll was probably higher.

The government blamed the *cordobazo* on "extremists" and "subversives."[4] Both the CGT and the CGT of the Argentines called a one-day general strike. On June 4, Onganía made a television and radio speech deploring the violence in Córdoba and announcing that he had dismissed his entire cabinet.

The spasm was not quite over. On June 2, three days before the scheduled arrival of Nelson Rockefeller on a fact-finding mission to Latin America, terrorists burned thirteen supermarkets belonging to a corporation in which the Rockefeller family held a controlling interest. Then, at the very moment Richard Nixon's special envoy was meeting with President Onganía at the Casa Rosada, the swirl of events reached its grisly climax.

At 11:30 A.M., on Monday, June 30, inside the Buenos Aires headquarters of the metalworkers' union, Augusto Vandor was just finishing a telephone conversation when he heard noise outside his second-floor office. Opening the door to investigate, he found himself face to face with an armed stranger. The man pumped five shots from a .45-caliber pistol at the startled Vandor, who slumped to the floor. A second intruder dashed into the office and put a package under a desk. He told a group of gaping onlookers that it was a bomb set to explode in five minutes. In a matter of seconds the assailants had fled to a nearby automobile and disappeared. Several of Vandor's friends dragged him out of the building before the explosive detonated, but he was dead on arrival at the hospital.[5]

The murder forced Onganía to declare a state of siege. The authorities made no headway in efforts to solve the crime. There was speculation that the killers were linked to the CGT of the Argentines, which had called a general strike for July 1, since Vandor had refused to support it. Others surmised that this was but another episode in a bloody tradition of power struggles within organized labor.[6] Finally, there were whispers that the perpetrators were newly emerging Peronist revolutionaries who regarded Vandor as a traitor to the movement, even though he and Perón had recently patched up their differences.[7]

The *conductor* sent a floral wreath to the wake. Later, statements were attributed to him claiming that he had warned Vandor that the game he was playing could result in his death. The risky conduct to which Perón supposedly referred was Vandor's alleged involvement with the Onganía regime, the U.S. embassy and the Central Intelligence Agency; Perón told El Lobo that he could not serve two masters (the Peronist movement and its enemies); if one side didn't kill him, the other would.[8]

The most interesting aspect of these admonitions is the suggestion that Perón had foreseen a Peronist assassination attempt. He was first reported to have commented on the murder in an interview published in a left-wing Uruguayan weekly in early 1970. After recounting his advice to El Lobo, he went on to describe his method of handling traitors within the movement. Likening them to microbes, he noted that "when a traitor appears, I don't expel him. I say 'Take care of him, he's useful; he's generating antibodies.' "[9]

In this sense, Perón regarded the Peronist movement as a living organism, subject to biological forces. If a microbe spawned antibodies that in turn destroyed it, who could argue with the laws of nature?

Yet in the same interview the *conductor* insisted that he controlled all the disparate elements of the Peronist movement. With rhetoric he often used when addressing leftist audiences or when seeking to worry the Casa Rosada and the U.S. State Department, he advocated the liberation of Argentina by means of a Cuban-style upheaval. Until the actual revolutionary moment arrived, he observed that his task was to coordinate forces. One of the units he had placed in the field was political, under orders to dialogue with the government. Another was an activist sector to which he gave the euphemistic designation "special formations." In the context in which he spoke, he had to be referring to the growing numbers of guerrillas engaged in paramilitary operations against the regime.

If a Peronist group had murdered Vandor, Perón might have ordered them to do it. The microbe-antibody theory would then provide a smoke screen to obscure his responsibility. It is also conceivable that Vandor was murdered by individual Peronists or a Peronist group trying to anticipate Perón's wish as a way to curry favor with him or enhance their standing within the movement. If so, then the microbe-antibody theory served to obscure his lack of control over the "special formations."

The nature of the relationship between Perón and his "special formations" remains controversial. His concept of leadership required him to maintain the impression that all Peronist groups responded to his directives, yet he also had to avoid responsibility for the burgeoning violence that might one day force a political settlement on terms favorable to him.

The new militants served his purposes by fomenting unrest and by professing allegiance to him. What gave this process an intriguing twist was the fact that many of the revolutionaries were trying to utilize Peronism as a vehicle for the spread of left-wing radicalism within the working class.

Onganía somehow survived the *cordobazo* and a subsequent smaller-scale uprising in Rosario during September. But the armed forces were by now deeply apprehensive about the worsening climate of violence and the inability of the regime to deal with it. The crisis intensified in 1970, as the various guerrilla organizations staged a series of robberies, kidnappings and attacks on police and military installations. The theft of weapons increased.[10]

The president did not grasp what was happening to the country. In late May he told a group of generals that the Argentine Revolution would require fifteen or twenty years to realize its goals, and that subversion against his regime was under control.[11] Several days later, he was disabused of this idea.

On the morning of May 29, 1970, Army Day and the first anniversary of the *cordobazo*, two men dressed in army uniforms appeared at the unguarded apartment of retired General Pedro E. Aramburu. Shortly afterward, he left quietly with them. By early afternoon, the news broke that terrorists had abducted the sixty-seven-year-old ex-president.

In a communiqué that evening, the kidnappers announced they were submitting Aramburu to "revolutionary justice" under charges including the execution of General Valle in 1956, the profanation of the body of Eva Perón, the nullification of social gains achieved by workers under Juan Perón and the betrayal of the national patrimony to foreign interests. The phrase "Perón or Death" punctuated the message. The perpetrators identified themselves as the Juan José Valle Command of an organization called the Montoneros.* A subsequent communiqué released on May 31 declared that Aramburu had been found guilty and would be put to death.[12]

The kidnapping stunned the nation and baffled the regime. To make matters worse for the Casa Rosada, friends of Aramburu began to whisper that "Fascists" within the government had eliminated the former president because he had turned against the administration and had made himself available as a replacement for Onganía.[13]

Aramburu's disappearance emphasized the impotence of the Onganía regime to a degree that exceeded the tolerance of its military supporters. On June 8, the commanders in chief of the armed forces deposed their hapless colleague, formed a junta and took charge of the government. Several days later they announced that the new president would be Gen-

---

* In Argentine history the montoneros were gauchos and peasants who fought on the side of Rosas during the civil strife of the nineteenth century.

eral Roberto M. Levingston, army attaché at the Argentine embassy in Washington.

He was such an unknown that the junta had to distribute to the press his photograph and a curriculum vitae. In the words of historian Félix Luna, it was "the first time in the course of Argentine history that the president had to be introduced to the public in a manner customarily employed to identify new subsecretaries of a ministry,"[14] not an auspicious beginning for the new man in the Casa Rosada.

47

The Turmoil Continues

As the Argentine Revolution collapsed, Perón was entering one of the most dramatic phases of his long political career. The instability of the military regime made it vulnerable to the sorts of pressures he was now in a position to apply. The vast experience he had accumulated and the tactical skills he had honed over the years made this his moment of supreme opportunity, and a fierce desire for self-justification impelled him to seize it. But his physical condition, weakened by age-induced weariness, made him susceptible to the influence of those around him. This in turn has called into question his responsibility for what ensued.

In March 1970, the discovery of traces of blood in his urine took him back to Dr. Puigvert's clinic in Barcelona. Tumors were found growing in his urethra, the membranous canal through which urine is discharged from the bladder. The surgeon removed them with an endoscope and pronounced his patient in excellent condition.[1] But news of the *conductor*'s health problem touched off speculation regarding the future of the Peronist movement.[2] Although Perón recuperated quickly, he now had physical needs requiring constant attention. The person who eagerly volunteered to provide these services was José López Rega.

Parlaying his presence inside the house at Puerta de Hierro with an ability to manipulate Isabel, Daniel had slipped quietly into the vacant post of private secretary to Perón. He saw to a myriad of minor details and continued to perform menial duties such as bringing coffee to Perón and his guests. It was but a small step for him to assume what amounted to the role of male nurse.

The way in which the *conductor* had delegated authority to Evita and had utilized her to further his own ends demonstrated how masterful he could be in turning to his own advantage the ambitions of those close to him. In the same vein it is possible to detect a certain tolerance on his part for the machinations of Isabel and her new ally. But old age would greatly impede his ability to keep them in check.

López Rega and Isabel were determined to take control over access to Perón and eliminate competitors from the inner circle. They were clever enough to extend their tentacles gradually. Daniel used his position in the household to gain a grip on the telephone and the mail. Emilio Romero, the right-wing Spanish editor who had formed a close friendship with Perón, was an early casualty.[3] Later, despite his long years of faithful service, Jorge Antonio suffered banishment from Puerta de Hierro at the hands of Isabel.*

While Isabel and López Rega were thus extending their influence, Perón continued to display his mastery of political gamesmanship. An interview published in a Parisian magazine quoted him in top revolutionary form, calling for a violent upheaval in Argentina and suggesting that if he regained power he might dismantle certain reactionary institutions, such as the army.[4] Peronist politicians were quick to cast doubt upon the authenticity of the article, despite its textual similarity to an interview published elsewhere by the same author several months earlier, or to insist that the *conductor* was speaking for dramatic effect only.[5] Peronist revolutionaries, however, must have been delighted by their leader's fiery pronouncements.

At the same time, moderate Peronists were encouraged by a soft-line policy Perón was simultaneously pursuing. His new personal representative was Jorge D. Paladino, who took over the job after Remorino's death in late 1968. Paladino, a young, handsome, personable politician, projected an aura of reasonableness and respectability. He participated in negotiations that resulted in the formation of a coalition called La Hora del Pueblo ("The Hour of the People"), bringing together Peronists, Radicals and several other parties in an effort to pressure the regime into permitting political activity to resume. He also held private talks with government officials and military leaders. The resignation of Alberte as Perón's delegate and the downgrading of Vicente's role in Montevideo

---

* Antonio's version of the incident is that under instructions from Perón he was negotiating with some Argentine military officers, including the army attaché at the Madrid embassy, when word reached Puerta de Hierro that the navy attaché was about to attempt to assassinate the *conductor*; his army contact assured Antonio that the rumor was baseless, but when the latter relayed this to Perón, Isabel accused him of participating in the "plot" and angrily expelled him from the house. E. Peicovich, *El Ultimo Perón,* p. 134. Perón remained in touch with Antonio and often visited his apartment, but he made no effort to overrule Isabel's edict. His acquiescence might have evidenced the dominance Isabel and López Rega exercised over him, but it was also consistent with the indifference he had always manifested toward friends.

helped Paladino, but the dislike (and perhaps jealousy) he generated among some veteran Peronists impeded his maneuverability.

On the labor front, Perón also veered to the right. The militant CGT of the Argentines had enjoyed few successes and had been weakened by repressive measures taken by the regime. At a July 1970 congress named for the late Augusto Vandor, the dissident confederation disbanded and delegates elected José Rucci from the metalworkers' union as secretary-general of a unified CGT. Diminutive, feisty and voluble, Rucci was an orthodox Peronist and the *conductor*'s personal choice for the post. He would carry out a policy of keeping organized labor subservient to Perón's dictates and out of Marxist hands.

In late September, Paladino announced that Perón would come back to Argentina before the end of the year.[6] In the light of past experience, few people took this as a serious declaration of intent, but it kept Perón in the news (there was much talk, on the occasion of his seventy-fifth birthday on October 8, about the possibility of his eventual return), and gave the regime fresh cause for concern.

This sequence of tactical thrusts by the *conductor* occurred at a time when the "special formations" were continuing to feed the unrest plaguing Argentina. On July 1, a group of terrorists briefly seized a small town in the province of Córdoba. The authorities drove off the intruders and captured several of them. Police fatally wounded one suspect during a subsequent raid. He turned out to have been a Montonero and one of Aramburu's kidnappers.

It was now possible to secure an ideological fix on the Montoneros.[7] Most of those identified as members came from middle-class Catholic backgrounds. (Indeed, the militant Catholicism they shared with prominent officials of the Onganía regime refueled the suspicion that the latter were to blame for the kidnapping of Aramburu.) They drew inspiration from the example of Camilo Torres, the Colombian guerrilla-priest killed when he took up arms against his government, as well as from the writings of John William Cooke.[8] Their Marxism was submerged in the rhetoric of revolutionary Peronism, which they viewed as authentically Argentine and the only vehicle for radical change in their country. They specialized in dramatic action with political significance comprehensible to the masses—propaganda by the deed. This was the motivation for the Aramburu abduction, the stunning effect of which was repeated on July 16, when the lifeless body of the ex-president was finally discovered.

The Montoneros would become the most important of the clandestine groups seeking to overthrow the government. Their outspoken loyalty to Perón, militant nationalism and audacious tactics brought them considerable influence within the Peronist Youth (Juventud Peronista, or JP), a federation of youth organizations at which Perón aimed his talk of a *trasvasamiento generacional*. The *conductor* never denounced the Montoneros and welcomed to Puerta de Hierro visitors who had ties to the group. They seemed to be his favorite "special formation."

This predilection would produce endless complications. On the morning of August 27, 1970, José Alonso fell victim to an assassin's bullets as he was being driven from his home by an associate. That afternoon a communiqué distributed to the press declared that a Montonero unit had handed the labor leader his just deserts for having betrayed the fatherland, the working class and the Peronist movement.[9]

The murder of Alonso set off shock waves among moderate Peronists. The identity of the killers remains a mystery. They may well have been the same individuals who sent Vandor to the Chacarita cemetery, but whether they belonged to the Montoneros is still unknown.

The proliferation of groups committed to revolution made it difficult to know which one was responsible for the acts of violence fast becoming commonplace. To distinguish one from another and to comprehend the subtle ideological differences between them was not an easy task. Changes in strategy and temporary alliances further complicated the internal-security problems besetting the regime. Thus, in addition to the Montoneros and the Peronist Armed Forces (Fuerzas Armadas Peronistas, or FAP), there emerged: the Revolutionary Armed Forces (Fuerzas Armadas Revolucionarias, or FAR), a Marxist-Leninist organization inspired by the model of Che Guevara and later gravitating toward Peronism; the Armed Forces of Liberation (Fuerzas Armadas de Liberación, FAL), also a Marxist-Leninist organization; and the People's Revolutionary Army (Ejército Revolucionario del Pueblo, or ERP), originally the military wing of a small Trotskyist party.[10] The ERP, which at some point seems to have absorbed the FAL, rejected Peronism from the start and sought to develop a revolutionary consciousness within the working class, first in the cities of the interior and later in the countryside.

President Levingston had neither the talent nor the temperament to counter the subversion. To add to his woes, the CGT demanded wage increases commensurate with the rising cost of living and called two general strikes during October. The government lifted the lid on salaries and interest rates in an attempt to galvanize the economy but succeeded only in stimulating inflation. Civilian impatience with military rule emulated the inflation rate. In an effort to develop a "political plan" by the end of the year, Levingston announced he would meet with his predecessors in the Casa Rosada (except, of course, the man in Madrid). Illia and Onganía refused to cooperate. The president ended up consulting with Frondizi, Guido, and a genuine fossil, General Farrell.[11] As he engaged in these meaningless gestures, he steadfastly refused to legalize the political parties or to set a date for elections.

As the ship of state drifted, knowledgeable porteños wondered how long the armed forces would tolerate Levingston. The identity of the gen-

eral in line to replace him seemed obvious, as the commander-in-chief of
the army had emerged as the dominant figure within the military establishment and its last best hope to find a way out of the crisis.

Alejandro A. Lanusse had participated in the ill-starred Menéndez revolt of 1951 and the price he paid for it—imprisonment in Patagonia for
the rest of the Perón era—gave him impeccable anti-Peronist credentials.
Lonardi made him chief of the grenadiers regiment, the crack mounted
unit used for ceremonial occasions and as the president's guard. In the
early 1960s Lanusse was an *azul*, in favor of constitutional rule and supportive of General Onganía. But when the Argentine Revolution became
increasingly authoritarian and, in his view, seemed to be taking the nation
toward a form of Fascism, he did not hesitate to lead the movement to
oust the president. The scion of a wealthy landowning family, Lanusse
was a liberal in the Argentine sense of the term, which meant that he
favored political democracy, laissez-faire economics and an internationalist
foreign policy. Yet he was quintessentially military—tall and erect, with
piercing eyes, accustomed to giving commands with a resonant voice and
expecting prompt obedience.[12]

On March 1, 1971, Levingston appointed as governor of Córdoba a
staunch conservative who immediately provoked the radical workers and
students of the province by calling them vipers and announcing that he
was going to crack down on them. Within days a series of violent strikes,
dubbed the *viborazo*, once again brought the city of Córdoba to the brink
of chaos, and the army had to declare it an emergency zone. Although
the president withdrew his governor, he still refused to accelerate preparations for elections. Moreover, he challenged the junta of commanders-
in-chief by firing its secretary, an officer who had been working on plans
for a political solution. The junta responded by quickly removing Levingston from office and installing as Argentina's next president Alejandro
Lanusse.

He came to the Casa Rosada with a commitment to restore constitutional
government. Yet he was also keenly aware that there was no way to oc-
complish that goal without dealing with Perón. He therefore resolved to
open the door to the Peronists, a decision that would lead to a confrontation
that was to fascinate the nation for the next two years.

48

Lanusse vs. Perón: Phase 1

Shortly after accepting the presidential sash, Alejandro Lanusse pledged to bring about free elections and an orderly transition to civilian rule. Knowing that vague promises garnished by lofty pronouncements would only feed the deep-seated skepticism and distrust with which most Argentines now viewed the military men who had been governing the country for the past five years, he resolved to take some decisive measures to demonstrate both his good faith and his willingness to explore fresh approaches to the political impasse that had frustrated the nation since 1955.

In a matter of days he made his first move by offering the Interior Ministry, which under the Argentine system has responsibility for the regulation of both political activity and elections, to a prominent member of the Radical party.[1] Dr. Arturo Mor Roig had been president of the Chamber of Deputies during the Illia administration. The respect he enjoyed among his peers and his preference for the politics of consensus made him well suited to execute Lanusse's strategy. Having first assured himself that service in the cabinet would in no way compromise his party, he agreed to undertake the difficult task of preparing the way for a return to democracy.

On April 1, Mor Roig announced that the ban Onganía had imposed on the political parties would be lifted. A fortnight later Lanusse declared that he would relinquish power to a constitutional government within three years.[2] These were bold steps, but what created a real sensation during these heady days were the president's initiatives toward the Peronists.

In an interview published in the *New York Times* in early April, Lanusse signaled his willingness to sit down and talk with Perón.[3] Shortly afterward the chief executive met Peronist labor leaders in the Casa Rosada and told them: "On this problem of Juan Perón I intend to go beyond what you dare to hope."[4] He elaborated by hinting that the government might return Eva Perón's body to Argentina. In addition, Lanusse made it clear that he would include Jorge Paladino, Perón's delegate, in the political discussions upon which he was about to embark.

For sixteen years the various occupants of the Casa Rosada had treated Perón as a nonperson. This had permitted him to obstruct the government with the formidable resources at his disposal and at the same time to remain wrapped in a mystique which time and distance enhanced. Lanusse wanted to force him into negotiations that would bind him to a positive course of action. The president's hope was that this would isolate him from the revolutionary left and drive the special formations out of the Peronist movement. It would also let the faithful see Perón as he really was—a tired old man in failing health.

Yet there were flaws in Lanusse's plan. To open the democratic process to the Peronists meant running the risk they would reject any conditions on their right to present candidates. Thus they would be free to nominate Perón, which would open up old wounds and expose the president to pressure, if not overt resistance, from anti-Peronists. Thus Lanusse would have to find a way to eliminate the candidacy of Perón without driving the Peronists out of the consensus that was a prerequisite to the holding of truly free elections. Firmly convinced that Perón did not want to be president again, he was confident at the outset that he could negotiate a solution to the Perón problem.

The *conductor* fully understood Lanusse's game and its implications. His response was to take special care not to unglue the Peronist movement or weaken his capability to keep the regime on the defensive. To abandon weapons such as the "special formations" and the threat of his own candidacy would have been serious tactical blunders.

Perón's prescription for maintaining cohesion was the same formula he had applied throughout his political career: preach unity while cultivating chaos. As an astute journalist reported: "Nobody can say that Perón hides it. He repeats it frequently. 'It is in the midst of confusion that I handle myself best, and if none exists one must create it. The art of politics is not to govern order but disorder.' "[5] The divide-and-rule doctrine promoted unity only to the extent that it left loyalty to the *conductor* as the only common ground for Peronists. What made Perón's playing of one subordinate against another an extraordinary tour de force was his simultaneous deployment of them against Lanusse.

Even before the president's overtures, disagreements about political strategy had begun to roil Peronist waters. Elements within organized labor expressed distaste for Peronist participation in the Hora del Pueblo and antipathy for Jorge Paladino.[6] It was yet another manifestation of the age-old rivalry between Peronist labor leaders and politicians.

When Lanusse made known his willingness to deal with the Peronists, a response from Madrid became imperative. Beginning on April 13, Peronist leaders converged upon the Spanish capital for what one magazine referred to as "Peronism's biggest conclave in the past ten years."[7] Reporters swarmed about Puerta de Hierro and the various hotels housing Peronist officials. It was therefore quite remarkable that the *conductor* was able to meet clandestinely with a high-ranking representative of the Lanusse regime. On April 22 at 6:00 P.M., Colonel Francisco Cornicelli managed to slip unnoticed into Perón's residence.

The meeting was more symbolic than substantive. Cornicelli merely repeated what Lanusse had already said in public and stressed the president's sincerity in promising a *juego limpio*, or "clean game." But the fact that the regime was dealing directly with Perón amounted to an important concession.

The conversation lasted for more than four hours. Perón did his usual lecturing on Argentine history and the accomplishments of his administration. Cornicelli brought up the subject of terrorism and suggested circumspectly that the *conductor* openly disavow those who were invoking his name as they robbed and killed. Perón insisted that conditions in Argentina were provoking the violence; if conditions changed, the trouble would disappear. This would remain a point of major disagreement between the Lanusse regime and Perón.

Both Cornicelli and Perón had their dialogue taped on separate recorders.[8] They agreed to keep the meeting a secret. Cornicelli lived up to his part of the deal. In return for his good faith he would achieve a perverse notoriety when Perón, in his inimitable style of ridicule, began to talk about his visit from a certain "Colonel Vermicelli."[9]

Jorge Paladino emerged from the Madrid conference as the newest, brightest star in the Peronist firmament. The *conductor* decided to accept Lanusse's offer and gave Paladino the go-ahead to enter into negotiations with Mor Roig.[10] José Rucci took back to Argentina instructions that the unions cool their antagonism toward the government. Unhappy at Paladino's preemption of center stage, the secretary-general of the CGT nonetheless left Madrid with his leadership of the Peronist labor wing firmly established.[11]

The green light he flashed to Paladino did not mean that Perón was terminating the Peronist offensive against the regime. While dispatching his personal delegate to the negotiating table, he was also instructing other Peronist politicians to continue to "hit hard" against the government.[12]

Nor did the *conductor* stop encouraging his young leftist supporters. This period saw the formation of several youth organizations advocating a radical brand of Peronism. Perón kept in close touch and sent them tapes and letters. This was an audience to which he channeled talk of "national socialism," praise for Castro's Cuba and Allende's Chile, and the promise of a *trasvasamiento generacional*. A new breed of leaders began to emerge, such as Rodolfo Galimberti, an articulate twenty-three-year-old graduate of the Tacuara,[13] and Dardo Cabo, a second-generation Peronist whose father was a metalworkers' union official once active in the resistance.[14]

In late June several of these youth groups participated in a conference that issued a warning against an "electoral farce," demanded Perón's physical presence in Argentina and expressed solidarity with guerrillas killed in action against the regime. The degree to which these organizations backed the special formations was readily apparent. A poster at the meeting declared: "If Evita were alive, she'd be a Montonero." At the close of the session a recorded message from someone identified as a Montonero claimed that FAP, FAR and the Montoneros were recruiting a "people's army" to fight a "people's war" in the name of Evita.[15]

Meanwhile, in Madrid, Perón gave a filmed interview in which he quoted Mao Tse-tung, dispensed revolutionary rhetoric and talked about antibodies and the international synarchy. He called elections a mere tactic and gave unmistakable approval to the use of violence to further the Peronist cause. He concluded by saluting those who had lost their lives in the struggle and sending his best wishes to "all of the comrades who are presently in prison."[16] The film was widely exhibited and its text published.

Young people attracted to Peronism by Perón's promise of a revolution like the one Castro had achieved and Allende would attempt tended to be ignorant of or to rationalize away the *conductor*'s past,[17] and discounted the fact that he welcomed into his fold elements from the other end of the political spectrum. For example, one of the youth groups he cultivated, the Guardia de Hierro, or "Iron Guard," brought together anti-Marxist militants who believed Perón when he talked about the international synarchy.[18] Moreover, the inner circle at Puerta de Hierro harbored individuals with extreme-right political views—López Rega and Milo Bogetich, a Croatian in charge of security at the residence.

The truth of the matter was that Perón had incredible success in his use of a political mirror. As one witness described it, "People visiting Puerta de Hierro would often stop by my apartment afterward. Many of them had diametrically opposing views, but every one of them would tell me how Perón agreed with them. It was very confusing to my wife. 'I just don't understand what this *justicialismo* is,' she would say."[19]

The ERP (the People's Revolutionary Army) was one group that refused to look at the *conductor* through a rose-tinted lens. At a clandestine press conference staged in late June, an ERP spokesman called Perón "the last hope for the Argentine middle class and a counterrevolutionary."[20] During this period the ERP was establishing a reputation as one of the more effective guerrilla groups. Its members not only stole and stockpiled large quantities of weapons but also pulled off a spectacular kidnapping of a director of the Swift Company meatpacking plant in Rosario. They released their victim, who also happened to be the honorary British consul, after Swift yielded to the demand that it distribute $62,500 worth of food to the city's poor.

In addition to negotiating with the regime, prodding hard-line Peronist politicians and stoking the flames of revolutionary Peronism, Perón opened up what might be termed a military offensive by wooing army officers who seemed vulnerable to the temptation to overthrow Lanusse. The possibility that yet another coup might produce a nationalist-populist military government like the one now ruling in Perú intrigued the *conductor*. His approach to the armed forces was as multidimensional as the other elements of his overall strategy. Francisco Licastro, a top student at the military academy until his expulsion in 1969 for conspiring against the regime, had recently converted to Peronism and developed contacts with young officers with leftist sympathies.[21] Retired Lieutenant Colonel Jorge Osinde, chief of intelligence during Perón's second presidency and an ultra-right-winger, took on the task of cultivating conservative anticommunist officers.[22]

The complex, at times contradictory, tactical thrusts launched from Puerta de Hierro converged toward the simple goal of restoring Perón to power. Lanusse, on the other hand, did not possess the luxuries of complete freedom of action and a clear objective. He had to account to his military peers. Moreover, his promise of a clean game could not stand as an end in itself if it meant an assumption of the risk of a Peronist victory at the polls and a triumphal return of the fugitive tyrant.

Lanusse's solution was the Grand National Accord, which he defined as a pre-election consensus to be reached by the major institutions of the country concerning the type of government to succeed him.[23] Lanusse's argument was that a leap into the void posed dangers as great as, if not greater than, a perpetuation of the status quo. He wanted to forge an agreement that would provide a political, social and economic framework conducive to both stability and progress.

A Grand National Accord would impose explicit limitations, beyond those spelled out in the constitution, upon future occupants of the Casa Rosada. Moreover, it not only numbered the armed forces among the participating institutions but also conferred upon them the duty to police compliance with the accord. Lanusse found it much more difficult to enthuse the major political parties about the need for a consensus than about his clean game. Indeed, the more he pushed for the former, the more he jeopardized the latter. Naturally, suspicious politicians became even more wary as speculation increased that the accord was really a vehicle for Lanusse's political ambitions. Self-proscription from the promised elections could have stilled these fears, but the president refrained from eliminating himself. He later explained that to do so would have jeopardized his effort to prepare the way for a transition to civilian rule.[24]

Lanusse kept his dream of an accord on a back burner during the tough negotiations, beginning in May, with Paladino. It would have been premature and improvident to press the Peronists on this point at a time when the president was trying to lure them into the clean game. The situation now called for some concrete gestures on the part of the regime to placate Perón and his followers.

In July a new Argentine ambassador, Air Force Brigadier Jorge Rojas Silveyra, arrived in Madrid. One of his first official acts was to make contact with Perón. The two men met secretly at Puerta de Hierro and Lanusse's envoy disclosed that the government would pay Perón the presidential pension accruing to him since he left office in 1955.[25]

This was a major concession, part of a pattern which included an announcement that Perón's bust would soon be placed in the Casa Rosada alongside those of other presidents, the dropping of the statutory rape charge against him and the first public disclosure that the Vatican had lifted his excommunication. But what the Peronist faithful longed for more than anything else was the return of Evita's body.

On Thursday, September 22, Rojas Silveyra telephoned Perón with the news that the corpse was finally on its way. Postponing his appointments for the rest of the week, the *conductor* began an anxious vigil that ended at 9:00 P.M. on Friday when the ambassador drove up to the house. Moments later, a van escorted by two police jeeps turned into the driveway. Colonel Mario Cabanillas, the Army Information Service chief who had taken custody of the body in 1956, stepped out of one of the jeeps and supervised the unloading of a black wooden coffin, which was carried into the living room. Perón, Isabel and two monks gathered around as López Rega and Paladino prepared to open the casket. Daniel used a small blowtorch to break the metal seal—a witless measure, since the preservatives used in the embalming were highly flammable.[26] Paladino then pried open the lid and cut his finger. According to one witness, Perón displayed no visible sign of emotion.[27] There was a moment of silence, and then Perón said only, "It's Evita."[28] The contents of the coffin were in a state of dishevelment attributable to careless handling. The shroud was damp and stained. But except for a flattening of the nose, Dr. Ara's masterpiece was remarkably intact.

Rojas Silveyra took Perón aside and described to him the route the corpse had taken in its long journey from Buenos Aires to Madrid. President Aramburu had made the decision to ship Evita's remains abroad. Colonel Cabanillas accompanied the coffin to a cemetery in Milan, Italy, and had it buried (some say with the cooperation of the Vatican, though ecclesiastical authorities deny it) in a grave marked with the name Maria Maggi. When the time came to give the body back to Perón, Cabanillas returned to the cemetery. Posing as a relative of the deceased, he had the coffin exhumed and set out by truck across southern France into Spain.[29] Perón's only response to the ambassador's disclosures was the terse comment: "I spent many happy years with this woman."[30] He then signed a paper acknowledging receipt of the body.

On Saturday, Dr. Ara, who was living in Madrid, examined the remains. He found the minor damage to be easily reparable.[31] Isabel washed the corpse and arranged its hair. Evita's sisters, flying to Spain immediately upon notification of the delivery, made a new shroud.

The problem of what to do with the body now rested with Perón. The sisters preferred that it be entombed in Madrid. But Evita's remains had too much symbolic value. Young left-wing Peronists had already appropriated her. They pointed to her violent tirades against the oligarchy, her repeated voicing of the cry "Perón or Death" and the fact that she once tried to purchase arms for her descamisados as proof that she harbored genuinely revolutionary impulses. Their hope was to transform "Evita the Saint" into "Evita the Guerrilla."

At the same time Puerta de Hierro's resident warlock had his own designs on Eva Perón's remains. López Rega opposed the burial of the body and had it moved to a room on the second floor.[32] Later, a fantastic story—entirely credible in light of his proven esoteric bent—began to circulate: he had Isabel lie on top of the coffin while he burned candles and uttered incantations for the purpose of raising Evita's spiritual essence from the corpse to the psyche of her would-be successor.[33]

Perón, meanwhile, seemed perfectly content to keep the body in his home. Some view this as indicative of the degree of control López Rega was exercising over the household, yet it also squares with an attitude of disinterest on the part of the *conductor*, who paid little more than lip service to the memory of Evita.

Two weeks after the return of the body, Lanusse fixed a date for general elections. The balloting was to take place on March 11, 1973, and the new government would take power on May 25 of that year. The regime had now locked itself into a timetable reasonably close to what Peronists were demanding.

There was now a distinct momentum to the president's campaign to extricate the country from its political impasse. In early October several army units staged an abortive coup in an effort to head off the process leading to elections. With the backing of a broad cross section of society, including the CGT and the Hora del Pueblo, Lanusse easily defeated the dissidents, whom he called members of the "Fascist far right."[34] His goal of national unity had never seemed more within reach. What he needed most at this point was a positive sign from Madrid. Instead, he received a double dash of cold water. Within the space of a few weeks Jorge Paladino resigned as Perón's delegate and the *conductor* appointed Héctor Cámpora to replace him.

The circumstances surrounding Paladino's downfall remain opaque to this day. Many Peronists believe López Rega masterminded the change in delegates as part of his bid to monopolize power. A doctoral dissertation written by a U.S. diplomat stationed in Buenos Aires during the early 1970s argues that Lanusse precipitated the defenestration by creating the impression, in the wake of his popular victory over the military rebels, that he really intended to be the presidential candidate of his Grand National Accord.[35]

While López Rega did oppose Paladino at every turn, the degree of control El Brujo exercised over Puerta de Hierro did not extend to decisions of this magnitude. At best he contributed to conditions that may have influenced Perón to make the sudden switch. Putting the blame on López Rega has become an escape for Peronists unwilling to confront Perón's responsibility for the events of the last years of his life. Indeed, it is altogether likely that the *conductor* used his private secretary as a check upon Paladino. He sent López Rega on a mission to Buenos Aires in July 1971 to perform tasks that tended to undercut his delegate.[36]

The theory that Lanusse caused Paladino's removal rests upon Perón's supposed reaction to several of the conciliatory gestures launched in his direction and to moves the president made after crushing the October coup. According to this interpretation, the *conductor* took offense at the government's decision to pay him his pension not in a lump sum but in installments; Lanusse's increased emphasis upon the accord aroused his deepest suspicions; then, immediately after the unsuccessful revolt, several cabinet changes and public hints by Lanusse intimates that he consider running for president convinced Perón that the negotiations were an effort to trap the Peronists in a new political movement headed by Lanusse; the *conductor* therefore sacked his negotiator and switched to a tough line.[37]

Assigning to Lanusse blame for what befell Paladino puts too narrow a focus on the struggle between Perón and the military regime. The political thrusts and parries were but one aspect of a complex scenario that also required the *conductor* to manipulate his followers in order to control them. Paladino had become quite controversial within Peronist ranks. The left, for example, abhorred him. John William Cooke's widow called him a "traitor to the fatherland and the working class" and gave voice to a charge that would be repeated many times: Paladino was not Perón's delegate to Lanusse but rather Lanusse's delegate to Perón.[38] Rodolfo Galimberti feuded openly with Paladino.[39] The CGT hierarchy had little use for him.[40] Rogelio Frigerio, maintaining a close epistolary contact with Perón, expressed misgivings about Paladino.[41] Furthermore, the beleaguered delegate took a stab in the back from unknown members of Lanusse's staff. They sent Perón a copy of a secret tape of a Lanusse-Paladino conversation in which the latter made a derogatory reference to his *conductor*.[42]

Thus the ground under Paladino had been trembling for some time. Rumors of his impending dismissal, moreover, intensified just *prior* to the October coup.[43] Expendability walked hand in glove with the position he held. His days as delegate were clearly numbered long before Lanusse's alleged indiscretions.

Every Perón subordinate who acquired independent prestige ended up on the scrap heap. Paladino had become a personality in his own right, respected by non-Peronist leaders, supported by admirers within the Peronist movement and vulnerable to the charge that he was interested in something other than the best interests of his chief. Why should his fate have differed from that suffered by Domingo Mercante and others?

Moreover, the implication is dubious that if the president had acted more prudently, he would have won Perón's consent to elections that at best would have led to an assumption of power by a government espousing "Peronism without Perón" under preset limitations on its authority. This overlooks the *conductor*'s dictum that elections were but one tactic in the battle he was waging. A shift from dialogue to intransigence more likely was yet another application of pendular politics.

Finally, to fault Lanusse assumes that Perón was not bent upon returning to the Casa Rosada. Indeed, there were many who took him at his word when he would tap himself on the chest and say "I'm like an automobile that looks good on the outside but inside the motor is broken down."[44] His lifelong aversion to veracity suggests that this was a smoke screen. As his friend Jorge Antonio has observed, "If you don't understand his goal was to return to power, you are an illiterate."[45]

The choice of Héctor Cámpora as delegate is consistent with this reading of Perón's intentions. The former president of the Chamber of Deputies had been politically inactive since his escape from Ushuaia. The newspaper *La Opinión* recalled his fabled obsequiousness to Perón and reported that when a Peronist deputy once proposed that the most important plaza in every Argentine town be renamed "President Perón," Cámpora took the floor to urge that *every* plaza in *every* town bear the names of Perón and Evita.[46]*

Perón had exchanged an intelligent, respected lieutenant for a mindless acolyte. The new ground rules for political activity in Argentina required the parties to reorganize by means of internal elections. Paladino had favored an open, democratic competition that he felt would revitalize the movement. Cámpora, acting on Perón's orders, would seek to reinstate verticality—in contemporary slang, *dedocracia*, or "finger-ocracy," the exercise of power by pointing the finger—by permitting the nomination of only one officially approved candidate for each party position to be filled. This responded to Perón's need to retain absolute control over his flock, and ought to have given pause to those who were predicting and counting upon the *conductor*'s semiretirement.

* According to a popular anecdote, once when Cámpora went to the residence Perón called him upstairs to the bathroom while he was shaving. The *conductor* asked him what time it was. "Any time you wish, General," Cámpora replied.

49

Lanusse vs. Perón:
Phase 2

A small brass band struck up the refrain of "*Los muchachos peronistas*" as the Aerolíneas Argentinas jet taxied down the runway at the Ezeiza Airport outside Buenos Aires. A crowd numbering in the neighborhood of 10,000 packed the roof terrace and milled about the approaches to the terminal building. All eyes strained for a glimpse at one of the arriving passengers, María Estela Martínez de Perón, who had been dispatched from Puerta de Hierro on her second political mission to Argentina.

The stated purpose of the visit, which began on the morning of December 7, 1971, was to promote "unity, organization and solidarity within the Peronist movement."[1] Perón had sounded this theme to prepare his followers for intra-party elections scheduled for early 1972. While not nearly of the magnitude of the threat posed by Vandor five years earlier, an expected challenge by supporters of Jorge Paladino might undermine the monolithic front the *conductor* felt he needed in the struggle with Lanusse. He was not taking any chances.

Although Isabel received a warm welcome as she stepped from the plane, the undercurrents of discord that quickly surfaced suggested that Perón had reason to worry, but not because of Paladino. The slogans on most of the banners and placards were those of the Peronist left. "FAP and the Montoneros are our comrades," roared one group of young militants, while another kept repeating "Evita, Perón, Revolution."[2] Bass drums, a staple at Peronist rallies, punctuated the chants.

While the left dominated the rank and file, the right controlled physical access to Isabel. Lieutenant Colonel Osinde directed a squad of retired army men who guarded her so efficiently that the police remained out of sight. López Rega never left her side.

Héctor Cámpora led the welcoming committee, which included delegates from all sectors of the movement. One of Evita's sisters provided a symbolic link to the past. The brief ceremonies unfolded without incident.

On the heels of Paladino's removal, Perón had shuffled his *consejo superior*, or high council, Peronism's top consultative body. Among those he added were: Héctor Cámpora; Rodolfo Galimberti and Francisco Licastro, whose presence gave the first trace of fulfillment to the often-promised *trasvasamiento generacional*; Jorge Osinde, a counterweight from the right; and Isabel.[3] López Rega did not make the list, but his vantage point as Perón's private secretary and his influence over Isabel more than compensated for the omission. Daniel also helped launch *Las Bases*, a Peronist magazine that would gain official status in January. Before long he was editing the publication, with help from daughter Norma and Raúl Lastiri, a minor Peronist functionary soon to become his son-in-law.

Isabel and López Rega spent three months in Argentina. The *conductor*'s wife visited various Peronist organizations and echoed her husband's pronouncements on the virtues of unity. In one notable radio interview she ranged even further afield, urging her compatriots to follow the teachings of the church, go to mass regularly and love one another across class lines.[4]* Her entreaties went for naught, as intramural differences continued to flare. Coincidental with her sojourn was the emergence of Rodolfo Galimberti as the movement's enfant terrible. He feuded noisily with labor leaders and right-wing youth groups such as the Guardia de Hierro. On the eve of Isabel's departure, he even denounced López Rega.[5]

These discordant notes did not deter the *conductor* from orchestrating other elements of his grand strategy. He welcomed non-Peronist leaders to Puerta de Hierro and worked to put together a political front for the forthcoming elections. Rogelio Frigerio visited him in January. Shortly thereafter Perón issued a document drafted in large part by Frigerio and advocating some of the latter's ideas regarding economic development.[6] This paved the way for a meeting between Perón and Arturo Frondizi, who traveled to Madrid in March and for the first time sat down with his former adversary. Their historic encounter bore fruit in the form of the Frente Cívico de Liberación Nacional (Civic Front for National Liberation), or FRECILINA, an electoral alliance composed of the Peronists, Frondizi's MID and several small political parties.

Another aspect of Perón's plan called for the formulation of wage and price measures that would be both acceptable to the "vertebral column" of his movement—the working class—and consistent with the overall economic policy he had in mind for Argentina. The mechanism for which he opted was a formal agreement, dubbed the "social contract," between labor and management. It would bind workers to a short-term voluntary wage freeze and business to price controls. In exchange for acquiescence,

---

* She also listed Charlton Heston and Charles Bronson as her favorite actors and revealed she had seen the movie *The Ten Commandments* seven times. *La Opinión*, January 19, 1972.

the labor movement was to receive an assurance that wages would eventually increase at a rate that would redistribute income in the workers' favor.[7]

Astute enough to realize how much political mileage he could obtain from a "social contract," the *conductor* brought labor and management representatives together in 1972 to begin hammering out a consensus. José Rucci, the CGT's secretary-general, served as chief negotiator for the unions. The man who sat on the other side of the table was José Ber Gelbard, soon to become a key and highly controversial figure in the resurgence of Peronism.

A Jewish immigrant from Poland, Gelbard as a child sold trinkets on the streets of the city of Catamarca. He later made his mark as an astute, energetic entrepreneur and helped found the Confederación General Económica (General Economic Confederation), or CGE, during Perón's second presidency. The CGE represented small businessmen, mostly from northwestern Argentina, who supported the regime and sought government subsidies in return. Now in his third term as head of the CGE, Gelbard vigorously promoted the "social contract" among his peers. He had constant access to Perón, though he was not a Peronist. His enemies accused him of many things (for example, he was linked to a business scandal allegedly involving Lanusse and had a shadowy relationship with López Rega).[8] In 1971 CGE economists began drafting a framework for the "social contract," the idea for which derived from Perón's notion of the "organized community."

The plague of political violence continued to ravage Argentina. Perón did not control it, but he profited immensely from the general climate of unrest, the operations of the various guerrilla groups and the embattled regime's inability to cope with the problem. Strikes, often culminating in bloodshed, were becoming almost daily occurrences. In the tradition of the *cordobazo*, demonstrators paralyzed Mendoza and forced the army to occupy the city in early April 1972. Protests spread to other large metropolitan areas in June.[9]

At the same time the guerrillas stepped up their robberies, bombings and kidnappings. In late March an ERP commando unit seized and held for ransom the president of the Italian-owned FIAT automotive industries in Argentina. The government refused to meet a demand for $1 million and the release of certain political prisoners. Shortly afterward, during a police raid on their hideout, the terrorists shot and killed their captive. On the very same day the general who commanded the army's Second Corps in Rosario fell victim to machine-gun fire as he rode to work. The ERP and the FAR claimed joint responsibility for the latter assassination.[10]

The authorities seemed helpless to prevent these outrages. Reports of torture of prisoners by the police and military attested to a growing sense of frustration and in turn gave further impetus to the widespread discontent.[11] An even more ominous development was an increase in reprisal attacks upon Peronists and leftists by individuals suspected of having ties to the police and the armed forces.

Now approaching its second year, the match between Alejandro Lanusse and Juan Perón played itself out against this bloodstained backdrop. As the situation worsened, time became one of Perón's most important allies. He refused to let himself be drawn into any sort of commitment on Lanusse's terms, which sought his voluntary withdrawal from the forthcoming elections and his help against the terrorist menace. The president found himself in a hole that deepened with each passing month, as it became less likely by the moment that he could reverse the process of democratization he had begun.

During this same period Ambassador Rojas Silveyra was pressuring Perón to make a public denunciation of the murders of the FIAT executive and the army general.[12] The kidnapping of the businessman could not have pleased the *conductor*; he had close ties to Italian industrialists and the perpetrators were from a non-Peronist guerrilla group. But even though CGT officials and other prominent Peronists deplored the incidents, their leader maintained his silence. Later he explained, "I have made no declaration because I think the people's violence is being provoked by violence on the government's part."[13] After Perón's refusal to speak out, Rojas Silveyra never again visited Puerta de Hierro.

At this point Perón seemed to be hardening his position. In response to speculation that both he and his adversary in the Casa Rosada were going to withdraw from the elections, he sarcastically noted that "Lanusse's proscribing himself as a presidential candidate is like my removing myself from the running for the throne of England."[14] To an Italian journalist he reiterated the dire warning that the regime was leading Argentina toward civil war, and disclosed that Lanusse had been sending emissaries to Puerta de Hierro, the first public reference to his contacts with Cornicelli and Rojas Silveyra.[15] This put the president on the defensive and forced him to release a transcript of the Perón-Cornicelli dialogue. On June 25 a Peronist party conference nominated Perón as its candidate for president.

Elements within the armed forces now began to express disgruntlement with Lanusse, and rumors of an impending coup circulated in early July.[16] In addition, the CGT announced plans for a new wave of strikes. The Casa Rosada suspected the worst, an *argentinazo* that would dwarf the 1969 Córdoba uprising. The president felt he had to take some decisive action. He chose the occasion of the July 7, 1972, armed forces comradeship dinner to launch a counteroffensive.

Anyone wishing to qualify as a candidate for president in 1973, he announced, would have to be physically present in Argentina before August 25, 1972. Further, any major government official who intended to run for president would have to resign by that date.[17] Thus, the regime would not proscribe Perón's candidacy; he had the option of returning by August 25 or taking himself out of the race. The fact that Lanusse gave himself a similar choice created an impression of fairness that he hoped would lead the public (and especially the Peronist rank and file) to accept the new ground rules.

Perón had no intention of permitting the regime to dictate the terms of his return or to force him to declare his candidacy before he judged the time to be ripe. Calling Lanusse's conditions arbitrary and not conducive to bringing peace to Argentina, he indicated that he would not accept them.[18]* Peronist leaders echoed their *conductor* and refused to join in negotiations Mor Roig was attempting to revive in an effort to forge an agreement with the political parties about the 1973 elections. Moreover, Cámpora, in a blatant effort to drive a wedge between Lanusse and the armed forces, suggested that the president was no longer in tune with the true sentiments of his fellow officers.[19]

Lanusse's response was volcanic. In a July 27 speech at the military academy he unleashed a personal attack upon Perón. Insisting that he would put no obstacles in the way if Perón wanted to return before August 25—he would even give him money for the trip, if that were necessary—the president opined that his adversary would remain in Madrid because "he doesn't have the balls to come back."[20] This aspersion on Perón's manhood was a rare public expression of a familiar slur.

The speech was more than a temper tantrum. Lanusse made a big point of emphasizing his respect for the Peronist party and its right to participate in the restoration of civilian government. If Perón thought he could separate the president from his military constituency, Lanusse would now demonstrate that he could similarly divide the Peronist movement.

The immediate Peronist rejoinder, albeit not planned as such, came during a rally staged by the left-wing youth sector in honor of Eva Perón. On July 28 a large crowd roared revolutionary slogans, cheered Rodolfo Galimberti as he lauded the "special formations" and heard Cámpora promise "a new seventeenth of October this year with Perón in the Plaza de Mayo."[21]

But if the Peronist left thought Lanusse's insults would radicalize Perón, they were mistaken. He waited several days and then issued a mild, enigmatic statement leaving the door ajar for further negotiations.[22] The sudden appearance of his bust (and Frondizi's) in the presidential gallery of the Casa Rosada in August further befuddled observers.

The best explanation for this turn of events derives in some measure from Lanusse's belief that he had Perón caught between having to accept

---

* This did not discourage a Uruguayan newspaper from printing a fanciful report that he intended to fly to the British Falkland Islands, which Argentines claimed as their territory, in order to be in technical compliance with the residence requirement. *La Opinión,* July 28, 1972, p. 11.

or reject the regime's ground rules; if he said yes, he would lose face; if he said no, he risked defections from Peronists unwilling to sit on the political sidelines. Whichever alternative he chose, the president would appear victorious, and the placing of the bust merely symbolized his mood of confidence.

Perón's patience paid off sooner than he perhaps expected. He summoned Cámpora to Madrid for a conference beginning August 4. Only five days later, one of Lanusse's civilian ministers resigned, citing political differences with the president, and on the next day the commander of the air force made a speech criticizing the regime's economic policies. Meanwhile, Mor Roig was making a last-ditch effort to bring the leaders of the various parties together in order to work out an agreement on the restoration of democracy. His labors foundered. The gusty winds that had filled Lanusse's sails in July were gone by mid-August.

It was at this precise moment that the president took a hit from the revolutionary left and from his antagonist in Madrid. On August 15 a guerrilla band attacked an army maximum-security prison in the Patagonian town of Rawson as its inmates mutinied. Twenty-five prisoners, members of the ERP, FAR and the Montoneros, escaped to the airport at the nearby city of Trelew and hijacked a commercial jet. Six of them, including the Harvard-educated ERP leader, Roberto Santucho, boarded the plane and flew to Chile, where they asked the Allende government for political asylum. Security forces recaptured the rest of the escapees and took them to a navy prison in Trelew.

By coincidence, on that same day Cámpora told a Madrid press conference that Juan Perón, though rejecting the August 25 deadline, would definitely return to Argentina before the end of 1972.[23] A flurry of rumors that Perón was about to turn up in Uruguay, Paraguay, Panamá or Perú had circulated from the time Cámpora arrived in Spain. Now, as he was departing for Ezeiza, the dentist-delegate lent a degree of substance to the speculation.

Within the week Perón's new strategy became apparent. At a meeting of Peronist leaders in a Buenos Aires hotel Cámpora released a document bearing his signature along with the *conductor*'s. Entitled "To the People of Argentina and to the Armed Forces," it made a direct pitch to the military: the regime did not represent the armed forces, but rather the "economic-financial power structure"; Lanusse was putting the military on a collision course with the people; it was not too late for the men in uniform to avoid this conflict by reaching an accommodation with Perón, who embodied the hopes of a majority of Argentines.[24]

Fortune, at Perón's side throughout the month, then struck yet another blow for him. Sixteen of the guerrillas who had been brought to the Trelew prison after the hijacking were shot to death outside their cells, and three others were wounded.[25] The government claimed they had attempted to escape, but the explanation had a false ring to it. The captives had been under heavy security, and the navy enjoyed a reputation for brutality. There were inconsistencies in official versions of the incident. A survivor later testified that guards lined up the prisoners and then mowed them down with automatic weapons.[26] The bloodbath at Trelew unified the revolutionary left, since the victims had been members of several different groups. It also produced a wave of public revulsion against the regime.

Lanusse's dream of a Grand National Accord had collapsed, social unrest was as widespread as ever, the subversives were growing more brazen by the day and the Perón problem had not disappeared. The regime may have proscribed him as a candidate, but it had been unable to impose conditions upon the 1973 elections. Lanusse now faced the unpalatable alternatives of rigging the elections, calling them off, or permitting events to run their course.

It is difficult to discern which of these scenarios Perón really preferred. In preparation for the possibility of elections he directed Cámpora to try to work out some kind of joint program with the Radicals through the Hora del Pueblo, but he also pursued his courtship of the armed forces. Thus if Lanusse attempted to go back on his promise of a clean game, the popular protest and terrorist violence certain to follow could trigger a military coup. The *conductor*'s hope may have been that nationalist officers sympathetic to him would then take power and pave the way for his return.

Cámpora had no success with the Radicals, who balked at his request that the Hora del Pueblo issue a statement denouncing the August 25 residency requirement.[27] Balbín and company seemed hesitant to make common cause with the Peronists, in part because of their hope of attracting Peronist support for Balbín's candidacy in the event the regime vetoed a Peronist presidential nominee, in part because they disapproved of Peronist overtures toward the military. In addition, Perón's reluctance to spell out his intentions, while an effective tactic in his contest with the regime, was hardly conducive to winning the confidence of the nation's second-largest political party.

While efforts to engage the Radicals faltered, Perón was preparing an unexpected move, the negotiation of an agreement with the regime itself. In mid-September, he drafted his own program for normalization. Gelbard is thought to have acted as a contact with the Casa Rosada in an attempt to reach a consensus about the terms of the program.[28] The final version was relayed to Cámpora, who formally presented it to the government on September 29.

The document contained two parts, a broad Agreement for National Reconstruction and a ten-point plan detailing its terms.[29] Some of the points were vague (for example, a call for the determination of what role the armed forces would play and for the political parties to reach an accord about the national elections); others were quite specific—the appointment of a military officer as interior minister to guarantee fair elections and the release of all political prisoners.

The moderate tone of the Peronist proposal and the regime's positive response to it evidenced prior consultation between Puerta de Hierro and the Casa Rosada.[30] Both sides seemed to be on the verge of a deal. But Cámpora insisted upon talking with representatives of the military commanders-in-chief. The government insisted that he sit down with the special commission that formed to work out the transition to civilian rule. Cámpora refused, whereupon the whole process disintegrated, as suddenly as it had begun.[31]

One explanation for these strange events puts the blame on Héctor Cámpora's ambition to become the Peronist candidate.[32] Speculation about a Cámpora candidacy had already surfaced.[33] There is some evidence that he may have impeded negotiations between Perón and the Radical party to secure the *conductor*'s blessing on a ticket to be composed of Balbín and a Peronist to be named later.[34] He knew the military would exclude him in any agreement they reached with Perón.

But Cámpora's fabled servility had not flagged and he had never before betrayed the slightest glimmer of political acumen. If he did intentionally keep Perón and the regime from an accord, it is more likely that others were manipulating him. Later he would clearly be acting under the influence of the Peronist left. Whether they had already begun to use him is uncertain. It is also possible that he simply misunderstood Perón and botched things. The fact that Cámpora had gone to Madrid for Perón's birthday on October 8 makes it conceivable that he was following Perón's instructions when he returned and demanded to confer directly with the armed forces.

Why would the *conductor* want to abort a process he himself had set in motion? The most logical inference to be drawn is that he meant the Agreement for National Reconstruction to be no more than a feint, perhaps to raise false hopes, perhaps to keep the regime in the dark about his intentions. He had to return to Argentina in 1972 in order to keep his word and also prove he still had the balls to do it. Yet he never entertained the slightest desire to work out a compromise that would relegate him to a secondary status. He often spoke as though he would be satisfied to become an elder statesman, but this was what many of his listeners wanted to hear.

By late October all negotiations between Perón and the regime had apparently ceased, but the preparations for the *conductor*'s return had gathered a seemingly irreversible momentum. An Alitalia jet had been chartered for mid-November. A return committee was arranging for a large delegation to meet him in Rome and accompany him back to Buenos Aires. There were the usual doubts and diversions. Perón told a correspondent for the French paper *Le Figaro* that he would return only if he could bring peace to Argentina and that conditions at the moment did not favor national reconciliation.[35] This disheartened the faithful to such a degree that López Rega disavowed the story and falsely claimed the reporter did not understand Spanish well.[36] There were rumors that Perón would fly to a nearby country. Confusion reigned. Perón had his *quilombo*.

50

A Leap into the Void

It was hardly a "Peronist day." A torrential rain soaked the verdant fields around Ezeiza and fed vast puddles that swamped the runways. A trio of helicopters hovered anxiously nearby. In the dense gloom their crews could barely discern traces of the 35,000 troops, tanks and artillery that had fanned out from the airport to form an impenetrable ring. A carefully screened crowd of 300 spectators and 1,500 media representatives braved the downpour in order to witness the historic occasion. After seventeen years and fifty-two days in exile, Juan Domingo Perón was coming home.[1]

The aircraft touched down at 11:15 A.M., not the fabled black plane but a white Alitalia DC-8, baptized the "Giuseppe Verdi," bearing a curious potpourri of Peronist politicians, labor leaders, retired military officers, businessmen, economists, priests, physicians, figures from the sports world and entertainers. They had crossed the ocean three nights earlier so that they might accompany their *conductor*, his wife and his private secretary on the flight from Rome.

The commander of the Ezeiza air base was the first Argentine official to board the jet. He found Perón in shirt-sleeves, seated in the first-class compartment.

"Good morning, sir," he greeted the ex-president.

"Good morning, Brigadier."

"Commodore, sir." The officer proceeded to explain the security measures that had been taken at the airport and told Perón that he and three other persons might leave the plane immediately.

"Thank you very much, Brigadier," needled Perón.

"Commodore, sir," came the cool rejoinder.[2]

Isabel, López Rega and Cámpora joined the *conductor* as he descended the gangplank and set foot on Argentine soil. In the words of a *Washington Post* reporter, he "looked astonishingly fit and scarcely tired for a man of his seventy-seven years."[3] The foursome clambered into a cream-colored Ford Fairlane, which slowly headed toward the airport hotel. A cordon of police cars and motorcycles quickly surrounded them. As the convoy passed the throng of welcomers, the Fairlane halted and Perón emerged to greet his cheering, rain-drenched followers. José Rucci suddenly dashed out from behind a restraining barrier, embraced his leader and lifted an umbrella over Perón's head. Both arms aloft in a familiar salutation, the onetime fugitive tyrant beamed his classic smile and then ducked back into the car.

The definitive word on the 1972 return of Juan Perón had issued from Héctor Cámpora on November 7, when he disclosed that Perón would arrive at Ezeiza on the morning of the seventeenth.[4] Lanusse reacted quickly with an assurance that the government would guarantee his physical security.[5] In the ten days separating the formal announcement and the actual event, Argentina experienced a veritable orgy of uncertainty.

On one level there were many who embraced the so-called Golden Vision, a belief that Perón was coming to sign a "grand national accord" with the military commanders and the leaders of the other parties, withdraw himself as a presidential candidate and fly back in triumph to Madrid, there to live out the rest of his days, an even greater national hero than San Martín.[6] The ex-president fed this expectation during talks with a non-Peronist politician in Madrid. The latter brought back to Buenos Aires a document prepared in Puerta de Hierro and spelling out a version of the "Golden Vision" which even floated the possibility of a Peronist-backed Lanusse candidacy.[7] But as the departure date drew near, one could detect no sign of any serious preparation for the fashioning of an agreement to which Perón, the junta and the political parties might subscribe.

Another conviction held by many was that Perón and the Casa Rosada had reached a secret understanding about the terms of his visit.[8] Lanusse categorically denied this, but people found it difficult to believe that Perón would step off a plane at Ezeiza without prior categorical assurances that he would not be turned back or taken into custody. A meeting between Lanusse and Gelbard on November 9 strengthened speculation that a deal had been made.[9] However, Gelbard later admitted to a U.S. diplomat that no prior agreement had been worked out, and that Perón hoped that a mass demonstration of popular support would force the military to meet his demands.[10]

How Perón might use his "special formations" and how they would greet his arrival greatly preoccupied the Casa Rosada. In late October the ex-president appointed as secretary-general of the Peronist movement Juan Abal Medina, a young man whose brother had been killed by police in a raid on terrorists allegedly involved in the Aramburu kidnapping. To some this looked like a tilt toward the Peronist left.[11]

On November 9 during a speech in Buenos Aires, Rodolfo Galimberti had compounded the anxiety by telling a student audience that they should be on hand at Ezeiza to welcome Perón; "those who have stones should bring stones," he added; "those who have something more should bring something more"; he urged listeners who could not reach the airport to occupy factories, neighborhoods and the university.[12] It sounded like a call for open insurrection. Moderate Peronists disclaimed his remarks, Lanusse made much of them, and Galimberti later claimed that the press had "misinterpreted" him.[13] From Madrid Perón reiterated his desire to bring peace to Argentina but did not specifically direct his followers to stay home on November 17.[14]

The weight government and military officials attached to the possibility Perón might at the last moment decide not to return gave a separate dimension to a panorama that was growing more suspenseful by the day. Lanusse later claimed he became convinced in late October that Perón would come,[15] but in a speech to a group of generals on November 11 he was still hedging his bets. He reported speculation that his adversary would visit the Pope and then claim the Holy Father had urged him not to go back to Argentina; this would serve as a face-saving pretext for the postponement of the trip. The president also indicated that Perón might try to incite his people to commit disturbances that would force the regime to keep him from entering the country.[16] A high-ranking Argentine army officer told U.S. military-intelligence personnel in late November that Peron's return caught Lanusse by surprise.[17]

Nothing Perón did in the days prior to his scheduled departure bespoke an impending change of plans. On November 14, Paraguayan passport in hand, he flew to Rome in a chartered twin-engine, French-built executive jet. Looking dapper in a dark gray suit, his camel's-hair coat casually draped over one arm, he stepped off the plane with Isabel at his side and grinned at the herd of reporters awaiting him. It was his first trip to the Eternal City since before World War II. He relished the chance to show off his fluency in Italian and to reminisce about his prior visit.[18]

Nothing of particular consequence came from the *conductor*'s sojourn in Rome. On the afternoon of the fourteenth he had a private conversation with Italy's Premier Giulio Andreotti in the latter's office, but they merely exchanged pleasantries and opinions. An archbishop from the Vatican called upon the ex-president at his hotel the next day and afterward told reporters that Perón had decided to forgo seeking an audience with Paul VI. The Pope's reluctance to become involved in the domestic politics of Argentina had been discreetly communicated to the *conductor* and he did not press the matter.[19] Finally, Perón met with an official from the Rumanian embassy and requested permission to visit Bucharest at some future date.

Meanwhile, on the home front the Lanusse regime was taking extraordi-

nary security precautions. Friday the nineteenth would be a paid holiday
for workers. All schools and universities were to recess. No crowds would
be allowed to gather. Only persons with special passes would be admitted
to Ezeiza. Heavily armed troops had already begun to converge upon the
airport.

The arrival of a plane filled with Peronists who were to accompany
their leader on the Rome–Buenos Aires flight and the frenzy generated
by swarms of journalists transcended mere confusion as the moment of
departure drew near. Pushing and shoving culminated in an exchange of
blows when a reception for Perón and his swollen entourage commingled
with a news conference at which the *conductor* was scheduled to appear.

That evening they filed aboard the Alitalia jet, 154 passengers in all,
a curious elite that embraced obvious choices from Peronism past and
present (Antonio Cafiero, Raúl Matera, Juana Larrauri, retired General
Ernesto Fatigatti, Alfredo Gómez Morales), a couple of non-Peronist
politicians, and a miscellany featuring a boxer, a tango singer, a model, a
film director, a historian and a poet. In the first-class cabin with Perón
and Isabel were López Rega, Isabel's maid, Perón's Croatian chief bodyguard, Cámpora, Raúl and Norma Lastiri (López Rega's son-in-law and
daughter) and several veteran Peronists who had organized the charter.
Noticeably missing from the plane were representatives of the JP (Peronist
Youth).

Shortly before midnight the DC-8 roared off the runway and set a course
toward Dakar on the west coast of Africa. After a brief refueling stop,
the airliner headed across the South Atlantic in the direction of the Río
de la Plata estuary. The journey from Rome to Ezeiza would take fifteen
and a half hours.

In the meantime groups of young people were gathering in Buenos
Aires and the suburbs for a march on Ezeiza. With bass drums and banners
they set out to defy the regime and welcome their *conductor*, leaving behind quiet, empty streets that gave the capital the look of a ghost town.
A steady rain fell as they converged upon the approach routes to the airport, some heading toward the main access highway, others making their
way along railroad tracks. But before they could reach even the environs
of Ezeiza, a massive concentration of troops supported by armor and
artillery discharged ample quantities of tear gas to repulse them. The demonstrators were as unsuccessful as the navy men who staged a brief rebellion that morning at the mechanics's school to protest Perón's return.

A pronounced age differential separated those who tried to win the
street for Perón and those admitted to the airport. The official welcomers
were orthodox politicians and labor leaders, and such relics as Domingo
Mercante and Carlos Aloé. The frustrated marchers, for the most part,
were too young to remember the last Peronist government.

Once inside the hotel at Ezeiza, Perón discovered that he was not free to leave. A controversy erupted as Cámpora accused the army of holding his *conductor* prisoner, while the regime preferred to term his status protective custody. Political leaders from FRECILINA, including Arturo Frondizi, were permitted to meet with Perón in the hotel, but as darkness fell, the situation remained tense and uncertain. At one point during the night soldiers aimed a machine gun at the front entrance, as if to emphasize the army's determination to keep Perón confined. Yet the military officers at the airport did not seem to be following any plan, an indication of the regime's lack of preparation for the event.[20] Lanusse had seen fit to leave town late in the day on a trip to the south to inaugurate a petrochemical complex. A delegate from the military junta was assigned to negotiate with Perón, and at dawn on Saturday the eighteenth the *conductor* finally secured his release.

During her prior visit to Argentina Isabel had picked out the house to which he now repaired.[21] It was located on Gaspar Campos Street in the municipality of Vicente López, which sits on the northwest edge of Buenos Aires between the capital and Olivos along the Río de la Plata. The bank of the river rises to heights attracting upper-middle-class refugees from the pollution of Buenos Aires and its industrial suburbs. Gaspar Campos Street runs parallel to the river far enough away from and above the heavily traveled Avenida Libertador, yet with easy access to the capital.

Perón's new residence fit nicely into its lush environs. A pair of rubber trees shaded the front of the white-brick, red-tiled dwelling. The entrance bore a shield belonging to the original owner and bearing the Latin inscription *Nec temere nec timide* ("Neither rashly nor timidly"). The design of the rear of the house suggested a nautical motif, with a second-floor bedroom (to be occupied by Isabel) rounded like a ship's cabin.

When word spread that Juan Perón was now in Vicente López, the spell he had always cast upon a large segment of the Argentine populace began to work its magic. By mid-morning small groups were filing by the house on Gaspar Campos Street.[22] The rain had abated and the spring foliage, in full bloom, lent vivid splashes of color to the spontaneous procession. At first the police attempted to limit access to the neighborhood, but by afternoon they abandoned the scene, apparently in response to Perón's complaint that the regime was keeping people away from him. The first bass drums arrived shortly after two, and by four-thirty a crowd had inundated the area.

The *conductor* himself began to make hourly appearances at a window under a gable overlooking the street. (He was so regular that the neighbors jokingly referred to him as "The Cuckoo.") He would gesture and say a few words, and the faithful would chant his name. At one point he turned up clad in blue pajamas. The sight of an enthusiastic throng moved him deeply. For more than a decade the opportunity to commune with a mass audience had been like mother's milk to him, and the isolation forced upon him by his lengthy expatriation had been difficult to endure. But today the calendar had been turned back for him and he loved it.

Isabel stood by him when he greeted the crowd and would occasionally substitute for him. Her routine consisted of exhibiting an enlarged photograph of Eva Perón and leading the now-familiar Peronist chant *"Se siente/Se siente/Evita está presente"* ("We feel it/We feel it/Evita is present").

The mood on the street was festive. Ice cream vendors pushed their wares as spectators climbed plane trees and roofs to get a better view. The bass drummers kept up a steady beat for the entire weekend, pausing only when Perón spoke and from three to six on Sunday morning. Young people from the Peronist left camped out for the night on a nearby lot and left their spray-painted calling cards on the walls of adjacent houses. The words "FAR," "Montoneros," "Five for One" and "Remember those shot at Trelew" greeted the Sunday pilgrims to Gaspar Campos Street. The atmosphere remained civil, however, and at midnight the police cleared the area without any incidents.

The carnival on Gaspar Campos Street reaffirmed the almost mystical bond between the *conductor* and his mass. The long years in exile had made him more appealing than ever, a paternal figure who projected wisdom and understanding, a messenger of peace, a symbol of hope, the incarnation of enduring myths. The Juan Perón of 1972 evoked the radiant legends of Peronism's past: the seventeenth of October, the emergence of the Argentine working class, the defeat of Spruille Braden, Evita and her social aid programs. His mind was still quick, his hair still black, his smile still captivating. Yet he was also an elderly man, bearing not only the physical signs of aging, like mottled skin and a wart against the bridge of his nose slightly above his right eye, but also the infirmities and vulnerabilities of his years.

One could already hear talk that the *conductor* was being manipulated by others. In his speech to the generals on November 11, Lanusse referred to reports that Perón was "less coherent and less lucid than he has been in his whole life and as never before gives the impression of being led." He added his own conclusion that "Perón is surrounded and no longer in any way controls the leadership of the 'movement.' "[23]

Lanusse did not name names, but the view was gaining currency that López Rega and Isabel now dominated the *conductor*.[24] They appeared constantly at his side. It was difficult to reach Perón without first securing the nod from Daniel. There were whispers that El Brujo and Isabel would keep the old man in isolation and refuse to talk with him, in order to impose their will upon him.[25] Perón was said to have been a completely different, much more relaxed person when his private secretary was not with him.[26] Rogelio Frigerio has reported that when he visited Perón in Vicente López shortly after his arrival, the ex-president tried to give him his unlisted phone number, but López Rega rudely snatched the piece of paper upon which Perón had written the number and claimed the phone was out of order.[27]

López Rega was easy to dislike. The man possessed no Peronist credentials save those he had invented for himself. What he lacked in intelligence he made up for in shrewdness and drive. From time to time what he wrote in *Las Bases* afforded insights into his peculiarly primitive mentality. Occasionally he caused embarrassment, as when in a series of articles entitled "Anatomy of the Third World" he linked the national socialism Great Britain, the U.S. and the U.S.S.R. had joined forces to defeat in World War II with the "national socialism" toward which the contemporary world was supposedly tending.[28] Since Perón had equated *justicialismo* with "national socialism," this amounted to an open admission that Peronism was "Nazi-Fascist." The article caused a minor flap and spread consternation in Peronist ranks.[29] The incident was yet another demonstration of the looking-glass quality of Peronism, since López Rega's explication reflected his own political preference.

On the other hand, a CIA report indicated that at this point in time the old man had "full command of his mental faculties."[30] Indeed, an examination of his behavior during his stay in Argentina demonstrates that Perón never stopped being Perón.

For example, he still knew how to play one subordinate off against another. He obtained the services of Juan Esquer as his personal bodyguard. A retired sergeant-major in the army veterinary corps, Esquer had taken care of Perón's horses during his second term. Honest and trustworthy, he became a counterforce to and enemy of López Rega.

The inner circle was now the setting for what the U.S. embassy termed a "Byzantine struggle," as various Peronists jockeyed for power and influence that was the *conductor*'s to dispense.[31] But Perón was still pulling the strings.

He kept his distance from the Peronist left. Rodolfo Galimberti reportedly received a dressing down from him for his "impudent and provocative acts and words."[32] At a press conference he praised the Peronist youth movement but refused to endorse John William Cooke's interpretation of Peronism as an authentic expression of class struggle in Argentina, despite the fact that young Peronist radicals treated the writings of his onetime dauphin-designate (now deceased) as gospel.[33]

The tactical moves emanating from Gaspar Campos Street likewise undercut the proposition that others were calling political shots for the *conductor*. These various maneuvers all bore the distinctive stamp of Juan Perón. Thus while the crowds were swarming to Gaspar Campos Street on the weekend of November 18–19, the *conductor* conferred with leaders from the other political parties. One of these sessions produced a historic encounter between Perón and Ricardo Balbín, old enemies embracing for the first time. El Chino, like Perón, symbolized the gerontocracy that has long hardened the arteries of Argentine politics. He was facing a challenge to his control over the Radical party but had not lost his touch (a powerful one-on-one presence, in the style of Yrigoyen) and gave no indication of wanting to step aside and make room for younger men.

The conversations during the weekend were but a prelude to a conclave held on Monday the twentieth at the Nino Restaurant nearby. Representatives from almost all the parties assembled with Perón and his top lieutenants to discuss the possibility of forming a political front. The *conductor* addressed the need for national unity. Peronist officials then called for the issuance of a manifesto denouncing the August 25 residency requirement, and for the designation of a joint committee to explore ways to execute Perón's ten-point program. At this juncture the gathering began to look like an effort to line up the other parties behind the Peronists. Balbín took the floor and expressed reluctance to fight the residency requirement, which in his view proscribed only those who had freely chosen not to be in the country by August 25. He also suggested that the parties urged to support a joint program be permitted to help draft it. Sensitive to Balbín's position, Perón quickly accepted his proposal that a joint committee be formed to prepare a new program for the political normalization of Argentina.[34]

The *conductor* finally had his private meeting with Balbín on the day after the Nino conference. The two old warriors hit it off splendidly. Their conversation was private, but Balbín's subsequent comments to the press conveyed satisfaction with Perón's quest for national reconciliation. Gaining the confidence of Argentina's most prestigious non-Peronist politician was crucial for Perón. He was apparently toying with the idea of a Peronist-Radical ticket, but Balbín indicated that his party would not enter into any electoral pacts. However, he did leave open the possibility of cooperating with the Peronists in a future civilian government.[35]

The encounters with Balbín produced one unexpected side effect, the gradual forging of a personal bond between Perón and his former antagonist. Perhaps because of a deepening distrust of those around him, the *conductor* would turn more frequently to Balbín for counsel and a sympathetic shoulder on which to lean. Theirs was a unique fellowship based upon the shared experience of a lifetime in the exercise of political leadership, Argentine style. It was the closest Perón would come to genuine friendship in his twilight years.

Although Perón had success in nudging the parties toward a united front, he made no headway in the direction of an accommodation with either Lanusse or the armed forces. At a press conference on November 22 the president commented favorably on Perón's presence in the country,[36] yet he would not invite the *conductor* to the Casa Rosada. Perón on his part would not request a meeting. Both men seemed to let pride stand in the way of an opening gesture. Perón stubbornly objected to the residency requirement. He refused to permit the regime to control his future course of action and created the impression that he would renounce his candidacy only after the lifting of the requirement. The military, however, feared that if they abrogated the requirement before Perón renounced, he might then try to exact other conditions in return for his withdrawal.[37]

There were still those who clung to the hope that Perón meant to outdo the president by forming his own "grand national accord," a civilian-military consensus that would bring peace, unity and prosperity to Argentina. Yet to fulfill this golden vision, the *conductor* would have to step aside. His failure to make any effort to approach Lanusse supports the view that he really did not want to put himself out to pasture. At his press conference for foreign journalists he fortified this supposition by gratuitously insulting the Argentine army.

It was in response to a question about Paraguay that Perón made his controversial remark: "I have the honor of being a citizen of this noble country and a general of its army, the most glorious of the entire continent."[38] The tone of his voice led the U.S. embassy to speculate that it was a throwaway line, delivered carelessly and without regard to its probable consequences.[39] A right-wing Peronist has claimed that afterward Perón explained "The closer you are to peace, the more you have to fire your cannons."[40] By mistake or design, the *conductor* succeeded in outraging the chauvinistic sensibilities of the Argentine officer corps. As commander-in-chief of the army, Lanusse felt obliged to aim a verbal volley back at him.[41] The incident had a decidedly negative impact upon the possibility of a deal between Perón and the armed forces.

The committee organized in the wake of the Nino conclave put together a six-point plan for the restoration of civilian rule and a rather vague economic program for national recovery. But efforts to negotiate with the junta stalled, and the political parties represented at Nino's never managed to endorse the committee's economic proposals. Because of deadlines the government had set for the naming of candidates and the registration of coalitions, time expired on the initiatives Perón had launched at the restaurant. The Radical party nominated Balbín for president, and in the first week of December the Peronists joined with several small parties, including those led by Frondizi and Solano Lima, to create the Frente Justicialista de Liberación (Justicialist Liberation Front), or FREJULI. The new entity immediately designated Perón as its nominee, a symbolic gesture that would make it possible for him to step aside for the candidate of his choice.

Perón was now reported to be on the verge of departing Argentina, but when he would take his leave and where he would go remained anyone's guess. There were reports that he would stop in Chile, Paraguay, Perú, Panamá and Cuba, and that he would even visit China.[42] The speculation about his selection of candidates for the FREJULI ticket intensified. The optimistic view was that he would tap a "respectable" Peronist for the presidential nomination. Among those prominently mentioned were Antonio Cafiero, Alfredo Gómez Morales, Jorge Taiana (a distinguished surgeon who was once Eva Perón's physician) and Antonio Benítez (former president of the Chamber of Deputies).[43]

The situation clarified somewhat when it was announced from Vicente López that Perón would fly to Paraguay on December 14. A Peronist party congress scheduled for the following day was to be the setting for the official nomination of the movement's candidate. The assumption was that the *conductor* would communicate his decision to the congress in time for his followers to ratify it.

In a formal statement issued just prior to his departure, Perón declined the FREJULI nomination.[44] On that same evening the word began to circulate that the *conductor* had decided upon a candidate, and that it was none other than Héctor Cámpora.[45]

The news sent shudders through Peronist circles. Cámpora elicited neither support nor minimal esteem from any of the various factions. But efforts by labor leaders and others to block or delay the nomination at the congress foundered against an immovable barrier, Perón's word. Verticality triumphed. Amid a cacophony of jeers the congress dutifully accepted the dentist as the party nominee, which automatically made him the FREJULI candidate.[46] Cámpora, who had accompanied Perón to Paraguay and then had immediately returned to Buenos Aires, let it be known that his leader's preference for the vice-presidential slot was Vicente Solano Lima, and once again the delegates applied a rubber stamp.

Most Peronists blame López Rega for Cámpora's nomination. One version holds that he and Isabel conspired to pressure Perón to put his delegate at the head of the ticket.[47] According to a slightly different account, El Brujo, Isabel and Cámpora announced that Perón had picked Cámpora, but in fact the *conductor* wanted the party congress to choose the nominee; López Rega prevented anyone from reaching Perón for confirmation. Daniel promoted Cámpora, these Peronists aver, as part of his master plan to take over the movement.[48]

It is difficult to believe that Perón would want to leave such a critical decision to an open convention. Never before had he exhibited any trust in the democratic process. Moreover, Cámpora was exactly the type of person Perón would tap to run in his place. The dentist wore his servility like a ribbon of honor and posed no threat to the *conductor*'s ascendancy. Since Cámpora had no constituency, his nomination could not be perceived as a tilt in favor of any particular faction and therefore would not upset the distribution of forces that Perón had always kept in careful equipoise.

Another explanation, consistent with the view that the choice of Cámpora best served Perón's interests, is that Perón believed that Cámpora's candidacy would provoke the military into canceling the elections or proscribing the Peronists. It was no secret that the men in uniform held Perón's delegate in supreme distaste. If the thought of Cámpora in the Casa Rosada was more than they could bear, they might call a halt to the "clean game" and thereby trigger a new round of convulsions.[49]

Perón might have had both possibilities in mind: an electoral victory by a candidate under his thumb, or military interference in the campaign. Of course this also meant running the risk that Cámpora might lose. The *conductor* constantly complained that the regime was stacking the deck against FREJULI, while he maintained the fiction that he had nothing to do with the choice of Cámpora, a disclaimer underscored by his failure to make a public appearance in Argentina with his arm around the nominee.[50]

Perón's departure on the evening of December 14 was a relatively low-key affair attended by three hundred well-wishers. He joined Isabel, López Rega and Cámpora on a commercial flight to Asunción for a reunion with his old friend Alfredo Stroessner.

Paraguay's most distinguished honorary citizen arrived to a warm welcome. Hugging the sixty-year-old Stroessner, Perón complimented him on his youthful looks. "The years have strengthened me," replied the president.[51]

A visit to Paraguay, under the heel of South America's longest-running dictatorship, was unlikely to enhance the image to which Perón aspired, that of a hemispheric statesman.* Therefore, after four relaxing, uneventful days in Asunción, the *conductor* proceeded to Lima, where he called upon Peruvian President Juan Velasco Alvarado. The two men conferred for forty-five minutes. Nothing of substance came from their exchange of views, but at least Perón could now point to the fact that he had met with a Latin American leader generally regarded as progressive. Later he held a press conference during which he came out on record against insurrection or civil war in Argentina and described himself as a "vegetarian lion."[52]

As Perón returned to Madrid, the political parties prepared for Argentina's first presidential campaign in a decade. Cámpora and Balbín were the main contenders. Seven other candidates completed the field, and

* A French newspaper expressed amazement that Perón could confer in Buenos Aires with Third World priests who ministered to Paraguayan refugees living in slums in the Argentine capital, and then a few days later embrace the man who drove them into exile. Article in *Le Monde*, quoted in *La Nación*, December 16, 1972.

several were expected to do reasonably well. Under the rules set by the regime, if no contestant won 50 percent of the votes, there would be a second round confined to those candidates who had received 15 percent or more of the total. The electorate would also choose a new Congress and governors for all the provinces.

The dismay provoked by Cámpora's nomination gradually abated and most Peronist luminaries fell in line, albeit reluctantly, behind their standard-bearer. At a press conference in late December, representatives of the JP (Peronist Youth) sounded a theme that would reverberate throughout the forthcoming campaign when they launched the slogan "Cámpora to the Government, Perón to Power."[53] The new watchwords conveyed an image of Perón as a political godfather, like the title character of the movie, depicted in advertising posters as pulling the strings from behind the scenes. For the young people who stood ready to energize the FREJULI campaign, Cámpora would become El Tío ("The Uncle"), a kindly, indulgent figure to whom they could rally with enthusiasm.

The role Perón would play in the campaign remained vaguely defined. As he departed from Argentina, he had promised to return in January, but there is cause to suspect he may not have wanted to make another transatlantic jaunt at this time. On December 31 he told a news conference in Madrid that "If I were fifty years younger, it wouldn't be hard to understand if I went around planting bombs and taking justice into my own hands."[54] A couple of weeks later a Peronist newspaper attributed to him a tirade in which he referred to the military as a "band of gangsters."[55] In early February he called them "beasts."[56] The regime reacted by barring him from the country until after the election. Thus he could now complain that the government was continuing to persecute him, and in addition he was spared the physical ordeal, as well as the political risk, of campaigning with Cámpora.

He was now at liberty to make his trip to Rumania. Flying to Bucharest, by way of Rome, he spent four days by the Danube and met with President Nicolas Ceaucescu, with whom he discussed international politics.[57] It was his first journey to an Iron Curtain country.*

The Casa Rosada had reason to feel concern about Perón's violent statements. In late December the FAR assassinated a high-ranking naval officer. In mid-February the ERP attacked a military installation in Córdoba and escaped with a truck loaded with guns and ammunition. At the same time a series of kidnappings netted millions of dollars in ransom payments.[58]

---

* The most widely bruited explanation for the visit was his desire to undergo treatments at the Aslan Clinic, a mecca for wealthy men and women seeking rejuvenation. But there is no evidence that he actually went there, and a spokesman for the clinic declared that the treatments required a much longer investment of time than Perón's brief stay in the Rumanian capital. See *Panorama*, February 15, 1973, p. 14; Meeker (Bucharest) to secretary of state, 0504, February 12, 1973.

Equally disturbing was the FREJULI campaign opener, a rally in Cámpora's hometown. The crowd chanted "Five for One" and other slogans associated with the Peronist left.[59] This was not what the military had had in mind when they lifted the ban on political activity.

As the campaign progressed, the regime resorted to a series of legal measures designed to harass the FREJULI ticket. Perhaps the specter of a Peronist victory now overwhelmed Lanusse, for he seemed to abandon his devotion to democracy and to toy with the idea of calling off the elections. But his fellow generals stood firm and refused to abort the process. The violence a cancellation would inevitably spawn weighed heavily in their minds.

Lanusse's shortcomings as a politician were now painfully apparent. The campaign brought to the surface the deep dissatisfaction felt by the great majority of Argentines toward military rule. By attacking FREJULI, the president called attention to the fact that the armed forces regarded the Peronists as their principal antagonists. This played directly into the hands of the latter, for it enabled them to capitalize on the antimilitary mood of the country. They could also frame the issue in terms that stirred memories of the 1946 campaign. Instead of "Braden or Perón," it was now "Lanusse or Perón."

Cámpora rose to the occasion by running a steady race and avoiding mistakes. He and Balbín behaved civilly toward each other, to the extent that the Radicals forfeited the support they might otherwise have received from anti-Peronist voters. The Peronist Youth campaigned vigorously for FREJULI. Organized labor had but to remind the rank and file of benefits workers had reaped under Peronist rule.

Several days before the election, Lanusse committed a final gaffe by delivering a televised speech that all but besought the electorate to reject the FREJULI candidates.[60] The voters responded in unequivocal terms. Cámpora defeated Balbín resoundingly. FREJULI captured all but one governorship, 45 of 69 Senate seats and 142 of 243 seats in the Chamber of Deputies.

Since Cámpora took only 49.56 percent of the ballots (with Balbín trailing far behind with 21.29 percent), the regime could have required a second round. But Lanusse announced that the FREJULI ticket had come so close to 50 percent that he would recognize it as the winner. The Radicals did not object.

Juan Perón's John the Baptist was now president-elect of Argentina.[61] After eighteen years in the wilderness the Peronists were about to regain power.

Part VII

The
Third
Presidency

(1973-1976)

51

Cámpora in the Casa Rosada

Alejandro Lanusse regards it as "perhaps the most difficult day of my life."[1] Apologists for the military regime that took power in March 1976 call it the day Marxist subversives took control of the Casa Rosada.[2] For progressive Peronists hoping for an end to violence, stagnation and economic dependence, it was the dawn of a new day.[3]

Billed as a "people's festival," the inauguration of Héctor Cámpora on May 25, 1973, brought the Peronist left into public view as never before.[4] The Plaza de Mayo sprouted an unruly forest of placards and banners heralding not only political organizations such as the JP but also the guerrillas of the FAP, FAR and the Montoneros. Even the red star symbolizing a faction of the ERP made an appearance. Someone painted the words "Montonero House" on the side of the Casa Rosada. The slogan chanters saluted "national socialism," "the rifles of Perón," "El Tío in the government, Perón in power," Chile and Cuba. One of the shouts was "Long live the Montoneros who killed Aramburu." Some observers viewed the spectacle with horror; others, more optimistic, saw it as a positive sign, an indication that young people who had resorted to terrorism were now willing to put down their weapons, come out into the open and work legally to bring about change.

Although photographers focused upon the militants, the latter were but a part of the immense throng. Groups representing the Peronist unions also made a strong showing.[5] The fact that the left appeared to have "won the street" could not have pleased orthodox labor leaders. There was nothing they could do about it now, but they would have other opportunities to display their muscle.

Following tradition, Cámpora began the inauguration ceremonies by appearing before a joint session of Congress. He read a three-and-a-half-hour speech, mercifully interrupted by a thirty-minute intermission. As expected, his flattery of Juan Perón and Evita soared to giddy heights. He paid tribute to "a marvelous youth [that] knew how to answer violence with violence," but then reassured listeners with the prediction that "The violence will decay." He clothed his pronouncements on foreign policy with familiar Third Position rhetoric, which included praise for the Vietnamese people and a promise to restore relations with Cuba (a measure echoing Perón's recognition of the Soviet Union in 1946).[6] Nothing he said was inconsistent with the dicta of his *conductor*.

Yet in the context of the day, some of Cámpora's statements created the impression that he was tilting to the left, the direction toward which the Peronist Youth was pushing. Unruly elements in the Plaza de Mayo set fire to a couple of automobiles and prevented military units from parading. When the commander-in-chief of the navy approached the Casa Rosada, shouts demanding vengeance for the Trelew massacre and the threatening behavior of the crowd provoked the admiral's bodyguards to discharge their guns. Several youths were wounded.

The situation grew so chaotic that Cámpora had to take a helicopter from the Congress to the roof of the Government House for the second part of the inauguration. Of the many foreign dignitaries in attendance, the only ones who were able to reach the Casa Rosada were presidents Salvador Allende of Chile and Cuba's Osvaldo Dorticós, whom the multitude cheered and let pass.

The transfer of the symbols of the presidency from the members of the junta to Héctor Cámpora climaxed the formalities. Lanusse and his two colleagues performed their duties and left as the jubilant throng in the White Room sang the national hymn and the Peronist march. The military officials of the outgoing regime boarded a helicopter on the roof—all except Lanusse, who declared "I will leave by the same door I came in"[7] and strode out the front entrance through the pressing mob to a waiting limousine. It was a remarkable display of fortitude. No one laid a hand on him as he made his dramatic exit.

Now that "Comrade President," as they liked to address him, had formally assumed office, the youthful activists in the plaza had one final scene to play. They marched through the streets of Buenos Aires due west to the far edge of the city, where hundreds of militants imprisoned for subversive or terrorist activities awaited them in the Villa Devoto jail. Perón had advocated an amnesty, a majority of Argentines may have favored it and Congress had been preparing an amnesty bill that would have freed political prisoners. Nevertheless, the inaugural celebrants could not wait. The inmates had already begun a mutiny. By eight-thirty a large crowd surrounded the building, which was draped with the banners of the various guerrilla groups. Several federal deputies, Peronist Youth representatives and Juan Abal Medina tried to calm the demonstrators and negotiate a solution. The pressure was too much for Cámpora, who on that very same night decreed a broad pardon, effective immediately.[8] The quick concession created an impression of weakness that did not augur well for El Tío and helped saddle him with a reputation for weather-vane decision-making.

Perón remained conspicuously absent during Cámpora's inauguration. Although the latter had insisted, in a burst of post-election euphoria, that "I will not be president even one day if General Perón is not in Argentina,"[9] the *conductor* had declined to attend the ceremonies or even to send Isabel, because he said it was Cámpora's show.[10] He even referred to himself, in a singular display of self-effacement, as a "soldier of Cámpora, just another subordinate."[11] This enabled him to distance himself from his surrogate whenever the occasion demanded and to shelter his own prestige from any blunders El Tío might commit.

Perón's conduct during the transition period was hardly that of a mere soldier. He began to essay exercises in diplomacy aimed at reducing Argentina's economic dependence upon the United States and strengthening her links with the Third World. He sought to counterbalance the heavy U.S. investment in Argentina with fresh infusions of Western European capital. He also made personal contacts in Paris with representatives from North Vietnam and Mexican President Luis Echeverría, and dispatched Isabel and López Rega on a trip to the People's Republic of China and North Korea in early May. These were quintessential applications of the pendular politics Perón had always practiced in the conduct of foreign affairs.

On the other hand, it soon became apparent that the slogan "Cámpora to the Government, Perón to Power" did not mean the *conductor* was going to assume the same degree of control he wielded during the halcyon years of his first presidency. His limited physical endurance pointed toward a need for him to alter his style of leadership. The clear and orderly delegation of authority to trusted lieutenants might have been a solution, but this had never been his way of doing things. He was too contemptuous of his subordinates, too reluctant to risk creating potential competitors, too accustomed to manipulate through the cultivation of disarray. With control of the Casa Rosada at stake and a Peronist power vacuum developing, the internal struggles grew much more intense. In the past the *conductor* had been able to stay on top of them and to use them to his advantage. Now he was finding it difficult to do this.

The fact that Perón did not name all the men who would serve in Cámpora's cabinet demonstrated that even in matters of consequence he was not exercising full command. The full list was not made public until inauguration day. Some of the selections bore the Perón brand. Others did not, although he probably had an opportunity to veto them. Thus José Gelbard, appointed to head the Ministry of the Economy, was so much in the "self-made man" mold of Miguel Miranda that Perón must have designated him. Orthodox Peronists Antonio Benítez and Jorge Taiana, slated for Justice and Education respectively, were exactly the type of men Perón would have chosen. But the nominations of Juan Carlos Puig as minister of foreign relations and Esteban Righi as interior minister were surprises. Both seemed much too young and obscure for the positions to which they were appointed. Puig's friendship with Cámpora's nephew and Righi's association with one of Cámpora's sons suggested that the president-elect had his own inner circle.[12]

A nomination that would have untold implications gave the Ministry of Social Welfare to José López Rega. His inclusion in the cabinet was, to say the least, preposterous, yet no one objected openly, not even when an official press release issued on inauguration day and containing biographical data on the new ministers referred to him as "one of the founders, along with Perón, of the National Justicialist Movement."[13] How he maneuvered himself into the cabinet is unknown. He may have taken advantage of his proximity to Perón, he may have struck a deal with Cámpora, or he may have utilized the backing of labor leaders unfriendly to El Tío. On the surface, Cámpora's stated intention to revive the Eva Perón Foundation, in which Isabel would be expected to play a major role, gave what passed for plausibility to the promotion of her principal collaborator to head the Social Welfare Ministry. But this was a slender fig leaf.

In addition to his job as Perón's private secretary, López Rega now had the wherewithal to build an independent power base. He would control appointments to the ministry and the enormous funds within its jurisdiction. His influence was to extend even further as a result of the election of his son-in-law as president of the Chamber of Deputies.

The elevation of Raúl Lastiri to a position that put him third in the order of succession to the presidency of the republic (after the vice-president and the president of the Senate) was in its way much more absurd than López Rega's ministerial appointment. Lastiri had no credentials save his family tie to El Brujo. He was a playboy who would one day boast to a magazine interviewer that he owned three hundred neckties and would permit himself to be photographed with his wife in their lavish boudoir.[14] According to one Peronist deputy, the selection of Lastiri was attributable to the party's tradition of verticality; a labor leader announced to a meeting of the Peronist bloc that Lastiri was Perón's choice and the legislators meekly accepted his word.[15] If true, the incident was a classic example of *dedocracia*.

Intramural squabbles had been so long part of the warp and woof of Peronism that it was difficult to imagine a Peronist movement at peace with itself. The emergence of a generation of young militants eager to utilize what Perón represented as a means of achieving a radical transformation of Argentine society added a new front to the turbulence. Having been instrumental in the FREJULI triumph, they had every right to look forward to a major role in the latest version of a "new Argentina." Indeed, shortly after the elections Perón was quoted as reiterating his promise of a *trasvasamiento generacional*: "The future now belongs to the *muchachos*. . . . They are organized, they have clear ideas, they have suffered persecution, they know what they want. They have prepared themselves all these years. . . . I tell them . . . you command and I'll set you straight."[16]

Yet apart from the words of the *conductor*, there was no evidence that the *muchachos* were moving into positions of real authority. The candidates who had ridden the FREJULI bandwagon to victory came mostly from the political and trade-union sectors of the movement. A mere handful of federal deputies and several governors could be said to sympathize with the JP. The only real success enjoyed by the young leftists was in obtaining mid-level positions in the federal and provincial bureaucracies. Within the Peronist movement itself, only Juan Abal Medina held what might be considered an important post, but whether he wielded any actual influence is questionable.

Despite their underrepresentation, the Peronist Youth militants had no intention of backing off in their quest for a place in the sun. They interpreted FREJULI's stunning victory as a mandate for their vision of radical change. Hubris pushed aside sound judgment and seduced them into a series of provocative acts in late April. They pressed upon Cámpora their own ten-point political program spelling out specific measures his administration should implement.[17] They formed two new organizations, the Peronist University Youth and the Peronist Working Youth, the latter for the purpose of competing with the CGT and its young-worker component, the Peronist Syndical Youth.[18] But the last straw was a proposal put forward by Rodolfo Galimberti, with the apparent approval of Juan Abal Medina, who was present at the time, for the creation of an "Argentine youth militia for national reconstruction."[19]

Although efforts were made to interpret Galimberti's words as a suggestion for the launching of a sort of domestic Peace Corps,[20] no amount of textual exegesis could undo the damage caused by his use of the term "militia." It summoned memories of the call for "workers' militias" in 1955 and left the impression, in the minds of some, that a member of the Peronist leadership wanted to nationalize the Montoneros. At a time when there were still lingering doubts that the armed forces would permit the Peronists to take office, a threat to the institutional status of the army was the last thing the *conductor* wanted to hear.

Galimberti and Abal Medina were immediately summoned to Madrid. Perón made no effort to hide his displeasure but refused to take personal responsibility for passing judgment on his wayward *muchachos*. Instead, he convened an ad hoc tribunal and presided over a stormy hearing that resulted in Galimberti's resignation from the high council.[21] Abal Medina somehow survived, perhaps through the intercession of Cámpora. Galimberti faded quietly away. His colleagues in the Peronist Youth did not protest his ouster and reaffirmed their allegiance to Perón.[22]

The sacking of Galimberti might have given comfort to Argentine moderates, but it was more than offset by the continuation of terrorist activity during the interim between the elections and the inauguration. Guerrilla groups were accumulating vast sums of money from what had become a highly profitable enterprise, the collection of extortion payments from foreign businesses and ransom for kidnapped foreign executives. The ERP made clear its intention to keep waging war against the Argentine armed forces and the multinational corporations. On May 1, one of its hit squads killed a navy admiral. Three weeks later the assassination of an orthodox Peronist union official by an armed left-wing Peronist organization stirred memories of the murders of Vandor and Alonso.[23] Labor leaders who once used overweight ex-boxers as bodyguards were now beginning to hire underworld characters adept at handling weapons.[24]

Perón and his subalterns had often reiterated their belief that once Cámpora assumed the presidency the plague of terrorism would lose its raison d'être and vanish.[25] It soon became apparent that this was wishful thinking in the extreme. True to its word, the ERP refused to suspend operations. The other armed left-wing groups, while refraining from paramilitary sorties, stepped up efforts to extend their influence within the Peronist movement.

The Peronists now bore responsibility for dealing with the violence and the subversion. Perón himself gave the first clue as to an approach that would be taken when shortly after the inauguration he blamed the "Trotskyists" (meaning the ERP) for the May 25 disturbances.[26] His strategy was to isolate the ERP from avowedly Peronist militants such as the Montoneros. This would permit him to distinguish between terrorists he could denounce as foreign-inspired and those whom he once called his "special formations." A few days later a shadowy organization calling itself the Central Security Command of the Peronist movement threatened to execute "one Communist for every 1,000 pesos demanded by the ERP for releasing its hostages."[27] Taking its cue from the *conductor*, the orthodox wing seemed to be preparing to wage war upon the extreme left. How long they would respect a distinction between the "Trotskyists" and other left-wing Peronists was another matter.

Within the Peronist movement itself, the most serious threat posed by the left centered in a struggle that had been going on for nearly two decades between union leaders concerned with bread-and-butter issues—

the "Vandorists," "labor bureaucrats" and "traitors to the working class," as their enemies called them—and militants who saw all labor issues in the larger context of Marxist doctrine. Perón fully recognized the danger posed by efforts to convert the support he had always enjoyed from his "vertebral column" into an instrument for the radical transformation of Argentine society. This prompted his decision to hand the universities over to the Peronist left, in the hope that they could be enticed away from the trade unions and confined to the groves of academe. It was a foolish tactic. The militants gladly accepted higher education as their own preserve but did not abandon their penetration of the labor movement. Minister of Education Taiana, who carried out Perón's directive, would pay a stiff price.*

Peronist control over organized labor was of critical importance to the economic policy adopted by the new administration. On June 8 the government, the CGE and the CGT signed a "social pact" intended to restrain inflation and eventually to redistribute income. In the short run the agreement committed labor and management to a wage and price freeze. The long-range objective was to adjust wages so as to increase, over a four-year period, the share of national income devoted to salaries from 40 percent (the 1973 level) to 50 percent (the level reached during the first Perón presidency).[28] Worker acceptance of the "social pact" was vital. Agitation by leftist elements within the unions could destroy it.

Turbulence marred the first three weeks of the Cámpora era as Peronism's left and right wings fought furious turf battles. Occupations of public buildings, workplaces and classrooms became daily occurrences. Interior Minister Righi pronounced himself against police suppression of initiatives taken by the "people" and thereby tied the hands of law-enforcement officials.[29] Cámpora made no attempt to end the turmoil. Indeed, he even met with representatives of the Montoneros and other guerrilla organizations in the Casa Rosada.

There now remained but one hope for those who wished to avoid revolutionary upheaval as well as for those who sought progressive but orderly change. Juan Perón was coming back. He was scheduled to arrive at Ezeiza on June 20.

With the Casa Rosada in Peronist hands, it was inevitable that the *conductor* would be tendered a properly triumphal return to Argentina. The anarchy into which the nation was sliding lent an urgency to the perceived need for Perón's presence. In the minds of the great majority of his compatriots, he alone could bring peace to his movement and a sense

---

* Arrested shortly after the 1976 coup, Dr. Taiana languished for five years behind prison bars. Though no formal charges were levied against him, Argentina's military rulers apparently held him responsible for the subversion of the universities during 1973 and 1974.

of unity to the political landscape. How he would do this seemed of secondary importance.

Having placed a messianic mantle on his shoulders, the Argentine people refused to consider the implications of his advanced age and fragile health. There was little public discussion of his physical condition. Even before the inauguration there were rumors, vigorously denied by Peronist sources, that he had suffered a heart attack.[30] In late May the press reported that some fruit juice of poor quality had given him gastric problems.[31] One could detect, however, a reluctance to believe that anything serious could be wrong with him.

In reality, the wear and tear of old age was taking its toll. Shortly before his departure, the reappearance of blood in his urine necessitated another visit to Barcelona, where Dr. Puigvert performed an operation for the removal of polyps of the prostate gland.[32] While there he complained of chest pains. Dr. Puigvert examined him with a stethoscope. He found nothing amiss but advised his patient to have his heart and lungs checked and to give up smoking.[33] A Buenos Aires heart specialist subsequently discovered that in late 1972 Perón had sustained a minor, undetected heart attack.[34] The damage had healed, but the possibility of further stress-induced seizures persisted.

It is difficult to know the extent to which the health factor figured in Perón's decision to return. According to some, he went back because he did not want to die, like Rosas, in exile. Others take at face value his professed ambition to become a roving ambassador who would unify Latin America. Yet the modest dealings he had with Chile and Paraguay during his second presidential term must have taught him something about the difficulty of moving beyond the rhetoric of inter-American union. Hemispheric problems had now grown much more complicated.

What had to have been on Perón's mind was the crisis facing Peronism in Argentina. Cámpora was plainly not up to the task of governing. Although he often insisted he harbored no wish to be president again, the *conductor* did not have many options. Indeed, the hypothesis that he did want the presidency one more time is compelling. There was no better way for him to attain the personal and historical vindication he had been pursuing relentlessly for eighteen years. The choice of an incompetent surrogate could only fuel the demand for him. He had recently postulated that "Like in chess, to win the game one must sacrifice pieces; except for the king, everything can be gambled to reach the final objective."[35] Cámpora was just another piece on the board. The goal was power, which only the king could wield.

When Cámpora flew to Madrid on June 15 for the purpose of bringing his leader back to Buenos Aires, Perón humiliated him openly. No one from Puerta de Hierro was at the airport to greet him. Franco scheduled a gala reception for him on the evening of the sixteenth and invited Perón. The *conductor* did not even bother to reply.* Wearing evening clothes and the presidential sash, Cámpora rushed to Puerta de Hierro in the hope he could persuade his chief to accompany him to the affair. He found Perón relaxing in a *guayabera* shirt. The *conductor* would not even embrace his emotionally distraught visitor, and excused himself on the ground that he was dining that evening with some friends.

Perón's insulting behavior persisted for the length of Cámpora's stay. He ignored the various ceremonies which marked the presidential visit until the day of departure, when he was present at the signing of a joint declaration by Franco and Cámpora at the airport. He had several meetings with his ex-delegate and is reported to have expressed great annoyance at what was happening in Argentina.[36]

There are several possible explanations for Perón's degrading treatment of Cámpora in Madrid. He may have been upset that El Tío insisted on coming to Spain, since the Spanish government was certain to welcome the Argentine president with all the honors due a chief of state. This meant that the *conductor* would be relegated to a secondary position. His ego would not permit him to play such a role.

He may also have been genuinely upset by Cámpora's performance in the Casa Rosada. Yet public humiliation was not likely to enhance the president's capacity to govern. Perhaps Cámpora thought that appearing at Perón's side in Madrid would strengthen his political hand. Yet the *conductor* was unwilling to lend him help—a negation that would also be consistent with a decision to undermine him.

Perón was now ready to make his ultimate return. Both his movement and his country were in disarray. But if he really believed conditions were propitious for the exercise of his manipulatory skills, he had underestimated the divisive forces at war within Peronism and overestimated his own physical capabilities. The Argentina of 1973 was not the Argentina of 1955, nor was the Perón of 1973 the Perón of 1955. His first seven days at home would make this painfully clear.

---

* Throughout his long exile in Madrid, Perón had had no personal contact with Franco, even though the latter's sister was a frequent visitor to Puerta de Hierro and on very friendly terms with Isabel. Interview with Pilar Franco, Madrid, July 7, 1977. The *caudillo* probably did not want to jeopardize Spain's relations with Argentina. Perón was not happy with his treatment by Franco. He met the *generalísimo* for the first time during a brief visit to Madrid by Cámpora shortly after the March 1973 elections.

52

The Final Return

Winter solstice as well as Argentine Flag Day, June 20 marked the occasion of the return of Juan Domingo Perón and the official termination of his exile. It was to be an encounter in the Peronist tradition of October 17, 1945, and the *cabildo abierto* of August 22, 1951.

Not hundreds of thousands but millions were expected to be on hand to greet him. The airport itself was too confined an area, so the broad access highway that linked Ezeiza to Buenos Aires would be used. Workmen erected a large platform atop an overpass located not far from the airport entrance, facing toward the capital. A thirty-meter-high photo of Perón, flanked by smaller likenesses of Isabel and Evita, provided the backdrop.

According to the schedule of events, the chartered Aerolíneas Argentinas jet carrying the *conductor* and his party would touch down at Ezeiza at 3:00 P.M. A helicopter would then transport Perón, Isabel, López Rega and Cámpora to a landing area near the overpass. A symphony orchestra would play the national hymn and the Peronist march, there would be a moment of silence for Evita and the "fallen comrades," and doves would be released. Perón would make the only speech.[1] He would stand behind bulletproof glass for the first time in his career.

Jorge Osinde made arrangements for security. The retired lieutenant colonel had been named secretary of sports within López Rega's Social Welfare Ministry, a curious appointment for Perón's onetime intelligence chief and top bodyguard. Osinde's ultra-conservative political persuasion indicated which wing of the movement had control over the official homecoming.

Since the Peronist left was excluded from the reception committee, its leaders decided to resort to the one tactic at which they excelled, mass mobilization. The Peronist Youth prepared to form impressive columns, complete with banners and bass drums, and converge directly in front of the platform. Thousands of its members would act as marshals and assume responsibility for crowd control.[2]

A time bomb was ticking but no one wanted to hear it. The authorities decided not to use the police or the army. They feared that the sight of uniforms might provoke violence from militant elements in the crowd, as had occurred on May 25. Plainclothesmen would be present but were under orders not to intervene.[3] The naive view predominated that this was a Peronist celebration, a joyous occasion, a day for people to express love for a father figure who was returning to them.

The government declared a holiday and offered free transportation to Ezeiza from anywhere in the country. Loudspeakers were set up along the entire length of the access highway. The Ministry of Social Welfare installed sanitation facilities and secured a fleet of tank trucks filled with water. Wood for more than a thousand campfires was stacked at various points on the side of the road. Temporary shelters were raised at the municipal auto racetrack.

At midday on the nineteenth the first arrivals staked out choice locations near the platform and prepared for a cold night under the stars. A radio broadcast of a junior lightweight boxing match from Tokyo, where an Argentine challenger lost a decision to the Japanese world champion, helped the evening hours pass. In the early morning an exchange of insults between groups huddled around fires produced gunshots. One person was reported to have been killed.

Meanwhile, on the other side of the Atlantic, Juan Perón was taking leave of a plethora of pleasant memories, several filing cabinets stuffed with correspondence and Evita's body, which had never been removed from the second floor of his home. Isabel and López Rega joined him in a black limousine for the drive to the airport. Francisco Franco, in his *generalísimo*'s uniform, was on hand to bid farewell to the man whose presence he had ignored for thirteen years. The formal ceremonies were longer than expected and delayed the departure of the jet. At long last Perón and Cámpora boarded the aircraft and joined the committee of dignitaries selected to participate in the flight.

The crowds streamed toward Ezeiza—women, children, the elderly, the healthy and the handicapped, the faithful and the curious, workers, peasants and students, in the largest gathering in Argentine history.[4] Vendors sold sausages, hot drinks, banners and buttons. People chanted Perón's name over and over again. For many it was a quasi-religious experience, as October 17, 1945, had been for the descamisados.

By mid-morning it was virtually impossible to approach the platform from the highway. For those at a distance from the overpass, unable to see or hear what was transpiring ahead of them, the day unfolded peacefully and uneventfully. It was not until later that they learned, from radio,

TV, newspapers and word-of-mouth reports, what had happened. Those who thought themselves fortunate to be at the front of the gigantic assembly would experience a nightmare.

Throughout the morning tension mounted. Clashes between members of the JP and the right-wing Peronist Syndical Youth became more frequent. The latter, part of the security force Osinde had put together, had taken up positions on and around the platform. At 10:30 A.M. a few shots were fired.

The sun made its appearance at 1:00 P.M. and it began to look like a "Peronist day." Many in the crowd shed coats and sweaters. Folk music blared through the loudspeakers. The Peronist Youth had set up a first-aid station near the platform. Already a number of spectators had required treatment for fainting and eye irritations caused by smoke from bonfires still smoldering on the shoulders of the highway. The master of ceremonies for the occasion, film director Leonardo Flavio, took the microphone from time to time in an effort to keep things calm and under control.

But the situation was simply too volatile, and at about two-thirty all hell broke loose. Both sides have advanced their own versions of what precipitated the disaster. Whatever the cause, a great quantity of blood, much of it innocent, irrigated the grassy environs of the intersection.

Orthodox Peronists tell the following story: the ERP, the FAR and the Montoneros were planning to assassinate Perón and had stationed snipers with high-powered rifles in trees to the right of the stage. As part of a coordinated plan, a huge column of militants from La Plata approached the overpass from a side road. Their intention was to surround the platform and occupy the area in front of the stage. They brought with them a bus filled with weapons, its windows covered, holes drilled in the side of the chassis. The defenders of the platform opened fire on the column and the snipers in a preemptive strike. Leftist sources, on the other hand, deny the existence of an assassination plot and claim that the right launched an unprovoked attack. Independent witnesses report that the shooting erupted during a frenzied battle of words, as the JP chanted "Perón, Evita, the Socialist Fatherland," and right-wing groups replied with "Perón, Evita, the Peronist Fatherland."

Those caught in the crossfire could not have cared less who started it. Members of the symphony orchestra dropped their instruments and lay flat on the platform as bullets whizzed over them. The crowd stampeded. Many fell and were trampled. Not everyone panicked: an old man stood his ground, insisting "Everything's all right, everything's all right," and tried to sell lemonade. Bodies fell from trees. Someone on the stage began releasing doves. People ran past and through an empty municipal swimming pool, and took shelter in nearby homes and a church. The parish priest, clad in vestments, tried to find help for refugees who had been wounded or were suffering from shock.

The acting president of Argentina, Vicente Solano Lima, was lunching at the airport when he received word of the shooting. He tried to drive to the scene but had to stop when he reached the combat zone. Returning to Ezeiza, he learned that eight deaths had been confirmed and that non-fatal casualties were mounting. He decided to divert Perón's jet away from Ezeiza.[5]

Meanwhile, aboard the charter the mood was one of subdued happiness. The *conductor* occasionally visited the tourist-class section and chatted with its occupants. The only news relayed from Argentina described the size of the crowd awaiting him and generated a sense of satisfaction among the passengers.[6] At some point during the trip he suffered pains in his upper abdomen. Raúl Lastiri administered some whiskey, improper treatment for stomach problems but appropriate medication for a heart attack. Whether Lastiri knew what he was doing or chose the correct remedy by mistake, Perón quickly recovered.[7]

As the plane passed over southern Brazil, Solano Lima made radio contact with it and spoke directly with Héctor Cámpora. He told him what was happening and suggested that the jet land at the air force base in Morón.

"But this is the general's big day," Cámpora protested. "We've gone to so much trouble to arrange the welcome. What will happen if people don't get to see the general?"

"Look," declared the acting president, "if you land here you'll be shot. Everything is out of control. The responsibility is mine and I order you to land at Morón."[8]

For Cámpora, fresh from his humiliation in Madrid, it was a cruel blow. He did not relish having to break the news to Perón.

Solano Lima immediately took a helicopter to the air base and was on hand to greet the *conductor* as he stepped from the charter. Eyewitnesses report that Perón bore an expression of displeasure.[9] Cámpora, whose stock with Perón must have been at an all-time low, made a brief radio speech blaming the disturbances on "elements who are against the country."[10] After remaining for an hour at Morón, Perón boarded a helicopter and took off in the direction of Buenos Aires.

The shooting at the overpass had abated somewhat and medical personnel were trying to carry off the wounded when the rival groups resumed their antagonistic chanting and another heavy exchange of gunfire erupted. As the afternoon wore on, it became obvious that Osinde's troops had superior weapons and were routing the JP militants. Giving no quarter, the right-wingers hunted down their adversaries, even to the point of raiding first-aid stations, and mercilessly beat anyone unlucky enough to fall into their hands. Prisoners were taken to the hotel at the airport and tortured.

To this day no one knows how many people lost their lives in what has come to be known as the Ezeiza Massacre. The newspapers initially put the figure at twenty, but later unconfirmed reports indicate that there may have been as many as several hundred fatalities. "Perón or Death" was the legend on many of the banners and posters. As an anti-Peronist writer has observed, they should have read "Perón *and* Death."[11]

In retrospect, it seems unlikely that any of the terrorist groups would have planned to kill Perón. Because of the bulletproof glass on the platform, they would have had to shoot down his helicopter or pick him off as he made his way to the stage, a very difficult and risky attempt. Nor did an assassination make much political sense, since the extreme left did not really control the Cámpora government and would not have had uncontested control over Argentina or the Peronist movement in the event of the *conductor*'s death.[12] Eliminating Perón would have set off an immediate clash, but the left, while armed, had nowhere near the firepower necessary to defeat the right at Ezeiza. They were simply not prepared for a pitched battle, as events demonstrated.

Whether the right had planned to provoke a shoot-out is likewise unclear. The many photographs of the event establish that the guardians of the platform were carrying automatic weapons. It is conceivable that they were merely prepared for trouble rather than seeking to start it. On the other hand, they may also have been looking for the political dividends likely to flow from the infliction of a decisive defeat on the left.

Finally, one cannot discard the possibility that a random spark ignited the battle. Someone on the stage may have thought he saw snipers. Osinde's men may have become enraged when the JP appeared to be on the verge of winning the street in front of the stage. A person in the crowd—a hot-headed member of the Peronist Youth, a deranged individual, a provocateur—may have fired the first shot. Given the level of emotions, it would not have taken much to unleash the furies.

The government appointed an investigating commission but no findings were ever released. Rumors abounded, the most intriguing of which was that Osinde had imported some French Algerians to do his dirty work.[13] The left blamed the right, the right blamed the left, the JP blamed the CIA, López Rega blamed Interior Minister Righi[14] and the CGT blamed the "international synarchy."[15] A noted psychiatrist called it a ritualistic slaughter of the young.[16] No one suggested that it might have been a case of antibodies destroying microbes.

On the evening of the twentieth Juan Perón made a brief address that was broadcast and telecast to the nation. His purpose was to thank those who had come from near and far to welcome him and to allay fears that some harm might have befallen him. Speaking from the presidential residence in Olivos, he barely alluded to the horrors of the day.[17] He spent the night in familiar surroundings, the guest of Héctor Cámpora, before moving to his Gaspar Campos Street house on the next day.

His luggage not yet unpacked, the *conductor* acted quickly to make his political presence felt. He chose the next evening to deliver a major speech to the nation. Seated between Cámpora and Isabel, with López Rega and Lastiri standing behind him, he spelled out the direction in which he wanted the Peronist administration to proceed. It was a clarion call for law and order, discipline and hard work, tolerance and unity, a statesman's vision designed to please moderate Peronists as well as fair-minded non-Peronists.[18] His words must have surprised those listeners whose impressions of him derived from the 1943–1955 period. This was a different Perón, more mellow, more mature, broader in outlook and apparently tempered by his European experience.

The discourse contained very little from which the Peronist left could take comfort. The *conductor* denounced both the violence-prone terrorists and the purveyors of alien doctrines who thought they could infiltrate Peronist ranks. While mentioning no names, he was clearly cautioning the militants of the JP and the Montoneros.

Perón's next move was a visit to the Radical party's suite of offices in the Congress on the following day for a conference with Ricardo Balbín. It was more than just a courtesy call. The two leaders talked privately for more than an hour. Afterward Balbín told the press he was in fundamental agreement with Perón's grand design for the nation, though he reserved the right to differ on ways to implement goals.[19] Thus Perón seemed to be heading in the direction of a broad consensus between Argentina's two great political parties. Behind the scenes Perón was also acting with dispatch. He asked Gelbard to set up for him a small staff to draft legislation and executive decrees. It operated out of a secret downtown office, the entrance to which was electronically protected.[20]

The decisive leadership the *conductor* was asserting raised questions about the fate of Héctor Cámpora. Much in the speech of June 21 could be interpreted as criticism of the president. El Tío delivered his own message to the nation on June 25, but it was a feeble echo of Perón's pronouncement. As a U.S. embassy official has noted, astute observers were now saying that Cámpora's days in office were numbered.[21]

This prediction came to pass when Cámpora resigned from the presidency on July 13. The engineering of Cámpora's ouster is surely one of the most enigmatic episodes of Perón's career. What makes it so difficult to understand is the fact that during this crucial period Perón suffered a mild heart attack that was kept secret and raised serious doubts about his capacity to handle physical and emotional strain.

Within a week of Perón's arrival, Mario Amadeo encountered him at an office in downtown Buenos Aires. He had a melancholy look on his face and seemed preoccupied with his health. "This weather is killing me," he complained. The chilly dampness of the Argentine winter was causing him great discomfort.[22]

But worse was to come. On the morning of the twenty-sixth, in his Vicente López home, Perón began to feel abdominal pains. Dr. Pedro Cossio, the nation's premier heart specialist, was summoned to the residence and diagnosed Perón as being on the verge of a heart seizure.[23] On the afternoon of the twenty-eighth, violent chest pains made it difficult for him to breathe and signaled the onslaught of the attack, which a CIA report termed a "myocardial infarct."[24] With the help of a team of physicians headed by Dr. Cossio, Perón recovered rapidly. In less than a week's time he was able to get out of bed and spend the day in an easy chair. The public knew nothing of what had happened and heard only that the ex-president had a bad case of the grippe.

At some point after Perón's initial recuperation, Cámpora offered to resign. There are four versions of what occurred. According to Cámpora, he had understood from the very beginning that he would step down so that Perón could assume the presidency; Perón's illness delayed his withdrawal, but on July 4 he told both his *conductor* and the cabinet that he was going to give up his office.[25] Perón himself later echoed this account.[26] Firsthand testimony from Defense Minister Angel Robledo holds that by early July Perón had resolved to dump Cámpora, but he used Isabel and López Rega to carry out his decision: at a cabinet meeting in the residence on July 6, Isabel inquired what role Perón would play in the administration, and she declared that if he were merely to perform ceremonial functions she would take him back to Puerta de Hierro. Stunned, Cámpora indicated that Perón could have any role he wanted and that he was prepared to resign at any moment. López Rega immediately congratulated Cámpora for his magnanimous offer to step down and urged that the cabinet accept it. After some debate the matter was left hanging until the following day, when López Rega, Cámpora and Taiana went upstairs to the bedroom to ask Perón how he felt about the issue. As sphinx-like as ever, Perón simply stated he would do what the people wanted. The three returned to the rest of the cabinet, assembled below, and the decision was made to accept Cámpora's resignation.[27] A slightly different version, emanating from the same source several months later[28] and supported by Gelbard,[29] is similar in detail, except that Perón had nothing to do with the ouster. It was the idea of Isabel and López Rega, who became panicked by Perón's heart attack. They knew that if Perón should die, they could easily lose the power they had accumulated. Acting quickly, they lured the unsuspecting Cámpora into expressing his willingness to resign. Perón had no choice but to leave the door open for a third presidency. Finally, a newspaper article suggested that Perón decided to get rid of Cámpora as a result of a private conversation with army commander Jorge Carcagno on July 10; General Carcagno told Perón that Cámpora had failed to act on a decree, ready for his signature, restoring to the ex-president his military rank and privileges; Perón became furious when Cámpora could not give a satisfactory explanation for the delay and "fired" him.[30]

The first and the last of these versions do not withstand close scrutiny. Cámpora may well have initially viewed himself as a temporary president, but nothing he did in early June reflected either a desire or an intention to give up the office. Perón was openly upset with him in Madrid, and what he found in Argentina displeased him even more. According to one cabinet minister, he was openly critical of El Tío at a dinner shortly after his return.[31] A Peronist labor leader has reported that during this same period he expressed grave preoccupation with what was happening within the government.[32] Perón might also have been irritated with Cámpora because of the latter's failure to resign of his own accord. Cámpora may have misread his chief, as Domingo Mercante had done two decades earlier, and failed to realize what Perón really wanted him to do. Or he may have begun to enjoy being president. Perón's subsequent ratification of Cámpora's account was merely a face-saving political gesture.

It seems highly unlikely that Cámpora's tardiness in restoring Perón's military rank would have caused his demise. There were too many better reasons for eliminating him. Moreover, Robledo's insistence that the decision had already been made and supporting testimony from Solano Lima[33] totally undercut the notion that Carcagno's visit provoked the ouster.

Two possibilities remain: either Perón or López Rega and Isabel toppled Cámpora. The most compelling argument pointing to Perón is that the ejection would have been a natural consequence of his unconcealed dissatisfaction with Cámpora. Moreover, the subtle manner in which El Tío was discarded was altogether typical of the Perón style. Bramuglia, Mercante, Paladino and others had fallen from grace under circumstances that had similarly obscured their leader's responsibility. López Rega and Isabel appeared to be blameworthy, just as Evita had once served as a cover for Perón. Attributing Cámpora's fall to them is of a piece with the view that they arranged the ouster of Paladino and the nomination of El Tío, hypotheses that have been shown to be dubious.

The one complicating factor is the heart attack. Dr. Cossio insists that what occurred on June 28 was not a massive seizure.[34] Perón may not have taken it seriously and may have discounted any warnings given to him, since he had always felt he knew more than any doctor about the healing arts. He probably made the decision to remove Cámpora before the twenty-eighth. The heart attack may have given him slight pause, but he did recuperate quickly.

On July 11 Cámpora finally signed the executive decree restoring Perón to the army at the rank of lieutenant general. There remained only the question of when and how to make the resignation public. The matter came to a head unexpectedly that same afternoon when Victorio Calabró, the vice-governor of Buenos Aires Province, let the proverbial cat out of the bag by declaring publicly: "Now that Perón is in the country, nobody more than he can be president of the Argentines."[35] Once this obvious proposition had been spoken aloud, the Peronist movement had no alternative but to clear the way for Perón's return to the Casa Rosada.

Final arrangements for Cámpora to step down were made on the following day. As the house on Gaspar Campos Street buzzed with activity, eight buses filled with chanting metalworkers circled the block. José Rucci suggested mobilizing the descamisados in the Plaza de Mayo for a symbolic replay of October 17, 1945.

There was something appropriate in the choice of Friday the thirteenth for Héctor Cámpora's swan song. That morning he and Solano Lima announced to the Congress their intention to resign. At 10:00 P.M. from his home in Vicente López, Juan Perón directed words of reassurance to the nation.[36] It was his first public appearance since the heart attack. His eyes were clouded, his appearance that of an elderly man in precarious health.[37] He pledged to carry out the will of the people.

Late in the day Cámpora and Solano Lima delivered their resignations to the Congress, which immediately voted to accept them. Under the law the presidency was now supposed to pass to the president of the Senate. But Alejandro Díaz Bialet suddenly discovered that he had to leave on a temporary overseas mission. His precipitous departure, some said, was due to his ties to the Cámpora people (his daughter was married to Cámpora's nephew). He was on a plane to Madrid as Raúl Lastiri took the oath of office and promised elections in the very near future. One of his first presidential acts was to remove Interior Minister Righi and Foreign Minister Puig and replace them with old-line Peronists.

The ship of state had definitely starboarded. *El Descamisado*, a slick weekly published by the Peronist left, tried to cheer up its readers by equating the resignation of El Tío with Evita's heroic renunciation. Editor Dardo Cabo insisted that the desires of the Argentine people, rather than the machinations of the CGT bureaucrats, were pushing Perón toward the presidency.[38]

The militants were now reiterating the charge that Perón was a prisoner of his inner circle and that the chief villain was López Rega. On July 21 the JP organized a march on Gaspar Campos Street to "break through the warlock's blockade," as a headline in *El Descamisado* put it.[39] Some thirty thousand orderly demonstrators chanted the usual revolutionary slogans (except for the provocative "socialist fatherland," which was prudently replaced by "national socialism, as the general demands"). They also called López Rega a "son of a bitch."[40] Perón met with a quartet of JP leaders for nearly two hours and heard them ask for direct access to him, without intermediaries. Afterward the government press office announced that his exclusive contact person with the Peronist Youth would be . . . José López Rega.

The militants claimed that Perón had nothing to do with the appointment.[41] But the *conductor* kept his silence, and within a week López Rega was meeting with representatives of a new group called the Peronist Youth of the Argentine Republic, led by a hitherto unheard-of Social Welfare Ministry functionary named Julio Yessi. The organization had been cut from the same cloth as the Peronist Syndical Youth. Created to counterbalance the left, it pledged to respect verticality. The gambit bore a remarkable similarity to the way new trade unions loyal to Perón had come into being in 1944 and 1945.

The government scheduled a new presidential election for September 23. Immediately there was earnest talk of a Perón-Balbín ticket, the realization of the "Golden Vision."[42] A cryptic comment made by Perón himself on July 13 encouraged the speculation.[43] On the last day of the month he met again with Balbín and expectations heightened.

Factions within the Peronist movement were simultaneously putting forward their own candidates for vice-president. On the left the JP struggled to resurrect Héctor Cámpora.* Orthodox Peronists began to promote Isabel. Moderates mentioned Taiana. There were also rumors of a Peronist-military alliance, to be embodied in a Perón-Carcagno slate. Balbín's vice-presidential candidacy attracted little enthusiasm within Peronist ranks.

The forging of a joint ticket with the Radicals would have required delicate negotiations between the parties, but in fact nothing of the sort was taking place. Indeed, neither at their meeting on June 24 nor during their July 31 conversation did Perón and Balbín even mention the matter.[44] Moreover, Perón was considering other methods of institutionalizing national unity. In early August he proposed to a group of political leaders, including Balbín, the creation of a council of state. It would be an advisory body composed of representatives from the various parties and interest groups and designed to provide a point of access that would link the president and elements outside his own political orbit. Balbín would be an obvious candidate for membership on the council.

While the ideas of a Perón-Balbín ticket and a council of state may have intrigued and even excited many Argentines, reality would disappoint them. Peronist party delegates filed into the ornate Cervantes Theater in downtown Buenos Aires on August 4 to nominate candidates. The convention brought together the political and CGT-dominated labor wings of the party. The Peronist Youth was excluded. That Perón would be chosen by acclaim

---

* Realizing how the Peronist Youth was using Cámpora, Perón would subsequently dispatch him as ambassador to México.

was beyond doubt. The important issue to be resolved was what to do about the vice-presidency.

The Peronist party had fashioned no procedures for sober debate, either before or during the convention, on the merits of the various candidates.[45] Indeed, there was confusion as to the agenda to be followed, with some delegates acting under the impression that the slot would be left open for Perón to fill at his leisure. From its inception the party had grown accustomed to ratifying decisions presented as Perón's, and this would be no exception. The nomination would go to the person at whom someone purporting to act in the *conductor*'s name pointed a finger.

After the convention gave its delirious approval to Perón's candidacy, a delegate jumped up and nominated Isabel for vice-president. Her candidacy had been rumored and had not been withdrawn. How could it not bear Perón's approval? Who could possibly be against Perón's wife? The assemblage approved her by acclamation. The whole business took about twenty-five minutes.

The lieutenant general stayed away from the convention and withheld his acceptance. Isabel, however, did not imitate his coyness. Hurrying to the theater, she declared her unqualified willingness to run and told the delegates that Perón always did what his people wanted.[46]

If any single event was to stamp Argentine history over the next decade, it was the nomination of Isabel. The ex-dancer had now achieved something that had eluded the beloved Evita. How did it happen? Did Perón want her on the ticket with him? Or was this a master stroke of Isabel and her cunning warlock, as many Peronists firmly believe?

Perón may have decided that Isabel's nomination made good political sense. There was resistance to Balbín among Peronists. The left looked down upon him as a representative of bourgeois interests. The politicians realized that a deal with Balbín meant some sharing of the spoils of victory with the Radicals. Few followers of Perón could have been happy with the prospect of Balbín's assumption of the presidency in the event of their *conductor*'s death. In the short run Balbín's presence on the ticket was inessential. Perón was doing a fine job nullifying him as a political opponent by encouraging talk of a joint candidacy, floating the idea of a council of state and, most importantly, securing his rival's concurrence in a grand design for Argentina. Balbín would be more useful as a worthy yet beatable adversary at the polls. Finally, Peronism had always been a multifaceted movement, with Perón balancing labor, elements of the middle and entrepreneurial classes and the military. The selection of a running mate identified with the middle class might be viewed as an excessive tilt to one side. Everyone could rally behind a vice-presidential candidate presented as an extension of Perón himself.

However, most Peronists today hold fast to the conviction that Perón preferred Balbín and did not want Isabel, but López Rega and his allies stampeded the convention into nominating her.[47] Once the old man had been presented with a fait accompli, he could not very well reject his wife, they insist, emphasizing Perón's supposed lack of willpower and physical stamina to fight against the intrigues of Isabel and her mentor. The *conductor* possessed a completely lucid mentality and could formulate ideas about what he wanted done, but he lacked the capacity to execute them. He had to rely upon others, and López Rega was able to cut him off from those who might have faithfully carried out his wishes.

This interpretation is appealing because it not only absolves Perón from blame but also suggests a fulfillment of poetic justice. Perón, the manipulator who used people like chess pieces in his pursuit of power, reached a degree of physical helplessness that reduced him to a pawn in the hands of his third wife and her mentor.

A contemporary CIA cable noted that "Perón has lucid periods, interrupted by periods of depression during which he becomes a dependent old man. In these latter periods, [he] refuses to consider any problems or talk to anyone other than his wife . . . and . . . López Rega . . . upon whom he becomes very dependent." But the report went on to state that "despite the foregoing, Perón is acting as president of the country, making all major decisions and ratifying all government appointments."[48]

Because the truth impacts upon contemporary Argentine politics, it is virtually impossible to find disinterested testimony regarding Isabel's rise to power. Perón probably tolerated his wife as the least objectionable vice-presidential candidate available to him. His primary goal was the vindication that a lopsided victory in the September elections would bring. He needed a running mate who would not hurt him, who could not claim any credit for his triumph, and who would thereafter be a ceremonial vice-president—in short, another Hortensio Quijano. He may have responded to a combination of factors including his own political judgment, pressures from Isabel and López Rega, and the backing his wife had attracted from orthodox labor leaders who threw their lot in with her when no one from their ranks emerged as a viable candidate.

Whichever version one adopts, Perón cannot escape responsibility. If he wanted her on the ticket or simply decided not to block her, he was callously indifferent to the survival of Peronism and the fate of Argentina in the event of his death in office. He knew who she was and upon whom she would depend if she inherited the presidency. He later stressed the need to reorganize the movement so that it could carry on effectively after his demise,[49] yet he had advocated restructuring the movement for decades without ever lifting a finger to make it capable of existing, let alone functioning smoothly, without him. In his old age he would continue to talk about reorganization and do nothing. It is difficult to avoid the conclusion that he simply did not care.

If Isabel's ambition and the machinations of López Rega imposed her upon Perón against his will, this was a deadly side effect of his style of authoritarian leadership. The imposition of verticality, with its emphasis upon unquestioning obedience, left his followers helpless to resist when old age caught up to their *conductor*, and López Rega and Isabel stepped into the void. This was also the bitter fruit of his lifelong preference for mediocre underlings. He had always populated his inner circle with buffoons. At this critical juncture, his chief court jester happened also to be a madman.

The nomination of Isabel stunned the Peronist Youth. The disaster at Ezeiza, the ouster of Cámpora and now the bestowal of the vice-presidential candidacy upon someone known to be under the influence of the hated López Rega constituted a string of defeats for the left. Yet the young militants reaffirmed their loyalty to Perón. Rationalizations were forthcoming, the most ingenuous of which was that they were witnessing a historical reenactment in which Isabel would emulate Evita and give up her position on the ticket.[50] There were even some who expected to hear this announced at a rally sponsored by the JP on August 22 to commemorate the Trelew massacre and Evita's renunciation.[51]

Juan Perón formally accepted his party's nomination on August 18. At the very beginning of his speech he assured the delegates that he fully realized the physical and mental strains that went with the presidency. He then read a document signed by Cossio and Taiana, affirming that he had recovered from the condition for which he had been treated on June 16 (a reference to his visit to Dr. Puigvert) and adding the opaque declaration that "His future activity ought to take into account his age and the [urological] affliction he suffered." Perón pronounced the report "for me sufficiently satisfactory."[52]

A CIA report on Perón's health at this time told quite a different story. His heart condition was chronic, requiring digitalis drugs to control the fibrillation, or rapid contractions of the heart muscle, and nitroglycerin tablets for anginal pain. He was also suffering from a moderately severe vascular disease that caused him pain when walking and climbing. In addition, his urinary bleeding occasionally recurred. The report quoted an unidentified source as opining that Perón had twelve to eighteen months to live.[53]

The health issue had been swept under the rug, but it may have been on some people's minds on August 31, when the CGT mobilized its hosts for a march in support of the Perón-Perón ticket. The confederation's purpose was to do what had been attempted unsuccessfully at Ezeiza—bring the *conductor* into contact with his people. For Perón it would be a challenge, an opportunity to demonstrate not only his physical endurance but also his ability to impose order upon his movement. The JP intended to participate en masse. A repeat of the Ezeiza violence would shatter the claim that Perón was Argentina's last hope for national reconciliation.

The event proved a dazzling success for the lieutenant general. Standing for long stretches at a time, he spent eight hours on a balcony of the CGT headquarters as nearly one million of the faithful paraded by him. The fabled Perón charisma had lost none of its magic. "All of us in the march had the feeling he was looking right at us as we passed" was the way one participant described it.[54] Not a single untoward incident marred the day. The unions and the Peronist Youth maintained discipline. The image of Peronist unity, badly shattered on June 20, underwent a much-needed refurbishing.[55]

From the deft way he handled the young militants during the campaign, it was clear that neither his political genius nor his luck had abandoned him. Having veered decidedly to the right after his arrival, he knew he must now tend to his opposite flank. In early September he met with Mario Firmenich, a top Montonero (who would later admit to participating in the Aramburu assassination) and Roberto Quieto, a FAR leader. Both pledged continuing support to the *conductor* and a suspension of paramilitary operations.[56] López Rega dropped from public view. With the election less than a fortnight away, fortune smiled upon Perón in a perverse sort of way. For some time, in response to youthful critics who wanted to speed up the revolutionary process in Argentina, he had pointed to the serious difficulties Salvador Allende was facing in his effort to build socialism in Chile.[57] Pressured by his extreme left followers, resisted by the middle class and destabilized by the CIA, Allende finally fell victim to a military coup that cost him his life on September 11. The bloodbath that followed made a prophet out of Perón and must have had a sobering effect on many of his *muchachos*.

The political campaign was dull and anticlimactic. Perón made no trips around the country and did not exert himself. Balbín took the high road and refrained from attacking him. The only question was by how much the *conductor* would better Cámpora's performance. When the votes were tallied, Perón had captured more than 60 percent.

Eighteen years before he had been a refugee on a Paraguayan gunboat. Now he was about to return in triumph to the Casa Rosada. He had won over the military, the church, large segments of the middle and upper classes—the same people who had driven him into exile in 1955. Even Washington looked upon him with favor. It was a truly astonishing achievement.

Two days after the election, Peronist euphoria turned to shock as unidentified gunmen pumped a hail of bullets into José Rucci. The CGT's general secretary had been spending his nights in various houses around town as a security measure. This did not spare him from the fate suffered by Vandor, Alonso and others. The police blamed the ERP, which the government had declared illegal on the previous day, but a communiqué from that organization later disclaimed responsibility.[58] Within twenty-four hours of Rucci's murder, a member of the Peronist Youth fell victim to assassins' bullets.

According to Arturo Frondizi, on the day of Rucci's funeral he received a call from Perón. The *conductor*'s voice conveyed deep concern. "What am I going to do about all this violence?" he asked. "I could put an end to it if I became a dictator, but I'm too old to be a dictator."[59]

On the dawn of his third term, Juan Perón confronted the dilemma of having to fulfill the conflicting expectations of millions of voters. For them his restoration was a triumph of faith, fed by the expectation that a sick old man who had been away for eighteen years could solve the nation's problems, and demonstrating the capacity of Argentines to believe in miracles.

53

"Perón to Power"

Elation wreathed the face of Lieutenant General Juan Domingo Perón as he stepped from his residence on the morning of October 12, 1973, four days after his seventy-eighth birthday.[1] He was on his way to be inaugurated as president of Argentina, but more importantly, this marked the first time in nearly two decades that he was appearing in a military uniform.

He had steadfastly endured the rigors of expatriation and the vilification heaped upon him for so many years. But the one arrow that had pierced him most deeply was the treatment he had received from his military peers. His comeback would not have been complete without the expunction of the stain on his military record. Though his rank and privileges had been restored, proper rehabilitation called for the wearing of the uniform in public. That he chose the inaugural ceremonies told more about his self-image than many of his followers, especially the young, wanted to know.

From the doorway he saluted a small crowd of applauding neighbors. Isabel, dressed in white, accompanied him to a waiting limousine as López Rega stood off to one side and gestured directions. The excitement of the occasion produced a charming vignette worthy of a silent comedy. The couple entered, exited and walked around the rear of the vehicle, nearly colliding in confusion over who was to sit on which side. At last they stationed themselves properly and drove off, a caravan behind them. Last in line was a Dodge pickup that had been transformed into an ambulance.

The festivities attending Perón's formal assumption of the presidency were low-key, especially in contrast to Cámpora's boisterous inauguration. Once again the movement's warring factions observed a truce. In his first platform appearance in the Plaza de Mayo since the infamous "five for one" diatribe of August 31, 1955, the *conductor* delivered a surprisingly perfunctory address. He promised to return on the first of May, in conformity with an old Peronist custom, to ask the people whether his performance in office satisfied them. Little more than a pastiche of generalities, the speech did contain a specific reference to the nation's young people, whom the president urged to work and prepare for leadership roles.[2] His brief exhortation masked the deep concern he felt toward the most serious problem he faced.

The tactic of encouraging the paramilitary escapades of his "special formations" had served him well during the exile period. Now it was proving difficult to harness the forces he had unleashed. The young men and women who had risked their lives in the struggle against the various military regimes had much more in mind than Perón's personal vindication. All wanted a new Argentina. To some this meant the attainment of an idealized vision of social justice, economic independence and a Third Position foreign policy. Others saw Peronism as a means to achieve some form of Marxist society. Still others openly rejected Peronism and espoused armed revolution.

The challenge posed by the youthful militants was a complex one. The non-Peronist ERP, its war chest bulging with ransom money, pressed forward the goal of a violent overthrow of the government. Most of the Peronist guerrillas had suspended illegal operations, but they were busily organizing workers, students and slum dwellers at the grass-roots level. The Montoneros were now in virtual control of the JP.

The left also appeared to be gaining ground in the two most important provinces of the country. Oscar Bidegain, the governor of Buenos Aires, was an old-line Peronist and onetime admirer of Mussolini.[3] Influenced by his wife and daughter, he had developed a sympathetic attitude toward the Peronist Youth and appointed a number of them to positions in his administration. In Córdoba, Governor Ricardo Obregón Cano also sympathized with the left. His vice-governor, Atilio López, came from the highly radicalized provincial labor movement that several years earlier had produced the *cordobazo*.

Though he may have been slow to realize the dimensions of the challenge, once he turned his attention to it the *conductor* demonstrated he had not lost his touch. He stepped up his efforts to isolate the ERP, this time linking them to the Trotskyists who he said were behind the May 1968 student uprising in France. "I was in Paris," he would intone, "exactly at the time of the barricades and I have talked with people who were there and who were on the barricades and I am well aware of what set those events in motion."[4] He was displaying his customary indifference to truth. The ERP had long since disclaimed any Trotskyist affiliation.[5] Though one Trotskyist faction did participate prominently in the Paris rebellion, the Trotskyists did not precipitate it. And finally, from all available evidence Perón was not in Paris at the time. Nonetheless, he sought to convince listeners that local conditions had nothing to do with the violence perpetrated by the ERP; it was orchestrated from abroad as part of a worldwide conspiracy. He would also insist that this kind of subversion was a police problem,[6] a proposition scornfully rejected when made by Lanusse.

A separate prong of his strategy was to urge that all young Peronists organize into one unit, a General Confederation of Youth as he envisioned it in a meeting with youth leaders on September 8. A close reading of the transcript of the session indicates that his real purpose was to try to depoliticize the young, or at least to make them more manageable from above. His fond recollections of the golden days of the UES and the various sports programs his government had sponsored implied that he would like to revive them. He suggested that his listeners hold a congress and unite all youth groups calling themselves Peronist into an equivalent of the CGT.[7] It was yet another manifestation of his dream of the "organized community." Of course the new confederation would be bound by the principle of verticality. The *muchachos* would have to obey or leave. The Montonero Firmenich and other young leftists in attendance did not openly oppose the idea, but they would subtly resist it.

Talk of sports and a General Confederation of Youth was a carrot that Perón extended to his young followers. The stick had come into view in early October when the Peronist high council, newly purged of its left-wing members, issued a "reserved document" declaring war upon the "Marxist terrorists and subversives" who were attacking the Peronist movement and its leaders. Every avowedly Peronist organization was to affirm its repudiation of Marxism and enlist in the struggle. The directive placed no limitations upon methods to be used, save that they be effective. It did not single out the ERP. According to *La Opinión*, which published the text, Perón gave his full approval to the document.[8]

These inflammatory instructions coincided with a rash of killings and bombings apparently sparked by Rucci's murder and reaching epidemic proportions during subsequent weeks. The majority of the victims were left-wing Peronists.[9] The antibodies were once again in deadly pursuit of the microbes. Those who did not share Perón's passion for medical analogies would soon suspect that "death squads" composed of off-duty police were doing much of the dirty work and that López Rega, an old hand at law enforcement, was somehow involved.

What responsibility did Perón bear for the bloodshed? He apparently sanctioned the "reserved document," which all but signaled an open hunting season upon heretics and subversives. His administration then took no action to reduce right-wing violence. At a press conference in February, Ana Guzzetti, a leftist reporter, cited an increasing number of "Fascist attacks" upon "popular militants" and asked him how he planned to deal with what she referred to as "para-police groups of the extreme right." In a rare display of public anger, Perón declared that it was a matter for the ultra-left and ultra-right to settle between themselves, and instructed the Ministry of Justice to initiate legal proceedings against *her*.[10] The mellowness that he had acquired in Europe apparently did not extend to aggressive questioning by journalists.

Perón was obviously essaying a policy of polarization. He wanted to force the Peronist left to choose between the ERP or its ilk and orthodox Peronism. The militants who had cast their lot with his movement resisted. They labored mightily to retain their standing as Peronists, while grumbling in private or telling jokes such as: Perón's limousine reaches a fork in the road. The chauffeur asks "Which way, General?" "The same as usual," Perón replies. "Signal left and turn right."

One of the more imaginative countermoves devised by the left was an attempt to indoctrinate army draftees. In October the Peronist Youth convinced the army to participate in a joint project for the repair of flood damage in Buenos Aires Province. Young soldiers worked shoulder to shoulder with young militants, some of whom may have once engaged in guerrilla operations against the government. At best it was a public-relations success for the JP. Perón kept his silence. In December a colonel who had helped organize the project failed to receive a promotion to general despite army commander-in-chief Carcagno's recommendation.*

Though Perón and his orthodox followers lumped all Marxist subversives and terrorists together, there is actually scant indication that the hard-liners of the ERP were making common cause with the Peronist left at this time. The ERP remained clandestine and kept kidnapping foreign businessmen. Extreme right-wing Peronists could not find them, so they directed their acts of retribution against the JP and other leftist groups that operated openly. Thus the ERP furnished the provocation and the Peronist left took the punishment.

An excellent example of this phenomenon gave Perón a pretext to terminate a struggle in Buenos Aires Province between supporters of Oscar Bidegain, the left-leaning governor, and Vice-Governor Victorio Calabró, an orthodox labor leader from the metalworkers' union. On January 19, the ERP staged its boldest operation yet, an armed assault on an army tank garrison in the city of Azul. The guerrillas engaged troops in a seven-hour firefight. On the following night, a grim-faced, uniformed Perón appeared on television not only to denounce the attack

---

* Carcagno himself then resigned, to be replaced by a general believed more sympathetic to the Peronist government. The fact that he was suspected of harboring political aspirations may have caused his demise. See J. Kandell, "Perón Replaces Two Military Chiefs," *New York Times*, January 4, 1974, p. 4; R. Terragno, *Los 400 días de Perón*, pp. 68–69.

but also to blame provincial authorities for tolerating subversion.[11] This direct criticism from the *conductor* made Bidegain's position untenable and he immediately resigned. Calabró assumed the governorship and embarked on a purge of Peronist Youth elements from the provincial government.

The incident at Azul had other negative effects upon the Peronist left. In Congress the majority bloc introduced a tough anti-subversive law so broad in scope that it could be used to repress any dissent. It aroused opposition not only from leftists but also from members of the Radical party, who remembered how the Peronists enforced similar legislation during the 1946–1955 period.[12] Eight deputies who belonged to or sympathized with the JP asked for a meeting with the president. According to a top aide, Perón remarked, "I'm going to fix those boys,"[13] and he gave them an appointment for what they thought would be a private talk. When they arrived, they found him waiting with live TV cameras and radio microphones. The *conductor* refused to let them draw him into a debate over the merits of the bill, but instead repeated his conviction that the ERP terrorists were part of a global conspiracy radiating from Paris. He insisted that the place to argue about legislation was within the Peronist bloc; since the bloc had made its decision, there was nothing he could do.[14] The deputies thereupon resigned and left the JP virtually without representation in Congress.

Córdoba presented an even bigger headache. The provincial labor movement was split between the orthodox and militant factions. The local heads of the powerful auto workers' and light and power unions were not only non-Peronist and Marxist, but were also honest, effective leaders highly respected by the rank and file. The ERP and the Montoneros were well organized in the province.

Governor Ricardo Obregón Cano, like Cámpora, was an old-line, conservative Peronist swept leftward by the political tide. Vice-Governor Atilio López, a left-wing Peronist from the transport workers' union, was directly participating in both a struggle for control of the regional CGT and a disruptive transportation strike. Obregón Cano backed López, and rumors that the federal government would intervene intensified. Once the situation in Buenos Aires Province had stabilized, all eyes turned to Córdoba, where labor unrest was now posing a distinct threat to the "social pact."

Perón publicly insisted that it was up to the Cordobans to settle their own problems.[15] They proceeded to do so in a manner unusual even by Argentine standards. The provincial police staged an insurrection on February 27 and overthrew the government.

The perpetrator of the putsch was Antonio Navarro, a retired army officer and the chief of police. When Obregón Cano accused him of supplying arms to right-wing groups and ordered his removal, Navarro had his men arrest both the governor and López. The police stormed the Government House in downtown Córdoba and seized several radio stations. Immediately an announcement went out on the airwaves that the purpose of the uprising was to eradicate the "Marxist coterie of Obregón Cano." The voice explained that since Perón had said Córdoba's difficulties should be resolved by the Cordobans themselves, that was exactly what they were doing.[16] The orthodox Peronist labor unions declared a strike in favor of Navarro (so quickly that observers suspected collusion[17]) and members of the Peronist Youth of the Argentine Republic took to the streets with automatic weapons. A journalist from *La Opinión* described the scene as reminiscent of Barcelona in 1937 during the Spanish Civil War.[18]

The provincial chamber of deputies met in an emergency session and swore in its president as acting governor. Meanwhile, the police released Obregón Cano and López, who fled to an unknown location and asked for help from a contingent of 230 federal police who had arrived in the city.

As gunshots reverberated throughout Córdoba, President Perón maintained a prudent silence. Indeed, in the midst of the crisis he found time to receive a visit from his old friend Hans-Ulrich Rudel, the former Luftwaffe ace whom he had not seen since his stay in the Dominican Republic.[19] Meanwhile, Chief Navarro accused Obregón Cano of distributing arms to "Marxist elements," the acting governor scheduled new provincial elections for September, and the fugitive governor asserted that he still had the backing of the federal authorities.[20] Total confusion reigned. On March 5 the Senate approved a law, forwarded by Perón, intervening the province. The issue was no longer in doubt. Two days later, Obregón Cano and López resigned.

Whether Perón merely tolerated what came to be known as the *navarrazo*, approved it or conceived it remains disputed. One view is that he personally gave the order for the coup.[21] A source close to Jorge Osinde claims that the president told his former intelligence chief that something had to be done about the problem in Córdoba.[22] A person like Osinde would not need any further instructions. He knew Navarro (they both were retired army lieutenant colonels) and traveled to Córdoba several times prior to the *navarrazo*. There is other evidence that Perón knew what was going on and could have called off the insurrection at any time.[23] On the other hand, Peronist sources have insisted that Perón did not want a revolt, but Osinde and his colleagues misinformed the president about what they were doing.[24]

None of these hypotheses about Perón's role does him credit. He let matters get beyond his control, or he delegated excessive authority to the ultra-rightists within his entourage, or he blatantly abused his constitutional authority.

Although the lieutenant general displayed flashes of the tactical brilliance that was uniquely his in countering subversion and terrorism, on the economic and foreign-policy fronts it was more difficult to produce results. An increase in international meat and grain prices helped slow down the rate of inflation, but the world oil crisis quickly nullified those gains. When some unions quietly negotiated wage agreements beyond the limitations set by the "social pact," rank-and-file pressure on the CGT began to mount and threatened the consensus that formed the bedrock of the Peronist recovery program.[25]

As had occurred during the first Perón era, the Third Position proved easier to talk about than to execute. The only real success the *conductor* scored was in developing a $1.2 billion trade agreement with the Cubans, to whom Argentina contracted to sell motor vehicles and other manufactured goods, in defiance of the U.S. effort to impose an economic blockade upon the island.[26]

There was much discussion of a possible trip by Perón to New York for a speech to the United Nations and a meeting with President Richard M. Nixon.[27] But this major diplomatic offensive never left the planning stage. Shortly after a helicopter flight to Argentina's aircraft carrier, anchored ninety miles at sea, and a brief meeting in Montevideo with Uruguayan President José María Bordaberry, Perón fell victim to yet another health crisis, the most serious to date, and survived it by the sheerest of good fortune.

It happened at the Gaspar Campos Street residence in the early morning hours of November 21, when he suddenly encountered great difficulty breathing. Incredibly, no doctor was on duty in the house. Several custodial employees frantically drove to the nearby home of Dr. Julio A. Luqui Lagleyze and roused him from bed. Returning with them, he found the president on the verge of asphyxiation and López Rega helping him breathe with an oxygen tube. Perón had been stricken with pulmonary edema, the abnormal accumulation of fluid in the lungs. Without immediate treatment, he could not have survived. Dr. Luqui Lagleyze administered an injection that saved his life. On the next day the government press office announced that the president had been stricken with bronchitis.[28]

Once again the *conductor* bounced back quickly, a testament to his strong constitution. Two days after his brush with death he appeared on television to assure the nation that he was well.[29] A CIA cable, however, reported that "his heart is still weak . . . [and] has very little excess strength in reserve."[30]

In January the cabinet sat down to an informal lunch at the home of one of the ministers to listen to a briefing from Dr. Taiana on the condition of the president. What he had to say shocked them. The chief executive, he confided to them, was suffering from a serious heart ailment and at best had six months to live. López Rega dissented, insisting that

Perón was in good health and that the doctors were exaggerating. "I can say this better than anyone," he declared, "because when the general's not well, I'm sick too."[31]

Despite what was known about the president's health, surprisingly little was done to limit his activity and exposure to both stress and the elements. In an off-the-record interview granted in January 1974 and published late in 1976, Dr. Cossio deplored the aircraft-carrier visit, which required the seventy-eight-year-old chief executive to climb metal ladders and endure the lash of winds of almost a hundred kilometers per hour. The pressures of appearing before large crowds, of speaking often to groups of Peronists demanding access to their *conductor*, and of resolving a myriad of petty problems were putting an excessive strain upon him, the heart specialist complained.[32]

A combination of factors undoubtedly contributed to the failure to adopt measures that might have prolonged Perón's life. His followers liked to put him in a class with other elderly statesmen like Mao, Franco and De Gaulle, and tended to make the simplistic assumption that if these old men could govern, so could he. The political crisis that enabled him to return to power now required careful, sustained attention and the exercise of leadership skills he alone possessed, especially in matters of internal security, Peronist-movement unity and economic policy. The problems he had to confront would have severely tested him in his prime. The style with which he had always governed included an extreme reluctance to delegate and to say no. Old age had deprived him of the willpower necessary to impose rational restraints upon his time. The principle of verticality made it impossible for subordinates to put such badly needed restraints into effect. Jealous of his position next to the throne, López Rega stood ready to prevent others from intruding.

Perón functioned well in the mornings but often tired and lost interest in what he was doing later in the day.[33] His regular routine was to work in the Casa Rosada until lunch and then return to Olivos or Gaspar Campos Street, where he would remain for the rest of the day. From December to mid-April, the hottest part of the summer, he spent virtually all his time in Olivos.

When well-rested, the *conductor* appeared to be physically sound. This was the impression of General Vernon Walters, deputy director of the U.S. Central Intelligence Agency, who made a top-secret visit to Perón in April. According to Walters, the president came to the door to meet him and shook hands firmly; his gait betrayed no hint of unsteadiness; his ankles were not swollen. They talked alone for three hours and Perón had no trouble hearing, never lost the thread of the conversation and did not even once have to go to the bathroom. He was totally relaxed. Upon his return to Langley, General Walters relayed these positive indications to the CIA medical specialists who debriefed him. They had better information than their deputy director, however. They told him that Perón would probably not live for more than a couple of months.[34]*

Despite his condition, the old man could still charm or impress visitors. His acting skills had not waned. A correspondent who talked with him early in 1974 describes how he spent most of the interview discoursing on the subject of conservation. "He sounded like a senior Jerry Brown," the reporter noted.[35]

He exercised by strolling about the grounds of the Olivos residence. He liked to drive, although for security reasons he remained within the gates. Once, when Isabel and López Rega were out of town, he strayed beyond the spacious confines of Olivos. Nattily dressed, he turned up unexpectedly on Gaspar Campos Street in a Fiat, greeted the employees at his home and the neighbors, and then disappeared.[36]†

In a sharp departure from past practices, the Peronists refrained from heaping honors upon their *conductor* and from putting his name on provinces, plazas, railroad stations, et cetera. Since the upper echelons of the movement harbored as many flatterers as ever, one suspects that it was Perón himself who passed the word that these excesses were not to be repeated.

Perón retained much of what for three decades had made him a singularly appealing personality. A novel element to which his compatriots had to adjust was the presence of José López Rega. The astrologer was not merely a constant shadow at the president's side, an almost "organic extension of Perón," as one observer put it,[37] but also a political force increasingly to be taken into account.

Daniel had always been a fertile source of amusement. Perón liked to poke fun at his idiosyncrasies, such as his fondness for burning incense ("It keeps the bugs away," the *conductor* would quip[38]). *La Prensa* once reported in a news item that he attended a "witches' conference" in Spain.[39] El Brujo did not let any of this bother him. He would soon transcend absurdity and teach his fellow Argentines what lay beyond.

---

* Walters states that the purposes of his trip were to give Perón his word as a soldier that current rumors of U.S. participation in a plot to overthrow him were false, and to express U.S. concern about a possible turn to the far left in Argentina. (Perón assured him that would not transpire.) The general, an uncanny linguist with long experience in Latin America, stayed at the Plaza Hotel and rode by himself in the subway. His presence in Buenos Aires went totally unnoticed. Interview with General Vernon Walters, Washington, May 12, 1977.

† According to Dr. Cossio, he was once involved in a minor auto accident while driving a Fiat on the highway that rings the capital. B. Neustadt, *La Argentina y los argentinos,* p. 304; interview with Dr. Pedro Cossio, Buenos Aires, May 3, 1978. Whether the mishap occurred on the same day as his surprise visit to Gaspar Campos Street is unknown.

As social welfare minister and private secretary to the president, he had his hand in many things. His pet project and personal brainchild, to which he devoted inordinate time and energy, was the "Altar of the Fatherland." This lineal descendant of the monument to Eva Perón, a gigantic pantheon of marble and granite, was to be constructed next to the University of Buenos Aires Law School on the Avenida Libertador, not far from the site of the former presidential residence.[40] The warlock hoped to unite the country by putting all its heroes in one burial place. San Martín, Rosas, Yrigoyen, Aramburu, Evita, the unknown soldier and eventually Juan Perón himself would lie together in perfect harmony. It was necrophilia transformed into public policy.

López Rega never forgot his days as a humble policeman. Perón had regained his former rank in the institution dearest to his heart, but Daniel entertained grander designs. In early May an executive decree promoted him to commissioner general of police, twelve grades above the rank at which he retired.[41] In addition to increasing his pension benefits and permitting him to wear a fancy new uniform, the promotion strengthened his links to the police. Later he revealed the real motive behind his return to law enforcement. The armed forces each derived inspiration from a great hero of the past. "The army has San Martín," he explained, "the navy has Brown and the air force Newbery. The police don't have anybody. . . . Now they have me."[42]

Perón was not reluctant to post López Rega on special assignments. The most notable was a trade mission to Libya, where he signed an agreement for the importation of petroleum. He also accompanied Isabel on a trip to Europe later in the year. On his return he described Pope Paul VI, with whom they had met, as a "man with very high moral values."[43]

López Rega continued to live with Perón and Isabel. He watched over the *conductor* with ceaseless vigilance, to the point of installing a listening device next to Perón's bed so that he could be alert to any unusual sounds during the night.[44] El Brujo was convinced that he was better qualified than any physician to decide what was best for Perón. Dr. Taiana has related how, when the doctors prescribed complete rest after one of the president's heart seizures, López Rega told Perón to get out of bed and walk, in order to keep his legs from drying up.[45] From time to time the attending physicians told him to stop meddling and he would withdraw without protest. But he always returned.

When he spoke about Perón's physical condition he went far beyond the bounds of rationality. Once he disclosed to listeners that the *conductor* had died in Madrid and that he had resurrected him.[46] During a presidential health crisis he insisted that as long as he stayed near Perón, everything would be fine because it was he who gave the general life.[47]

These were not isolated utterances.[48] Perhaps those who heard them did not take them seriously at first and dismissed him as a harmless eccentric. By the time enough people realized his pursuit of power was in earnest, it may have been too late to stop him. The left opposed him from the start but had no influence upon what went on in Perón's inner circle. Peronist politicians never had much leverage. The only sector of the movement with muscle of its own, the unions, probably did not perceive Daniel as a threat to their interests, and he was clever enough to cultivate orthodox labor leaders.

Did Perón deplore what El Brujo was doing?* Although lucid enough to deal with important problems, was the *conductor* too old and exhausted to put a stop to the petty and not-so-petty excesses his private secretary was committing? Or did he simply not care? The patterns of behavior he had followed all his life suggest the latter explanation. Daniel's rise to power was symptomatic of one of Peronism's fundamental weaknesses, a quasi-monarchical structure that permitted the king to impose not only his queen but also his court jester upon a country that in other respects was the most politically sophisticated in Latin America.

The violence that flared after Rucci's murder and the issuance of the "reserved document" gave no indication of abating in 1974. Right-wing attacks on groups and individuals linked to the Peronist left increased. On March 23, Juan Abal Medina was wounded in a narrow escape from an assassination attempt. On the occasion of a state visit to Buenos Aires by Uruguayan President Bordaberry in February, police arrested dozens of left-wing Peronists for allegedly plotting to kill Perón, Isabel and their guest. A federal judge later ordered the release of the person charged with masterminding the conspiracy on a finding that the government's evidence against him was insufficient.[49] However, a number of bombings and killings during this period could legitimately be attributed to the Peronist left. The ERP continued its kidnappings, the most spectacular of which extracted $14.2 million from Exxon for the return of one of its refinery managers. They also wounded, abducted and then released the director of the U.S. Information Service in Córdoba.

Perón renewed his efforts to agglutinate all his youthful supporters into a single, disciplined organization. The JP and other Peronist-left groups balked, sensing that his ultimate goal was to impose someone like Julio Yessi upon them. At one point he put army colonel Vicente Damasco in charge of bringing the *muchachos* together. Colonel Damasco invited leaders of the JP and Yessi's Peronist Youth of the Argentine Republic to an *asado* (an outdoor meal of roasted meat), where he hoped they would play soccer against each other.[50] The JP stayed away, reluctant to socialize with people who were shooting and bombing them.[51] The colonel's next initiative was to compose a "March for Argentine Youth."[52] As

---

* The only solid evidence of discontent is in a letter Perón sent to Jorge Antonio on October 19, 1973: "Crazy López Rega creates every class of problems for me . . ." J. Antonio, *Ahora o nunca,* p. 135.

methods of achieving unity, these ideas ranked second only to the "Altar of the Fatherland."

In a speech to right-wing youth leaders on February 7, the president hammered away at those who had "infiltrated" the movement. He called them "idiots" and "deceivers." "What are they doing in *justicialismo*?" he asked. "If I were a Communist, I'd go to the Communist party."[53]

The answer was not long in coming. In an editorial in *El Descamisado*, Dardo Cabo took issue with his *conductor*, indirectly yet unmistakably. "So now we are infiltrators," he complained. "Yesterday we were the *muchachos*, emotionally hailed by the chief of the movement for our struggle. Our dead were honored. And now . . . they say there are other 'socialist' parties where we can go if we like. Why didn't they tell us that before, when we were fighting?"[54]

Things finally came to a head on May 1, the day of the "plebiscite" Perón had promised at his inauguration.[55] The *muchachos* wanted a dialogue between the *conductor* and his people. Perón and those around him wanted a May Day in the style which had evolved during his second presidency, complete with a beauty contest and entertainment. The JP sought to mobilize a huge crowd in the Plaza de Mayo. The organizers did their best to discourage militant groups from coming. Banners and placards were forbidden. The Peronist Youth smuggled cans of spray paint and rolls of cloth material into the plaza. At an appropriate moment they painted their slogans and raised their banners. The theme of the rally was "National Unity." By mid-afternoon the first Montonero chant bounced off the surrounding buildings and drew a response from the CGT participants and right-wing youth groups. From their positions in the plaza the left and right exchanged hostile gestures. At 4:25 someone burned a Montonero flag, to the applause of the orthodox sector.

Perón arrived by helicopter and appeared in a Casa Rosada balcony at 5:10. Isabel crowned the beauty queen and the JP shouted "There's only one Evita." A military band played the national hymn and for the only time in the day the crowd stood silent. When the president began to speak from behind a bulletproof glass enclosure, the left-wing youths kept interrupting him with chants asking, for example, "Why is the people's government full of gorillas?"

A dialogue of the deaf ensued, Perón heaping praise upon organized labor and the old-line leaders who had been assassinated, the JP hurling insults at Rucci and Vandor. Perón denounced "mercenaries at the service of foreign money." The *muchachos* kept shouting. Perón called them "stupid" and "beardless youths." His face now contorted with rage, he lost his composure. As he spewed forth venom, the JP contingents, comprising perhaps half of a crowd of 100,000, turned their backs on him and walked away.

Perón cut short his speech. As he uttered his closing remarks, waves of workers and right-wing youths attacked the withdrawing columns with poles and stones. "There goes unity," observed a bystander as a pitched battle broke out in front of the cathedral.[56] The leftists were once again caught by surprise and came out second best. Many fled in panic down the adjoining streets. Dozens required medical treatment.

When the situation demanded it, Juan Perón had used his young followers as shock troops. The "special formations" helped destabilize regimes that were hostile to him and paved the way for his triumphal return. His vague promises, couched in terms like "national socialism" and "*trasvasamiento generacional*," were calculated tactics.

Although many young Peronists believed him, some of the leaders of left-wing Peronist youth groups must have known in their hearts that he really was not a proto-Castro. Yet they also realized that the Argentine working class was solidly Peronist, and therefore the only way to bring about legitimate socialism was to influence, if not take control of, the Peronist movement. They were trying to make of Peronism something it never was, and in this respect Perón was justified in calling them infiltrators. They thought they could exploit him in the same manner he was exploiting them. But the old man was still the master manipulator, and in the end deserved them as much as they deserved him.

54

The Death of
the Conductor

It bore the hallmarks of a sentimental journey, a state visit to the country that had sheltered him in his hour of greatest need. His doctors advised against the trip to Paraguay.[1] According to several accounts, he wanted to postpone it, but López Rega pressured him to go and he yielded.[2]*

President Stroessner insisted that he arrive by boat so that a big crowd could greet him at the dock. On June 6 Perón flew to a port in northern Argentina, where he boarded a minesweeper for a cruise upriver. A heavy rain was falling as the Paraguayans gave him a tumultuous welcome. The gunboat upon which he had taken refuge in 1955 fired a twenty-one-gun salute. Standing beneath a canopy that did not protect him completely from the steady precipitation, he reviewed troops from the army in which he was an honorary general. Despite the brevity of his stay, he seemed exhausted when he returned to Buenos Aires.

These were trying times for the *conductor*. Although stung by his public denunciation, the Peronist left announced on May 6 that it would remain loyal to Perón.[3] The lieutenant general could not seem to get rid of them. In a speech on May 13 he attacked their "revolutionary infantilism" and accused them of trying to provoke a civil war that would cost a million Argentine lives. He once again invoked the microbe-antibody theory and assured his audience that the workers would develop their own self-defense mechanisms.[4] Right-wing terrorists, both active and potential, undoubtedly grasped the message.

* José María Rosa, historian and Argentine ambassador to Paraguay at the time, claims that the trip's principal purpose was to patch up relations that had become strained during negotiations with Paraguay for a joint hydroelectric project of vital importance to Argentina. Interview with José M. Rosa, Buenos Aires, May 1, 1978; see also P. Hernández, *Conversaciones con José M. Rosa*, pp. 174–92.

The subversion problem sorely vexed him but cracks in the "social pact" were even more worrisome. The lid on prices was creating shortages of staple goods, which in turn gave rise to a black market providing food and other necessary items at inflated prices. Workers were pressuring their unions for wage increases. Labor leaders in turn sought Perón's approval of deviations from the limits set by the "social pact." Scattered strikes erupted and the CGT began to criticize Gelbard. Caught in the middle, the president voiced bitter complaints, to the point of privately threatening to "go home" to Madrid.[5]

Shortly after his return from Paraguay, Perón met with Balbín in the Casa Rosada. The president seemed worn out both in body and spirit. "I'm dying," he told his visitor. Balbín gave him a number of political suggestions. The *conductor* took extensive notes.[6]

On the morning of Wednesday, June 12, the face of Juan Perón appeared on the nation's television screens. In unusually blunt language he took to task those who were threatening the "social pact" and denounced what he called a "psychological campaign" of "deliberate provocation." He also made it clear he was not criticizing the political opposition. He singled out businessmen and labor leaders, as well as "certain oligarchical daily newspapers" that kept publicizing shortages. Invoking a hoary precedent, he obliquely threatened to resign.[7]

The CGT immediately declared a strike and summoned workers to the Plaza de Mayo. By late afternoon a huge crowd had gathered in front of the Casa Rosada and was clamoring for Perón. He appeared on the balcony at 5:15 and raised his arms in a familiar gesture. The temperature fell below 10 degrees C. (50 degrees F.) as he delivered a short speech thanking the workers for their support and promising to stay on the job. Theater once again substituted for statesmanship. He concluded by asking God to bestow upon his listeners the good fortune and happiness they deserved. "I carry in my ears what to me is the most remarkable music of all, the voice of the Argentine people."[8] It sounded like a farewell message.

For the rest of the week he engaged in his normal activities. On Saturday, he went to the Morón air base to see Isabel off; she was departing for Geneva, where she would address the International Labor Organization. López Rega went with her on the trip, which was to include visits to Rome and Madrid. Over the weekend the president manifested cold symptoms, the worst of which was a persistent cough.

The leadership of the CGT met with him in the Casa Rosada on Monday morning. He told them he would approve a bonus to be paid to workers as an offset against the rising cost of living. According to a North American economist, this "appeared to make a mockery out of the government's fight against . . . inflation."[9] But other problems may have been distracting him.

He returned to Olivos by way of Dr. Cossio's office, where he received a thorough physical examination. Cossio advised total rest.[10] The president decided to remain at the residence but he continued to work. The press office announced he was not going to the Casa Rosada because he had contracted the grippe. On Wednesday the nineteenth Dr. Taiana noted that Perón's condition was not improving and began to worry. He telephoned López Rega in Rome to suggest that he return home immediately.[11] The social welfare minister arrived the following day and assured reporters that the president had no more than a simple cold.[12]

López Rega now took charge at the residence. He, Gelbard and Taiana, who was one of the physicians attending the president, were the only ministers who saw Perón regularly. It was during this period that El Brujo disclosed that Perón was really a pharaoh who should have been mummified ten years ago. In response to a question about the vice-president, he explained that "Isabel does not exist. She is a creation of mine."[13]

Official sources insisted that the president was recuperating from the grippe and attending to matters of state.[14] Cossio and Taiana, however, realized he had not shaken off his bronchial infection, which under normal circumstances should have begun to abate after forty-eight hours, and increased the dosages of antibiotics they had prescribed.[15] Meanwhile, the noodle-makers' union declared a strike, the first work stoppage since Perón's June 12 appeal, and the Congress approved a bill for the construction of the "Altar of the Fatherland."

On June 25 Héctor Cámpora unexpectedly arrived in Buenos Aires from México, where he had been serving as ambassador. The ostensible purpose of his trip was to make arrangements for a forthcoming visit by Mexican President Echeverría. His efforts to see Perón met with frustration.

On Thursday the twenty-seventh López Rega spoke words of reassurance to the press.[16] But on the next day Isabel cut her trip short and flew back home. The official announcements for the first time hinted that the president's condition was serious. In the late afternoon a bulletin signed by Cossio and Taiana stated that he required "absolute rest."[17]

On Saturday morning, still confined to bed, Juan Perón signed his last two presidential decrees. The first accepted the resignation of Héctor Cámpora; the second temporarily delegated the presidency to Isabel. According to Jorge Garrido, the government notary public who was present at the time, Perón was completely lucid.[18]

The armed forces, the church, the CGT, the Congress and even the Peronist Youth rallied behind Isabel in this moment of crisis. Balbín declared that he would "back the constitutional president whether in trousers or in a skirt."[19]

On Sunday, June 30, an army chaplain administered the sacraments of penance and holy communion to Perón. Cossio and Taiana issued a bulletin stating that his condition had not changed in the past twenty-four hours and that he still required complete rest. The press office, clinging to a false optimism, announced he was improving.[20] At 3:00 A.M. on Monday, an electrocardiograph registered disturbances in his heart rhythms.[21]

Perón spent a comfortable night and seemed much better the next morning. He sipped some tea and had a lively conversation with his wife. López Rega and Gelbard visited him briefly. At 10:00 A.M. Isabel called a meeting of the cabinet to order in one of the ground-floor rooms. Outside it was a gorgeous "Peronist day."

Suddenly the sound of cries and doors slamming interrupted the meeting. A maid rushed downstairs and called to Taiana: "Doctor, come quickly! The general's gotten worse." Hurrying to Perón's bedroom, Taiana found him sprawled on the bed. "I'm going," he told the physician, his body convulsing, and then he lapsed into unconsciousness. Taiana's diagnosis was that he had suffered a cardiac arrest. It was nearly 10:30 A.M.[22]

The medical team massaged Perón's chest and applied mouth-to-mouth resuscitation, but to no avail. At 12:30 López Rega decided to try his hand. He grabbed Perón by the ankles and uttered some incomprehensible phrases. His pharaoh did not respond. "I can't do it . . . I can't . . . ," López Rega mumbled. "For ten years I did it, but now I can't . . ."[23] Taiana and Cossio put on their jackets and retired to an adjoining room, where they began to draft a bulletin. At 1:15 the doctors ordered that efforts to revive Perón cease and they declared him officially dead.

It was left to Isabel to break the news to the nation. Shortly before 2:00 P.M., seated at a table and with the cabinet lined up behind her, she videotaped the official announcement. López Rega stood by her right shoulder, his hands on her chair. With a voice shaking with emotion she lamented the passing of "a true apostle of peace and nonviolence."[24] Several hours after the television and radio networks carried her message, López Rega himself unexpectedly took to the airwaves to repeat the news.

The ceremonies for the departed *conductor* were relatively brief, at least in comparison with the marathon of mourning that followed Evita's death. One limitation was Perón's personal request that his body not be embalmed. On Tuesday morning the coffin was transported from Olivos to the cathedral for a funeral mass, and then to the Congress for the wake.

The public outpouring of grief was intense. A huge multitude surrounded the Congress building and impatiently waited for the viewing to begin. There was a tremendous crush at the front gates and a number of people fainted. Cries of "Here comes a body" would reverberate as an unconscious form would be lifted aloft and passed from hand to hand to the edge of the plaza where ambulances were waiting.[25]

When at last the doors opened, visitors walked one by one along a passageway lined with police and union members in work clothes. They were directed to the Blue Room, an octagonal enclosure between the Senate and the Chamber of Deputies, where the uniformed, flag-draped corpse of Juan Perón lay in an open coffin. Those who were standing watch kept repeating "Don't faint," "It's all right," and "Don't touch the body." When mourners gave signs of succumbing to emotion, attendants would quickly move in from behind and grab them by the elbows.[26]

The lines stretched for block after block. On Wednesday the rains came but had no effect on the crowds. Security was tight but there were no problems. The Peronist Youth militants, grieving like everyone else, were on their best behavior. Mario Firmenich and other prominent Montoneros passed by the coffin and gave their beloved old man a V-for-victory salute.[27]

Though thousands were still waiting outside, the gates were closed early Thursday morning. The casket was moved to the Chamber of Deputies, where at 8:15 A.M. a throng of officials and dignitaries listened to a dozen orations paying tribute to the deceased president. All but one ranged from the ordinary to the forgettable. It was Ricardo Balbín who stole the show.

When they invited him to speak he hesitated, wondering whether it was at all proper for him to participate. On his way to the Congress he still had not decided. At the last moment he agreed. "I was supposed to be the eleventh speaker," he recalled in 1980, "but they called me seventh. I was thinking about something else and was surprised to hear my name."[28] The veteran politician arose, put his hands in his pocket and improvised a sentimental, tango-like farewell, invoking long years of conflict that had ripened into a relationship of mutual understanding and trust. "This old adversary," he concluded, "bids goodbye to a friend."[29] It was the finest moment of Balbín's long career.

At the close of the ceremonies the casket was sealed and placed in a hearse, which slowly returned to Olivos. The crypt of a tiny chapel on the grounds of the residence would serve as the lieutenant general's resting place.

55

Aftermath

"Perón's only successor will be the Argentine people, who in the last analysis will be the ones who ought to decide." These were the words of the *conductor* himself, speaking to the nation on the morning of June 12.[1] If he intended them to be a political testament, he ought to have been much more specific.

In the aftermath of the funeral a report circulated to the effect that just before his death he had asked one of his assistants to determine whether it would be legally permissible to transfer the presidency to Balbín.[2] The story excited Radicals but the Peronists ignored it. The assistant later denied that the conversation ever took place.[3]

Speculation that Isabel would be an interim chief executive or would share authority with some kind of council of state came to naught. Interior Minister Benito Llambí set the matter straight when he declared: "Verticality was Perón's. Now that the leader has died, this verticality is exercised by the person the people elected with him, the president herself."[4] The full powers of the office now belonged to Isabel. How she would exercise them should have become apparent on the day of Perón's death. The commander-in-chief of the army came to her with a decree providing for certain security measures to take effect until after the funeral. She called López Rega and asked him what to do. He told her to sign and she signed.[5]

On the day after Perón's body was put to rest in the chapel, his widow convened an extraordinary meeting at the residence. Summoned to Olivos were the entire cabinet, the three commanders of the armed forces, the presidents of the Senate and Chamber of Deputies, the heads of the CGT and the CGE, and Ricardo Balbín. No agenda had been announced beforehand.

Isabel went straight to the point. With a grim expression on her face, she said it had come to her attention that serious charges had been raised against López Rega. Recalling that Perón considered him "like a son," she praised the social welfare minister warmly and then threw the floor open to discussion.

Several of those present, known to be allies of the warlock, echoed her appreciation of him. Others gave eloquent or long-winded speeches devoid of substance. Only Robledo, Taiana, Admiral Emilio Massera and Balbín spoke out against Daniel. The Radical leader criticized him for involving himself in matters far afield from his ministry and even accused him of organizing armed bands. At the close of the discussion Isabel observed that "what was good for Perón will be good for me, just as what was bad for Perón will be bad for me."[6] Shortly after the meeting, the press office announced that López Rega would continue as private secretary to the president.

According to Heriberto Kahn, the journalist who has written the best account of the meeting, Isabel had not made up her mind beforehand but was inclined to go with the majority; if those who really opposed El Brujo had had the courage to speak up, she might have dismissed him.[7] If true, this amounts to a terrible indictment of those who remained silent.

By mid-August López Rega had solidified his position. Robledo and Taiana resigned from the cabinet. Balbín's influence upon the government had all but evaporated. Massera, with the armed forces behind him, survived.

The tranquility produced by the funeral of Perón did not last very long. A mere week after his passing a young woman from the Peronist Youth was raped and beaten to death. On July 15 a vile and senseless murder shocked the nation. Assailants burst into a restaurant where Arturo Mor Roig was lunching and gunned him down. The former interior minister had retired from politics and was working as a legal advisor to a small company. It was never determined who killed him. A Montonero rally in late July cheered a reference to his assassination. But no one explained what purpose it served.

Terrorist activity intensified. On July 31 Rodolfo Ortega Peña, the most prominent leftist still serving in the Chamber of Deputies, was machine-gunned on a downtown Buenos Aires street. A group styling itself the Argentine Anti-Communist Alliance, or the Triple A, took credit.[8] A deadly rhythm of violence and reprisal was now developing. The Triple A quickly became the most feared of the right-wing para-police squads. Among its victims were a brother of ex-President Frondizi, a former deputy police chief of Buenos Aires Province and Atilio López. The group also released a blacklist of intended victims, including a number of luminaries from the Peronist left, several entertainers, three Radical legislators and Dr. Taiana.

The ERP, meanwhile, mounted more assaults on military units, its members now wearing uniforms when they went into action. The organization would soon open up a front in the hilly sugar-growing region of Tucumán Province and engage the Argentine army in guerrilla warfare.

On September 4 *La Causa Peronista*, a Montonero magazine, ran an article by Firmenich and one of his colleagues describing in lurid detail how they had kidnapped and murdered Aramburu. The government closed down the publication, whereupon the Montoneros announced they would resume clandestine paramilitary operations.

Their first splashy venture was the kidnapping of the Born brothers, directors of the huge grain-trading conglomerate Bunge and Born.[9] The ransom netted them $50 million. On the eve of October 17, as Isabel prepared for her first Loyalty Day without Perón, the Montoneros demonstrated they had lost none of their flair for bizarre publicity. They stole Aramburu's body from its tomb and said they would keep it until the government brought Evita's remains back to Argentina.

Isabel gave an impression of helplessness that confirmed the worst fears of those who had shuddered when her husband put her on the ticket with him. The sad truth was that Perón had done nothing to prepare her for the job she now held. She depended totally upon López Rega, whose strange antics were not likely to build public confidence in the new administration. In August a leftist daily reprinted a photo from a Brazilian newspaper which showed him participating in the rites of a spiritist cult in Pôrto Alegre.[10] He made periodic unexplained visits to southern Brazil, which gave rise to rumors that he sought inspiration from his cult and he was investing Social Welfare Ministry funds in Brazil.[11] He had a habit of mouthing Isabel's words as she delivered speeches.[12] According to one anecdote, when asked why he did this, he replied that he was serving as intermediary between the president and Perón, who was speaking through his widow from the grave. The most startling of the Isabel/López Rega stories describes how a military aide caught him slapping the president and threatening to shoot her. He is supposed to have claimed that the pressures of office had made her hysterical and that he was merely bringing her to her senses.[13] Whether or not these incidents ever occurred, they were the subject of endless speculation and formed an integral part of the backdrop of Isabel's presidency.

López Rega was less effective at policymaking than he was at consolidating his grip upon the government. As terrorism mounted and the economy collapsed, his idea of a response was to fly secretly to Madrid and bring Evita's body back with him. His carefully staged arrival on November 17—and the subsequent return of Aramburu's remains by the Montoneros—diverted public attention, but only momentarily. Dr. Ara's masterpiece went on display, next to Perón's closed casket, in the Olivos chapel. When the novelty wore off, the crowds of visitors diminished, perhaps because of the elaborate security precautions and the growing unpopularity of the regime.

One of López Rega's triumphs was the October 21 resignation of the cabinet member who had become his chief rival. The departure of José Gelbard marked the death knell for the "social pact." The new economy minister, veteran Peronist Alfredo Gómez Morales, utilized more traditional measures to stem the inflation, but to no avail. With wage contracts up for renewal in mid-1975, a crisis of major proportions loomed.

López Rega's solution was to replace Gómez Morales with one of his intimates and apply austerity measures. This meant an abandonment of Perón's consensus approach and the use of the coercive powers of the government to impose a sudden shock treatment on Argentina's ailing economy.[14] Since one aspect of the treatment would be a wage freeze, the Peronist administration had placed itself in an adversary relationship with its "vertebral column," organized labor.

On June 27, for the first time ever, workers staged a massive protest march on a Peronist-controlled Casa Rosada.[15] The claim of labor leaders that they were "supporting" Isabel fooled no one. Despite a government plea that the unions keep their members at home and a heavy morning rain, the historic plaza was filled to capacity. The crowd chanted obscenities against López Rega. Within a fortnight the CGT followed up with a two-day general strike. Isabel had to give in and approve wage contracts with substantial increases. Inflation soared.

The armed forces looked on with growing concern. Terrorism and the guerrilla war in Tucumán were disastrous enough, but the element of labor unrest was potentially explosive. The Montoneros and other left-wing Peronist militants were busily organizing in the factories in the hope of exploiting the situation. Memories of the *cordobazo* haunted the generals.

It was at this point that the military joined the CGT and the politicians in reaching a consensus that the first step toward resolving the crisis was to remove José López Rega. The June 27 rally turned out to be the beginning of the end for Isabel's Rasputin.

He had become the most powerful and the most feared person in Argentina. People were looking at him with the paralyzed fascination of rabbits facing a python. The suspicion that para-police groups carried out his commands grew stronger by the day. In May 1975 alone, twenty-nine murders were attributed to the Triple A.[16] Lawyers, priests, workers, journalists, students and teachers found themselves targeted for extinction. The government made no effort to stop the carnage.

Yet on June 27 the demonstrators in the plaza cursed him and made fun of him and he was helpless to respond. The aura of omnipotence around him suddenly vanished, and his enemies took heart. Politicians began to call for his resignation. Newspapers began to print unfavorable references to him. *La Opinión*'s Heriberto Kahn reported that the army had charged him with organizing and directing the Triple A and cited facts to back up the accusation.[17]

López Rega had reached the end of the line. The armed forces demanded his removal and Isabel had no choice but to accede. On July 20, after the president had made him a "special ambassador" without assignment, he flew first to Rio de Janeiro, then to Madrid, and shortly thereafter vanished from the face of the earth.

The elimination of López Rega turned out to have no perceptible impact upon the economy or internal security. The president, her tenacity matching her incompetence, refused to step aside. The slogan "Isabel is Perón," coined in a bid to shore her up, now militated against any organized Peronist move to replace her. Those who had her ear were devoid of any fresh ideas that might have halted the slide. The next elections were several years away.

For months on end rumors of an impending military coup dominated political conversation. There was no doubt that the armed forces would intervene; the only question was when. Yet the troops remained in their barracks. The generals were biding their time, apparently wanting to let things reach such dire straits that Peronism would be forever discredited and the entire country would welcome them as saviors.

The hour of the sword struck shortly after midnight on March 25, 1976. A helicopter that was taking Isabel from the Casa Rosada to the Olivos residence developed "engine trouble" and diverted to the military section of the downtown airport. When it landed, armed soldiers stepped aboard, took her into custody and put her on an air force plane bound for the Andean lake country, where she was placed under house arrest in a luxurious chalet belonging to the provincial government.[18]

A military junta took over and installed one of its members as president. The new regime thereupon set out to exterminate the threat of subversion and cure the economy. Yet another new era was about to dawn.

Dealing with the ERP in Tucumán was relatively simple. The army deployed superior forces and annihilated them. The Montoneros and their allies presented a different problem. For two years a "dirty war" ravaged Argentina as the armed forces, the police and armed bands for whom the regime denied responsibility hunted down, captured, tortured and summarily killed thousands of suspected subversives. Victims ranged from ERP leader Mario Santucho, Montonero Dardo Cabo and former Perón delegate Bernardo Alberte to innocent bystanders of every description.[19] Argentine political exiles flocked to other countries. Admiral César Guzzetti, the new foreign minister, explained to the United Nations that the right-wing terrorism rampant in his country was the work of antibodies that the microbes of left-wing subversion had created.[20]

Out of the carnage came the revolting euphemism *desaparecido*, the "disappeared," a person who has ceased to exist. The government attempted to create the impression it had no control over the unidentified groups that carried out this mass liquidation and that it knew nothing of the fate of the "disappeared." The fact that few Argentines—least of all the families of the victims—believe this will be a destabilizing element in Argentine politics for at least a generation, since the armed forces have taken the position that no victorious army ever permits its own Nuremberg.

The new government repressed wage demands, overvalued the peso in order to encourage imports and eliminated controls over many areas of the economy. These measures put a brake on inflation, stimulated foreign investment and brought a temporary recovery benefiting certain segments of the middle and upper classes. Free competition brought with it a spate of bankruptcies, as local manufacturers could not survive against a flood of imported goods produced more cheaply in Japan and elsewhere. Moreover, the artificially high rate at which the peso was pegged proved ruinous to Argentine exporters, who received undervalued dollars for their sales abroad. Prices skyrocketed, making Buenos Aires one of the most expensive cities in the world. By 1981 the peso had undergone a series of dramatic devaluations and another economic crisis loomed.

The junta appeared to have made a conscious decision not to repeat the most egregious mistakes of the Liberating Revolution. No campaign was launched to denigrate the memory of Perón, nor were the Peronists singled out for reprisals.* The government quietly delivered Evita's body to her sisters, who buried it in the family crypt at the Recoleta Cemetery. Perón's remains found their way to the tomb of his mother and grandfather in La Chacarita.

Isabel, charged with embezzlement, languished under house arrest; the regime could not seem to decide what to do with her. Since she was a divisive force among Peronists, it would have made sense to let her go after a brief period of confinement. Instead, the government kept her in isolation, first at a military installation in Azul and later in Perón's country house in San Vicente. Agitation for her release then became a banner to which a fractured Peronist movement could rally. It was not until July 6, 1981, that she gained her freedom, whereupon she flew immediately to Spain.

In their fourth turn at the helm since the 1930 revolution, the armed forces demonstrated that they were as incapable as ever of providing

---

* Several Peronist officials were imprisoned for varying terms. Héctor Cámpora, who had the bad luck to return to Buenos Aires a few days before the coup, took refuge, along with his sons and Juan Abal Medina, in the Mexican embassy. He was not permitted to leave until November 1979 and he died of cancer in Mexico City on December 19, 1980. In August 1981 Abal Medina broke the Latin American record for the longest period of asylum in an embassy, previously held by Peruvian Víctor Haya de la Torre, who once spent 1,219 days in the Colombian embassy in Lima. *Latin American Weekly Report,* August 14, 1981, p. 8.

more than interim leadership. General replaced general in the Casa Rosada, labor unrest intensified, and the families of the "disappeared" demanded an accounting.

The Argentine invasion of the Falklands (Malvinas) in April 1982, a diversionary gambit designed to unite the country behind the regime, turned into a bloody disaster, exposing monumental diplomatic and military misjudgments on the part of the high command. The resulting moral bankruptcy of the armed forces, which (except for the air force) had fought as badly as they had governed, threatened to create a power vacuum and intensified pressure for a return to civilian rule.

Both before and during the fighting in the South Atlantic, there were clear signs that Peronism had survived. Peronist politicians made declarations, Peronist labor leaders kept the CGT alive, and the Peronist faithful chanted their slogans whenever mass gatherings were permitted. But the movement was still divided, with verticalists, in search of a new *conductor*, pitted against those who would build from Peronism an ideology closer to the European social-democratic model.

The Peronists' ability to contribute in a positive way to their country's future may depend upon how they come to terms with their departed leader. Juan Perón created a distinctively Argentine brand of authoritarian populism straddling both sides of the political spectrum. A Peronism based upon some form of social democracy could not embrace the heterogeneous elements he was able to bring together. His unique genius in understanding, reflecting and manipulating Argentina is not likely to reappear in the near future, if ever. Perón shaped his movement to suit talents he alone possessed. While he lived, he did much to assure his own niche in Argentine history and little to institutionalize Peronism. Indeed, he may not have wanted Peronism to flourish without him, in order to magnify his historical image.

There is much to dislike in Perón—the cynicism, the utter disdain for truth, the lack of principle, the selfishness, the irresponsibility. His willingness to condone violence, his distorting of truth beyond recognition and his rejection of accountability set sorry examples which the military rulers succeeding Isabel duplicated with tragic consequences.

Beyond Argentina's borders he will be remembered for the high drama of his career rather than his exercise of statesmanship. His greatness was contextual only. Even within his native land his stature owes much to the mediocrity of his competitors and those who came after him.

To his credit he legitimized the aspirations of millions of Argentines previously excluded from civil life. He gave the working class an enduring self-awareness and cohesiveness, brought social welfare to the poor, and permitted women to see in the roles he assigned to his second and third wives new possibilities of self-fulfillment. In this latter respect he departed from the deep-rooted machismo of his fellow countrymen.

He also was a pacifist at heart, despite his occasional use of violent rhetoric and his acceptance of terrorism that favored his cause, a curious contradiction at the essence of his nature. He steadfastly rejected violence as an open instrument of policy. His record, while far from perfect, stands in sharp contrast to the torture and killing that traumatized Argentina in the late 1970s. Moreover, it is undeniable that the man once reviled as a South American Hitler would never have plunged or blundered his country into war.

For Argentines, understanding Perón is a prerequisite to understanding themselves. There is more truth than hyperbole to the popular saying that "If Argentina were an orange, Perón would be the juice." But he must be accepted as he was, the sum total of all his parts, rather than an idealized epitome of good or evil. To mythologize him will lead only to opportunistic manipulation of what he represented and produce the same kind of endless, diversive debate inspired by Rosas.

A nation that cannot resolve its past will have difficulty working out its destiny.

Bibliography

BOOKS

Acossano, Benigno. *Eva Perón: Su verdadera vida*. Buenos Aires: Editorial Lamas, 1955.

Aizcorbe, Roberto. *Argentina: The Peronist Myth*. Hicksville, N.Y.: Exposition Press, 1975.

Alende, Oscar. *Entretelones de la trampa*. Buenos Aires: Santiago Rueda, 1964.

Alexander, Robert J. *Communism in Latin America*. New Brunswick: Rutgers University Press, 1957.

―――. *An Introduction to Argentina*. New York: Frederick A. Praeger, 1969.

―――. *Juan Domingo Perón: A History*. Boulder, Col.: Westview Press, 1979.

―――. *Labor Relations in Argentina, Brazil, and Chile*. New York: McGraw-Hill, 1962.

―――. *The Perón Era*. New York: Columbia University Press, 1951.

―――. *Trotskyism in Latin America*. Stanford: Hoover Institution Press, 1973.

Aloé, Carlos, *Gobierno, proceso, conducta*. Buenos Aires: private printing, 1969.

Alonso Piñeiro, Armando. *La dictadura peronista*. Buenos Aires: Editorial Prestigio, 1955.

Altuve Carrillo, Leonardo. *Yo fuí embajador de Pérez Jiménez*. Caracas: Libroven, S.R.L., 1973.

Amadeo, Mario. *Ayer, hoy, mañana*. Buenos Aires: Ediciones Gure, 1956.

Antonio, Jorge. *Ahora o nunca*. Buenos Aires: private printing, 1975.

―――. *Y ahora qué?* Buenos Aires: Ediciones Verum et Militia, 1966.

Ara, Pedro. *El caso Eva Perón*. Madrid: CVS Ediciones, 1974.

Araujo, Enrique Dias. *La conspiración del '43: El GOU, una experiencia militarista en la Argentina*. Buenos Aires: Ediciones La Bastilla, 1971.

Arciniegas, Germán. *The State of Latin America*. Translated by Harriet de Onis. New York: Alfred A. Knopf, 1952.

Areilza, José María de. *Así los he visto*. Barcelona: Editorial Planeta, 1974.

Arena, Luis. *Alelí*. Buenos Aires: Editorial Estrada, 1954.

Arenas Luque, Fermín V. *Juan Domingo Perón: El segundo hijo de Dios*. Buenos Aires: private printing, 1969.

Badanelli, Pedro. *Perón: La iglesia y un cura.* Buenos Aires: Editorial Tartessos, 1960.

Baily, Samuel L. *Labor, Nationalism, and Politics in Argentina.* New Brunswick: Rutgers University Press, 1967.

Balvé, Beba, Juan Carlos Marín, and Miguel Murmis. *Lucha de calles, lucha de clases: Elementos para su análisis (Córdoba 1971–1969).* Buenos Aires: Ediciones La Rosa Blindada, 1973.

Baquerizas, José. *Porqué se creyó en Perón?* Buenos Aires. private printing, 1957.

Barager, Joseph R., ed. *Why Perón Came to Power: The Background to Peronism in Argentina.* New York: Alfred A. Knopf, 1968.

Barnes, John. *Evita, First Lady: A Biography of Eva Perón.* New York: Grove Press, 1978.

Barrau, Miguel Angel. *Historia del regreso.* Buenos Aires: private printing, 1973.

Barrios, Américo. *Con Perón en el exilio.* Buenos Aires: Editorial Treinta Dias, 1964.

Beals, Carleton. *Latin America: World in Revolution.* London: Abelard-Schuman, 1963.

Becke, Carlos von der. *Destrucción de una infamia.* Buenos Aires: private printing, 1956.

Beladrich, Norberto O. *El parlamento suicida.* Buenos Aires: Ediciones Depalma, 1980.

Belloni, Alberto. *Del anarquismo al peronismo: Historia del movimiento obrero argentino.* Buenos Aires: A. Peña Lillo, 1960.

Benedetti, Antonio. *Perón y Eva: Trayectoria y fin de un régimen.* Mexico City: Editores Panamericanos Asociados, 1956.

Berger, Raoul. *Impeachment: The Constitutional Problems.* Cambridge: Harvard University Press, 1973.

Beveraggi Allende, Walter. *El partido laborista, el fracaso de Perón y el problema argentino.* Montevideo: private printing, 1954.

Blanksten, George I. *Perón's Argentina.* Chicago: University of Chicago Press, 1953.

Blum, John Morton, ed. *The Price of Vision: The Diary of Henry A. Wallace, 1942–1946.* Boston: Houghton Mifflin, 1973.

Boizard, Ricardo. *El caso Kelly.* Buenos Aires: Ediciones Andes, 1957.

———. *Esa noche de Perón.* Santiago: private printing, 1955.

Borrero, José María. *La Patagonia trágica.* Buenos Aires: Editorial Americana, 1967.

Borroni, Otelo, and Roberto Vacca. *La vida de Eva Perón,* Vol. 1. Buenos Aires: Editorial Galerna, 1970.

Botana, Helvio I. *Memorias tras los dientes del perro.* Buenos Aires: A. Peña Lillo, 1977.

Bourne, Richard. *Political Leaders in Latin America.* Baltimore: Penguin Books, 1969.

Bowers, Claude G. *Chile through Embassy Windows, 1939–1953.* New York: Simon & Schuster, 1958. Republished, Westport, Conn.: Greenwood Press, 1977.

Braden, Spruille. *Diplomats and Demagogues.* New Rochelle, N.Y.: Arlington House, 1971.

Bradford, Saxton E. *The Battle for Buenos Aires.* New York: Harcourt, Brace, 1943.

Brady, Frank. *Onassis: An Extravagant Life.* Englewood Cliffs, N.J.: Prentice-Hall, 1977.

Bruce, George. *La Evita de los "descamisados."* Translated by Lope Alberti. Barcelona: Ediciones Picazo, 1976.

Bruce, James. *Those Perplexing Argentines.* New York: Longmans, Green, 1953.

Bryce, James. *South America: Observations and Impressions.* New York: Macmillan, 1912.

Buela, Alberto E. *La sinarquía y lo nacional.* Buenos Aires: Ediciones Marcos, 1974.

Bustos Fierro, Raúl. *Desde Perón hasta Onganía.* Buenos Aires: Ediciones Octubre, 1969.

Buzio, Victorio Alberto. *Aquello se llamó justicialismo.* Buenos Aires: Editorial Indice, 1958.

Cabot, John Moors. *Toward Our Common American Destiny.* Freeport, N.Y.: Books for Libraries Press, 1955.

Cafiero, Antonio F. *Cinco años después . . .* Buenos Aires: private printing, 1961.

Cámpora, Héctor J. *El mandato de Perón.* Buenos Aires: Ediciones Quehacer Nacional, 1975.

————. *La revolución peronista.* Buenos Aires: Editorial Universitaria de Buenos Aires, 1973.

Carril, Bonifacio del. *Crónica interna de la Revolución Libertadora.* Buenos Aires: private printing, 1959.

Casas, Nelly. *Frondizi: Una historia de política y soledad.* Buenos Aires: Ediciones La Bastilla, 1973.

Cavallo, Miguel Angel. *Puerto Belgrano, hora o: La marina se subleva.* Bahía Blanca: Edición Diario "Democracia," 1955.

Chávez, Fermín, *Perón y el peronismo en la historia contemporánea.* Buenos Aires: Editorial Oriente, 1975.

Cincuenta y tres periodistas argentinos. *Libro azul y blanco de la prensa argentina.* Buenos Aires: O.N.P.A., 1951.

Ciria, Alberto. *Estados Unidos nos mira.* Buenos Aires: Ediciones La Bastilla, 1973.

————. *Parties and Power in Modern Argentina (1930–1946).* Translated by Carlos A. Astiz with Mary F. McCarthy. Albany: State University of New York Press, 1974.

————. *Perón y el justicialismo.* Buenos Aires: Siglo Veintiuno, 1971.

Codovilla, Victorio. *Batir al nazi-peronismo: Para abrir una era de libertad y progreso.* Buenos Aires: Editorial Anteo, 1946.

Collier, David, ed. *The New Authoritarianism in Latin America.* Princeton University Press, 1979.

Collier, Peter, and David Horowitz. *The Rockefellers: An American Dynasty.* New York: Holt, Rinehart and Winston, 1976.

Colom, Eduardo. *17 de octubre: La revolución de los descamisados.* Buenos Aires: La Epoca, 1946.

Comisión Argentina por los Derechos Humanos. *Argentina: Proceso al genocidio.* Madrid: Elias Querejeta, 1977.

Concatti, Rolando. *Nuestra opción por el peronismo.* Buenos Aires: Publicaciones del Movimiento Sacerdotes para el Tercer Mundo de Mendoza, 1972.

Confalonieri, Orestes D. *Perón contra Perón*. Buenos Aires: Editorial Antygua, 1956.

Cooke, John W. *Peronismo e integración*. Buenos Aires: Editorial Aquarius, 1972.

———. *Peronismo y revolución*. Buenos Aires: Ediciones Papiro, 1971.

Corbiere, Emilia J. *Conversaciones con Oscar Alende*. Buenos Aires: Hachette, 1978.

Córdoba, Tomás. *La Argentina: Perón y después*. Buenos Aires: Editorial Los Andes, 1976.

Cowles, Fleur. *Bloody Precedent*. New York: Random House, 1952.

———. *Friends and Memories*. New York: Reynal & Co., 1978.

Crassweller, Robert D. *Trujillo: The Life and Times of a Caribbean Dictator*. New York: Macmillan, 1966.

Crespo, Alfonso. *Eva Perón: Viva o muerta*. Lima: Editorial Studium, 1978.

Cristensen, Sven. *Es el coronel Perón nazi-fascista?* Tucumán: Editorial La Raza, 1945.

Custodio Figueroa, A. *La verdadera intención del coronel Juan D. Perón*. Buenos Aires: Editorial Verdad, 1944.

Cutolo, V., and V. Risolia. *Tomás L. Perón: Grandeza e infortunio de una vida*. Buenos Aires: Ministerio de Salud Pública, 1953.

Damonte Taborda, Raúl. *A donde va Perón? De Berlin a Wall Street*. Montevideo: Ediciones de la Resistencia Revolucionaria Argentina, 1955.

———. *Ayer fué San Perón*. Buenos Aires: Ediciones Gure, 1955.

Dehesa, José Alberto. *Marzo 23, hora 24*. Buenos Aires: private printing, 1977.

Delich, Francisco J. *Crisis y protesta social: Córdoba, mayo de 1969*. Buenos Aires: Ediciones Signos, 1970.

Descartes (pseud. for Juan D. Perón). *Política y estrategia*. Buenos Aires: República Argentina, 1951.

Díaz, Fanor. *Conversaciones con Rogelio Frigerio*. Buenos Aires: Hachette, 1977.

Diez periodistas argentinos. *Así cayó Perón: Crónica del movimiento revolucionario triunfante*. Buenos Aires: Editorial Lamas, 1955.

Domínguez, Nelson. *Conversaciones con Juan J. Taccone*. Buenos Aires: Hachette, 1977.

Duggan, Laurence. *The Americas: The Search for Hemisphere Security*. New York: Henry Holt and Co., 1949.

Dulles, J.W.F. *Unrest in Brazil: Political-Military Crises, 1955–1964*. Austin: University of Texas Press, 1970.

———. *Vargas of Brazil*. Austin: University of Texas Press, 1967.

Editors of *La Prensa*. *Defense of Freedom*. New York: John Day, 1952.

Eisenhower, Milton. *The Wine Is Bitter: The United States and Latin America*. New York: Doubleday, 1963.

Ejército Argentino, Escuela de Suboficiales. *Manual del aspirante*. Campo de Mayo, 1925.

Escobar, Justo, and Sebastián Velázquez. *Examen de la violencia argentina*. México: Fondo de Cultura Económica, 1975.

Falcoff, Mark, and Ronald H. Dolkart, eds. *Prologue to Perón: Argentina in Depression and War, 1930–1943*. Berkeley: University of California Press, 1975.

Farago, Ladislas. *Aftermath*. New York: Simon and Schuster, 1974.
Fayt, Carlos S. *Naturaleza del peronismo*. Buenos Aires: Viracocha, 1967.
Ferla, Salvador. *Martires y verdugos*. Buenos Aires: private printing, 1964.
Fernández Alvarino, Próspero Germán. *Z. argentina: El crimen del siglo*. Buenos Aires: private printing, 1973.
Ferns, H.S. *Argentina*. New York: Praeger, 1969.
Ferrero, Roberto A. *Del fraude a la soberanía popular*. Buenos Aires: Ediciones La Bastilla, 1976.
Fillol, Tomás Roberto. *Social Factors in Economic Development: The Argentine Case*. Cambridge: MIT Press, 1961.
Firpo, M. Eduardo. *Péron y los peronistas*. Buenos Aires: Alberdi, 1965.
Flores, María (pseud. for Mary Main). *The Woman with the Whip*. Garden City: Doubleday, 1952.
Franco Salgado-Araujo, Francisco. *Mis conversaciones privadas con Franco*. Barcelona: Editorial Planeta, 1976.
Frank, Waldo. *South American Journey*. New York: Duell, Sloan and Pearce, 1943.
Fraser, Nicolas, Philip Jacobson, Mark Ottaway and Lewis Chester. *Aristotle Onassis*. New York: J.B. Lippincott, 1977.
Fraser, Nicholas, and Marysa Navarro. *Eva Perón*. New York: W.W. Norton, 1980.
Frigerio, Rogelio. *Las condiciones de la victoria: Manual de política argentina*. Montevideo: A. Monteverde, 1963.
Fuchs, Jaime. *La penetración de los "trusts yanquis" en la Argentina*. Buenos Aires: Editorial Cartago, 1958.
Furtado, Celso. *Economic Development of Latin America: A Survey from Colonial Times to the Cuban Revolution*. Translated by Suzette Macedo. Cambridge: Cambridge University Press, 1970.

Gambini, Hugo. *El 17 de octubre*. Buenos Aires: Centro Editor de América Latina, 1971.
————. *El peronismo y la iglesia*. Buenos Aires: Centro Editor de América Latina, 1971.
————. *El primer gobierno peronista*. Buenos Aires: Centro Editor de América Latina, 1971.
García-Zamor, Jean-Claude. *Public Administration and Social Change in Argentina: 1943–1955*. Rio de Janeiro: private printing, 1968.
Gasparri, Petrus, ed. *Codex Juris Canonici*. Rome: Vatican Press, 1957.
Gazzera, Miguel, and Norberto Ceresole. *Peronismo: Autocrítica y perspectivas*. Buenos Aires: Editorial Descartes, 1970.
Germani, Gino. *Authoritarianism, Fascism, and National Populism*. New Brunswick, N.J.: Basic Books, 1978.
Ghioldi, Américo. *De la tiranía a la democracia social*. Buenos Aires: Ediciones Gure, 1956.
Godio, Julio. *La caída de Perón: De junio a setiembre de 1955*. Buenos Aires: Granica, 1973.
Goldwert, Marvin. *Democracy, Militarism, and Nationalism in Argentina, 1930–1966: An Interpretation*. Austin: University of Texas Press, 1972.
González, Ernesto. *Que fué y que es el peronismo*. Buenos Aires: Ediciones Pluma, 1974.
González Sastrol, C. *Porque estoy con el coronel Perón*. Buenos Aires: Editorial Lista Blanca, 1945.

González Trejo, Horacio, and Carlos Pérez, eds. *Argentina: Tiempo de violencia*. Buenos Aires: Carlos Pérez, 1969.
Goodrich, Leland M., and Marie J. Carroll, eds. *Documents on American Foreign Relations: July 1943–June 1944*, Vol. 6. Boston: World Peace Foundation, 1945.
————, eds. *Documents on American Foreign Relations: July 1944–June 1945*, Vol. 7. Boston: World Peace Foundation, 1947.
Graham-Yooll, Andrew. *A Matter of Fear: Portrait of an Argentinian Exile*. Westport, Conn.: Lawrence Hill, 1982.
————. *The Press in Argentina, 1973–78*. London: Writers and Scholars Educational Trust, 1979.
————. *Tiempo de tragedia: Cronología de la revolución argentina*. Buenos Aires: Ediciones de la Flor, 1972.
Greenup, Ruth, and Leonard Greenup. *Revolution before Breakfast: Argentina, 1941–1946*. Chapel Hill: University of North Carolina Press, 1947.
Griffis, Stanton. *Lying in State*. New York: Doubleday, 1952.
Guardo, Ricardo C. *Horas difíciles*. Buenos Aires: Private printing, 1963.
Guemes, Gontran de. *Así se gestó la dictadura*. Buenos Aires: Ediciones Rex, 1956.
Gunther, John. *Inside Latin America*. New York: Harper & Row, 1940.
————. *Inside South America*. New York: Harper & Row, 1966.

Halperin Donghi, Tulio. *Argentina: La democracia de masas*. Buenos Aires: Editorial Paídos, 1972.
Hamill, Hugh M., Jr., ed. *Dictatorship in Spanish America*. New York: Alfred A. Knopf, 1965.
Haney, Lynn, *Naked at the Feast: A Biography of Josephine Baker*. New York: Dodd, Mead, 1981.
Hennert, Danielle, and Alex Roudene. *Mata Hari, Eva Perón*. Paris: Editions Rombaldi, 1974.
Hernández, José. *The Gaucho Martín Fierro*. Translated by C.E. Ward. Albany: State University of New York Press, 1967.
Hernández, Pablo J. *Conversaciones con José M. Rosa*. Buenos Aires: Colihue/ Hachette, 1978.
Hernández Arregui, Juan José. *Peronismo y socialismo*. Buenos Aires: Ediciones Corregidor, 1973.
Herron, Francis. *Letters from the Argentine*. New York: G.P. Putnam's Sons, 1943.
Hodges, Donald C. *Argentina, 1943–1976: The National Revolution and Resistance*. Albuquerque: University of New Mexico Press, 1976.
Hull, Cordell. *The Memoirs of Cordell Hull*, Vol. 2. New York: Macmillan, 1948.

Imaz, José Luis de. *Los que mandan (Those Who Rule)*. Translated by Carlos A. Astiz. Albany: State University of New York Press, 1970.
————. *Promediados los cuarenta*. Buenos Aires: Editorial Sudamericana, 1977.
Irazusta, Julio. *Perón y la crisis argentina*. Buenos Aires: La Voz del Plata, 1956.

James, Daniel. *Che Guevara: A Biography*. New York: Stein and Day, 1969.
Jassen, Raúl. *Jorge Antonio: Un argentino frente a la oligarquía*. Buenos Aires: Ediciones ALPE, 1961.

Johnson, John J. *Political Change in Latin America: The Emergence of the Middle Sectors*. Stanford: Stanford University Press, 1958.
Josephs, Ray. *Argentine Diary: The Inside Story of the Coming of Fascism*. New York: Random House, 1944.

Kahn, Heriberto. *Doy fe*. Buenos Aires: Editorial Losada, 1979.
Kandel, Pablo, and Mario Monteverde. *Entorno y caída*. Buenos Aires: Editorial Planeta, 1976.
Kelly, David. *The Ruling Few*. London: Hollis and Carter, 1952.
Kirkpatrick, Jeane. *Leader and Vanguard in Mass Society: A Study of Peronist Argentina*. Cambridge: MIT Press, 1971.
Kohl, James, and John Litt. *Urban Guerrilla Warfare in Latin America*. Cambridge: MIT Press, 1974.

Lack, John. *Eva Perón*. Buenos Aires: private printing, 1958.
Lafiandra, Felix (h), ed. *Los panfletos: Su aporte a la Revolución Libertadora*. Buenos Aires: Editorial Itinerarium, 1955.
Lamas, Raúl. *Los torturadores: Crímenes y tormentos en la cárceles argentinas*. Buenos Aires: Editorial Lamas, 1956.
Lanusse, Alejandro A. *Mi testimonio*. Buenos Aires: Lasserre Editores, 1977.
Latin American Studies Association. *La represión en Argentina, 1973–1974*. México City: Universidad Nacional Autónoma de México, 1978.
Lipset, Seymour M. *Political Man: The Social Bases of Politics*. Garden City: Doubleday, 1960.
Loge, Leo. *El camino de la muerte: Perón a través de sus palabras*. Buenos Aires: private printing, 1955.
Lombille, Roman J. *Eva, la predestinada: Alucinante historia de éxitos y frustraciones*. Buenos Aires: Ediciones Gure, 1956.
Lonardi, Luis Ernesto. *Dios es justo*. Buenos Aires: Francisco A. Colombo, 1958.
Lonardi, Marta. *Mi padre y la revolución del 55*. Buenos Aires: Ediciones Cuenca del Plata, 1980.
López Rega, José. *Alpha y omega: Un mensaje para la humanidad*. Buenos Aires: Editorial "Rosa de Libres," 1963.
———. *Astrología esotérica*. Buenos Aires: Editorial "Rosa de Libres," 1962.
———. *El sabio hindú*. New York: Karuna Press, 1977.
Luca de Tena, Torcuato, Luis Calvo, Esteban Peicovich, eds. *Yo, Juan Domingo Perón: Relato autobiográfico*. Barcelona: Editorial Planeta, 1976.
Lucero, Franklin. *El precio de la lealtad*. Buenos Aires: Editorial Propulsión, 1959.
Luna, Félix. *Argentina de Perón a Lanusse, 1943–1973*. Buenos Aires: Editorial Planeta, 1974.
———. *El 45*. Buenos Aires: Editorial Sudamericana, 1975.
———. *Diálogos con Frondizi*. Buenos Aires: Editorial Desarrollo, 1963.
———, ed. *El peronismo*, Vol. I. Buenos Aires: Todo Es Historia, 1976.
Lux-Wurm, Pierre. *Le Peronisme*. Paris: Librairie Générale de Droit et de Jurisprudence, 1965.

Madier, Nelly. *Mis amores con Perón*. Buenos Aires, Ediciones B.M., 1955.
Maggi, Ginna. *Patria y traición: Confabulación Ibáñez-Perón*. Buenos Aires: Ediciones Gure, 1957.
———. *Tres presidentes en un andén*. Buenos Aires: private printing, 1954.

Magnet, Alejandro. *Nuestros vecinos justicialistas.* Santiago: Editorial del Pacífico, 1953.
Malerga Pittaluga, Alcides. *Verdad y mentira de Perón.* Buenos Aires: Ediciones Observador, 1955.
Marsal S., Pablo. *Perón y la iglesia.* Buenos Aires: Ediciones Rex, 1955.
Martínez, Pedro Santos. *La nueva Argentina,* 2 vols. Buenos Aires: Ediciones La Bastilla, 1976.
Martínez, Rodolfo. *Grandezas y miserias de Perón.* México City: private printing, 1957.
Martínez, Tomás Eloy. *La pasión según Trelew.* Buenos Aires: Granica Editor, 1973.
Martins, Mario. *Perón: Um confronto entre Argentina e o Brasil.* Rio de Janeiro: Edições do Povo, 1950.
Mendé, Raúl A. *El justicialismo: Doctrina y realidad peronista.* Buenos Aires: Guillermo Kraft, 1951.
Mende, Tibor. *L'Amérique Latine entre en scène.* Translated by Jeanne N. Mathieu. Paris: Editions du Seuil, 1952.
Mercier Vega, Louis. *Autopsia de Perón: Balance del peronismo.* Translated by Menene Gras. Barcelona: Tusquets Editor, 1975.
Meyer, Doris. *Victoria Ocampo: Against the Wind and the Tide.* New York: George Braziller, 1979.
Ministerio de Relaciones Exteriores y Culto. *La República Argentina ante el "Libro Azul."* Buenos Aires: República Argentina, 1946.
Molinari, Aldo Luis. *Caso Duarte.* Buenos Aires: private printing, 1958.
Montemayor, Mariano. *Claves para entender a un gobierno,* 2d ed. Buenos Aires: Editorial Concordia, 1963.
Montgomery, Paul L. *Eva, Evita: The life and Death of Eva Perón.* New York: Pocket Books, 1979.
Monzalvo, Luis. *Testigo de la primera hora del peronismo.* Buenos Aires: Editorial Pleamar, 1974.
Moore, Archie, and Leonard B. Pearl. *Any Boy Can: The Archie Moore Story.* Englewood Cliffs, N.J.: Prentice-Hall, 1971.
Morales Salazar, Carlos. *Por que volverá Perón.* Santiago: private printing, 1959.
Morrison, DeLesseps S. *Latin American Mission: An Adventure in Hemisphere Diplomacy.* New York: Simon and Schuster, 1965.
Mujica, Carlos. *Peronismo y cristianismo.* Buenos Aires: Editorial Merlin, 1973.
Murmis, Miguel, and Juan Carlos Portantiero. *Estudios sobre los orígenes del peronismo,* Vol. 1. Buenos Aires: Siglo Veintiuno, 1971.

Nadra, Fernando. *Perón, hoy y ayer.* Buenos Aires: Editorial Polémica, 1972.
Naipaul, V.S. *The Return of Eva Perón.* New York: Alfred A. Knopf, 1980.
Navarro Gerassi, Marysa. *Los nacionalistas.* Buenos Aires: Editorial Jorge Alvarez, 1968.
Neustadt, Bernardo. *La Argentina y los argentinos.* Buenos Aires: Emecé Editores, 1976.
Newton, Jorge. *Perón el visionario.* Buenos Aires: Guillermo Kraft, 1955.
Nudelman, Santiago I. *Proceso contra la dictadura,* 2 vols. Buenos Aires: private printing, 1953, 1955.
————. *El régimen totalitario.* Buenos Aires: Private printing, 1960.
Núñez Arca, P. *Perón, hombre de América: Biografía de un gran gobernante.* Private printing, undated.

O'Connor, Harvey. *World Crisis in Oil*. New York: Monthly Review Press, 1962.

Odena, Isidro J. *Libertadores y desarrollistas*. Buenos Aires: Ediciones La Bastilla, 1977.

Olivieri, Aníbal O. *Dos veces rebelde*. Buenos Aires: Ediciones Sigla, 1958.

Orona, Juan V. *La dictadura de Perón*. Buenos Aires: private printing, 1970.

―――. *La logia militar que derrocó a Castillo*. Buenos Aires: private printing, 1966.

―――. *La revolución del 16 setiembre*. Buenos Aires: private printing, 1970.

Owen, Frank. *Perón: His Rise and Fall*. London: The Cresset Press, 1957.

Panaia, Marta, Ricardo Lesser and Pedro Skupch. *Estudios sobre los orígenes del peronismo*, Vol. 2. Buenos Aires: Siglo Veintiuno, 1973.

Pastor, Reynaldo. *Frente al totalitarianismo peronista*. Buenos Aires: Bases Editorial, 1959.

―――. *La otra faz de la segunda dictadura*. Buenos Aires: Bases Editorial, 1960.

Pavón Pereyra, Enrique. *Coloquios con Perón*. Madrid: Editores Internacionales Técnicos Reunidos, 1973.

―――. *Conversaciones con Juan D. Perón*. Buenos Aires: Colihue/Hachette, 1978.

―――. *Perón: Preparación de una vida para el mando, 1895–1942*. Buenos Aires: Ediciones Espino, 1952.

―――. *Perón tal como es*. Buenos Aires: Editorial Macacha Guemes, 1973.

―――. *Los últimos días de Perón*. Buenos Aires: Ediciones La Campana, 1981.

―――. *Vida de Perón*. Buenos Aires: Editorial Justicialista, 1965.

Paz, Alberto Conil, and Gustavo Ferrari. *Argentina's Foreign Policy, 1930–1962*. Translated by John J. Kennedy. Notre Dame: University of Notre Dame Press, 1966.

Peicovich, Esteban. *Hola Perón*. Buenos Aires: Jorge Alvarez, 1965.

―――. *El último Perón*. Madrid: Cambio 16, Mundo Actual, 1975.

Pendle, George. *Argentina*, 2d ed. London: Oxford University Press, 1961.

Peña, Milciades. *El peronismo: Selección de documentos para la historia*. Buenos Aires: Ediciones Fichas, 1972.

Perelman, Angel. *Como hicimos el 17 de octubre*. Buenos Aires: Editorial Coyoacan, 1961.

Perina, Emilio. *Detrás de la crisis*. Buenos Aires: Editorial Periplo, 1960.

Perón, Eva. *Historia del peronismo*. Buenos Aires: Editorial Freeland, 1973.

―――. *My Mission in Life*. Translated by Ethel Cherry. New York: Vantage Press, 1953.

Perón, Juan D. *Actualización política y doctrinaria para la toma del poder*. Buenos Aires: Pevuel Ediciones, undated.

―――. *Apuntes de historia militar*. Buenos Aires: República Argentina, 1951.

―――. *La comunidad organizada*. Buenos Aires: Secretaria Política de la Presidencia de la Nación, 1974.

―――. *Conducción política*. Buenos Aires: Editorial Freeland, 1974.

―――. *Del poder al exilio: Como y quienes me derrocaron*. Buenos Aires: Ediciones Argentinas, 1974.

―――. *El frente oriental de la Guerra Mundial en 1914*. Buenos Aires: Instituto Geográfico Militar, 1931.

―――. *La fuerza es el derecho de las bestias*. Buenos Aires: Ediciones Síntesis, 1976.

————. *La hora de los pueblos*. Buenos Aires: Editorial Pleamar, 1973.

————. *Juan Perón, 1973–1974: Todos sus discursos, mensajes y conferencias completos*, 2 vols. Buenos Aires: Editorial de la Reconstrucción, 1974.

————. *Latinoamérica: Ahora o nunca*. Buenos Aires: Ediciones Síntesis, 1973.

————. *Libro azul y blanco*. Buenos Aires: Editorial Freeland, 1973.

————. *El pensamiento político de Perón*. Buenos Aires: Abel del Río, 1972.

————. *Perón-Cooke correspondencia*, 2 vols. Buenos Aires: Granica Editor, 1973.

————. *Peronist Doctrine*. Buenos Aires: República Argentina, 1952.

————. *El pueblo quiere saber de qué se trata*. Buenos Aires: Editorial Freeland, 1973.

————. *El pueblo ya sabe de qué se trata*. Buenos Aires: Editorial Freeland, 1973.

————. *La realidad de un año de tiranía*. Private printing, 1958.

————. *La tercera posición argentina*. Buenos Aires: Ediciones Argentinas, 1974.

————. *Tres revoluciones militares*. Buenos Aires: Ediciones Síntesis, 1974.

————. *Los vendepatria*. Buenos Aires: Editorial Freeland, 1972.

Peterson, Harold F. *Argentina and the United States, 1810–1960*. New York: State University of New York, 1964.

Petras, James. *Politics and Social Structure in Latin America*. New York: Monthly Review Press, 1970.

Pinedo, Jorge. *Consignas y lucha popular en el proceso revolucionario argentino, 1955–1973*. Buenos Aires: Editorial Freeland, 1974.

Pineiro, Armando Alonso. *Crónica de la subversión en la Argentina*. Buenos Aires: Ediciones Depalma, 1980.

Pizarro Miguens, Raúl A. *La justicia nacional resolvió "El Caso Duarte."* Buenos Aires: Ediciones Gure, 1959.

Plater, Guillermo D. *Una gran lección*. La Plata: Editorial Almafuerte, 1956.

Poppen, James L. *Perón, the Man*. Private printing, undated.

Potash, Robert A. *The Army and Politics in Argentina, 1928–1945: Yrigoyen to Perón*. Stanford: Stanford University Press, 1969.

————. *The Army and Politics in Argentina, 1945–1962: Perón to Frondizi*. Stanford: Stanford University Press, 1980.

Prieto, Ramón. *Correspondencia Perón-Frigerio, 1958–1973*. Buenos Aires: Editorial Macacha Guemes, 1975.

————. *De Perón a Perón: De 1946 a 1973*. Buenos Aires: Ediciones Macacha Guemes, 1974.

————. *El pacto: Ocho años de política argentina*. Buenos Aires: Editorial En Marcha, 1963.

————. *Treinta años de vida argentina*. Buenos Aires: Editorial Sudamericana, 1977.

Pujades, Pablo. *El justicialismo de Perón*. Bogotá: Minerva, 1958.

Quinterno, Carlos A. *Militares y populismo: La crisis argentina de 1966 a 1976*. Buenos Aires: Editorial Temas Contemporáneos, 1978.

Rabinovitz, Bernardo. *Sucedió en la Argentina, 1943–1956: Lo que no se dijo*. Buenos Aires: Editorial Gure, 1956.

Ramos, Jorge Abelardo. *Adiós al coronel*. Buenos Aires: Editorial Epoca, 1976.

————. *La era del bonapartismo, 1943–1973*. Buenos Aires: Editorial Plus Ultra, 1973.

————. *Revolución y contrarrevolución en la Argentina: Nueva historia de los argentinos.* Buenos Aires: La Reja, 1961.

Randall, Laura. *An Economic History of Argentina in the Twentieth Century.* New York: Columbia University Press, 1978.

Rangel, Carlos. *Del buen salvaje al buen revolucionario.* Barcelona: Libros de Monte Avila, 1976.

Ratier, Hugo. *El cabecita negra.* Buenos Aires: Centro Editor de América Latina, 1971.

Real, Juan José. *Treinta años de historia argentina.* Buenos Aires: Ediciones Crisol, 1976.

Reiner, Silvain. *Eva Perón.* Paris: Flammarion, 1960.

Rennie, Ysabel F. *The Argentine Republic.* New York: Macmillan, 1945.

Repetto, Nicolás, *Mi paso por la política: De Uriburu a Perón.* Buenos Aires: Santiago Rueda, 1957.

República Argentina. *Casos de la segunda tiranía,* Vol. 1. Buenos Aires: Editorial Integración, 1958.

————. *Libro negro de la segunda tiranía.* Buenos Aires: República Argentina, 1958.

Revista *Gente. Fotos, hechos, testimonios de 1035 dramáticos días.* Buenos Aires: Editorial Atlantida, 1976.

Reyes, Cipriano. *Que es el laborismo.* Buenos Aires: Ediciones R.A., 1946.

————. *Yo hice el 17 de octubre.* Buenos Aires: GS Editorial, 1973.

Rivera, Enrique. *Peronismo y frondizismo.* Buenos Aires: Editorial Patria Grande, 1958.

Robertson, S.R. *Making Friends for Britain: An Incursion into Diplomacy.* Buenos Aires: Guillermo Kraft, 1948.

Rock, David, ed. *Argentina in the Twentieth Century.* Pittsburgh: University of Pittsburgh Press, 1975.

————. *Politics in Argentina, 1890–1930: The Rise and Fall of Radicalism.* London: Cambridge University Press, 1975.

Rodríguez Monegal, Emir. *Jorge Luis Borges: A Literary Biography.* New York: E.P. Dutton, 1978.

Rom, Eugenio R. *Así hablaba Juan Perón.* Buenos Aires: Peña Lillo, 1980.

Romero, Emilio. *Argentina entre la espalda y la pared.* Madrid: private printing, 1963.

Romero, José Luis. *A History of Argentine Political Thought.* Translated by Thomas F. McGann. Stanford: Stanford University Press, 1963.

Romualdi, Serafino. *Presidents and Peons: Recollections of a Labor Ambassador in Latin America.* New York: Funk & Wagnalls, 1967.

Rottjer, Aníbal. *El llanto de las ruinas: La historia, el arte y la religión ultrajados en los templos de Buenos Aires, 16–17 de junio de 1955.* Buenos Aires: Librería Don Bosco, 1955.

Sábato, Ernesto. *Claves políticas.* Buenos Aires: Rodolfo Alonso Editor, 1971.

————. *El otro rostro del peronismo: Carta abierta a Mario Amadeo.* Buenos Aires: Private printing, 1956.

Sacquard de Belleroche, Maud. *Eva Perón: La Reine des Sans Chemises.* Paris: La Jeune Parque, 1972.

Sánchez Zinny, E.F. *El culto de la infamía: Historia documentada de la segunda tiranía argentina.* Buenos Aires: private printing, 1958.

Santander, Silvano. *Técnica de una traición: Juan D. Perón y Eva Duarte, agentes del nazismo en la Argentina.* Buenos Aires: Editorial Antygua, 1955.

Santayana, Mauro. *Tragédia argentina: Poder e violência de Rosas ao peronismo.* Rio de Janeiro: Francisco Alves, 1976.

Sava, George. *Mourning Becomes Argentina.* London: New Horizon, 1978.

Schiffer, Irvine. *Charisma: A Psychoanalytic Look at Mass Society.* New York: The Free Press, 1973.

Scobie, James R. *Argentina: A City and a Nation.* New York: Oxford University Press, 1964.

————. *Buenos Aires: Plaza to Suburb, 1870–1910.* New York: Oxford University Press, 1974.

Sebrelli, Juan José. *Eva Perón: aventurera o militante?* Buenos Aires: Editorial La Pleyade, 1971.

Selser, Gregorio. *El onganiato,* 2 vols. Buenos Aires: Carlos Samonta, Editor, 1973.

————. *Diplomacia, garrote y dólares en América Latina.* Buenos Aires: Editorial Palestra, 1962.

Senen González, Santiago. *Breve historia del sindicalismo argentino, 1957–1974.* Buenos Aires: Alzamor Editores, 1974.

————. *El sindicalismo después de Perón.* Buenos Aires: Editorial Galerna, 1971.

Silvert, Kalman H. *The Conflict Society: Reaction and Revolution in Latin America.* New Orleans: Hauser Press, 1961.

Sindicato de Luz y Fuerza. *Cien años contra el país.* Buenos Aires: Colección Cuadernos CEES, 1970.

Skidmore, Thomas E. *Politics in Brazil, 1930–1964: An Experiment in Democracy.* New York: Oxford University Press, 1967.

Smith, O. Edmund, Jr. *Intervención yanqui en Argentina.* Translation by Amelia Aguado. Buenos Aires: Editorial Palestra, 1965.

Snow, Peter G. *Argentine Radicalism: The History and Doctrine of the Radical Civic Union.* Iowa City: University of Iowa Press, 1965.

Sobel, Lester A., ed. *Argentina and Perón, 1970–75.* New York: Facts on File, 1975.

Straffer, Fritz. *Perón y Eva: Unidos en la vida y en la muerte.* Barcelona: Producciones Editoriales, 1975.

Szmullewicz, Efraím. *Así huyó Kelly!* Buenos Aires: Editorial Andina, 1957.

Szulc, Tad. *Twilight of the Tyrants.* New York: Henry Holt, 1959.

Taccone, Juan J. *Crisis: Respuesta sindical.* Buenos Aires: Private printing, 1971.

Taylor, J.M. *Eva Perón: The Myths of a Woman.* Chicago: University of Chicago Press, 1979.

Terragno, Rodolfo. *Los 400 días de Perón.* Buenos Aires: Ediciones de la Flor, 1974.

Theroux, Paul. *The Old Patagonia Express: By Train Through the Americas.* New York: Houghton Mifflin, 1979.

Timerman, Jacobo. *Prisoner Without a Name, Cell Without a Number.* Translated by Tony Talbot. New York: Alfred A. Knopf, 1981.

Tosco, Agustín. *La lucha debe continuar.* Buenos Aires: Libros para el Tercer Mundo, 1975.

Urondo, Francisco. *La patria fusilada.* Buenos Aires: Ediciones de Crisis, 1973.

Urrutia, Federico de. *Perón.* Madrid: NOS, 1946.

Vicepresidencia de la Nación, Comisión Nacional de Investigaciones. *Documentación, autores y cómplices de las irregularidades cometidas durante la segunda tiranía,* 5 vols. Buenos Aires: República Argentina, 1958.

Villar Araujo, Carlos. *Argentina: De Perón al golpe militar.* Madrid: Ediciones Felmar, 1976.

Vincent, Frank. *Around and About South America: Twenty Months of Quest and Query.* New York: D. Appleton, 1890.

von Lang, Jochen (with the assistance of Claus Sibyll). *The Secretary: Martin Bormann, The Man Who Manipulated Hitler.* Translated by Christa Armstrong and Peter White. New York: Random House, 1979.

Walsh, Rodolfo J. *Operación masacre.* Buenos Aires: Continental Service, 1964.

————. *Quién Mató a Rosendo?* Buenos Aires: Editorial Tiempo Contemporáneo, 1969.

Walter, Richard J. *Student Politics in Argentina: The University Reform and Its Effects, 1918–1964.* New York: Basic Books, 1968.

Weil, Felix J. *Argentine Riddle.* New York: John Day, 1944.

Weil, Thomas E. *Area Handbook for Argentina.* Washington: Department of the Army, 1974.

Weisbrot, Robert. *The Jews of Argentina: From the Inquisition to Perón.* Philadelphia: The Jewish Publication Society of America, 1979.

Welles, Sumner. *Where Are We Heading?* New York: Harper, 1946.

Whitaker, Arthur P. *Argentina.* Englewood Cliffs, N.J.: Prentice-Hall, 1964.

————. *Argentine Upheaval: Perón's Fall and the New Regime.* New York: Praeger, 1956.

————. *The United States and Argentina.* Cambridge: Harvard University Press, 1954.

Wright, Winthrop R. *British-Owned Railways in Argentina: Their Effect on Economic Nationalism, 1854–1948.* Austin: University of Texas Press, 1974.

Wynia, Gary W. *Argentina in the Postwar Era: Politics and Economic Policy Making in a Divided Society.* Albuquerque: University of New Mexico Press, 1978.

Zabala, Arturo J. *La revolución del 16 de setiembre.* Buenos Aires: Ediciones Debate, 1955.

DISSERTATIONS

Chaffee, Lyman G. "Political Bargaining and the Opposition in Argentina: The Case of the Confederación General del Trabajo." Ph.D., University of California at Riverside, 1969.

De Hoyos, Ruben J. "The Role of the Catholic Church in the Revolution against President Juan D. Perón." Ph.D., New York University, 1970.

Deiner, John T. "ATLAS: A Labor Instrument of Expansion under Perón." Ph.D., Rutgers University, 1970.

Dobson, J. Michael. "Religious Innovation and the Politics of Argentina: A Study of the Movement of Priests for the Third World." Ph.D., Indiana University, 1974.

James, Daniel. "Unions and Politics: The Development of Peronist Trade Unionism, 1955–1966." Ph.D., University of London, 1979.

Kenworthy, Eldon G. "The Formation of the Peronist Coalition." Ph.D., Yale University, 1970.

Lewis, Irving S. "American Press Opinion of Argentina, 1939–1949." M.A., Georgetown University, 1951.

Little, Walter. "Political Integration in Peronist Argentina, 1943–1955." Ph.D., Fitzwilliam College, Cambridge University, 1971.

McGeagh, Robert. "Catholicism and Sociopolitical Change in Argentina, 1943–1973." Ph.D., University of New Mexico, 1974.

Pyle, Norman R. "A Study of U.S. Propaganda Efforts and Pro-Allied Sentiments in Argentina During World War II." Ph.D., Georgetown University, 1968.

Smith, Wayne S. "The Argentine Elections of 1973: Demilitarization and the Struggle for Consensus." Ph.D., George Washington University, 1980.

Taylor, Julie M. "Myth and Reality: The Case of Eva Perón." Ph.D., St. Anthony's College, Oxford University, 1973.

Notes

Diplomatic and military intelligence documents through the end of 1949 may be found in the National Archives, Washington, D.C., except those marked as from Suitland. The latter are stored in the National Records Center, Suitland, Maryland.

Post-1949 diplomatic, military intelligence and Central Intelligence Agency materials were obtained under the Freedom of Information Act. Copies are on file with the author.

Unless otherwise noted, all cited diplomatic and intelligence documents originated in Argentina.

CHAPTER ONE

1. For descriptions of the earthquake, see *Ahora*, January 21, 1944; *La Prensa*, January 17, 1944; *Inter-American Monthly*, February 1944; *New York Times*, January 17, 1944; *Newsweek*, January 24, 1944, p. 33; *Primera Plana*, January 14, 1969, p. 72; R. Josephs, *Argentine Diary*, pp. 331–35; U.S. embassy to secretary of state, 835.48/17, January 18, 1944.
2. The speech is reprinted in J. Perón, *El pueblo quiere saber de qué se trata*, pp. 39–41.
3. *Primera Plana*, January 14, 1969, p. 72. (Unless otherwise noted, all translations are by the author.)
4. *La Prensa*, January 17, 1944.
5. Armour to secretary of state, 835.00/2272, January 21, 1944; R. Josephs, *supra* note 1, p. 335.
6. The most reliable accounts appear in "La historia del peronismo—II," *Primera Plana*, June 22, 1965, pp. 46–47; O. Borroni and R. Vacca, *La Vida de Eva Perón*, pp. 71–72; R. Tettamenti (pseudonym), "Eva Perón," in *Los hombres de la historia*, No. 161, July 1971, p. 200; N. Fraser and M. Navarro, *Eva Perón*, pp. 32–33.
7. T. Luca de Tena, *Yo, Juan Domingo Perón*, p. 51.
8. "Testimonios: Juan Perón habla de Eva Perón," *Panorama*, April 21, 1970, p. 66.

9. Editorial by Emilio Romero in the Madrid newspaper *Pueblo*, reprinted in E. Peicovich, *El último Perón*, p. 108.
10. See E. Pavón Pereyra, *Conversaciones con Juan D. Perón*, p. 91.
11. The parallel with Huey Long is suggested in A. Ciria, *Estados Unidos nos mira*, pp. 201–202. A State Department biographical sketch went even further by calling Perón "a South American combination of the Kingfish and President Roosevelt." Division of Biographic Information, Department of State, August 30, 1949 (copy on file with author).

CHAPTER TWO

1. J. Bryce, *South America*, p. 323.
2. See G. Pendle, *Argentina*, pp. 11–13.
3. Ibid., pp. 13–15.
4. See J. Romero, "Buenos Aires: Una historia," *Polémica*, No. 64, August 1971, p. 90.
5. Ibid., p. 91.
6. See H. Ferns, *Argentina*, p. 94.
7. F. Vincent, *Around and About South America*, p. 153.
8. "Argentina," *Fortune*, July 1938, p. 27 (anonymous article written by Archibald MacLeish).
9. See G. Pendle, *supra* note 2, p. 4.
10. J. Bryce, *supra* note 1, p. 328.
11. G. Pendle, *supra* note 2, p. 55.
12. For an exploration of the links between the spirit of *Martín Fierro* and the rise of Peronism, see P. Winn, "From Martín Fierro to Peronism: A Century of Argentine Social Protest," *The Americas*, Vol. 35, July 1978, p. 89.
13. J. Gunther, *Inside South America*, p. 171.
14. See J. Scobie, *Argentina*, p. 276; T. Weil, *Area Handbook for Argentina*, p. 48.
15. See T. Weil, *supra* note 14, p. 51.
16. See J. Scobie, *supra* note 14, p. 276.
17. See T. Weil, *supra* note 14, p. 52.
18. See R. Alexander, *An Introduction to Argentina*, p. 122.
19. See T. Weil, *supra* note 14, p. 78.
20. Ibid., p. 72.
21. See J. Bruce, *Those Perplexing Argentines*, p. 100.
22. See, generally, R. Weisbrot, *The Jews of Argentina*.
23. See T. Weil, *supra* note 14, p. 89.
24. See G. Pendle, *supra* note 2, p. 171.
25. See J. Bruce, *supra* note 21, pp. 47–49.

CHAPTER THREE

1. The description of Lobos is based upon the author's visit to the town on July 12, 1980.
2. See *Panorama*, September 29, 1970, p. 26.
3. See R. Pastor, *Frente al totalitarianismo peronista*, p. 50.
4. The author had access to the dossier at the Bureau of Historical Studies of the Argentine army in Buenos Aires on August 1, 1980.

5. See T. Luca de Tena, *supra* Ch. 1, note 7, p. 19.
6. See V. Cútolo and V. Risolia, *Tomás L. Perón*; T. Luca de Tena, *supra* Ch. 1, note 7, p. 20.
7. See E. Pavón Pereyra, *Perón*, p. 245.
8. See E. Pavón Pereyra, "Perón: El hombre del destino," No. 1, November 1973, p. 2 (series of magazines).
9. Interview with Luis Ratti (a physician from Lobos), Buenos Aires, September 23, 1977.
10. "Las memorias de Juan Perón (1895–1945)," *Panorama*, April 14, 1970, p. 20 (hereinafter cited as "Las memorias").
11. Ibid., p. 21.
12. In the 1920s the government brutally suppressed a peon revolt in Patagonia. See J. Borrero, *La Patagonia trágica*.
13. See T. Luca de Tena, *supra* Ch. 1, note 7, p. 20.
14. "Las memorias," p. 20.
15. Ibid., p. 21.
16. Ibid.
17. See T. Luca de Tena, *supra* Ch. 1, note 7, p. 22.
18. See R. Potash, *The Army and Politics in Argentina, 1928–1945*, pp. 2–4.
19. Interview with Colonel Emilio A. Bidondo, director of historical studies of the Argentine army, Buenos Aires, July 18, 1980.
20. See F. Chávez, *Perón y el peronismo en la historia contemporánea*, p. 22.
21. Interview with Colonel Bidondo, *supra* note 19.
22. Personal dossier of Juan D. Perón, *supra* note 4.
23. Ibid.
24. Ibid.
25. Interview with Carlos V. Aloé, Buenos Aires, December 1976.
26. Columbia Oral History Collection (series of interviews from the early 1970s, on file at Columbia University and the Instituto Torcuato Di Tella, Buenos Aires).
27. Quoted in E. Pavón Pereyra, *supra* note 8, No. 4, November 1973, p. 66.
28. J. Perón, "Higiene militar," in Ejército Argentino, *Manual del aspirante*, Ch. F.
29. Quoted in E. Pavón Pereyra, *Perón tal como es*, p. 30.
30. Confidential biographic data, U.S. embassy, Buenos Aires, January 20, 1944 (copy on file with author).
31. See, e.g., E. Pavón Pereyra, *supra* note 8, No. 4, November 1973, p. 55.
32. See "Las memorias," p. 22.
33. Perón is quoted as having told the anecdote in A. Barrios, *Con Perón en el exilio*, p. 23.
34. See M. Bracker, "Perón: Evolution of a Strong Man," *New York Times Magazine*, February 22, 1948.
35. See R. Potash, *supra* note 18, p. 3.
36. Interview with Julián Sancerni Jiménez, Buenos Aires, May 6, 1977.
37. See E. Pavón Pereyra, *supra* note 8, No. 5, December 1973, pp. 95–97.

CHAPTER FOUR

1. See J. Scobie, *supra* Ch. 2, note 14, pp. 104–105.
2. See H. Ferns, *supra* Ch. 2, note 6, p. 94.
3. See D. Rock, *Politics in Argentina, 1890–1930*, p. 53.

4. S. Welles, *Where Are We Heading?*, p. 189.
5. See R. Potash, *supra* Ch. 3, note 18, p. 35.
6. For an excellent account of the events leading up to the 1930 coup, see ibid., pp. 29–54.
7. "Las memorias," p. 23.
8. Interview with Julián Sancerni Jiménez, Buenos Aires, May 6, 1977.
9. The primary source for Perón's attitude toward and participation in the 1930 coup is a report he wrote early in 1931. See J. Perón, *Tres revoluciones militares*, pp. 13–82.
10. Ibid., p. 19. In a taped interview with Mark Falcoff in Madrid on July 27, 1968, Perón presented a somewhat derogatory description of General Uriburu ("He was a good person, but he wasn't made for governing").
11. J. Perón, *supra* note 9, p. 77.
12. Ibid., pp. 81–82.
13. See E. Pavón Pereyra, *supra* Ch. 3, note 8, No. 6, August 1974, pp. 114–16.
14. See M. Goldwert, *Democracy, Militarism, and Nationalism in Argentina, 1930–1966*, pp. 35–44.
15. G. Pendle, "Para escribir sobre Perón," *Mundo Nuevo*, July 1968, p. 77.
16. See, generally, E. Pavón Pereyra, *supra* Ch. 3, note 7, pp. 129–48; E. Pavón Pereyra, *supra* Ch. 3, note 8, No. 6, August 1974, pp. 119–20.
17. Dossier, *supra* Ch. 3, note 4, vol. 7.
18. Ibid., Vol. 8.
19. See J. Perón, *Apuntes de historia militar*, p. 139.
20. Ibid., pp. 139–43.
21. See, e.g., G. Maggi, *Patria y traición*, pp. 22–23; F. Owen, *Perón*, p. 11; R. Damonte T., *A donde va Perón?*, p. 168; see also Congress of Industrial Organizations, Committee on Latin American Affairs, *The Argentine Regime: Facts and Recommendations to the United Nations Organization* (1946), p. 100.
22. S. Ross, "Perón: South American Hitler," *The Nation*, February 16, 1946.
23. "Dark Shadows Surrounding the Departure of Colonel Perón from Our Country," *Ercilla*, November 24, 1943. See also C. Bowers, *Chile Through Embassy Windows*, pp. 139–40.
24. G-2 Report, 2271-L-32, No. 5785, April 20, 1938.
25. See J. de Imaz, *Promediados los cuarenta*, p. 143.
26. G-2 Report, *supra* note 24.
27. See F. Luna, *El 45*, p. 58.
28. Dossier, *supra* Ch. 3, note 4, vol. 8.
29. See E. Pavón Pereyra, *supra* Ch. 3, note 7, pp. 200–201; "Las memorias," p. 23.
30. See E. Pavón Pereyra, *supra* Ch. 3, note 8, No. 8, August 1974, p. 157.
31. "Las memorias," p. 23; T. Luca de Tena, *supra* Ch. 1, note 7, p. 27.
32. Falcoff tape, *supra* note 10.
33. See T. Luca de Tena, *supra* Ch. 1, note 7, pp. 28–29.
34. See E. Peicovich, *supra* Ch. 1, note 9, p. 39.
35. Falcoff tape, *supra* note 10.
36. See E. Pavón Pereyra, *supra* Ch. 3, note 7, pp. 209–10.
37. Quoted in F. Luna, *supra* note 27, p. 60. For a slightly different version given by Perón, see "Las memorias," p. 23.
38. See E. Pavón Pereyra, *supra* Ch. 3, note 7, pp. 222–23.

CHAPTER FIVE

1. See, generally, A. Ciria, *Parties and Power in Modern Argentina (1930– 1946)*, pp. 35–48.
2. There is impressive footage of the funeral procession in the documentary film *Ni vencidores ni vencidos?* (1972).
3. See Y. Rennie, *The Argentine Republic*, p. 232.
4. See "Argentina," *Fortune, supra* Ch. 2, note 8, p. 32.
5. See M. Navarro Gerassi, *Los nacionalistas*, p. 121; Y. Rennie, *supra* note 3, p. 271.
6. See M. Navarro Gerassi, *supra* note 5, p. 118.
7. For an interesting profile of Ortiz, See J. Gunther, *Inside Latin America*, pp. 284–90.
8. See A. Whitaker, *The United States and Argentina*, p. 109.
9. See ibid., pp. 112–13.
10. See J. Gunther, *supra* Ch. 2, note 13, p. 120.
11. See, generally, S. Bradford, *The Battle for Buenos Aires*.
12. See R. Potash, *supra* Ch. 3, note 18, pp. 172–74.
13. See K. Loewenstein, "Legislation against Subversive Activities in Argentina," *Harvard Law Review*, Vol. 56, 1943, p. 1261.
14. See E. Días Araujo, *La conspiración del '43*, p. 67; A. Ciria, *supra* note 1, p. 73; Y. Fisk and R. Rennie, "Argentina in Crisis," *Foreign Policy Reports*, Vol. 20, No. 4, May 1, 1944, p. 34.
15. See F. Herron, *Letters from the Argentine*, p. 285.
16. For a contemporary profile of General Justo, see V. de Pascual, "Argentina's Man of Destiny?" *Inter-American Monthly*, November 1942, p. 15.
17. For the most authoritative account of the birth of the GOU, see R. Potash, *supra* Ch. 3, note 18, pp. 184–90; see also F. Chávez, *supra* Ch. 3, note 20; E. Días Araujo, *supra* note 14; J. Orona, *La logia militar que derrocó a Castillo*.
18. See R. Potash, *supra* Ch. 3, note 18, p. 185. For corroborative evidence, see F. Luna, *supra* Ch. 4, note 27, p. 57. On the other hand, Perón himself insisted that the lodge already existed when the colonels who founded it approached him and asked him to join. Ibid., p. 60; "Las memorias," p. 24.
19. Y. Rennie, *supra* note 3, p. 305.
20. See R. Potash, *supra* Ch. 3, note 18, pp. 193–94.
21. J. Perón, *supra* Ch. 4, note 9, p. 112. Potash has concluded from the tone of the manifesto and from the testimony of others that Perón merely co-authored it. R. Potash, *supra* Ch. 3, note 18, p. 196.
22. Quoted in "Historia del peronismo—II," *Primera Plana*, August 24, 1965, p. 42.
23. T. Luca de Tena, *supra* Ch. 1, note 7, p. 36.
24. R. Potash, *supra* Ch. 3, note 18, p. 196.
25. Quoted in "Historia del peronismo—IV," *Primera Plana*, July 6, 1965, p. 42.
26. Quoted in R. Alexander, *Juan Domingo Perón*, pp. 158, 159.
27. Ibid., p. 159.
28. B. del Carril, *Crónica interna de la Revolución Libertadora*, pp. 27–28.
29. Quoted in "Historia del peronismo—XI," *Primera Plana*, August 24, 1965, p. 42.
30. Quoted in F. Luna, *supra* Ch. 4, note 27, pp. 57–58.
31. Reprinted in J. Orona, *supra* note 17, pp. 110–11.
32. See, for example, R. Alexander, *The Perón Era*, pp. 12–13.

33. R. Potash, *supra* Ch. 3, note 18, p. 196, n. 33.
34. Cabot to secretary of state, 835.00/1-1546, 1-1746, 1-3046, January 15, 16 and 30, 1946; see also FBI memo, 835.00/1-946, January 9, 1946.
35. F. Luna, *supra* Ch. 4, note 27, pp. 21–22.
36. Braden to secretary of state, 835.00/7-1745, July 17, 1945.
37. V. Codovilla, *Batir al nazi-peronismo*, pp. 106–107.
38. See R. Potash, *supra* Ch. 3, note 18, p. 192, n. 22. For corroboration, see B. del Carril, *supra* note 28, p. 26.
39. J. Perón, *supra* Ch. 4, note 9, p. 89.

CHAPTER SIX

1. For what appears to be the first profile of him, complete with photos, in a popular magazine, see *Ahora*, June 29, 1943.
2. Hoover to Berle, 835.00/2289, December 28, 1943.
3. E. Peicovich, *supra* Ch. 1, note 9, pp. 39–40.
4. See R. Potash, *supra* Ch. 3, note 18, p. 211.
5. Reprinted in C. Fayt, "Naturaleza del peronismo," *Aportes*, July 1966, pp. 99–105.
6. R. Potash, *supra* Ch. 3, note 18, p. 215.
7. The letter is reprinted in L. Goodrich and M. Carroll, eds., *Documents on American Foreign Relations: July 1943–June 1944*, Vol. 6, pp. 525–28.
8. E. Kenworthy, "The Formation of the Peronist Coalition," Ph.D. dissertation, 1970, p. 117.
9. Reprinted in L. Goodrich and M. Carroll, *supra* note 7, pp. 528–34.
10. E. Smith, *Intervención yanqui en Argentina*, p. 106.
11. See F. Luna, *supra* Ch. 4, note 27, p. 24.
12. See M. Navarro Gerassi, *supra* Ch. 5, note 5, p. 179.
13. See L. Goodrich and M. Carroll, *supra* note 7, p. 534.
14. See F. Weil, *Argentine Riddle*, pp. 52–54.
15. Interview with Eduardo Colom, Columbia Oral History Collection.
16. Perón went so far as to offer to Radical leader Amadeo Sabattini the vice-presidential nomination on a ticket headed by the colonel, but Sabattini refused. See F. Luna, *supra* Ch. 4 note 27, pp. 116–17; interview with Ricardo Guardo, Columbia Oral History Collection.
17. For an account of the origin of FORJA, see M. Navarro Gerassi, *supra* Ch. 5, note 5, pp. 138–39.
18. *La Nación*, November 13, 1943.
19. *La Razón*, November 20, 1943.
20. A detailed description of the affair is contained in Federal Bureau of Investigation, "German Espionage in Latin America," June 1946, pp. 172–77 (copy on file with author).
21. See *Latin American Political Report*, October 12, 1979, pp. 316–17.
22. The FBI report, *supra* note 20, pp. 180–83, presents the case against Argentina for its complicity in the coup.
23. See C. Beals, *Latin America*, p. 142.
24. See R. Potash, *supra* Ch. 3, note 18, p. 231.
25. Ibid.
26. See Ibid., p. 223.
27. See R. Woods, "Hull and Argentina: Wilsonian Diplomacy in the Age of Roosevelt," *Journal of Inter-American Studies and World Affairs*, Vol. 16, August 1974, p. 367.

28. See R. Potash, *supra* Ch. 3, note 18, p. 234.
29. U.S. Department of State, *Foreign Relations of the United States: Diplomatic Papers, 1944*, Vol. VII, pp. 251–52 (hereinafter cited as *Diplomatic Papers*).
30. Translation in enclosure no. 1 to dispatch no. 12,576 of August 7, 1945, U.S. embassy, Santiago, Chile (copy on file with author).
31. T. Luca de Tena, *supra* Ch. 1, note 7, pp. 37–38.
32. See E. Kenworthy, *supra* note 8, p. 128.
33. See "La caída del Presidente Ramírez," *Primera Plana*, February 18, 1969, p. 33.
34. Quoted ibid.
35. Reprinted ibid.
36. See G. de Guemes, *Así se gestó la dictadura*, p. 93.
37. "La caída del Presidente Ramírez," *supra* note 33, p. 33.
38. See B. del Carril, *supra* Ch. 5, note 28, pp. 31–32.
39. For Perón's comments on the affairs, see *La Nación*, March 20, 1944.
40. See "La historia del peronismo—IV," *Primera Plana*, July 6, 1965, pp. 44–45. The author had access to a photocopy of the original oath, which is part of the private archive of Juan Perón.
41. Office of Strategic Services, R&A No. 1959, March 2, 1944.
42. For more of the same, see 800, weekly stability report, John W. Long, brigadier general, U.S. military attaché, Buenos Aires, April 11, 1944 (Suitland). According to a more sympathetic U.S. observer "Farrell . . . reminded me of nothing so much as a big, friendly St. Bernard dog. He was about as glamorous as an old shoe." R. and L. Greenup, *Revolution before Breakfast*, p. 17.
43. See B. del Carril, *supra* Ch. 5, note 28, p. 112.

CHAPTER SEVEN

1. Interview with Lucio Bonilla, textile worker, Columbia Oral History Project.
2. Quoted in "Historia del peronismo—VIII," *Primera Plana*, August 3, 1965, p. 44.
3. On the history of the Argentine labor movement, see A. Belloni, *Del anarquismo al peronismo*; see also S. Baily, *Labor Nationalism and Politics in Argentina*; M. Murmis and J. Portantiero, *Estudios sobre los orígenes del peronismo*, Vol. 1; L. Chaffee, "Political Bargaining and the Opposition in Argentina: The Case of the Confederación General del Trabajo," Ph.D. dissertation, 1969.
4. See R. Alexander, *Communism in Latin America*, Ch. 9.
5. See H. Ratier, *El cabecita negra*.
6. "Argentina," *supra* Ch. 2, note 8, p. 108.
7. Y. Rennie, *supra* Ch. 5, note 3, p. 311.
8. Quoted in F. Weil, *supra* Ch. 6, note 14, p. 75.
9. See S. Baily, *supra* note 3, p. 70.
10. J. Perón, *Conducción política*, p. 52.
11. Quoted in Bohan to secretary of state, 835.00/1561, June 12, 1943.
12. Quoted in "Historia del peronismo—IX," *Primera Plana*, August 10, 1965, p. 44.
13. Interview with Domingo A. Mercante (son), Buenos Aires, May 5, 1977.
14. Interview with L. Bonilla, *supra* note 1.

15. L. Monzalvo, *Testigo de la primera hora del peronismo*, p. 70.
16. Quoted in "Historia del peronismo—XI," *Primera Plana*, August 24, 1965, p. 44. For the U.S. embassy's report of the incident, see Reed to secretary of state, 835.00/1955, October 4, 1943.
17. See H. Gambini, *El 17 de octubre*, p. 13.
18. For Perón's account, see E. Peicovich, *supra* Ch. 1, note 9, pp. 40–41; "Las memorias," p. 24. For Mercante's account, see "Historia del peronismo —XI," *Primera Plana*, August 24, 1965, pp. 44–45. For the U.S. embassy's interpretation, ascribing political motivations to Perón's move, see memo, Fishburn to Bohan, 850.4, November 10, 1943, and Fishburn, "1943 Argentine Labor Developments," 850.4, February 1944 (Suitland).
19. See A. Cortesi, "Argentina Sets Up Labor Department," *New York Times*, December 1, 1943, p. 9:1.
20. Interview with Francisco J. Figuerola (son), Buenos Aires, May 9, 1977. A U.S. embassy dispatch said of Figuerola: "A highly competent statistician, his political beliefs are a curious mixture of nearly all known types of authoritarianism." Reed to secretary of state, 835.504/147, December 8, 1943.
21. Reprinted in J. Perón, *supra* Ch. 1, note 2, p. 29.
22. Ibid., p. 95.
23. J. Perón, *El pueblo ya sabe de qué se trata*, p. 119.
24. See Armour to secretary of state, 835.00/2257, December 30, 1943.
25. Reprinted in J. Perón, *supra* Ch. 1, note 2, p. 157.
26. See, generally, W. Little, "Political Integration in Peronist Argentina, 1943–1955," Ph.D. dissertation, 1971, pp. 22–36; interviews with Lucio Bonilla, Francisco Pérez Leirós and Juan Rodríguez, Columbia Oral History Project; "Historia del peronismo—XII," *Primera Plana*, August 31, 1964, pp. 42–46; see also R. Alexander, *supra* Ch. 5, note 32, pp. 20–32.
27. Most of the decrees affected specific categories of employment and did not apply to the entire work force. See W. Little, *supra* note 26, p. 27.
28. See interview with L. Bonilla, *supra* note 1.
29. Ibid. See interview with Rafael Ginocchio, Columbia Oral History Project.
30. See interview with L. Bonilla, *supra* note 1.
31. See ibid.; "Historia del peronismo—XII," *Primera Plana*, August 31, 1965, pp. 42–46.
32. See P. Smith, "Social Mobilization, Political Participation, and the Rise of Juan Perón," *Political Science Quarterly*, Vol. 84, March 1969, pp. 42–47.
33. See C. Reyes, *Yo hice el 17 de octubre* (autobiography); interview with Cipriano Reyes, Columbia Oral History Project.
34. See interview with L. Bonilla, *supra* note 1.
35. See W. Little, *supra* note 26, p. 32.
36. See L. Chafee, *supra* note 3, pp. 51–53.
37. Quoted in E. Peicovich, *supra* Ch. 1, note 9, p. 41.
38. See F. Chávez, *supra* Ch. 3, note 20, p. 234, n. 43.

CHAPTER EIGHT

1. The speech was reprinted in *La Prensa*, June 11, 1944.
2. See Office of Strategic Services, R&A Report No. 2304, July 4, 1944.
3. *La Prensa*, June 11, 1944.
4. The author of a generally excellent study of U.S.-Argentine relations reflected this reaction by claiming that "Perón declared that it was not a

matter of great moment to Argentina whether the Allies or the Axis won the war," an unfortunate distortion of what the colonel actually said. A. Whitaker, *supra* Ch. 5, note 8, p. 130.

5. *Supra* note 2.
6. Confidential biographic data, U.S. embassy, Buenos Aires, January 20, 1944 (copy on file with author).
7. For an early sample of Griffiths' reporting on Perón, see Griffiths to Reed, 835.00/2208, November 23, 1943.
8. See J. Fishburn, "1943 Argentine Labor Development," 850.4, February 1944 (Suitland).
9. See secret report from Brigadier General J. Lang, 835.00/9-1644, September 16, 1944.
10. D. Kelly, *The Ruling Few*, p. 288.
11. See R. Woods, "Hull and Argentina: Wilsonian Diplomacy in the Age of Roosevelt," *Journal of Inter-American Studies and World Affairs*, Vol. 16, August 1974, p. 350.
12. S. Welles, *supra* Ch. 4, note 4, p. 201.
13. U.S. embassy cable cited in R. Potash, *supra* Ch. 3, note 18, p. 242.
14. *Diplomatic Papers, 1944*, Vol. VII, pp. 260–62.
15. The State Department was fully apprised of this struggle. See, for example, Armour to Department of State, 800, March 28, 1944 (Suitland).
16. A speech he made to officers at the Campo de Mayo garrison on March 13 exemplifies his effort to navigate these shoals. He stressed Argentine devotion to democratic ideals and his own perplexity at U.S. distrust. The country was not leaning toward Fascism, he insisted, nor would it yield to Allied pressures. He accused most Argentine nationalists of unwittingly and mistakenly taking a trend toward Nazism. The FBI obtained a detailed paraphrase of the speech and transmitted it to the State Department. See Hoover to Berle, 835.00/2813, April 21, 1944.
17. See *Diplomatic Papers, 1944*, Vol. VII, pp. 276–77.
18. See E. Smith, *supra* Ch. 6, note 10, p. 133.
19. See D. Kelly, *supra* note 10, p. 305.
20. See E. Peffer, "Cordell Hull's Argentine Policy and Britain's Meat Supply," *Inter-American Economic Affairs*, Vol. 10, Autumn 1956, p. 13.
21. *Diplomatic Papers, 1944*, Vol. VII, p. 333.
22. Ibid., p. 284.
23. See ibid., p. 355.
24. Ibid., p. 285.
25. L. Goodrich and M. Carroll, eds., *Documents on American Foreign Relations: July 1943–June 1944*, Vol. 7, p. 584.
26. See S. Welles, *supra* Ch. 4, note 4, p. 206.

CHAPTER NINE

1. Interview with Arturo Jauretche, Columbia Oral History Project.
2. See confidential biographic data, U.S. embassy, Buenos Aires, January 20, 1944, p. 3 (copy on file with author). For an obviously fictionalized account of his love life in Italy, see F. Straffer, *Perón y Eva*, pp. 31–54.
3. T. Luca de Tena, *supra* Ch. 1, note 7, pp. 101–102. See also E. Peicovich, *supra* Ch. 1, note 9, p. 12. Jorge Antonio has confirmed that he was the source of this anecdote. Interview with Jorge Antonio, Buenos Aires, October 4, 1977.

4. See "La historia que contó Perón," *Redacción*, April 1978 (Supp.), pp. 13–14.
5. *Time*, April 24, 1944.
6. V. de Pascual, "Strong Man of Argentina," *Inter-American Monthly*, May 1944.
7. *Radiolandia*, December 25, 1943, cited in O. Borroni and R. Vacca, *supra* Ch. 1, note 6, p. 70.
8. See "La historia del peronismo—II," *Primera Plana*, June 22, 1965, p. 47.
9. Interview with Enrique Pavón Pareyra, Buenos Aires, April 1977.
10. Interview with Julián Sancerni Jiménez, Buenos Aires, May 6, 1977.
11. The best of the Evita biographies is N. Fraser and M. Navarro, *supra* Ch. 1, note 6. The Borroni-Vacca book, *supra* Ch. 1, note 6, contains a wealth of generally reliable information. J. Taylor, *Eva Perón*, contributes valuable insights.

    Much of the writing about Eva Perón relies heavily upon M. Flores (pseudonym for Mary Main), *The Woman with the Whip*, a one-sided account drawn from sources hostile to Evita.
12. See O. Borroni and R. Vacca, *supra* Ch. 1, note 6, p. 26.
13. Quoted in "Eva Duarte: Los años difíciles," Part 1, *Radiolandia*, March 21, 1980, p. 62.
14. Quoted in J. Capsitski, "Prehistoria de Eva Perón," *Todo Es Historia*, No. 14, June 1968, p. 14.
15. N. Fraser and M. Navarro, *supra* Ch. 1, note 6, p. 26.
16. See ibid., pp. 22–23.
17. For the recollections of the film's director, see M. Soffici, "Cuando la actriz eligió la revolución," *La Opinión*, July 22, 1973, p. 4.
18. See M. Navarro, "The Case of Eva Perón," *Signs*, Vol. 3, Autumn 1977, p. 231.
19. Interview with José María Rosa, Buenos Aires, October 21, 1976.
20. See "Historia del peronismo—III," *Primera Plana*, June 29, 1965, p. 43.
21. Quoted in "Historia del peronismo—III," *supra* note 20, p. 42.
22. Reed to secretary of state, 835.00/9-644, September 6, 1944.

CHAPTER TEN

1. See, generally, M. Moyano, "Submarinos alemanes en Mar del Plata," *Todo Es Historia*, No. 72, April 1973, p. 37.
2. S. Santander, *Técnica de una traición*.
3. See L. Farago, *Aftermath*, pp. 244–47; article by A. Pujol in *Le Figaro*, September 1, 1970, cited in "La fortuna de Perón," *Redacción*, November 1976, p. 22. Perón's supposed involvement with the Nazis was graphically depicted in the NBC-TV mini-series *Evita*, February 23–24, 1981.
4. See S. Santander, *supra* note 2, p. 28.
5. See ibid., pp. 47, 52.
6. See R. Potash, *supra* Ch. 3, note 18, pp. 252–53.
7. Quoted in T. Luca de Tena, *supra* Ch. 1, note 7, p. 87; F. Luna, *supra* Ch. 4, note 27, p. 55.
8. Interview with agent, February 13, 1978 (subject was Dutch citizen at the time and was working for U.S. military attaché, Brigadier General J. Lang).
9. Quoted in T. Luca de Tena, *supra* Ch. 1, note 7, p. 86.
10. See "La fortuna de Perón," *supra* note 3.
11. Falcoff tape, *supra* Ch. 4, note 10.

12. Interview with Mario Amadeo, Buenos Aires, July 26, 1980.
13. See J. Perón, *supra* Ch. 1, note 2, p. 108.
14. See, e.g., statements quoted in T. Luca de Tena, *supra* Ch. 1, note 7, pp. 28–29, and F. Luna, *supra* Ch. 4, note 27, pp. 58–59.
15. J. Perón, *supra* Ch. 1, note 2, p. 160.
16. Memo by Second Secretary Edward P. Moffitt, 835.00/4-1145, April 11, 1945.
17. Falcoff tape, *supra* Ch. 4, note 10.
18. See, e.g., T. Luca de Tena, *supra* Ch. 1, note 7, p. 28.
19. See Cabot to secretary of state, 835.00/12-445, December 4, 1945.
20. See T. Luca de Tena, *supra* Ch. 1, note 7, pp. 88, 90.

CHAPTER ELEVEN

1. On student opposition to Perón, see R. Walter, *Student Politics in Argentina*, Ch. 6.
2. See Office of Strategic Services, R&A 1306.21, June 6, 1945 (copy on file with author).
3. See Reed to secretary of state, 835.00/4-2345, April 23, 1945 (text of Perón's statement).
4. See F. Luna, *supra* Ch. 4, note 27, pp. 74–75.
5. See R. Walter, *supra* note 1, pp. 122–24.
6. On Rockefeller's role, see P. Collier and D. Horowitz, *The Rockefellers*, pp. 237–38. Rockefeller's own version of the events is contained in an interview in the Columbia Oral History Project, but has not yet been released for attribution.
7. See S. Braden, *Diplomats and Demogogues*, p. 319.
8. See S. Welles, *supra* Ch. 4, note 4, p. 215. In a speech later that year, Rockefeller declared that he had recommended Braden's appointment. See *New York Times*, August 25, 1945.
9. On the Warren mission, see Warren to secretary of state, 711.35/4-1845, April 18, 1945; Reed to secretary of state, 711.35/4-1945, April 19, 1945; State Department to U.S. embassy (Bogotá), 711.35/4-1945, April 19, 1945. See also T. McGann, "The Ambassador and the Dictator: The Braden Mission to Argentina and Its Significance for U.S. Relations with Latin America," *Centennial Review*, Vol. VI, Summer 1962, pp. 347–48.
10. See S. Braden, *supra* note 7, p. 320.
11. Quoted in L. Vega, *Autopsia de Perón*, p. 113.
12. See A. Schlesinger, Jr., "Good Fences Make Good Neighbors," *Fortune*, August 1946, p. 163.
13. The best source on Spruille Braden is his autobiography, *supra* note 7.
14. Interview with John Moors Cabot, Washington, D.C., March 2, 1979.
15. See M. Scenna, "Braden y Perón," *Todo Es Historia*, No. 31, October 1969, p. 13.
16. A. Schlesinger, Jr., *supra* note 12, p. 131.
17. Braden to secretary of state, 711.35/7-1145, July 11, 1945.
18. D. Kelly, *supra* Ch. 8, n. 10, p. 307.
19. Interview with John Moors Cabot, *supra* note 14. For criticism of Cortesi's reporting from Argentina, see A. Vannucci, "United States-Argentine Relations, 1943 to 1948: A Case Study in Confused Foreign Policy-Making," Ph.D. dissertation, 1978, pp. 304–306.
20. Braden to secretary of state, 711.35/5-2345, May 23, 1945.

21. In addition to the Department of State archival materials now available, the best sources on the Braden-Perón clash are S. Braden, *supra* note 7; F. Luna, *supra* Ch. 4, note 27; M. Scenna, *supra* note 15; H., Gambini, "Braden cuenta su historia," *Redacción*, July 1976, p. 28 (Braden's retrospection thirty-one years after the events).

22. Braden to secretary of state, 711.35/5-2345, May 23, 1945.

23. For Braden's detailed account of the meeting, see *Diplomatic Papers, 1945*, Vol. IX, pp. 380–85.

24. S. Braden, *supra* note 7, p. 325.

25. Ibid., p. 326.

26. *Diplomatic Papers, 1945*, Vol. IX, p. 385.

27. Ibid.

28. *New York Herald-Tribune*, June 11, 1945.

29. See F. Luna, *supra* Ch. 4, note 27, pp. 79, 124–25; *Diplomatic Papers, 1945*, Vol. IX, p. 507 (Braden's report of visit).

30. *Diplomatic Papers, 1945*, Vol. IX, p. 507.

31. Quoted ibid., pp. 124–25.

32. Published in *La Prensa* and *La Nación*, June 16, 1945.

33. See S. Braden, *supra* note 7, p. 333.

34. See *Diplomatic Papers, 1945*, Vol. IX, pp. 508–11; see also S. Braden, *supra* note 7, pp. 328–30.

35. Perón was particularly incensed by a front-page article published in the *New York Herald-Tribune* on June 24 and reporting on a plot to unseat him. He called it "false from beginning to end." *La Nación*, June 25, 1945. Braden, on the other hand, was delighted with the article. In a cable to Washington he stated that it was "entirely factual *or merely reported what is generally being said and assumed to be true here*" (emphasis added). Thus the ambassador approved the publication of widely repeated yet unsubstantiated rumors that undermined his adversary. Braden to secretary of state, 811.91235/6-2545, June 25, 1945.

36. *Diplomatic Papers, 1945*, Vol. IX, p. 511.

37. Ibid., p. 512.

38. Ibid.

39. Reprinted in *La Nación*, July 3, 1945, and in J. Perón, *supra* Ch. 7, note 23, pp. 114–15. He made a similar statement to a Cuban journalist, who reprinted it in *Diario Ilustrado*, Santiago, Chile, July 6, 1945.

40. *Diplomatic Papers, 1945*, Vol. IX, pp. 518–19.

41. See ibid., pp. 514–17.

42. See F. Luna, *supra* Ch. 4, note 27, pp. 122–24. For an early report of this version, see memo by J. Griffiths, "Colonel Perón at Dinner on October 30 with Local Nazis," November 15, 1945 (Suitland).

43. See T. Luca de Tena, *supra* Ch. 1, note 7, pp. 81–82; E. Pavón Pereyra, *supra* Ch. 3, note 29, p. 47; E. Pavón Pereyra, "Diálogos con Perón," *Siete Días*, May 7, 1973, p. 17.

44. J. Edgar Hoover darkly warned the State Department that "it is believed that if the meeting takes place the mob will be uncontrollable and might even turn against the present Government." Hoover to Lyon, 835.00/7-1245, July 12, 1945.

45. See F. Luna, *supra* Ch. 4, note 27, pp. 147–48.

46. Braden to secretary of state, 835.5043/7-1445, July 14, 1945.

47. See F. Luna, *supra* Ch. 4, note 27, pp. 149–50.

48. For Braden's description of the attacks, see *Diplomatic Papers, 1945*, Vol. IX, pp. 396–97.

49. See M. Scenna, *supra* note 15, p. 20.
50. See, e.g., T. Luca de Tena, *supra* Ch. 1, note 7, p. 76.
51. Interview with John Moors Cabot, an eyewitness, *supra* note 14; see also M. Scenna, *supra* note 15, p. 20.
52. See F. Luna, *supra* Ch. 4, note 27, pp. 102–104.
53. See ibid., pp. 70–71.
54. Report by Brigadier General A. Harris, August 22, 1945 (Suitland).
55. Quoted in F. Luna, *supra* Ch. 4, note 27, p. 98 (Américo Ghioldi).
56. Félix Luna has called Perón's flowery, awkwardly phrased speech "one of the loudest gaffes of his career." F. Luna, *supra* Ch. 4, note 27, p. 171. For a sampling of the hostile reaction to which the colonel exposed himself, see *La Nación*, August 28, 1945.
57. *New York Times*, August 29, 1945.
58. S. Braden, *supra* note 7, p. 333.
59. The entire speech is reprinted in F. Luna, *supra* Ch. 4, note 27, pp. 132–35.
60. Interview with John Moors Cabot, *supra* note 14.

CHAPTER TWELVE

1. The following account is based upon an eyewitness description by Colonel Santiago Menéndez, one of Perón's adjutants, in the Colombia Oral History Project. See also Brigadier General A.R. Harris, "Comment on Current Events," No. 271, September 8, 1945 (Suitland).
2. See "Historia del peronismo—XIV," *Primera Plana,* September 14, 1965, p. 38.
3. See "Historia del peronismo—XV," *Primera Plana*, September 21, 1965, p. 40.
4. F. Luna, *supra* Ch. 4, note 27, p. 199.
5. See ibid., pp. 177–79.
6. Reprinted in J. Perón, *supra* Ch. 7, note 23, p. 165.
7. See F. Luna, *supra* Ch. 4, note 27, p. 201; "Historia del peronismo—XIV," *Primera Plana*, September 14, 1965, p. 42.
8. "Braden cuenta su historia," *Redacción*, July 1976, p. 32.
9. See "Historia del peronismo—XIV," *Primera Plana*, September 14, 1965, p. 42.
10. See "Historia del peronismo—XV," *Primera Plana*, September 21, 1965, p. 40.
11. See F. Luna, *supra* Ch. 4, note 27, p. 208.
12. Griffiths to Braden, 835.00/9-3045, September 30, 1945.
13. Cabot to secretary of state, 835.00/9-3045, September 30, 1945.
14. See "Treinta años de política argentina (1943–73)—II," *Redacción*, October 1977, pp. 25–26.

CHAPTER THIRTEEN

1. Quoted in O. Borroni and R. Vacca, *supra* Ch. 1, note 6, p. 85.
2. Colonel S. Davis, "Comment on Current Events," No. 254, May 12, 1945 (Suitland).
3. U.S. embassy, Buenos Aires, to secretary of state, No. 202, August 3, 1945, OSS File 140129.

4. Quoted in "Historia del peronismo—XIX," *Primera Plana*, October 19, 1965, p. 41.
5. See "Historia del peronismo—III," *Primera Plana*, June 29, 1965, p. 43.
6. Ibid., p. 42.
7. See O. Borroni and R. Vacca, *supra* Ch. 1, note 6, p. 89.
8. See M. Firpo, *Perón y los peronistas*, p. 204; F. Lucero, *El precio de la lealtad*, p. 27.
9. See R. Potash, *supra* Ch. 3, note 18, p. 262.
10. The following account of the events leading up to October 17, 1945, is drawn principally from: F. Luna, *supra* Ch. 4, note 27, pp. 216 ff.; "Historia del peronismo—XVI, XVII," *Primera Plana*, September 28, 1965, p. 40, October 5, 1965, p. 50; "Events Which Have Taken Place in Campo de Mayo Between the 6th and 19th of October, 1945," Office of Legal Attaché, U.S. embassy, Buenos Aires, December 5, 1945 (translation of description written by two Argentine colonels who participated in the events; document was furnished to legal attaché; copy on file with author). An indispensable but self-serving account was written by Perón and later published under the pseudonym "Bill de Caledonia." It is reprinted in M. Firpo, *supra* note 8, p. 196. The original, of which a copy is in the author's possession, is contained in Perón's private archive.
11. Written statement by Oscar Igounet (participant), Buenos Aires, September 1977.
12. See F. Lucero, *supra* note 8, p. 29.
13. For an account of the conspiracy, see R. Potash, *supra* Ch. 3, note 18, p. 268.
14. Interview with Santiago Menéndez, Perón's adjutant, Columbia Oral History Project.
15. See R. Potash, *supra* Ch. 3, note 18, p. 270.
16. Quoted in F. Luna, *supra* Ch. 4, note 27, p. 227.
17. See Cabot to secretary of state, 835.00/10-1045, October 10, 1945.
18. F. Luna, *supra* Ch. 4, note 27, p. 228.
19. See J. Torre, "La CGT y el 17 de octubre de 1945," *Todo Es Historia*, No. 105, p. 72.
20. A cable to Washington from the U.S. embassy erroneously characterized the speech as the "usual demagogic line." Cabot to secretary of state, 835.00/10-1045, October 10, 1945.
21. The speech is reprinted in J. Perón, *supra* Ch. 7, note 23, p. 182.
22. See H. Gambini, *El 17 de octubre*, pp. 24–25.
23. See F. Luna, *supra* Ch. 4, note 27, pp. 238–39. A dispatch from the U.S. embassy reached the same conclusion. See Cabot to secretary of state, 835.00/10-1245, October 12, 1945.
24. Quoted in F. Luna, *supra* Ch. 4, note 27, p. 245.

CHAPTER FOURTEEN

1. The text of the admiral's speech, along with the interruptions by the crowd, is reprinted in F. Luna, *supra* Ch. 4, note 27, pp. 327–28.
2. See "Historia del peronismo—XVIII," *Primera Plana*, October 12, 1965, p. 44.
3. Quoted in "Historia del peronismo—XVII," *Primera Plana*, October 5, 1965, p. 52 (source: D'Andrea).

4. Quoted in F. Luna, *supra* Ch. 4, note 27, p. 246 (source: Mercante). For a description of Perón's trip to the gunboat, see *La Nación*, October 14, 1945.
5. See A. Belloni, *supra* Ch. 7, note 3, p. 53.
6. See *supra* Ch. 13, note 10.
7. Reprinted in F. Luna, *supra* Ch. 4, note 27, pp. 335–37.
8. Reprinted ibid., pp. 337–38.
9. Reprinted ibid., p. 336.
10. Cabot to secretary of state, 835.00/10-1545, October 10, 1945.
11. The minutes of the meeting are reprinted in "La CGT y el 17 de octubre de 1945," *Pasado y Presente*, July–December 1973, p. 403.
12. For Reyes' account, see C. Reyes, *supra* Ch. 7, note 33.
13. See F. Luna, *supra* Ch. 4, note 27, p. 271.
14. Quoted in "Historia del peronismo—XVII," *Primera Plana*, October 5, 1965, p. 53.
15. Quoted in "Historia del peronismo—XVIII," *Primera Plana*, October 12, 1965, p. 46.
16. See "Historia del peronismo—XVII," *Primera Plana*, October 5, 1965, p. 53.

CHAPTER FIFTEEN

1. The following account is based in large part upon articles in *La Epoca, La Nación* and *La Prensa*; E. Colom, *17 de octubre*; H. Gambini, *supra* Ch. 13, note 22; F. Luna, *supra* Ch. 4, note 27; Angel Perelman, *Como hicimos el 17 de octubre*; "Historia del peronismo—XVIII, XIX," *Primera Plana*, October 12, 19, 1965, p. 40; J. Torre, *supra* Ch. 13, note 19; "Fusil, machete, el viejo 17," *Primera Plana*, October 13, 1970, p. 76.
2. *Ahora*, October 20, 1945. This illustrated magazine, published thrice weekly, contains many valuable photos of the events of October.
3. Quoted in "Historia del peronismo—XIX," *Primera Plana*, October 19, 1965, p. 42.
4. Quoted in "Fusil, machete, el viejo 17," *supra* note 1, p. 80 (source: Farrell).
5. Photo in *Ahora*, October 20, 1945.
6. Quoted in E. Colom, *supra* note 1, p. 95.
7. D. Kelly, *supra* Ch. 8, note 10, p. 309–10.
8. For the student's testimony, see "Una historia escrita en la calle," *Siete Días*, October 14, 1974, pp. 34–35.
9. *La Nación*, October 18, 1945.
10. See F. Luna, *supra* Ch. 4, note 27, p. 343 (interview with Perón).
11. The speech is reprinted in J. Perón, *supra* Ch. 7, note 23, p. 185.
12. See "Historia del peronismo—XX," *Primera Plana*, October 26, 1965, pp. 29–30.
13. Interview with Santiago Menéndez, Columbia Oral History Project.
14. For an exhaustive and illuminating exploration of the subject, see M. Navarro, "Evita and the Crisis of 17 October 1945: A Case Study of Peronist and Anti-Peronist Mythology," *Journal of Latin American Studies*, Vol. 12, May 1980, p. 127.
15. See, e.g., interview with Pedro Otero, Columbia Oral History Project; A. Perelman, *supra* note 1.

16. See "Historia del peronismo—XVIII," *Primera Plana*, October 12, 1965, p. 46 (testimony of Dr. Mazza).
17. Quoted in F. Luna, *supra* Ch. 4, note 27, p. 307.
18. Quoted in J. Real, *Treinta años de historia argentina*, pp. 93–94.
19. Cabot to secretary of state, 835.00/10-1845, October 18, 1945 (noon).
20. Cabot to secretary of state, 835.00/10-1845, October 18, 1945 (6:00 P.M.).
21. Cabot to secretary of state, 835.00/10-1945, October 19, 1945.
22. *New York Times*, October 19, 1945.
23. *London Times*, October 19, 1945.
24. Secretary of state to U.S. embassy, Argentina, 835.00/10-204, October 20, 1945.
25. S. Romualdi, "Argentine Labor and Perón," *American Federationist*, December 1945.

CHAPTER SIXTEEN

1. See O. Borroni and R. Vacca, *supra* Ch. 1, note 6, p. 117.
2. Evita's birth certificate, which recorded her actual date of birth (May 7, 1919) and the name "Eva María Ibarguren," was destroyed at some point during 1945. See N. Fraser and M. Navarro, *supra* Ch. 1, note 6, pp. 69–70.
3. See F. Luna, *supra* Ch. 4, note 27, pp. 394–402.
4. Interview with Dr. Ricardo Guardo, Buenos Aires, October 10, 1977.
5. See F. Luna, *supra* Ch. 4, note 27, pp. 346–53.
6. See Military Intelligence Division, W.D.G.S., "Military Attaché Report, Argentina," BID No. 7221, OSS File XL 3522, Rep. No. R-3-46, January 2, 1946. On Mosca, see ibid., OSS File XL 35224, Rep. No. R-4-46, January 2, 1946.
7. F. Luna, *supra* Ch. 4, note 27, p. 364.
8. See *Newsweek*, November 5, 1945.
9. See S. Braden, *supra* Ch. 11, note 7, p. 356.
10. Byrnes to Hoover, 835.00/10-2245, October 22, 1945.
11. See "Review of Political Developments," U.S. embassy, Buenos Aires, November 14, 1945 (Suitland).
12. Memo of conversation, State Department, 835.00/11-2645, November 26, 1945.
13. Military Intelligence Division, W.D.G.S., "Military Attaché Report: Uruguay," BID No. 3144.0600, OSS File XL 34115, Rep. No. R-484-45, December 18, 1945.
14. Cabot to secretary of state, top-secret telegram, January 21, 1946.
15. Cabot to secretary of state, top-secret telegram, January 25, 1946.
16. Military Intelligence Division, W.D.G.S., "Military Attaché Report: Uruguay," BID No. 3144.0600, OSS File XL 43214, Rep. No. R-69-46, February 12, 1946.
17. See *La Vanguardia*, November 6, 1945.
18. Quoted in F. Luna, *supra* Ch. 4, note 27, p. 412.
19. For a description of the incident, see Military Intelligence Division, W.D.G.S., "Military Attaché Report: Argentina," BID No. 3143.0100, OSS File XL 336053, Rep. No. R-804-46, December 18, 1945.
20. For a profile of Quijano, see F. Luna, ed., *El peronismo* (Vol. I), pp. 147–49.
21. Quoted in F. Luna, *supra* Ch. 4, note 27, p. 447.

22. See ibid., pp. 406–10; see also "Historia del peronismo—XX," *Primera Plana*, October 26, 1965, p. 32.
23. See *La Prensa*, January 30, 1946.
24. See *La Nación*, January 26, 1946.
25. See F. Luna, *supra* Ch. 4, note 27, pp. 425–26.
26. Interview with Raúl Bustos Fierro, Buenos Aires, October 10, 1977.
27. See *La Prensa*, February 9, 1946.
28. Ibid., February 21, 1946.
29. *New York Times Magazine*, February 3, 1946.
30. For a Peronist's description of the photographer, see R. Bustos Fierro, *Desde Perón hasta Onganía*, pp. 38–39.
31. See Cabot to secretary of state, 835.00/1-1646, January 16, 1946.
32. *Look*, March 5, 1946, pp. 38–39.
33. See S. Braden, *supra* Ch. 11, note 7, p. 356.
34. *Diplomatic Papers, 1946*, Vol. XI, pp. 197–98.
35. Ibid., p. 201.
36. Ibid., pp. 201–202.
37. Ibid., pp. 203–204.
38. Ibid., p. 204.
39. *New York Times*, February 13, 1946.
40. See J. Perón, *Libro azul y blanco*.
41. *Diplomatic Papers, 1946*, Vol. XI, p. 219.
42. For an exhaustive treatment of the subject, see R. McGeagh, "Catholicism and Sociopolitical Change in Argentina," Ph.D. dissertation, 1974, Ch. III.
43. Interview with Dr. Ricardo Guardo (eyewitness), Buenos Aires, 1978.
44. *La Prensa*, February 13, 1946.
45. Reprinted in J. Perón, *supra* Ch. 7, note 23, p. 188.
46. Interview with Dr. Ricardo Guardo, Buenos Aires, 1978.
47. *La Orientación*, February 27, 1946, p. 1.
48. *Diplomatic Papers, 1946*, Vol. XI, pp. 228–29.
49. Ibid., p. 229. According to Cabot, the embassy sent about thirty of its people to polling places all over the country. None of them saw any evidence of pressure being exerted on voters. Interview with John Moors Cabot, Washington, March 2, 1979. For a detailed report on the elections, see Republica Argentina, Ministerio del Interior, *Las fuerzas armadas restituyen el imperio de la soberanía popular* (2 vols.).
50. See R. Potash, *The Army and Politics in Argentina, 1945–1962*, p. 45.
51. See F. Luna, *supra* Ch. 4, note 27, p. 470.
52. Ibid., p. 471.
53. See, e.g., G. Blanksten, *Perón's Argentina*, pp. 67–69.
54. See E. Kenworthy, *supra* Ch. 6, note 8, Ch. 6.
55. H. Herring, "Can We Run Argentina?" *Harper's*, October 1946, p. 298.

CHAPTER SEVENTEEN

1. The speech is reprinted in J. Perón, *supra* Ch. 7, note 23, p. 202.
2. See "La primera presidencia—II," *Primera Plana*, May 10, 1966, p. 39.
3. See N. Fraser and M. Navarro, *supra* Ch. 1, note 6, pp. 76–77.
4. For a profile of Bramuglia, see F. Luna, *supra* Ch. 16, note 20, pp. 146–47.
5. For a profile of Miranda, see ibid., pp. 138–41.
6. On the new cabinet, see "La primera presidencia—II," *Primera Plana*, May 10, 1966.

7. Interview with Ricardo Guardo, Buenos Aires, May 5, 1977.
8. See Reed to secretary of state, 835.00/12-2244, December 22, 1944.
9. Interview with Peronist official, Buenos Aires, 1977 (name withheld by request).
10. See, e.g., *La Prensa*, May 31, 1953, p. 2; June 1, 1953, p. 3; June 2, 1953, p. 3; *Democracia*, June 2, 1953, pp. 1, 3.
11. The photo is reproduced in N. Fraser and M. Navarro, *supra* Ch. 1, note 6, between pp. 38 and 39.
12. See O. Borroni and R. Vacca, *supra* Ch. 1, note 6, pp. 132–33.

CHAPTER EIGHTEEN

1. Cabot to secretary of state, 835.00/4-2446, April 24, 1946.
2. See "La primera presidencia—III," *Primera Plana*, May 17, 1966, pp. 37–39; Brigadier General C. H. Caldwell, military attaché, "Estimate of the Situation," April 30, 1946 (Suitland).
3. See J. Orona, *La dictadura de Perón*, p. 41.
4. For details on how the decision was reached, see R. Bustos Fierro, *supra* Ch. 16, note 30, pp. 57–62.
5. Interviews with Ricardo Guardo, Buenos Aires, April 27, 1977; José María Rosa, Buenos Aires, October 21, 1976.
6. See S. Quintana, "Comparison of the Constitutional Basis of the United States and Argentine Political Systems," *University of Pennsylvania Law Review*, Vol. 9, 1947, pp. 654–56.
7. See "La primera presidencia—IV," *Primera Plana*, May 31, 1966, p. 36.
8. See Congreso Nacional, *Diario de sesiones de la Cámara de Diputados*, Vol. I (1947), p. 294.
9. Messersmith to secretary of state, 835.00/7-346, July 3, 1946 (enclosing memo by R.K. Oakley).
10. Interview with Ricardo Guardo, Buenos Aires, September 29, 1977.
11. See "La primera presidencia—V," *Primera Plana*, June 7, 1966, p. 42.
12. See R. McGeagh, *supra* Ch. 16, note 42, p. 120.
13. Interview with Antonio Benítez, Buenos Aires, July 24, 1980.
14. For profiles of the justices, see Office of Strategic Services, R&A No. 2801, January 5, 1945.
15. See, generally, "La primera presidencia—VIII," *Primera Plana*, July 5, 1966, p. 36; A. Leonhard, "The 1946 Purge of the Argentine Supreme Court of Justice," *Inter-American Economic Affairs*, Vol. 17, 1964, p. 73; G. Blanksten, *supra* Ch. 16, note 53, pp. 122–32.
16. For a summary of the charges, see O'Donoghue to secretary of state, 835.00/7-1946, July 19, 1946.
17. *Supra* note 14.
18. See Burrows to secretary of state, 835.00/11-1446, November 14, 1946.
19. G. Blanksten, *supra* Ch. 16, note 53, p. 111.
20. See R. Berger, *Impeachment*, pp. 252–96.

CHAPTER NINETEEN

1. On the economic program of Perón's first presidency, see G. Wynia, *Argentina in the Postwar Era*, pp. 43–70; E. Chambers, "Some Factors in the Deterioration of Argentina's External Position, 1946–1951," *Inter-*

American Economic Affairs, Vol. 8, 1954, p. 27; D. Easum, "Justicialismo in Retrospect: Failure of the Peronista Timetable," *Inter-American Economic Affairs*, Vol. 6, 1952, p. 32; E. Kenworthy, "Argentina: The Politics of Late Industrialization," *Foreign Affairs*, Vol. 45, April 1967, p. 463; O. Holmes, "Perón's 'Greater Argentina' and the United States," *Foreign Policy Reports*, December 1, 1948, p. 158.

2. See, e.g., J. Perón, *Juan Perón, 1973–1974*, Vol. 1, p. 26.

3. See, e.g., República Argentina, *Libro negro de la segunda tiranía*, pp. 155–59.

4. See "La primera presidencia—IX," *Primera Plana*, July 12, 1966, p. 36; J. Oyuela, "Los planes quinquenales," *Polémica*, No. 86, January 1972.

5. C. Furtado, *Economic Development of Latin America*, p. 158. On IAPI, see "La primera presidencia—X," *Primera Plana*, July 19, 1966, p. 40.

6. See "La primera presidencia—XIII," *Primera Plana*, August 9, 1966, p. 34.

7. Quoted in O. Confalonieri, *Perón contra Perón*, p. 218.

8. Quoted in "La primera presidencia—XI," *Primera Plana*, July 26, 1966, p. 34.

9. See W. Wright, *British-Owned Railways in Argentina*, p. 249.

10. See N. Bowan, "The End of British Economic Hegemony in Argentina: Messersmith and the Eady-Miranda Agreement," *Inter-American Economic Affairs*, Vol. 28, Spring 1975, p. 3.

11. See W. Wright, *supra* note 9, p. 251.

12. See Ray to ambassador, 850, June 28, 1948 (Suitland) ("I am convinced the Argentines were fully justified in expecting that substantial quantities [of agricultural products used by the Marshall Plan] would be purchased here").

13. Quoted in secret memorandum, "Instances of Apparent Discrimination by ECA against Argentina," State Department, January 25, 1949, p. 6 (copy on file with author).

14. See, e.g., D. Easum, *supra* note 1, pp. 38–48; O. Holmes, *supra* note 1, p. 162.

15. See A. Whitaker, *supra* Ch. 5, note 8, p. 181.

16. See G. Wynia, *supra* note 1, pp. 68–69.

17. See Ray to secretary of state, 835.00/2-1549, February 15, 1949; see also Bruce to Armour, 850, January 2, 1948 (Suitland) (reference to Miranda's "unscrupulous actions").

18. Interview with Alfredo Gómez Morales, Columbia Oral History Project.

19. Quoted in F. Kluckhorn, "Portrait of Argentina's 'Strong Man,'" *New York Times Magazine*, December 1, 1946.

20. See A. Potash, *supra* Ch. 16, note 50, pp. 61–62; O. Holmes, *supra* note 1, p. 167.

CHAPTER TWENTY

1. See S. Baily, *supra* Ch. 7, note 3, p. 99.

2. Ibid., pp. 102–104.

3. The law was also used to decimate small Catholic syndicates that responded to the social teachings of the church. See R. McGeagh, *supra* Ch. 16, note 42, pp. 55–57.

4. See W. Little, *supra* Ch. 7, note 26, Ch. III.

5. See "Historia del peronismo—XLIV," *Primera Plana*, May 16, 1967, p. 43.

6. Interview with Luis Gay, Columbia Oral History Project.

7. See, generally, J. Torre, "La caída de Luis Gay," *Todo Es Historia*, No. 89, October 1974; Watrous to secretary of state, "Visit to Argentina of Members of the American Federation of Labor and Railway Labor Executives Association," 835.5043/2-1347, February 13, 1947.
8. See S. Romualdi, *Presidents and Peons*, Ch. II (autobiography).
9. S. Romualdi, *supra* Ch. 15, note 25.
10. See J. Torre, *supra* note 7, p. 86; Watrous, *supra* note 7, p. 5.
11. S. Romualdi, *supra* note 8, p. 56.
12. T. Luca de Tena, *supra* Ch. 1, note 7, p. 185.
13. See S. Romualdi, *supra* note 8, p. 56.
14. T. Luca de Tena, *supra* Ch. 1, note 7, p. 185.
15. O'Donoghue to secretary of state, 835.5043/1-2247, January 22, 1947.
16. See Watrous, *supra* note 7, p. 9.
17. See "La primera presidencia—XLIV," *Primera Plana*, May 16, 1967, p. 44.
18. See J. Torre, *supra* note 7, p. 92.
19. After a brief period of hiding, Gay returned home but had difficulty finding work. In 1950, the blacklisting came to an end for unknown reasons, and he was permitted to live out the rest of the Perón era in tranquility. See ibid., p. 93.
20. Reprinted in *The Congressional Record*, Vol. 93, Pt. 11, p. A 1486.
21. Portions reprinted in S. Romualdi, *supra* note 8, pp. 60–61.
22. See J. Torre, *supra* note 7, p. 93.
23. See "La primera presidencia—XLIV," *Primera Plana*, May 16, 1967, pp. 44–45. On Espejo's lack of qualifications, see interview with Rafael Ginocchio (CGT leader), Columbia Oral History Project.

CHAPTER TWENTY-ONE

1. Interview with John Moors Cabot, Washington, March 2, 1979.
2. *Diplomatic Papers—1946*, Vol. XI, pp. 270–78.
3. See T. McGann, *supra* Ch. 11, note 9, p. 344.
4. Messersmith to Braden, 835.00/2-1646, February 16, 1946.
5. See J. Blum, ed., *The Price of Vision*, pp. 611–12.
6. See S. Braden, *supra* Ch. 11, note 7, p. 361.
7. See C. Burrows, Memorandum of conversation with Carl Speth, 835.00/8-1646, August 16, 1946; *Diplomatic Papers—1946*, Vol. XI, p. 303.
8. Messersmith to Acheson, 835.00/10-1646, October 16, 1946.
9. See *Diplomatic Papers—1946*, Vol. XI, pp. 327–37.
10. Braden to Messersmith, 800, November 27, 1946 (Suitland).
11. See *Diplomatic Papers—1946*, Vol. XI, pp. 327–29.
12. *Diplomatic Papers—1947*, Vol. VIII, pp. 196–97.
13. See J. Perón, *El pensamiento político de Perón*, p. 57 (UP interview, July 30, 1946).
14. See "La primera presidencia—V," *Primera Plana*, June 7, 1966, pp. 43–45.
15. See A. Whitaker, *supra* Ch. 5, note 8, p. 218.
16. See P. Santos Martínez, *La nueva Argentina*, Vol. 1, pp. 241–43.
17. See ibid., pp. 254–56. The speech is reprinted in J. Perón, *Peronist Doctrine*, p. 399.
18. See E. Pavón Pereyra, *supra* Ch. 3, note 8, No. 24, April 1974, pp. 163–64.
19. See A. Ciria, *Perón y el justicialismo*, pp. 168–69; "La primera presidencia—VII," *Primera Plana*, June 21, 1966, p. 39.

20. See H. Warren, "Diplomatic Relations Between the United States and Argentina," *Inter-American Economic Affairs*, Vol. 8, Winter 1954, p. 63.
21. A. Moore and L. Pearl, *Any Boy Can*, p. 219.
22. See *Noticias Gráficas*, April 9, 1949.
23. One reason Perón gave for Bramuglia's ouster was that the latter had not kept the president informed of attitudes and opinions of the U.S. government, as reported by the Argentine ambassador in Washington. See Bruce to secretary of state, 350/361.2, August 15, 1949 (Suitland).

CHAPTER TWENTY-TWO

1. Quoted in O. Borroni and R. Vacca, *supra* Ch. 1, note 6, p. 137.
2. Ibid., p. 135.
3. Reprinted in *La Nación*, February 13, 1947.
4. See O. Borroni and R. Vacca, *supra* Ch. 1, note 6, p. 135.
5. See J. Taylor, *supra* Ch. 9, note 11, p. 42.
6. Interview with Ricardo Guardo, Buenos Aires, May 5, 1977.
7. Reprinted in E. Peicovich, *supra* Ch. 1, note 9, p. 118.
8. Quoted in P. Santos Martínez, *supra* Ch. 21, note 16, p. 87.
9. Quoted in J. Areilza, *Así los he visto*, p. 192.
10. Quoted ibid., p. 194.
11. *Washington Post*, May 26, 1947, p. 7B. Ambassador Messersmith sent the State Department an indignant cable denying Pearson's allegations. 800, May 29, 1947 (Suitland).
12. Quoted in O. Borroni and R. Vacca, *supra* Ch. 1, note 6, p. 160.
13. See U.S. embassy to secretary of state, "Departure of Mrs. Perón for Europe," 835.0011/6-1347, June 13, 1947.
14. Quoted in "La primera presidencia—XXIII," *Primera Plana*, December 6, 1966, pp. 36–37.
15. Reprinted in E. Peicovich, *supra* Ch. 1, note 9, p. 118.
16. Quoted in O. Borroni and R. Vacca, *supra* Ch. 1, note 6, p. 164.
17. Quoted in "La primera presidencia—XXIII," *Primera Plana*, December 6, 1966, p. 38.
18. See N. Fraser and M. Navarro, *supra* Ch. 1, note 6, p. 94.
19. Interview with Lilián Lagomarsino de Guardo, Buenos Aires, July 15, 1980.
20. Quoted in O. Borroni and R. Vacca, *supra* Ch. 1, note 6, pp. 168–69.
21. Memo, Box 536, "E" File, 800, June 20, 1947 (Suitland).
22. See telegram from U.S. embassy, London, June 3, 1947.
23. See telegram from U.S. embassy, London, June 13, 1947; N. Fraser and M. Navarro, *supra* Ch. 1, note 6, pp. 94–95.
24. See telegram from U.S. embassy, London, June 20, 1947.
25. See telegram from U.S. embassy, London, July 10, 1947.
26. Quoted in "La primera presidencia—XXIV," *Primera Plana*, December 13, 1966, p. 38.
27. U.S. embassy to secretary of state, 735.51/7-2847, July 28, 1947, p. 2.
28. *France Dimanche*, July 27, 1947.
29. See L. Farago, *supra* Ch. 10, note 3, pp. 244–45.
30. Interview with source, Buenos Aires, October 21, 1977 (name withheld by request).
31. *Time*, July 14, 1947.
32. Interview with Raúl Salinas, Buenos Aires, September 29, 1977.

33. See memo for the ambassador, 800, June 4, 1947 (Suitland).
34. See Oakley, "Recent Political Development," 800, October 6, 1947 (Suitland).
35. See J. Taylor, *supra* Ch. 9, note 11, p. 118.
36. E. Perón, *My Mission in Life*, p. 190.
37. Ibid., p. 42.
38. See J. Taylor, *supra* Ch. 9, note 11, p. 67.
39. J. Perón, "Juan Perón habla de Eva Perón," *Panorama*, April 21, 1970, p. 66.
40. E. Perón, *supra* note 36, p. iii.
41. Interview, 1977, Washington, D.C. (name withheld by request).
42. See T. Luca de Tena, *supra* Ch. 1, note 7, pp. 144–45.
43. Interview with Arturo Jauretche, Columbia Oral History Project. The poet José María Castiñeiro de Dios confirmed the story. Interview, Buenos Aires, July 17, 1980.
44. See E. Perón, *supra* note 36, p. 41.
45. Interview with Percy Foster (foreign correspondent), Buenos Aires, July 2, 1980.
46. Bruce to secretary of state, 800, January 20, 1948 (copy on file with author).

CHAPTER TWENTY-THREE

1. Quoted in R. Bustos Fierro, *supra* Ch. 16, note 30, p. 123.
2. G. Blanksten, *supra* Ch. 16, note 53, p. 73.
3. See "La primera presidencia—XLVIII," *Primera Plana*, June 13, 1967, p. 38.
4. See ibid., p. 40; A. González Arzac, "La Constitución 'Justicialista' de 1949," *Todo Es Historia*, Supp. No. 41, undated, pp. 16–17.
5. Quoted in Maleady to secretary of state, 835.00/10-2048, October 20, 1948.
6. See "Report on Argentine Labor," U.S. embassy, Buenos Aires, 850.4/800, November 1948 (Suitland), for a description of the unequal campaign.
7. The expression used was *malandrófilo*, literally "fond of bad men." Name of Peronist withheld by request.
8. See "Historia del peronismo—XLIX," *Primera Plana*, June 20, 1967, p. 36.
9. Biographical report, U.S. embassy, Buenos Aires, 350.3/350, March 31, 1949 (Suitland).
10. Quoted in "Historia del peronismo—XLVIII," *Primera Plana*, June 13, 1967, p. 44. See also A. González Arzac, "Vida, pasión y muerte del Artículo 40," *Todo Es Historia*, No. 31, November 1969, pp. 42–45.
11. See P. Santos Martínez, *supra* Ch. 21, note 16, p. 131.
12. See R. Scott, "Argentina's New Constitution: Social Democracy or Social Authoritarianism?" *Western Political Quarterly*, Vol. 4, December 1951, p. 572.
13. See, generally, A. González Arzac, *supra* note 10.
14. See *Diplomatic Papers—1949*, Vol. II, pp. 485–86.
15. Ibid., p. 486.
16. Ibid.
17. See ibid., pp. 491–93.
18. See L. Ilsley, "The Argentine Constitutional Revision of 1949," *Journal of Politics*, Vol. 14, 1952, p. 236; R. Scott, *supra* note 12, pp. 574–75.

CHAPTER TWENTY-FOUR

1. Reprinted in *La Nación*, August 22, 1947.
2. See I. Schieffer, *Charisma*, pp. 37–39.
3. See "La primera presidencia—XL," *Primera Plana*, April 18, 1967, p. 36.
4. Ibid.
5. Interview with David Bléjer (Sammartino's law partner at the time and an eyewitness), Buenos Aires, April 1977.
6. See A. Ciria, "La Argentina dividida: Peronistas y antiperonistas" *Polémica*, No. 85, November 1971, p. 121.
7. Quoted in *La Opinión*, November 10, 1971.
8. See R. Alexander, *supra* Ch. 5, note 32, pp. 68–70.
9. See "La primera presidencia—XLI, XLII," *Primera Plana*, April 25, 1967, p. 40, May 2, 1967, p. 32.
10. See, e.g., secret memorandum of G. Ray, U.S. embassy, Buenos Aires, April 28, 1948 (copy on file with author), reporting on conversation with Perón. For a collection of Perón's statements on the subject, see J. Perón, *supra* Ch. 21, note 17, p. 421.
11. See R. Alexander, *supra* Ch. 7, note 4, pp. 173–76.
12. Quoted in O. Confalonieri, *Perón contra Perón*, p. 181.
13. See "La primera presidencia—XXXII, XXXIII," *Primera Plana*, February 21, 1967, p. 34, February 28, 1967, p. 36.
14. See C. Aloé, *Gobierno, proceso, conducta*, pp. 248–52.
15. See ibid., pp. 214–16.
16. See A. Blanksten, *supra* Ch. 16, note 53, pp. 205–208.
17. Quoted in editors of *La Prensa, Defense of Freedom*, p. 25.
18. See ibid., p. 31.
19. For a vivid description of the attack, see *La Prensa*, January 25, 1947.
20. See N. Pyle, "A Study of U.S. Propaganda Efforts and Pro-Allied Sentiments in Argentina During World War II," Ph.D. dissertation, 1968, p. 122.
21. See *Diplomatic Papers—1947*, Vol. VIII, pp. 319–25.
22. Ibid., p. 325.
23. See "La primera presidencia—XLIII," *Primera Plana*, May 9, 1967, p. 36.
24. See G. Blanksten, *supra* Ch. 16, note 53, pp. 211–13.
25. See W. Little, *supra* Ch. 7, note 26, p. 64.
26. See Hoover to Berle, 835.00/11-546, November 5, 1946.
27. Watrous, "Attitudes and Activities of Cipriano Reyes," November 26, 1946 (Suitland).
28. See "La primera presidencia—XLVI," *Primera Plana*, May 30, 1967, p. 36.
29. The speech is translated in enclosure no. 2 to dispatch no. 546, U.S. embassy, Buenos Aires, September 9, 1948 (copy on file with author).
30. For a detailed description, see Maleady, "September 24 Plot to Assassinate the Peróns," 835.00/10-148, October 1, 1948, excerpted in *Diplomatic Papers—1948*, Vol. IX, p. 292.
31. For an account by one of the accused conspirators, see W. Beveraggi Allende, *El partido laborista, el fracaso de Perón y el problema argentina*, p. 54. See also Dearborn to Tewksbury, 835.00/10-1948, October 19, 1948.
32. See *Diplomatic Papers—1948*, Vol. IX, p. 295.
33. See Ray to secretary of state, 835.00/9-2848, September 28, 1948.
34. Ibid.
35. See Acheson to U.S. embassy, Buenos Aires, 835.00/1-2149, January 21, 1949.

36. See Ray to secretary of state, 835.00/12-1749, December 17, 1949.
37. Griffiths' allegations are accepted as true in L. Farago, *supra* Ch. 10, note 3, pp. 46–54. A more recent biography of Bormann presents convincing evidence that the Nazi official died in 1945. J. von Lang, *The Secretary*.
38. See "La primera presidencia—XLVI," *Primera Plana*, May 30, 1967, p. 36.
39. Quoted ibid., p. 37.
40. Philip Hamburger, "A Reporter in Argentina: Love, Love, Love," *The New Yorker*, June 26, 1948, p. 32.

CHAPTER TWENTY-FIVE

1. J. Perón, *La comunidad organizada*.
2. J. Perón, *supra* Ch. 21, note 17, pp. 86–87.
3. J. Perón, *supra* note 1, p. 54.
4. On *justicialismo*, see G. Blanksten, *supra* Ch. 16, note 53, pp. 276–305; R. Mendé, *El justicialismo*; G. Pendle, "President Perón's 'Philosophy,'" *Fortnightly*, April 1954.
5. R. Damonte Taborda, *A donde va Perón?* p. 251.
6. For convincing support of this proposition, see G. Germani, *Authoritarianism, Fascism, and National Populism*; see also K. Silvert, "The Costs of Anti-Nationalism: Argentina," in K. Silvert, ed., *Expectant Peoples*; E. Kenworthy, "The Function of the Little-Known Case in Theory Formation or What Peronism Wasn't," *Comparative Politics*, October 1973, p. 17. The case for regarding Peronism as a form of Fascism is made in S. Lipset, *Political Man*, pp. 170–73. For a recent article renewing the argument, see P. Lewis, "Was Perón a Fascist? An Inquiry into the Nature of Fascism," *Journal of Politics*, Vol. 42, February 1980, p. 242.
7. See G. Wynia, *supra* Ch. 19, note 1, p. 55.
8. Quoted in *La Nación*, September 6, 1950.
9. Reprinted in J. Perón, *La tercera posición argentina*, p. 97.
10. See J. Perón, *supra* Ch. 7, note 10, pp. 21, 168.
11. See ibid., p. 266.
12. See ibid., pp. 66, 70.
13. Ibid., p. 126.
14. Ibid., p. 52.
15. See ibid., p. 15.
16. See ibid., pp. 52–53.
17. Ibid., p. 32.
18. Lecture by Arturo Sampay, Buenos Aires, November 10, 1976.
19. J. Perón, *supra* Ch. 7, note 10, p. 265.
20. Interview with Antonio Benítez, Buenos Aires, July 24, 1980.
21. Interview with Ricardo Guardo, Buenos Aires, May 5, 1977.
22. Interview with Ricardo Guardo, Buenos Aires, 1978.
23. See M. Bracker, "Perón: Evolution of a Strong Man," *New York Times Magazine*, February 22, 1948.
24. See "La primera presidencia—XVI, XVII," *Primera Plana*, September 6, 1966, p. 40, September 13, 1966, p. 38.
25. The sources for the dental episode are a secret U.S. embassy memorandum, A-566, December 17, 1948 (copy on file with author), and an interview with Ricardo Guardo, Buenos Aires, October 1977.
26. "La primera presidencia—LIV," *Primera Plana*, August 1, 1967, p. 36;

República Argentina, *Casos de la segunda tiranía*, Vol. I, p. 43; R. Pastor, *Frente al totalitarianismo peronista*, p. 409.

27. See Franklin to Department of State, 935.7137/3-2651, March 26, 1951; Urruela to secretary of state, 935.7137/3-2851, March 28, 1951.
28. See *Crítica*, March 25, 1951.
29. See Martindale to Department of State, 935.7137/7-551, July 5, 1951.
30. See P. Santos Martínez, *supra* Ch. 21, note 16, Vol. I, pp. 237–38.
31. Franklin to Department of State, dispatch no. 656, October 31, 1950 (copy on file with author).
32. R. Damonte Taborda, *Ayer fué San Perón*, pp. 58–59.
33. T. Luca de Tena, *supra* Ch. 1, note 7, pp. 188–89.

CHAPTER TWENTY-SIX

1. See H. Gambini, "Cuando Perón y Evita estaban en la cima," *Visión*, November 20, 1970, p. 49; "La primera presidencia—LVII," *Primera Plana*, August 29, 1967, pp. 47–48.
2. See "La historia del peronismo—XL," April 18, 1967, p. 38.
3. See G. Wynia, *supra* Ch. 19, note 1, p. 69.
4. See *Diplomatic Papers—1950*, Vol. II, p. 721.
5. See *La Nación*, May 2, 1950.
6. See B. Rabinovitz, *Sucedió en la Argentina, 1943–1956*, p. 122.
7. See "La primera presidencia—VII," *Primera Plana*, June 21, 1966, p. 38.
8. Quoted ibid., p. 39.
9. Quoted ibid.
10. For the U.S. ambassador's reaction, see *Diplomatic Papers—1950*, Vol. II, pp. 732–33.
11. See H. Peterson, *Argentina and the United States, 1810–1960*, pp. 478–79.
12. Quoted in W. Little, *supra* Ch. 7, note 26, p. 64.
13. See "La primera presidencia—XLV," *Primera Plana*, May 23, 1967, p. 36.
14. Quoted in W. Little, *supra* Ch. 7, note 26, p. 96.
15. See "La primera presidencia—XLV," *Primera Plana*, May 23, 1967, p. 40.
16. E. Perón, *supra* Ch. 22, note 36, p. iii.
17. See M. Navarro, "Apuntes para una historia de la Fundación," *La Opinión*, July 22, 1973, p. 6; "La primera presidencia—XXVI," *Primera Plana*, December 27, 1966, p. 36.
18. J. Bruce, *supra* Ch. 2, note 21, pp. 187–88.
19. See F. Cowles, *Bloody Precedent*, pp. 188–89.
20. E. Perón, *supra* Ch. 22, note 36, pp. 125–26.
21. There were several documented instances in which firms refusing to contribute to the foundation suffered harassment. See N. Fraser and M. Navarro, *supra* Ch. 1, note 6, pp. 118–19; R. Weisbrot, *supra* Ch. 2, note 22, pp. 233–36.
22. See W. Little, *supra* Ch. 7, note 26, p. 60, n. 3.
23. See J. Taylor, *supra* Ch. 9, note 11, p. 46.
24. Quoted in R. Tettamanti, "Eva Perón," *Los hombres de la historia*, No. 161, July 1971, p. 213.
25. Quoted in O. Borroni and R. Vacca, *supra* Ch. 1, note 6, p. 244.
26. See "La primera presidencia—XXVII," *Primera Plana*, January 3, 1967, p. 38.
27. See J. Taylor, *supra* Ch. 9, note 11, p. 95.

28. Interview with Raúl Salinas, Buenos Aires, October 26, 1977.
29. Apodaca to ambassador, 800, September 2, 1947 (Suitland).
30. *Democracia*, July 12, 1948.
31. Memo from Colonel C. Clarke, 350, August 30, 1949 (Suitland).
32. J. Areilza, *supra* Ch. 22, note 9, p. 202.
33. *Supra* note 28.
34. Interview with Nini Montiam, Madrid, June 27, 1977.
35. J. Perón, *Del poder al exilio*, p. 77.
36. See Griffis to secretary of state, 735.00/1-1050, January 10, 1950 (source: Canadian ambassador).
37. P. Ara, *El caso Eva Perón*, p. 46.
38. See O. Borroni and R. Vacca, *supra* Ch. 1, note 6, p. 237.
39. Quoted ibid., p. 303.
40. Quoted ibid., p. 299.
41. T. Luca de Tena, *supra* Ch. 1, note 7, p. 182.
42. For a published version of the joke, see A. Agostinelli, "Juan Perón por dentro," *Siete Dias*, December 2, 1968.
43. See O. Confalonieri, *supra* Ch. 24, note 12, pp. 268–70.
44. See Franklin to secretary of state, 735.00/10-2450, October 24, 1950; 735.00/10-3150, October 31, 1950.

CHAPTER TWENTY-SEVEN

1. For descriptions of the *cabildo abierto*, see "La primera presidencia— XXVII," January 10, 1967; T. Mendé, *L'Amérique Latine entre en scène*, pp. 145–48.
2. See N. Fraser and M. Navarro, *supra* Ch. 1, note 6, pp. 142–43.
3. See B. Rabinovitz, *supra* Ch. 26, note 6, p. 136.
4. A Puerto Rican newspaper reported that a military delegation had visited Perón to inform him that the army looked with disfavor upon his wife's political ambitions. *El Imparcial*, San Juan, P.R., August 3, 1951.
    Professor Potash was unable to find evidence that any such meeting ever took place, but suggests that there were other methods the officer corps might have used to communicate their displeasure. See R. Potash, *supra* Ch. 16, note 50, p. 130.
5. See, e.g., F. Owen, *supra* Ch. 4, note 21, p. 195.
6. See A. Rouquié, "Adhesión militar y control político del ejército en el régimen peronista (1946–1955)," *Aportes*, January 1971, p. 88.
7. See "La primera presidencia—LIII," *Primera Plana*, July 25, 1967, p. 39.
8. See F. Lucero, *supra* Ch. 13, note 8, p. 41.
9. Quoted in *La Nación*, August 23, 1951.
10. J. Taylor, "Myth and Reality: The Case of Eva Perón," Ph.D. dissertation, 1973, p. 74.
11. Quoted in *La Nación*, August 23, 1951.
12. Her speech, Perón's speech and the dialogue between Evita and the crowd are reprinted ibid. There are also phonograph records and tapes of the event.
13. Reprinted in *La Nación*, September 1, 1950.
14. See, e.g., *New York Times*, September 1, 1951; *El Tiempo* (Bogotá), September 21, 1951.

CHAPTER TWENTY-EIGHT

1. See O. Borroni and R. Vacca, *supra* Ch. 1, note 6, p. 266.
2. On the Menéndez coup, see "La primera presidencia—LIII," *Primera Plana*, July 25, 1967, p. 38; D. Tussie and A. Federman, "El golpe de Menéndez," *Todo Es Historia*, November 1972, p. 8; R. Potash, *supra* Ch. 16, note 50, pp. 123–33; J. Orona, *supra* Ch. 18, note 3, p. 97; Bunker to Department of State, 735.00/10-151, October 1, 1951.
3. J. Orona, *supra* Ch. 18, note 3, p. 105.
4. Quoted in "La primera presidencia—LIII," *Primera Plana*, July 25, 1967, p. 41.
5. Quoted in J. Orona, *supra* Ch. 18, note 3, p. 108.
6. Ibid., pp. 108–109.
7. Reprinted in *La Nación*, September 28, 1951.
8. Quoted in O. Borroni and R. Vacca, *supra* Ch. 1, note 6, p. 267.
9. Reprinted in *La Nación*, September 30, 1951, p. 4.
10. See O. Borroni and R. Vacca, *supra* Ch. 1, note 6, pp. 267–68.
11. Quoted in *Hispanic American Report*, Vol. 4, August 1951, p. 38.
12. See A. Rouquié, *supra* Ch. 27, note 6, p. 88.
13. Quoted ibid., pp. 269–70.
14. Quoted ibid., pp. 270–72.
15. J. Barnes, *Evita, First Lady*, p. 153.
16. On the 1951 election, see "La primera presidencia—LVII, LVIII, LIX," *Primera Plana*, August 29, 1967, p. 46, September 5, 1967, p. 36, September 12, 1967, p. 36.
17. The *London Times*, Ed. Supp., November 17, 1951, described the elections as "a sandwich with a very thin filling of correct, democratic practice enclosed between two indigestible hunks of violence and intimidation in the worst authoritarian tradition."
18. See P. Snow, *Argentine Radicalism*, p. 69.
19. For a good description of Peronist propaganda during this period, see "Z," "Argentina in the Tunnel," *Foreign Affairs*, April 1952, p. 401.
20. Quoted in *La Nación*, November 10, 1951.
21. Quoted in O. Barroni and R. Vacca, *supra* Ch. 1, note 6, p. 296.
22. Quoted in "La primera presidencia—LVIII," *Primera Plana*, September 5, 1967, p. 38.

CHAPTER TWENTY-NINE

1. See "La primera presidencia—XXIX," *Primera Plana*, January 17, 1967, p. 36.
2. Ibid., p. 38.
3. E. Perón, *supra* Ch. 22, note 36, p. 176.
4. Ibid., p. 11.
5. Ibid., p. 214.
6. Ibid., p. 203.
7. Ibid., p. 195.
8. Ibid., p. 189.
9. Ibid., p. 60.
10. Ibid., p. 85.

11. See *La Nación*, June 12, 17 and 18, 1952.
12. See G. Wynia, *supra* Ch. 19, note 1, p. 70, fn. 41.
13. See interview with Alfredo Gómez Morales, Columbia Oral History Project.
14. See Mallory to Department of State, 735.11/3-62, March 6, 1952.
15. See Martindale to Department of State, 735.11/4-2852, April 28, 1952.
16. For a dramatic photo, see J. Taylor, *supra* Ch. 9, note 11, between pp. 102–103.
17. Reprinted in O. Borroni and R. Vacca, *supra* Ch. 1, note 6, pp. 278–79.
18. See ibid., p. 280.
19. See ibid., p. 282.
20. See N. Fraser and M. Navarro, *supra* Ch. 1, note 6, p. 157.
21. See "La segunda presidencia—I," *Primera Plana*, May 7, 1968, pp. 70–71.
22. See O. Borroni and R. Vacca, *supra* Ch. 1, note 6, pp. 287–89; "La segunda presidencia—V," *Primera Plana*, June 4, 1968, p. 48.
23. See República Argentina, *supra* Ch. 19, note 3, p. 47.
24. Dr. Ara has written a book detailing his involvement. P. Ara, *supra* Ch. 26, note 37.
25. Quoted in O. Borroni and R. Vacca, *supra* Ch. 1, note 6, p. 316.
26. Quoted ibid.
27. R. Boizard, *Esa noche de Perón*, p. 63.
28. The following description is taken from accounts in *La Nación*, July 28, 1952, and August 11, 1952, newsreel footage and the documentary film *Ni vencidores ni vencidos?* (1972).
29. Quoted in J. Taylor, *supra* Ch. 9, note 11, p. 65 (source: Raúl Apold, Peron's press secretary).

CHAPTER THIRTY

1. For a sketch of the scene, see A. Molinari, *Caso Duarte*, p. 9.
2. Reprinted in "La segunda presidencia—IX," *Primera Plana*, July 2, 1968, pp. 46–47.
3. Reprinted in O. Borroni and R. Vacca, *supra* Ch. 1, note 6, pp. 284–87.
4. See *Primera Plana*, May 23, 1967.
5. Martindale to Department of State, 735.11/10-152, October 1, 1952.
6. See O. Confalonieri, *supra* Ch. 24, note 12, p. 86.
7. See G. Plater, *Una gran lección*, p. 209.
8. See *Time*, April 20, 1953.
9. T. Luca de Tena, *supra* Ch. 1, note 7, p. 191.
10. See "La segunda presidencia—X," *Primera Plana*, July 9, 1968, p. 46.
11. A. Molinari, *supra* note 1.
12. R. Pizarro Miguens, *La justicia nacional resolvió "El Caso Duarte."*
13. See *New York Times*, September 19, 1951.
14. See *London Times*, May 1, 1953.
15. Quoted in "La segunda presidencia—XIX," *Primera Plana*, October 1, 1968, p. 49.
16. The speech is excerpted ibid. pp. 49–50.
17. See "La segunda presidencia—XX," *Primera Plana*, October 8, 1968, p. 48; República Argentina, *supra* Ch. 19, note 3, pp. 227–33.
18. Interview with eyewitness (name withheld by request), Buenos Aires, 1976.
19. Ibid.
20. Quoted in *Hispanic American Report*, Vol. 6, May 1953.

21. The net was so wide it took in Victoria Ocampo, one of Argentina's best-known intellectuals, who was confined for twenty-six days in a woman's prison. See D. Meyer, *Victoria Ocampo*, pp. 154–66.
22. See "La segunda presidencia—XXIX," *Primera Plana*, December 17, 1968.

CHAPTER THIRTY-ONE

1. See, e.g., E. Pavón Pereyra, *supra* Ch. 3, note 29, p. 294.
2. For the study of the use of Argentine labor attachés to spread *justicialismo* abroad, see J. Deiner, "ATLAS: A Labor Instrument of Expansion Under Perón," Ph.D. dissertation, 1970.
3. See D. Bray, "Peronism in Chile," *Hispanic American Historical Review*, February 1967, p. 38; "La segunda presidencia—XXIII," *Primera Plana*, October 29, 1968, p. 44.
4. Quoted in *La Nación* (Santiago), February 15, 1953; translated in Hall (Santiago) to Department of State, 735.11/2-1653, February 16, 1953.
5. See Hall (Santiago) to Department of State, 735.11/3-253, March 2, 1953, p. 6.
6. See Hall (Santiago) to Department of State, 735.11/3-1153, March 11, 1953; C. Bowers (U.S. ambassador to Chile), *supra* Ch. 4, note 23, p. 359.
7. Martindale to Department of State, 735.11/3-1253, March 12, 1953.
8. See "La segunda presidencia—XXIV," *Primera Plana*, November 5, 1968, p. 51.
9. See P. Santos Martínez, *supra* Ch. 21, note 16, Vol. I, pp. 300–301.
10. J. Perón, *La hora de los pueblos*, p. 85.
11. See J. Dulles, *Vargas of Brazil*, p. 316.
12. See T. Skidmore, *Politics in Brazil, 1930–1964*, p. 150; J. Dulles, *Unrest in Brazil*, pp. 23, 27.
13. See hearings before the Committee on Foreign Relations, U.S. Senate, 89th Congress, 2nd Session, February 7, 1966, pp. 7, 34 (testimony of Lincoln Gordon); see also T. Skidmore, *supra* note 12, pp. 211, 295, 324.
14. See "La segunda presidencia—XXVI," *Primera Plana*, November 26, 1968, p. 59.
15. See M. Eisenhower, *The Wine Is Bitter*, p. 65.
16. Interview with John Moors Cabot, Washington, March 2, 1979.
17. Ibid.
18. See "La segunda presidencia—XXV," *Primera Plana*, November 12, 1968, p. 47.
19. M. Eisenhower, *supra* note 15, p. 65.
20. Ibid., p. 255.
21. J. Cabot, *Toward Our Common American Destiny*, pp. 91–92.
22. Quoted in Hanna (Asunción) to Department of State, 735.11/10-553, October 5, 1953.

CHAPTER THIRTY-TWO

1. See "La segunda presidencia—XIII," *Primera Plana*, August 13, 1968, p. 50.
2. See A. Cafiero, *Cinco años después . . .*, Ch. XVII.
3. See J. Antonio, *Y ahora qué?* (autobiography); R. Jassen, *Jorge Antonio*.
4. See "La segunda presidencia—XVIII," *Primera Plana*, September 24, 1968, p. 50.

5. T. Luca de Tena, *supra* Ch. 1, note 6, p. 210.
6. D. Morrison, *Latin American Mission*, p. 211.
7. The following account is based upon an interview with Lloyd Cutler, Washington, June 30, 1979. Its accuracy has been confirmed by one of the other Kaiser attorneys involved. Letter of V.A. Rodriguez to author, July 12, 1979.
8. See P. Santos Martínez, Vol. 2, *supra* Ch. 21, note 16, pp. 116–17.
9. See, e.g., O. Confalonieri, *supra* Ch. 24, note 12, pp. 223–24.
10. See "La segunda presidencia—XIV," *Primera Plana*, August 20, 1968, p. 54.
11. For a report on the speech, see *New York Times*, April 20, 1954; see also Vaky to Department of State, 835.2553/4-2754, April 27, 1954.
12. For a summary of each group's proposals, see Walstrom to Department of State, 835.2553/6-254, June 2, 1954; Vaky to Department of State, 835.2553/6-1854, June 18, 1954; 835.2553/7-1654, July 16, 1954; 835.2553/7-2254, July 22, 1954.
13. See Vaky to Department of State, 835.2553/9-1554, September 15, 1954; 835.2553/9-2254, September 22, 1954.
14. See Nufer to secretary of state, 835.2553/1-2355, January 23, 1955.
15. Copy of letter on file with author.
16. For a summary of the terms of the contract, see Vaky to Department of State, 835.2553/5-255, May 2, 1955.
17. See "La segunda presidencia—XVI," *Primera Plana*, September 10, 1968, p. 49.
18. For a description of how the opposition distorted the actual terms of the contract, see Hopkins to Department of State, 835.2553/8-1055, August 10, 1955.
19. See G. Wynia, *supra* Ch. 19, note 1, p. 73.

CHAPTER THIRTY-THREE

1. Quoted in R. Pastor, *La otra faz de la segunda dictadura*, p. 70.
2. Quoted ibid., p. 66.
3. L. Arena, *Alelí*, p. 15.
4. See "La segunda presidencia—VI," *Primera Plana*, June 11, 1968, p. 48.
5. Ibid.
6. República Argentina, *Casos de la segunda tiranía*, Vol. 1, p. 108, reprinted from Vice Presidencia de la Nación, Comisión Nacional de Investigaciones, *Documentación, autores y cómplices de las irregularidades cometidas durante la segunda tiranía*, Vol. II, p. 222.
7. República Argentina, *supra* note 6, p. 107.
8. Interview, Buenos Aires, 1977 (name withheld by request).
9. V. Gheorgiu, "La hora 25 de Perón," *Clarín*, October 24, 1955.
10. República Argentina, *supra* note 6, p. 106.
11. See "La segunda presidencia—VI," *Primera Plana*, June 11, 1968, p. 50.
12. For a contrary view, see Siracusa to Department of State, 735.11/11-554, November 5, 1954, arguing that Perón was working almost as hard as ever. Regarding Perón's sports activities, the writer noted that "Perón is actually performing a valuable piece of work for Peronism in terms of securing the support of coming generations for that system."
13. See "La segunda presidencia—VII," *Primera Plana*, June 18, 1968, p. 48.
14. T. Luca de Tena, *supra* Ch. 1, note 7, p. 102.

15. See ibid., p. 12.
16. Quoted in "La segunda presidencia—VII," *supra* note 13, p. 47.
17. República Argentina, *supra* note 6, p. 108.
18. See "La segunda presidencia—VII," *supra* note 13, p. 47.
19. See *La Prensa*, July 26, 1953.
20. See O. Confalonieri, *supra* Ch. 24, note 12, p. 129.
21. See A. Barrios, *supra* Ch. 3, note 33, p. 64.
22. See *Time*, February 19, 1954; *Excelsior* (Mexico City), February 16, 1954.
23. Dulles to U.S. embassy, Buenos Aires, 735.11/5-455, May 4, 1955.

CHAPTER THIRTY-FOUR

1. The speech is reprinted in *La Nación*, November 11, 1954.
2. R. De Hoyos, "The Role of the Catholic Church in the Revolution against President Juan D. Perón," Ph.D. dissertation, 1970, p. 116.
3. See J. Orona, *supra* Ch. 18, note 3, pp. 191–92.
4. See ibid., pp. 192–95; Franklin to Department of State, 735.00/10-2450, October 24, 1950; R. McGeagh, *supra* Ch. 16, note 42, pp. 123–43. 158–65.
5. See R. McGeagh, *supra* Ch. 16, note 42, p. 164; see also O. Confalonieri, *supra* Ch. 24, note 12, pp. 275–76.
6. Quoted in H. Gambini, *El peronismo y la iglesia*, p. 75.
7. See R. De Hoyos, *supra* note 2, pp. 108–109.
8. See ibid., pp. 110–11.
9. For a detailed discussion of various hypotheses, see ibid., pp. 125–41.
10. See Sandifer to Department of State. 735.00/7-2955, July 29, 1955.
11. See "La segunda presidencia—XXX," *Primera Plana*, December 24, 1968, p. 62.
12. Reprinted in *La Nación*, November 24, 1954.
13. Reprinted ibid.
14. Quoted in J. Orona, *supra* Ch. 18, note 3, p. 203.
15. Quoted ibid., p. 204.
16. See ibid., p. 208; R. De Hoyos, *supra* note 2, pp. 178–79; P. Marsal, *Perón y la iglesia*, pp. 99–107.
17. Interview with Antonio Cafiero, Washington, November 18, 1977.
18. Quoted in *La Nación*, February 12, 1955.
19. See J. Orona, *supra* Ch. 18, note 3, p. 210.
20. See R. Walter, *supra* Ch. 11, note 1, pp. 143–46.
21. See R. De Hoyos, *supra* note 2, p. 170.
22. For a complete collection of these pamphlets, see F. Lafiandra, *Los panfletos*.
23. For photos and diagrams, see ibid., pp. 369–70.
24. See ibid., p. 257.
25. Quoted in H. Gambini, *supra* note 6, p. 84.
26. Quoted in "La segunda presidencia—XXXI," *Primera Plana*, December 31, 1968, p. 82.
27. See R. De Hoyos, *supra* note 2, p. 288.
28. The following account is taken from "La segunda presidencia—XXXI," *supra* note 26; R. De Hoyos, *supra* note 2, pp. 291–96.
29. Quoted in "La segunda presidencia—XXXI," *supra* note 26, pp. 82–83.
30. See R. De Hoyos, *supra* note 2, pp. 296–303.

31. See F. Lafiandra, *supra* note 22, pp. 198, 208. An investigating commission formed after Perón's ouster reached the same conclusion. See República Argentina, *supra* Ch. 33, note 6, pp. 169–83.
32. Interview with Oscar Albrieu, Columbia Oral History Project, confirmed in interview with Oscar Albrieu, Buenos Aires, September 20, 1977.
33. The controversy has not yet been put to rest. In 1980 a retired navy captain presented to the ruling military junta what he said was the genuine "burnt flag." His claim was later disputed. See *La Prensa*, July 9, 1980, p. 1; *La Nación*, July 12, 1980.
34. See *Hispanic American Report*, Vol. 8, July 1955.
35. For the text of the decree, see F. Lafiandra, *supra* note 22, pp. 200–201.

CHAPTER THIRTY-FIVE

1. See M. Amadeo, *Ayer, hoy, manana*, pp. 48–50.
2. See F. Lucero, *supra* Ch. 13, note 8, pp. 79–81.
3. Nufer, memorandum: ambassador's meeting with Perón on June 16, attached to Siracusa to Department of State, 835.413/6-2255, June 22, 1955. Nufer's real reason for seeing Perón was to discuss the issue of profit remittances for U.S. firms in Argentina.
4. See R. De Hoyos, *supra* Ch. 34, note 2, pp. 303–306.
5. See M. Amadeo, *supra* note 1, pp. 45–46; R. Potash, *supra* Ch. 16, note 50, p. 187.
6. For descriptions of the bombing, see "La segunda presidencia—XXXII," *Primera Plana*, January 7, 1969, p. 32; "De Perón a Onganía—I," *Panorama*, October 22, 1968, p. 72; Siracusa to Department of State, *supra* note 3; Siracusa to Department of State, 735.00/7-655, July 6, 1955 (reports of Office of U.S. Air Attaché); *La Nación*, June 17, 1955.
7. Interview with employee, Hurlingham, Argentina, 1977 (name withheld by request).
8. Interview with aide, Buenos Aires, May 15, 1978 (name withheld by request).
9. Quoted in "De Perón a Onganía—I," *supra* note 6, p. 74.
10. Quoted ibid.
11. A CGT official had broadcast a call for workers to go into the streets. The strategy was to block troop movements, as had been attempted during the Menéndez coup. The CGT apparently did not realize that the army had remained loyal to Perón. It was not until 4:00 P.M. that the confederation received word of Perón's displeasure that workers were coming to the Plaza de Mayo, but by then effective communication was impossible. See Reichard to Department of State, 735.00/6-2455, June 24, 1955.
12. See *La Nación*, June 17, 1955.
13. For descriptions of the burnings, see "La segunda presidencia—XXXIII," *Primera Plana*, January 14, 1969, p. 41; "De Perón a Onganía—II," *Panorama*, October 29, 1968, p. 14; A. Rottjer, *El llanto de las ruinas*.
14. Quoted in "De Perón a Onganía—II," *supra* note 13, p. 77.
15. See, e.g., F. Lafiandra, *supra* Ch. 34, note 22, p. 201.
16. Quoted in R. De Hoyos, *supra* Ch. 34, note 2, p. 315; P. Santos Martínez, *supra* Ch. 21, note 16, Vol. 2, p. 225.
17. See J. Orona, *supra* Ch. 18, note 3, p. 232.
18. J. Perón, *La forza es el derecho de las bestias*, p. 94.
19. J. Perón, *Del poder al exilio*, p. 17.

20. T. Luca de Tena, *supra* Ch. 1, note 7, p. 217; see also R. De Hoyos, *supra* Ch. 34, note 2, p. 315 (1966 interview with Perón).
21. See "La segunda presidencia—XXXIII," *supra* note 13, p. 44.
22. See República Argentina, *supra* Ch. 33, note 6, pp. 183–92.
23. See "De Perón a Onganía—II," *supra* note 13, p. 76.
24. See "La segunda presidencia—XXXIII," *supra* note 13, p. 44.
25. Excerpted in J. Orona, *supra* Ch. 18, note 3, p. 232.
26. See A. Whitaker, *Argentine Upheaval*, p. 10; "La segunda presidencia—XXXIV," *Primera Plana*, January 21, 1969, p. 21.
27. See F. Lucero, *supra* Ch. 13, note 8, p. 112.
28. Interview with Oscar Albrieu, September 20, 1977.
29. See J. Orona, *supra* Ch. 18, note 3, pp. 242–45.
30. See H. Gambini, *supra* Ch. 34, note 6, p. 103.
31. The speech is excerpted in J. Orona, *supra* Ch. 18, note 3, pp. 245–47.
32. Nufer to secretary of state, 735.11/7-1955, July 19, 1955.
33. "La segunda presidencia—XXXV," *Primera Plana*, January 28, 1969, p. 20.
34. See ibid., pp. 21–22; "De Perón a Onganía—II," *Panorama*, November 5, 1968, pp. 74–75.
35. Ibid., p. 76.
36. For the text of the "resignation," see J. Orona, *supra* Ch. 18, note 3, pp. 259–60.
37. Siracusa to Department of State, 735.11/9-255, September 2, 1955, p. 3.
38. Interview, Buenos Aires, May 15, 1978 (name withheld by request).
39. Interview with Oscar Albrieu, *supra* note 28.
40. The speech is reprinted in República Argentina, *supra* Ch. 19, note 3, p. 263.
41. See Siracusa to Department of State, *supra* note 37, p. 2.

CHAPTER THIRTY-SIX

1. See F. Lafiandra, *supra* Ch. 34, note 22, p. 283; R. De Hoyos, *supra* Ch. 34, note 2, p. 247.
2. See R. Potash, *supra* Ch. 16, note 50, p. 196.
3. See ibid., pp. 196–97.
4. See "La caída y el exilio—I," *Primera Plana,* May 6, 1969, pp. 47–48.
5. Interview with Oscar Albrieu, Columbia Oral History Project.
6. Quoted in "La caída y el exilio—I," *supra* note 4, p. 46.
7. See R. De Hoyos, *supra* Ch. 34, note 2, pp. 369–70.
8. For a detailed account of General Lonardi's role, see L. Lonardi, *Dios es justo.*
9. See interview with Oscar Albrieu, *supra* note 5.
10. See F. Lucero, *supra* Ch. 13, note 8, p. 132.
11. T. Luca de Tena, *supra* Ch. 1, note 7, p. 230.
12. Interview with Oscar Albrieu, *supra* note 5.
13. The literature on the Liberating Revolution is voluminous. Especially useful were: "La caída y el exilio—VI, VII," *Primera Plana*, June 10, 1969, p. 56, June 17, 1969, p. 43; "De Perón a Onganía—V, VI," *Panorama*, November 19, 1968, p. 73, November 26, 1968, p. 75; R. Potash, *supra* Ch. 16, note 50, pp. 200–202; J. Orona, *La revolución del 16 de setiembre.*
14. Quoted in L. Lonardi, *supra* note 8, p. 70.
15. V. Gheorgiu, *supra* Ch. 33, note 9, Part II, October 25, 1955.
16. Quoted ibid., Part III, October 26, 1955.
17. Quoted ibid., Part IV, October 27, 1955.

18. L. Lonardi, *supra* note 8, p. 121.
19. Interview with Oscar Albrieu, *supra* note 5.
20. J. Perón, *supra* Ch. 35, note 18, p. 105.
21. Interview with Oscar Albrieu, *supra* note 5.
22. The text is reprinted in J. Orona, *supra* Ch. 18, note 3, pp. 294–95.
23. J. Perón, *supra* Ch. 35, note 18, p. 108.
24. Interview with Hugo Gullamón, Buenos Aires, October 14, 1977.
25. J. Perón, *supra* Ch. 35, note 18, p. 108.
26. J. Perón, *Perón-Cooke correspondencia*, Vol. 1, p. 8.
27. See Siracusa to Department of State, 735.11/9-2655, September 26, 1955.
28. T. Luca de Tena, *supra* Ch. 1, note 7, p. 230.
29. See "La caída y el exilio—XII," *Primera Plana*, July 29, 1969, p. 36; "De Perón a Onganía—VIII," *Panorama*, December 10, 1968, p. 74.
30. See F. Lucero, *supra* Ch. 13, note 8, p. 169.
31. Quoted in "El exilio de Perón," *Redacción* (Supp. No. 5), July 1973, p. 3.
32. Ibid.
33. See *La Nación*, September 24, 1955.
34. See J. Perón, *supra* Ch. 35, note 18, pp. 56–57.
35. Interview with aide, Buenos Aires, October 17, 1977 (name withheld by request).
36. Siracusa to Department of State, *supra* note 27.
37. See P. Ara, *supra* Ch. 26, note 37, pp. 167–77.
38. Interview with Patricio Kelly, Buenos Aires, May 3, 1977.
39. See "De Perón a Onganía—IX," *Panorama*, December 17, 1968, p. 74.
40. E. Sábato, *El otro rostro del peronismo*, p. 40.
41. The letter is reprinted in *Clarín*, October 1, 1955.

CHAPTER THIRTY-SEVEN

1. See M. Amadeo, *supra* Ch. 35, note 1, pp. 66–68.
2. For Perón's denial of the rumors, see J. Perón, *supra* Ch. 35, note 19, pp. 80–81.
3. See E. Pavón Pereyra, *supra* Ch. 3, note 8, No. 31, June 1974, pp. 5–14.
4. See C. Ross, "Perón: El comienzo del exilio," *Todo Es Historia,* No. 69, January 1973, p. 12; "El exilio de Perón," *Redacción*, Supp. No. 5, July 1973, pp. 5–6.
5. See C. Ross, *supra* note 4, pp. 10–13.
6. J. Perón, *supra* Ch. 35, note 19, pp. 65–66.
7. J. Gunther, *supra* Ch. 2, note 13, p. 238.
8. See *La Nación*, October 4, 1955; U.S. embassy (Asunción) to Department of State, 734.00/10-755, October 7, 1955.
9. The interview is reprinted in J. Perón, *supra* Ch. 35, note 18, pp. 12–17.
10. For the text of Teisaire's statement, see *La Nación*, October 5, 1955.
11. See Wardlaw (Asunción) to Department of State, 735.00/10-1155, October 11, 1955.
12. See H. Gambini, "La odisea de un presidente," *Panorama*, September 15, 1970, p. 44.
13. See M. Montemayor, "Perón en el Paraguay," *Esto Es*, October 18, 1955.
14. Interview with Mariano Montemayor, Buenos Aires, July 31, 1980.
15. Quoted in "La caída y el exilio—XIII," *Primera Plana*, August 5, 1969, p. 52.

16. Quoted ibid.
17. See E. Pavón Pereyra, *supra* Ch. 3, note 8, No. 32, January 1975, pp. 25, 36–40.
18. For the tribunal's judgment, see República Argentina, *supra* Ch. 19, note 3, p. 268.
19. See T. Luca de Tena, *supra* Ch. 1, note 7, p. 236.
20. See Ageton (Asunción) to secretary of state, 735.00/11-255, November 2, 1955.
21. See T. Luca de Tena, *supra* Ch. 1, note 7, p. 237.
22. Quoted in *El Comercio* (Lima), November 5, 1955.
23. See *La Crónica* (Lima), October 10, 1955.
24. See "De Perón a Onganía—X," *Panorama*, December 24, 1968, p. 43.
25. See "De Perón a Onganía—XI," *Panorama*, December 31, 1968, p. 66.
26. On Lonardi's fall, see R. Potash, *supra* Ch. 16, note 50, pp. 214–24; "De Perón a Onganía—XII, XIII," *Panorama*, January 7, 1969, p. 66, January 14, 1969, p. 66; "La caída de Lonardi," *Primera Plana*, November 10, 1970, p. 80.

CHAPTER THIRTY-EIGHT

1. See H. Gambini, *supra* Ch. 37, note 12, p. 46.
2. Weise (Colón) to Department of State, 735.00/5-1456, May 5, 1956, p. 2.
3. Interview with José Dominador Bazán, Panamá, May 26, 1981.
4. Telephone interview with Gwen Bagni, Los Angeles, November 21, 1978.
5. The U.S. consul in Colón referred to his "propensity for indiscriminate companionship." *Supra* note 2.
6. See *La Epoca*, January 25, 1956.
7. The source for this episode is R. Martínez, *Grandezas y miserias de Perón*, pp. 38–40.
8. Ibid., p. 38.
9. See "El caso Isabel—Segunda parte," *Somos*, January 14, 1977, p. 45; E. Pavón Pereyra, *supra* Ch. 3, note 8, No. 33, June 1974, p. 55.
10. Sources for the initial encounter of Perón and Isabel are R. Martínez, *supra* note 7, pp. 49–50; "El caso Isabel—Segunda parte," *supra* note 9, p. 44; H. Gambini, *supra* Ch. 37, note 12, p. 46.
11. See "El caso Isabel—Segunda parte," *supra* note 9, p. 49; "La verdadera historia de Isabel Perón," *Radiolandia 2000*, January 20, 1978, p. 11.
12. CIA information report, 00-3,084, 250, July 17, 1957.
13. R. Martínez, *supra* note 7, p. 48.
14. See *La Nación*, January 15, 1956.
15. See Department of State, memorandum of conversation, 735.00/12-1655, December 16, 1955.
16. See Nufer to secretary of state, 735.00/1-1256, January 12, 1956.
17. *New York Herald-Tribune*, January 17, 1956, p. 1.
18. See memorandum for the files, 735.00/2-2456, February 24, 1956.
19. See R. Martínez, *supra* note 7, pp. 37–38.
20. Weise (Colón) to Department of State, 735.00/6-2256, June 22, 1956, p. 2.
21. See *La Epoca*, January 25, 1956.
22. See *New York Herald-Tribune*, January 23, 1956.
23. T. Luca de Tena, *supra* Ch. 1, note 7, p. 239.
24. See R. Martínez, *supra* note 7, pp. 103–104.

25. See "De Perón a Onganía—XIV, XV," *Panorama*, January 21, 1969, p. 67, January 28, 1969, p. 66; F. Luna, *De Perón a Lanusse, 1943–1973*, pp. 101–108; R. Potash, *supra* Ch. 16, note 50, pp. 226–30.
26. For the best account of the concealment of the body, see N. Fraser and M. Navarro, *supra* Ch. 1, note 6, pp. 175–78.
27. See O. Borroni and R. Vacca, *supra* Ch. 1, note 6, pp. 341–42.
28. See G. Wynia, *supra* Ch. 19, note 1, pp. 147–50.
29. For early reports of the violence, see *Hispanic American Report*, Vol. 9, March 1956.
30. Quoted in R. Prieto, *El pacto*, p. 57.
31. *Supra* note 15.
32. R. Martínez, *supra* note 7, p. 189.
33. On the Valle revolt, see "De Perón a Onganía—XVI, XVII," *Panorama*, February 4, 1969, pp. 66; February 11, 1969, p. 66; P. Ochoa, "Los fusilamientos de 1956." *Primera Plana*, June 8, 1971, p. 38; J. Orona, *supra* Ch. 36, note 13, pp. 99–144; R. Potash, *supra* Ch. 16, note 50, pp. 230–36.
34. A U.S. embassy official witnessed the shootings in La Boca. Interview, November 3, 1981 (name withheld by request).
35. The incident is described in S. Ferla, *Martires y verdugos* and R. Walsh, *Operación masacre*.
36. Interview with Oscar Albrieu, Buenos Aires, May 12, 1977; C. Morales Salazar, *Por que volverá Perón*, pp. 264–65.
37. J. Perón, *supra* Ch. 36, note 26, p. 7.
38. See L. Altuve Carrillo, *Yo fuí embajador de Pérez Jiménez* (account of Perón's stay in Managua by Venezuelan ambassador to Nicaragua).

CHAPTER THIRTY-NINE

1. For a profile of Pérez Jiménez, see T. Szulc, *Twilight of the Tyrants*, p. 249.
2. See Chaplin (Caracas) to Department of State, 735.00/8-1356, August 13, 1956.
3. Interview with Pablo Vicente, Buenos Aires, October 27, 1977.
4. R. Martínez, *supra* Ch. 38, note 7, p. 10.
5. J. Perón, *supra* Ch. 36, note 26, Vol. I, p. 170.
6. For descriptions of Perón's life in Caracas, see E. Pavón Pereyra, *supra* Ch. 3, note 8, No. 36, July 1974, p. 101; *Visión*, April 26, 1957; A. Barrios, *supra* Ch. 3, note 33; R. Galán, "Perón y yo," *Así 2da*, April 13, 1973, pp. 3–4. Another source was the interview with Pablo Vicente, *supra* note 3.
7. CIA information report, *supra* Ch. 38, note 12.
8. R. Martínez, *supra* Ch. 38, note 7, p. 87.
9. See J. Perón, *supra* Ch. 36, note 26, Vol. I, p. 170.
10. See Hall (Caracas) to Department of State, 735.00/3-2456, March 24, 1956.
11. See Fisher (Caracas) to secretary of state, 735.00/4-2957, April 29, 1957.
12. See D. James, "Power and Politics in Peronist Trade Unions," *Journal of Interamerican Studies and World Affairs*, Vol. 20, February 1978, pp. 3, 21.
13. See "De Perón a Onganía—XX," *Panorama*, March 4, 1969, p. 34.
14. For the text of Perón's letter appointing Cooke as his heir, see J. Perón, *supra* Ch. 36, note 26, Vol. II, p. 375.

15. For a biographical sketch of Cooke, see *La Opinión*, September 9, 1973.
16. See *Hispanic American Report*, Vol. 10, February–March 1957.
17. The following account is based upon: J. Antonio, *supra* Ch. 32, note 3, pp. 279–309; *O Cruzeiro Internacional*, December 1, 1959; *Excelsior* (Mexico City), May 22, 1973; interview with José Espejo, Buenos Aires, October 13, 1977.
18. See article by Gabriel García Márquez, undated clipping from *Cuestionario*, p. 11, supplied to author by Patricio Kelly.
19. For Cooke's complaint about charges he was "pro-communist," see J. Perón, *supra* Ch. 36, note 26, Vol. I, p. 62.
20. Cooke complained of this in a letter to Perón. See ibid., p. 192.
21. For a description of this process, see R. Martínez, *supra* Ch. 38, note 7, p. 48. A prominent Peronist gave a similar account. Interview, November 18, 1977 (name withheld by request).
22. T. Luca de Tena, *supra* Ch. 1, note 7, p. 250; see also A. Barrios, *supra* Ch. 3, note 33, p. 13.
23. See Fisher (Caracas) to Department of State, 735.00/6-457, June 4, 1957 (conflicting opinions within Venezuelan government regarding whether agents of Argentine government or Peronists planted bomb); see also A. Barrios, *supra* Ch. 3, note 33, pp. 14–15.
24. See Vaky, memorandum of conversation, 735.00/3-2257, March 22, 1957.
25. See McIntosh to secretary of state, 735.00/7-1257, July 12, 1957.
26. See R. Guardo, *Horas difíciles*, pp. 88–90.
27. See E. Perina, *Detrás de la crisis*, pp. 127–31.
28. For Prieto's version of the Perón-Frondizi accord, see R. Prieto, *supra* Ch. 38, note 30.
29. See J. Perón, *supra* Ch. 36, note 26, Vol. II, p. 46.
30. See ibid., Vol. I, p. 37.
31. See R. Prieto, *supra* Ch. 38, note 30, p. 110.
32. Quoted in N. Casas, *Frondizi*, p. 293.
33. See T. Szulc, *supra* note 1, p. 300.
34. For a photo of the headline, see E. Pavón Pereyra, *supra* Ch. 3, note 8, No. 37, August 1974, p. 122.
35. See R. Galán, *supra* note 6, pp. 4–5.
36. See A. Barrios, *supra* Ch. 3, note 33, pp. 21–24.

CHAPTER FORTY

1. T. Luca de Tena, *supra* Ch. 1, note 7, p. 259.
2. Ibid., p. 262.
3. A. Barrios, *supra* Ch. 3, note 33, p. 71.
4. Ibid., p. 44.
5. Ibid., p. 51.
6. Ibid., p. 30.
7. Ibid., pp. 101–102.
8. Interview with Henry Raymont, Washington, January 11, 1980.
9. See J. Perón, *supra* Ch. 36, note 26, Vol. II, p. 386.
10. See R. Potash, *supra* Ch. 16, note 50, p. 267.
11. See F. Díaz, *Conversaciones con Rogelio Frigerio*, pp. 43–44.
12. Interview with Arturo Frondizi, Buenos Aires, October 18, 1977.
13. See F. Luna, *Diálogos con Frondizi*, p. 40.

14. See R. Potash, *supra* Ch. 16, note 50, pp. 263–69. For Frondizi's denial, see J. Orona, *supra* Ch. 36, note 13, p. 197.
15. See R. Prieto, *supra* Ch. 38, note 30, pp. 120–21.
16. See "De Perón a Onganía—XXV," *Panorama*, April 22, 1969, p. 66.
17. See G. Wynia, *supra* Ch. 19, note 1, pp. 85–88.
18. Ibid., p. 88.
19. For accounts of Frondizi's performance during 1958, see R. Potash, *supra* Ch. 16, note 50, pp. 282–99; F. Luna, *supra* Ch. 38, note 25, pp. 123–26; I. Odena, *Libertadores y desarrollistas*, pp. 107–29.
20. See *Hispanic American Report*, Vol. II, November 1958.
21. See R. Potash, *supra* Ch. 16, note 50, pp. 299–30.
22. J. Perón, *supra* Ch. 36, note 26, Vol. II, p. 65.
23. Ibid., p. 95.
24. Ibid., p. 127.
25. See D. James, *supra* Ch. 39, note 12, p. 21.
26. See *La Nación*, July 21, 1959.
27. See E. Pavón Pereyra, *supra* Ch. 3, note 8, No. 38, August 1974, pp. 159–60; J. Perón, *supra* Ch. 36, note 26, Vol. II, pp. 79, 105–109.
28. Interview with Delia Parodi, Buenos Aires, July 3, 1980; Perón warned Cooke to be cautious in dealing with the women's branch. See J. Perón, *supra* Ch. 36, note 26, Vol. II, pp. 55–56.
29. See R. Prieto, *supra* Ch. 38, note 30, p. 190, for an unsympathetic view of Cooke's involvement.
30. See D. Hodges, *Argentina 1943–1976*, p. 39.
31. M. Gazzera and N. Ceresole, *Peronismo*, p. 113.
32. Interview with David Bléjer, Buenos Aires, April 1977.
33. Interview with Ramón Prieto, Buenos Aires, September 29, 1977.
34. Roberto Galán approached the U.S. embassy and inquired whether Perón might obtain a visa to the United States. Secretary of State John Foster Dulles instructed the embassy to discourage the application. See Dulles to U.S. embassy Dominican Republic, February 20, 1958 (copy on file with author).
35. Interview with Hipólito Paz, Buenos Aires, August 18, 1980.
36. See Bernbaum to Department of State, 735.00/12-3059, December 30, 1959; Lodge (Madrid) to secretary of state, 735.00/1-2060, January 20, 1960.
37. For descriptions of the departure, see A. Barrios, *supra* Ch. 3, note 33, pp. 113–18; E. Pavón Pereyra, *supra* Ch. 3, note 8, No. 39, August 1974, pp. 178–80.

CHAPTER FORTY-ONE

1. For descriptions of Perón's arrival, see A. Barrios, *supra* Ch. 3, note 33, pp. 119–20; Braggiotti (Seville) to Department of State, 735.00/1-2860, January 28, 1960.
2. Quoted in F. Salgado-Araujo, *Mis conversaciones privadas con Franco*, p. 95.
3. See R. Alexander, *supra* Ch. 5, note 26, p. 165.
4. For the text of the decision of the Supreme Court of Justice upholding the confiscation, see República Argentina, *supra* Ch. 19, note 3, p. 278; see also *New York Times*, November 26, 1956.

5. A cable from the embassy in Buenos Aires reports a source as claiming that Perón had made substantial investments in Venezuela and Cuba but had lost everything with the overthrows of Pérez Jiménez and Batista. U.S. embassy to secretary of state, October 31, 1964 (copy on file with author).

6. According to a CIA report written during Perón's Dominican stay, he "is now absolutely without funds and unable at present to tap deposits in Switzerland which are in the name of Evita Perón, his deceased wife." CIA information report, 3/345, 784, February 19, 1958.

7. See J. Taylor, *supra* Ch. 9, note 11, pp. 67–68. Percy Foster, the source for this claim, confirmed his version in an interview in Buenos Aires on July 2, 1980, but could offer no substantiation.

8. See *supra* note 5.

9. A Barrios, *supra* Ch. 3, note 33, pp. 102, 113–14. A CIA report confirms that an Argentine businessman who may have been giving Perón money was living in Switzerland at the time. CS-3/429, 815, March 7, 1960.

10. *Supra* note 1.

11. See A. Barrios, *supra* Ch. 3, note 33, p. 126.

12. Interview with Nini Montiam, Madrid, June 27, 1977.

13. T. Luca de Tena, *supra* Ch. 1, note 7, p. 107.

14. Interviews with Eduardo Colom, Buenos Aires, May 9, 13, 1978.

15. See A. Agostinelli, *supra* Ch. 26, note 42.

16. Interview with Nini Montiam, Madrid, July 7, 1977.

17. The term appears on the marriage certificate. Copy on file with author. For an authoritative account of the wedding, see A. Puentes, "Verdad y mentira sobre el matrimonio Perón-Isabel Martínez," *Siete Días*, August 12, 1976, p. 10.

18. An indispensable account appears in an article on spiritism in *Siete Días*, November 14, 1967, p. 58; see also "El caso Isabel—Segunda parte," *supra* Ch. 38, note 9; "La verdadera historia de Isabel Perón," *supra* Ch. 38, note 11, p. 4; *Primera Plana*, October 19, 1965.

19. Quoted in "El caso Isabel—Segunda parte," *supra* Ch. 38, note 9, p. 44.

20. See *Primera Plana*, May 18, 1965; see also *La Razón*, December 27, 1961.

21. See E. Pavón Pereyra, *supra* Ch. 3, note 8, No. 40, August 1974, p. 185; E. Romero, *Argentina entre la espada y la pared*, pp. 54–55.

22. See P. Gasparri, ed., *Codex Juris Canonici* §§ 1557, 2227, 2232.

23. See *La Opinión*, August 13, 1971.

24. See *La Nación*, January 27, 1960.

25. See *Hispanic American Report*, Vol. 14, March 1961, p. 70 (Juan Bramuglia defends "Peronism without Perón").

26. See R. Potash, *supra* Ch. 16, note 50, pp. 336–50; "De Perón a Onganía—XXXV," *Panorama*, July 15, 1969, p. 74; I. Odena, *supra* Ch. 40, note 19, pp. 287–331.

27. See A. Paz and G. Ferrari, *Argentina's Foreign Policy, 1930–1962*, pp. 194–97.

28. See F. Luna, *supra* Ch. 38, note 25, p. 205.

29. See P. Snow, *supra* Ch. 28, note 18, p. 93.

30. Perón's initial preference for abstention is confirmed by a written statement supplied to the author by Raúl Matera; and interviews with Antonio Cafiero, Buenos Aires, July 28, 1980, and Miguel Unamuno (labor leader), Buenos Aires, July 5, 1980. See also R. Guardo, *supra* Ch. 39, note 26, pp. 349–50.

31. See *La Nación*, January 27, 1962.
32. See A. Whitaker, "Left and Right Extremism in Argentina," *Current History*, February 1963, p. 86.
33. See R. Potash, *supra* Ch. 16, note 50, p. 363.
34. See I. Odena, *supra* Ch. 40, note 19, pp. 348–51.
35. See M. Gazzera and N. Ceresole, *supra* Ch. 40, note 31, p. 120.

CHAPTER FORTY-TWO

1. The author had the opportunity to see the passport during an interview with Delia Parodi, Buenos Aires, May 4, 1977.
2. Quoted in E. Pavón Pereyra, *supra* Ch. 3, note 8, No. 41, August 1974, p. 215.
3. See *Primera Plana*, July 14, 1964.
4. See M. Goldwert, *supra* Ch. 4, note 14, pp. 188–93.
5. See Communiqué No. 150, reprinted ibid., pp. 191–92.
6. See *Hispanic American Report*, Vol. 16, August 1962. See also McClintock (Madrid) to Department of State, 735.00/8-462 (report of pro-Peronist Argentine bishop that "Framini . . . has definitely turned to left under instructions from Perón").
7. Their position was embodied in the "Program of Huerta Grande," reprinted in *Cuadernos de Marcha*, No. 71, 1973, p. 33.
8. Quoted in *Hispanic American Report*, Vol. 15, December 1962.
9. Cooke, as might be expected, had a low opinion of Villalón. See J. Perón, *supra* Ch. 36, note 26, Vol. II, pp. 304–307.
10. Solano Lima met Perón for the first time on his return from Jerusalem after covering the Adolf Eichmann trial for a Buenos Aires newspaper. Hans Rudel, the famed Stuka pilot, arranged the encounter. Interview with Vicente Solano Lima, Buenos Aires, September 27, 1977.
11. See J. Rowe, "The Argentine Elections of 1963: An Analysis," Election Analysis Series No. 1, Institute for the Comparative Study of Politics, undated, pp. 17–18.
12. See G. Wynia, *supra* Ch. 19, note 1, pp. 112–35.
13. As a Peronist labor leader recalled, "We fought for power." Interview, Buenos Aires, July 22, 1980 (name withheld by request).
14. See letter from Perón to Frigerio, reprinted in R. Prieto, *Correspondencia Perón-Frigerio*, p. 53.
15. See "El plan de lucha de la CGT," *Polémica, 1962–1972*, No. 5, 1972; M. Lopez Olaciregui, "1964 operación retorno," *Todo Es Historia*, No. 94, March 1975, p. 83.
16. See *Hispanic American Report*, Vol. 17, March 1964.
17. See recorded message from Perón, quoted in *La Razón*, October 25, 1964, and interview in *Marcha* (Montevideo), February 27, 1970.
18. Interview, Buenos Aires, July 28, 1980 (name withheld by request).
19. See T. Martínez, "El exilio en Madrid," *La Opinión*, August 29, 1972, reprinted July 2, 1974.
20. See E. Rom, *Así hablaba Juan Perón*, p. 137.
21. See E. Peicovich, *supra* Ch. 1, note 9, p. 31.
22. Reprinted in *La Razón*, August 22, 1964.
23. Quoted ibid.
24. See U.S. embassy to secretary of state, 350, September 11, 1964.

25. See "El retorno de Perón," *Polémica 1962–1972*, No. 6, 1972, p. 166.
26. See *Hispanic American Report*, Vol. 17, November 1964.
27. An Uruguayan magazine had quoted Perón as claiming: "I asked de Gaulle to go to Latin America." *Marcha*, August 3, 1964, quoted in Rusk to U.S. embassy, August 7, 1964. A French diplomat informed the U.S. embassy in Paris that "de Gaulle considers Perón attempt to ride coattails in Third World ridiculous." U.S. embassy (Paris) to secretary of state, September 19, 1964. There is no evidence that de Gaulle was ever in direct contact with Perón.
28. See *Primera Plana*, October 27, 1964.
29. Quoted in Walker (Madrid) to secretary of state, 1853, November 3, 1964.
30. See U.S. embassy (Asunción) to Department of State, 193, November 12, 1964.
31. See U.S. embassy to Department of State, 657, November 12, 1964.
32. Interview with Alberto Iturbe, Buenos Aires, May 12, 1978.
33. See J. Antonio, *Ahora o nunca*, pp. 48–49.
34. Ibid., p. 50.
35. Walker (Madrid) to secretary of state, 675, December 1, 1964.
36. Interview with Alberto Iturbe, *supra* note 32.
37. The following description is based upon the accounts in E. Peicovich, *supra* Ch. 1, note 9, pp. 23–29; *Primera Plana*, December 8, 1964, p. 6; interview with Alberto Iturbe, *supra* note 32; interview with Delia Parodi, *supra* note 1; letter by Juan Perón, reprinted in E. Pavón Pereyra, *supra* Ch. 3, note 29, pp. 199–207; J. Antonio, *supra* note 33, pp. 50–53.
38. According to Illia, he left the decision to his ministers and accepted full responsibility for it. Interview with Arturo Illia, Buenos Aires, May 15, 1978.
39. Iturbe was the first to make this charge. See U.S. embassy to secretary of state, 904, January 8, 1965. See also J. Antonio, *supra* note 33, p. 52. Even if the United States had pressured Brazil to stop Perón, the idea that an easily identifiable North American officer would let himself be seen and heard by the detained Peronists is absurd on its face. General Vernon Walters, U.S. army attaché in Rio de Janeiro at the time, insists that North American military and diplomatic personnel had orders not to go anywhere near the airport. Interview, Washington, May 12, 1977.
40. Letter from Perón to the Provisional Commission for the Return of Perón, December 12, 1964 (copy furnished author by a member of the commission).

CHAPTER FORTY-THREE

1. *Time*, December 12, 1964.
2. J. Goodsell, "Perón Influence Reassessed," *Christian Science Monitor*, December 18, 1964, p. 11.
3. See Woodward (Madrid) to secretary of state, 717, December 15, 1964.
4. See P. Ranis, "*Peronismo* Without Perón Ten Years After the Fall (1955–1965)," *Journal of Inter-American Studies*, Vol. 8, January 1966, p. 121.
5. See E. Pavón Pereyra, *supra* Ch. 3, note 29, p. 275.
6. Interview with Jorge Antonio, Buenos Aires, October 7, 1977.
7. See *Primera Plana*, October 5, 1965; Rabenold to Department of State, A-163, August 21, 1963.

8. For descriptions of Isabel's stay at the hotel, see *Primera Plana*, October 19, 1965, p. 8; *Gente*, October 12, 1965; *La Nación*, October 13, 1965.
9. Quoted in *Gente*, October 12, 1965.
10. See U.S. embassy to secretary of state, 551, October 18, 1965.
11. See *Primera Plana*, November 9, 1965, p. 16.
12. See M. Gazzera and N. Ceresole, *supra* Ch. 40, note 31, pp. 130–33.
13. Reprinted in *Ultima Hora*, November 17, 1965.
14. See *Primera Plana*, November 23, 1965.
15. Quoted ibid., December 14, 1965.
16. Quoted ibid., December 21, 1965.
17. This portion of the letter is paraphrased in E. Pavón Pereyra, *supra* Ch. 3, note 8, No. 42, August 1974, p. 237.
18. Quoted in *Primera Plana*, March 8, 1966, p. 17.
19. See ibid., March 8, 1966, p. 12.
20. Reprinted in E. Pavón Pereyra, *supra* Ch. 3, note 29, p. 266.
21. Interview with Augusto Vandor by Professor Robert Alexander, Buenos Aires, June 22, 1966.
22. Interview with Enrique Corvalán Nanclares (Perón's candidate), Buenos Aires, July 24, 1980.
23. See *Primera Plana*, May 24, 1966, p. 82.
24. See G. Bra, "El derrocamiento de Illia," *Todo Es Historia*, No. 109, June 1976, p. 6.
25. See G. Wynia, *supra* Ch. 19, note 1, pp. 128–29.

CHAPTER FORTY-FOUR

1. See Revista *Gente, Fotos, hechos, testimonios de 1035 dramáticos días*, pp. 146–47.
2. Interview with Pablo Vicente, Buenos Aires, October 27, 1977; see also M. Santayana, *Tragédia Argentina*, p. 124.
3. See *La Nación*, July 10, 1966. A cable from the U.S. embassy referred to him as "José López Regui." Duke (Madrid) to Department of State, A-23, July 16, 1966.
4. Sources for biographical information about López Rega are: "López Rega: Su increible historia," *Somos*, October 29, 1976, p. 10; J. Kandell, "Perón Aide Is Prominent in the Corridors of Power," *New York Times*, July 6, 1974, p. 3.
5. See Revista *Gente, supra* note 1, p. 135.
6. *P.B.T.*, January 14, 1955, p. 40.
7. Interview with wife's acquaintance, Buenos Aires, July 1980 (name withheld by request).
8. The anecdote was related to the author by an embassy official in Buenos Aires in 1976. It appears in H. Kahn, *Doy Fe*, p. 80.
9. See "López Rega," *supra* note 4, p. 12.
10. See M. Santayana, *supra* note 2, pp. 122–23.
11. See *Primera Plana*, November 19, 1963, pp. 32–33.
12. J. López Rega, *Astrología esotérica*, p. 13.
13. J. López Rega, *Alpha y omega*, pp. 68–79; the cow chapter is reprinted in *Cuestionario*, September 1973.
14. Interview with wife's acquaintance, *supra* note 7.
15. Interview with Jorge Rojas Silveyra (Argentine ambassador to Spain), Buenos Aires, July 29, 1980.

16. Interview with Jorge Antonio, Buenos Aires, July 23, 1980; see also T. Eloy Martínez, "El ascenso, triunfo, decadencia y derrota de José López Rega," *La Opinión*, July 22, 1975, p. 24.

CHAPTER FORTY-FIVE

1. Perón is said to have exchanged letters in April with some of the generals who were preparing the coup and to have encouraged them to go ahead with their plans. Interview with courier, Buenos Aires, July 1980 (name withheld by request).
2. Quoted in *Primera Plana*, July 12, 1966, p. 18.
3. See *Primera Plana*, July 5, 1966.
4. Quoted in *New York Times*, July 15, 1966, p. 9.
5. See H. Ferns, *supra* Ch. 2, note 6, p. 231.
6. See ibid., pp. 231–32.
7. See K. Johnson, "Argentina's Mosaic of Discord, 1966–1968," Political Studies Series No. 6, Institute for the Comparative Study of Political Systems, 1969, pp. 27–30.
8. See G. Wynia, *supra* Ch. 19, note 1, pp. 169–72.
9. See *La Nación*, December 14, 1966; *Primera Plana*, January 10, 1967, p. 18.
10. Interview with Jorge Antonio, Buenos Aires, October 7, 1977.
11. Ibid.
12. Interview with Hipólito Paz, Buenos Aires, August 18, 1980.
13. Interview with David Bléjer, Buenos Aires, April 1977.
14. See article in *Extra*, December 1968.
15. An excellent sampling is found on the Falcoff tape, *supra* Ch. 4, note 10, which records him asserting, *inter alia*, that he won 80 percent of the vote in the 1946 elections, that Braden organized the Communists against him, and that Britain and the United States supplied the Argentine navy with ammunition during the 1955 Liberating Revolution.
16. J. Peron, *Latinoamérica*, p. 71.
17. Ibid., pp. 35, 55, 58. For an apparently serious description of the synarchy, see A. Buela, *La sinarquía y lo nacional*. A tongue-in-cheek treatment appears in *Cuestionario*, p. 16 (undated clipping on file with author).
18. J. Perón, *supra* note 16, pp. 54, 61.
19. See, e.g., his "Letter to the Movement" on the occasion of Che Guevara's death, reprinted in *Militancia*, August 30, 1973.
20. Quoted in E. Peicovich, *supra* Ch. 1, note 9, p. 46.
21. See *Primera Plana*, April 2, 1968.
22. See "Declaracion de Tucumán," reprinted in *Cuadernos de Marcha*, No. 71, 1973, p. 36.
23. See M. Gazzera and N. Ceresole, *supra* Ch. 40, note 31, p. 151.
24. See *Primera Plana*, April 2, 1968.
25. See J. Perón, *supra* Ch. 36, note 26, Vol. II, p. 39.
26. See D. Hodges, *supra* Ch. 40, note 30, pp. 40–41; C. Velazco, "Revolución o muerte," *Panorama*, August 1965, p. 52.
27. See J. Kohl and J. Litt, *Urban Guerrilla Warfare in Latin America*, p. 324.
28. For a history of the Tacuara, see M. Gerassi, *supra* Ch. 5, note 5, pp. 255–32.
29. For a portrait of Joe Baxter, see *Panorama*, April 6, 1972.

30. See, generally, J. Dobson, "Religious Innovation and the Politics of Argentina: A Study of the Movement of Priests for the Third World," Ph.D. dissertation, 1974.

CHAPTER FORTY-SIX

1. See G. Wynia, *supra* Ch. 19, note 1, p. 186.
2. For the views of the most prominent of these leaders, see A. Tosco, *La lucha debe continuar.*
3. The following account is based upon "Mayo de 1969: Tropelias de Cain," *Primera Plana*, May 30, 1972, p. 19; *Primera Plana*, May 27, 1969, p. 11, June 3, 1969, p. 10; *Panorama*, June 3, 1969, p. 6; "El cordobazo," *Polémica, 1962–1972*, No. 15, July 1972; F. Delich, *Crisis y protesta social*; "Quince días que sacudieron al país" (undated pamphlet).
4. See *Washington Post*, June 1, 1969, p. A25.
5. On the murder of Vandor, see *Primera Plana*, July 8, 1969, p. 13; *Panorama*, July 8, 1969, p. 9; *El descamisado*, February 26, 1974 (first-person account supposedly written by one of the killers); M. Gazzera and N. Ceresole, *supra* Ch. 40, note 31, pp. 165–67; R. García, *Patria sindical versus patria socialista*, pp. 73–83.
6. See *Primera Plana*, July 8, 1969, p. 13.
7. See *New York Times*, July 1, 1969, p. 1.
8. Quoted in *Panorama*, June 30, 1970, p. 67.
9. Interview in *Marcha* (Montevideo), February 27, 1970.
10. See *Panorama*, April 27, 1970, p. 14.
11. See F. Luna, *supra* Ch. 38, note 25, p. 205.
12. The kidnappers of Aramburu described how they did it in *La Causa Peronista*, September 3, 1974, reprinted in Revista *Gente, supra* Ch. 44, note 1, p. 93.
13. See *New York Times*, June 9, 1970, p. 10.
14. F. Luna, *supra* Ch. 38, note 25, p. 207.

CHAPTER FORTY-SEVEN

1. See Hill (Madrid) to Department of State, A-88, March 11, 1970; *La Razón*, March 6, 1970.
2. See U.S. embassy to Department of State, A-268, July 3, 1970; "Después de Perón, Qué?" *Confirmado*, May 6, 1970.
3. Interview with Emilio Romero, Madrid, July 7, 1977.
4. See *La Nación*, July 6, 1970, quoting extensively from the article, which appeared in *Africasia*.
5. See Lodge to Department of State, A-287, July 12, 1970.
6. See *Panorama*, September 29, 1970, p. 10.
7. See *Panorama*, July 14, 1970, p. 10.
8. See D. Hodges, *supra* Ch. 40, note 30, p. 54.
9. See *Panorama*, September 1, 1970, p. 8; *Periscopio*, September 1, 1970, p. 12; *La Causa Peronista*, August 27, 1974 (a supposedly firsthand account by the perpetrators).
10. See, *generally*, J. Kohl and J. Litt, *supra* Ch. 45, note 27, Part 4; D. Hodges, *supra* Ch. 40, note 30, pp. 52–57.

11. See "Levingston Presidente," *Polémica, 1962–1972*, July 1972, p. 217.
12. For profiles of Lanusse, see W. Smith, "The Argentine Elections of 1973: Demilitarization and the Struggle for Consensus," Ph.D. dissertation, pp. 152–53; B. Collier, "Argentina's Lanusse under the Long Shadow of Perón," *New York Times Magazine*, August 20, 1972, p. 12; "Man in the News," *New York Times*, March 25, 1971, p. 14. An indispensable source is A. Lanusse, *Mi testimonio* (autobiography).

CHAPTER FORTY-EIGHT

1. See A. Lanusse, *supra* Ch. 47, note 12, pp. 217–24.
2. See L. Sobel, ed., *Argentina and Perón, 1970–75*, pp. 27–28.
3. *New York Times*, April 7, 1971, p. 27.
4. A. Lanusse, *supra* Ch. 47, note 12, p. 232.
5. *Panorama*, June 22, 1971.
6. See U.S. embassy to secretary of state, 1554, April 7, 1971.
7. *Confirmado*, April 21, 1971, p. 14.
8. For the published transcript of the meeting, see *Las Bases*, July 18, 1972, p. 34; *La Nación*, July 4, 1972, p. 1.
9. Interview with Francisco Cornicelli, Buenos Aires, July 25, 1980.
10. See Lodge to Department of State, A-208, May 2, 1971, p. 2.
11. See ibid.
12. Quoted in *Confirmado*, April 21, 1971, p. 14; see also *La Nación*, May 6, 1971.
13. See *Panorama*, July 6, 1971, p. 10.
14. Cabo was one of a group of nationalist youths who hijacked an Argentine airliner and flew it to the British-held Falkland Islands, which the Argentines claim and call the Malvinas, to protest a state visit of Prince Philip. See *Primera Plana*, October 4, 1966, p. 19.
15. See *Panorama*, July 6, 1971, p. 10.
16. J. Perón, *Actualización política y doctrinaria para la toma del poder*, p. 47.
17. In addition to countless statements demonstrating a strong antipathy to communism, one could point to Perón's failure to oppose the right-wing coup that deposed leftist President Jácobo Arbenz of Guatemala in 1954. As CIA-backed rebel troops invaded the country, Perón told Ambassador Nufer he had no sympathy for the besieged government and supported the U.S. goal to eliminate communism from the hemisphere. Siracusa to Department of State, 714.00/6-2154, June 21, 1954.
18. Interview with member of Guardia del Hierro, Buenos Aires, July 7, 1980 (name withheld by request).
19. Interview, Madrid, June 27, 1977 (name withheld by request).
20. See *Panorama*, July 6, 1971, p. 12.
21. See ibid., May 18, 1971, p. 9.
22. See Lodge to Department of State, A-667, November 29, 1971, p. 3.
23. See A. Lanusse, *supra* Ch. 47, note 12, pp. 238–40; see also W. Smith, *supra* Ch. 47, note 12, pp. 168–70. It is curious that Jorge Antonio had used the term "Grand National Accord" several years earlier to describe a rapprochement the Peronists ought to propose to Onganía. See *Primera Plana*, October 29, 1968, p. 15.
24. See A. Lanusse, *supra* Ch. 47, note 12, p. 239.
25. Interview with Jorge Rojas Silveyra, Madrid, July 29, 1970.

26. Ibid.
27. Interview with Jorge Paladino, Buenos Aires, May 4, 1977.
28. Interview with Jorge Rojas Silveyra, *supra* note 25.
29. For a contemporary account of the odyssey of Evita's body, see Lodge to Department of State, A-557, October 8, 1971.
30. Interview with Jorge Rojas Silveyra, *supra* note 25.
31. See P. Ara, *supra* Ch. 26, note 37, pp. 264–69.
32. Interview with Jorge Paladino, September 20, 1977.
33. See M. Santayana, *supra* Ch. 44, note 2, p. 124.
34. A. Lanusse, *supra* Ch. 47, note 12, p. 250.
35. See W. Smith, *supra* Ch. 47, note 12, pp. 176–80.
36. See R. Prieto, *supra* Ch. 42, note 14, pp. 141–43; Lodge to Department of State, A-512, September 17, 1971, p. 4.
37. W. Smith, *supra* Ch. 47, note 12, pp. 176–83.
38. Quoted in *Panorama*, July 27, 1971, p. 15.
39. See ibid., October 5, 1971, p. 17.
40. See Lodge to Department of State, *supra* note 36, p. 6.
41. See R. Prieto, *supra* Ch. 42, note 14, p. 141.
42. See W. Smith, *supra* Ch. 47, note 12, p. 183.
43. See *La Opinión*, October 6, 1971; *Panorama*, October 5, 1971, p. 17. For a useful chronology, see *La Opinión*, November 4, 1971.
44. Interview with Jorge Paladino, Buenos Aires, 1976.
45. Interview with Jorge Antonio, October 4, 1977.
46. *La Opinión*, November 10, 1971.

CHAPTER FORTY-NINE

1. See *Panorama*, December 14, 1971, p. 14.
2. See ibid., p. 12.
3. See Lodge to secretary of state, 642, December 2, 1971.
4. *La Opinión*, January 19, 1972.
5. See *La Opinión*, February 5, March 2, 1972.
6. The document, entitled "La única verdad es la realidad" ("Reality is the only truth"), is reprinted in "La Crisis Argentina," Supp. to *Reconstrucción* (undated).
7. See G. Wynia, *supra* Ch. 19, note 1, pp. 213–17.
8. Sources on Gelbard include: interview, Washington, March 3, 1977; *La Nación*, October 5, 1977, p. 1 (obituary); *Militancia*, November 1, 1973, p. 36, November 22, 1973, p. 34 (unproven intimations by left-wing magazine); *Siete Días*, October 3, 1977, p. 12 (unproven intimations by right-wing magazine).
9. See L. Sobel, *supra* Ch. 48, note 2, pp. 46–48.
10. See ibid., pp. 52–53.
11. See ibid., pp. 51, 53–54.
12. Interview with Jorge Rojas Silveyra, Buenos Aires, July 29, 1980.
13. Quoted in *La Opinión*, May 28, 1972.
14. Quoted in *Panorama*, April 27, 1972, p. 14.
15. *La Opinión*, June 29, 1972.
16. See W. Smith, *supra* Ch. 47, note 12, p. 201.
17. See *La Opinión*, July 8, 1972.
18. See *La Opinión*, July 9, 1972.
19. See *La Nación*, July 26, 1972.

20. The speech is excerpted in U.S. embassy to secretary of state, 708, July 28, 1972. For Lanusse's version of the motivations behind the speech, see A. Lanusse, *supra* Ch. 47, note 12, pp. 293–96.
21. See *Panorama*, August 3, 1972, p. 16.
22. See *La Opinión*, August 1, 1972, p. 10.
23. See ibid., July 16, 1972.
24. See ibid., July 23, 1972, p. 8.
25. For accounts of what later came to be known as the Trelew Massacre, see *Washington Post*, August 23, 1972, p. A-22; T. Martínez, *La pasión según Trelew*.
26. See L. Diuguid, "Argentina Curbs News about Killings," *Washington Post*, September 24, 1972, p. A-29.
27. See W. Smith, *supra* Ch. 47, note 12, pp. 228–29.
28. See ibid, p. 234; W. Smith, memorandum of conversation with José Gelbard, 736, October 11, 1972.
29. The document is reprinted in *La Opinión*, October 5, 1972, p. 8.
30. See Lodge to secretary of state, 6011, September 26, 1972 (two visiting Spanish generals, thought to be carrying a message from Perón, met with Lanusse); U.S. embassy to secretary of state 6156, October 2, 1972 ("It is now clear that Junta had prior knowledge of Perón's new 'plan' ").
31. See Lodge to secretary of state, 6501, October 17, 1972; Lodge to secretary of state, 6615, October 19, 1972.
32. See W. Smith, *supra* Ch. 47, note 12, p. 241.
33. See *La Opinión*, September 29, 1972, p. 8.
34. Interview with Enrique Vanoli (Radical politician), Buenos Aires, July 4, 1980.
35. See *La Opinión*, October 28, 1972, p. 10.
36. See Lodge to secretary of state, 6958, November 3, 1972.

CHAPTER FIFTY

1. Sources for the November 1972 return include: *Panorama*, November 23, 1972, pp. 16–21; *Confirmado*, November 21, 1972, pp. 14–15; *La Opinión*, November 18, 1972; *La Opinión*, November 11, 1973, p. 2 (cultural section); M. Barrau, *Historia del regreso*.
2. Quoted in *Confirmado*, November 21, 1972, p. 14.
3. L. Diuguid, "Perón Returns to Argentina," *Washington Post*, November 18, 1972, p. A1.
4. See *La Opinión*, November 8, 1972.
5. See ibid.
6. See *Panorama*, November 9, 1972, pp. 11–12.
7. The politician, Rodolfo Martínez, furnished the author with a copy of the document.
8. See W. Smith, *supra* Ch. 47, note 12, p. 245; Lodge to secretary of state, 7030, November 7, 1972; Lodge to secretary of state, 7078, November 8, 1972, p. 3.
9. See Lodge to secretary of state, 7149, November 10, 1972.
10. See W. Smith, memorandum of conversation with José Gelbard, January 15, 1973.
11. On the other hand, Abal Medina's appointment could also have been viewed as a moderating influence, since he apparently disliked Galimberti. See Lodge to secretary of state, 7650, December 1, 1972.

12. Quoted in *La Opinión*, November 11, 1973, p. 4 (cultural section).
13. See Lodge to secretary of state, 7181, November 13, 1972.
14. Message reprinted in M. Barrau, *supra* note 1, pp. 133–34.
15. See República Argentina, *Declaraciones y conferencias de prensa del presidente de la nación Teniente General Alejandro Agustín Lanusse en el país*, Vol. I (March–December 1971), p. 278 (Lanusse statement at press conference, November 11, 1972).
16. The text of the speech is reprinted in M. Barrau, *supra* note 1, Appendix.
17. Cable to U.S. Defense Intelligence Agency, 28248, November 22, 1972.
18. See *La Nación* and *La Opinión*, November 15, 1972.
19. See Stabler (Rome) to secretary of state, 6799, November 10, 1972; 7028, November 18, 1972.
20. See W. Smith, *supra* Ch. 47, note 12, p. 248.
21. The house was purchased in Isabel's name on September 25, 1972 (copy of title on file with author).
22. Sources for the description of the events outside Perón's house include: interview with eyewitness, Buenos Aires, May 9, 1978 (name withheld by request); extensive motion-picture footage (source withheld by request); *Panorama*, November 23, 1972, pp. 16–17; Lodge to secretary of state, 7341, November 19, 1972.
23. See M. Barrau, *supra* note 1, Appendix.
24. See *Ultima Clave*, November 23, 1972.
25. Interview with non-Peronist politician, Buenos Aires, July 17, 1980 (name withheld by request).
26. Interview with neighbor, Vicente López, July 1980 (name withheld by request).
27. Interview with Rogelio Frigerio, Buenos Aires, July 10, 1980.
28. J. López Rega, "Anatomía del Tercer Mundo," *Las Bases*, August 3, 1972, p. 40.
29. See *La Opinión*, August 9, 1972, p. 10.
30. CIA intelligence information cable, 314/09054-72.
31. See Lodge to secretary of state, 7653, December 1, 1972.
32. See ibid.
33. See C. Roper, "Perón Breathes Little Fire," *Manchester Guardian Weekly*, December 2, 1972, p. 5.
34. See W. Smith, *supra* Ch. 47, note, 12, pp. 251–52; Lodge to secretary of state, 7409, November 21, 1972, 7438, November 22, 1972; interview with Ricardo Balbín, Buenos Aires, July 31, 1980.
35. See *Panorama*, November 30, 1972, p. 12; Lodge to secretary of state, 7434, November 22, 1972.
36. See L. Diuguid, "Lanusse Hails Perón Return," *Washington Post*, November 23, 1972, p. A30.
37. See W. Smith, *supra* Ch. 47, note 12, p. 258.
38. J. Perón, *supra* Ch. 19, note 2, Vol. I, p. 30.
39. Lodge to secretary of state, 7552, November 28, 1972.
40. Interview, Buenos Aires, July 22, 1980 (name withheld by request).
41. See Lodge to secretary of state, *supra* note 39.
42. See Lodge to secretary of state, 7846, December 11, 1972.
43. See W. Smith, *supra* Ch. 47, note 12, p. 271.
44. For the text of his statement, see J. Perón, *supra* Ch. 19, note 2, Vol. I, p. 31.
45. See Lodge to secretary of state, 7960, December 14, 1972.

46. See Lodge to secretary of state, 8010, December 18, 1972.
47. Interview with Angel Robledo, Buenos Aires, May 3, 1977.
48. See W. Smith, *supra* Ch. 47, note 12, pp. 278–79.
49. Interview with Jorge Antonio, Buenos Aires, October 24, 1977. See also A. Lanusse, *supra* Ch. 47, note 12, p. 277.
50. See, e.g., Perón's directives to FREJULI and the Argentine electorate, reprinted in J. Perón, *supra* Ch. 19, note 2, Vol. I, p. 35; See also Lodge to secretary of state, 8185, December 26, 1972, p. 2 of Section 2.
51. Quoted in *La Opinión*, December 16, 1972.
52. See Belcher (Lima) to secretary of state, 7703, December 21, 1972.
53. See *La Opinión*, December 21, 1972.
54. Quoted in *Panorama*, January 4, 1973, p. 13.
55. Quoted in *Mayoría*, January 14, 1973.
56. Quoted in *La Opinión*, February 6, 1973.
57. See Stabler (Rome) to secretary of state, 1156, February 13, 1973.
58. See L. Sobel, *supra* Ch. 48, note 2, pp. 55, 70–72.
59. For a description of the rally, see W. Smith, *supra* Ch. 47, note 12, pp. 331–32.
60. See *La Opinión*, March 10, 1973.
61. The phrase is Richard Gott's. See R. Gott, "Argentina's John the Baptist," *Manchester Guardian Weekly*, March 3, 1973, p. 5.

CHAPTER FIFTY-ONE

1. A. Lanusse, *supra* Ch. 47, note 12, p. 328.
2. See, e.g., "Cuando la subversión fué poder," *Somos*, December 3, 1976, p. 10.
3. See, e.g., E. Marín, "El 25 de mayo de 1973: Cámpora al gobierno," *Transformaciones en el Tercer Mundo*, No. 24, February 1974.
4. The description of Cámpora's inauguration is based upon: E. Marín, *supra* note 3; *Panorama*, May 31, 1973, pp. 14–16; *La Opinión*, May 26, 1973; Revista *Gente, supra* Ch. 44, note 1, pp. 4–17; interview with Alejandro Lanusse, Buenos Aires, October 20, 1977; W. Smith, *supra* Ch. 47, note 12, pp. 403–10.
5. See photograph in E. Pavón Pereyra, *supra* Ch. 3, note 8, No. 46, September 1974, pp. 16–17.
6. The speech is reprinted in H. Cámpora, *La revolución peronista*, p. 76.
7. Quoted in *Washington Post*, May 30, 1973, p. A17.
8. For descriptions of the Villa Devoto incident, see *La Razón*, May 26, 1973; *Panorama*, May 31, 1973, pp. 16–18; Revista *Gente, supra* Ch. 44, note 1, pp. 22–23; W. Smith, *supra* Ch. 47, note 12, pp. 410–12.
9. Quoted in *New York Times*, March 14, 1973, p. 1.
10. Interview with official of Cámpora administration, Buenos Aires, May 4, 1978 (name withheld by request).
11. Quoted in *La Opinión*, March 17, 1973.
12. On Cámpora's cabinet, see *Panorama*, May 31, 1973, pp. 20–21; W. Smith, *supra* Ch. 47, note 12, pp. 412–13. Puig was a career civil servant who had written speeches for Cámpora during the campaign. Interview with Juan Carlos Puig, Washington, May 23, 1979.
13. See *La Nación*, May 26, 1973.
14. See Revista *Gente, supra* Ch. 44, note 1, pp. 46–48.

15. Interview, Buenos Aires, October 19, 1977 (name withheld by request).
16. Quoted in *La Prensa*, March 21, 1973.
17. See W. Smith, *supra* Ch. 47, note 12, pp. 387–89.
18. See R. García, *supra* Ch. 46, note 5, pp. 22–24; *La Opinión*, April 22, 1973.
19. See *La Opinión*, April 21, 1973.
20. See *La Opinión*, April 22, 1973 (Galimberti claimed what he really meant to advocate was the formation of "militias for volunteer work").
21. See *Panorama*, May 3, 1973, pp. 14–16.
22. See *La Opinión*, May 9, 1973.
23. See R. García, *supra* Ch. 46, note 5, pp. 91–97.
24. See ibid., p. 27.
25. See, e.g., *La Opinión*, March 15, 1973 (Perón quoted as saying "I think that, rationally considered, the problem of guerrilla warfare does not escape a natural law which holds that once causes have disappeared, their effects ought to disappear").
26. Quoted in *La Opinión*, May 31, 1973.
27. See *Panorama*, June 7, 1973, p. 13; *Manchester Guardian Weekly*, June 16, 1973, p. 15.
28. See G. Wynia, *supra* Ch. 19, note 1, pp. 214–17.
29. See W. Smith, *supra* Ch. 47, note 12, p. 416.
30. See *Panorama*, May 24, 1973, p. 16.
31. See *La Opinión*, May 31, 1973.
32. CIA intelligence information cable, 314/05317-73: "Perón's recent operation, although it went well, took a toll on Perón's overall health. [Source deleted] speculates that Perón will live a year to eighteen months."
33. See E. Peicovich, *supra* Ch. 1, note 9, pp. 143–44 (interview with Dr. Puigvert).
34. See B. Neustadt, *La Argentina y los argentinos*, p. 302 (interview with Dr. Pedro Cossio).
35. Quoted in *La Opinión*, May 4, 1973, p. 18.
36. Sources for the description of Perón's treatment of Cámpora in Madrid include interview with Mario Amadeo, Buenos Aires, September 23, 1977; interview with high Peronist official who witnessed some of the events, Buenos Aires, October 21, 1977 (name withheld by request); *La Prensa*, June 16–19, 1973; Revista *Gente, supra* Ch. 44, note 1, pp. 30–33.

CHAPTER FIFTY-TWO

1. For the detailed program, see *La Razón*, June 19, 1973.
2. For instructions to JP members, see *El Descamisado*, June 19, 1973.
3. Interview with Vicente Solano Lima, Buenos Aires, November 1976.
4. Sources for the description of the events of June 20 include: *La Razón*, June 20, 1973 (excellent, detailed reporting); *La Nación*, June 21, 1973; interviews with numerous eyewitnesses (names withheld by request); "La matanza de Ezeiza," *Gente*, June 12, 19, 1980 (right-wing version); *El Descamisado*, June 26, July 3, 10, 1973 (left-wing version; eyewitness accounts and photos); Revista *Gente, supra* Ch. 44, note 1, pp. 36–43 (photos).
5. Interview with Vicente Solano Lima, *supra* note 3.
6. Interview with Marcelo Sánchez Sorondo (passenger), Buenos Aires, July 8, 1980.

7. Interview with Dr. Pedro Cossio, Buenos Aires, May 3, 1978; see also B. Neustadt, *supra* Ch. 51, note 34, p. 303 (interview with Dr. Cossio).

8. Interview with Vicente Solano Lima, Buenos Aires, May 12, 1977; see also "La matanza de Ezeiza," *supra* note 4 (interview with V. Solano Lima).

9. Interviews with Mario Amadeo, Buenos Aires, September 23, 1977, and Marcelo Sánchez Sorondo, *supra* note 6.

10. The text is reprinted in *La Nación*, June 21, 1973, p. 1.

11. R. Aizcorbe, *Argentina*, p. 242.

12. For a convincing argument that the Cámpora government was hardly a Marxist regime, see W. Smith, *supra* Ch. 47, note 12, pp. 412–15.

13. Solano Lima claims that he questioned the Algerian ambassador, who denied that any Algerians were involved. Interview with Vicente Solano Lima, *supra* note 8.

14. See R. de Casabellas, "Una crisis con matices que no tiene parangón en la historia argentina," *La Opinión*, July 17, 1973.

15. See *La Opinión*, June 22, 1973, p. 12.

16. See article by Dr. Arnaldo Rascovsky in *La Opinión*, July 1, 1973.

17. The text is reprinted in J. Perón, *supra* Ch. 19, note 2, Vol. I, p. 47.

18. The speech is reprinted ibid., p. 49.

19. See *Panorama*, June 26, 1973, p. 5.

20. Interview with Gustavo Caravallo, Buenos Aires, July 9, 1980 (member of staff).

21. See W. Smith, *supra* Ch. 47, note 12, p. 430.

22. Interview with Mario Amadeo, *supra* note 9.

23. See B. Neustadt, *supra* Ch. 51, note 34 (interview with Dr. Cossio).

24. CIA intelligence information report, 321/26651-73, September 28, 1973.

25. See H. Cámpora, *El mandato de Perón*, pp. 83–84.

26. See Perón's speech of July 13, 1973, reprinted in J. Perón, *supra* Ch. 19, note 2, Vol. I, p. 53.

27. See W. Smith, *supra* Ch. 47, note 12, pp. 431–33.

28. Interview with Angel Robledo, Buenos Aires, May 3, 1977.

29. Interview with José Gelbard, Washington, March 3, 1977.

30. See *La Opinión*, July 13, 1973, p. 5.

31. Interview with Antonio Benítez, Buenos Aires, July 24, 1980.

32. See N. Domínguez, *Conversaciones con Juan J. Taccone*, pp. 170–71.

33. See W. Smith, *supra* Ch. 47, note 12, p. 431 (interview with Vicente Solano Lima).

34. Interview with Pedro Cossio, Buenos Aires, May 3, 1978.

35. Quoted in *La Opinión*, July 13, 1973.

36. The speech is reprinted in J. Perón, *supra* Ch. 19, note 2, Vol. I, p. 53.

37. Interview with eyewitness, Washington, February 1982 (name withheld by request). See also Krebs to secretary of state, 5033, July 14, 1973 ("Perón looked tired and drawn, his voice was somewhat hoarse . . .").

38. *El Descamisado*, July 17, 1973, pp. 2–3.

39. See ibid., July 24, 1973 (front-page headline).

40. See ibid., pp. 4–7.

41. See Krebs to secretary of state, 5368, July 24, 1973.

42. See W. Smith, *supra* Ch. 47, note 12, pp. 444–48.

43. Quoted in Krebs to secretary of state, 5032, July 14, 1973 ("I have great respect for Dr. Balbín and would go anywhere with him").

44. Interview with Ricardo Balbín, Buenos Aires, July 31, 1980.

45. Interview with Peronist deputy, Buenos Aires, October 19, 1977 (name withheld by request).

46. See *La Opinión*, August 5, 1973; *La Nación*, August 5, 1973; *La Prensa*, August 5, 1973.
47. E.g., interview *supra* note 45; A. Robledo, *supra* note 28.
48. CIA intelligence information cable, 314/06243-73.
49. See W. Smith, *supra* Ch. 47, note 12, pp. 461–64.
50. See *El Descamisado*, August 14, 1973 (editorial by Dardo Cabo).
51. Interview with official in Cámpora administration, Buenos Aires, May 1, 1978 (name withheld by request).
52. The speech is reprinted in J. Perón, *supra* Ch. 19, note 2, Vol. I, p. 75.
53. CIA intelligence information report, *supra* note 24.
54. Interview with foreigner who marched in parade, Buenos Aires, 1976 (name withheld by request).
55. For descriptions of the march, see *New York Times*, September 1, 1973, p. 5; *Washington Post*, September 1, 1973, p. A12; for extraordinary photos of the event, see *El Descamisado*, September 4, 1973 (special supplement).
56. See *La Opinión*, September 7, 1973; Lodge to secretary of state, 6653, September 10, 1973.
57. See *La Opinión*, September 11, 1973.
58. See *La Nación*, September 27, 1973; *Panorama*, September 27, 1973, p. 4; R. García, *supra* Ch. 46, note 5, p. 99; Revista *Gente*, *supra* Ch. 44, note 1, pp. 60–63 (photos); *La Opinión*, December 30, 1973.
59. Interview with Arturo Frondizi, Buenos Aires, October 18, 1977.

CHAPTER FIFTY-THREE

1. The author viewed motion-picture footage of Perón's departure from Gaspar Campos Street.
2. The speech is reprinted in J. Perón, *supra* Ch. 19, note 2, Vol. I, p. 207.
3. See *Panorama*, May 31, 1973, p. 15. Perón admitted that he had ordered Bidegain's candidacy. See ibid., May 3, 1973, p. 14.
4. J. Perón, *supra* Ch. 19, note 2, Vol. I, p. 69.
5. On the history of the ERP, see *Primera Plana*, April 4, 1972, p. 10; *Estrella Roja*, August 15, 1973; J. Petras, "Urban Guerrillas in Argentina," *New Left Review*, January–February 1972, p. 51; C. Russell et al., "Urban Guerrillas in Argentina: A Select Bibliography," *Latin American Research Review*, Vol. 9, No. 3, 1974, pp. 69–77.
6. See J. Perón, *supra* Ch. 19, note 2, Vol. I, p. 213.
7. For a transcript of the meeting, see ibid., p. 140.
8. See *La Opinión*, October 2, 1973.
9. See L. Sobel, *supra* Ch. 48, note 2, pp. 98–101.
10. See J. Perón, *supra* Ch. 19, note 2, Vol. 2, pp. 77–78.
11. The speech is reprinted ibid., p. 31.
12. See J. Kandell, "Argentina Enacts Contested Curbs on Terrorism," *New York Times*, January 26, 1974, p. 9.
13. Interview with aide, Buenos Aires, July 11, 1980 (name withheld by request).
14. The transcript of the meeting is reprinted in J. Perón, *supra* Ch. 19, note 2, Vol. 2, p. 33.
15. Ibid., p. 90.
16. See *La Opinión*, March 1, 1974.

17. See J. Kandell, "Right-Wing Policemen End Revolt in Argentine City," *New York Times*, March 2, 1974, p. 2.
18. *La Opinión*, March 1, 1974.
19. See ibid., March 2, 1974.
20. See ibid.
21. See Hill to secretary of state, 1942, March 18, 1974, p. 3.
22. Interview, Buenos Aires, July 22, 1980 (name withheld by request).
23. Interview, *supra* note 13; Defense Minister Angel Robledo, who insists that López Rega instigated the revolt, believes that Perón was kept informed of developments. Interview, Buenos Aires, March 3, 1977.
24. See "Situation in Córdoba," memorandum of conversation between U.S. embassy officials and Peronist representatives, March 29, 1974.
25. See G. Wynia, *supra* Ch. 19, note 1, pp. 221–22.
26. See *New York Times*, February 26, 1974, p. 6.
27. See *La Opinión*, November 1, 1973, p. 1. The Argentine foreign minister, Alberto Vignes, discussed with a U.S. embassy official the possibility of a Perón-Nixon meeting in Key Biscayne, Florida, on Perón's return from New York. Krebs to secretary of state, 8414, November 16, 1973.
28. See J. Luqui Lagleyze, "Yo salvé la vida a Perón," *Todo Es Historia*, No. 104, January 1976, p. 71; B. Neustadt, *supra* Ch. 51, note 34, pp. 305–306 (Dr. Cossio's version).
29. See *La Opinión*, November 24, 1973.
30. CIA intelligence information cable, 314/09479-73, p. 8.
31. Quoted in H. Kahn, *supra* Ch. 44, note 8, p. 28.
32. See Revista *Gente, supra* Ch. 44, note 1, pp. 71–73.
33. See E. Peicovich, *supra* Ch. 1, note 9, p. 153 (interview with Dr. Taiana).
34. Interview with Vernon Walters, Washington, May 12, 1977.
35. Interview with Henry Raymont, Washington, January 11, 1980.
36. Interview with neighbor, Vicente López, May 9, 1978 (name withheld by request).
37. See *New York Times*, July 6, 1974, p. 3.
38. Interview, *supra* note 13.
39. See *La Prensa*, September 23, 1972.
40. The press secretary in the Casa Rosada published a slick brochure containing sketches of the planned monument. See República Argentina, "Altar de la Patria," September 1974 (copy on file with author).
41. See *La Prensa*, May 11, 1974.
42. Quoted in H. Kahn, *supra* Ch. 44, note 8, p. 87.
43. Quoted in *New York Times*, July 6, 1974, p. 3.
44. See E. Peicovich, *supra* Ch. 1, note 9, pp. 155–56 (interview with Dr. Taiana).
45. Ibid., p. 154.
46. Interview, *supra* note 13.
47. Ibid.
48. See, e.g., T. Eloy Martínez, *supra* Ch. 44, note 16, p. 1.
49. See Hill to secretary of state, 1158, February 13, 1974 (plot termed a phony).
50. Interview with Perón aide, Buenos Aires, July 16, 1980 (name withheld by request).
51. See *La Opinión*, February 2, 1974.
52. See R. Terragno, *Los 400 días de Perón*, pp. 78–79.
53. The speech is reprinted in J. Perón, *supra* Ch. 19, note 2, Vol. 2, p. 69.

54. *El Descamisado*, February 12, 1974, pp. 2–3.
55. Sources for the description of the May 1 rally include: *La Opinión*, May 2, 1974 (reprint of complete transcript of Perón's speech); J. Kandell, "Perón Criticizes His Leftist Supporters," *New York Times*, May 2, 1974, p. 2 (excellent eyewitness account); *El Peronista*, May 4, 1974 (leftist version; excellent photos); Revista *Gente, supra* Ch. 44, note 1, pp. 110–13 (photos).
56. Quoted in *La Opinión*, May 2, 1974.

CHAPTER FIFTY-FOUR

1. See E. Peicovich, *supra* Ch. 1, note 9, p. 158 (interview with Dr. Taiana).
2. See E. Pavón Pereyra, *Los últimos días de Perón*, p. 158; "La verdadera muerte de Perón—I," *La Semana*, July 27, 1978, p. 22.
3. See J. Kandell, "Leftists to Back Perón Despite Rebuff," *New York Times*, May 7, 1974, p. 2.
4. The speech is reprinted in J. Perón, *supra* Ch. 19, note 2, Vol. 2, p. 203.
5. See *La Opinión*, August 9, 1975 (interview with Dr. Taiana).
6. Interview with Ricardo Balbín, Buenos Aires, July 31, 1980.
7. The speech is reprinted in J. Perón, *supra* Ch. 19, note 2, Vol. 2, p. 270.
8. The speech is reprinted ibid., p. 275.
9. G. Wynia, *supra* Ch. 19, note 1, p. 222.
10. See "La verdadera muerte de Perón—I," *supra* note 2, p. 25.
11. See E. Peicovich, *supra* Ch. 1, note 9, p. 159 (interview with Dr. Taiana).
12. See *La Opinión*, June 21, 1974.
13. Quoted in H. Kahn, *supra* Ch. 44, note 8, pp. 31–32.
14. See *La Opinión*, June 28, 1974.
15. See "Como murió Perón—II," *La Semana*, July 19, 1978, p. 60.
16. See *La Opinión*, June 28, 1974 ("The general is recovering well, thank God . . .").
17. See ibid., June 29, 1974.
18. Interview with Jorge Garrido, Buenos Aires, October 14, 1977.
19. Quoted in *New York Times*, June 30, 1974, p. 11.
20. See *Washington Post*, July 1, 1974, p. A16.
21. See "Como murió Perón—III," *La Semana*, July 12, 1978, p. 28.
22. See E. Peicovich, *supra* Ch. 1, note 9, pp. 161–63 (interview with Dr. Taiana).
23. Quoted in *Ultima Clave*, September 11, 1974. Dr. Taiana has stated for attribution only that López Rega "took Perón by the ankles with the intention of helping him, while he murmured something." Quoted in E. Peicovich, *supra* Ch. 1, note 9, p. 163.
24. Her speech is reprinted in *La Opinión*, July 2, 1974, p. 3.
25. Interview with foreign journalist, Buenos Aires, June 16, 1975 (name withheld by request).
26. Ibid. For the best collection of photographs of the mourning, see *La Causa Peronista*, July 9, 1974, pp. 9–39.
27. See *Noticias*, July 4, 1974, p. 1 (photo).
28. Interview with Ricardo Balbín, Buenos Aires, July 31, 1980.
29. A copy of the speech was furnished to the author by Enrique Vanoli, Radical party official, on July 4, 1980, in Buenos Aires.

CHAPTER FIFTY-FIVE

1. J. Perón, *supra* Ch. 19, note 2, Vol. 2, p. 273.
2. See H. Kahn, *supra* Ch. 44, note 8, pp. 37–38.
3. Interview with Gustavo Caravallo, Buenos Aires, July 9, 1980.
4. Quoted in P. Kandel and M. Monteverde, *Entorno y caída*, p. 13.
5. Interview with Perón aide, Buenos Aires, July 11, 1980 (name withheld by request).
6. An authoritative description of the meeting is found in H. Kahn, *supra* Ch. 44, note 8, pp. 39–43. Its authenticity has been confirmed by Defense Minister Angel Robledo, interview, Buenos Aires, May 17, 1978, and Admiral Emilio Massera, interview, Washington, June 7, 1979.
7. H. Kahn, *supra* Ch. 44, note 8, p. 43. Dr. Robledo agrees with Kahn's hypothesis. Interview, *supra* note 6.
8. See L. Sobel, *supra* Ch. 48, note 2, pp. 118–19.
9. For a detailed description, with diagram, see *La Nación*, September 20, 1974.
10. See *Noticias*, August 6, 1974.
11. See H. Kahn, *supra* Ch. 44, note 8, pp. 66–67.
12. See *Newsweek*, March 10, 1975, p. 32.
13. The author heard this anecdote for the first time in Buenos Aires in July 1975, and many times thereafter.
14. See G. Wynia, *supra* Ch. 19, note 1, pp. 223–24; D. Della Costa, "El rodrigazo," *Todo Es Historia*, No. 121, June 1977, p. 39.
15. The author was present in the Plaza de Mayo during the demonstration.
16. See L. Sobel, *supra* Ch. 48, note 2, p. 145.
17. *La Opinión*, July 6, 1975, p. 1; see also H. Kahn, *supra* Ch. 44, note 8, pp. 90–91.
18. On the fall of Isabel, see J. Dehesa, *Marzo 23, hora 24*; "Lo que jamás se contó sobre la caída de Isabel Perón," *Gente*, March 10, 1977, p. 4, March 17, 1977, p. 4.
19. The sorry record of human-rights violations in Argentina during this period is documented in Organización de los Estados Americanos, Comisión Interamericana de Derechos Humanos, "Informe sobre la situación de los derechos humanos en Argentina," April 11, 1980. For the classic account of torture in an Argentine prison, see J. Timerman, *Prisoner Without a Name, Cell Without a Number*. A. Graham-Yooll, *A Matter of Fear*, contains a fascinating collection of horror stories journalists could not publish during this period.
20. See V. Naipaul, *The Return of Eva Perón*, p. 172; see also J. Neilson, "Murder Most Natural?" *Buenos Aires Herald*, October 12, 1976, p. 8.

Index